T0297795

Introduction to Modeling in Physiology and Medicine

Introduction to Modeling in Physiology and Medicine

Second Edition

Claudio Cobelli

Department of Information Engineering, Università di Padova, Italy

Ewart Carson

Emeritus Professor of Systems Science in the School of Mathematics, Computer Science and Engineering at City, University of London, United Kingdom

Academic Press is an imprint of Elsevier
125 London Wall, London EC2Y 5AS, United Kingdom
525 B Street, Suite 1650, San Diego, CA 92101, United States
50 Hampshire Street, 5th Floor, Cambridge, MA 02139, United States
The Boulevard, Langford Lane, Kidlington, Oxford OX5 1GB, United Kingdom

British Library Cataloguing-in-Publication Data
A catalogue record for this book is available from the British Library

Library of Congress Cataloging-in-Publication Data
A catalog record for this book is available from the Library of Congress

ISBN: 978-0-12-815756-5

For Information on all Academic Press publications
visit our website at https://www.elsevier.com/books-and-journals

Publisher: Mara Conner
Acquisition Editor: Mara Conner
Editorial Project Manager: Leticia Lima
Production Project Manager: R. Vijay Bharath
Cover Designer: Christian J. Bilbow

Typeset by MPS Limited, Chennai, India

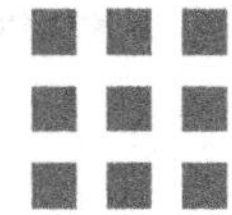

Contents

Preface to the second edition

A number of changes have been introduced in this second edition. First, clearer guidance is provided regarding the mathematical prerequisites in order to achieve the maximum benefit from the material, particularly in the later chapters. The basic structure of the book remains unchanged, while a number of the chapters providing details of the basic approaches to modeling have been enhanced. In the light of developments over recent years, the range of case study material included in this book has been substantially increased, including two new extensive examples drawn from recent research experience.

Our thanks go to Martina Negretto for assistance with preparation of the manuscript.

We would also like to thank members of the Elsevier team who have encouraged and helped us in bringing this second edition into fruition, particularly Leticia Lima and Mara Conner.

Claudio Cobelli and Ewart Carson
Padova, Italy and Ludlow, United Kingdom
August 2019

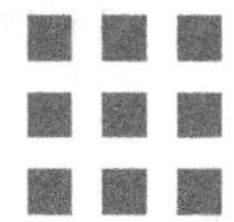

Preface to the first edition

Mathematical modeling is now widely applied in physiology and medicine to support life scientists and clinical workers. Our aim in writing this book is to provide an introduction to this topic, presenting the underlying principles of good modeling methodology together with numerous examples, indicating the way in which such modeling is finding application in physiology and medicine.

Mathematical modeling finds application in medical research, in education, and in supporting clinical practice. In the research context, the use of models can, for example, yield quantitative insights into the manner in which physiological systems are controlled. In the educational setting, medical students can use computer model simulation to explore the dynamic effects of pathophysiological processes or of drug therapy. In the clinical arena, mathematical models can enable estimates to be made of physiological parameters that are not directly measurable—useful for example in diagnosis, as well as enabling predictions to be made as to how changes in drug therapy will impact on variables of clinical importance, such as blood pressure or blood glucose concentration.

This book is directed at a broad readership across a wide range of student and practitioner backgrounds. In terms of the student readership, it is designed to appeal to biomedical engineers and to those studying physical and engineering sciences, and biological and life sciences. It should also appeal to medical students who wish to enhance their quantitative understanding of the physical and chemical processes that underpin physiology and medicine. Further, this book should be of interest to practitioners of all professions who have an interest in quantitative aspects of physiology and medicine.

This book begins by exploring some of the complexities of physiology that lend themselves to modeling in order that their quantitative features may be better understood. The concepts of mathematical modeling are then introduced, showing that models can be used for a wide range of purposes: to gain insights, to support processes of measurement, to make predictions of future behavior, and in a variety of ways assist in enhancing clinical research and practice. A number of approaches to developing mathematical models are then considered, with each being illustrated by a range of examples. The remainder of the text then focuses on issues associated with making estimates of model parameters and addressing the problem of ensuring that a mathematical model is valid; that is to say fit for its intended purpose. The final chapter comprises a number of case studies which demonstrate, in detail, how the modeling concepts, methods, and techniques that have been described and discussed earlier can be applied to real-world problems in physiology and medicine.

Lastly, we wish to express our thanks to a number of our colleagues who have worked with us in developing the examples and case studies, including: Alessandra Bertoldo, Chiara Dalla Man, Giovanni Sparacino, Gianna Toffolo, and Peter Weller; and to Andy Morrison for his assistance in the preparation of the figures. We are also indebted to those who over many years have offered us encouragement and support in our modeling ventures, including Riccardo Bonadonna, Derek Cramp, Ludwik Finkelstein, Roman Hovorka, David Kelley, Antonio Lepschy, Robert Rizza, Abdul Roudsari, and Peter Sönksen. Finally, we should like to express our gratitude to Jonathan Simpson and all his colleagues at Academic Press/Elsevier for their encouragement, support, and tolerance during the lengthy gestation of this book.

Claudio Cobelli, Ewart Carson

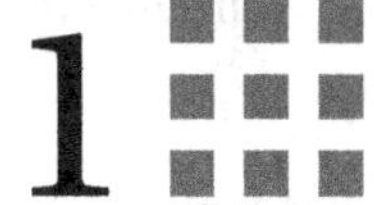

Introduction

1.1 Introduction

Over the past few decades there has been a considerable increase in the application of quantitative methods to the study of physiological systems. New techniques for making physiological measurements are being constantly developed and applied, and there has been a corresponding increase in the methods available for the analysis and interpretation of such experimental data.

Improvements have occurred in both the quality and quantity of experimental data that are now available from studies in the intact organism and on the isolated organ. Advances in instrument technology and biochemical laboratory methods have significantly contributed to these improvements.

In parallel, there have been substantial advances in terms of concepts, methods, and techniques for the study of dynamic systems; advances that have originated in control and systems theory. These are increasingly finding their way into physiological investigations, and in associated investigations in the clinical sciences and medicine. An additional driver for all of this is, of course, the availability of more computing power. Harnessing all of these together results in an increase in the use of mathematical modeling techniques in physiological investigations.

The increasing application of modeling and dynamic systems analysis offers benefits for the physiology, control and systems science, and biomedical engineering. For control and systems science there is opportunity to examine the structure and behavior of complex physiological systems which function effectively. Moreover, such systems provide a test bed for examining the merits and limitations of techniques of modeling and dynamic systems analysis, originally developed largely for technological applications.

For the physiologist, the appropriate use of mathematical models offers many potential benefits. They provide a concise description of complex dynamic processes, indicate ways in which improved experimental design could be achieved, and enable hypotheses concerning physiological structure to be tested. Furthermore, they allow estimates to be made of parameters (physiological quantities) that are otherwise not directly accessible to measurement. Although initially most modeling applications have been in the areas of physiological and medical research, they are now increasingly being used as aids in the diagnosis and treatment of disease.

If these benefits are to be realized, there is clearly a need for a greater awareness and understanding of modeling methodology and techniques, together with their strengths and limitations. This book has been devised to address those issues, provide insight into the why

Introduction to Modeling in Physiology and Medicine. DOI: https://doi.org/10.1016/B978-0-12-815756-5.00001-1

and how of modeling, the need for models, what they can do, how to build them, and how to use them.

The concepts, problems, and approaches are illustrated with examples and case studies drawn both from literature within the field and from our own extensive experiences gained over many years of endeavor. The illustrations cover a broad range of physiological topics, demonstrating the wide applicability of the approaches being described.

1.2 The book in context

This book forms a part of the series of volumes in *Biomedical Engineering.* However, physiological modeling is very much an interdisciplinary subject. Hence the topic is also central to a range of related disciplines including biomathematics, medical and health informatics, and systems physiology.

Significant activity in the field of mathematical modeling of physiological systems stretches back more than 100 years. Texts in the field have been produced for more than 50 years. Milsum (1966) and Milhorn (1966) were among the first to produce such texts. Additionally, an early, biomathematics classic was created by Riggs (1963), while Talbot and Gessner (1973) produced a definitive text having a systems physiology focus. Since then dynamic modeling of physiological systems has been a major component of many biomedical engineering texts. Examples include Bronzino (2000), and Enderle, Blanchard, and Bronzino (2000), Keener and Sneyd (1998), Hoppensteadt and Peskin (2002), Edelstein-Kehset (2004), Ottesen *et al.* (2004), and DiStefano (2013). For a more advanced treatment of modeling methodology, the reader should consult Carson and Cobelli (2014).

Other volumes have focused on particular approaches to modeling or on specific areas of physiology. For example, volumes on compartmental modeling have been produced by Atkins (1969) and Godfrey (1983), among others. The analysis of data yielded by dynamic tracer experiments has been the subject of volumes by Jacquez (1972, 1996) and Cobelli *et al.* (2000). The modeling of metabolic and endocrine systems has been described by McIntosh and McIntosh (1980) and by Carson *et al.* (1983). The related subject of physiological modeling and control has been dealt with extensively by authors such as Carson and Cramp (1985), Khoo (2000), and Northrop (2000).

In addition to textbooks on the subject, there are readily available modeling software packages. Some such as MATLAB and SIMULINK are generic modeling packages for dynamic systems. Others have been designed for a specific physiological application. Examples include SAAM II, NONMEM, and Jsim which is extensively used in the physiome project.

However, there have been remarkably few attempts to produce entry-level texts on the topic of modeling of physiological systems; the earlier volume by Finkelstein and Carson (1985) being one of the few. The focus of this present volume is to provide a comprehensive introduction to the modeling of dynamic, physiological systems. The emphasis is placed firmly on developing sound modeling methodology, with numerous examples and case studies being included as illustrations.

1.3 The major ingredients

In general terms, a model is a representation of reality. However, it is also an approximation of that reality since not all the ingredients of that reality can be incorporated into any model. Hence the models that we are concerned with in the chapters that follow will all, in their various ways, provide approximate representations of the particular physiological systems under consideration. What is crucial is that the form of model developed is appropriate for its purpose. As already hinted at, there can be a wide range of possible purposes for modeling. For instance, the form of a model adopted for the purpose of understanding some of the complexities of the control of breathing might be different from one adopted as an aid for weaning an intensive care unit patient off a ventilator. This is the case even though in both examples the physiological focus is the respiratory system.

The way in which we develop a model will be dependent on our knowledge of the relevant physiology and the availability of relevant experimental data. So in essence the process of building a model can be regarded as a mapping of physiological knowledge and experimental data into the model. In the case of a model that is essentially a representation of the experimental data available; it is those data that dominate in this mapping process. On the other hand, if the model is designed to provide a representation of the physiology more explicitly, then it will be the physical and chemical knowledge of that physiological system that dominates in the building of the model.

The overall process of modeling involves a number of interrelated ingredients. These are model building, model identification, simulation, and model validation. Used appropriately in conjunction with each other, they provide a methodology for developing a model that will be fit for its intended purpose.

Model building involves formulating equations that provide an adequate representation of either the experimental data (in the case of a data-driven model) or the underlying physiology (in the case of a model that explicitly represents the underlying physiology). Once the model has been built, identification can take place which includes making estimates of those parameters (physiological quantities) in the model that cannot be measured directly, using the available input/output experimental data.

Simulation involves solving the model equations to predict output behavior. Such computer simulation might, for instance, be used to predict the time course of a patient's blood glucose concentration in the case of a model designed to explore relationships between insulin dosage and blood glucose in a diabetic patient. The fourth ingredient is that of model validation; this involves examining (in the case of two or more competing models) which is the best in relation to the modeling purpose. In the case of a single model it involves examining whether that model is good enough in relation to its purpose. This validation process involves the use of statistical tests as well as examining other features of the behavior of the model.

All are vital ingredients of the modeling exercise and are very much interrelated. One point that will be stressed in the following chapters is the iterative nature of the modeling process. Just as any design process is very much iterative in nature—only very rarely will it be right first time—the same applies with modeling. Usually, several iterations through the cycle of ingredients will be needed before an acceptable end product is produced.

1.4 Readership and prerequisites

This book describes the development of models of physiological systems; models that can be used in a variety of ways, including as aids to understanding, as means of supporting clinical processes, and for educational purposes among others. Given that the level of this text is essentially an introductory guidebook, it is aimed at students of biomedical engineering and related disciplines. Such students may be undergraduates, or may be following more specialized master's programs in the subject.

However, one of the fascinations of the subject of physiological modeling is its very interdisciplinary nature. As such, it is an activity undertaken not only by those with technical backgrounds in biomedical engineering and health informatics, but also by many in the clinical and life sciences. Thus this text will also be relevant to the needs of physiologists, biologists, and clinical scientists and practitioners interested in quantitative approaches and results.

In terms of prerequisites for those with a clinical or life sciences background, it is helpful to have a basic understanding of the fundamental concepts of dynamic systems and their representation by differential equations. In Chapter 2, Physiological complexity and the need for models, some examples are included which offer a resume of the dynamics of first-order systems; showing how such systems can be represented mathematically, and the nature of the solutions of such equations.

1.5 Organization of the book

As indicated above, the aim of this book is to provide an introduction to the modeling of physiological systems. However, before proceeding to the actual modeling process, it is worth understanding a little about the fundamentals of physiology itself. This is important if modeling is to be undertaken successfully. In the normal healthy individual, the physiological systems provide an almost incredible array of functions necessary for the maintenance of life. In doing so, they exhibit a variety of forms of complexity. Chapter 2, Physiological complexity and the need for models, thus provides some insights into the nature of physiological complexity.

Physiological complexity is discussed in terms of function and behavior (which we wish to access), and measurements (which are available). Complexity manifests itself in terms of concepts such as hierarchy and feedback, and each is considered in the physiological context. As a result of complexity it is often not possible to directly measure (*in vivo*) the quantities of interest. Only indirect measures of such quantities may be possible. This complexity of physiological systems, coupled with limitations in measurement means that models have to be adopted as a means to aid understanding.

Chapter 3, Models and the modeling process, introduces the concepts of model and modeling process. It describes what is meant by a model, the variety of models, why modeling (i.e., modeling purpose), and the nature of the modeling process. There are many possible purposes for modeling. These can range from investigating the physical or chemical structure and associated parameters of the physiological system in question to the development of clinical models for either diagnosis or patient management. This is followed by a description of the modeling process, stressing the need for good modeling methodology. The basic ingredients of model formulation, model identification, model validation, and model simulation are described.

Following on from the first three introductory chapters, Chapter 4, Modeling the data, starts the detailed examination of approaches to modeling. Here the focus is modeling the data. The aim of this chapter is to describe data modeling approaches as representations of physiological dynamics. The chapter describes what we mean by modeling the data, when such approaches are applicable and how it should be done (i.e., a description of the principal types of data-driven (black box) models). Approaches include modeling both continuous and discrete time signals, adopting both time domain and frequency domain methods.

In contrast, Chapter 5, Modeling the system, focuses on modeling the system. The aim of the chapter is to describe approaches to modeling the physiology, showing that it can be done at different levels and that the approach adopted depends on available *a priori* knowledge and assumptions made. The approaches adopted compare and contrast the following cases: static versus dynamic, deterministic versus stochastic, time-invariant versus time-varying, lumped versus distributed, linear versus nonlinear and continuous versus discrete. As with the previous chapter, extensive examples are included as illustrations of the approaches available, demonstrating how modeling can be carried out for a wide range of physiological processes and situations.

We need a complete model of the physiological system under consideration. By this stage we shall have at least one candidate model, but possibly more than one with the need to choose between them. Focusing on a single model, if it is incomplete this will be due to some of the parameter values being unknown. This is true whether the modeling approach has been data driven or driven by the physiology of the system. We may be dealing with the whole model or just part of it. Chapter 6, Model identification, aims to provide a framework for dealing with this situation (whether the model is data driven or physiologically based). To solve this problem we need data. Data sometimes occur from the intrinsic dynamics of the system (e.g., spontaneous oscillations or noise), but usually we must design experiments. Chapter 6, Model identification, discusses what experiments need to be designed to yield appropriate data.

Chapter 7, Parametric modeling—the identifiability problem, and Chapter 8, Parametric models—the estimation problem, address the problem of identifying models that include parameters, whether these are input/output models or models that explicitly correspond to the physiology of the system under investigation. Chapter 7, Parametric modeling—the identifiability problem, considers the problem of identifiability. That is, whether it is theoretically possible to make unique estimates of all the unknown parameters of the model on the basis of those input/output experiments, which it is proposed to perform as a means of acquiring experimental data. Having addressed this problem of identifiability, techniques for estimating the unknown parameters are then discussed in Chapter 8, Parametric models—the estimation problem. Emphasis is placed upon linear least squares and nonlinear least squares techniques, though brief reference is made to maximum likelihood and Bayesian estimation.

The focus of Chapter 9, Nonparametric models—signal estimation, is nonparametric models. These are defined and methods are outlined for estimating functions, rather than parameters. Available techniques include raw deconvolution and deterministic regularization.

Chapter 10, Model validation, considers the issue of model validation, that is to say whether a particular model is good enough for its intended purpose, or in the case of a number of competing models, which of them is best. Having defined what is meant by model validity, an overall framework, together with associated methods, for the validation process is presented. The chapter ends with some recommendations for good modeling practice. Finally Chapter 11, Case studies, illustrates the methods and techniques that have been discussed in relation to validation through a series of case studies.

Throughout the text, numerous illustrations, examples, and case studies are included; demonstrating how the methodology and techniques described can be applied across a wide range of physiological examples. All of these illustrations are appropriately referenced. With regard to the basic methodology described in this book, only essential references are included. Readers who wish to engage in a deeper study of modeling methodology are encouraged to consult our companion volume (Carson & Cobelli, 2014), which includes extensive referencing to all methodological issues and detail.

2 Physiological complexity and the need for models

2.1 Introduction

Before moving on to the modeling activity that forms the bulk of this book, it is worth devoting attention to the nature of the physiological systems that we shall be modeling. In various ways all physiological systems are characterized by their complexity. In this chapter we shall examine the nature of this complexity in physiology. It is important to understand this complexity, since by definition any model that we create will be a simplification, an approximation of that complex reality. By understanding something of this complexity we shall be in a better position to make the simplifying assumptions that correspond to the particular model formulation that we shall adopt. In essence, the model that we develop needs to have taken into account both the inherent complexity that we have simplified and the availability of measurement data which will be used in estimating the parameters of our model.

Fig. 2–1 shows a schematic representation of the human organism. In effect, this is a conceptual model that gives a flavor of the complexity of human physiology. Although quite a complex figure, it is clearly a very simplified and approximate representation of all the physiological detail. Nevertheless, it does capture the essence of the dynamic processes that are present within the living organism. It depicts the human organism as a complex multi-input, multi-output system, with linkages involving an array of physicochemical processes. Finally, it includes many of the standard functions found in any complex control system; that is sensing, decision making and control, actuating or effecting, and the feeding back of information. Some of the ingredients of complexity in this physiological context are considered in later sections of this chapter. However, let us first examine some of the attributes of complexity in a more general sense.

2.2 Complexity

Complexity manifests itself in a number of ways. First, in general, the greater the number of components or elements there are in a system, the greater its complexity will be. The greater the number of neurons in a central nervous system or the larger the number of intermediate substances in a metabolic pathway, the greater the complexity will be. However, complexity is associated not only with the number of elements, but also with their interconnectivity (Flood & Carson, 1993). In the case of the central nervous system this would correspond to the number of interconnections between neurons.

Introduction to Modeling in Physiology and Medicine. DOI: https://doi.org/10.1016/B978-0-12-815756-5.00002-3

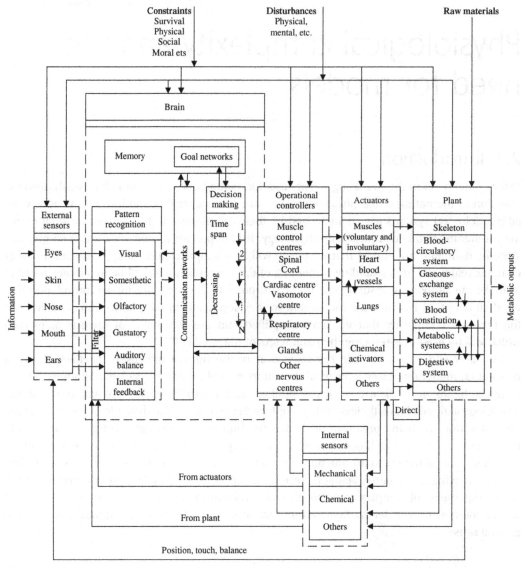

FIGURE 2–1 The human organism as a complex system. *Source: Adapted from Janes, F. R., & Carson, E. R. (1971). Modelling biological systems.* IEE Electronics and Power, 17, *110–116.*

These concepts of numbers of elements and interactions form part of a framework for complexity that has been proposed by Yates (1978). Yates suggested that complexity arises when one or more of five attributes are found which, in addition to the two already referred to, include nonlinearity, asymmetry, and nonholonomic constraints.

Nonlinear systems occur when at least one element in the system relates to and varies in a nonlinear way with another. It would be represented graphically by a curved rather than a straight line. Nonlinear systems are, in general, much more difficult to analyze and comprehend than linear systems; that is, they are more complex. Almost all physiological systems are inherently nonlinear, even if from a modeling perspective it may be possible, and indeed reasonable, to treat them as if they were linear under specific conditions. This is a concept that will be considered in detail later in the book.

Asymmetry occurs when symmetry in a system's relationships no longer holds. Consider the following example. A single cell after fertilization multiplies to become two cells, and then four, and then eight, and so on. Eventually, this produces an organism in the mold of its parents. During the developmental process, the single cell becomes a distinct organism or creature due to organization and differential growth. Differential growth is a type of asymmetry, and without it the process of growth described above would result in nothing more than a very large number of cells. Due to the differential growth, the results in the specialization give rise to the emergence of specific organs within the overall organism, such as the liver.

Holonomics relate to the integrity of systems, so that holonomic constraints are constraints that relate to laws affecting an entire organism. The obverse of this is nonholonomic constraints. These relate to parts of a system that are temporarily outside central control and which, in essence, go off and do their own thing. This applies significantly in the physiological context. The central nervous system would not be able to cope with the myriad of regulatory functions that take place within the human organism, for instance. As such, the human organism has evolved and adapted in such a manner that there is very considerable local regulation and control. For example, large numbers of metabolic processes are regulated at the local level (as will be described later), without recourse to centralized neural control. Complexity arises in situations where there is a high degree of freedom in parts of a system. In other words, the behavior and control of the parts cannot easily be predicted just on the basis of knowledge of the overall system characteristics.

Complexity also arises as a consequence of stochastic and time-varying dynamic effects. These will be considered in later chapters. Three key concepts that will aid our understanding of physiological complexity are feedback, control, and hierarchy and these will be discussed in later sections of this chapter. However, before doing so a review some of the basic concepts of dynamic systems and their mathematical representation which will underpin much of the modeling to be described later in the book.

2.3 System dynamics

To gain an understanding of the nature and behavior of dynamic systems, such as are to be found throughout the human organism, it is convenient at the outset to examine the simplest type of system, namely those modeled by first-order differential equations with constant, or time-invariant coefficients. As an approximation, many real systems can be represented satisfactorily by such simple models. Moreover, these simple models exhibit clearly some of the basic phenomena of system dynamic behavior.

2.3.1 First-order linear time-invariant systems

Fundamentally, a first-order linear time-invariant dynamic system is one in which the rate of change of the response variable is, in the absence of a forcing input, directly proportional to the instantaneous value of the variable itself. The nature of such systems can be illustrated by deriving the equations in the examples that follow. Other examples will be presented in Chapter 5, Modeling the system, in the context of modeling the system. Here the intention is to use two examples to illustrate the nature of the mathematical representation and the solution of the relevant differential equations.

2.3.2 The dynamic behavior of first-order linear time-invariant systems—solution by integration

By the behavior of a dynamic system we mean the variation of the response variable with time, resulting either from the application of a forcing input or from starting from some initial state, which is not an equilibrium state. To analyze the behavior it is necessary to solve the appropriate differential equation to obtain the response variable as a function of time. Consider first a simple system in the absence of any forcing function. The equation of such a system can be solved by simple integration.

As an example consider a population, the magnitude of which is measured at convenient time intervals, Δt apart (see Fig. 2–2). If P_{n-1} and P_n are the levels of population at times t_{n-1} and t_n respectively.

$$\frac{(P_n - P_{n-1})}{\Delta t} = \frac{\Delta P}{\Delta t} \tag{2.1}$$

As the time interval $\Delta t = t_n - t_{n-1}$ becomes very small, $\Delta P/\Delta t$ approximates more closely to the instantaneous rate of change of the population with respect to time, dP/dt.

The rate of change of population dP/dt is equal to the difference between the birth rate N_b and the death rate N_d. Hence:

$$\frac{dP}{dt} = N_b - N_d \tag{2.2}$$

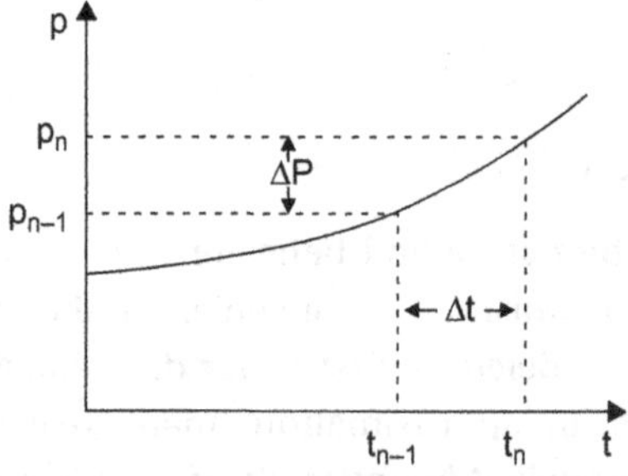

FIGURE 2–2 Graph of population, P, as a function of time.

Suppose that both birth rate and death rate are proportional to the existing population, but with different constants of proportionality k_b and k_d such that $N_b = k_b \cdot P$ and $N_d = k_d\ P$. Therefore:

$$N_b - N_d = k_b\ P - k_d\ P = (k_b - k_d)\ P = kP \tag{2.3}$$

Substituting for $N_b - N_d$ in (2.2)

$$\frac{dP}{dt} = kP \tag{2.4}$$

Rearranging (2.4) we have:

$$\frac{dP}{P} = k \times dt \tag{2.5}$$

Integrating both sides of this equation:

$$\begin{aligned} &\int (1/P) \cdot dP = \int k \cdot\ dt, \ \text{ that is} \\ &\log_e P = k\,t + C \end{aligned} \tag{2.6}$$

where C is the constant of integration. When $t = 0$, $P = P_0$. Therefore $C = \log_e P_0$. Hence:

$$\log_e P - \log_e P_0 = k\,t \tag{2.7}$$

Rearranging: $\log_e (P/P_0) = k\,t$. Hence:

$$\frac{P}{P_0} = e^{kt} \text{ or } P = P_0 e^{kt} \tag{2.8}$$

So the solution is an exponential function of time, the magnitude of which depends on P_0, the initial value of P.

The general form of response is dependent upon k, the rate constant. The two real forms of solution are those with P_0 being positive and k being either positive or negative. With k positive, the birth rate is greater than the death rate, and the plot of P against time results in a positive exponential (see Fig. 2–3). With k negative, the death rate is greater than the birth rate, and the plot gives a negative (decreasing) exponential. The time constant T, which is the reciprocal of the rate constant k governs the speed of the system response. For example, if k is small, there is a slow response since T is then large. As shown in Fig. 2–3, the time constant may be found graphically by drawing the tangent to the curve at any point Z and measuring the distance between the point where the tangent cuts the time axis and the point where the vertical projection through Z cuts the time axis.

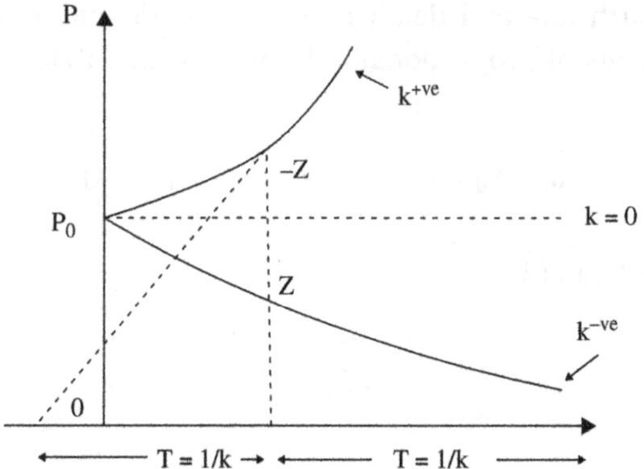

FIGURE 2–3 Graph depicting the dynamics of population as a function of the value of the population rate constant, k.

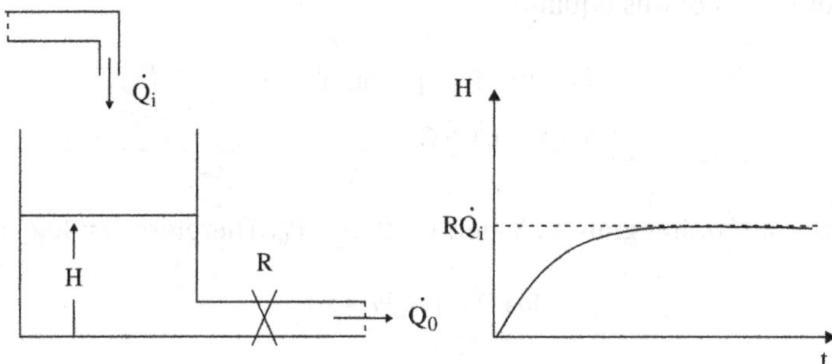

FIGURE 2–4 Representation of a first-order tank system, including the dynamics of the head of liquid in the tank, H, as a function of time in response to a step change in flow input, F_i.

2.3.3 The classical solution for a first-order system

Consider now the dynamic response of a first-order, linear time-invariant system, subjected to a forcing input. To illustrate the classical method of analyzing such a problem consider the tank system shown diagrammatically in Fig. 2–4. This example is a useful analog of many important biological systems, such as a compartment, loss from which is a function of the substance contained.

The flow rate of liquid into the tank is F_i, with an output flow rate of F_o through a valve of resistance R. It is assumed that the valve has a linear characteristic such that F_o is proportional to the head of water H. The rate of change of volume of liquid in the tank, V, is thus:

$$\frac{dV}{dt} = F_i - F_o \tag{2.9}$$

But,

$$F_o = \frac{H}{R} \tag{2.10}$$

and,

$$\frac{dV}{dt} = A\,\frac{dH}{dt} \tag{2.11}$$

where A is the cross sectional area of the tank. Substituting (2.10) and (2.11) in (2.9) gives

$$A\,\frac{dH}{dt} = F_i - \left(\frac{H}{R}\right) \tag{2.12}$$

which is first-order linear differential equation relating H to F_i.

Let the tank initially be empty, such that H, the height of the liquid in the tank is zero at $t = 0$.

Further, let a step input of flow rate, F_i, be applied at $t = 0$, that is, let the input rate of liquid be zero for $t < 0$ and F_i (a constant value) for $t \geq 0$. Eq. (2.12) can then be solved to determine the response of H to the input F_i. The solution has two parts; a free or natural response H_n, and a forced response H_f. The total solution or response is the sum of these two, $H = H_n + H_f$. The natural response is the response exhibited in the absence of a forcing function, as a result of a disturbance from equilibrium. This is given by the solution of

$$A\left(\frac{dH}{dt}\right) + \frac{H}{R} = 0 \tag{2.13}$$

which can be rewritten as

$$\frac{dH}{dt} = -\frac{H}{AR} \tag{2.14}$$

From the previous discussion it can be seen that the solution is an exponential form. This can also be seen from the fact that the solution must be a function that remains in the same form when differentiated. Let us try the solution

$$H = C\,e^{at} \tag{2.15}$$

Substituting for H and dH/dt in (2.13) we have

$$a\,C\,e^{at} + \left(\frac{1}{AR}\right) C\,e^{at} = 0 \tag{2.16}$$

Hence,

$$a + \left(\frac{1}{AR}\right) = 0 \tag{2.17}$$

Therefore $H = C\,e^{at}$ is a solution of (2.13) if a is a root of (2.16) which is known as the auxiliary equation, that is if $a = -1/(AR)$

We can write $T = 1/(AR)$, so that $a = -1/T$. The natural response is thus

$$H_n = C\,e^{-t/T} \tag{2.18}$$

Since the exponential function decays with time, the free response can, in this case, be described as a transient response.

We can now write the complete solution as

$$H = H_f + C\,e^{-t/T} \tag{2.19}$$

The response H_f can now be seen as the ultimate steady-state response, the part which remains after the transient response has decayed, in other words when $dH/dt = 0$.

Substituting $dH/dt = 0$ in (2.12) we have

$$H_f = R\,F_i \tag{2.20}$$

so that

$$H = RF_i + C\,e^{-t/T} \tag{2.21}$$

To evaluate C, which determines the magnitude of the natural response, it is necessary to consider initial conditions. When $t = 0$, $H = 0$, and substituting this in (2.21) we have

$$0 = RF_i + C \tag{2.22}$$

Hence,

$$C = -RF_i \tag{2.23}$$

The total response is then, as shown in Fig. 2–4

$$H = R\,F_i(1 - e^{-t/T}) \tag{2.24}$$

2.3.4 General case of a first-order linear system

Let us apply this approach to the general first-order system, as shown in Fig. 2–5, which can be described by the first-order, time-invariant differential equation:

$$T \cdot \left(\frac{dy}{dt}\right) + y = m(t) \tag{2.25}$$

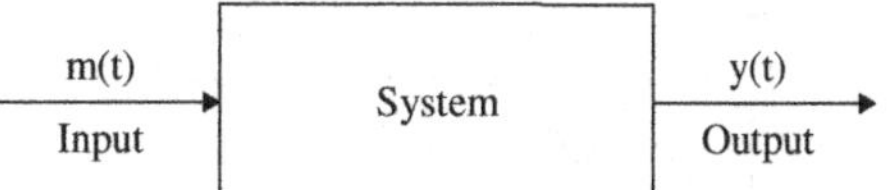

FIGURE 2–5 General representation of a first-order system with input m(t) and output y(t).

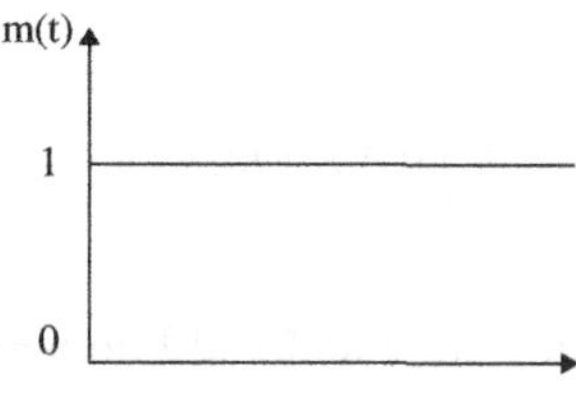

FIGURE 2–6 Forced component of response of a first-order system with a step input.

The natural or free response, y_n, depends upon the dynamics of the system itself and is found by solving (2.25) with the input equal to zero:

$$T \cdot \left(\frac{dy}{dt}\right) = -y \tag{2.26}$$

The solution, derived in a manner parallel to that developed in Section 2.3.2 is:

$$y_t = C\,e^{-t/T} \tag{2.27}$$

For a physical system the constant T is generally positive, so that the natural response is transient. The constant C depends on the initial conditions of the system as shown below.

The forced response, y_i, depends upon the particular input of the system and is usually the same form as the input for the case where the input is a unit step function (see Fig. 2–6). The forced response is obtained by finding a value of y which satisfies the equation:

$$T \cdot \left(\frac{dy}{dt}\right) + y = 1 \tag{2.28}$$

where the right-hand side of the equation is the particular input applied. The solution (cf. (2.20)) is:

$$y_t = 1 \tag{2.29}$$

The complete response is found by adding the natural and forced responses:

$$y = y_f + y_n = 1 + C\,e^{-t/T} \tag{2.30}$$

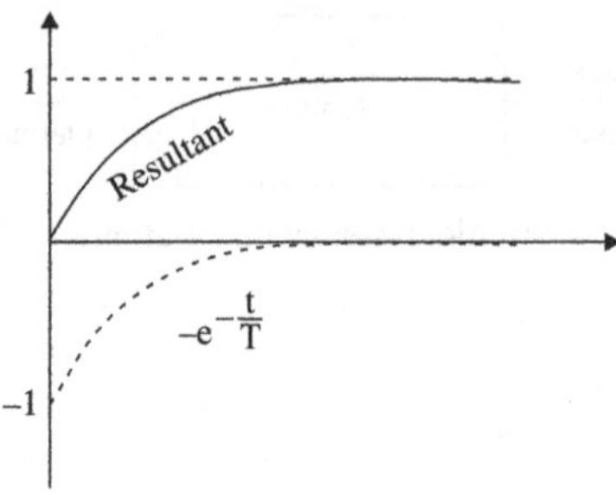

FIGURE 2–7 Resultant response (free + forced) of a first-order system to a unit step input.

The constant C can be found from the initial conditions. If at $t = 0$, $y = 0$, then from (2.30) $C = -1$. Therefore as shown in Fig. 2–7:

$$y = 1 - e^{-t/T} \tag{2.31}$$

The response of the system will vary depending on the specific form of the input applied. The most commonly used input, in addition to the step, is the impulse, which can be regarded as the first derivative of the step: In the context of this book, the injection of a drug could be regarded as an impulse input, whilst a constant infusion could be regarded as a step input.

For a system that can be described by a first-order, linear time-invariant differential equation, the rate at which the process proceeds is completely described by specifying the value of the time constant, rate constant, or half-life of that process.

The time constant is the value of time that makes the power to which the number e is raised equal to -1 in (2.31). For a step input it is the time taken to reach 63.2% of the final value.

That is in (2.31), let $t = T$. Then,

$$y = 1 - e^{-1} = 0.632 \tag{2.32}$$

The time constant is the reciprocal of the rate constant (which therefore has the dimension of time^{-1}).

Alternatively, a first-order linear process may be characterized by its half-life. This is particularly appropriate when examining the exponential decrease observed in the output variable of a first-order linear process following the application of an impulse input. The half-life is the time required for the output variable to be reduced to half of its initial value. Consider the output variable which is characterized by

$$y(t) = y_0\, e^{-t/T} = y_0\, e^{-kt} \tag{2.33}$$

where T is the time constant of the process and k is the corresponding rate constant.

Starting at time $t_0 = 0$, there is a time $t_{1/2}$ at which y has decayed to half its initial value, that is:

$$y(t_{1/2}) = \tfrac{1}{2}\, y_0.$$

Substituting for $t_{1/2}$ in (2.33):

$$y\,(t_{1/2}) = \tfrac{1}{2}\, y_0 = y_0\, e^{-t_{1/2}T} = y_0\, e^{-kt_{1/2}}$$

Solving for $t_{1/2}$ by taking logarithms to the base e yields:

$$t_{1/2} = T\,\ell n\, 2 = \frac{1}{k}\,\ell n\, 2 \tag{2.34}$$

The half-life, $t_{1/2}$, depends only upon the time constant of the system and is independent of the magnitude of the initial value. Hence for any general time, t_1, on the response curve with a value of y_1, the value of y at time $(t = t_1 + t_{1/2})$ will be $\tfrac{1}{2}\, y_1$.

2.4 Feedback

Feedback is a fundamental feature of all physiological systems. It is vital in terms of ensuring physiological regulation and control. It is an ingredient of the complexity that characterizes physiological systems.

At its simplest, feedback can be regarded as a mutual causality, whereby variable X has an effect on variable Y, and in turn variable Y has an effect on variable X. If an increase in variable X brings about an increase in variable Y, and that increase in variable Y brings about a decrease in variable X, the process is referred to as negative feedback.

2.4.1 Negative feedback

Glucose metabolism provides us with examples of such negative feedback. For instance, in a normal individual, an increase in blood glucose concentration (variable X), brought about by the ingestion of the carbohydrate component of a meal, causes an increase in the secretion of insulin (variable Y). The effect of this increased insulin level is to bring about a reduction in the blood glucose concentration toward a normal value. This negative feedback process is inherently regulatory, seeking to enhance the control of blood glucose concentration. Physiologically the effects of insulin on glucose are achieved by processes that include the chemical conversion of glucose into glycogen that is stored in the liver.

2.4.2 Positive feedback

On the other hand, positive feedback corresponds to the situation in which variable X causes an increase in variable Y, which in turn, brings about a further increase in X. An example

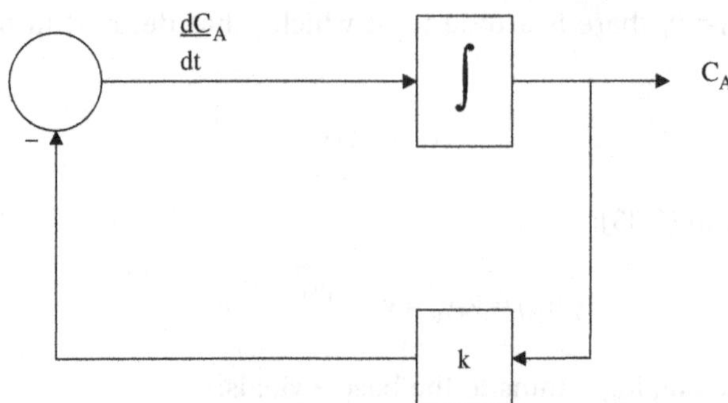

FIGURE 2–8 Signal flow diagram illustrating inherent negative feedback.

outside the physiological domain is the wage-price spiral. An increase in wages causes price increases that in turn act as a catalyst for further wage increases. This is clearly a destabilizing phenomenon.

2.4.3 Inherent feedback

The examples of feedback considered above relate to control systems in which the feedback link takes the form of a flow of material or information. There is, however, a further form of feedback that needs to be considered, namely inherent feedback.

Consider the case of a metabolic system. Suppose that in a simple chemical reaction, it can be assumed that the rate of concentration decrease of chemical A, taking part in the reaction, is directly proportional to its concentration. Mathematically this can be expressed as:

$$\frac{dC_A}{dt} = -k\,C_A \tag{2.35}$$

where C_A is the concentration of chemical A, and k is the rate constant for the reaction. Eq. (2.35) can be expressed in the form of a signal flow diagram (see Fig. 2–8). This shows the integration of dC_A/dt to yield C_A. This is then fed back, being multiplied by k and by −1 to yield dC_A/dt. This is effectively a negative feedback connection. In other words, there is an inherent regulatory effect exhibited in this chemical reaction despite the fact that there is no physical feedback link. This phenomenon of inherent feedback that has been revealed is contained in any dynamic process that can be described mathematically in this way in differential equation form.

2.4.4 Combining negative and positive feedback

Both positive and negative feedback can be seen in a simple model of population dynamics, as already considered in terms of the mathematics involved in Section 2.3.2. This is a model that could apply, for instance, in relation to the number of humans or animals in a particular location, or equally in the context of cell populations within an organism.

Suppose that the birth rate in a population is assumed to be directly proportional to the number of individuals in the population and let k_b be the rate constant that defines this relationship. Mathematically we can represent this by the following differential equation which indicates that the rate of change of population occurs in a positive manner at a rate proportional to the number of individuals making up the population (P):

$$\frac{dP}{dt} = k_b \, P \tag{2.36}$$

In a similar way we could assume that the death rate in this population (P) is directly proportional to P, being characterized by a rate constant k_d. Mathematically this could be represented as:

$$\frac{dP}{dt} = -k_d \, P \tag{2.37}$$

where the negative sign indicates that this is a process causing a negative rate of change in the population (in contrast to the birth effect).

Combining (2.36) and (2.37) gives us an overall model for the dynamics of this population:

$$\frac{dP}{dt} = k_b \, P - k_d \, P \tag{2.38}$$

Graphically we can describe this by the signal flow diagram shown in Fig. 2–9, where the symbols and terminology adopted are the same as in the previous figure. This clearly indicates the presence of both positive and negative feedback loops, providing another illustration of inherent feedback.

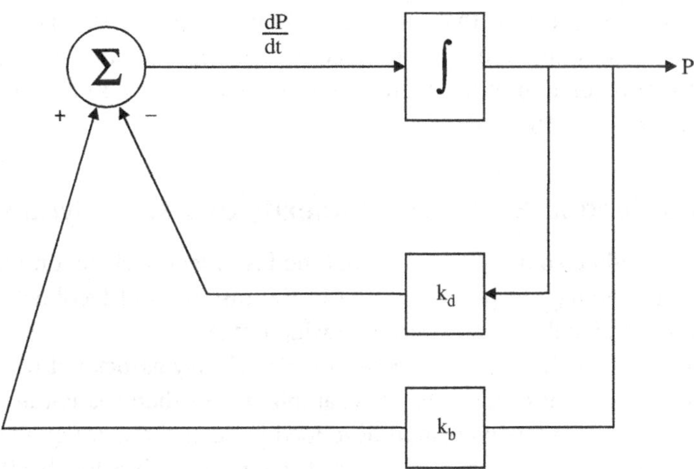

FIGURE 2–9 Signal flow diagram of population growth model.

The death rate is negative feedback regulating population growth. The birth rate is positive inherent feedback; it tends to lead to population instability that is explosive exponential population growth. The relative strengths of these opposing feedback processes (e.g., due to disease, medical intervention, famine, etc.) will determine the overall complexity of the patterns of population dynamics that are observed.

2.4.5 Derivative and integral feedback

In the examples considered so far, it has been assumed that the feedback effect has been directly proportional to the variable that brings about this effect. Other forms of feedback are possible, however. It can be shown that reliance on proportional feedback and control alone can result in delay in achieving the desired regulatory effect, often with oscillations being apparent before the desired steady state is achieved.

One way of improving dynamic response is to incorporate feedback where there is not only a sensing of change in variable X, but also a sensing of its rate of change (dX/dt). There is some evidence that this occurs in the case of carbohydrate metabolism, for instance. In other words, insulin is being secreted not only in response to elevation of glucose concentration, but also to positive rate of change of glucose concentration. The incorporation of such derivative (rate of change) feedback and control brings about a more speedy response within the control loop and a more rapid achievement of the desired regulation.

In addition to proportional and derivative feedback, there are systems in which there appears to be integral feedback. One of the problems with control based on proportional and derivative feedback is that there can be an error in the final steady state that is achieved once the correcting feedback has taken its effect. A means of overcoming this problem is to include control action whereby there is a feedback signal employed which is proportional to the integral between the desired value of the variable being controlled and its actual value. A number of studies have suggested that a number of physiological systems behave as if such integral feedback was in operation. For instance, in an early example Saratchandran *et al.* (1976) proposed that regulation of the thyroid hormones is achieved through a combination of proportional and integral feedback.

2.4.6 Effects of feedback on the complexity of system dynamics

The sections above outline some of the principal modes of feedback action that are found in the complexity of physiology. In practice many of the instances of feedback are even more complicated. Moreover, feedback can result in a wide range.

Changes occurring with feedback processes are also closely associated with the transition from the healthy state to that of disease. For example, type I diabetes is the result of a total failure of the glucose/insulin feedback loop described in Section 2.5.3. Equally, type II diabetes is at least in part the consequence of a partial failure of such a feedback loop, with the parameters involved changing from their normal values.

Feedback is intimately related not only to the manner in which physiological systems are regulated, but also the patterns of dynamic behavior that they exhibit. It can affect stability and speed of response. Some of the behavioral features will be examined in examples that will be considered in later chapters.

2.5 Control in physiological systems

2.5.1 General features

The study of control in physiological systems reveals a range of manifestations of complexity. A central feature is homeostasis at various levels in the hierarchy, from intracellular mechanisms to mechanisms operating at the level of the whole organism. Much of the major focus is related to the internal environment of the intact physiological organism, but control systems also feature prominently in relation to the way we deal with externally sensed information (via the eyes, ears, etc.).

The patterns of regulation and control occurring within physiological systems are many and varied. Static and dynamic equilibrium, linear and nonlinear regulation, weak and highly stable rhythmicity (oscillating systems) are all instrumental in the maintenance of the living state. In most engineering applications of feedback control, the focus is temporal control, studying and seeking to minimize transient errors in the approach to a goal value. In the physiological state, however, in addition to such temporal aspects, control also involves geometric or functional patterns (in the context of neural control) and the minimization of their deviations from normal resting values (Talbot & Gessner, 1973). This involves control action. For example, in the visual system, color and contrast involve spatial rather than time integrals and time derivatives. Equally the maintenance of the set of steady-state operating points for flows and concentrations in the circulatory or respiratory systems provides examples of functional pattern control.

Let us return now to chemical regulation and control within the physiological system and examine some of its dynamic features. A range of regulatory mechanisms is involved, both in the maintenance of the environment within the individual cell and in their aggregation into the behavioral patterns of the entire organism. Some of the major processes occurring within the cell are shown in Fig. 2–10. This is a very simplified representation aimed at illustrating some of the complexities of regulation found within the functioning human organism.

Control is evident at each level. For example, within each and every cell at the lowest level there is both transcriptional and translational control involved in protein synthesis, incorporating genetic effects transmitted via RNA. Feedback features in all these control mechanisms. Proteins may either be incorporated into the cellular structure bringing about structural change or may, as enzymes, be involved in subsequent chemical reactions occurring within the cell. Control is in turn exerted upon cellular activity by feedback mechanisms outwith the cell stemming from hormonal secretions of the endocrine and neuroendocrine glands. The neuroendocrine glands receive stimuli from the brain which in turn received

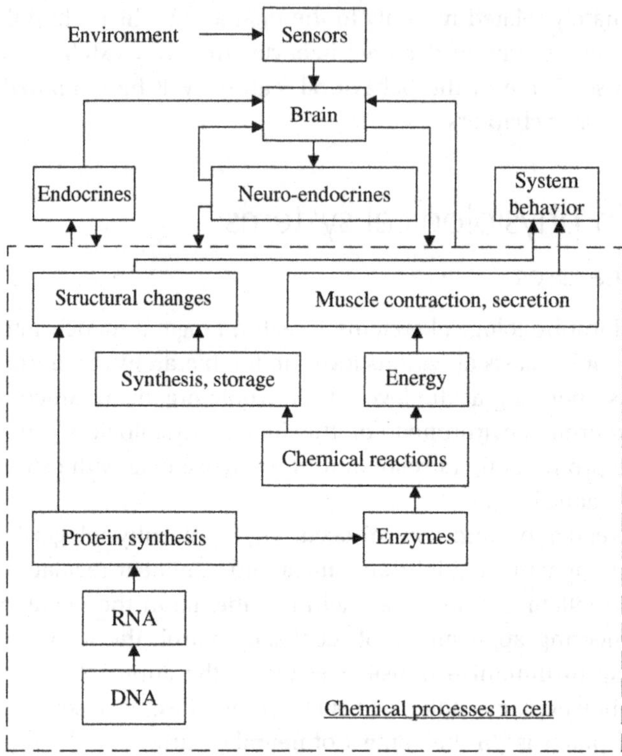

FIGURE 2–10 Major processes occurring within the cell and their integration into total system behavior.

feedback signals from both endocrines and neuroendocrines as depicted in the figure. Brain signals impacting on neuroendocrine activity are also influenced by signals sensed from the external environment as indicated.

2.5.2 Enzymes

The rate of chemical changes in physiological systems is generally controlled by enzymes, which act as biological catalysts. In the simplest enzyme controlled reaction, an enzyme (E) and chemical substrate (S) form an enzyme-substrate complex (X) which in turn decomposes into the original enzyme (E) and the product of the reaction (P). This system of reactions can be represented by the equation:

$$E + S \leftrightarrow X \rightarrow E + P \tag{2.39}$$

Assuming first-order reactions, such that rate of change is directly proportional to the concentration of the ingredients of the reaction, the mass transfer equations for the system are given by:

$$\frac{dE}{dt} = -k_{EX}\ E\ S + k_{XE}\ X \tag{2.40}$$

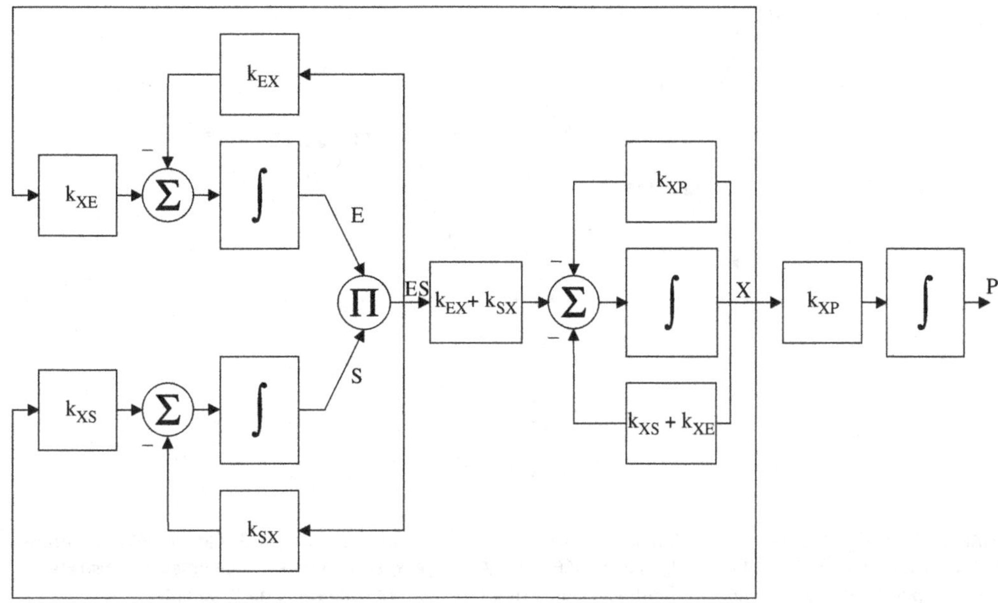

FIGURE 2–11 Signal flow diagram for a simple enzymic reaction.

$$\frac{dS}{dt} = -k_{SX}\ E\ S + k_{XS}\ X \tag{2.41}$$

$$\frac{dX}{dt} = (k_{EX} + k_{SX})\ E\ S - (k_{XS} + k_{XE})\ X - k_{XP}\ X \tag{2.42}$$

$$\frac{dP}{dt} = k_{XP}\ X \tag{2.43}$$

where E, S, X, and P are the quantities of free enzyme, substrate, complex, and product respectively. The k values are the rate constants for the appropriate reactions, so that for instance k_{XP} is the rate constant relating rate of production of product to the quantity of complex.

A signal flow diagram for this system is shown in Fig. 2–11, where the representation adopts the same format as in Figs. 2–8 and 2–9. The symbols Σ and Π represent summation and product respectively. As seen, the dynamics resulting even from this very simple process are complex and nonlinear. For instance, the reversible reaction $E + S \leftrightarrow X$ gives rise to two negative feedback loops tending to regulate E and S. On the other hand the regenerative cycle $E \rightarrow X \rightarrow E$ leads to a positive feedback loop which has a potentially reinforcing effect.

This simplistic treatment has neglected many of the features that occur in more realistic enzymic reactions. For example, reaction rates frequently depend upon the presence of a substance other than enzyme or substrate to activate or inhibit the process. A typical reaction

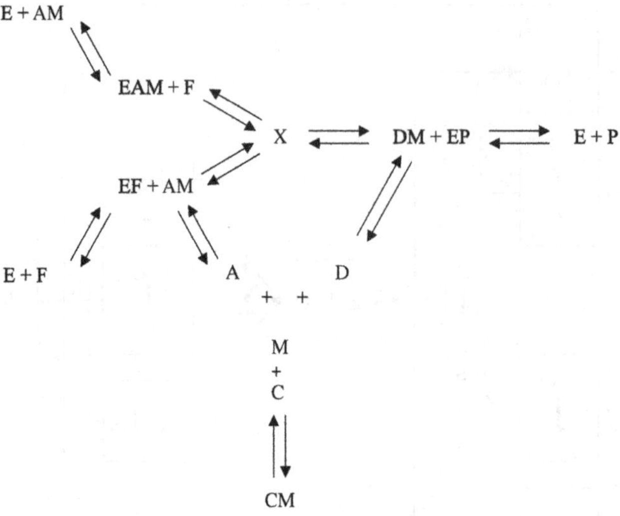

FIGURE 2–12 Phosphofructokinase (PFK) reactions. The nomenclature adopted is: A, ATP; AM, Mg-ATP; C, citrate; CM, ATP-citrate; D, ADP; DM, Mg-ADP; E, enzyme (PFK); EAM, complex; EF, complex; EP, complex; F, substrate (fructose-6-phosphate); M, Mg (magnesium); P, product (fructose 1,6 diphosphate); and X, complex.

involving the enzyme phosphofructokinase which occurs in glucose metabolism is shown in Fig. 2–12. The many pathways available give rise to even more complex patterns of regulatory behavior.

2.5.3 Hormones

Control in such chemical reactions, however, is not confined to the action of enzyme systems. For example, there are a large number of chemical reactions that form a part of glucose metabolism taking place in a manner that are under enzyme control. However, this set of reactions is also controlled by a range of hormones, including insulin, glucagon, adrenalin, cortico-steroids, growth hormone, and the thyroid hormones. Hormones are powerful chemical agents secreted by endocrine glands such as the pancreas and the thyroid gland.

Three types of hormonal action are evident from a control perspective. The first type of action is associated with hormones that act on smooth muscle or other cells to stimulate an effect such as muscle contraction (Fig. 2–13). These are sometimes referred to as kinetic hormones. The consequence of this action is perceived by a neural detector. For example, arterial baroreceptors monitor changes in blood pressure following the secretion of adrenalin from the adrenal medulla. The fact that neural transmission is involved in the feedback pathway from the site of the kinetic action to the particular endocrine gland ensures that within seconds the appropriate changes in hormonal output can occur.

The second type of hormonal action manifests itself in the change in blood concentration of a particular chemical (see Fig. 2–14). Hormones bringing about such action are

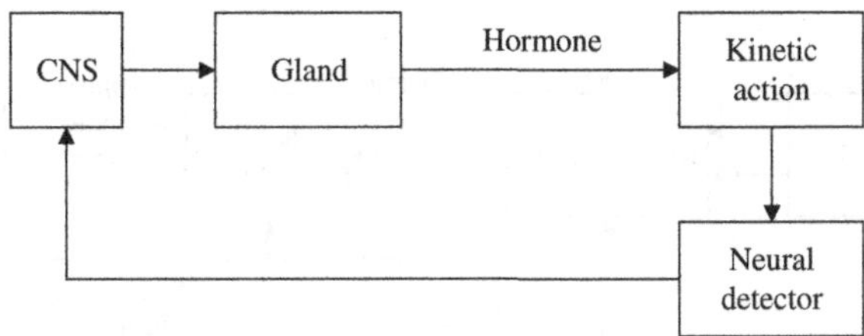

FIGURE 2–13 Hormonal action on smooth muscle or other cells to stimulate an effect such as muscle contraction.

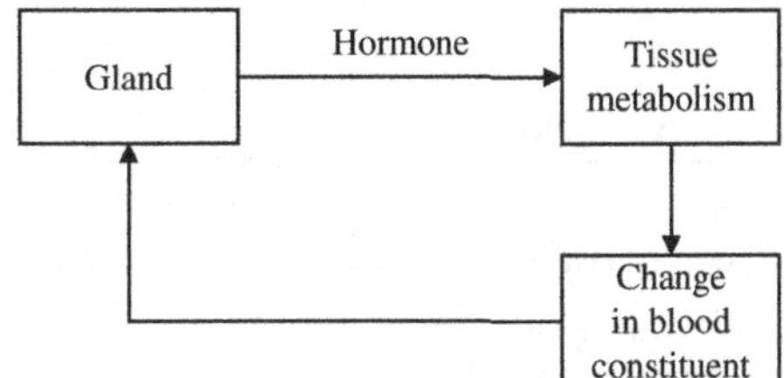

FIGURE 2–14 Hormonal action manifesting itself in the change in blood concentration of a particular chemical.

sometimes referred to as metabolic hormones. For example, insulin secreted in the pancreas brings about a decrease in the level of blood glucose. This may be due either to its direct allosteric effect in an enzyme system or to its mediation of a transport process. By allosteric, we mean that the regulation of the enzyme is by the binding of an effector molecule at a site other than the enzyme's active site. The feedback in this case is chemical, the lower level of blood glucose in the blood perfusing the pancreas being recognized and inhibiting further insulin secretion. The limitation of this type of control stems from the fact that this local chemical feedback has an effective time constant which is typically of the order of tens of minutes.

The third type of hormonal control involves endocrino-kinetic or trophic hormones (sometimes also known as endocrine-kinetic hormones). These are produced by one gland which, in turn, controls the activity of another (see Fig. 2–15). For example, ACTH is a trophic hormone secreted by the anterior pituitary which, in turn, acts upon the adrenal cortex in controlling the rate of secretion of cortico-steroids. The actions of such target gland hormones are complex, multiple, and slow. The effects of cortico-steroids, for instance, are such that their actions on peripheral tissues cannot be monitored by changes in a single blood constituent. It is therefore the concentration of the steroid itself that is used as the feedback signal. Also, the feedback effects are more complex for this type of hormone. Pathways to both hypothalamus and pituitary may be present, affording greater flexibility in the system's response to a particular perturbation. Moreover, target gland activity can change very rapidly in response to a changed external environment. Disturbances such as stress or seasonal changes are detected and fed into the hypothalamus via the central nervous system.

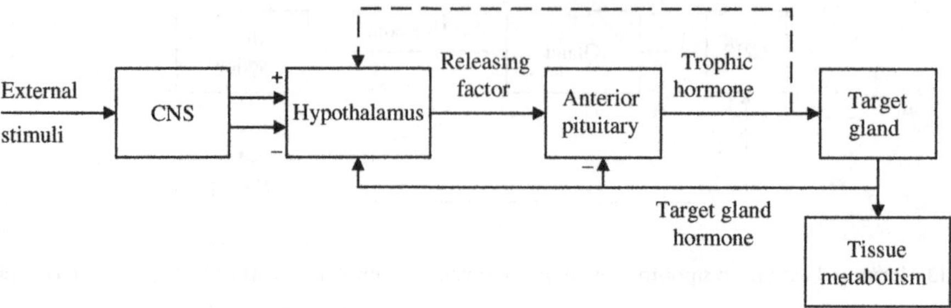

FIGURE 2–15 Trophic (endocrino-kinetic) hormone.

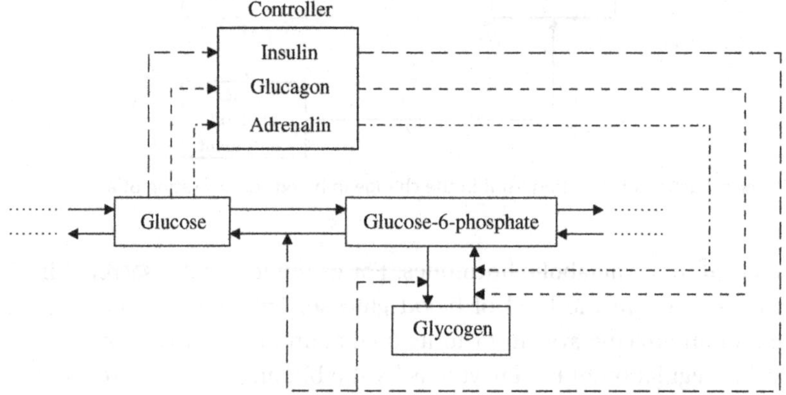

FIGURE 2–16 Hormonal control of chemical reactions.

From a systems perspective, a number of interesting features are apparent if we consider a portion of the liver glucose system. The reactions by which glucose is converted into glucose-6-phosphate and glycogen involve complex enzyme systems. Some of these, in turn, are under hormonal control (see Fig. 2–16). For example, if the blood glucose level is high, insulin is secreted, thus facilitating the conversion of glucose-6-phosphate into glycogen and hence bringing about a decrease in the glucose level. The hormone glucagon, however, is also secreted in response to the same stimuli as applied to insulin. Yet its metabolic effect is in direct opposition of insulin in that it tends to raise glucose levels. Glucagon, however, is more sensitive than insulin and modulates reactions promoted by insulin thereby bringing about better control action.

Here we have an antagonist pair of metabolic hormones acting in a manner parallel to that occurring in locomotion, where muscle extension is achieved by active contraction of an antagonist.

The overall control of the chemical processes of physiology involves the nervous system as well as hormones. Many of these are still not very well understood, though considerable advances in understanding have taken place in some areas; for instance, relating to the vagal control of breathing.

Nevertheless, it is clear that a complex array of control actions is involved in the totality of chemical processes to be found in the intact physiological organism. At a simple level there is strong local control action. This enables many of the chemical processes to be regulated without recourse to higher levels of control. This is due to the fact that chemical reaction rates are generally concentration-dependent, giving rise to inherent negative feedback. This, together with the sophisticated array of enzymic, hormonal, and nervous system mechanisms involving both chemical and neural transmission, provides a degree of flexibility and adaptability that constitutes an excellent example of effectively functioning control.

2.6 Hierarchy

From the foregoing descriptions it is clear that feedback and control in physiological systems offer many examples of functioning complexity. However, in our treatment of feedback and control a further feature of system complexity has become apparent: hierarchy.

The structure of the overall human organism offers itself to analysis in hierarchical terms; from genes, through cellular subsystems, cells, organelles, organs to the intact physiological organism. At each level there is feedback and control action of a variety of modes. Equally each level of organization is aggregated into the next level up in this organizational hierarchy (e.g., cellular subsystems aggregate into cells and organs into the intact organism).

Examining the control of organ systems a number of mechanisms are evident. As we have already seen, in many processes there is strong, local low level chemical control. This is particularly appropriate for the situation in which disturbances to the metabolic process are unlikely to be large in magnitude. On the other hand, for the likes of carbohydrate metabolism where gross perturbations occur daily, through the feeding process, hormonal mechanisms form an integral component of the regulatory process.

We can define a hierarchy of regulatory mechanisms in terms of intrinsic chemical, enzymic, hormonal and neural control. This multitude of controllers ensures that the organ systems and the organism as a whole are able to withstand disturbances normal and abnormal both in terms of magnitude and time scale.

2.7 Redundancy

One more feature that characterizes the complexity of human physiology is redundancy. The most obvious examples of redundancy relate to the provision of pairs of organs: two eyes, ears, lungs, and kidneys. In the case of the sensory organs, this permits an increased sophistication in sensory perception, such as binocular vision. The duplication of lung and kidney function provides the ability to cope with extremes of operating conditions that would tax the single organ. Moreover, the kidney, whilst of prime importance in the regulation of the body's water balance, also has a limited capacity to act as a chemical plant and can therefore provide a limited degree of back-up for the major chemical plant—the liver.

A degree of redundancy is also apparent in the organ control systems. For example, a number of hormonal control loops are involved in the maintenance of blood glucose levels. Glucagon, adrenalin, growth hormone, and cortico-steroids are all capable in several ways of remedying low glucose levels. This is not to say that all these hormones are specific in their action, for many hormones mediate a variety of metabolic effects. Nevertheless, a high level of reliability is afforded in the correction of a deficiency in blood glucose. On the other hand there is only a single control loop capable of lowering elevated glucose levels—the insulin controller. This is, however, a robust controller in the healthy individual, thus offsetting to a degree the absence of any back-up system from a system design perspective.

Redundancy is also apparent in the nervous system. In many instances a small fraction of the available information needing to be transmitted is carried by each of a large number of units. In this way immunity to large scale loss of information is provided, even though small numbers of the central neurons are dying every day.

Organisms with a higher nervous system are capable of responding selectively to a vast number of specific combinations of sensory stimuli. This ability has led to the hypothesis that information from the dense organs is progressively re-coded to higher levels in a less redundant form. Since the transmission lines—the number of fibers in a sensory pathway—are fairly constant, this reduction process would occur in terms of reduced average activity in the sensory centers, that is economy of pulses. Great economy can be achieved by this recoding, providing of course that it occurs with the minimum sacrifice of information.

2.8 Function and behavior and their measurement

From the foregoing sections it is clear that physiological systems exhibit complexity in a variety of forms. The integration of the system components, the manner in which they are interconnected, and the mechanisms by means of which they are regulated and controlled give rise to the functional and behavioral patterns that are to be found in the functioning physiological organism. Fig. 2–1 provided us with one simplified representation of some of this overall physiological complexity. It is these functional and behavioral patterns which are of interest to us as physiological modelers.

However, in order to be able to quantify the dynamic processes and effects that are occurring within the complexity of our physiological systems, we must be able to take measurements. This is where many challenges lie; there are limits as to what can be measured in living organisms. There are constraints, both practical and ethical.

For example, it is generally not possible to take invasive measurements on the organs, nor in the tissues, nor of the secretion of the glands of the intact physiological organism. This has traditionally meant that, in terms of chemical variables in the body, measurements have been limited to those that could be derived from blood, urine, or breath samples. More is now possible, however, due to technological advance. Making use of advanced imaging modalities it is now possible to derive measurements of glucose in the brain, assuming that the organ in question (brain, liver, or kidneys for example) can be precisely identified from the images in question.

At an experimental level, our ability to access and hence potentially understand physiological complexity is limited. We are constrained by measurement technology and methodology as to what may be measured directly (*in vivo*). As far as accessing information regarding other quantities is concerned, the only way forward is by using indirect or inferential methods. This means using models, which will be explained below.

2.9 Challenges to understanding

Physiology is complex and the availability of measurements to access the dynamics of this complexity is limited. It is this tension between complexity and measurement that is one of the major drivers for modeling activity and the manner in which it should be undertaken. As we shall see in the chapters that follow, modeling enables us to maximize the information that can be gained from measurements. It also aids our understanding of complexity. Quantitative models in essence are vehicles for relating our quantitative measurements to features of physiological behavior.

For instance, in the circulatory system we can measure blood pressure and flow rate. If we postulate, in the form of a mathematical model, that pressure is equal to the product of flow and compliance, then measurements of pressure and flow will enable us to make estimates of compliance in the blood vessel under consideration. The measurements may enable us to assume that compliance is constant over a specified range of pressures and flow rates. We could then use this model to explore how changes in vessel compliance, due say to disease processes of arteriosclerosis, would alter these pressure/flow relationships. In this way models can aid our understanding.

This particular example illustrates the idea of a model as a means of indirect or inferential measurement. We cannot directly measure the compliance of a blood vessel. However, we can estimate its value, by inference, from the available measures of pressure and flow and the mathematical relationship between them that we have postulated in terms of the parameter that is in compliance. So models can increase our understanding of physiological complexity. This is one reason why we might wish to develop a model of some aspect of physiology. The following chapter will explore the idea of why we might wish to formulate and use mathematical models, outlining a range of possible purposes for such physiological modeling.

2.10 Exercises and assignment questions

1. Give a summary of some of the main ways in which complexity manifests itself in physiological systems.
2. Feedback is an essential ingredient of functioning physiological systems. Using appropriate diagrammatic representations, illustrate some of the different modalities in which feedback may occur.
3. Describe briefly the ways in which hormones can exert a controlling action in the regulation of physiological systems.
4. List some of the different ways in which the concept of redundancy can be observed in functioning physiological systems.

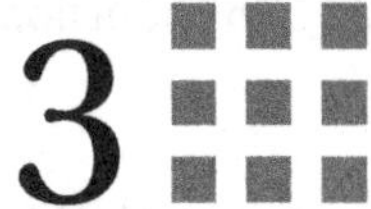

Models and the modeling process

3.1 Introduction

The aim of this chapter is to show what is meant by a model, the variety of models, why modeling (i.e., modeling purpose), and the nature of the modeling process. A number of examples are included to illustrate these fundamental modeling concepts, which constitute the building blocks for the more detailed treatment that will follow in later chapters.

3.2 What is a model?

What do we mean by the term model? In essence, a model is a representation of reality involving some degree of approximation. Models can take many forms. They can be iconic, symbolic, or analagous. They can be quantitative or qualitative. For the most part, however, this book will focus upon mathematical models; quantitative representations of physiological reality that are expressed in the form of mathematical equations, whereby these equations provide a symbolic representation of the physiology.

Our mathematical model will only be an approximation to reality though. For instance we can formulate equations that represent the way in which blood is pumped around the circulatory system by the heart. A completely realistic model would require us to represent mathematically every molecule of the heart muscle. This would clearly result in a totally intractably large set of equations. In practice we are likely to adopt a simpler formulation that might include the four heart chambers (ventricles and atria) as entities in our model, but excluding detail at the molecular level. In this way our model is an approximation of the true situation, but one that is likely to be of sufficient detail for the purpose for which we are building the model (see below).

Reverting to the model classification of iconic, symbolic, or analagous, an anatomical dummy is an iconic model, being representative in form of the human body, but not in terms of full working detail. Nevertheless it is helpful as a teaching aid in anatomy. A length of flexible tubing provides an analog of a blood vessel and may, for instance, be useful on the basis of its parameters in understanding some of the dynamics of viscous fluids including blood. In the context of medical research, a mouse or rat is another example of an analogous model. For instance it might be assumed that pharmacokinetic and/or pharmacodynamic effects observed in that animal might be scaled up to indicate what might be expected to be observed in the human subject.

Introduction to Modeling in Physiology and Medicine. DOI: https://doi.org/10.1016/B978-0-12-815756-5.00003-5

Other classifications of models exist. We can have conceptual, mental, verbal, physical, statistical, logical, graphical models etc. For instance, a standard textbook of physiology may typically include a description of the inhalation of air that results in oxygen entering the bloodstream via the lungs, and the corresponding removal of carbon dioxide that is exhaled back into the atmosphere. That description may well extend to some thousands of words. This is, in fact, a verbal model of part of the respiratory system. It is a qualitative model. In contrast, many of these physiological processes could equally well be captured by a quantitative, mathematical model, such as by the adoption of an appropriate set of differential or algebraic equations. It can be represented by two different modeling modalities; a verbal description or a mathematical one. Each though will just be an approximation of the full complexities of the respiratory dynamics and their controlling mechanisms.

In another modality, we can use a graph to represent the way in which a drug is cleared from the bloodstream. Suppose that the process can be approximated as a first order one, which is the rate of clearance of the drug is directly proportional to the concentration of the drug in the bloodstream. We could represent this process by plotting graphically the concentration of the drug on the y-axis against time, plotted on the x-axis. The result would be an exponentially decaying curve (one which if plotted semi-logarithmically would yield a straight line). This exponential plot of drug concentration versus time can be regarded as a graphical model of the drug clearance process.

Thus, in essence, a model is a representation of the physiological system of interest. Deriving the model is a transformation process, as depicted in Fig. 3–1, where this transformation is brought about using an appropriate modeling methodology which will be described later.

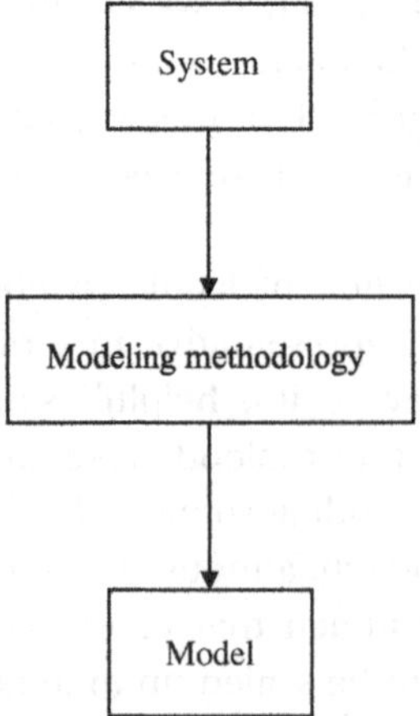

FIGURE 3–1 Modeling methodology: a means of transforming a system into a model. *Adapted from Carson, E. R., & Cobelli, C. (Eds.). (2014).* Modelling methodology for physiology and medicine *(2nd ed.). Amsterdam: Elsevier.*

3.3 Why model? The purpose of modeling

The way in which we formulate a model, and the degree of detail that is incorporated into it, are determined principally by its intended purpose. From a basic scientific perspective, the four general types of purpose for which models are developed correspond to the four classical categories of descriptive, interpretive, predictive, and explanatory models.

The descriptive use of mathematical models is the expression of quantitative relationships in terms of equations. These equations provide a concise and economic description of the system under consideration, and facilitate ease of analysis and handling of data. For example, if a variable in a system is directly proportional to another (say a relationship between pressure and volume), then a linear equation relating the two is more concise and easy to handle rather than a graphical or verbal description.

Models can also be used for interpreting experimental results. For example, a single exponential decay, as a mathematical expression, provides a compact representation of data that approximate to a first-order process. A first-order process, for example, meaning the rate of loss of a substance is directly proportional to the quantity or concentration of that substance in the pool or compartment from which it is being lost. This could apply to the rate of drug clearance from the bloodstream. In other words, if a sequence of blood samples were analyzed for the concentration of a particular drug, the changing drug concentration over time could be approximated as an exponential decay, the rate constant of which provided information regarding the rate of clearance of that drug. In a similar fashion, a mathematical model can be used to interpret data collected as part of a lung function test.

A third general category of purpose is prediction. Here we are addressing the question as to how a system would respond to a stimulus or to a change in the system. An example would be predicting how the human organism, or a specific physiological organ system, might respond to the injection or infusion of a drug. Suppose that a mathematical model has been formulated which includes the processes that are affected by a particular drug. The model can then be used, in simulation mode, by applying a stimulus to it corresponding to the drug injection or infusion. In the model, one can observe how the drug concentration in the body changes with time, or how blood pressure changes over time following the administration of a drug that is designed to reduce blood pressure.

In another situation, one might use a model to simulate the way in which the time course of urea and creatinine in the bloodstream changes as a result of a change in kidney function. This kidney function change would typically be simulated by changing the value of an appropriate parameter in the model.

Finally, models can be used for explanatory purposes. For example, if the model's parameters correspond to explicit physiological processes or effects, then changes in observed behavior can be interpreted in terms of changing parameter values. This means that the model can be used to help provide a physiological explanation for observed dynamic effects. In this way a model can, for instance, be used to help understand how changes in physiological parameters can bring about changes in the uptake of substances, including drugs, by various body organs.

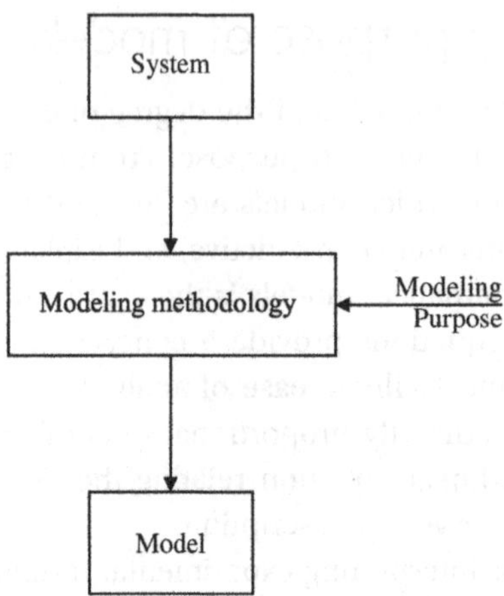

FIGURE 3–2 The purpose of the model: driving the modeling process. *Adapted from Carson, E. R., & Cobelli, C. (Eds.). (2014).* Modelling methodology for physiology and medicine *(2nd ed.). Amsterdam: Elsevier.*

The purpose of the modeling process is a key driver of good modeling methodology, as shown in Fig. 3–2. Whilst descriptive, interpretive, predictive, and explanatory are the four classical categories of model purpose, more specific purposes can be identified in the context of physiological systems. These include: aiding understanding, hypothesis testing, inferential measurement, teaching, simulation, and experimental design.

For example, competing models, constituting alternative hypotheses as to the nature of the physiological processes taking place, can be examined to determine which are compatible with physiological or clinical observation. Moreover, a model of the relevant metabolic processes, when taken together with measurements of a metabolite made in the bloodstream, can be used to infer the value of the metabolite in the liver. This use of models as a means of indirect measurement can avoid the need to resort to invasive techniques that might be difficult or ethically problematic.

Models can also assist in the educational process. Through simulation of a model, students can be exposed to a wider range of physiological and pathophysiological situations rather than what would be possible in a conventional laboratory setting. Models can also play an important role in relation to experimental design. For example, if the number of blood samples that can be taken from a patient in a given period of time is limited, models can be used to determine the times at which blood samples should be extracted in order to obtain the maximum information from the experiment. This is particularly relevant in the context of pharmacokinetic or pharmacodynamic effects.

Models can also play key roles in relation to diagnosis and patient management. For instance, if a model includes a parameter that corresponds to the rate of uptake of a substance by the liver, then estimation of that parameter can provide a diagnostic indicator of the effectiveness of that uptake process, and for example whether there might clinically be some degree of obstruction. Equally, model simulation can be used to compare the likely dynamic effects resulting from different routes of drug administration or of different dosage levels in terms of their expected effects on key clinical variables.

3.4 How do we model? The modeling process

In developing a mathematical model, two fundamentally distinct approaches are possible.

The first is based on experimental data and is essentially a data-driven or black-box modeling approach. In essence, this means seeking quantitative descriptions of physiological systems based on input/output descriptions derived from experimental data collected on the system. These are mathematical descriptions of data that only correspond implicitly to the underlying physiology.

These data-driven models are particularly appropriate where there is a lack of knowledge concerning the underlying physiology. Also, they are appropriate where an overall input/output representation of the system's dynamics is all that is needed; that is, there is no need to know specifically how the physiological mechanisms gave rise to such input/output behavior.

The second approach, modeling the system, provides a clear contrast, as an attempt to explicitly represent the underlying physiology. However, as has already been indicated, any model is by definition an approximation of reality, so any model of a physiological system will involve a greater or lesser degree of approximation to the underlying physical and chemical processes. These models offer the advantage that features of dynamic behavior that are observed can be directly related to physiological parameters and variables that are explicitly incorporated into the model.

Regardless of the approach to modeling that is adopted, there is one common feature. A good model is dependent upon a clear and appropriate methodology being adopted for the modeling process. This provides the means by which the physiological system of interest is transformed into the model, as outlined in Fig. 3–1. The nature of this methodology in relation to the model building or formulation process is shown below.

3.5 Model formulation

In the case of a data-driven or black-box model, the methodology adopted in the model building process is summarized in Fig. 3–3. A full account is given in Chapter 4, Modeling the data. In essence, however, a model structure is chosen to provide an input/output description of the data obtained from the physiological system. There are several methods for formulating such models including time series analysis, transfer function analysis, etc. The degree of complexity of the mathematical formalism is chosen to be consistent with the intended purpose for the model. The parameters of this mathematical expression are then determined in the identification process as outlined in Section 3.6.

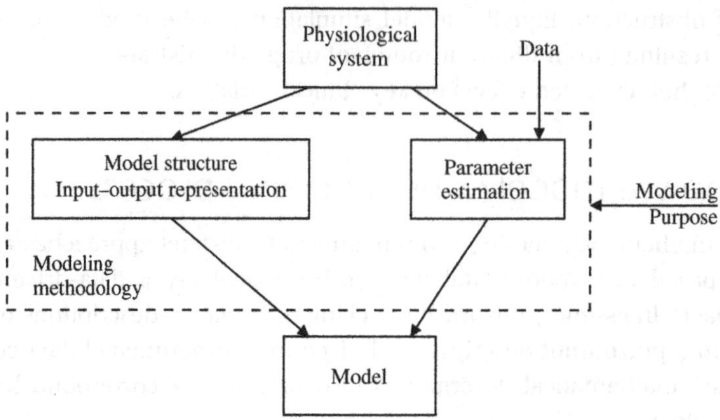

FIGURE 3–3 A methodological framework for modeling the data. *Adapted from Carson, E. R., & Cobelli, C. (Eds.). (2014).* Modelling methodology for physiology and medicine *(2nd ed.). Amsterdam: Elsevier.*

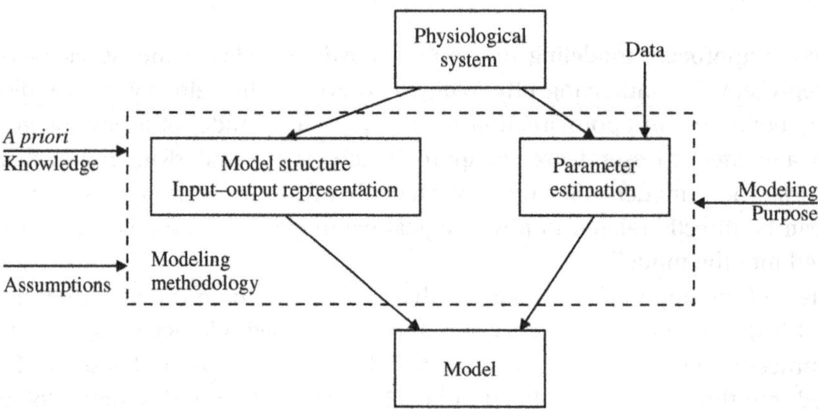

FIGURE 3–4 A methodological framework for modeling the system. *Adapted from Carson, E. R., & Cobelli, C. (Eds.). (2014).* Modelling methodology for physiology and medicine *(2nd ed.). Amsterdam: Elsevier.*

The modeling methodology for the situation where the model seeks to provide an explicit representation of the underlying physiology is depicted in Fig. 3–4. Here there are essentially three distinct components of the modeling process. These are formulation of a conceptual model, the mathematical realization of that conceptual model, and then the solution of the model to give the required relations between the variables of interest (this last component being achieved once the model identification process is complete). This approach to modeling is considered in detail in Chapter 5, Modeling the system.

The conceptual model is based on the physiological knowledge that it is proposed to have been represented by the model. However, since any model is an approximation of the underlying reality, a number of simplifying assumptions will need to be made. These can typically be categorized under the headings of aggregation, abstraction, and idealization.

Aggregation is typified by lumping together all of the extravascular space of the human organism and treating it as a single lumped compartment. Another example would be treating the kidney as a single lumped entity as opposed to providing distinct model representation of the different types of nephron in the kidney.

Abstraction is the degree to which only certain aspects of a system are considered in a model. For example, in modeling blood glucose regulation, the bloodstream is regarded as containing only glucose and the hormones involved in its regulation. In such abstraction other features that are important but do not relate directly to glucose regulation are neglected.

For the purpose of formulating a model, structures or behavior that is difficult to describe or treat can be approximated by simple idealized ones. For example, in a metabolic system the injection of a metabolite can be regarded as being instantaneously distributed throughout the system although, in fact, the distribution takes a finite time.

Having produced the conceptual model, equations are then constructed to provide a mathematical description of the components of the conceptual model. In a dynamic model, these equations will typically describe the manner in which one or more physiological variable varies as a function of time. The constants in the mathematical models are the parameters that specify the relationships between variables.

In general, we shall want to be able to obtain explicit relationships between variables and/or parameters in the model—in other words to solve the model. Within the model the relevant variables are commonly connected through complex mathematical relations such as differential equations. Obtaining the required explicit relations is commonly done by computer implementation of the model. In some cases the structure and parameter values of the model may be known *a priori*. The model can, therefore, be solved and its validity further assessed as discussed in Section 3.7. Often, however, there is uncertainty in the structure of the model and/or its parameters. In this situation, the solution is not possible directly, and identification of the model from input/output data must be carried out as described below.

3.6 Model identification

In order to complete the transformation from system to model as shown in Fig. 3–1, we need to have specified the structure of the model and to have fully determined all the parameters corresponding to that structure. In other words, the model needs to be complete so that it can be solved. In practice our model may not be complete because some of the parameter values are unknown. This may be the case regardless of whether our model is data-driven or an explicit model of the underlying physiology. At this stage an integrated identification framework is needed as shown schematically in Fig. 3–5.

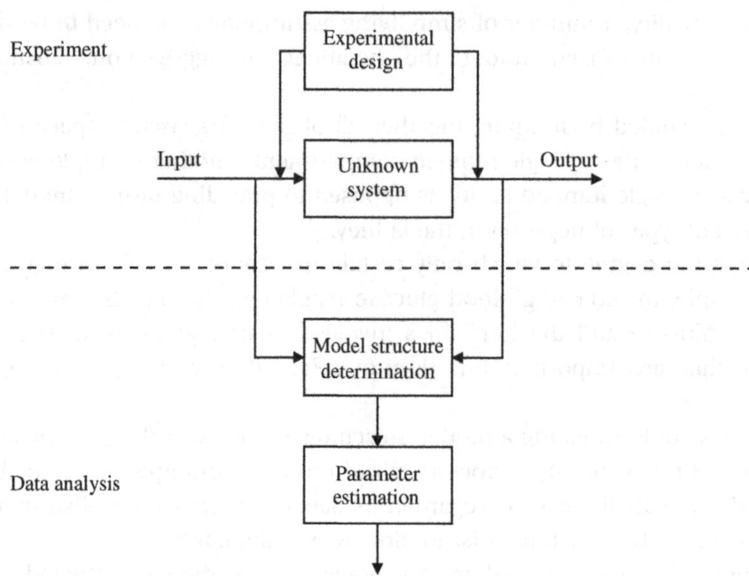

FIGURE 3–5 Model identification. *Adapted from Carson, E. R., & Cobelli, C. (Eds.). (2014).* Modelling methodology for physiology and medicine *(2nd ed.). Amsterdam: Elsevier.*

Solving this identification problem requires data. Sometimes data may be obtained from the intrinsic dynamics of the physiological system. Examples include electrophysiological signals relating to brain, muscle, or cardiac function. Such situations tend to be the exception, however, so in practice experiments usually need to be designed. These experiments involve applying some stimulus to the system and observing the dynamic response of one or more of the variables. Clearly, the input/output data from the experiment must contain that part of the model with the unknown parameter values. Typical input stimuli might involve the application of a trace quantity of a metabolite in the case of a metabolic system or a step change in the fraction of an inspired gas in the case of the respiratory system.

In the identification process, the first issue addressed is whether the experimental data are sufficiently rich enough to enable unique estimates to be made of all the unknown parameters. This is known as the identifiability problem. Problems of identifiability arise where there is a mismatch between the complexity of the model and the richness of the data. That is, the model is too complex (too many unknown parameters) for the experimental data, or the data are not sufficient for the model provided. In such cases, there is the need to explore whether the model might, in a manner that retains validity, be reduced (simplified), or whether the experimental design might be enriched. This could be achieved, for example, by making measurements of an additional variable.

If the model is uniquely identifiable, assuming perfect data, it is possible to proceed directly to estimating the unknown parameters. A range of techniques exist and will be discussed in detail in later chapters. Those that are most widely adopted use an approach based on linear or nonlinear least squares estimation.

3.7 Model validation

Validating a model is in the essence examining whether it is good enough in relation to its intended purpose. This assumes of course that it has been developed in such a way that it can reasonably be tested. A model is by definition an approximation of reality. As such, it will not be able to reproduce all the features of behavior that would be found in the real system. The question is can it reproduce those that matter in terms of how it is to be used in practice?

When working with a number of competing, candidate models, the validation process consists of determining which of these models is best in relation to its intended purpose. We can, therefore, define a valid model as one that has successfully passed through all the tests that form the validation process.

An important point to stress at the outset is that the validation process is very much an integral component of the modeling process overall. It is an activity that takes place whilst the model is being built as well as once the completed model is available. The issue of validity testing during the process of model formulation involves considering issues, such as whether the various ways in which the model is an approximation of reality are reasonable (given the intended purpose of the model).

Once the model is complete and all its parameters have been specified, the validation process can be summarized as shown in Fig. 3–6. Again it is important to emphasize that the validity issue is intimately related to model purpose. In other words, it is specific to the particular problem being dealt with. We are examining whether all the necessary ingredients are included in our model. For example, we might want to use our model to test the hypothesis that particular changes in vascular blood flow were linked to particular changes in the elastic properties of certain arteries. Suppose these changes in blood flow corresponded to the change from a healthy state to one of disease. We would then expect that by changing the elasticity parameters in a way which we knew corresponded to the disease process, we would see dynamic patterns of blood flow that were observed in the disease state. In other words the model would be reproducing the changes in blood flow pattern that we were expecting. This test provides evidence to support the validity of the model.

More generally we can say that, dependent upon purpose, some features of the model and the system output (i.e., experimental output data) must correspond sufficiently for the same input (an acceptably small difference between them). In relation to the domain of intended validity, we are testing whether our model is credible.

The basic approach when validating a single model is to compare the behavior of the model and the system, based upon appropriate output features of response. Any discrepancy between the system and model output should be analyzed for plausibility of behavior.

In some situations, as previously discussed, formal parameter estimation techniques will have been employed in developing the model. In such cases there are additional quantitative tools available for use in the validation process. These include examining the residuals of the mismatch between model and system response, and also examining the plausibility of the estimates of the parameters, where the parameters have a clear physiological meaning (e.g., elasticity of arteries).

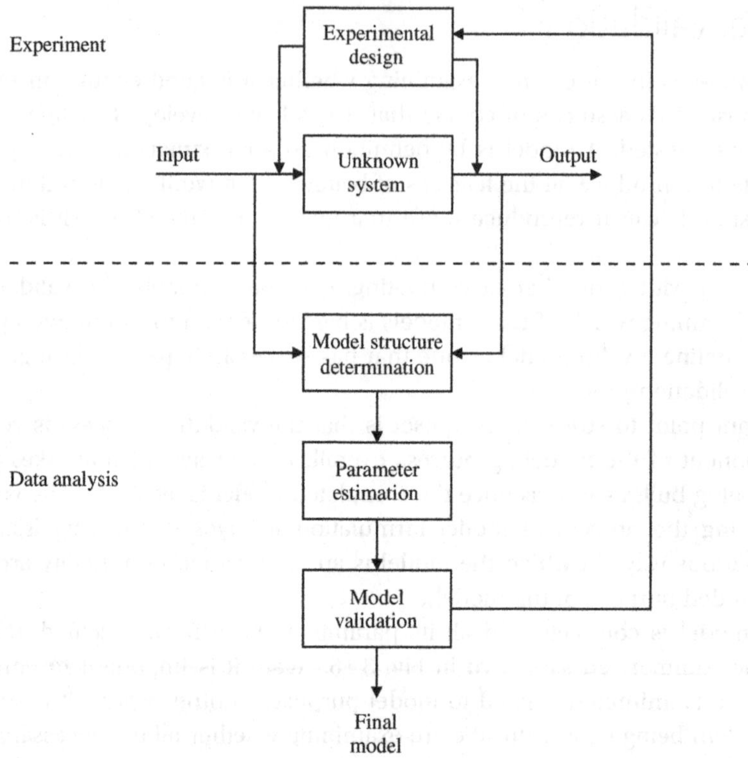

FIGURE 3–6 Validation of the complete model. *Adapted from Carson, E. R., & Cobelli, C. (Eds.). (2014). Modelling methodology for physiology and medicine (2nd ed.). Amsterdam: Elsevier.*

When choosing between a number of competing models, the choice can be aided by examining the parsimony of the models. In other words, if two models are equally acceptable in terms of their features of response, and are also both plausible, then the preferred model would be the one with a smaller number of parameters or the lowest order. In terms of models represented by differential equations, this would be the one that had the smaller number of such equations. In terms of curve fitting, a linear model would be of lower order than a quadratic or cubic model. Further details of such testing, and of the validation process overall, can be found in Chapter 10, Model validation.

As we have seen, there are many comparatively simple cases of structured, dynamic physiological processes that can be modeled with sets of first-order differential equations. In some situations it is possible to solve these equations analytically. However, there are many situations in which this is either not possible or not practicable. Hence an alternative approach is required.

The first difficulty is the particular problem of obtaining solutions for equations that are of a nonlinear form. The second difficulty relates to the tedious task of solving large sets of equations, corresponding to physiological processes where a large number of variables need to be incorporated into the model. Both of these factors may substantially hinder progress. In such situations it may be desirable to use digital computer simulation methods, given their widespread availability and ever-increasing computing power/cost ratio. The aim of the next section is to examine this arena of computer simulation and to provide an account of the what, when, why, and how of simulation.

3.8 Model simulation

Having derived a complete model, including estimating all unknown parameters and checking its validity in relation to its intended domain of application, it is now possible to use it as a simulation tool. Computer simulation involves solving the model (i.e., the equations that are the realization of the model) in order to examine its output behavior. This might typically be the time course of one or more of the system variables. In other words we are performing computer experiments on the model.

In fact simulation can be used either during the process of model building or with a complete model. During model building, simulation can be performed in order to clarify some aspects of behavior of the system or part of it in order to determine whether a proposed model representation seems to be appropriate. This would be done by comparison of the model response with experimental data from the same situation. Simulation, when performed on a complete, validated model, yields output responses that provide information regarding system behavior; information which, depending on the modeling purpose, assists in describing the system, predicting behavior, or yielding additional insights (i.e., explanation).

Why carry out computer simulation? The answer is that it might not either be possible, appropriate, convenient, or desirable to perform particular experiments on the system (e.g., it cannot be done at all, it is too difficult, too expensive or too dangerous, it is not ethical or it would take too long to obtain results). Therefore, we need an alternative way of experimenting with the system. Simulation offers an alternative that overcomes the previously mentioned limitations. Such experimenting can provide information that is useful in relation to our modeling purpose.

In order to perform computer simulation we first need a mathematical model that is complete in terms of all its parameters being noted and with initial conditions specified for all the variables. If the model is not complete in the sense of there being unspecified parameter values, then formal parameter estimation techniques must be employed to obtain such estimates (this estimation process will be described in Chapter 7, Parametric modeling—the identifiability problem). The model is then implemented on the computer. This assumes that the model equations cannot be, or are not being, solved analytically and that a numerical solution of the system is needed.

Therefore, the model is solved on the computer, this solution process producing the time course of the system variables. In technical terms, the computer implementation is done either by using standard programming languages or specialist simulation packages.

A number of practical issues arise in order to achieve successful simulation. These will be considered in some detail in Chapter 11, Case studies, where one of the case studies gives particular emphasis to the practical aspects of computer simulation.

An emerging branch of computer simulation is the *in silico* clinical trials (ISCT). In almost every other industrial sector where the cost of de-risking for mission-critical products is an issue, virtual prototyping has become the best solution; but for biomedical products the use of computer modeling and simulation is still somehow limited. There are signs that this situation is changing, albeit not as quickly as it could. Of course, all this is driven by the growing capability of simulation technologies to accurately simulate complex physiological processes; in particular the area of diabetes modeling has shown significant advancements in the last 20–30 years.

ISCT, defined as the use of individualized computer simulation in the development or regulatory evaluation of a medicinal product, medical device, or medical intervention (Viceconti *et al.*, 2017), aims to recreate the concept of an *in vivo* trial using an *in silico* approach, where a large number of individual patients is modeled. The key word is individual, that is, to enable realistic *in silico* experimentation one has to describe the inter-individual variability observed in the population under study. In other words average models are not appropriate since their capabilities are generally limited to predicting a population average that would be observed during a clinical trial. Given the large inter-individual variability, an average model approach cannot describe realistically the variety of individual responses to a treatment. Thus, to enable realistic *in silico* experimentation, e.g., in diabetes, it is necessary to have a simulation model equipped with a cohort of *in silico* subjects that sufficiently represent the well-known large inter-individual variability of key metabolic parameters in the diabetes population.

Another, often underappreciated, advantage of ISCT is based on the assumption that *in vivo* clinical trials work fine, and the motivation for replacing them is related to the risk, duration, or cost that the trial involves; but not to their ability to provide a reliable answer on the safety and/or efficacy of a new biomedical product. Unfortunately, this is not always the case. The prime mover of ISCT is the shortcomings of the current *in vivo* trials. The problem is the numerosity (intended as the number of patients enrolled in the trial), or better its relationship with the level of acceptable risk. In other words to test rare but not so rare events in a clinical trial one has to enroll a very large number of subjects and observe them for a long period of time with resulting increasing exponential costs. Here ISCT can play an important role because it is relatively easy to test a large number of extreme individuals, that is, belonging to the tails of the parameter probability distributions, in computer simulation.

After years of rejection, some regulators are now beginning to consider a possible role for computer modeling and simulation in the certification process for biomedical products. The US Food and Drug Administration (FDA) is leading this trend, worldwide. An important landmark was the acceptance by FDA of the type 1 diabetes simulator developed by the Universities of Virginia and Padova (Kovatchev *et al.*, 2009) which was accepted by FDA as a substitute to animal (pre-clinical) trials for testing certain insulin treatments including the artificial pancreas. This simulator and its recent developments (Dalla Man *et al.*, 2014; Visentin *et al.*, 2018) will be discussed in detail in case study eight to show the power of ISCT in artificial pancreas and glucose sensor research as well as in testing novel insulin formulations.

3.9 Summary

This chapter has provided an outline of the nature of models and the processes by which they are formulated, identified, and validated. The manner in which computer simulation can be performed has also been briefly discussed. All these ingredients form the basis of the modeling processes that will be described in greater detail in the following chapters. This book is designed to describe and promote the essence of modeling methodology. Readers who wishes to pursue particular aspects in greater detail should refer to our companion volume (Carson & Cobelli, 2014) and in our earlier work (Carson *et al.*, 1983). Having now outlined the principles of the modeling process, the next two chapters will provide a wide range of model building examples. Chapter 4, Modeling the data starts this process, focusing on models that are designed to provide descriptions of experimental data.

3.10 Exercises and assignment questions

1. Describe what is meant by the concept of a model of a physiological system and discuss the various forms that a model might take. Give an illustration of some of these forms in the context of physiology.
2. Discuss the range of possible purposes for which a model of a physiological system might be formulated. Give an example in each case.
3. Describe the process of formulating a model of a physiological system, discussing the way in which the particular formulation might be influenced by the availability of physiological knowledge.
4. Using appropriate examples, discuss how the processes of model formulation, model identification, and model validation are inter-related.
5. How might the process of simulation be useful in the physiological or clinical context?

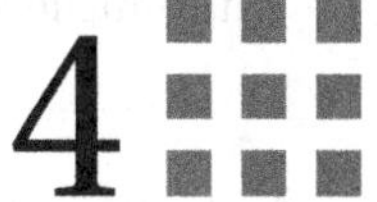

Modeling the data

4.1 Introduction

So far, we have talked in general terms about the modeling process and the need for good modeling methodology. In this chapter and the one that follows, we shall demonstrate how models can be developed as a means of representing physiological dynamics. This chapter focuses upon data modeling. Chapter 5, Modeling the system, will concentrate on models as representations of the underlying systems that give rise to physiological data.

We need to consider first of all what we mean when we say modeling data, and when such approaches are applicable. Having discussed these issues, we shall go on to discuss some of the ways in which data modeling can be performed. This will be done by means of a range of examples, considering the different ways in which physiological data can arise.

4.2 The basis of data modeling

Data modeling provides us with a means of representing the variables that characterize physiological dynamics as captured by the measurement process. These models are in essence black box models and as such are mathematical representations of our measurement data, having only implicit correspondence to the underlying physiology that gives rise to these measures. This contrasts with the approaches considered in Chapter 5, Modeling the system, where the models formulated are in their various ways explicit representations of the physiology.

These data models do, however, provide us with concise descriptions of physiological data. As such they offer advantages over purely graphical representations. Whilst the graph does have an immediate visual appeal, a mathematical description is concise and can be used as a basis for generalization from the specific data in terms of characterizing patterns or features contained within the data.

4.3 The why and when of data models

So when is it appropriate to adopt data models? First, they are useful in situations where there is a lack of knowledge of the underlying physiology; for example, as is the case in a number of areas of electrophysiology and neurophysiology. These are situations where the very complexity of the system in question gives rise to uncertainty in structure and behavior.

Introduction to Modeling in Physiology and Medicine. DOI: https://doi.org/10.1016/B978-0-12-815756-5.00004-7

A second possibility is an overall input/output description of the system dynamics, without needing to understand specifically how the physiological mechanisms gave rise to such input/output behavior. Typical situations include the control of a physiological variable; for example, by means of drug therapy.

4.4 Approaches to data modeling

In essence, there are two major types of approaches to data modeling. These correspond to treating the system as being either deterministic or stochastic. In both cases the output measurement will generally be corrupted by noise, but in the first case the system output is a deterministic function of the input. In the stochastic case the output is not a deterministic function of the input due to some unmeasurable disturbances (noise) within the system itself.

The stochastic modeling strategy is particularly important in electrophysiology and neurophysiology. However, this approach is not the subject of our book. Readers who are interested in the data modeling of such physiological signals should consult texts such as Marmarelis and Marmarelis (1978), Bruce (2000), or Westwick and Kearney (2003). This book will be focusing on the deterministic system approach.

The measurements that provide us with the physiological data can take a variety of forms. First, the measurements can be discrete or continuous. Usually the variables themselves are continuous, but we can choose whether to collect the data as sample values at discrete time points or as continuous signals. For instance, the blood glucose concentration of a diabetic patient is a continuous signal, but typically such a patient might decide to measure his or her blood glucose concentration, say between four and eight times a day, corresponding to events such as meal times and bedtime. So although the variables are continuous, we have a set of data corresponding to values measured at discrete times. On the other hand, we may have continuous data in the form of signals monitoring the cardiac status of a patient with heart or circulatory problems over a period of 24 hours.

Equally, even if the data are continuous, we can elect to analyze them as such or as a set of discrete data obtained by sampling the continuous record (usually at equispaced time intervals for convenience of analysis). On the other hand, whilst discrete data points are usually analyzed using discrete time methods, it is possible to convert such discrete data to continuous form by the adoption of appropriate interpolation and extrapolation methods.

The emphasis in this chapter is placed upon time domain data. Examples of frequency domain approaches are included though, together with means by which time domain data can be converted into frequency domain forms. For more in-depth treatments of frequency domain approaches to data modeling, readers should consult works such as Marmarelis and Marmarelis (1978) and Westwick and Kearney (2003).

Our discussion of approaches to data modeling will be grouped into four categories. These correspond to different types of physiological and clinical situations. The first, considered in Section 4.5, focuses on situations in which we are interested in a single, measurable variable that arises as a spontaneously occurring signal. Examples would include body temperature, urine potassium and electrical rhythms in the gastrointestinal tract.

Section 4.6 again focuses on a single variable, but this time on a signal that occurs as a direct response to some form of perturbation to the physiological system in question. The monitoring of the blood glucose concentration of a diabetic patient in response to a particular regimen of insulin injections would be one example of this case. Others could include evoked potential responses and the time course of arterial pressure in response to an antihypertensive agent administered in order to bring about its reduction.

The third case, treated in Section 4.7, considers the causal relationship between two variables. Examples include the relationship between glucose and insulin in the normal subject and the impact of water loading on the level of sodium in urine.

Whilst this third category has focused on situations whereby the relationship between the two variables is something that arises naturally within the normally functioning human organism, the last case, discussed in Section 4.8, deals with a situation in which there is explicit control. Examples include glucose/insulin relationships in the diabetic patient and the relationship between blood pressure and dosage of sodium nitroprusside administered to bring about its control.

The final example of data modeling that we shall discuss is the impulse response. This will be examined from a deconvolution perspective. We can either reconstruct the unknown input (e.g., hormone secretion) when we know the system output and the impulse response, or determine the impulse response when both input and output of the system are known. An example of such an impulse response might be the circulatory transport function of an organ from knowledge of arterial and venous concentrations of an intravascular indicator.

4.5 Modeling a single variable occurring spontaneously

As will be demonstrated in this and the sections that follow, a wide range of methods and techniques are available for providing quantitative descriptions of physiological and medical signals.

The first case to be considered is a single variable which can be regarded as having arisen spontaneously. In reality the signal that is observed will be the result of a range of interacting physical and chemical processes within the human body that give rise to the particular manifestation. Regarding the single variable as having arisen spontaneously is in effect a means of distinguishing this signal, essentially of endogenous origin, from one which arises as the explicit effect of having administered some test signal to the organism; for instance, a drug injection or the application of an electrical stimulus to the body.

The examples presented have been selected to demonstrate that the quantitative analysis (that is to say data modeling) is applicable across the broad range of physiological signals. Equally they show that such modeling can be applied to signals that are either nonperiodic, or are periodic with frequencies that range from cycle times measured in seconds to those of one or more months.

4.5.1 Temperature

The cyclic change in body temperature during the menstrual cycle of a woman is a typical example of a biological rhythm. The basic pattern of the rhythm is broadly consistent from one month to the next, though some variation occurs from one monthly cycle to the next in any particular individual. As a first approximation it is reasonable to model such temperature data by a sine wave function.

An example of the temperature variation in a woman, not taking oral contraceptives, measured orally on waking each morning is shown in Fig. 4–1. These are some of the data that were collected over a period of almost 1 year, with measurements being omitted on 94 days. They were modeled by the sine wave function given by (4.1) (McIntosh & McIntosh, 1980):

$$y = A_1 \sin\left[\frac{6.2832(A_2 + t)}{A_3}\right] + A_4 \tag{4.1}$$

where y is the dependent variable (temperature), and t is the independent variable (time). Parameter A_1 corresponds to the peak amplitude of the sinusoidal temperature variation, and A_2 is a parameter for synchronizing the phases of the model and the data. Parameter A_3 modifies the period or distance between peaks of the sinusoidal temperature variation, whilst A_4 represents the displacement of the central mean value from zero. Fig. 4–1 depicts the first 90 days of the experimental data, together with the fitted data model. In this case the fitted parameter values, together with their standard deviations (SD), are: $A_1 = 0.191°C \pm 0.011°C$, $A_2 = 12.85 \pm 0.47$ days, $A_3 = 27.07 \pm 0.07$ days, and $A_4 = 36.56°C \pm 0.008°C$.

Another approach, (which has been adopted in the analysis of this time series of temperature values) has been to calculate the correlation between all pairs of values of the

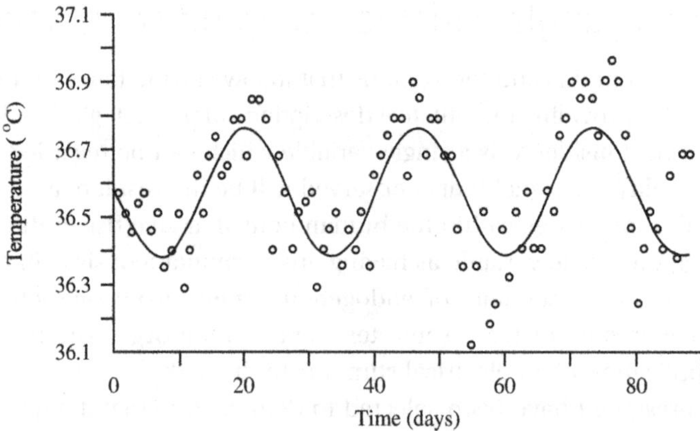

FIGURE 4–1 Temperature variation in a woman, not taking oral contraceptives, measured orally on waking each morning. Experimental data corresponding to the first 90 days are shown, together with the fitted data model. *Adapted from McIntosh, J. E. A., & McIntosh, R. P. (1980).* Mathematical modelling and computers in endocrinology. *Berlin: Springer-Verlag.*

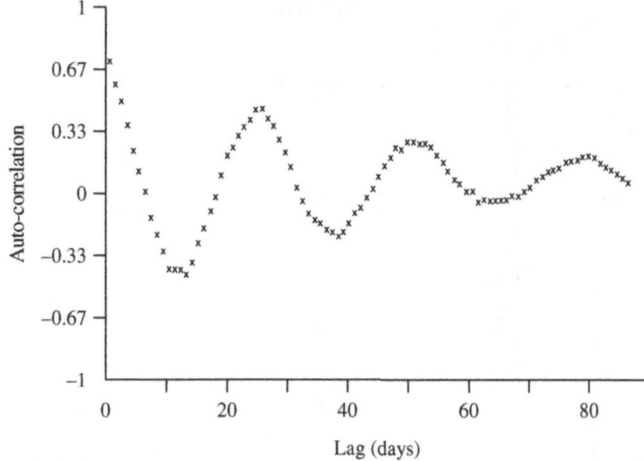

FIGURE 4–2 Correlation analysis on the temperature data showing the relationship between autocorrelation and lag. *Adapted from McIntosh, J. E. A., & McIntosh, R. P. (1980).* Mathematical modelling and computers in endocrinology. *Berlin: Springer-Verlag.*

temperature variable, *the autocorrelation coefficient,* at each different lag or time interval apart (McIntosh & McIntosh, 1980). This correlation coefficient is calculated from the covariance of the same variable displaced in time. The *correlogram* provides a graphical representation of the variation of correlation as a function of the lag. As previously discussed, if there is more than a single rhythm present in the time series, then a corresponding number of peaks will be found in the correlogram. Correlograms of time series displaying obvious cyclicity may not provide new information since they tend to closely mirror the rhythm of the data. Peaks may also occur at harmonics of the basic frequencies, and this can be confusing when interpreting the results obtained.

Performing this correlation analysis on the temperature data considered in this example results in the relationship between autocorrelation and lag as shown in Fig. 4–2. In the analysis, all values of lag up to a maximum corresponding to 170 days were included.

The values of the correlation coefficients between pairs of measurements separated by a range of lags or time intervals varied in a sinusoidal manner which clearly reflected the dominant cyclicity of the temperature data. The peak in the autocorrelation function at a lag of approximately 27 days shows that there was a mean correlation of 0.33 between all measurements separated by this interval. Equally, a correlation also existed between observations that were 54 days apart, and so on.

An alternative means of analyzing these rhythms is to describe them as the sum of an arbitrary number of sine waves of different frequencies, phases and amplitudes. A model consisting of a sum of sine waves is known as a *spectral representation.* From the spectral representation one can construct a *spectral density function,* which is a graph showing the contributions of each frequency to the observed process. This spectrum is the Fourier transform of the auto-covariance function from which autocorrelations are calculated. Carrying

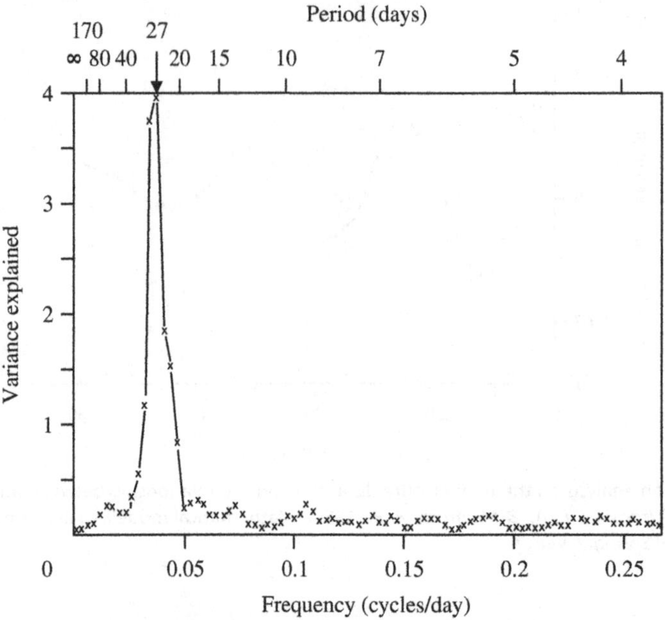

FIGURE 4–3 Spectral density function of the daily temperature data. *Adapted from McIntosh, J. E. A., & McIntosh, R. P. (1980).* Mathematical modelling and computers in endocrinology. *Berlin: Springer-Verlag.*

out this transformation for our example of the temperature data yields the spectral density function shown in Fig. 4–3 (McIntosh & McIntosh, 1980). The contributions of the different frequencies to the total variance about the mean of the data are represented as a function of the frequencies. In this figure the data are also expressed as periods. From this plot it can be observed that most of the variance is explained by a process with a period between 26 and 28 days.

4.5.2 Urine potassium

A second example relates to a series of measurements of the potassium concentration in a patient's urine. In our example, the data were collected once a day from a road traffic accident patient who remained in an intensive care unit for 27 days. A time series plot of the data is shown in Fig. 4–4.

The reference range for urine potassium concentration is 40–120 mmol/L. The time series plot shows two outliers (highlighted by circles), which may have arisen due to errors in measurement. These could be removed by changing their actual values to their expected values. However, physiologically large changes can occur. Hence it may be difficult to determine whether these experimental values are due to poor measurement technique or physiological changes. For this reason, the values were left unchanged. Moreover, there were three missing values, which were set to their expected values (Flood & Carson, 1993).

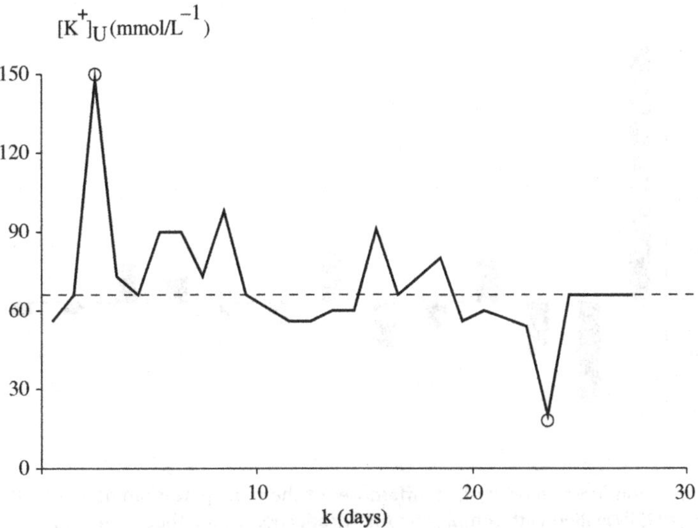

FIGURE 4–4 Time series plot of urine potassium. *Adapted from Flood, R. L., & Carson, E. R. (1993).* Dealing with complexity: An Introduction to the theory and application of systems science *(2nd ed.). New York: Plenum.*

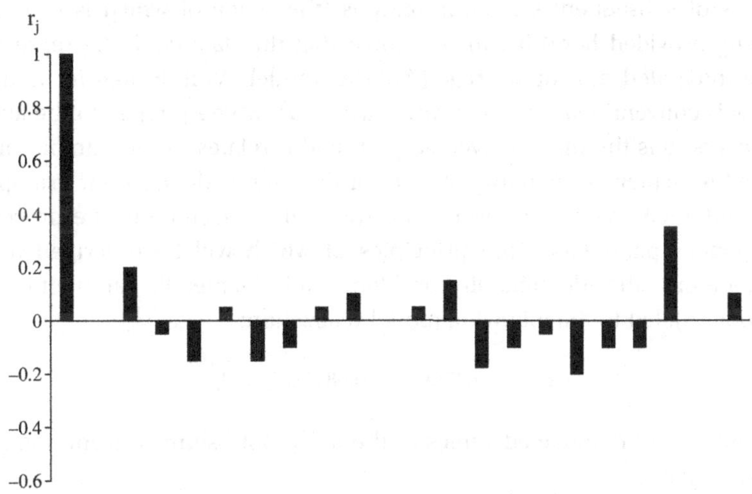

FIGURE 4–5 Correlogram of the urine potassium data. *Adapted from Flood, R. L., & Carson, E. R. (1993).* Dealing with complexity: An Introduction to the theory and application of systems science *(2nd ed.). New York: Plenum.*

The correlogram of the raw data is presented in Fig. 4–5. The autocorrelation function r_j clearly damps out slowly. This implies nonstationarity of the series which is not obvious from the basic time series data. Hence, the first differences of the series were taken. The autocorrelation function r_j of this is shown in Fig. 4–6.

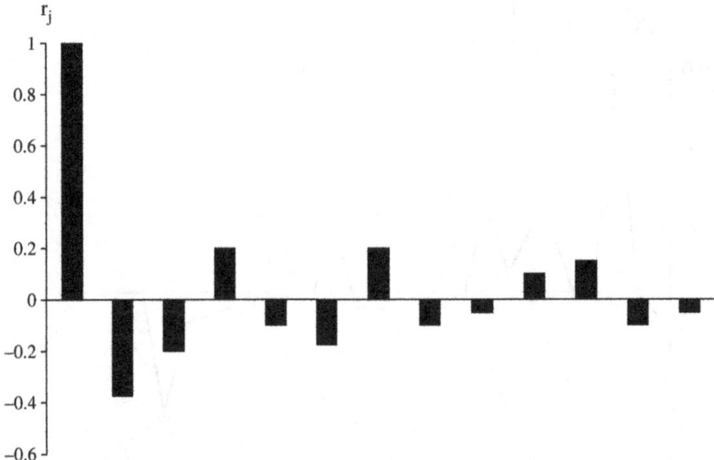

FIGURE 4–6 Autocorrelation function of the first differences of the urine potassium data. *Adapted from Flood, R. L., & Carson, E. R. (1993).* Dealing with complexity: An Introduction to the theory and application of systems science *(2nd ed.). New York: Plenum.*

On the basis of subsequent statistical analysis (the scope of which is beyond the basic exposition being provided here) it can be shown that the data could be represented by an autoregressive integrated moving average (ARIMA) model. As indicated in Section 4.7.2, an ARIMA process is conventionally written ARIMA(p, d, q), where p refers to the autoregressive part of the process, q is the moving average part, and d relates to the number of differences that are needed to achieve stationarity of a set of time series data. In our example here, the ARIMA model adopted was of the form ARIMA(2, 1, 0). Carrying out the processes of estimating this model's parameters (the principles of which will be described in Chapter 7: Parametric modeling—the identifiability problem, and Chapter 8: Parametric models—the estimation problem), led to the following model realization:

$$x_t = -0.6476x_{t-1} - 0.6817x_{t-2} + U_t \tag{4.2}$$

where the x values are the modeled values of the urine potassium concentration at the daily times of measurement.

This example illustrates how ARIMA modeling can be used in fitting time series data. In practice, however, this modeling approach can be difficult when the number of data points is comparatively low. In this case there were 27 clinical data points. General experience is that a time series of at least 50–100 values is needed if the errors in estimating the parameters of the ARIMA model are not to be unacceptably large. This modeling approach would be more applicable in situations where there was online patient monitoring with frequent sampling, rather than with the more restricted regimen of daily data derived from laboratory results.

4.5.3 Gastrointestinal rhythms

The third example returns to a case of rhythmic data, namely the electrical rhythms of the gastrointestinal system. This is a domain that has not received as much attention as, for instance, nerve-axon electrical potentials or the field of cardiac pacemakers. Reasons for this include the fact that smooth muscle (such as is found in the digestive system) does not have the dimensions and properties which lend them to easy measurement, unlike the physiological cellular measurements on nerve axons; nor are there specialized areas of tissue corresponding to the cardiac pacemaker concepts. Nevertheless, there is increasing interest in the role of these gut electrical rhythms, both in the healthy subject and in the disease state, an interest which is advanced by the use of models as a vehicle for aiding description and understanding of these phenomena.

Spontaneous electrical rhythms occur in all parts of the digestive tract below the middle of the stomach. These rhythms are commonly called slow waves. A schematic representation of the gastrointestinal tract, together with typical frequencies recorded in man, is given in Fig. 4–7 (Linkens, 1979). The frequency and wave shape of the slow waves varies considerably between the organ and the species being studied. For example, the canine stomach has narrow pulse-like waves of approximately 0.08 Hz, whereas the human stomach produces square-like waves of approximately 0.05 Hz. Fig. 4–8 shows typical recordings from normal and diverticular-diseased colons. In the case of disease, there is a tendency for these waves to have a component higher in frequency than normal. Equally, colonic waveforms are seen to be nearly sinusoidal with the occurrence of considerable variation in amplitude.

In terms of modeling these data, one widely adopted approach has been to represent them in terms of Van der Pol type dynamics as given by (4.3) which is in effect a coupled oscillator model:

$$\frac{d^2x}{dt} - \epsilon(\alpha^2 - x^2)\frac{dx}{dt} + \omega^2 x = 0 \tag{4.3}$$

in other words, a model of the form of a second order differential equation.

This equation as a model of the data has considerable advantages in that its three parameters ϵ, α, and ω approximately determine the wave shape, amplitude, and frequency of the nonlinear oscillation. These are the primary parameters under consideration in this slow wave modeling. Equally this equation has been treated extensively in nonlinear differential equation studies.

In order to produce a representation of the whole 240 cm of the small intestine, it is necessary to adopt up to 100 oscillators linked in a chain with each being represented by an equation of the form of (4.3) (Linkens, 1979).

4.5.4 Hormonal time series

Plasma concentrations of hormones exhibit cyclic behaviors which can range from seasonal to circadian to ultradian (hours) to rapid (minutes). It is worth noting that while seasonal

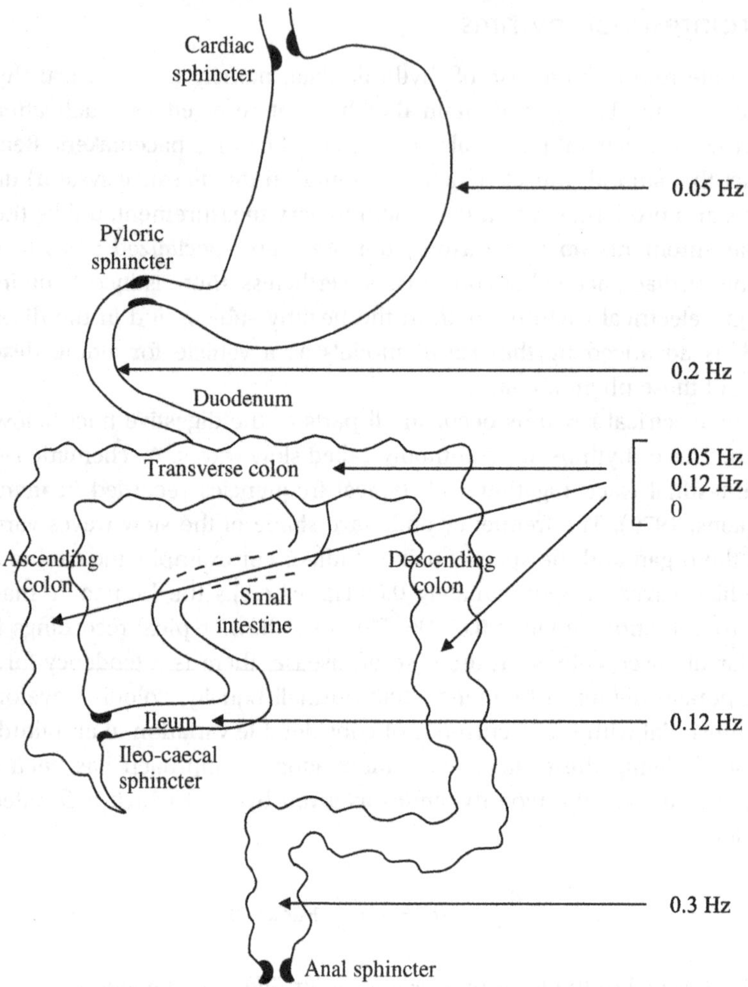

FIGURE 4–7 A schematic representation of the gastrointestinal tract, together with typical frequencies recorded in man. *Adapted from Linkens, D. A. (Ed.) (1979).* Biological systems, modelling and control. *Stevenage: Peter Peregrinus Press.*

and circadian rhythms have been known for some time, it is only since the 1970s and 1980s (with the advent of very sensitive radioimmunoassay methods) that both ultradian and rapid patterns have come to be understood. Three examples of hormonal time series are shown. Fig. 4–9 shows plasma cortisol concentration over a 24 hours window with uniform 15 minutes sampling: the circadian trend is shown by the dashed line and we can see on top of that the ultradian oscillations of smaller amplitude and period (3–5 hours). Fig. 4–10 shows C-peptide (a hormone secreted by the pancreas equimolarly with insulin, but not degraded by the liver) concentration in plasma measured every 10 minutes for 24 hours in a normal

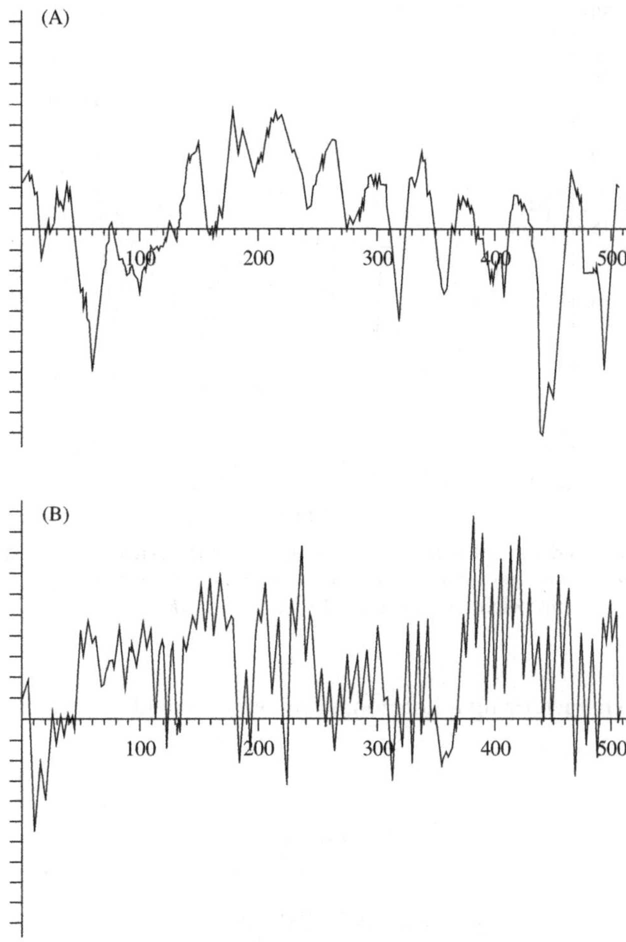

FIGURE 4–8 Typical recordings from (A) normal and (B) diverticular-diseased colons. *Adapted from Linkens, D. A. (Ed.) (1979).* Biological systems, modelling and control. *Stevenage: Peter Peregrinus Press.*

(upper panel) and a type 2 diabetic (lower panel) subject. Ultradian oscillations with a period of 90–180 minutes are apparent in the normal subject while the diabetic subject time series appears much more irregular. Fig. 4–11 shows an example of rapid oscillations: plasma C-peptide is sampled for 3 hours every 2 minutes, and 5–15 minutes oscillations can be seen. In both Figs. 4–10 and 4.11 the associated glucose oscillations are shown in the lower panels, (which will be commented on in Section 4.7.1).

The hormonal time series usually consists of a finite number of samples $\{y(t_k)\} = \{y(t_1), y(t_2), \ldots, y(t_N)\}$ where the generic sample $y(t_k)$ is related to the concentration $c(t_k)$ by

$$y(t_k) = c(t_k) + v(t_k) \tag{4.4}$$

where $v(t_k)$ is the measurement error at time t_k.

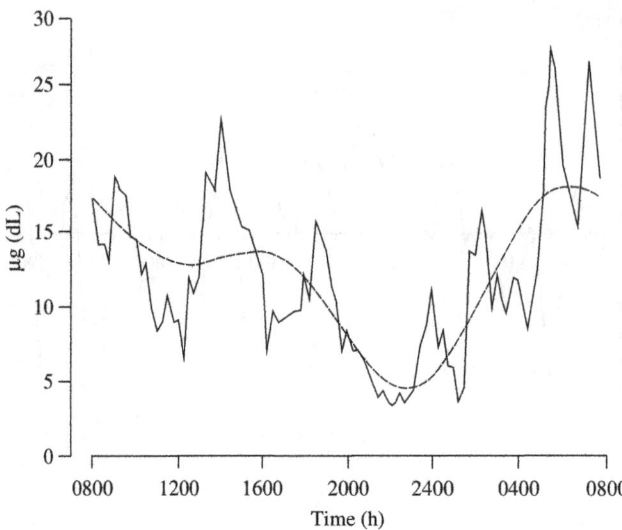

FIGURE 4–9 Time series of cortisol concentration measured every 15 min for 24 h in a normal subject. *Adapted from Van Cauter, E. (1990). Computer assisted analysis of endocrine rhythms. In G. Forti, V. Guardabasso, D. Rodbard (Eds.).* Computers in endocrinology: Recent advances *(pp. 59–70). New York: Raven Press.*

A first means of characterizing a hormonal time series could be in terms of its mean and variance:

$$\mu = \sum_{k=1}^{N} \frac{y(t_k)}{N} \tag{4.5}$$

$$\text{var} = \sum_{k=1}^{N} \frac{(y(t_k) - \mu)^2}{N - 1} \tag{4.6}$$

This has sometimes proven to be a useful representation. For example, it has enabled it to be shown that luteinizing hormone (LH) secretion in women is more variable in the luteinizing than in the follicular phase. However, this mean and variance model does not provide insight into the pulsatility features of the series, such as the number of secretory events and their amplitudes.

The recognition and analysis of peaks is not easy. For instance, one has to detect which are the true peaks and which are the spurious ones (due to measurement error). It is worth noting that classic pattern recognition techniques such as those used for QRS detection of ECG signals or for spike detection of EEG cannot be employed, given the nature of the data and the irregularity of secretory events. One possibility would be to recognize as true peaks only those whose levels are sufficiently greater, for example, three SD, than their previous minimum (Fig. 4–12). This rough model, however, can be criticized in a number of aspects. For example, it is very sensitive to outliers and does not take advantage of the future history.

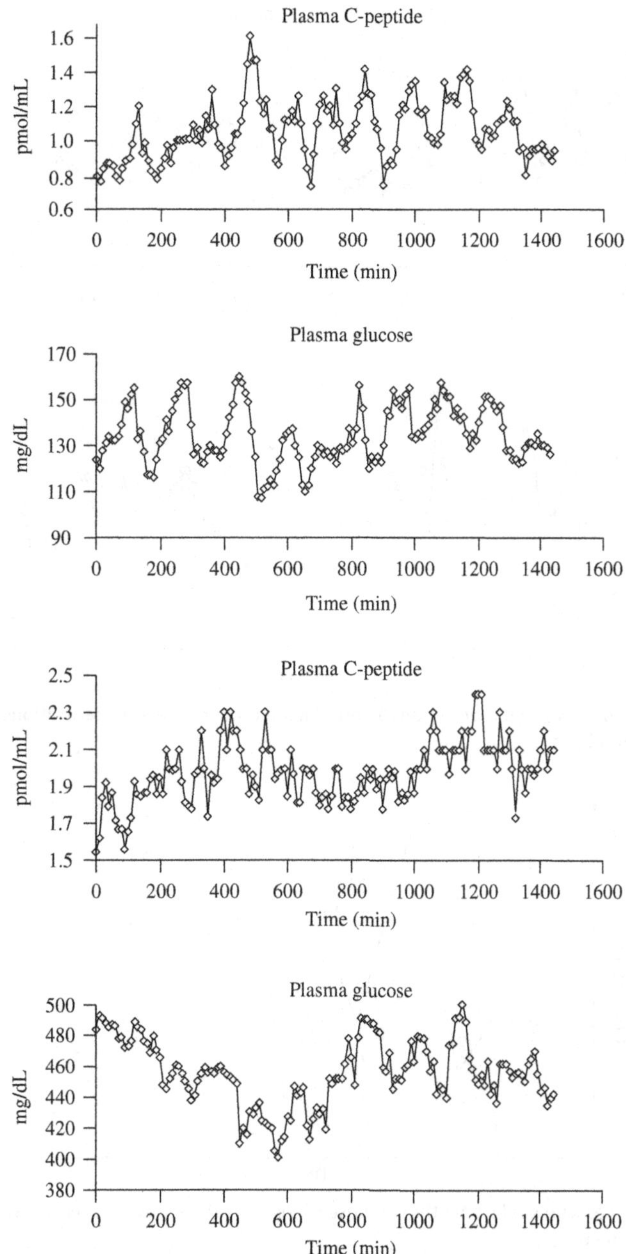

FIGURE 4–10 Time series of C-peptide (*upper panel*) and glucose (*lower panel*) concentrations measured every 10 min for 24 h in a normal subject. *Adapted from Sturis, J., Van Cauter, E., Blackman, J. D., & Polonsky, K. S. (1991). Entrainment of pulsatile insulin secretion by oscillatory glucose infusion.* Journal of Clinical Investigation, 87, *439–445.*

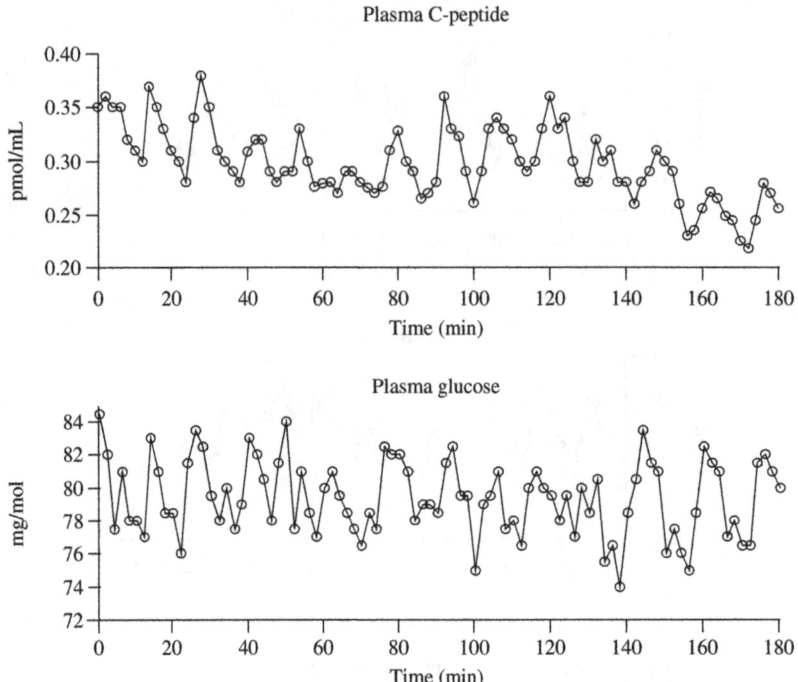

FIGURE 4–11 Time series of C-peptide (*upper panel*) and glucose (*lower panel*) concentrations measured every 2 min for 3 h in a normal subject.

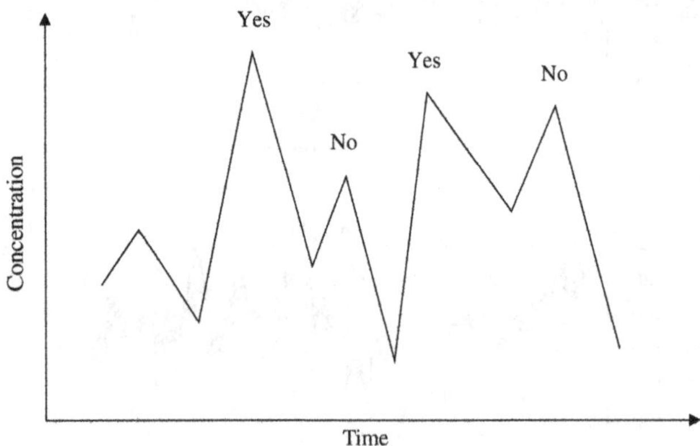

FIGURE 4–12 Recognition as true peaks only those whose levels are sufficiently greater, for example, three SD, than their previous minimum.

An interesting algorithm that was specifically developed for ultradian oscillations is ULTRA (Van Cauter, 1988). The idea is to polish the series by eliminating it from nonsignificant variations. A variation is assumed to be significant if it is sufficiently elevated, that is, greater than ρSD (where ρ is a parameter and SD is the standard deviation of measurement error), with

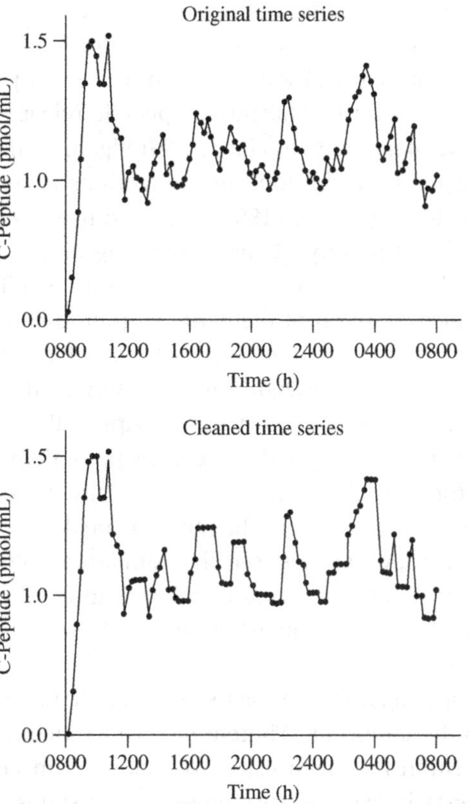

FIGURE 4–13 Performance of the algorithm. *Adapted from Van Cauter, E. (1990). Computer assisted analysis of endocrine rhythms. In G. Forti, V. Guardabasso, D. Rodbard (Eds.).* Computers in endocrinology: Recent advances *(pp. 59–70). New York: Raven Press.*

respect to the previous data point. More specifically, if $y(t_{k+1}) > y(t_k)$, then the increment is significant if $y(t_{k+1}) - y(t_k) > \rho SD$. If $y(t_{k+1}) < y(t_k)$, then the decrement is significant if $y(t_k) - y(t_{k+1}) > \rho SD$. Thus if the series has an increasing trend and one encounters a nonsignificant increment or a nonsignificant decrement, then either, respectively, one does nothing or maintains the value at the previous levels. The same applies if the series exhibits a decreasing trend and one encounters, respectively, a nonsignificant trend or a nonsignificant increment. An example of the algorithm performance is shown in Fig. 4–13. Clearly the critical point of this algorithm is the choice of ρ, but one easily appreciates that the detection of peaks is much easier on the polished series. However, in many situations where pulses are brief, small in amplitude, and irregular; peak detection is difficult.

Another widely used approach to study hormone pulsatility from plasma concentration time series is to look for cycles by time series spectral analysis, that is, by computing the autocorrelation function or Fourier transform (Veldhuis, Carlson, & Johnson, 1987; Veldhuis & Johnson, 1988). Unfortunately, spectral analysis is hard to apply when small length and noisy data sets are considered; in addition, it does not handle cycles whose timing is inherently irregular, which is the most common situation (Merriam & Wachter, 1982). Finally, since both peak detection and spectral analysis ignore the morphology of the pulse, they cannot detect changes in the pattern of hormone episodic release which characterize some physiological and pathophysiological states (Pincus, Mulligan, *et al.*, 1996).

A more recently developed powerful tool for the analysis of hormonal time series is the approximate entropy algorithm (Pincus, 1991). Approximate entropy provides a model-independent measure of the regularity of the underlying secretion process by calculating the logarithmic likelihood that patterns in the time series are similar on the next incremental comparison. Notably, such a notion of regularity is quite different from that usually considered in engineering, where, for a signal, regularity is meant as being synonymous with smoothness. The approximate entropy algorithm summarizes the time series into a single nonnegative number; ApEn: the higher the value of ApEn, the more irregular is the process. Approximate entropy is not intended to replace peak detection or spectral analysis, but is complementary to them. In fact, approximate entropy discerns changes in the pulsatile behavior that are not reflected in changes in peak occurrences or amplitudes. Moreover, approximate entropy focuses on the similarity between pulses and nearly ignores the quiescent intervals of the secretory release, thus relaxing the spectral analysis requirement of a dominant set of frequencies at which some patterns within the time series are repeated.

The approximate entropy algorithm appears well-suited to the clinical need of distinguishing the healthy from the abnormal. Therefore since its inception in the early 1990s, the approximate entropy algorithm has been extensively applied in endocrinology to study the pulsatility of many hormones in various pathophysiological states (e.g. Hartman *et al.*, 1994; Meneilly, Ryan, Veldhuis, & Elahi, 1997; Pincus, Gevers, *et al.*, 1996; Pincus, Mulligan, *et al.*, 1996; Schmitz *et al.*, 1997). Such a great interest in approximate entropy is motivated by the fact that many pathological or prepathological states are associated with an enhanced secretion disorder which ApEn was found able to successfully measure. For instance, in Hartman *et al.* (1994) time series of growth hormone (GH) plasma concentration were considered in normal and acromegalic subjects. The average value of ApEn in the normal subjects was shown to be lower than that in the pathological ones, suggesting that the pathology is characterized by an increased disorder of the secretion process.

Briefly, ApEn index can be defined as follows. Let $\{y(k)\} = \{y(1), y(2), \ldots, y(N)\}$ denote the N-size time series from which we want to calculate the ApEn index. Let r (a real) and m (an integer) be the two given positive parameters. In order to compute ApEn, let us first form the sequence of vectors x(1) through x(N − m + 1), where each x(i) is defined by:

$$x(i) = [y(i), y(i+1), \ldots, y(i+m-1)], \quad i = 1, 2, \ldots, N-m+1 \tag{4.7}$$

Vector x(i) contains m consecutive samples of the time series {y(k)}, commencing with the i-th point.

Define the distance d[x(i),x(j)] between vectors x(i) and x(j) as the maximum difference in their respective scalar components:

$$d[x(i), x(j)] = \max_{k=1,\ldots,m} |y(i+k-1) - y(j+k-1)| \tag{4.8}$$

Now compute, given r, for each $i \leq N - m + 1$ the number:

$$C_i^m(r) = \frac{\#\text{ of } j \text{ for which } d[x(i), x(j) \leq r]}{N - m + 1} \tag{4.9}$$

$C_i^m(r)$ values measure, within a tolerance r, the frequency, or regularity, of patterns similar to a given pattern of window of length m. Next, define $\Phi^m(r)$ as the average value of ln $C_i^m(r)$:

$$\Phi^m(r) = \frac{1}{N - m + 1} \sum_{i=1}^{N-m+1} \ln C_i^m(r) \tag{4.10}$$

Finally, define the ApEn index as:

$$\text{ApEn} = \Phi^m(r) - \Phi^{m+1}(r) \tag{4.11}$$

It is possible to demonstrate that ApEn measures the logarithmic likelihood that runs of patterns that are close (within a tolerance r), for windows of m observations remain close for windows of $m + 1$ observation. The greater the likelihood of remaining close (i.e., the regularity), the lower the value of ApEn.

ApEn depends on two positive parameters: m, an integer, and r, a real. While m gives the length of the compared runs, r represents the tolerance which determines if the runs are close enough. The choice of m and r is usually done by criteria based on statistical considerations and obviously influences the value of ApEn. To appreciate better the influence of m and r let us consider Fig. 4–14 where a portion of the time series {y(1),

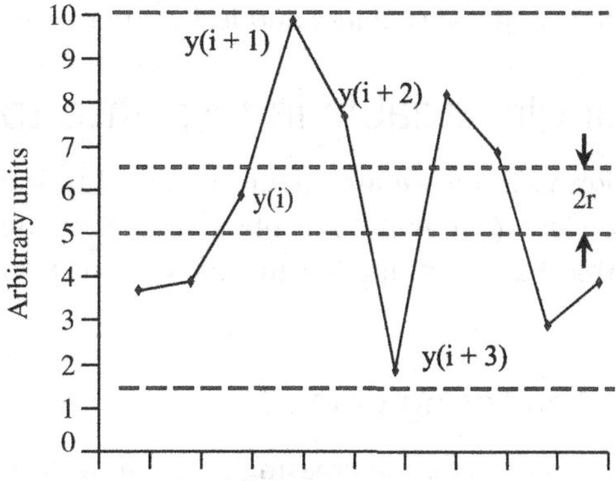

FIGURE 4–14 Role of the choice of the threshold r in ApEn calculation.

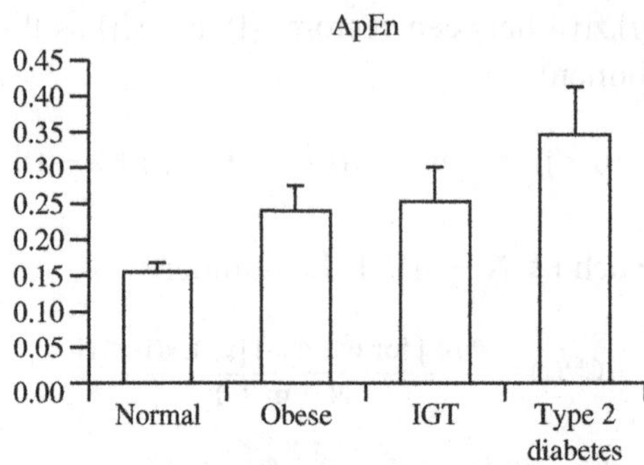

FIGURE 4–15 ApEn values (mean ± SD) in normal, obese, impaired glucose tolerant (IGT) and type 2 diabetic subjects. *Adapted from Sparacino, G., & Cobelli, C. (1998). Analisi di serie temporali. In C. Cobelli, & R. Bonadonna (Eds.).* Bioingegneria dei Sistemi Metabolici *(pp. 109–136). Bologna: Patron.*

y(2),..., y(i),..., y(N)} is shown. Assuming y(i) is the reference sample, we have to evaluate the samples that are similar to y(i) (within the tolerance band r). If r is too small (short dashed) no sample (except y(i)) will fall into the tolerance bands, ApEn will be small, and nonsignificant; if r is too large (long dashed lines) all samples will fall into the tolerance band and again ApEn will be useless as a means of distinguishing different signals (one will also consider as being similar samples which are not). In practice, since the number of data in endocrine-metabolic time series is not large, it is not possible to choose m too large and r too small. Available guidelines suggest for $N > 1000$ samples, $m = 2$ and $r = 0.1/0.25$ SD, where SD is the sample standard deviation of the series; for $N < 1000$ $m = 1$. The choice of r between 10% and 25% of signal SD is a compromise between the two case limits, that is, r too small or too large.

As an example, consider the case described in Sparacino and Cobelli (1998) where ApEn has been used to analyze the C-peptide series of Fig. 4–10 together with those of obese and glucose intolerant subjects (O'Meara, Sturis, Blackman, *et al.*, 1993; O'Meara, Sturis, Van Cauter, & Polonsky, 1993; Sturis, Van Cauter, Blackman, & Polonsky, 1991). Results are shown in Fig. 4–15. ApEn increases with the severity of the disease, that is, obese, impaired glucose tolerant and diabetic subjects have less and less regularity in ultradian oscillations.

4.6 Modeling a single variable in response to a perturbation

The second type of situation is when we are again interested in modeling a single variable. However, this time we are viewing it as the response of a physiological system to a specific stimulus or perturbation that has been applied to that system. Examples of such situations are presented below.

4.6.1 Glucose home monitoring data

With advances in telecare, it is becoming increasingly common for patients with chronic diseases to monitor their clinical and health status at home . The data can then be transmitted to a clinical center where they can be analyzed, and appropriate advice fed back to the patient. This is particularly relevant in the case of patients with type 1 diabetes who home-monitor their blood glucose concentration.

In many cases the diabetic patient will measure their blood glucose concentration up to four times a day. One approach to analyzing these data is to make use of structured time series modeling, an approach that has been widely adopted in the analysis of economic time series data (Harvey, 1989). This involves identifying patterns in these blood glucose time series as comprising four elements:

$$G_i = f(D_i, C_i, T_i, R_i) \tag{4.12}$$

where G_i refers to the observed blood glucose value at time t_i, whilst D_i, C_i, T_i, and R_i are the daily pattern, cyclical component, trend component, and random noise, respectively at time t_i. The explicit functional relationship, f, used to relate these four subpatterns, can take a variety of forms. The most straightforward, adopted here in this example, is additive; simply adding the elements (Deutsch *et al.*, 1994).

Trend patterns representing long-term behavior exist when there is a general increase in the blood glucose values over time. Daily patterns (which in time series analysis are generally known as seasonality) exist when the blood glucose data observed on different days fluctuate according to some daily rhythm (in other words, periodic fluctuations of constant length which repeat themselves at fixed intervals). This may be due to an internal diurnal rhythm or inadequacy in the current insulin therapy.

A cyclic pattern is similar to a seasonal pattern, but the length of a single cycle is generally longer. In the context of the diabetic patient, this could arise as a consequence of the difference between workdays and weekends, or from the menstrual cycle in women. Although randomness, by definition, cannot be predicted, once it has been isolated, its magnitude can be estimated and used to determine the extent of likely variation between actual and predicted blood glucose levels (Deutsch *et al.*, 1994).

Fig. 4–16 depicts blood glucose data obtained from an adult patient over a 21-day period by home monitoring. During this time the patient recorded four blood glucose measurements per day, together with details of his diet and insulin regimen. In addition, he provided a brief commentary on his social activities and general well-being, information that could be helpful in interpreting the results of the time series analysis. The results of the time series analysis are shown in Fig. 4–17 (Deutsch *et al.*, 1994).

4.6.2 Response to drug therapy—prediction of bronchodilator response

The clinical focus of this example is chronic obstructive pulmonary disease in which a bronchodilator drug such as theophylline is administered in order to attempt to open obstructed airways. The aim is to be able to predict the response to theophylline using a simple data-driven model (Whiting, Kelman, & Struthers, 1984). This then enables the drug dosage to be adjusted in order to achieve the target therapeutic concentration.

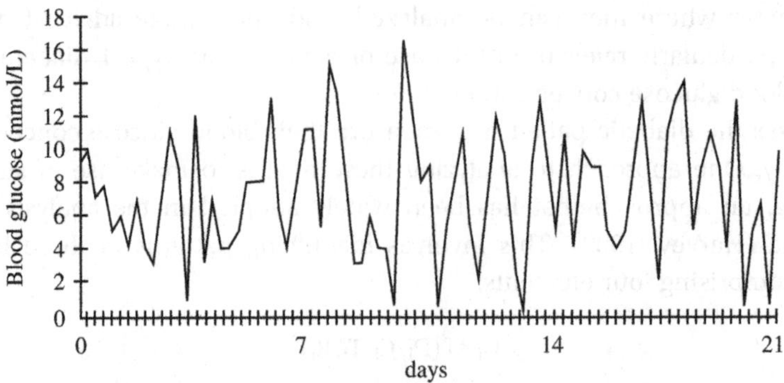

FIGURE 4–16 Home-monitored blood glucose measurements collected by a diabetic patient over a period of 21 days. *Adapted from Deutsch, T., Lehmann, E. D., Carson, E. R., Roudsari, A. V., Hopkins, K. D., & Sönksen, P. H. (1994). Time series analysis and control of blood glucose levels in diabetic patients.* Computer Methods and Programs in Biomedicine, 41, *167–182.*

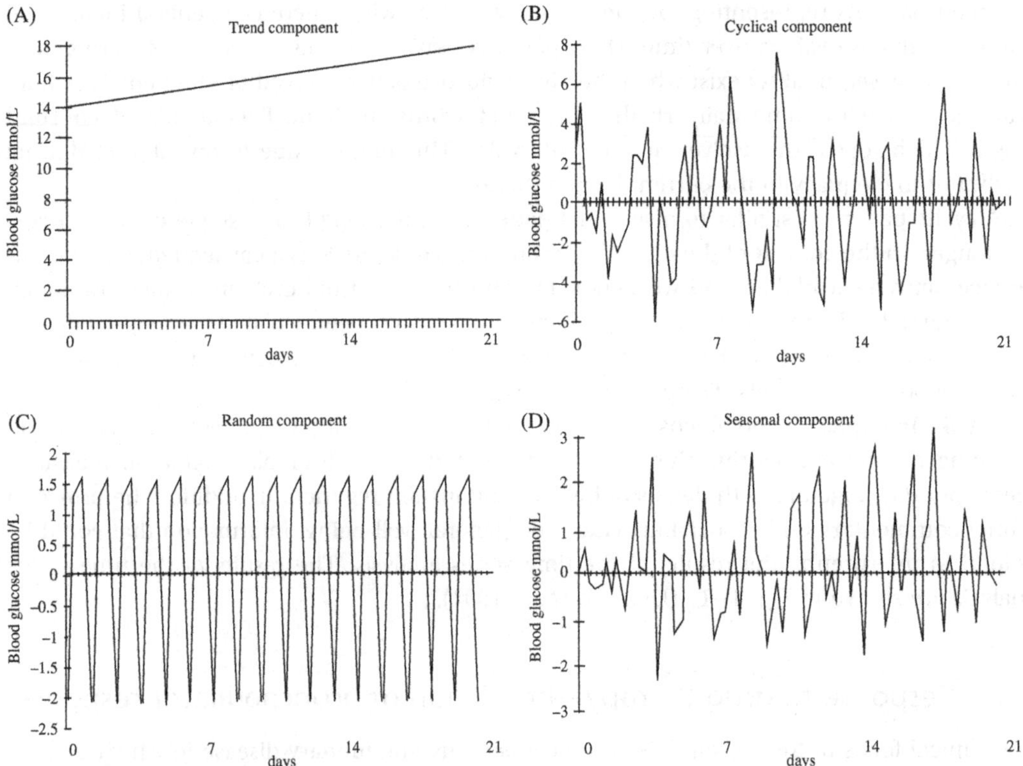

FIGURE 4–17 Analysis of the time series home-monitored blood glucose data in terms of (A) trend, (B) cyclical, (C) random, and (D) seasonal components. *Adapted from Deutsch, T., Lehmann, E. D., Carson, E. R., Roudsari, A. V., Hopkins, K. D., & Sönksen, P. H. (1994). Time series analysis and control of blood glucose levels in diabetic patients.* Computer Methods and Programs in Biomedicine, 41, *167–182.*

The model used to relate the drug effect on respiratory function to concentration in the steady state was of the form:

$$FVC = m\,Cp_{SS} + i \tag{4.13}$$

where FVC is the forced vital capacity, Cp_{ss} is the steady-state plasma concentration of theophylline, m ($1\,\mu g^{-1}$ mL) represents the sensitivity of an individual to theophylline and the intercept i is the untreated, baseline FVC. FVC values were used to assess ventilatory response since they closely reflected the extent to which the small airways were unobstructed. This linear (straight line) model of the data was assumed to provide an adequate representation over the range of concentrations encountered in the study.

Using Bayesian probability theory and maximum likelihood estimation, Whiting and colleagues were able to predict the response of an individual to any steady-state concentration of theophylline, provided that the mean values of the parameters m and i were known in a representative population of patients with chronic bronchitis.

Assuming that all the parameters are normally distributed and independent, and all measurements are also independent, the most likely set of values of m and i for an individual is obtained by minimizing the function M where:

$$M = \frac{(m - m_{mean})^2}{\sigma_m^2} + \frac{(I - i_{mean})^2}{\sigma_i^2} + \sum_{j=1}^{n}\left(\frac{(FVC_j - FVC_{j\,est})^2}{\sigma_{FVC}^2}\right) \tag{4.14}$$

and where σ_m^2 and σ_i^2 are the variances of the parameters m and i, σ_{FVC}^2 is the estimated variance of FVC and $FVC_{j\,est}$ is the expected value of FVC_j given by the equation:

$$FVC_{j\,est} = m\ Cp_{SS} + i \tag{4.15}$$

and n is the number of paired FVC–Cp_{ss} measurements. The estimates of the parameters m, σ_m^2, i, and σ_i^2 were subsequently obtained using the program NONMEM.

4.7 Two variables causally related

The third category is using input/output experimental data in order to establish quantitative relationships between two variables that are causally related. The underlying mechanisms can be different. For instance, two hormones may have their secretion controlled by the same factor, or the secretion of a hormone (e.g., testosterone) is under the control of another hormone (LH), or the same gland may simultaneously release two hormones. Also, substrate-hormone interaction can produce hormone and substrate concentration time series which are correlated, for example, in Figs. 4–10 and 4–11 glucose and C-peptide concentrations.

4.7.1 Hormone/hormone and substrate/hormone series

Cross-correlation and cross-spectrum (i.e., finding the maxima of the Fourier transform of the cross-correlation function) have been intensively applied to understand correlation in hormone/hormone, for example, testosterone/LH (Veldhuis *et al.*, 1987), LH/FSH (Veldhuis and Johnson, 1988), and substrate/hormone, for example, glucose/C-peptide concentration time series (O'Meara, Sturis, Blackman, *et al.*, 1993; O'Meara, Sturis, Van Cauter, *et al.*, 1993; Sturis *et al.*, 1991, 1992). These techniques suffer from a number of limitations, including those already mentioned, in discussing autocorrelation and spectral analysis for analyzing a single time series. In particular, the small number of data and measurement noise make results difficult to interpret. In addition, it is also possible that slow or large trends that are present in one of the series (or in both, but in opposite directions) can mask possible concordances of oscillations of smaller amplitude and period. Finally, a different measurement error in the two series may produce misleading results, for example, if measurement error variance in one series is sufficiently large so that spurious oscillations due to noise are comparable to true oscillations in the other series.

Another available approach is the extension of the single series peak detection, that is, one analyzes concordance of peak positions in the two series. Each series is analyzed separately with a peak detection algorithm, so that peak position and amplitude are obtained. Since concordance analysis only examines peak positions, usually one considers the two on–off quantized series (see Fig. 4–18). However, these two series cannot be looked at as such, that is, for each instantaneous event present in one or the other series, in both series or in none, because a number of coincidences can occur by chance (and this increases with pulse frequencies). The two on–off series can be analyzed with various techniques including a Monte Carlo simulation strategy (Clifton, Aksel, Bremner, Steiner, & Soules, 1988) and an analytical approach that calculates a specific concordance index (Guardabasso, Genazzani, Veldhuis, & Rodbard, 1991).

There are some intrinsic limitations in peak concordance analysis. First, peak amplitudes can only play a minor role in the analysis, for example, a very large peak in one series can easily be associated with a very small peak in the other series. Secondly, when concordance analysis, like cross-correlation or cross-spectral analysis, indicates a statistical concordance, this does not necessarily mean a functional concordance, that is, two hormones may be functionally independent, but can exhibit a high concordance due to the presence of a component of the same frequency, for example, ultradian.

Recently a new technique, cross-approximate entropy, has been introduced (Pincus, Mulligan, *et al.*, 1996). An index (Cross-ApEn) is provided, which measures the degree of synchrony between two series belonging to the same endocrine-metabolic axis, for example, two interacting hormones. The theory on which cross-approximate entropy is based on is the same behind approximate entropy. While single series regularity measured by ApEn refers to some relation existing in the signal between different time instants, Cross-ApEn assesses the synchrony of two signals with higher values of Cross-ApEn associated with increasingly asynchronous series.

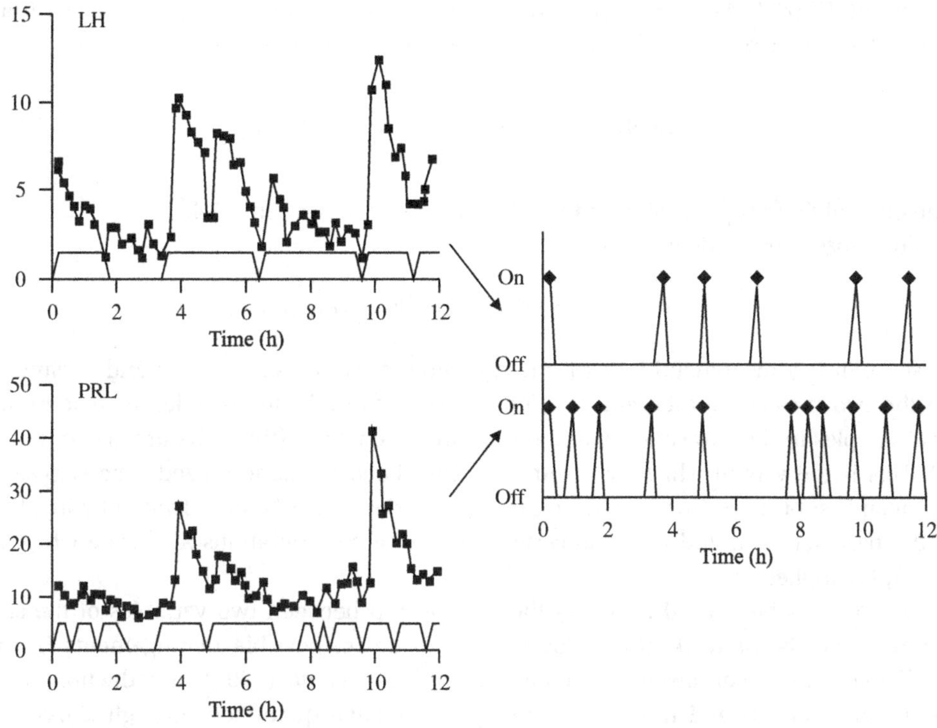

FIGURE 4–18 Time series of luteinizing (LH) and prolactin (PRL) hormone and their two-level quantized version: high level (on) when active secretion occurs and low level (off) at all other times. *Adapted from Guardabasso, V., Genazzani, A. D., Veldhuis, J. D., & Rodbard, D. (1991). Objective assessment of concordance of secretory events in two endocrine time series.* Acta Endocrinologica, 124, *208–218.*

Let $y = \{y(1), y(2),..., y(N)\}$ and $z = \{z(1), z(2),..., z(N)\}$ be two N-size time series. By using parameters r (a real) and m (an integer) we can build the sequence of $N - m + 1$ m-dimension vectors:

$$x(i) = [y(i),...,y(i + m - 1)] \tag{4.16}$$

$$s(i) = [z(i),...,z(i + m - 1)] \tag{4.17}$$

and can define for each i $(1 \leq i \leq N - m + 1)$:

$$C_i^m(r)(y||z) = \frac{\#\text{ of j for which } d[x(i)s(j)] \leq r}{N - m + 1} \tag{4.18}$$

where

$$d[x(i)s(j)] = \max_{k=1,2,...,m} |y(i + k - 1) - z(j + k - 1)| \quad j = 1,..., N - m + 1 \tag{4.19}$$

The terms $C_i^m(r)\ (u\|v)$ denote the fraction of $N-m+1$ vectors s(j) similar (within a tolerance r) to vector x(i) of similar lengths m. One can calculate the quantity:

$$\Phi^m(r)(y||z) = \frac{1}{N-m+1} \sum_{i=1}^{N-m+1} \ln\ C_i^m(r)(y||z) \tag{4.20}$$

The meaning of $\Phi^m(r)(y\|z)$ is similar to $\Phi^m(r)$ as defined in Section 4.5.4.

Finally, Cross-ApEn is defined as:

$$\text{Cross-ApEn} = \Phi^m(r)(y||z) - \Phi^{m+1}(r)(y||z) \tag{4.21}$$

Cross-ApEn is a meaningful index if the two series have the same mean and variance; in fact, if the two means are different, it is not possible to evaluate an index of synchronism because samples in the two series would never have been close (the same applies to the variance). This is the way in which Cross-ApEn is calculated on standardized time series, that is, the mean is subtracted from each sample of the series which is then divided by its SD. As far as the parameters m and r are concerned, the same considerations are made when discussing ApEn applies.

Cross-ApEn has been used to assess the relationship between two variables of the same endocrine-metabolic network, thus allowing one to detect possible derangements in their mode of interaction. For instance, in Pincus, Mulligan *et al.* (1996), a reduction in the synchrony between LH and testosterone in aging has been quantified through Cross-ApEn (in aging both LH and testosterone series are also more irregular as shown by ApEn). In Sparacino and Cobelli (1998), the relationship between the glucose and C-peptide time series already discussed in Section 4.5.4 has been studied with Cross-ApEn. Cross-ApEn results (see Fig. 4–19) show that, in moving from normal metabolism to diabetes, there is a significant deterioration in the synchronism between glucose and C-peptide oscillations with derangement already present in prediabetes states such as obesity and impaired glucose tolerance. In other words, the efficiency of the control system is progressively deteriorating.

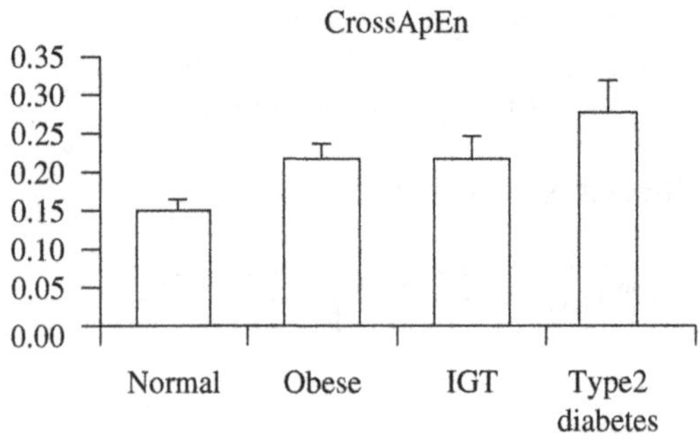

FIGURE 4–19 Cross-ApEn values (mean ± SD) in normal, obese, impaired glucose tolerant (IGT) and type 2 diabetic subjects. *Adapted from Sparacino, G., & Cobelli, C. (1998). Analisi di serie temporali. In C. Cobelli, & R. Bonadonna (Eds.).* Bioingegneria dei Sistemi Metabolici *(pp. 109–136). Bologna: Patron.*

4.7.2 Urine sodium response to water loading

Let us now consider a set of time series data that relate water intake as the input and urine sodium as the output. Physiologically the data are of interest as they provide insight as to the manner in which sodium is selectively excreted in the control of total body water. Fig. 4–20 shows these time series data with x_t being the water input and y_t the urine sodium output. The number of samples, n, is 100.

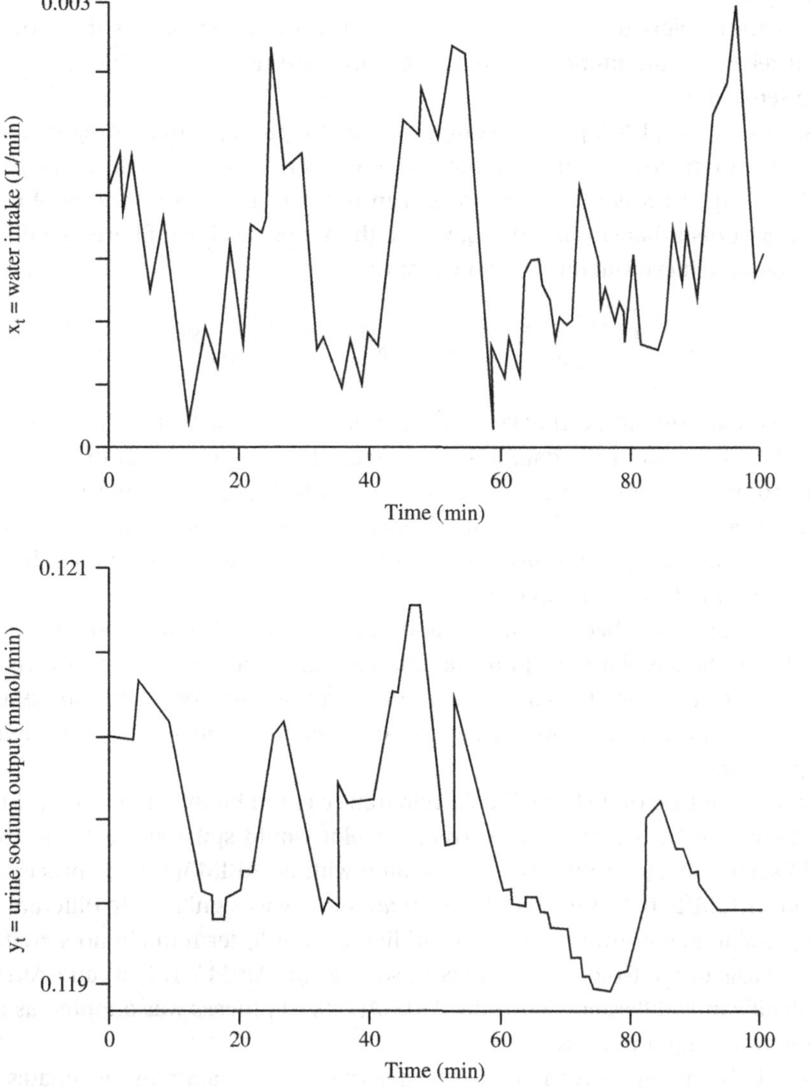

FIGURE 4–20 Time series plot of water intake and urine sodium output. *Adapted from Flood, R. L., & Carson, E. R. (1993).* Dealing with complexity: An introduction to the theory and application of systems science *(2nd ed.). New York: Plenum.*

The ARIMA model is adopted (Flood & Carson, 1993) and the modeling package MINITAB is used to assess the type and order of the input time series as an ARIMA process. MINITAB is a statistical software package (developed at Pond Laboratory, University Park, Pennsylvania 16802, United States), which supports this ARIMA modeling. The overall objective of an ARIMA modeling exercise is to build a model of a univariate time series, expressed in terms of past observations, and errors between current and past observations; so as to make predictions about a particular variable of interest, in this case urine sodium output.

As already discussed in Section 4.5.2, an ARIMA process is conventionally written ARIMA (p, d, q), where p refers to the autoregressive part of the process, q is the moving average part, and d relates to the number of differences that are needed to achieve stationarity of a set of time series data.

The essence of an ARIMA process is that we are integrating both autoregressive and moving average components. This means that a given observation in a time series generated by an ARIMA(p, d, q) process may be expressed in terms of past observations of order p, and current and past disturbances of order q, where the series has been filtered by differencing d times in order to achieve stationarity. So we have:

$$\begin{aligned} x_t = (1+\phi_1)x_{t-1} + (\phi_2-\phi_1)x_{t-2} + \cdots + (\phi_p - \phi_{p-1}) \\ -\phi_p x_{t-p-1} + \mu + u_t - \theta_1 u_{t-1} - \cdots - \theta_q u_{t-q} \end{aligned} \tag{4.22}$$

Initially the data should be checked for outliers, replacing actual outlier values with their expected values if errors in the data are suspected. The correlogram of the raw data is then inspected and assessed for stationarity. If the series displays nonstationarity, the first differences of the series are taken and these are inspected and assessed. If stationarity has still not been achieved, then the second has been identified as the number of times the differences have to be taken to achieve stationarity.

When stationarity has been achieved, and after the partial-autocorrelation function has been calculated, the standard errors of the autocorrelation and partial-autocorrelation functions are taken, so that the standard error values of these function plots can be assessed for significance. This enables an appropriate ARIMA process to be selected by identifying the time lags p and q.

In relation to our example here, if a correlogram were to be drawn it would show that the raw data decay slowly. A partial-autocorrelation plot would spike at lag 1 and then tail off. This would seem to suggest that we were dealing with an ARIMA(1, 0, 0) process. However, adopting an ARIMA(2, 0, 0) process, the estimate of ϕ_2 was significantly different from zero. Exploring possible higher order models by adding a ϕ_3 or θ_1 term made no significant difference on the basis of the t-ratios. The sums of squares for ARIMA(1, 0, 0) and ARIMA(2, 0, 0) were not significantly different. Hence the ARIMA(2, 0, 0) process was adopted as a representation of the water input process.

The MINITAB package was then used to derive the final parameter estimates for ϕ_1 and ϕ_2. Maximum likelihood estimation is used for this process (see Chapter 8: Parametric models—the estimation problem). Using these estimates, a series of transformations,

Table 4–1 Cross-correlation ($r_{\alpha\beta}$), standard error (SE), and impulse response (v_k) of urine sodium response to water intake represented by an ARIMA(2, 0, 0) process.

k	0	1	2	3	4	5	6	7	8	9	10
$r_{\alpha\beta}$	0.03	0.13	−0.14	0.13	0.36	0.14	0.28	0.30	0.26	0.14	−0.14
SE	0.10	0.10	0.10	0.10	0.10	0.10	0.10	0.10	0.10	0.10	0.10
v_k	0.10	0.05	−0.05	0.05	0.13	0.09	0.10	0.11	0.10	0.05	−0.02

cross-correlations ($r_{\alpha\beta}$), and impulse responses of urine sodium response were simulated. The standard error was assumed to be 0.1 ($n^{-1/2}$ evaluated for n = 100). The results of these simulations are shown in Table 4–1, in which k is the lag between input and output. If these results are then compared with examples given in the classic work of Box and Jenkins (1976), the model that best fits the data is (r, s, b) = (2, 1, 4), that is:

$$(1 - \delta_1 B - \delta_2 B^2)y_t = (\omega_0 - \omega_1 B)x_{t-4} \tag{4.23}$$

where x_t and y_t are respectively the water input and urine sodium output.

In order to complete this statistical transfer function model, it is necessary to add an appropriate noise model. Making use of techniques described in Box and Jenkins (1976), and implemented in the MINITAB package, a second order noise model was postulated and its parameters estimated.

This example has shown how a simple model may be adequate as a means of providing an adequate input/output representation. However, successful application of this ARIMA modeling is critically dependent upon an adequate set of time series samples; here there were 100 samples. Whilst this number may often be adequate, a figure of 200 or more is usually needed to ensure a successful modeling outcome.

4.8 Input/output modeling for control

The next type of model considered is one that corresponds to explicit physiological control systems. Here, models are to be formulated based on input/output experiments in order to obtain greater understanding in quantitative terms of the dynamics of such control systems. Examples are presented which include both a naturally occurring physiological control, such as the pupil light reflex, as well as situations corresponding to therapeutic control. One classic instance presented is insulin control of blood glucose in diabetes.

4.8.1 Pupil control

An example for adopting a frequency response approach to modeling an input/output situation for control purposes is provided by the classical pupil light reflex study of Stark and Sherman, as described by Toates (1975).

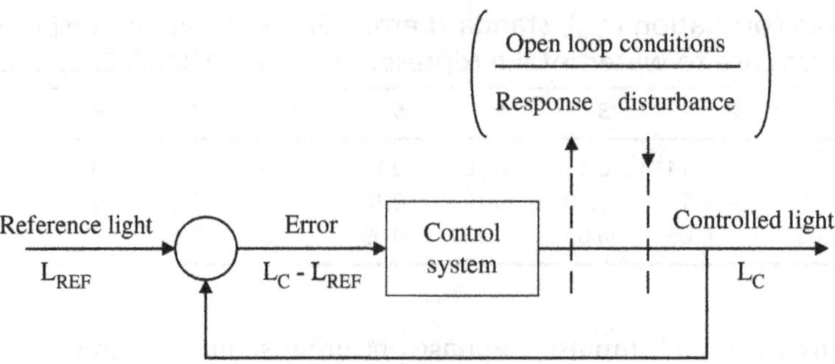

FIGURE 4–21 Simplified representation of the pupil light reflex system. *Adapted from Stark, L., & Sherman, P. (1957). A servo-analytical study of consensual pupil light reflex to light.* Journal of Neurophysiology *20: 17–26.*

The quantity of light reaching the retina is determined by the pupil aperture size. When the intensity of light is higher than desired, the pupil light reflex causes a contraction of the pupil so as to reduce the quantity of admitted radiation. Conversely, in dim illumination the aperture enlarges so that more light falls on the retina. This pupil light reflex was first modeled as a feedback control system by Stark and Sherman (1957).

A simplified representation of the system is shown in Fig. 4–21. The controlled variable is the quantity of light falling on the retina, L_c. There is also a reference light flux variable, L_{REF}, with which L_c is compared. The difference, or error $L_c - L_{REF}$, is the signal that operates the control system.

The experimental technique by which data were obtained for the purpose of building a mathematical model of the system involved measuring light stimulus and the pupil area. Stark and Sherman (1957) devised a method for opening the feedback loop without interfering with the system. This involved focusing the light stimulus so that the light entering the eye had a diameter that was smaller than the smallest diameter of the pupil. In this way any changes the pupil made were unable to influence the quantity of light falling on the retina. A disturbance was introduced at the output of the system by modulating the intensity of the light falling on the retina in a sinusoidal manner. The response, in the form of pupil changes, was measured. By ensuring that only small test signals were employed, it was reasonable to assume that linear analytical techniques would be valid.

By carrying out this input/output experiment over a range of frequencies, the open-loop frequency response was obtained, depicted as a Bode diagram in Fig. 4–22. From this frequency response it can be seen that the low frequency gain is 0.16 and that at high frequencies the gain falls off with a slope of −18 db/octave. Since a single exponential lag is responsible for −6 db/octave, Stark and Sherman estimated that three such lag elements must be present, each having a time constant of approximately 0.1 second. Hence the transfer function model proposed to describe the open-loop characteristic of the pupil is:

$$G(s) = \frac{0.16\ \exp(-0.18\ s)}{(1+0.1\ s)^3} \tag{4.24}$$

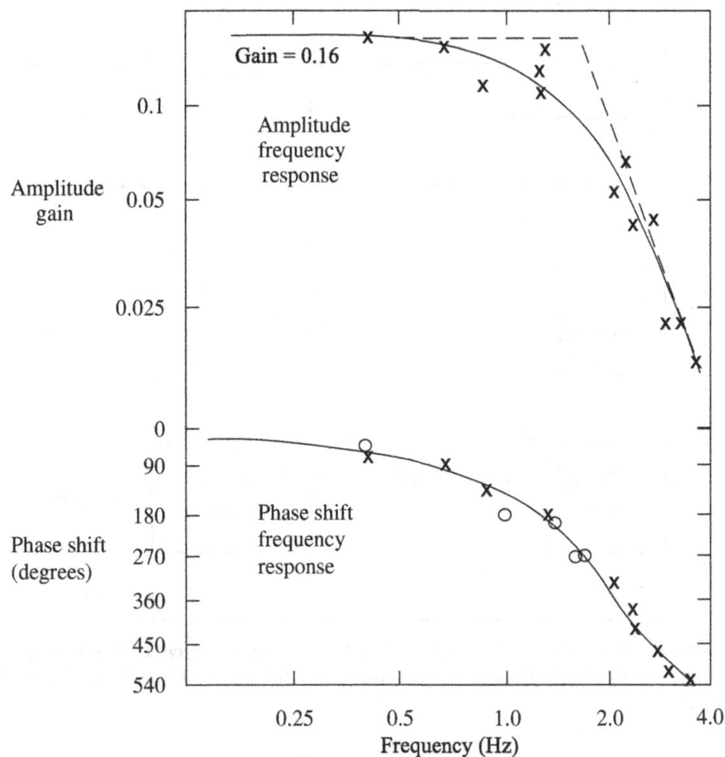

FIGURE 4–22 Open-loop frequency response of the pupil light reflex. *Adapated from Stark, L., & Sherman, P. (1957). A servo-analytical study of consensual pupil light reflex to light.* Journal of Neurophysiology *20: 17–26.*

The term $\exp(-0.18s)$ is the Laplace representation of the pure delay of 0.18 seconds, 0.16 is the gain constant, and $1/(1 + 0.1s)$ represents a lag, of which there are three present.

4.8.2 Control of blood glucose by insulin

In Type 1 diabetes pancreatic beta cell function is lost and must be replaced externally (see Fig. 4–23), that is, insulin must be infused exogenously. Advances in glucose sensing and the availability of fast-absorbing insulin analogs can potentially lead to a closed-loop insulin delivery system or artificial pancreas based on a subcutaneous site for glucose sensing and insulin delivery. One important ingredient of the artificial pancreas is the algorithm for calculating insulin delivery rate based on glucose measurements.

Various approaches have been proposed, which have been reviewed by Bequette (2005). Here we briefly discuss one relatively simple approach, based on an input/output model, the proportional-integral-derivative controller, PID, which is widely employed in industrial control systems. The PID controller responds to glucose with three components: a proportional component (P) that reacts to the difference between measured glucose and

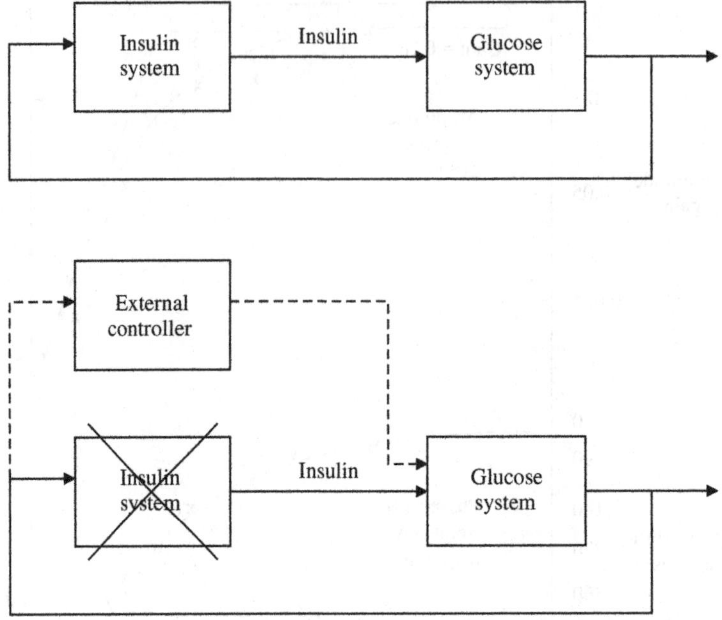

FIGURE 4–23 The glucose-insulin control system in a healthy (*upper panel*) and type 1 diabetic (*lower panel*) subject. In type 1 diabetes pancreatic beta cells do not secrete insulin, thus the physiological controller must be replaced by an external one.

basal glucose; an integral component (I) that reacts to persistent hyper- or hypo-glycemia; and a derivative component (D) that reacts to the rate of change in glucose. More precisely:

$$PID(t) = P(t) + I(t) + D(t); \quad PID \geq 0 \ \ \forall t \tag{4.25}$$

where

$$P(t) = Kp(G(t) - G_B) \tag{4.26}$$

$$I(t) = \frac{Kp}{T_I}\int_0^t (G(t) - G_B)dt; \quad I(0) = ID_B \tag{4.27}$$

$$D(t) = KpT_D \frac{dG(t)}{dt} \tag{4.28}$$

Kp determines the rate of insulin delivery in response to glucose above the target G_B, T_I the ratio of proportional to integral delivery, and T_D the ratio of derivative to proportional delivery.

This model has been used in diabetic dogs to show the feasibility of closed-loop insulin delivery using the subcutaneous route (Pantaleon, Loutseiko, Steil, & Rebrin, 2006). PID parameters were fixed from pilot-dog studies and from knowledge of the total daily dose of insulin that each dog required for open-loop glucose control. Glucose concentration was measured frequently in plasma, and continuous glucose concentration was calculated by linear extrapolation of measured values. Fig. 4–24 shows the performance of the PID controller in a 6-hour experiment with a meal given at the fourth hour for three different values of the gain Kp. A stable meal response for a wide range of gain can be observed.

One can note that, while preprandial glucose values are very similar for the different gains, the peak post-prandial glucose decreases significantly as the gain increases (Fig. 4–24, upper panel) due to a higher early-phase insulin delivery (Fig. 4–24, lower panel) which produces a higher insulin concentration (Fig. 4–24, middle panel).

4.8.3 Control of blood pressure by sodium nitroprusside

This example considers the situation in which the drug sodium nitroprusside is administered to lower the blood pressure of patients in the hospital (Slate & Sheppard, 1982). Closed-loop control methods are adopted, so that the drug infusion rate should be adjusted based on frequent measurements of arterial blood pressure. Feedback is needed to maintain pressure near a desired value because of disturbances that perturb pressure, the changing state of the patient and the wide range of response characteristics generally found amongst a population of patients.

In this study an automatic control system is adopted, with mean arterial pressure being controlled by a nonlinear proportional plus integral plus derivative (PID) controller as depicted in Fig. 4–25. For the purpose of testing and evaluating the design of the controller, a model of the arterial pressure related to features of the patient was developed. Such a model enables computer simulation studies to be performed as part of the controller evaluation process.

The model in this case is partly derived on the basis of experimental data, but also in part derived using some physiological and pharmacological concepts. Experimental data, for example, provide evidence of the patient's sensitivity to the drug and the lagged response resulting from uptake, distribution and biotransformation of the drug. The resulting patient model, represented in transfer function form, is shown in Fig. 4–26. A pseudo-random binary signal was used to program the drug infusion rate, and cross-correlation analysis was used to estimate the impulse response. This model was then incorporated in a simulation schema to examine a range of dynamic and control effects associated with this drug therapy.

4.9 Input/output modeling: impulse response and deconvolution

Another important input/output model is the impulse response of the system. The impulse response is not only useful for characterizing the system under study, but it is the key ingredient of the convolution integral. As we shall see, this forms the basis for solving by deconvolution a number of important inverse biomedical problems; that is to say estimating inputs to the system, for example, the secretion rate of a gland, which cannot be directly measured *in vivo*.

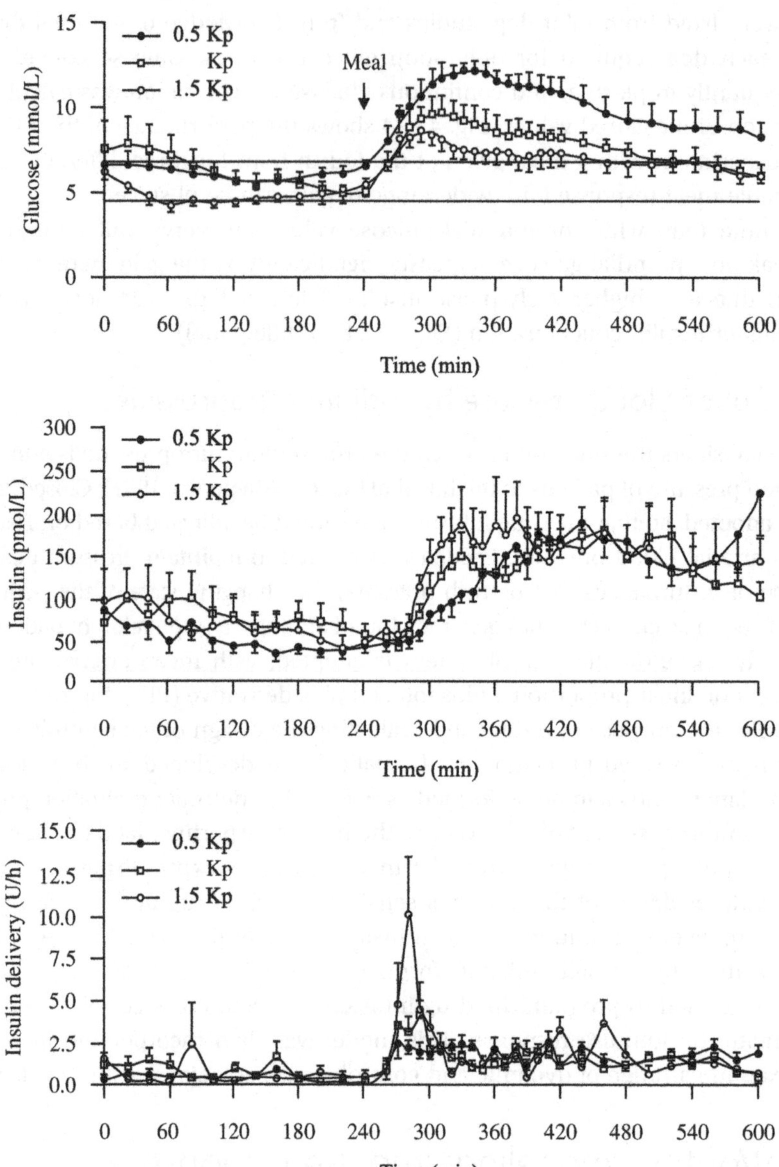

FIGURE 4–24 Blood glucose (*upper panel*), plasma insulin (*middle panel*), and PID algorithm insulin delivery (*lower panel*) during 10 h closed-loop control in diabetic dogs (n = 8) for three values of gain (Kp). Meal occurs at the fourth hour. *Adapted from Pantaleon, A. E., Loutseiko, M., Steil, G. M., Rebrin, K. (2006). Evaluation of the effect of gain on the meal response of an automated closed-loop insulin delivery system.* Diabetes, 55, *1995–2000.*

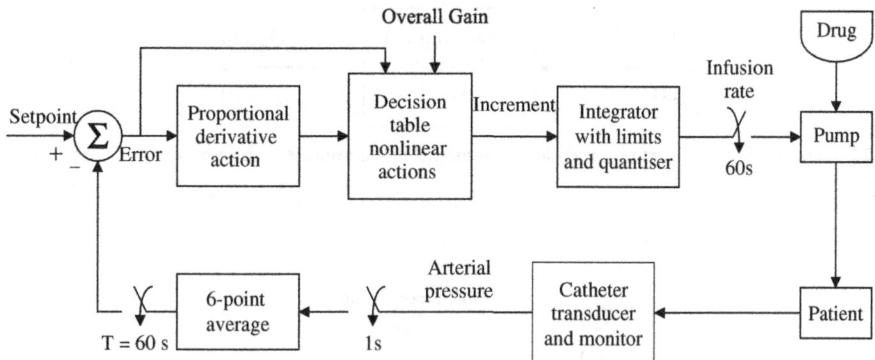

FIGURE 4–25 Automated system for the infusion of sodium nitroprusside using a nonlinear PID digital controller. *Adapted from Slate, J. B., Sheppard, L. C. (1982). Automatic control of blood pressure by drug infusion.* IEE Proceedings, 129 *(part A), 639–645.*

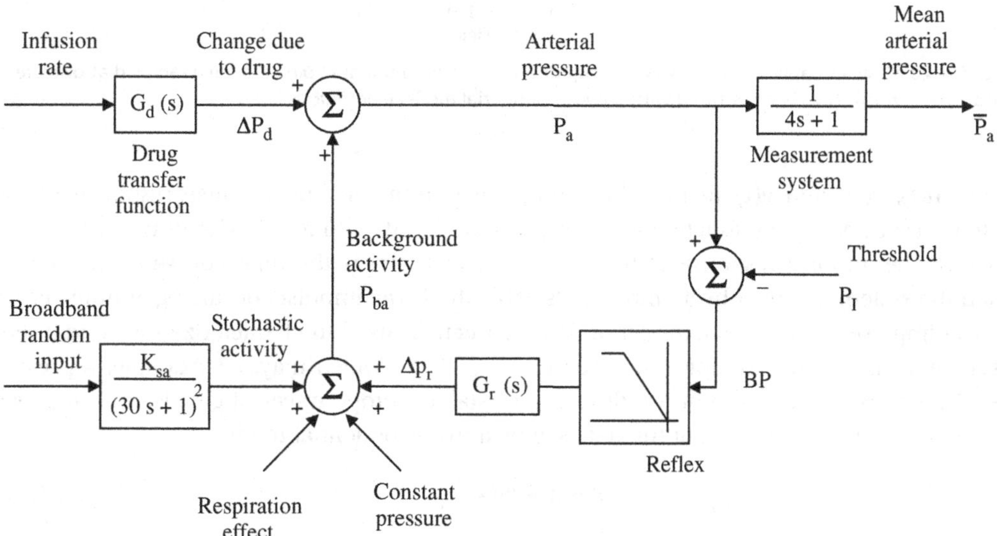

FIGURE 4–26 Model of a postsurgical cardiac patient developed to test drug dynamic and control effects. *Adapted from Slate, J. B., Sheppard, L. C. (1982). Automatic control of blood pressure by drug infusion.* IEE Proceedings, 129 *(part A), 639–645.*

4.9.1 Impulse response estimation

Consider the linear time-invariant dynamic system depicted in Fig. 4–27. One can write the integral equation:

$$c(t) = \int_{-\infty}^{t} g(t - \tau)u(\tau)d\tau \tag{4.29}$$

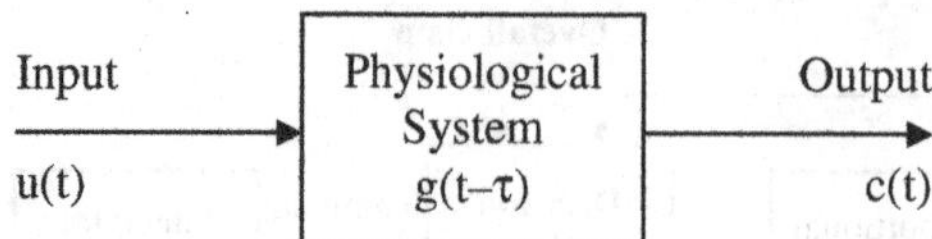

FIGURE 4–27 A linear time-invariant physiological system. g(t) is the impulse response, u(t) is the input, and c(t) is the output.

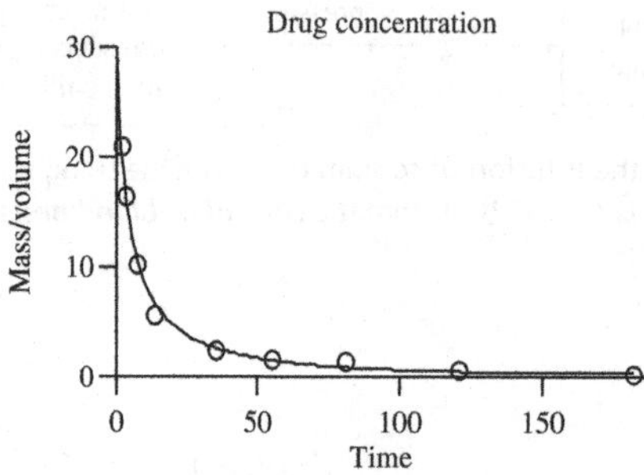

FIGURE 4–28 Plasma disappearance curve of a drug or a tracer after a unitary bolus at time 0 sampled at discrete times (*open circles*). The data are fitted with a two exponential model (*continuous line*).

where u(t), c(t), and g(t) denote the input, the output and the impulse response of the system, respectively. The function g(t) describes the input/output behavior of the system and is called the impulse response of the system. In fact, g(t) is the time course of the output when the system is forced by a unitary pulse δ(t), the Dirac impulse, occurring at time zero.

The impulse response is a model of data that can be used to characterize the system. For instance, consider the disappearance curve of Fig. 4–28 which may, for example, represent the disappearance of a drug or a radioactive or stable isotope tracer of glucose injected as a unit bolus at time 0. One can fit the data say by a two exponential model:

$$g(t) = A_1 e^{-\alpha_1 t} + A_2 e^{-\alpha_2 t} \tag{4.30}$$

From knowledge of g(t) one can calculate some parameters of the system, for example, the area under the curve, AUC:

$$\mathrm{AUC} = \int_0^\infty g(t)d\tau \tag{4.31}$$

or the initial distribution volume, V:

$$V = \frac{D}{g(0^+)}$$

where D is the dose amount, or the clearance rate, CR:

$$CR = \frac{1}{\int_0^{\infty} g(t)dt} = \frac{1}{AUC} \tag{4.32}$$

Since the system is linear, one can also work, instead of in time, in the Laplace domain. From (4.29), one has:

$$C(s) = G(s) \cdot U(s) \tag{4.33}$$

where G(s) is the transfer function of the system.

The impulse response is not only a model of data that is useful per se, but also because it is the key ingredient for solving the convolution and deconvolution problems.

4.9.2 The convolution integral

The integral (4.29) is called the convolution integral, that is, c(t) is the convolution of u(t) with g(t). Thus knowing g(t), we can use convolution for predicting the output response c(t) for a variety of known inputs u(t). For instance, we could investigate administering the drug as a bolus at different times during the day with the goal of reaching and maintaining therapeutic levels of its concentration. This is a direct problem: knowing the input and the impulse response, to predict the output.

The most powerful use of the convolution integral is in tackling what in the mathematics/physics/engineering literature is referred to as an inverse problem; that is, instead of following the cause-effect chain (direct problem), one follows the reversal of this chain. If the unknown signal is the input of the system, the inverse problem is an input estimation problem (Fig. 4–29) which is solved by deconvolution. This is very important because many signals of interest for the quantitative understanding of physiological systems are not directly measurable *in vivo*. Some examples include the secretion rate of a gland, the production rate of a substrate, or the appearance rate of a drug in plasma after oral administration. Very often, it is only possible to measure the causally related effects of these signals in the

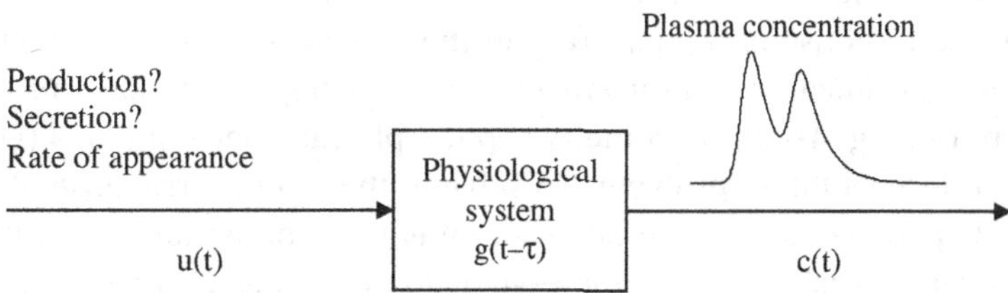

FIGURE 4–29 The input estimation problem: from knowledge of response of the system and of the output, for example, plasma concentration, reconstruct the input; for example, substrate production, hormone secretion rate or drug absorption rate.

circulation (e.g., the time course of plasma concentrations). Thus there is the need of reconstructing the unknown causes (e.g., hormone secretion rate) from the measured effects (e.g., hormone plasma concentration).

4.9.3 Reconstructing the input

Deconvolution is known to be ill-posed (i.e., the problem of reconstructing u(t) from the finite number of samples of c(t), which does not permit a unique solution), and ill-conditioned [i.e., a small percentage error in the measured effect (e.g., hormone concentration in plasma) can produce a much greater percentage error in the estimated cause (e.g., secretion rate)]. Moreover, dealing with physiological signals adds to the complexity of the problem, since they are often nonnegative and sampled at a nonuniform and/or infrequent rate. We shall discuss these problems and how to solve them in Chapter 9, Nonparametric models—signal estimation. Here the focus is on the basic concepts, illustrating by way of examples the potential of deconvolution for solving important biomedical problems.

Let us consider some examples taken from Sparacino, De Nicolao, and Cobelli (2001). Suppose we want to reconstruct insulin secretion rate from C-peptide concentration data (C-peptide is used instead of insulin because they are secreted equimolarly by the pancreas, but C-peptide does not, unlike insulin, undergo any extraction by the liver). In normal conditions, the pancreas releases C-peptide (and insulin) in an oscillatory fashion with at least two detectable modes: rapid pulses, with period between 8 and 15 minutes, which are superimposed on to slower and larger oscillations, named ultradian oscillations, whose period ranges between 90 and 150 minutes. If glucose concentration increases rapidly, for instance during an intravenous glucose tolerance test (IVGTT), the spontaneous oscillations are obscured by the response of the pancreas. A sudden and large secretory peak (first phase) is followed by a smooth release (second phase). The pancreatic secretion is not directly measurable and the only available information is the plasma concentration of C-peptide. Fig. 4–30 (upper panel) shows the C-peptide plasma concentration measured every 20 minutes for 12 hours in a normal subject (Sturis *et al.*, 1991).

The ultradian oscillatory pattern of the secretion (i.e., the cause) is evident from the measured concentration (i.e., the effect). The sampling rate is, however, insufficient to reveal the rapid pulses. Fig. 4–30 (lower panel) depicts the C-peptide plasma concentrations nonuniformly sampled for 4 hours in a normal subject during an IVGTT. The time series clearly reflects the biphasic response of the pancreas to the glucose stimulus. For both cases, since C-peptide kinetics are linear, the problem of reconstructing C-peptide (insulin) secretion rate (i.e., the input of Fig. 4–29) from the C-peptide plasma concentrations (i.e., the output of Fig. 4–29) is a deconvolution problem. To solve it, the impulse response of the system is required. In the C-peptide case, an ad hoc experiment can be performed in the same individual on a separate occasion. After suppressing the spontaneous pancreatic secretion by means of a somatostatin infusion, an intravenous bolus of C-peptide is administered and plasma concentration samples are collected frequently.

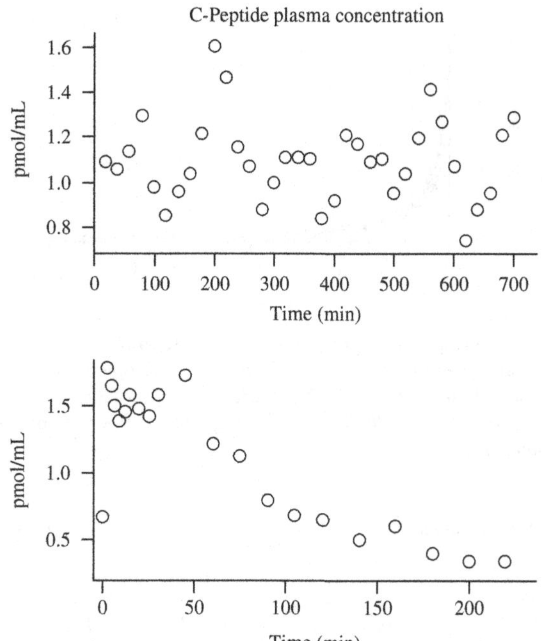

FIGURE 4–30 C-Peptide plasma concentration time series. *Upper panel*: Spontaneous ultradian oscillations. *Lower panel*: Intravenous glucose tolerance test (IVGTT). *Adapted from Sparacino, G., De Nicolao, G., Cobelli, C. (2001). Deconvolution. In E. Carson, C. Cobelli (Eds.).* Modelling methodology for physiology and medicine *(pp. 45–75). New York: Academic Press.*

The impulse response g(t) is obtained by fitting a sum of two exponentials to the data by nonlinear least squares. A representative data set with the model fit is reported in Fig. 4–31. Now, looking at (4.29), we know c(t) and g(t) and need to estimate u(t). By using the techniques discussed in Chapter 9, Nonparametric models—signal estimation, we can reconstruct insulin secretion for the two experimental situations of Fig. 4–30. Results are shown in Fig. 4–32: the left panels show the reconstructed insulin secretion (upper panel: ultradian oscillations; lower panel: IVGTT) while the right panels show the corresponding reconvolution, that is, with the estimated u(t), knowing g(t), we can solve (4.29) for c(t).

Another problem, which could be tackled similarly to the one discussed above, would be to use deconvolution on the C-peptide time series of Fig. 4–10 to quantitatively assess the derangement of the physiological control system in diabetes.

A further application is to study hormone secretion after a hormonal stimulus. For instance, an injection of growth hormone releasing hormone (GHRH) is given to adolescents to assess the ability of the pituitary gland to properly secrete GH. Plasma concentrations of GH are measured for 2 hours following the stimulus (Fig. 4–33). By using the GH impulse response we can reconstruct the GH secretion rate, thus being better informed with regard to designing a hormonal therapy that favors normal growth.

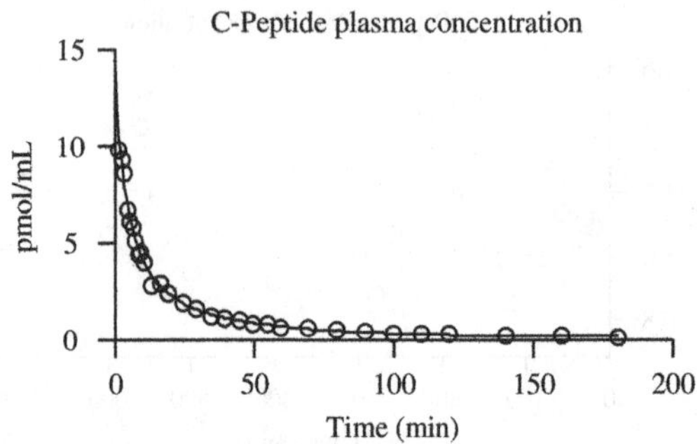

FIGURE 4–31 The C-peptide impulse response. A bolus of C-peptide is administered at time 0 (endogenous secretion has been suppressed) and plasma concentration is frequently sampled (*open circles*). A sum of two exponentials is filled against the data (*continuous line*). *Adapted from Sparacino, G., De Nicolao, G., Cobelli, C. (2001). Deconvolution. In E. Carson, C. Cobelli (Eds.).* Modelling methodology for physiology and medicine *(pp. 45–75). New York: Academic Press.*

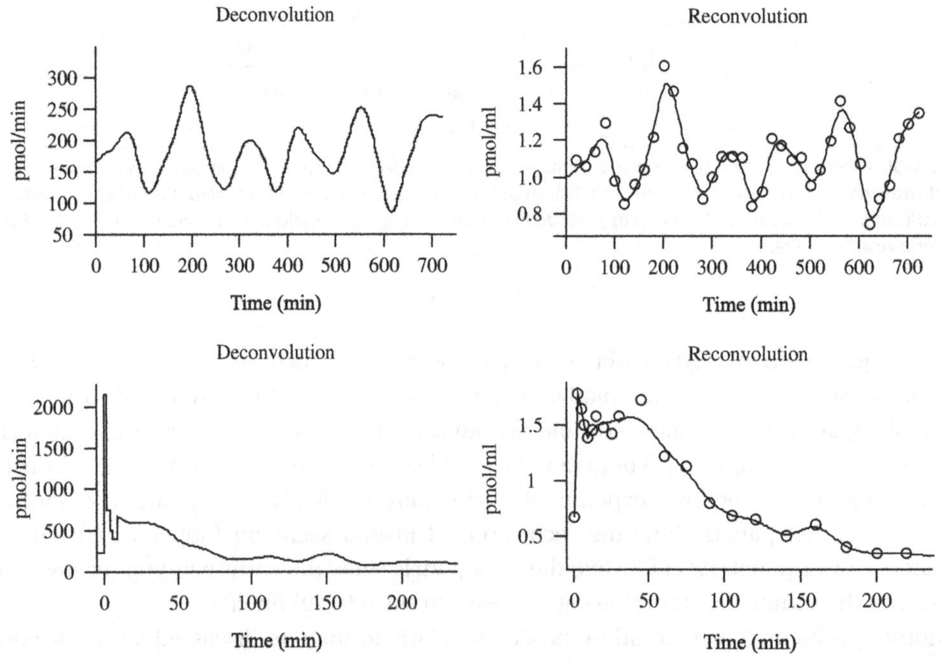

FIGURE 4–32 Estimation of insulin secretion rate by deconvolution. *Left panels*: Ultradian oscillations (*upper panel*) and IVGTT (*lower panel*). *Right panels*: Ultradian oscillations (*upper panel*) and IVGTT (*lower panel*) reconvolution against data. *Adapted from Sparacino, G., De Nicolao, G., Cobelli, C. (2001). Deconvolution. In E. Carson, C. Cobelli (Eds.).* Modelling methodology for physiology and medicine *(pp. 45–75). New York: Academic Press.*

A final example concerns using deconvolution to reconstruct the rate of appearance in plasma of a drug taken orally or injected subcutaneously. This could enable therapy to be optimized, or drug design enhanced, by improving the mechanisms by which the drug is absorbed and released. The only measurements available are those of the drug in plasma

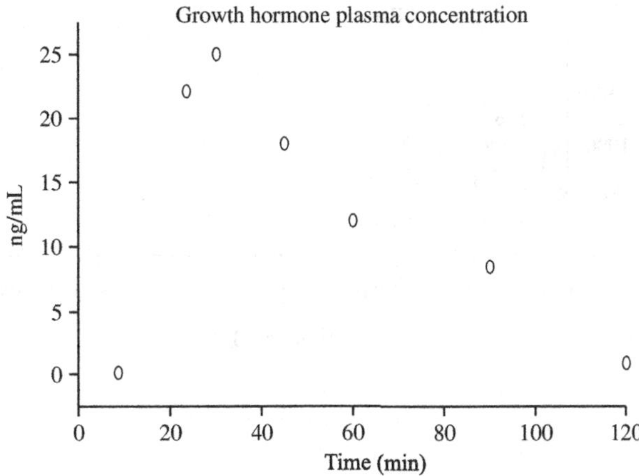

FIGURE 4–33 Plasma concentration of growth hormone (GH) after a bolus of growth hormone releasing hormone (GHRH) at time 0. *Adapted from De Nicolao, G., Liberati, D., Sartorio, A. (1995). Deconvolution of infrequently sampled data for the estimation of growth hormone secretion.* IEEE Transactions on Biomedical Engineering, *42, 678–687.*

(e.g., after an oral administration) (Fig. 4–34, upper panel). By using deconvolution we can reconstruct the drug rate of appearance (Fig. 4–34, lower panel), thus estimating a nonmeasurable key ingredient for therapy or drug design.

We conclude by noting that there are a number of biomedical applications of deconvolution, including hormone secretion/substrate production (Caumo & Cobelli, 1993; De Nicolao & Liberati, 1993; De Nicolao, Liberati, & Sartorio, 1995; Pilo, Ferrannini, & Navalesi, 1977; Polonsky *et al.*, 1986; Sartorio, De Nicolao, Pizzini, & Liberati, 1997; Sparacino & Cobelli, 1996, 1997; Veldhuis *et al.*, 1987); pharmacokinetics (Charter & Gull, 1991; Cobelli *et al.*, 1987; Cutler, 1978; Dix, Frazier, Cooperstein, & Riviere, 1986; Gillespie & Veng-Pedersen, 1985; Hovorka *et al.*, 1998; Iga, Ogawa, Yashiki, & Shimamoto, 1986; Pillonetto, Sparacino, & Cobelli, 2001; Tett, Cutle, & Day, 1992; Verotta, 1996; Vicini *et al.*, 1999); radiography (Hunt, 1971); tracer data processing (Bates, 1991; Commenges & Brendel, 1982; Sparacino *et al.*, 1997); and transport through organ studies (Bassingthwaighte, Ackerman, & Wood, 1996; Bronikowsky, Lawson, & Linehan, 1983; Clough *et al.*, 1993; Knopp, Dobbs, Greenleaf, & Bassingthwaighte, 1976; Nakai, 1981; Sparacino, Bonadonna, Steinberg, Baron, & Cobelli, 1998).

4.10 Summary

This chapter has examined the process of modeling experimental data. Four cases have been examined, namely: modeling a single variable occurring spontaneously; modeling a single variable in response to a perturbation; modeling two variables that are causally related; and input/output modeling for control. A range of examples has illustrated these four cases. Both time and frequency domain approaches to modeling have been demonstrated. The basis of convolution and deconvolution has also been outlined. The next chapter will go on to

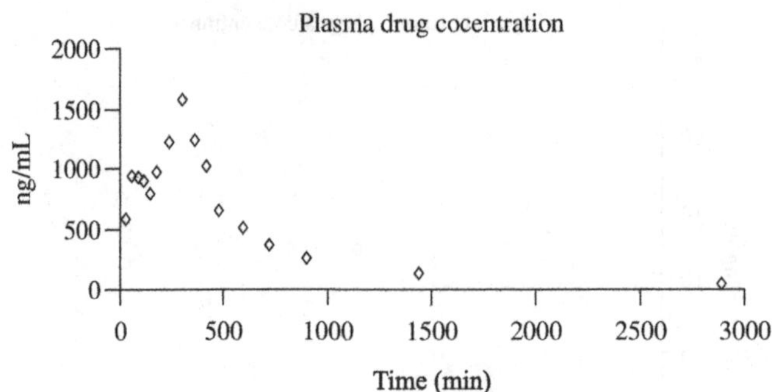

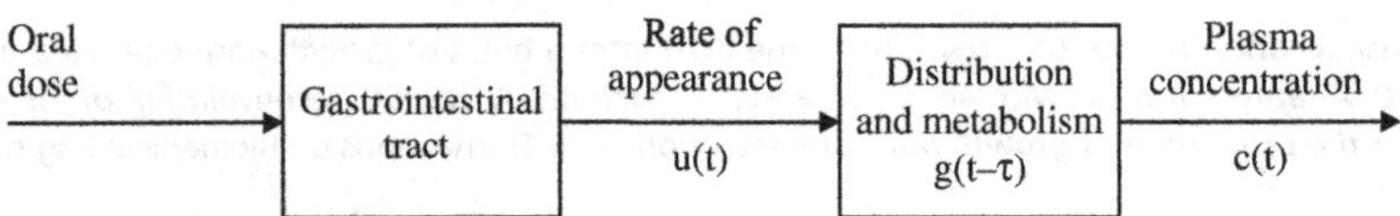

FIGURE 4–34 Estimation of the appearance rate of a drug in plasma. *Upper panel*: Plasma concentration of the drug after an oral administration at time 0. *Lower panel*: The pharmacokinetic system. From knowledge of drug plasma concentration c(t), and its distribution and metabolism (the impulse response, g(t)), it is possible to reconstruct by deconvolution the drug rate of appearance in the circulation.

illustrate approaches to model formulation, where the aim is to produce mathematical formalisms corresponding to the underlying physical and chemical mechanisms which are the basis of physiological systems.

4.11 Exercises and assignment questions

1. Discuss the nature of the relationship between physiological measurement and data modeling.
2. Data modeling can be applied to either a single variable or to two interrelated (input/output) variables, with or without control. Give some examples for each of these different situations.
3. Plasma concentrations of hormones exhibit a spontaneous cyclic behavior. Which are the most powerful modeling methods to analyze hormonal time series?
4. Input/output models are often needed either to understand quantitatively naturally occurring control in physiological systems, or to control a severely diseased physiological system. Give an example for each case.
5. The impulse response of the system is the key ingredient of the convolution integral. Define the deconvolution problem and discuss why it is important in physiology and medicine by also giving some examples.

5

Modeling the system

5.1 Introduction

The previous chapter showcased how models could be developed in such a way as to provide a correspondence with available physiological data. The objective was to produce a mathematical expression that was capable of describing the available data. In such situations successful modeling would be characterized primarily by a good fit of the model to the data (or of the data to the model, depending on one's perspective). However, such models do not necessarily correspond explicitly to the relevant underlying physiology.

Where there is a need for the model to correspond to the relevant physiology, then some other means of modeling are required, which is the theme of this chapter. The aim is to describe approaches to modeling the physiology (which can be regarded as the system of interest). It will be shown that this can be done at a number of levels. The particular approach to be adopted depends upon the available *a priori* knowledge that is available, and the extent to which it is reasonable to make simplifying assumptions regarding the physiology.

A number of approaches will be compared and contrasted. Comparisons will be made of static and dynamic, deterministic and stochastic, time-invariant and time-varying, lumped and distributed, linear and nonlinear, and continuous and discrete forms. Between them, these represent different levels of complexity of models. Some of the basic mathematics associated with linear first-order dynamic systems have already been discussed in Section 2.3. However, we shall begin with the simple static case and then systematically progress to more complex forms of dynamic representation.

5.2 Static models

Let us begin by considering a static model, a model of a system in which there is no change occurring over a period of time.

In the circulatory system, a relationship can be developed between the rate at which blood flows through a blood vessel and the pressure drop along that length of blood vessel. For simplicity, assume that there is a steady volume flow (Q) of blood along a blood vessel which is treated as being rigid, where the pressure drop along its length (L) is P, and let the internal diameter of the vessel be D. Then, given the assumptions stated earlier, the relationship between flow and pressure can be expressed as:

$$Q = \frac{KPD^4}{L} \tag{5.1}$$

Introduction to Modeling in Physiology and Medicine. DOI: https://doi.org/10.1016/B978-0-12-815756-5.00005-9

where K is the parameter which creates the equality. In fact, K varies with the viscosity of the fluid (in this case blood), which means that (5.1) can be rewritten as:

$$Q = \frac{(P_1 - P_2)\pi r^4}{8\rho L} \tag{5.2}$$

P_1 and P_2 are the pressures at the two ends of the blood vessel, r is the internal radius, and ρ is the viscosity of the blood. In other words, the ratio of the mean pressure gradient to mean flow is a measure of the extent to which the system resists flow. We can term this ratio as the vascular resistance R where:

$$R = \frac{8\rho L}{\pi r^4} \tag{5.3}$$

Therefore we can write the relation between pressure and flow as:

$$(P_1 - P_2) = RQ \tag{5.4}$$

Hence from measurement of mean values of pressure and flow, the resistance can be calculated. In the context of the circulatory system, if P_1 is the mean ascending aortic pressure, P_2 is venous pressure, and Q is the mean aortic flow (cardiac output), then R represents the total systemic peripheral resistance. If, in this model, the assumption can be made to neglect the effect of venous pressure (since it is only a few mmHg), then an estimate of the total peripheral resistance can be obtained from the ratio of mean ascending aortic pressure and cardiac output. This linear relationship is graphically depicted in Fig. 5–1.

The linear model above is a particular case of the more general model which states that pressure P is a function of flow Q. This can be expressed mathematically as:

$$P = f(Q) \tag{5.5}$$

where f( ) represents a general form of functional relationship.

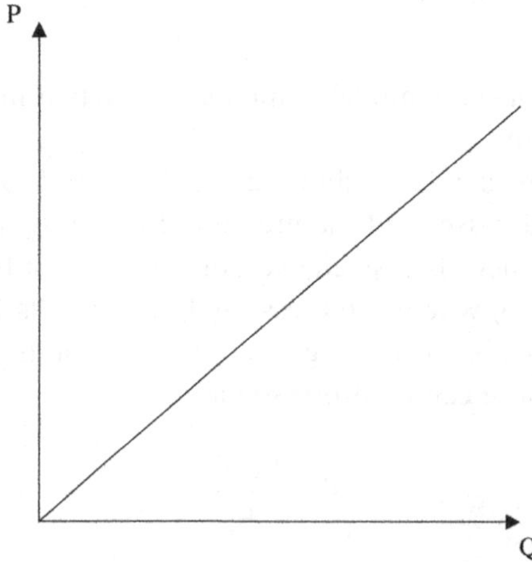

FIGURE 5–1 Graphical representation of a linear relationship between blood pressure, P, and blood flow, Q.

In the case of the airflow in the respiratory system, a linear model relationship between pressure and flow only applies in the case of laminar airflow. Where there is turbulent flow, the resistance to flow is no longer a constant, but is now a function of gas flow:

$$R = R_0 + R_1(Q) \tag{5.6}$$

R_0 corresponds to the value of resistance at zero flow and $R_1(\ )$ is the general nonlinear functional relationship defining the manner in which the resistance in the steady state increases with increase in airflow.

The turbulent flow that occurs in the upper respiratory tract at high flow rates, such as in the case of mechanical ventilation, can be reasonably approximated by a model of the form:

$$P = R_0Q + R_1Q^2 \tag{5.7}$$

This model is nonlinear, since in addition to the first term R_0Q—which is linear—there is a second term in which there is a component of pressure proportional to the square of the flow R_1Q^2.

Another example of a static, nonlinear model is provided by the Michaelis–Menten equation. This describes the steady-state (static) condition of an enzyme-controlled chemical reaction, the model being of the form:

$$v = \frac{V_{max}}{K_m + s} \tag{5.8}$$

The variable v is the rate or velocity, or flux, of the chemical reaction in the steady state and s is the concentration of the chemical substrate involved in the reaction. Two parameters characterize the effects of the enzyme involved in the reaction. V_{max} is the maximal rate of the chemical reaction as the substrate concentration becomes very large and tends toward infinity. The second parameter (K_m) corresponds to the concentration of chemical substrates for which the reaction velocity would be half of the maximum value of V_{max}. This model is nonlinear, since a doubling of the value of the substrate concentration s does not result in a doubling of the reaction of the chemical velocity v. The nonlinear nature of this model relationship is shown graphically in Fig. 5–2 where, in effect, the steady-state reaction velocity or flux saturates toward its maximal value as the substrate concentration tends toward infinity.

However, if one examines the form of this model as it would apply in the case of low values of substrate concentration, the relationship approximates to one in which the reaction velocity is directly proportional to the substrate concentration. In other words, for small values of s, the denominator of (5.8) approximates to K_m, since s is small compared to K_m, and so the model equation for reaction velocity can be written as:

$$v = \frac{V_{max}}{K_m} \tag{5.9}$$

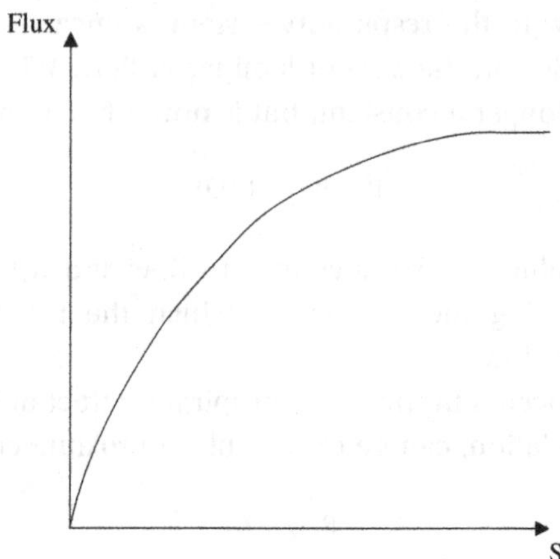

FIGURE 5–2 Nonlinear relationship between chemical flux and the concentration of the chemical substrates.

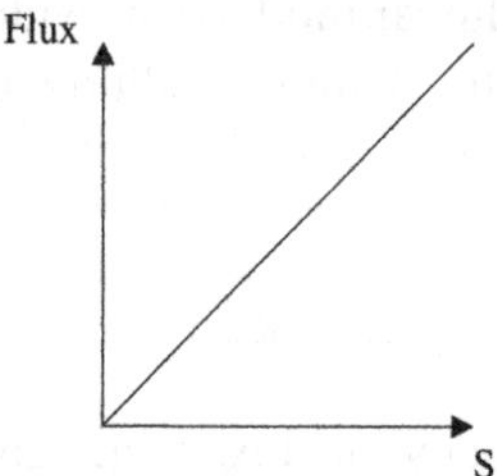

FIGURE 5–3 Linearized relationship between chemical flux and substrate concentration.

Under appropriate conditions, this is an example of being able to approximate a full nonlinear model by a linear one. It should be noted, however, that this model is only valid for small values of substrate concentration. Graphically, this linearized model would give rise to the relationship shown in Fig. 5–3.

5.3 Linear modeling

While analysis of the steady-state condition can provide some useful information regarding the characteristics of a physiological system, the extent of this information is necessarily limited. More often than not, one would wish to have some knowledge of the manner in which a particular system responds to a stimulus, not just being limited to knowledge of the final state that one or more of the variables ultimately achieve. This means that we must move from a static view of the world to one in which we examine the richness of dynamic behavior that a system may exhibit.

As we have already seen, a model is by definition an approximation of a system in terms of its representation. In other words, in modeling the dynamics of a system a number of assumptions are going to be made, and it is important that such assumptions should be made in an explicit manner. To begin with let us consider the simplest case. We shall assume that our system can be treated as being deterministic, linear, and time-invariant (that is to say, that the parameters are constant, rather than changing in some way over time). Furthermore, effects which in reality may be spatially distributed are treated as if they could be lumped together in a way that removes the need for this spatial dimension. As a first example we shall derive a simple dynamic model to represent a portion of the circulatory system.

5.3.1 The Windkessel circulatory model

In the Windkessel model, the arteries are treated as if they comprise an elastic reservoir with fluid storage capacity. The compliance of this reservoir is assumed to represent the total arterial compliance. The term compliance is the parameter that specifies the elastic nature of the blood vessels. It is defined as the incremental change in volume that would result from an incremental change in pressure. In other words:

$$C = \frac{\Delta V}{\Delta P} \tag{5.10}$$

where C is compliance, ΔP is the change in pressure, and ΔV is the change in the volume.

In terms of Fig. 5–4, blood enters the arterial reservoir as a result of ventricular ejection from the heart, and flows out at the other end of the reservoir through the peripheral resistance. A mathematical model of these dynamics can be formulated as follows. The input

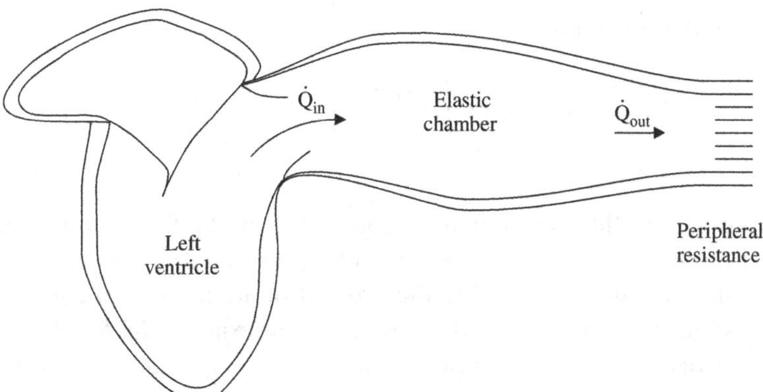

FIGURE 5–4 Representation of a portion of the circulatory system depicting the flow of blood from the left ventricle of the heart into the systemic circulation.

flow into the arterial system $\dot{Q}_{in}(t)$, is equal to the sum of the outflow $\dot{Q}_{out}(t)$ of blood from the arterial system into the venous system and the rate dV/dt of storage (the continuity equation):

$$\dot{Q}_{in}(t) = \frac{dV(t)}{dt} + \dot{Q}_{out}(t) \tag{5.11}$$

If one makes the assumption that there is a linear relationship between pressure and volume, then the total arterial compliance C will be constant throughout a heartbeat

$$C = \frac{dV(t)}{dP(t)} \tag{5.12}$$

Assuming that the outflow $\dot{Q}_{out}(t)$ is proportional to the arteriovenous pressure difference P(t), then:

$$\dot{Q}_{out}(t) = \frac{P(t)}{R} \tag{5.13}$$

where R is the total peripheral resistance. Substituting (5.12) and (5.13) into (5.11) yields:

$$\dot{Q}_{in}(t) = C\frac{dP(t)}{dt} + \frac{P(t)}{R} \tag{5.14}$$

Since there is flow into the arterial system only during ventricular systole, $\dot{Q}_{in}(t)$ is zero in diastole. If we define t* as the time at which ventricular ejection ends, and let T be the total duration of a cardiac cycle, the dynamic behavior of the system during any time interval during diastole can be described by:

$$C\frac{dP(t)}{dt} + \frac{P(t)}{R} = 0, \quad t* < t < T \tag{5.15}$$

The solution of this equation is:

$$P(t) = P \cdot \exp\left[-\frac{(t - t*)}{\tau}\right], \quad t* < t < T \tag{5.16}$$

where $\tau = RC$.

In other words, given the assumption that ascending aortic flow is zero during diastole, the Windkessel model describes the diastolic aortic pressure decay as a mono-exponential function with a time constant τ, equal to the product of arterial compliance and peripheral resistance. An estimate of τ can be made from fitting an exponential function to the plot of diastolic pressure decay. If cardiac output is measured, peripheral resistance can be computed from the ratio of mean pressure to cardiac output. Eventually, the ratio τ/R yields an estimate of the compliance, C. Eq. (5.16) is an example of the exponential response as a function of time which is the solution to any first-order, linear differential equation model.

5.3.2 Elimination from a single compartment

As a further example of a simple dynamic model, consider the elimination of a drug from the bloodstream. As an approximation it will be assumed that the bloodstream can be considered to be a single compartment, in which the drug is uniformly distributed. In other words, the concentration of the drug will be the same at all points within this bloodstream compartment. If the drug has been injected into the bloodstream, this assumption that there is a uniform concentration corresponds to neglecting the rapid mixing effects of the drug which would occur immediately following injection. Mathematically we can describe this model as follows:

$$\frac{dQ(t)}{dt} = -p_1 Q(t) + U(t), \quad Q(0) = 0 \tag{5.17}$$

$$C(t) = \frac{Q(t)}{V} \tag{5.18}$$

In (5.17), the variable Q represents the mass of drug in plasma as a function of time. The input variable U(t) is the mass of drug input into the bloodstream again as a function of time. The parameter (p_1) is the fractional rate constant for the drug, and V is the plasma distribution volume. In other words this equation states that the rate of change of mass of the drug is given by the difference between the flux of drug out of the compartment (the first term on the right-hand side of the equation) and the flux of drug into the compartment (the second term). The initial condition of this equation Q(0) is the mass of drug in the compartment at time zero.

For any value of input function U(t), the general solution of this pair of (5.17) and (5.18) can be shown to be the convolution integral:

$$C(t) = \frac{1}{V}\int_0^t \exp\left(-p_1(t-\tau)\right)U(\tau)d\tau \tag{5.19}$$

However, a simpler solution is obtained for the case where the drug is introduced rapidly as a brief pulse of unit magnitude, that is it approximates to a unit impulse, $U(t) = \delta(t)$. Now the solution becomes:

$$C(t) = \frac{1}{V_1}\exp(-p_1 t) \tag{5.20}$$

which is a single exponential decay characteristic of the response to an impulse for a lumped, linear, time-invariant, deterministic first-order system.

5.3.3 Gas exchange

As a further example of simple linear dynamic modeling, let us consider the process of gas exchange between the alveolus of the lung and the blood capillary (Flenley & Warren, 1988).

This takes place by passive diffusion across the alveolar–capillary membrane down a concentration gradient. For an inert solute in a single solvent, diffusion can be described by Fick's law as follows:

$$\frac{\Delta Q}{\Delta t} = -dA\frac{\Delta C}{l} \tag{5.21}$$

where the quantity of solute ΔQ diffusing per unit time Δt is a function of the cross-sectional area A and distance l over which diffusion is occurring. The concentration gradient is ΔC, and the diffusion coefficient is d, a physical rate constant which is dependent on properties of the system such as the molecular weight of the solute and the temperature and viscosity of the solvent. The quantity of the substance which is dissolved in the surface layers of the alveolar–capillary membrane, and hence the concentration gradient across the membrane, are determined by the product of the partial pressure of the substance in the adjoining compartment (alveolar or capillary) and the solubility coefficient α, for the substance in the membrane. Hence, we can rewrite Fick's law as follows:

$$\frac{\Delta Q}{\Delta t} = -\left[dA\frac{\alpha}{l}\right][P_A - P_C] \tag{5.22}$$

where P_A and P_C are the partial pressures that are exerted by the gas in the alveoli and capillaries respectively.

It might seem intuitively obvious that a thickening of the alveolar–capillary membrane; that is to say an increase in l, as can occur as a result of a disease process, should reduce the rate of diffusion. This would suggest that measurement of the diffusion rate would be a useful diagnostic tool. However, there are a number of complications when it comes to applying this simple Fick's law model to the lungs. First, the alveolar–capillary membrane consists of a layer of alveolar epithelial cells and capillary endothelial cells, both of which have a basement layer which in some areas are fused together, while in others are separated by a narrow interstitium. Hence the use of a single solubility coefficient cannot be justified. Moreover, the gases in question are not inert, but do in fact combine with hemoglobin in the capillary red blood cells. As such, the assumption that this chemical interaction is infinitely rapid and does not provide a rate limiting step in the gas exchange process is probably not valid. Finally, the total area involved in gas exchange and the thickness of the alveolar–capillary membrane vary with the degree of inflation of the lungs and cannot readily be measured. Hence, in clinical practice the term $-d\alpha\, A/l$ is replaced by the single term D, which is defined as the diffusing capacity of the lungs. Fick's equation can therefore be rewritten as:

$$\frac{\Delta Q}{\Delta t} = D(P_A - P_C) \tag{5.23}$$

This is the standard first-order linear model which is widely adopted in respiratory measurement.

5.3.4 The dynamics of a swinging limb

The next example is a freely swinging human limb. Specifically, let us consider the situation in which the leg swings freely under the action of gravity, after its release from contact with the ground in its rearward position by raising the toe. This situation depicted in Fig. 5–5 is the basis of the mathematical model that has been developed by Milsum (1966).

The model described here makes a number of simplifying assumptions. For instance, the complexities of leg shortening and hip raising necessary for the heel to be able to clear the ground are excluded. Equally the focus is on the controlled system, which means that the controlling effects arising from the neuromuscular feedback loops of the antagonistic pairs of effector muscles are not considered.

The angular motion of the leg is based on Newton's second law of motion:

$$T = J\frac{d^2\theta}{dt^2} = J\frac{d\omega}{dt} \tag{5.24}$$

where T is the net torque, or turning moment about the axis of rotation; J is the moment of inertia of the accelerating body about this axis; θ is the angle of rotation; and ω is the angular velocity of rotation.

As a further simplifying assumption in the modeling process, the leg will be assumed to be a stiff uniform cylinder as shown in Fig. 5–6 with the dimensions of:

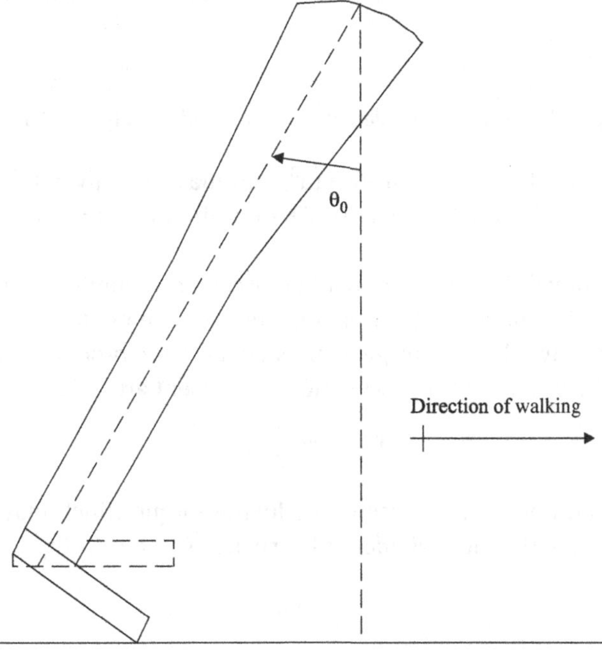

FIGURE 5–5 Model of swinging limb. *Adapted from Milsum, J. H. (1966).*

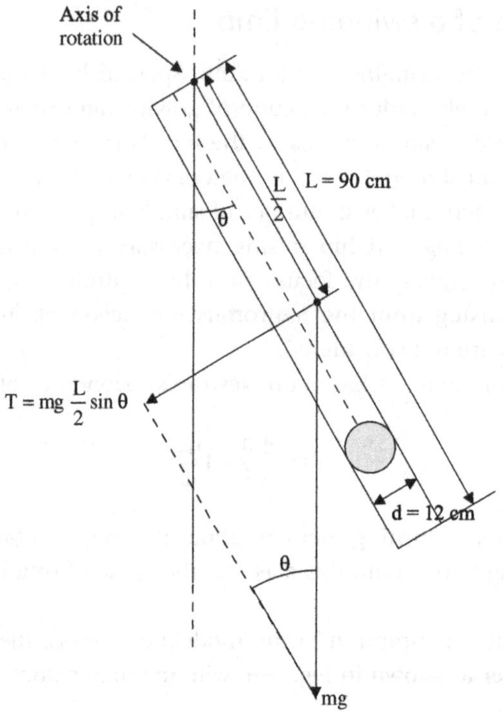

FIGURE 5–6 The leg modeled as a stiff uniform cylinder. *Adapted from Milsum, J. H. (1966).*

$$\text{Length, } L = 90\text{ cm; diameter, } d = 12\text{ cm; and density, } \rho = 1.1\text{g/cm}^2 \tag{5.25}$$

from which volume, $V = (\pi/4)d^2L = 10{,}300\text{ cm}^3$, and mass, $m = \rho V = 11.5$ kg, which approximates to a typical value for a 70 kg male subject despite the simplifying assumptions which have been made.

If it is further assumed that there are neither viscous nor nonlinear retarding torques due to joint stiffness, air friction, tissue deformation, etc. then the net torque is only that resulting from the forces of gravity. This net torque is thus equal to the product of the leg-weight component perpendicular to the leg (mg sin θ) and the moment arm L/2, as shown in Fig. 5–6:

$$T = -mg\frac{L}{2}\cdot\sin\theta \tag{5.26}$$

The right-hand term of (5.24) is termed the inertia torque which may be evaluated using the moment of inertia of the thin-cylindered leg swinging about its hip joint:

$$J = \frac{mL^2}{3} \tag{5.27}$$

Substituting (5.26) and (5.27) into (5.24) leads to the following second-order differential equation of motion:

$$\frac{d^2\theta(t)}{dt^2} + \left(\frac{3g}{2L}\right)\sin\theta(t) = 0 \tag{5.28}$$

Due to the presence of the term sin θ, (5.28) is in fact nonlinear. However, the equation may be linearized if the deflections of the limb may be considered as being small, in which case sin θ is approximately equal to θ (where θ is measured in radians).

Milsum (1966) had assessed the error associated with making such a small deflection, linearizing assumption. For a leg of length 90 cm, and with a half pace of 38 cm, θ is equal to 0.4 radians, whereas sin θ would be 0.39 radians. This implies a maximum error arising from this assumption of 2.5%, with the average error being much less than this figure. Hence (5.28) becomes:

$$\frac{d^2\theta}{dt^2} + \left(\frac{3g}{2L}\right)\theta = 0 \tag{5.29}$$

Solving this equation yields a sinusoidally varying pattern of angular position of the swinging limb, without there being any damping of the oscillations. In other words, the solution of this equation would correspond to unending sinusoidal oscillation as shown in Fig. 5–7. In reality, however, there are energy dissipation effects during working, which in the model can be included in the form:

$$T_b = -b\frac{d\theta}{dt} \tag{5.30}$$

This simple linear representation is, of course, an approximation to what in practice is probably a more complex effect. The negative sign indicates that this torque opposes the motion. This viscous friction causes the oscillatory response as depicted in Fig. 5–7 to decay, as shown by the dashed line, toward the terminal state of zero energy stored in the system. In steady walking the relevant muscles in the leg must pump in enough energy to

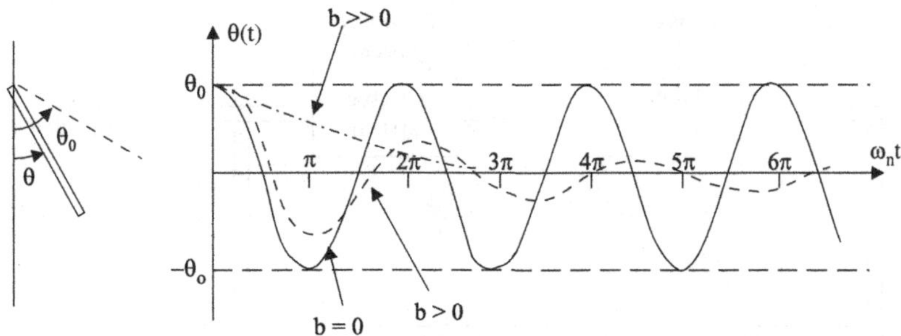

FIGURE 5–7 Dynamics of swinging limb model. *Adapted from Milsum, J. H. (1966).*

make up for this viscous dissipation as well as providing the various forces required in relation to posture which this simple model formulation has neglected (Milsum, 1966). It is therefore necessary to add an appropriate torque, $T_m(t)$, as a function of time, so that (5.24) becomes:

$$T_m - b\frac{d\theta}{dt} - mg\left(\frac{L}{2}\right)\theta = J\frac{d^2\theta}{dt^2} \tag{5.31}$$

or

$$J\frac{d^2\theta(t)}{dt^2} + b\frac{d\theta(t)}{dt} + k\theta(t) = T_m(t) \tag{5.32}$$

where the gravity coefficient has been defined as a generalized spring constant $k = mg(L/2)$. This equation represents a basic second-order linear system with an input forcing function and viscous damping in addition to the inertia and spring effects of the system modeled as (5.29). From an energy perspective, the spring stores potential energy, the inertia stores kinetic energy, and the viscous damping dissipates both.

5.3.5 A model of glucose regulation

The glucose regulatory system is a classic negative feedback system (Fig. 5–8) maintaining glucose homeostasis. When blood glucose concentration increases after a perturbation, for example, a meal, an oral glucose tolerance test (OGTT) or an intravenous infusion of glucose, the pancreas beta-cells secrete more insulin. The resulting increased plasma level of insulin, in turn, enables blood glucose to return to its basal concentration by enhancing glucose utilization by the tissues and inhibiting endogenous glucose production.

Let us assume that the glucose and insulin systems are each describable by a single compartment representation with, respectively, substrate and hormonal fluxes entering and outgoing from the compartment (Fig. 5–9). The next step then is to detail the control signals from the glucose to the insulin system and from the insulin to the glucose system. A general

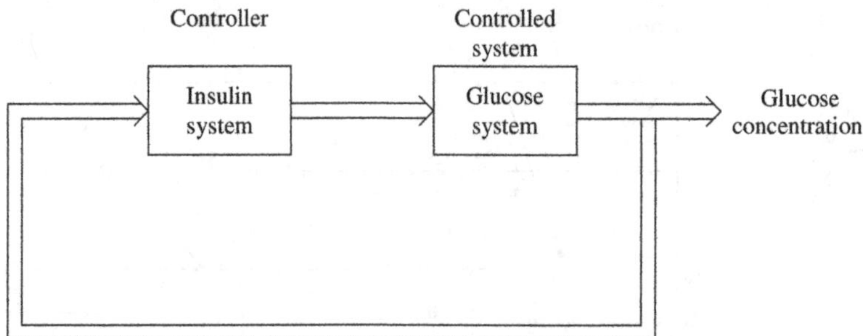

FIGURE 5–8 The glucose regulatory system depicted as a classic negative feedback system.

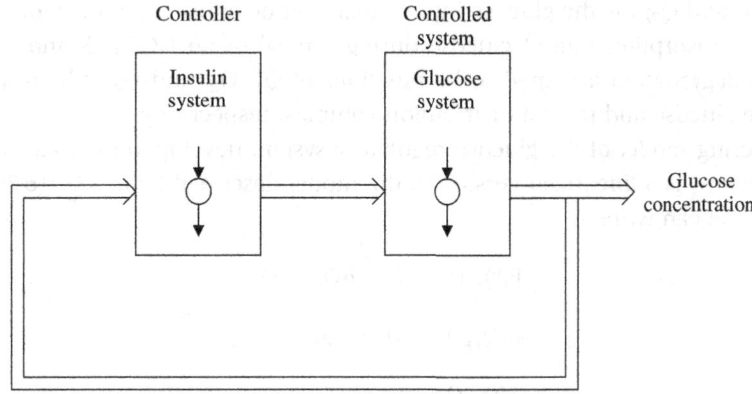

FIGURE 5–9 The glucose regulatory system depicting the compartmental structure of controller and controlled system.

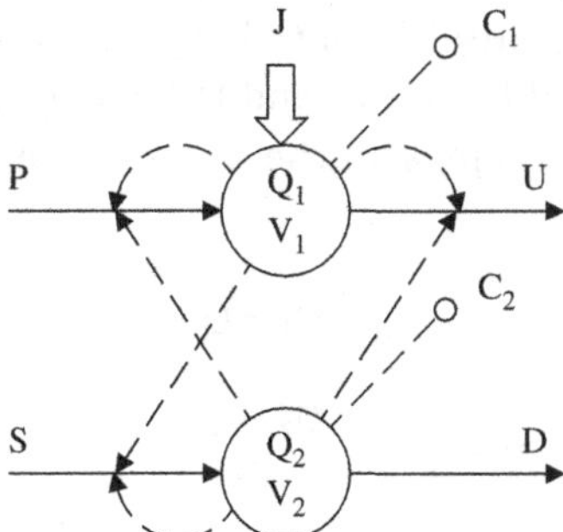

FIGURE 5–10 Glucose and insulin fluxes and their control following a glucose perturbation J. The measured concentrations of glucose C_1 and insulin C_2 are also shown.

scheme depicting the glucose and insulin fluxes of material and the control signals following a glucose perturbation is shown in Fig. 5–10. The model equations are:

$$\dot{Q}_1(t) = P(Q_1, Q_2) - U(Q_1, Q_2) + J(t) \quad Q_1(0) = Q_{10} \tag{5.33}$$

$$\dot{Q}_2(t) = S(Q_1, Q_2) - D(Q_2) \quad Q_2(0) = Q_{20} \tag{5.34}$$

$$C_1(t) = \frac{Q_1(t)}{V_1} \tag{5.35}$$

$$C_2(t) = \frac{Q_2(t)}{V_2} \tag{5.36}$$

where Q_1 and Q_2 denote glucose and insulin masses respectively, with the suffix "o" denoting the basal state; P and U are respectively glucose production and utilization assumed to be functions of Q_1 and Q_2; J is the glucose input which can be either an intravenous injection or infusion or the absorption rate of glucose during a meal or an OGTT; S and D are insulin secretion and degradation assumed to be functions of Q_1, Q_2, and Q_2 only, respectively; V_1 and V_2 are the glucose and insulin distribution volumes, respectively.

The pioneering model of the glucose regulatory system developed by Bolie (1961), which we describe below, is a linearized version of the model described by (5.33)–(5.36). To arrive at this model one can write:

$$P(Q_1, Q_2) = P_0 - \alpha Q_1 - \beta Q_2 \tag{5.37}$$

$$U(Q_1, Q_2) = U_0 + \gamma Q_1 + \delta Q_2 \tag{5.38}$$

$$S(Q_1, Q_2) = S_0 + \varepsilon Q_1 - \eta Q_2 \tag{5.39}$$

$$D(Q_2) = D_0 - \mu Q_2 \tag{5.40}$$

where α, β, γ, δ, ε, and μ are rate parameters ≥ 0 [the minus and plus signs in (5.37)–(5.40) denote the modalities of glucose–insulin control, e.g., insulin secretion is stimulated by glucose and inhibited by insulin] and P_0, S_0, U_0, and D_0 denote values in the basal state.

By defining the variables that represent the deviation of glucose and insulin from their basal values:

$$q_1 = Q_1 - Q_{10} \tag{5.41}$$

$$q_2 = Q_2 - Q_{20} \tag{5.42}$$

one has:

$$\dot{q}_1(t) = -p_1 q_1(t) - p_2 q_2(t) + J(t) \quad q_1(0) = 0 \tag{5.43}$$

$$\dot{q}_2(t) = -p_3 q_2(t) + p_4 q_1(t) \quad q_2(0) = 0 \tag{5.44}$$

$$c_1(t) = \frac{q_1(t)}{V_1} \tag{5.45}$$

$$c_2(t) = \frac{q_2(t)}{V_2} \tag{5.46}$$

where $p_1 = \alpha + \gamma$; $p_2 = \beta + \delta$; $p_3 = \eta + \mu$; $p_4 = \varepsilon$.

This linear model has been used in conjunction with intravenous injections or infusions (Bolie, 1961; Ceresa *et al.*, 1973; Segre *et al.*, 1973) and also during an OGTT (Ackerman *et al.*, 1964; Gatewood *et al.*, 1968a, 1968b) to obtain a four-parameter portrait of the glucose regulation system in various glucoses intolerance states including diabetes. For the intravenous inputs one has $J(t) = D \cdot \delta(t)$ for the injection and $J(t) = J[1(t) - 1(t - t_a)]$ for the infusion, where the term $\delta(t)$ is the Dirac function and $1(t - T)$ the Heaviside function

($=0$ for $t<T$ and 1 for $t\geq T$). For the oral input one has $J(t)=J[1(t)-1(t-t_a)][1-e^{-\beta(t-t_a)}]$.

An alternative simpler parameterization has also been used to characterize the glucose regulatory system. To do so, (5.43)–(5.46) have been recast as second-order differential equations in C_1 and C_2 by first writing (5.43) and (5.44) in terms of C_1 and C_2:

$$\dot{C}_1(t) = -m_1c_1(t) - m_2c_2(t) + J'(t) \quad C_1(0) = 0 \tag{5.47}$$

$$\dot{C}_2(t) = -m_3c_2(t) + m_4c_1(t) \quad C_2(0) = 0 \tag{5.48}$$

with $m_1 = p_1$, $m_2 = p_2V_2/V_1$, $m_3 = p_3$, $m_4 = p_4V_1/V_2$, and $J'(t) = J(t)/V_1$; and then differentiating (5.47) and (5.48) with respect to time. This leads, after some algebraic manipulation, to a pair of second-order equations:

$$\ddot{C}_1(t) + 2\alpha\dot{C}_1(t) + \overline{\omega}_0^2C_1(t) = S_1(t) \tag{5.49}$$

$$\ddot{C}_2(t) + 2\alpha\dot{C}_2(t) + \overline{\omega}_0^2C_2(t) = S_2(t) \tag{5.50}$$

where $\alpha = (m_1 + m_3)/2$, $\overline{\omega}_0^2 = m_1\, m_3 + m_2m_4$, $S_1(t) = m_3J'(t) + \dot{J}'(t)$, and $S_2(t) = m_4J'(t)$.

The linearity of the system allows us to obtain an analytical solution, if the input $J(t)$ is a simple function of time. For instance if $J(t)$ is such that:

$$S_1(t) = B \cdot \delta(t) \tag{5.51}$$

one has:

$$C_1(t) = \frac{B}{\overline{\omega}}e^{-\alpha t}\sin\overline{\omega} \tag{5.52}$$

where $\overline{\omega}^2 = \overline{\omega}_0^2 - \alpha^2$.

For situations in which (5.51) can be considered to be a good approximation for an intravenous infusion (certainly it is for an injection) and for an oral administration, interpreting glucose concentration measurement using (5.52) provides a two-parameter classification of the blood glucose control system. In particular $\overline{\omega}_0$ was suggested in Ackerman *et al.* (1964) as being the most significant parameter in distinguishing diabetics from normal subjects. Moreover, the natural period $T_0 = 2\pi/\overline{\omega}_0$ was used as a classification parameter: normal subjects showed T_0 values less than 3 hours, while diabetics were greater than 5 hours. However, a significant gray area was observed.

This linear model made a conceptually important contribution to work in this field in the 1970s. However, this linear description has been subsequently shown to be not valid, for example, if insulin is also measured and the model of (5.42)–(5.46) is fitted simultaneously to both glucose and insulin concentration data (and will be discussed later). This, in some sense, is not surprising since glucose and insulin concentrations hardly show a small change during an intravenous or an oral perturbation, thus violating the assumption that would justify linearization of the model of (5.33)–(5.36) that is, deviations from steady-state equilibrium are sufficiently small.

5.4 Distributed modeling

In many cases metabolic processes can be adequately represented in terms of a lumped model. This assumes that it is reasonable to consider that a chemical substance is uniformly distributed in a physical space treated as a single compartment. This was the assumption made in the example of drug elimination considered in Section 5.3.2. In that case the drug was assumed to be uniformly distributed throughout the bloodstream, resulting in the drug concentration at any particular time being of equal value throughout that space. Such a simple model clearly neglects the effects of blood flow and mixing during the early period following the drug injection.

In distributed modeling, no such assumption of homogeneity is made. This leads to a more complicated form of mathematical representation. The examples of lumped models presented in Section 5.3 gave rise to ordinary differential equations. These were equations in which the left-hand side of the equality took the form dx/dt, the rate at which the dependent variable x is changing with respect to time t, the independent variable. In other words, because a lumped model had been adopted, one only had to consider variation of drug concentration with respect to time. In a distributed model there would also be the need to represent the variation of drug concentration with respect to spatial position.

Mathematically this gives rise to equations involving two partial derivatives: for example, $\partial x/\partial z$, the partial derivative (rate of change) of x (say drug concentration) with respect to z, a spatial variable (say the distance along a particular blood vessel), as well as $\partial x/\partial t$, the partial rate of change of drug concentration with respect to time.

The solution for models realized as sets of partial differential equations is much more complicated than that of the ordinary differential equations of lumped models. Normally one has to resort to numerical computational techniques, the scope of which lies beyond this introductory text.

5.4.1 Blood–tissue exchange

An important area of distributed parameter modeling is transport and metabolism of a substance at the organ level. This is a topic that has been considered in detail by Vicini (2001) (extracts from these treatments are included here). Every organ *in vivo* is perfused by its own vascular tree, and capillaries are the most important elements since they allow exchange of substrates between blood and tissue through passive or active transport. The capillary–tissue unit is therefore the elementary functional unit discussed here, in order to describe transport and metabolism of a substance at the organ level. The substance that reaches the capillary is proportional to the flow that perfuses it. The flow to the system is partitioned in all the branches of the capillary network, and these partitions come together in the outlet vein. The flow subdivision is not uniform and is referred to as the heterogeneity of flow. As a result there is heterogeneity of metabolism in every capillary–tissue unit. This is shown schematically in Fig. 5–11. Every capillary–tissue unit is positioned between an arteriole and a venule. Blood reaches the capillaries through an arteriole and leaves them through a

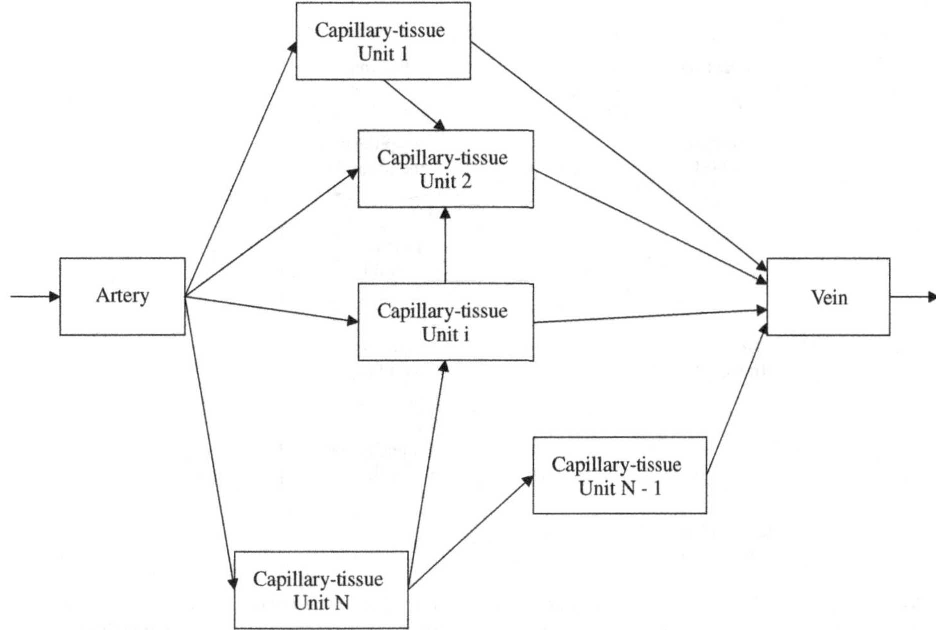

FIGURE 5–11 Schematic representation of the vascular network of an organ showing the heterogeneity of blood–tissue exchange. Transport and metabolism occur in the capillary–tissue unit.

venule, but from an arteriole, blood can be distributed to numerous meta-arterioles before reaching the capillary.

A typical capillary can be thought of as a thin wall tube (capillary membrane), formed by endothelial cells embedded in one another. The transport modality through the capillary membrane is twofold. Some substances are subject exclusively to passage through the small spaces between endothelial cells and endothelial gaps; this is especially true for smaller molecules (e.g., proteins). Other substances can also flow through the endothelial cells by means of facilitated diffusion or active transport. Fundamentally, blood–tissue exchange consists of the passage of molecules from the plasma, through the capillary membrane, to the interstitial fluid and, from there, through the cellular membrane or sarcolemma, to the parenchymal cell where metabolism takes place. An example of the elementary processes of blood–tissue exchange is shown in Fig. 5–12.

The experimental techniques for the study of blood–tissue exchange are based on the use of tracers and include multiple tracer dilution, positron emission tomography (PET), and nuclear magnetic resonance spectroscopy. Here we concentrate on multiple tracer dilution and will discuss PET and interpretative system models in Chapter 11, Case Studies.

This method consists of the simultaneous injection, upstream of the organ, of more than one tracer, each with different molecular characteristics. The simultaneous use of several differing tracers allows separate monitoring of the elementary processes of blood–tissue exchange. For example, consider the case when the objective of the experiment is the

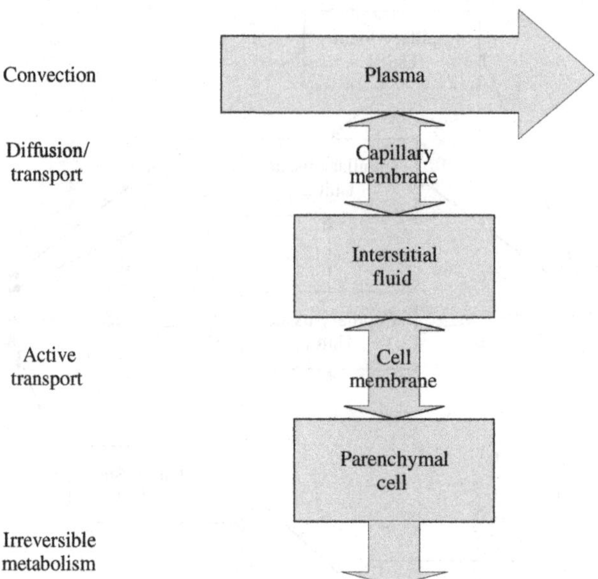

FIGURE 5–12 Basic steps of blood–tissue exchange. Glucose is transported via convection by plasma flow, diffuses in the interstitial volume, and from there is transported through the cell membrane, and is irreversibly metabolized there.

measurement of all the elementary processes (convection, diffusion, transport, and metabolism). In such a situation one can usually inject four tracers simultaneously upstream of the organ (in an artery that transports blood flow entering the organ), and then measure them downstream (from a vein that collects the flow leaving the organ).

The first tracer is distributed only in the capillary bed (intravascular tracer), the second is subject to the bidirectional exchange through the capillary membrane (extracellular tracer), the third, once subjected to the two previous steps, also permeates the cell through the sarcolemma (permeating not metabolizable tracer), and, finally, the fourth is also metabolized (permeating metabolizable tracer). These tracers must obviously be distinguishable from one another once they reach the organ outflow. The venous outflow curves (Fig. 5–13) must then be analyzed by means of plausible and physiologically reasonable mathematical models of the organ.

5.4.1.1 The single-capillary model

Consider a generic single tracer confined within the capillary. In the hypothesis of negligible radial diffusion (radius of capillary is small), the concentration of tracer (expressed, for example, in mmol/mL) will be defined by the surface c(x,t) (where x is the space coordinate and t the temporal coordinate). The fundamental equation of the distributed parameter

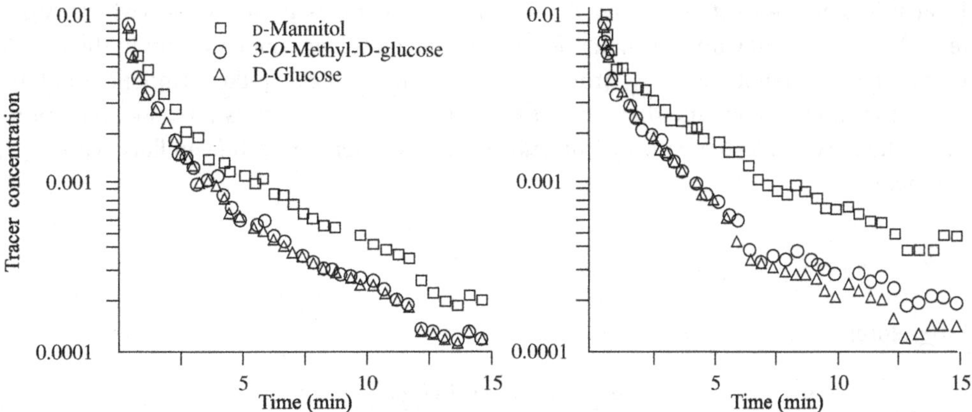

FIGURE 5–13 Multiple indicator dilution washout curves to measure glucose transport and phosphorylation in human skeletal muscle in the basal (left) and insulin stimulated (right) state. Three tracers are injected in the brachial artery, an extracellular D-[^{12}C]-mannitol), a transportable but not metabolizable (3-0-[^{14}C]-methyl-D-Glucose) and a metabolizable D-[^{3}H]glucose), and their concentration measured in a vein. *Adapted from Saccomani et al., 1996.*

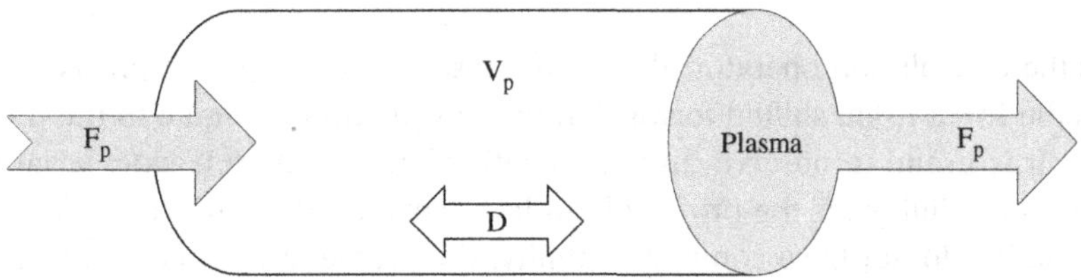

FIGURE 5–14 Single-region, single-capillary blood–tissue exchange model.

model for the single capillary (Fig. 5–14) is given by the classic equation describing convection and axial diffusion:

$$\frac{\partial c(x,t)}{\partial t} = -v(x)\frac{\partial c(x,t)}{\partial x} + D\frac{\partial^2 c(x,t)}{\partial x^2} \tag{5.53}$$

where v is the velocity of convection (cm/s) and D the diffusion coefficient (cm^2/s). At this point, we can introduce some simplifications. First, let us suppose that the system is in a steady state. Moreover, it is known that the presence of red blood cells creates, in the capillaries, inner spaces of purely convective transport (this is the plug flow): a limited error is then introduced if we neglect the effect of axial diffusion. Transport in the single capillary therefore remains defined by convection alone:

$$\frac{\partial c(x,t)}{\partial t} = -v(x)\frac{\partial c(x,t)}{\partial x} \tag{5.54}$$

If, at this point, we establish that the capillary diameter is uniform everywhere, we can write $v(x) = v$. From now on, we shall refer to the plasma tracer concentration in the capillary as $c_p(x,t)$. Let us denote with V_p (mL/g) the volume of the capillary (independent from the axial coordinate, since the diameter of the capillary is constant as a reasonable approximation), the flow of plasma with F_p (mL/min/g), and the length of the capillary with L (cm). We can write:

$$v = \frac{F_p L}{V_P} \tag{5.55}$$

and therefore:

$$\frac{\partial c_p(x, t)}{\partial t} = -\frac{F_p L}{V_p}\frac{\partial c_p(x, t)}{\partial x} \tag{5.56}$$

This is a first-order partial differential equation with boundary condition: $c_p(0,t) = u(t)$, where u(t) is the concentration profile (mmol/mL) at the capillary inlet. Its solution is:

$$c_p(L, t) = \delta\left(t - \frac{V_p}{F_p}\right) \otimes u(t) = u\left(t - \frac{V_p}{F_p}\right) \tag{5.57}$$

where $\otimes$ is the convolution operator. Briefly, the response of a single capillary to the generic input u(t) is the input itself, shifted forward in time by an amount equal to the transit time of the capillary. It is useful to observe that the length of the capillary L, since axial diffusion is negligible, does not influence the profile of outflow concentration. In agreement with the fact that the capillaries do not have contractile ability, the profile at the inlet is not deformed by passage through the capillary.

5.4.1.2 The capillary–interstitial fluid model

Suppose that the capillary is dipped in a homogeneous and stagnant medium (convection happens only in the capillary), the interstitial fluid, which in the microcirculatory system separates the capillary membrane from the cellular membrane. As we have already indicated, the capillary membrane is characterized by the presence of endothelial gaps, that is, fissures between the endothelial cells. The possibility that a generic substance will pass from one side of the membrane to the other will depend on many factors, including the width of the gaps and their distribution on the membrane. We now define the permeability of a membrane (Crone & Lassen, 1970) as:

$$P = \frac{\text{Flow through the membrane}}{\text{Membrane surface} \times \text{concentration gradient through the membrane}} \tag{5.58}$$

Let us now consider the concentration gradient through the capillary membrane. The concentration in the capillary is $c_p(x,t)$; and in the interstitial fluid (referred to as the interstitial volume, V_{isf}) is $c_{isf}(x,t)$. The dynamics of the concentration through the capillary membrane can therefore be described, as a function of the discontinuity of the concentration across the membrane, with the equation (first-order process):

$$\frac{\partial c_p(x,t)}{\partial t} = -\frac{S_g(x)}{V_P}[P_-(x)c_p(x,t) - P_+(x)c_{isf}(x,t)] \tag{5.59}$$

where $S_g(x)$ is the capillary membrane surface interested to the exchange (g indicates the endothelial pores, or endothelial gaps), $P_-(x)$ is the permeability in the direction leaving from the membrane (centrifuge permeability), $P_+(x)$ is the permeability in the direction entering the capillary (centripetal permeability) (Bassingthwaighte & Goresky, 1984).

At this point, we make the following hypotheses:

- the dimensions of capillary and tissue are uniform with respect to the axial direction; therefore the surface relating to the exchange is independent of the axial dimension: $S_g(x) = S_g$.
- the permeability is uniform in both the axial, $P(x) = P$, and the radial direction, $P_+ = P_- = P$; the product permeability-surface PS_g (mL/min/g) is therefore a constant.
- the radial diffusion in the interstitial fluid is fast; if the capillary is situated in a well-perfused organ (e.g., the cardiac tissue), the distance between the capillaries is usually small, so that the equilibrium time in the lateral direction of the concentration of the substance subject to diffusion is a negligible fraction of the transit time of the capillary.

We can now derive a simple two-region model that describes transcapillary transfer (Fig. 5–15). The explicit solution of this model was derived by Rose & Goresky (1976), Sangren & Sheppard (1953), and Sheppard (1962), while Bassingthwaighte *et al.* (1992) proposed efficient numerical algorithms.

The plasma region equation is the following:

$$\frac{\partial c_P(x,t)}{\partial t} = -\frac{F_p L}{V_p}\frac{\partial c_p(x,t)}{\partial x} - \frac{PS_g}{V_p}\left[c_p(x,t) - c_{isf}(x,t)\right] \tag{5.60}$$

and analogously for the interstitial fluid equation:

$$\frac{\partial c_{isf}(x,t)}{\partial t} = \frac{PS_g}{V_{isf}}\left[c_p(x,t) - c_{isf}(x,t)\right] \tag{5.61}$$

where V_{isf} is the volume of the interstitial fluid.

The system of two equations defined above describes transport through the endothelial gaps of the capillary membrane for a single capillary. One can show that the solution to this system is given, again for the boundary condition $c_p(0,t) = u(t)$, by this function:

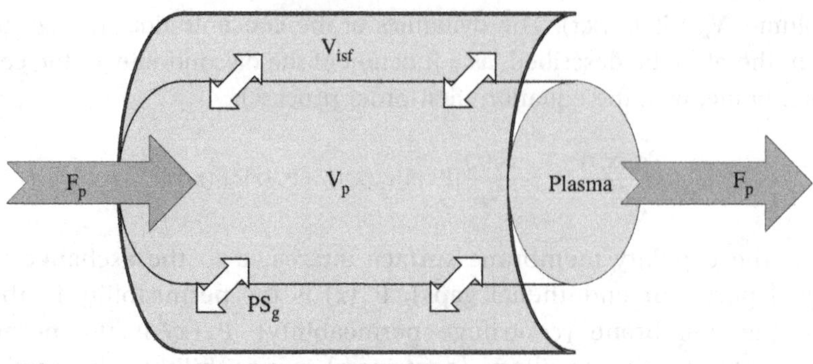

FIGURE 5–15 The two-region, single-capillary blood–tissue exchange model.

$$c_p(L, t) = e^{-PS_g/F_p}\left(t - \frac{V_p}{Fp}\right) + \sum_{n=1}^{+\infty} \frac{\left(\frac{V_p}{F_p}\frac{PS_g}{V_p}\frac{PS_g}{V_{isf}}\right)^n \left(t - \frac{V_p}{F_p}\right)^{n-1} e^{-PS_g/V_{isf}(t-V_p/F_p)-PS_g/F_p} 1(t-\tau)}{n!(n-1)!} \tag{5.62}$$

where $l(t-\tau)$ is the step function (zero before τ and one at and after τ). Eq. (5.62) can be written more conveniently if we define the auxiliary constants $\tau = V_p/F_p$, $k_a = PS_g/V_p$, $k_b = PS_g/V_{isf}$:

$$c_p(L, t) = e^{-\tau k_a}\delta(t-\tau) + \sum_{n=1}^{+\infty} \frac{(\tau k_a k_b)^n (t-\tau)^{n-1} e^{-k_b(t-\tau)-\tau k_a} 1(t-\tau)}{n!(n-1)!} \tag{5.63}$$

The first addendum (throughput fraction) represents the molecules of substance that flow directly through the capillary without ever leaving it and is, therefore, equal to the intravascular response of the single capillary, scaled by the factor $e^{-\tau ka}$. The second addendum (tail function) describes the return (backdiffusion) of the substance from the interstitial fluid to the capillary (Bassingthwaighte & Goresky, 1984).

5.4.1.3 The capillary–interstitial fluid-cell model

At this point, we can model the kinetics of a substance leaving interstitial fluid and entering the cell membrane through the parenchymal cell. The model (Fig. 5–16), a rather straightforward extension of the two-region model, is described by:

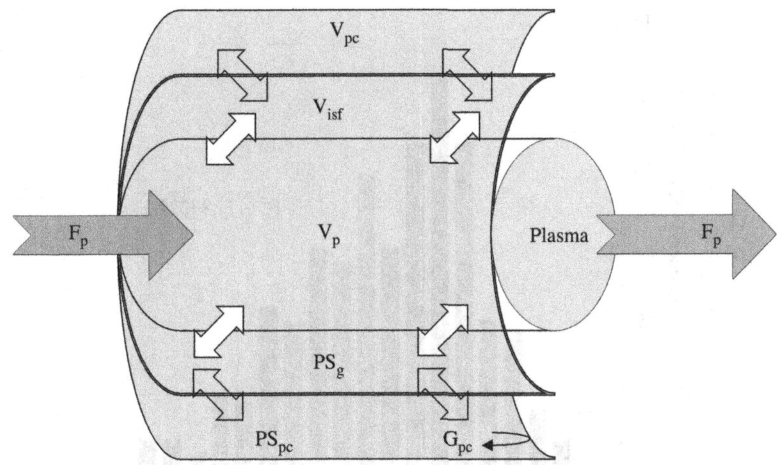

FIGURE 5–16 The three-region, single-capillary blood–tissue exchange model. *ISF*, Interstitial fluid; *PC*, parenchymal cell.

$$\begin{aligned}
\frac{\partial c_p(x,t)}{\partial t} &= -\frac{F_p L}{V_p}\frac{\partial c_p(x,t)}{\partial x} - \frac{PS_g}{V_p}\left[c_p(x,t) - c_{isf}(x,t)\right] \\
\frac{\partial c_{isf}(x,t)}{\partial t} &= -\frac{PS_g}{V_{isf}}\left[c_{isf}(x,t) - c_p(x,t)\right] \\
&\quad - \frac{PS_{pc}}{V_{isf}}\left[c_{isf}(x,t) - c_{pc}(x,t)\right] \\
\frac{\partial c_{pc}(x,t)}{\partial t} &= -\frac{PS_{pc}}{V_{pc}}\left[c_{pc}(x,t) - c_{isf}(x,t)\right] - \frac{G_{pc}}{V_{Pc}}c_{pc}(x,t)
\end{aligned} \tag{5.64}$$

where PS_{pc} (mL/min/g) is the permeability-surface product of the cell membrane, V_{pc} (mL/g) is the volume of the parenchymal cell, and G_{pc} (mL/min/g) is irreversible metabolism. The explicit solution is again due to Rose and Goresky (1976); an efficient numerical solution, also including the contribution from diffusion, is reported by Bassingthwaighte *et al.* (1992).

5.4.1.4 The whole-organ model

Until now, we have limited our analysis to the single capillary. In a more generalized setting, and as noted at the beginning of this chapter, an organ is characterized by a network of interconnected capillaries (King *et al.*, 1996). The total flow into the organ becomes divided between the capillaries in an unequal and nonuniform way. This is the spatial heterogeneity of flow (Bassingthwaighte & Goresky, 1984). Flow heterogeneity causes heterogeneity of the local capillary permeability, thus limiting the quantity of substances that can be exchanged between blood and tissue.

Knowledge of such a prominent phenomenon is very important for modeling blood–tissue exchange of substrates. In fact, neglecting flow heterogeneity can result in biased estimation of extravascular parameters (King *et al.*, 1996; Kuikka *et al.*, 1986). Thus the

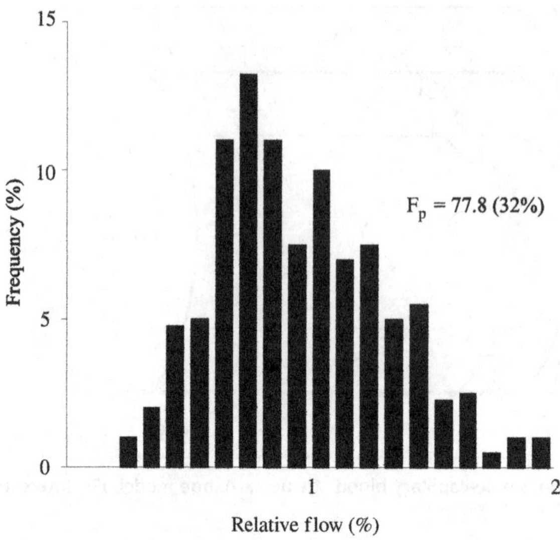

FIGURE 5–17 Example of a frequency histogram in a normal subject showing relative flow in human muscle in the basal state. Flow measurement was made with [^{15}O]-labeled water and positron emission tomography. In the abscissa the relative flow is normalized to the mean flow. The ordinate shows the frequency with which a given range of relative flows is observed. Mean flow (F_p, mL/min/g) and relative dispersion (expressed in %) of the distribution are also presented.

availability of a description of flow heterogeneity (even an approximate one) in the organ of interest is a prerequisite for physiologically sound kinetic modeling (Vicini *et al.*, 1998).

The most common approaches to assess flow heterogeneity in an animal, or in isolated and perfused tissue, are microsphere deposition (Bassingthwaighte & Goresky, 1984) and autoradiography (Stapleton *et al.*, 1995); both very invasive techniques that require sectioning of the organ under study. In contrast to animal studies, there is little knowledge about flow heterogeneity in humans. PET provides a potentially valuable tool for the assessment of regional flow heterogeneity (Vicini *et al.*, 1997; Utriainen *et al.*, 1997). In fact, the PET image of a given organ, when obtained with an appropriate marker such as [^{15}O] water, provides information not only of average flow in a region of interest but also of its spatial distribution (Fig. 5–17).

There are two landmark models to describe the heterogeneity of flow. The first is by Goresky and colleagues (see, for example, Rose & Goresky, 1976). The second is by Bassingthwaighte and colleagues (see for instance, King *et al.*, 1996). Below we describe the salient features of this second model, also referred to as the parallel capillary model or parallel network model (King *et al.*, 1996). Such an approach stems directly from the fact that, especially in muscle, capillaries are arranged in a more or less parallel fashion. However, the method assumes that the capillaries all end at the same point ($x = L$), and this can be a more difficult condition to satisfy (Jacquez, 1985). It is important to note that any parallel capillary heterogeneity model does not allow the description of phenomena, such as the

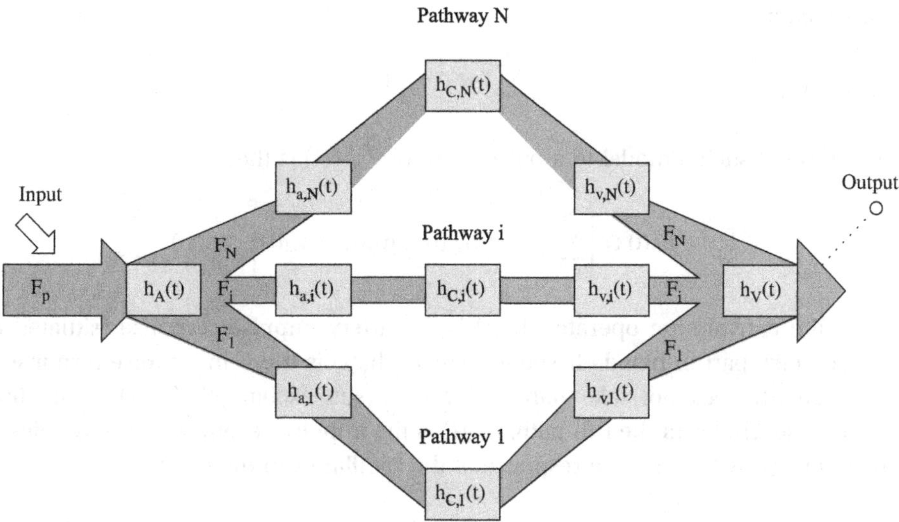

FIGURE 5–18 Structure of the distributed parameter organ model.

shunting between capillaries which may have a crucial importance on a correct description of the problem.

Let us suppose that the organ is describable with a number N of parallel pathways (Fig. 5–18), along which the blood–tissue exchange occurs. Every pathway represents a region of the organ characterized by a fraction F_i of the total input flow F and a fractional mass W_i. Based on this definition, a pathway is a compact description of subregions within the organ, each one characterized by the same flow for unit of tissue mass. It is useful to point out that these regions also do not need to be adjacent. Every pathway therefore is characterized from a regional relative flow, $f_i = F_i/F_p$, $i = 1, \ldots, N$, where F_p is the total input flow, and a fractional mass W_i, $i = 1, \ldots, N$ (which we define as the percentage of the organ's mass interested from the regional relative flow f_I). The output of the model is therefore given by the total outflow, which is the weighted sum of the single-capillaries responses.

Let us formally define the width of the i-th flow class Δf_i, $i = 1, \ldots, N$ for a generic flow distribution as:

$$\begin{aligned} \Delta f_1 &= f_2 - f_1 \\ \Delta f_i &= \frac{f_{i-1} + f_{i+1}}{2}, \quad i = 2, \ldots, N-1 \\ \Delta f_N &= f_N - f_{N-1} \end{aligned} \tag{5.65}$$

The distribution of relative flows has unitary area:

$$\sum_{i=1}^{N} w_i \Delta f_i = 1 \tag{5.66}$$

and unitary mean:

$$\sum_{i=1}^{N} f_i w_i \Delta f_i = 1 \tag{5.67}$$

The response of such a model to a pulse input $u(t) = \delta(t)$ is then:

$$h(t) = h_A(t) \otimes \left[\sum_{i=1}^{N} w_i f_i \Delta f_i h_{a,i}(t) \otimes h_{c,i}(t) \otimes h_{v,i}(t) \right] \otimes h_V(t) \tag{5.68}$$

where $\otimes$ is the convolution operator, $h_A(t)$ is the artery impulse response (situated at the inlet, does not take part in blood–tissue exchange), $h_V(t)$ is the vein impulse response (situated at the outlet, does not take part in blood–tissue exchange), $h_{a,i}(t)$ is the impulse response of the arterioles in the i-th path, $h_{v,i}(t)$ is the impulse response of the venules in the i-th path, and $h_{c,i}(t)$ is the impulse response of the capillaries in the i-th path.

$$h_{c,i}(t) = \delta(t - \tau_i) = \delta\left(t - \frac{V_p}{F_i}\right) \tag{5.69}$$

where V_p (volume per unit tissue) is capillary volume. Thanks to the associative and commutative property of convolution, we can simplify such a model:

$$h(t) = h_{AV}(t) \otimes \left[\sum_{i=1}^{N} w_i f_i \Delta f_i h_{av,i}(t) \otimes h_{c,i}(t) \right] \tag{5.70}$$

where $h_{AV}(t) = h_A(t) \times h_V(t)$ and $h_{av,i}(t) = h_{a,i}(t) \otimes h_{v,i}(t)$, $i = 1, \ldots, N$. This formulation is rather general. However, such parameter richness means that, for achieving identifiability of the physiologically relevant parameters, it is necessary to assume some characteristics of the model, such as flow heterogeneity and large vessel volumes, according to prior information (e.g., using labeled microspheres allows to measure flow heterogeneity). When this kind of information is available (e.g., the case of the isolated and perfused animal heart, where the model has been initially developed), the model is identifiable.

A classic application of this model has been to describe transport and metabolism of glucose in the isolated and perfused heart (Kuikka *et al.*, 1986). In this study, four tracers were injected into the aorta; an intravascular, an extracellular, a permeating not metabolizable, and a permeating metabolizable tracer. The four outflow dilution curves measured in the coronary sinus were interpreted with the model of Fig. 5–18 by using the capillary–interstitial–cell model of (5.64).

5.4.2 Hepatic removal of materials

Estimating the rate constants associated with the hepatic removal of materials from the circulation is a problem for clinicians as well as physiologists and pharmacologists. A large group of special interest compounds in this regard are extensively bound to plasma proteins

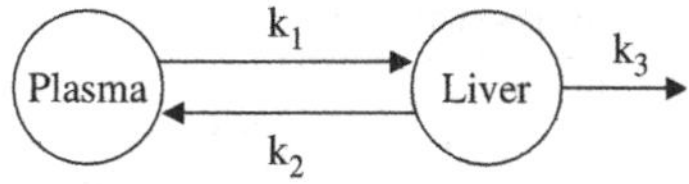

FIGURE 5–19 Lumped model for the estimation of hepatic transport.

with the result that they are removed almost exclusively by the liver. In the short interval during which this occurs, their extrahepatic distribution is largely confined to the vascular volume. Endogenous products such as bilirubin and bile acids, diagnostic agents such as indocyanine green, rose bengal, sulfobromophthalein (BSP) as well as many drugs are familiar examples.

The lumped model (Fig. 5–19) is a classic representation that allows the estimation of the rate constants for hepatic transport from the plasma disappearance curve of the material. The model specifically predicts that after an instantaneous injection of material into the plasma compartment, plasma concentration will decline as the sum of two exponentials whose slopes and intercepts are simple functions of the rate constant for hepatic uptake (k_1), the rate constant for the return of material from liver cells to plasma (k_2), and the rate constant for irreversible removal from liver cells (k_3). Experimentally determined disappearance curves are often closely approximated by two exponentials. Moreover, the initial volume of distribution determined by extrapolation of the plasma concentration to $t = 0$ is usually consistent with the model assumption of a single well-stirred plasma compartment. These observations together with the mathematical and experimental simplicity of the methods and its feasibility for human studies have led to its wide and continuing use ever since it was originally suggested for BSP removal by Richards *et al.* (1959).

This model, however, drastically simplifies the physiological variables in a living system. Specifically, the plasma volume is not a single well-stirred compartment, and liver cells are exposed to a profile of concentrations along the sinusoids—not as the model assumes to the mean concentration in the plasma volume as a whole. The model by Forker & Luxon (1978), which we describe below, has been principally developed to analyze the validity of the assumptions involved in treating the circulating plasma volume and liver cells as homogeneous compartments and deriving quantitative estimates of the errors that can occur as a result of this simplification.

The model is shown in Fig. 5–20 and is partly lumped and partly distributed. It is assumed that lumped compartmental representation is adequate for the heart and lungs, peripheral mixing and splanchnic mixing. However, the assumption of homogeneity which a lumped representation would imply is removed when describing the dynamics of the material in the liver. The model contains a small central compartment, P, which receives the pulse of injected material at $t = 0$. The volume of this compartment, V_p, represents a fraction of the total plasma volume considered to undergo instantaneous mixing and is visualized here as equivalent to the combined plasma volume of the heart and lungs. A splanchnic circuit receives plasma from and delivers it to P at the rate of hepatic plasma flow, F. Compartment R contains the remainder of the plasma volume, V_r, not contained in V_p or the

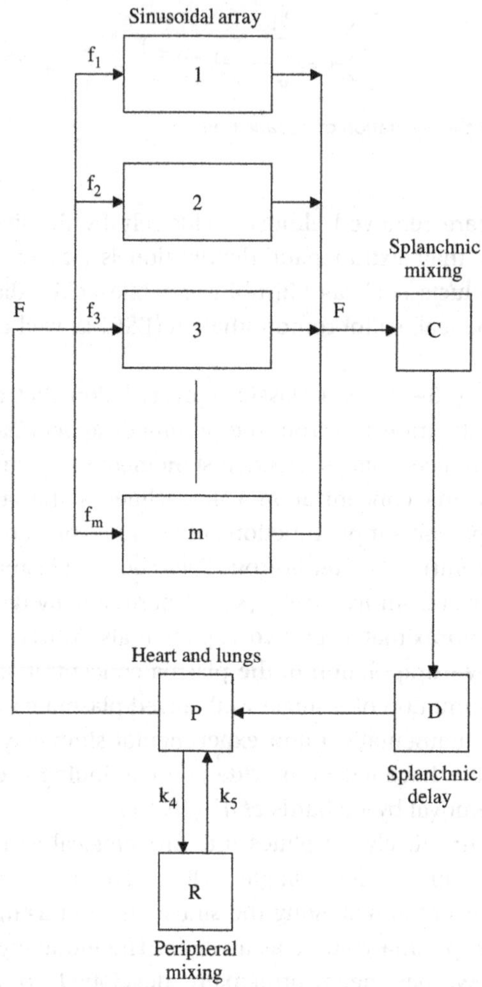

FIGURE 5–20 A hybrid (part lumped, part distributed) model. F denotes the total hepatic plasma flow, m is the total number of sinusoids, f_1, f_2, and f_m are respectively the plasma flows into the first, second, and m-th sinusoids, and k_4 and k_5 are the fractional transfer rate constants between compartments P and R. *Adapted from Forker & Luxon, 1978.*

splanchnic circuit and provides for delayed mixing in the peripheral circulation. Compartments R and P exchange with each other at a flow rate, H, equivalent to the cardiac output less the hepatic plasma flow. The splanchnic segment of the model contains a parallel array of liver sinusoids in series with a mixing compartment, C, and a simple delay represented by compartment D. The latter two compartments are included to simulate delay and dispersion in the extrahepatic portion of the splanchnic loop.

The sinusoidal array comprises many identical units whose liver cells all operate with the same rate constants, but the fraction of liver plasma flow assigned to individual sinusoids

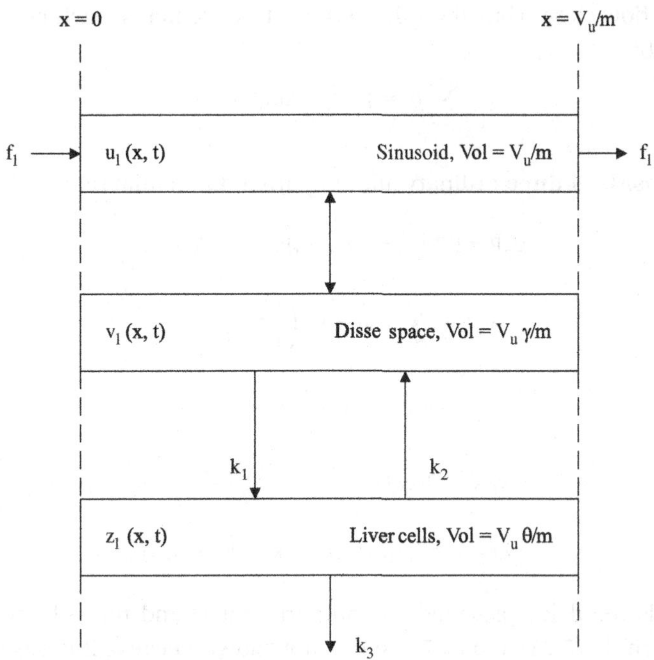

FIGURE 5–21 Representation of a liver sinusoid unit of the distributed model. x denotes the cumulative sinusoidal volume, V_u is the total volume of m identical sinusoids, f_l is the plasma flow to the l-th sinusoid, γ is the ratio of extravascular, extracellular volume to sinusoidal volume, θ is the ratio of intracellular volume to sinusoidal volume, and k_1, k_2, and k_3 are fractional transfer rate constants as indicated in the figure; u, v, and z denote concentrations in the indicated sites as functions of distance and time. *Adapted from Forker & Luxon, 1978.*

has been given a normal distribution to simulate the shape of hepatic indicator dilution curves. The model for the generic l-th sinusoid is shown in Fig. 5–21 and is based on the assumptions discussed by Goresky, Bach, and Nadeau (1973). Specifically the fractional transfer constants, k_1, k_2, and k_3, are first-order rate constants, flow-limited distribution of material to the cell surface is assumed, and axial diffusion is neglected so that dispersion at the outflow of the sinusoidal system is wholly attributable to delayed return of material from liver cells and to the nonuniform distribution of plasma flows. In Fig. 5–21, x (the location variable) is the cumulative vascular volume (instead of sinusoidal length—this simplifies the notation); u_l, v_l, and z_l denote the material concentration in the sinusoid, Disse space, and liver cells, respectively, V_u is the total volume of m identical sinusoids, f_l is the plasma flow to the l-th sinusoid, γ is the ratio of extravascular, extracellular volume to sinusoid volume, and θ is the ratio of intracellular volume to sinusoidal volume.

Consider m identical sinusoids grouped in n classes according to n values of f_l, the plasma flow per sinusoid. The flow distribution scheme assigns a fraction, α_l, of the m sinusoids to each flow class. Thus the i-th class has $m\alpha_i$ elements, each element is characterized by flow f_i with:

$$\sum_{i=1}^{n} \alpha_i = 1 \quad \sum_{i=1}^{n} m\alpha_i f_i = F \tag{5.71}$$

The model consists of three ordinary and 2n partial differential mass balance equations:

$$V_p\dot{P} = FC(t - \tau_d) + k_5 V_r R - (F + k_4 V_p)P \tag{5.72}$$

$$V_c\dot{C} = \sum_{i=1}^{n} (\alpha_i m f_i) u_i\left(\frac{V_u}{m}, t\right) - FC \tag{5.73}$$

$$V_r\dot{R} = k_4 V_p P - k_5 V_r R \tag{5.74}$$

$$\dot{u}_i(x,\ t) + \gamma\dot{v}_i(x,\ t) + \theta\dot{z}_i(x,\ t) + f_i \cdot \frac{\partial u_i(x,\ t)}{\partial x} = -\theta k_3 z_i(x,\ t) \tag{5.75}$$

$$\theta\dot{z}_i(x,\ t) = k_1\gamma v_i(x, t) - \theta(k_2 + k_3) z_i(x,\ t) \tag{5.76}$$

where $\tau_d = V_p/F$ is the delay provided by compartment D and the volume term Δx, which multiplies each term in (5.75) and (5.76) and is not shown because it drops out.

The initial conditions are:

$$P(0) = 1 \tag{5.77}$$

$$u_i(x,\ 0) = v_i(x,\ 0) = z_i(x,\ 0) = C(0) = R(0) = 0 \tag{5.78}$$

since an impulsive input of material at time $t = 0$ in P is assumed, with P being the concentration normalized to its initial value.

The auxiliary conditions are:

$$u_i(0, t) = P(t) \tag{5.79}$$

$$v_i(x,\ t) = u_i(x,\ t) \tag{5.80}$$

the first denoting that the input concentration to the sinusoids is P, while the second denotes that the material in Disse space is in rapid equilibrium with that in plasma sinusoids.

The model variable of interest is the time course of the concentration in the peripheral compartment, R. However, an analytical solution in closed form is not possible. The authors have obtained its Laplace transform, R(s), which was subsequently inverted numerically. Volumes and flows in the model were mostly assigned from published data on dogs (Table 1 in Forker & Luxon, 1978). Given these values, the lumped-distributed model generates plasma disappearance curves uniquely determined by the choice of the three hepatic rate constants k_1, k_2, and k_3. A wide range of rate constant values, all functionally significant, was examined.

The major findings of this simulation study can be summarized as follows. First, the lumped-distributed model generates disappearance curves that are fitted almost exactly by the sum of two exponentials. As a result, the clearance of material recovered by the lumped model has a small error. Similarly, the initial volume of distribution is only slightly (20%) lower than the lumped-distributed model. However, the picture changes when estimates of the rate constant of the lumped model are considered. Estimates of k_1 and k_2 were consistently lower with errors in the range of 4%−57% and 6%−73%, respectively, while a relatively minor underestimation error was encountered in k_3 estimate, ranging from 1% to 7%. Also of note is that errors in estimating k_1 and k_2 increase rapidly with increasing values of the initial extraction fraction. In fact, in the lumped-distributed model the plasma concentration of the material in the liver is less than in the periphery. The lumped model ignores this effect and compensates for this error by lowering the values of the rate constants. This underestimation effect is obviously more pronounced when the plasma disappearance curves vary more rapidly, and is thus amplified in the first portion of the disappearance curve. In effect k_1 and k_2, which are estimated from the first portion of the curve, have a greater error.

Although this lumped-distributed model cannot be used *in vivo* to estimate hepatic removal of substances, it provides a cautionary lesson when disappearance curves are analyzed with conventional lumped representation. It also stresses the importance of relying on entire disappearance curves and not just on initial slope estimates for hepatic removal, in order to ensure that estimates for clearance are robust.

5.4.3 Renal medulla

As a final example of distributed modeling, let us consider the development of a model of the medulla of the kidney which could be used to simulate human renal function. The model presented here focuses on the conservation of water and electrolytes and the production of urine within the medulla. The renal medulla is unusual in the degree to which its anatomical structure is essential to its function due to the transverse interactions between longitudinal flows in the parallel tubules. By formulating an appropriate mathematical model it is possible to provide a controlled and quantitative method of studying the contributions of the individual components of the kidney to the dynamic behavior of the overall system (Cage *et al.*, 1977).

A schematic diagram of the structure of the model is shown in Fig. 5−22, where this corresponds to the kidney anatomy. The mass of the cortex and the medulla is composed of many tubular structures. These are divided into four classes: the cortical nephrons, the juxtamedullary (JM) nephrons (since they are anatomically and functionally distinct), the collecting ducts, and the vasa recta. All members of a class are assumed to behave similarly and each class is simulated by tubes made up by a series of segments in which fluid flows from one segment to the next. A set of adjacent segments makes up a functionally distinct tube section, such as the thick ascending limb of the loop of Henle. The medulla is not treated as a continuous structure, but rather is modeled as a set of discrete terraces, recognizing the

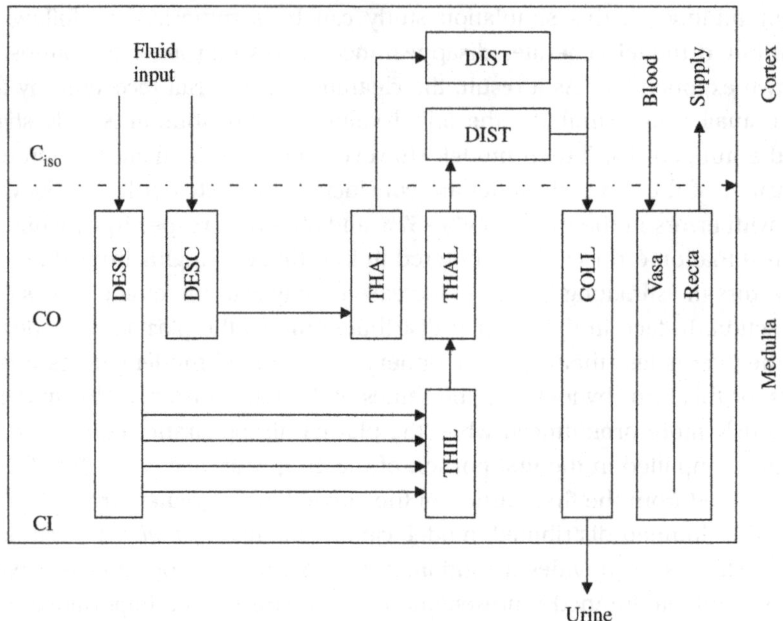

FIGURE 5–22 Schematic model of the renal medulla. C_{iso}, CO, and CI are total interstitial solute concentrations. *COLL*, Collecting duct; *DESC*, descending limb of the loop of Henle; *DIST*, distal convoluted tubule; *THAL*, thick ascending limb of the loop of Henle; *THIL*, thin ascending limb of the loop of Henle . *Adapted from Cage et al., 1977.*

distributed nature of flows in the kidney. A terrace contains segments of different sections and the depth of the terrace is the length of a single segment.

5.4.3.1 Model assumptions

A number of assumptions have been made in developing the model, and these can be stated explicitly as follows. First, all the segments within a section of tube are given the same values for area, volume, and permeability coefficients. The values for area and volume for each segment are the sum of the surface areas and volumes of all the members of a class within the depth of one terrace.

In the cortical nephrons, which make up 85% of the total, the loops of Henle pass only as far as the inner zone of the medulla (see Fig. 5–22). Concerning the JM nephrons, the effect of the reducing numbers of the loops of Henle toward the tip of the medulla is represented by reducing the numbers of tubes in this class, and by allowing a proportion of the fluid descending through each terrace to be passed directly to the ascending limb. The JM nephrons are reduced by a geometric process to 30% of their number by the medullary tips, equivalent to 4.5% of all nephrons.

The vasa recta are treated as if they act only as a passive drain for the medulla. Therefore they are modeled as a class of tubes that loop once through the entire length of the medulla. The flux of solutes for the vasa recta is treated as for other segments, except that the flow rate down the descending limbs is held constant and the ascending flow is determined directly from the other tubes. The ascending vasa recta are assumed to take up excess fluid from the interstitium.

The glomeruli and proximal tubules are part of a complex control system that supplies the nephrons with fluid. The effect of this early part of the nephron is represented by a fixed flow rate at the beginning of the descending limbs of the loops of Henle. By changing the value of this input to the model, it is possible to investigate how the medulla responds to changes in glomerular filtration rate and proximal resorption.

5.4.3.2 Principles of the mathematical formulation for the tubular structures

Consider an elemental segment of an individual tube, as shown in Fig. 5–23, which is assumed to be well mixed radially and to be unaffected by axial diffusion. The mass balance for water passing through this segment is given by:

$$\left(\pi R_j^2 \Delta x\right) \cdot \frac{\partial \rho(x,t)}{\partial t} = \rho(x-\Delta x,t)\cdot Q(x-\Delta x,t) - \rho(x,t)\cdot Q(x,t) - \left(2\pi R_j \Delta x\right)\cdot J(x,t) \quad (5.81)$$

where J is the water efflux rate per unit area, Q is the flow rate of water, R is the inner radius of tubule cross section, t is time in seconds, x is distance along the tubule, and ρ is fluid density. The term Δx represents a small increment of distance and the subscript j specifies the tubule section number.

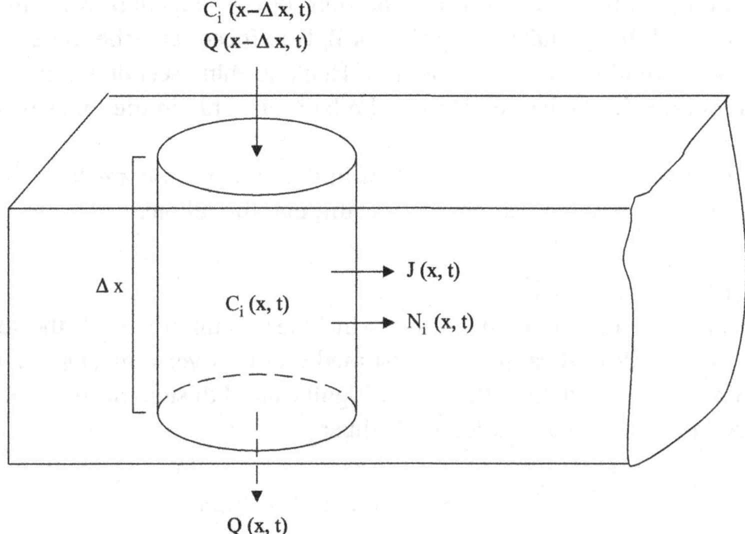

FIGURE 5–23 Diagram showing a segment within a terrace in the renal medulla. *Adapted from Cage et al., 1977.*

Assuming that the density of water remains constant at 1.0 g/cm^3, (5.81) can be simplified to:

$$Q(x,\ t) = Q(x - \Delta x,\ t) - (2\pi R_j \Delta x) \cdot J(x,\ t) \tag{5.82}$$

Since the concentration of solute does not remain constant, no equivalent simplification is possible. Hence the equation describing mass balance for solutes is:

$$\left(\pi R_j^2 \Delta x\right) \cdot \frac{\partial C_i(x,t)}{\partial t} = C_i(x - \Delta x, t) \cdot Q(x - \Delta x, t) - C_i(x,t) \cdot Q(x,t) - \left(2\pi R_j \Delta x\right) \cdot N_j(x,t) \tag{5.83}$$

where C is the concentration of solute and the subscript i defines the solute species.

To represent the various tubular structures which are simulated as a number of functionally distinct classes of tubes, the values for the areas and volumes of the segments are increased by the number of tubes in the class. The equations are rewritten, labeling the segment at distance x along the tube as n. Eq. (5.82) then becomes:

$$Q(n,t) = Q(n-1,t) - (2\pi\ R_j \Delta x B_j) \cdot J(n,\ t) \tag{5.84}$$

where B is the total number of nephrons in both kidneys. In a similar way, (5.83) becomes:

$$\left(\pi\ R_j^2 \Delta x B_j\right) \cdot \frac{dC_i(n,t)}{dt} = C_i(n-1,t) \cdot Q(n-1,\ t) - C_i(n,\ t) \cdot Q(n,\ t) - (2\pi\ R_j \Delta x B_j) \cdot N_i(n,\ t) \tag{5.85}$$

These equations can be modified to take account of the reduction in JM nephron numbers toward the tip of the medulla. The value of B_j is reduced, and the mass flows of water and solutes from descending limb of the loop of Henle to thin ascending limb of the loop of Henle are incorporated in the model. Hence, the loop of Henle in the inner medulla, B_j is a function of x.

Fluid flow in (5.84) and (5.85) is constrained in the model to be greater than or equal to zero so as to avoid the possibility of reverse flow through the tubule.

5.4.3.3 Interstitial compartment

The equation for the interstitial compartments includes assumptions for the tubular structures similar to those adopted earlier. It is assumed that transverse mixing results in homogeneity in each terrace, and that there is insignificant diffusion or mass flow between terraces. The equation for a solute at level p is thus:

$$V_p \cdot \frac{dC_i(p,t)}{dt} = \Sigma_n(2\pi\ R_m \Delta x B_m) \cdot N_i(m,t) \tag{5.86}$$

where V_p is the interstitial volume of terrace p and m is the number of different segments within the terrace.

5.4.3.4 Transmural flux

It is assumed that the layer of cells that constitutes a segment of a tube acts as a simple semipermeable membrane with specific permeabilities. The transmural flux rates for the solutes and solvent can then be calculated using Fick's law and the laws of osmosis. For the solvent, the volume efflux rate per unit area is given by:

$$J(n, t) = k_{wj} \cdot \Sigma_i (C_i(p, t) - C_i(n, t)) \tag{5.87}$$

where k is the reabsorption coefficient of the solute species. It is assumed that all the segments and terraces in the model have constant volume.

As stated earlier, the vasa recta flow is held constant in the descending vasa recta, and so J is set equal to zero in (5.87). The ascending vasa recta are assumed to remove all the excess fluid from the interstitium as the result of hydrostatic and oncotic forces acting on its very permeable membrane. Thus for the ascending limb:

$$J(p, t) = \Sigma_m J(m, t) \cdot (2\pi R_m \Delta x B_m) \tag{5.88}$$

where R_m and B_m are the radius and number of nephrons represented by segment m.

The equations for the solutes within the vasa recta are of the same form as for the other classes, but their permeability coefficients are very high, allowing the solutes to move easily into the vasa recta, which act as a drain for the medulla. When only passive diffusion is involved, the flux of solute is given by Fick's law:

$$N_i(n, t) = k_{ij}(C_i(n, t) - C_i(p, t)) \tag{5.89}$$

where N is the molar flux per unit area. In the sections where reabsorption of electrolyte in the nephron is caused by active transport, it is assumed that passive diffusion occurs in parallel with active transport and that the effects are additive:

$$N_e(n, t) = k_{ej}(C_e(n, t) - C_e(p, t)) + N_{active} \tag{5.90}$$

where the subscript e refers to electrolyte and N_{active}, the active transport component, is given by:

$$N_{active} = \begin{Bmatrix} a_{ej} \cdot C_e(n, t) & \text{for } C_e(n, t) < C_{e\ iso} \\ a_{ej} \cdot C_{e\ iso} & \text{for } C_e(n, t) \geq C_{e\ iso} \end{Bmatrix} \tag{5.90a,b}$$

with the subscript iso indicating that the electrolyte is isotonic to blood plasma.

Having formulated the mathematical model in this fashion, parameter values and boundary conditions can be inserted into the equations and simulation studies performed.

5.5 Nonlinear modeling

In Section 5.3 the examples presented were systems that were being modeled as if they exhibited linear dynamics. Mathematically the models were composed of linear, ordinary differential equations. This concept of linearity can be illustrated by considering the following equation:

$$\frac{dx(t)}{dt} = -a\,x(t) + b\,u(t) \tag{5.91}$$

The dynamics of the dependent variable x are being represented in this equation as a function of the independent variable time; u is the input variable and a and b are (constant) parameters. Examining the first term on the right-hand side of this equation, a doubling of the value of the dependent variable would result in a doubling of the value of that right-hand term since the parameter a is a constant.

In contrast, consider (5.92):

$$\frac{dx(t)}{dt} = -c\,x^2(t) + b\,u(t) \tag{5.92}$$

where c is a constant parameter. Now if we double the value of x, this first right-hand term is no longer doubled due to the presence of this x^2 term. In other words this x^2 term makes the equation, and hence the model, one that is nonlinear. Let us now consider some examples of nonlinear models.

5.5.1 The action potential model

Several cellular functions depend on the generation and propagation of the action potential. For instance, receptors convert chemical, thermal, and electrical signals into an action potential: signals that control muscle contraction and hormone secretion are action potentials. The action potential is an electrical signal which consists of the local depolarization of the cell membrane as a result of a stimulus (Fig. 5–24). Since the action potential is generated only if the stimulus is above a certain threshold, this perturbation of the electrical equilibrium of the membrane produces the depolarization of the adjacent region, thus allowing (in the case of a neuron) the propagation of the signal along the axon. The main advantage of this complex signal transmission system is that the signal is regenerated at each section of the membrane and is thus less sensitive to noise.

5.5.1.1 An electrical model of the cell membrane

The cell membrane lipid bilayer structure is an insulating component and also at rest there is a difference of potential between the intracellular and extracellular space. The simplest model to describe the electrical behavior of the membrane is thus a capacitance (Fig. 5–25). The model equation is:

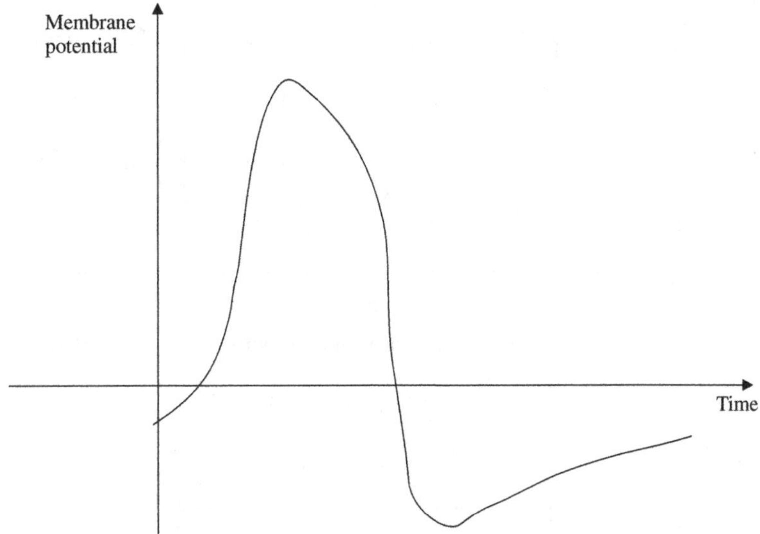

FIGURE 5–24 Dynamics of the action potential.

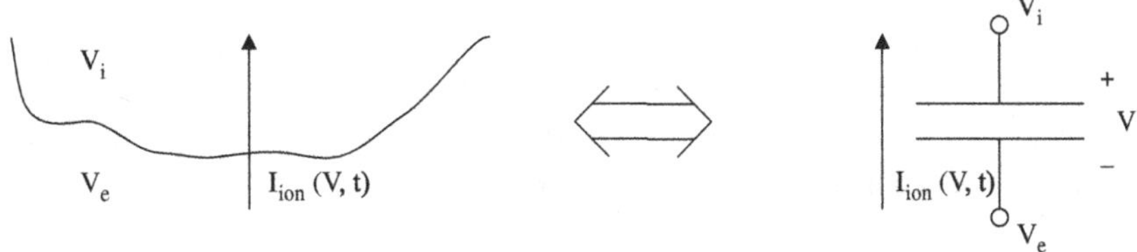

FIGURE 5–25 Capacitance model of the cell membrane. Note that $V = V_i - V_e < 0$.

$$C_m \frac{dV}{dt} + I_{ion}(V, t) = 0 \tag{5.93}$$

where $V = V_i - V_e$ (the intracellular and extracellular potentials respectively), C_m is the membrane capacitance, and I_{ion} are the ionic currents through the membrane, the most important being those of sodium (Na^+), potassium (K^+), and chloride (Cl^-).

One can now build on the schema of Fig. 5–25 by taking into account the following facts: (a) the ion fluxes occur along ion-specific channels each characterized by a certain resistance; (b) ions move along the channels due to a membrane potential (described by the Goldman equation which combines the Nerst potential of the individual ions); and (c) at equilibrium the different ion concentrations are maintained by an active pump which balances the passive fluxes of sodium and chloride into the cell and of potassium outside the cell.

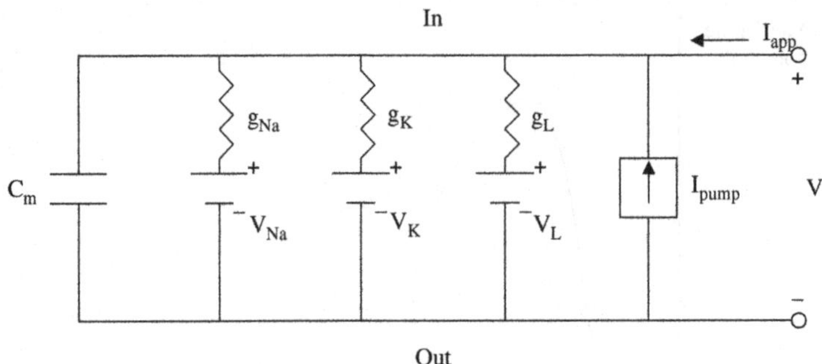

FIGURE 5–26 Expanded electrical analog model of the cell membrane. Note that $V_{Na} < 0$ and $V_K > 0$.

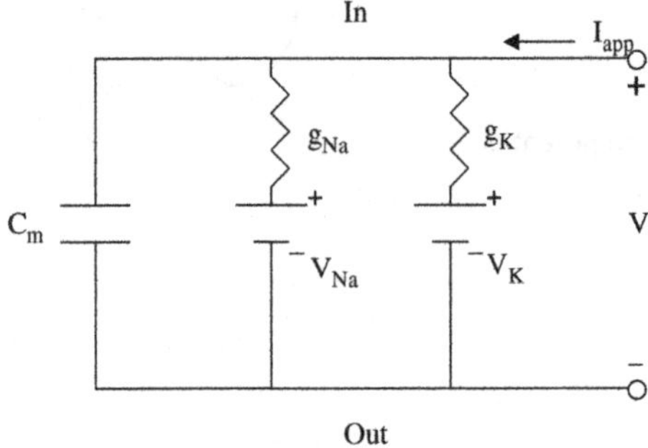

FIGURE 5–27 Membrane voltage in response to a small current.

The contribution of sodium and potassium ions to the action potential is explicitly considered, since it is assumed that it is predominant with respect to that of all the other ions, including chloride, which are lumped into a leakage current. With the above logic, (5.93) becomes:

$$C_m \frac{dV}{dt} + gNa(V - V_{Na}) + g_K(V - V_K) + g_L(V - V_L) = I_{pump} + I_{app} \tag{5.94}$$

where g_{Na}, g_K, and g_L are the channel conductances of sodium, potassium, and leakage; and V_{Na}, V_K, and V_L are the respective Nerst potentials of sodium, potassium, and all other ions. I_{pump} is the active pump current and I_{app} is the applied current stimulus. By incorporating these concepts, the electrical analog of the cell membrane becomes that shown in Fig. 5–26. This linear model is valid only if a small current is applied (Fig. 5–27), but we have seen that, with an elevated current, the system response is completely different (Fig. 5–24).

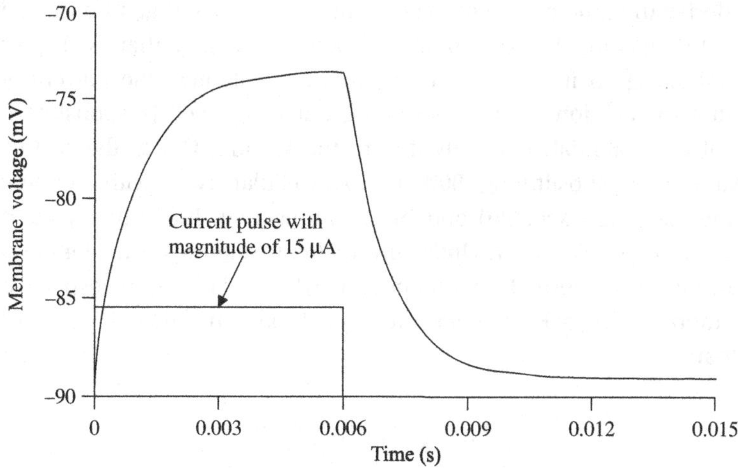

FIGURE 5–28 The model of Fig. 5–26 focusing on sodium and potassium ions only.

5.5.1.2 The Hodgkin–Huxley model

This model focuses on sodium and potassium ions only and does not consider the role of the active sodium pump (Fig. 5–28). Thus, the model equation becomes:

$$C_m \frac{dV}{dt} = -g_{Na}(V - V_{Na}) - g_K(V - V_K) + I_{app} \tag{5.95}$$

It is useful to define membrane potential at equilibrium, that is, when $I_{app} = 0$ (this is known as the Goldman equation and combines the Nerst potential of the individual ions):

$$V_{eq} = \frac{(g_K V_K + g_{Na} V_{Na})}{(g_K + g_{Na})} \tag{5.96}$$

The key piece of intuition which led to the formulation of this model was that the individual ion conductances of the cell membrane are not constant, but rather are a function of the membrane potential, that is, $g_{Na} = g_{Na}(V)$, $g_K = g_K(V)$, and $g_L = g_L(V)$. In addition, it was perceived that for an increase of the membrane potential, the permeability increases differently for various ions with the dominant ion being the one with the highest permeability.

Since the system is a closed-loop feedback system, that is, the membrane potential is a function of the ion conductances which in turn depend on the membrane potential, the only possibility to investigate the system experimentally was to open the feedback loop by maintaining a potential that was constant over time. For this purpose Hodgkin & Huxley (1952) developed the voltage clamp technique. This involved imposing step changes of the membrane potential (of different amplitudes) and measuring (at constant voltage) the ionic current in response to the stimulus, thus eliminating the dependence of the conductances from the membrane voltage.

In order to derive the time course of the conductances g_{Na} and g_K as a function of V, it has been necessary to separate the individual components of I_{Ion}, that is, I_{Na} and I_K. It was assumed that, following an increase in the membrane potential, the current going into the cell is mostly due to Na^+ ions, while that going out of the cell (responsible for the return to equilibrium of the potential) is mostly due to the K^+ ion. Hence the two components of I_{Ion} were separated by substituting 90% of extracellular Na^+ with coline (a substance which makes the axon nonexcitable) and by assuming that, immediately after the increase of V, the current is due to Na^+ only. Under these circumstances, let us denote by I^1_{Na} and I^2_{Na} the sodium current under normal conditions and when $[Na^+]_{ext} = 0$ respectively. Assuming also that the ratio $I^1_{Na}/I^2_{Na} = K$, a constant over time, and that $I^1_K = I^2_K$, one has from $I_{Ion} = I_{Na} + I_K$ that:

$$I^1_{Na} = \frac{K}{K-1}\left(I^1_{Ion} - I^2_{Ion}\right) \tag{5.97}$$

Fig. 5–29 shows the time course of I_{Ion} and of its components I_{Na} and I_K. It is now possible to determine the time course of $g_{Na} = I_{Na}/(V - V_{Na})$ and $g_K = I_K/(V - V_K)$ as functions of V.

Fig. 5–30A shows g_K for a step increase and decrease of V, while Fig. 5–30B and C show g_K and g_{Na} for various values of step increase of V. It should be noted that g_{Na}, for a step increase of V, first increases and then decreases.

5.5.1.3 Potassium conductance

By observing Fig. 5–30A and B, one notes that g_K increases after a step increase in V in a sigmoidal fashion. However, it decreases exponentially when the stimulus ends. Accordingly, the following description has been proposed for g_K:

$$g_K = g_K n^4 \tag{5.98}$$

where g_K is a constant and n obeys the differential equation:

$$\tau(v)\frac{dn}{dt} - n_\infty(v) - n = 0 \tag{5.99}$$

with $v = V - V_{eq}$. This can also be rewritten as:

$$\frac{dn}{dt} = \alpha_n(v)\,(1-n) - \beta_n(v)n \tag{5.100}$$

where:

$$\tau(v) = \frac{1}{\alpha_n(v) + \beta_n(v)}; \quad n_\infty(v) = \frac{\alpha_n(v)}{\alpha_n(v) + \beta_n(v)} \tag{5.101}$$

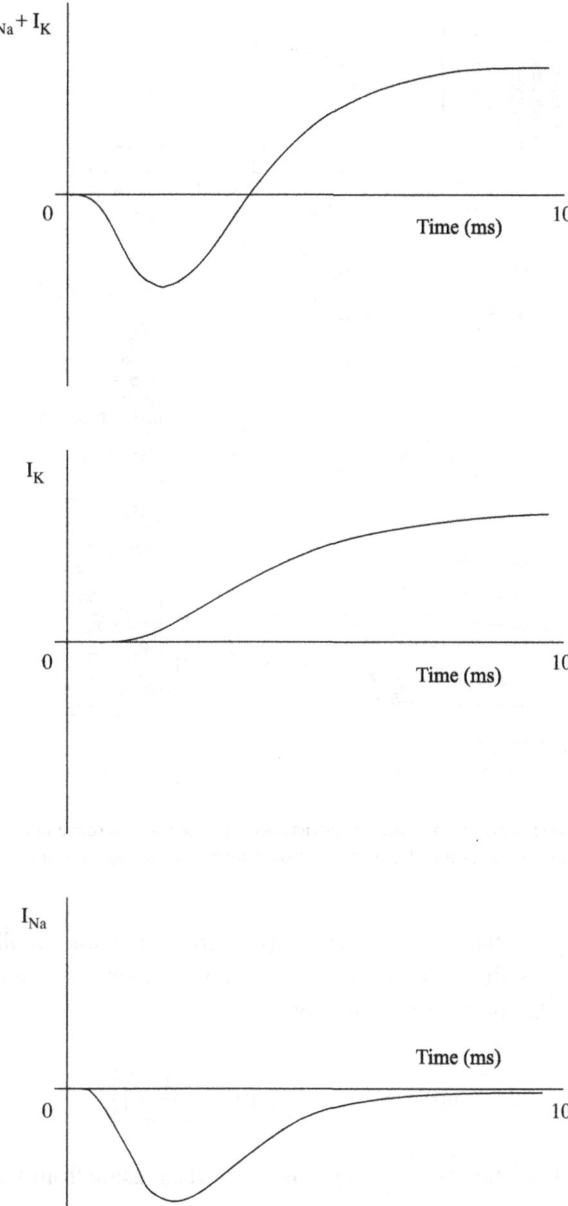

FIGURE 5–29 Time course of I_{Ion} and its components I_K and I_{Na}.

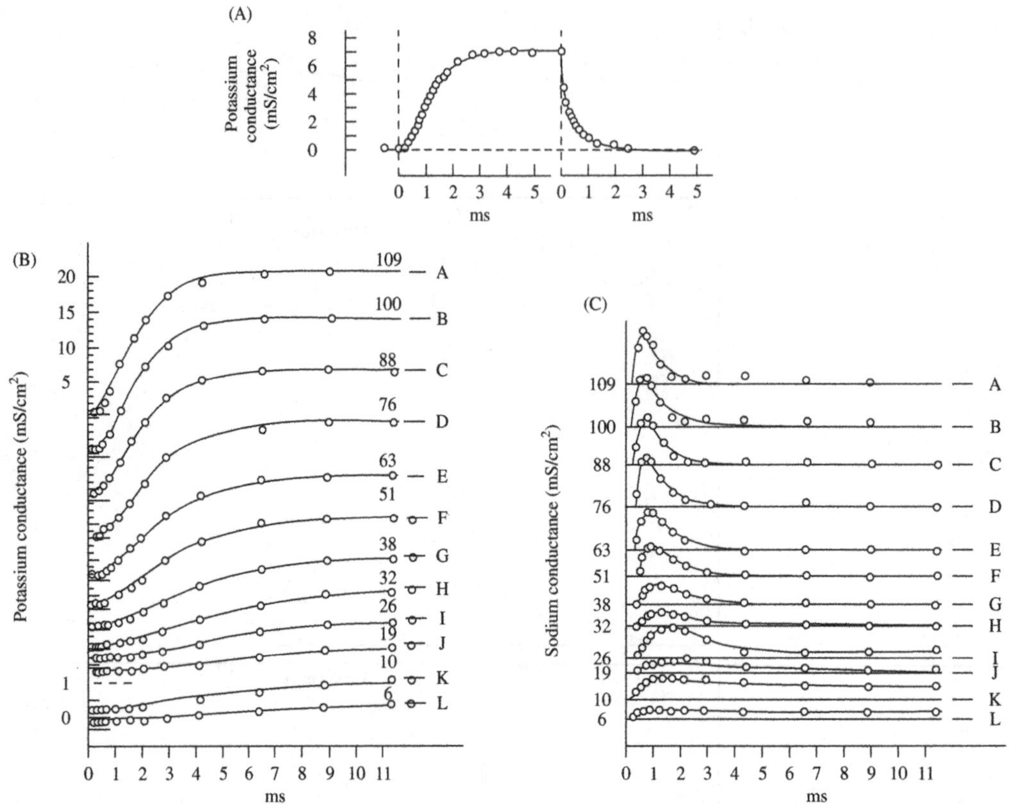

FIGURE 5–30 (A) Dynamic response of potassium conductance, g_K, for step increase and decrease of V; (B) and (C) dynamic response of potassium, g_K, and sodium, g_{Na}, conductances for various step increases in V.

For values of V higher than the threshold, n(t) increases exponentially toward its regimen value and, thus, activates the potassium current: n(t) is called the potassium activation. For V increasing from 0 to V_0, n(t) is described by:

$$n(t) = n_\infty(v_0)\left[1 - \exp\left(-\frac{t}{\tau_n(v_0)}\right)\right] \tag{5.102}$$

and $n^4(t)$ is a sigmoidal function (Fig. 5–31), while for V decreasing from V_0 to 0 n(t) is given by:

$$n(t) = n_\infty(v_0)\exp\left(-\frac{t}{\tau_n(v_0)}\right) \tag{5.103}$$

and $n^4(t)$ decreases exponentially.

One can estimate the values of α_n and β_n for each value of V of the step function by fitting the function to the data. Since the number of V values was finite, to obtain the values of α_n and β_n for every value of V a function was fitted to the α_n, β_n data (Fig. 5–32).

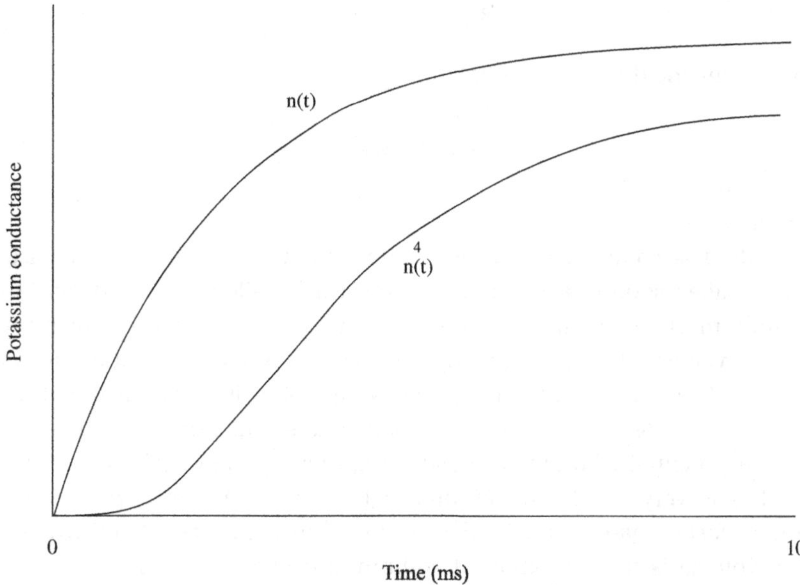

FIGURE 5–31 Dynamics of n(t) and $n^4(t)$ following a step increase in membrane voltage.

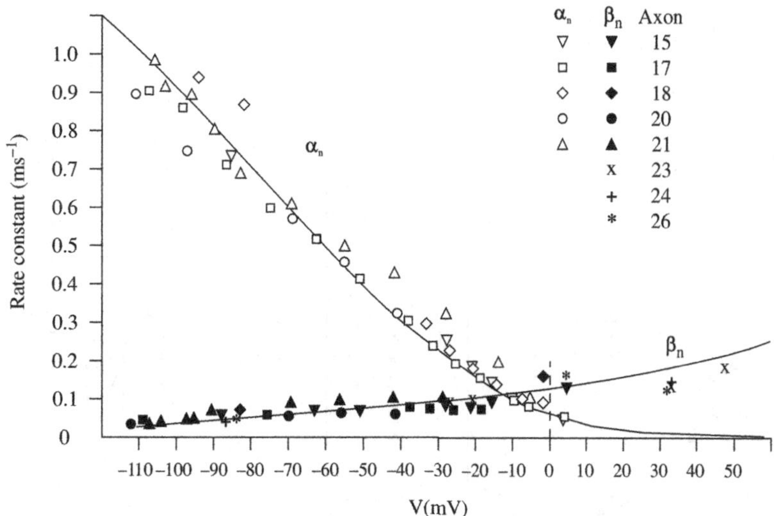

FIGURE 5–32 Fitted values of α_n and β_n.

5.5.1.4 Sodium conductance

By observing Fig. 5–30C it can be seen that, after a step increase in V, the sodium channels are first activated and then deactivated. The following description has been proposed for g_{Na}:

$$g_{Na}(v) = g_{Na}m^3h \tag{5.104}$$

where m and h obey the differential equation:

$$\frac{dw}{dt} = \alpha_w(1 - w) - \beta_w w \tag{5.105}$$

where w = m or w = h.

The value of m is small in the steady state, but it is the first to increase after the stimulus and is called sodium activation. The term h is called sodium deactivation (h = 0 means that sodium channels are not active). As with g_K, α_w and β_w are estimated first for the various values of step function after which a curve is fitted to the a_w, β_w data (Fig. 5–33). The components of g_{Na} following a step increase in membrane voltage are shown in Fig. 5–34, while Fig. 5–35 shows the function describing g_{Na} and g_K during an action potential with Fig. 5–36 showing their gating variables. It is worth noting that since $\tau_m(V)$ is very much greater than $\tau_n(V)$ and $\tau_h(V)$, m(t) responds to voltage variations much faster than n and h (Fig. 5–36). Thus, the first effect of a step change in membrane voltage is the activation of sodium currents. This process in turn causes a further increase in membrane potential. For elevated values of V, h tends to 0 and thus sodium currents are deactivated, while potassium currents are activated, hence returning the system to equilibrium.

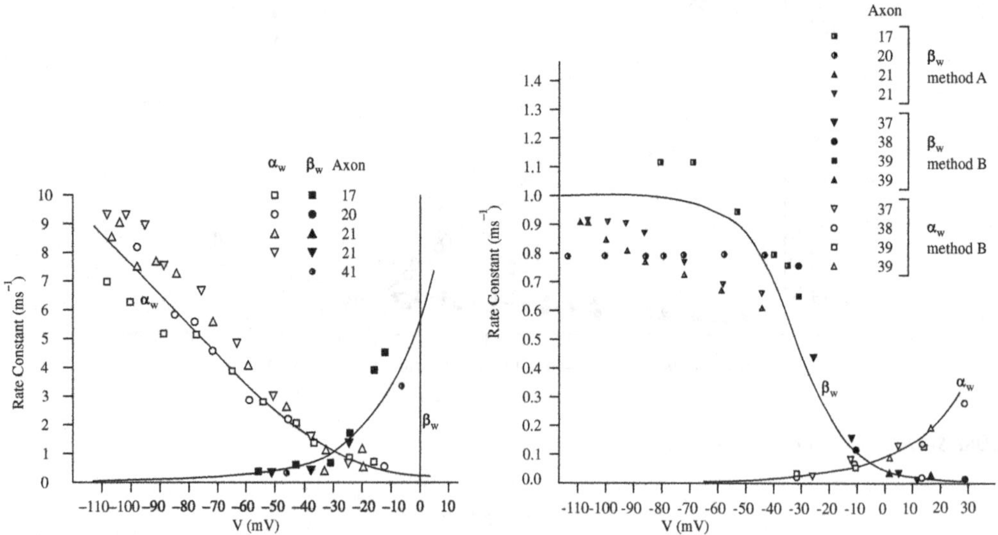

FIGURE 5–33 Curve fitting to the α_w and β_w data. α_w and β_w data were obtained by using two different methods A and B.

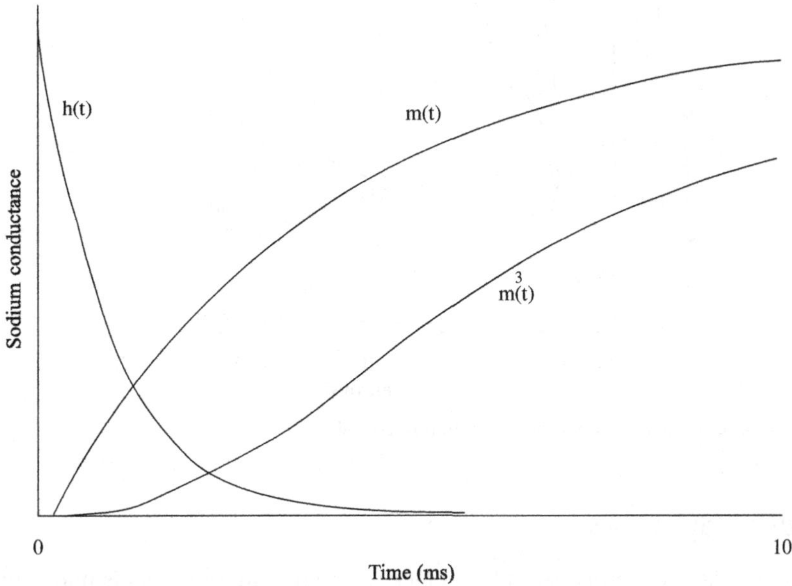

FIGURE 5–34 Components of g_{Na} following step increase in membrane voltage.

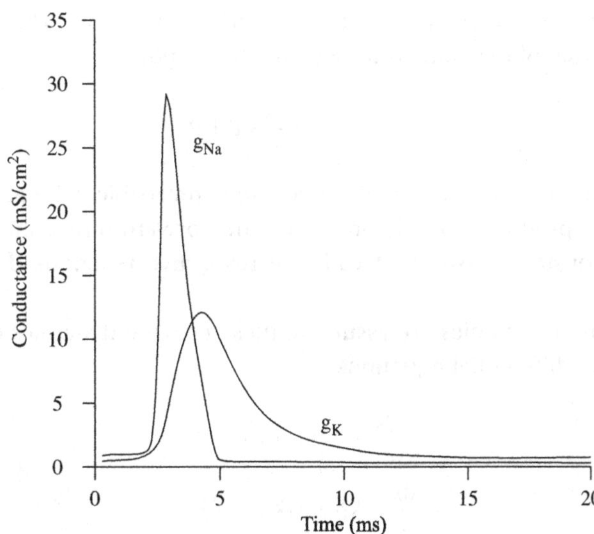

FIGURE 5–35 Conductances g_{Na} and g_K during an action potential.

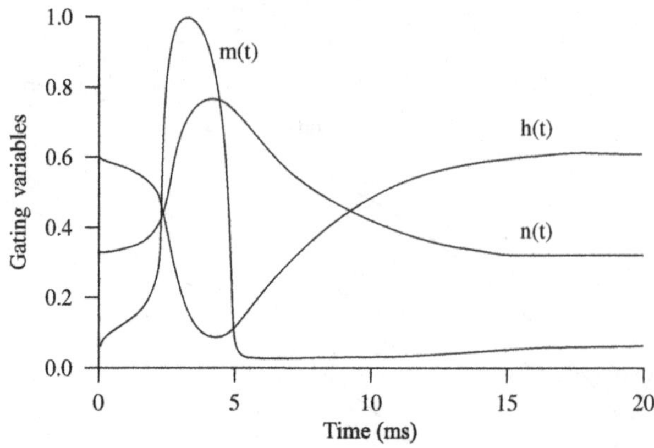

FIGURE 5–36 Responses of m, n, and h during an action potential.

5.5.2 Enzyme dynamics

The dynamics of chemical processes taking place within the human organism are complex, and only rarely can one truly consider such dynamics to be linear. The nonlinear form of mathematical models in this domain can be illustrated by examining a simple enzyme reaction.

In the simplest of enzyme reactions, an enzyme (E) and a chemical substrate (S) form an enzyme-substrate complex (X). In turn, this complex decomposes into the original enzyme (E) and the reaction product (P). In other words the enzyme acts as a catalyst in this chemical reaction, but remains unchanged at the end of the reaction. The standard chemical representation of this set of reactions is as depicted in (5.106):

$$E + S \underset{k_2}{\overset{k_1}{\longleftrightarrow}} X \overset{k_3}{\longrightarrow} E + P \tag{5.106}$$

In other words, the substrate to complex reaction is reversible, whereas the conversion of complex into reaction product can only proceed in the forward direction. The parameters k_1, k_2, and k_3 are the constants associated with the respective reactions defining the rates at which they proceed.

If first-order reaction dynamics are assumed, these enzyme dynamics can be represented by the following set of differential equations:

$$\frac{ds}{dt} = -k_1 se + k_2 x \tag{5.107}$$

$$\frac{dx}{dt} = k_1 se - (k_2 + k_3)x \tag{5.108}$$

$$\frac{de}{dt} = (k_2 + k_3)x - k_1 se \tag{5.109}$$

$$\frac{dp}{dt} = k_3 x \tag{5.110}$$

where s, x, e, and p are the concentrations of the chemical ingredients S, X, E, and P, respectively. The conservation equation:

$$e_0 = e + x \tag{5.111}$$

also applies, where the subscript refers to the initial concentration. In other words, the enzyme exists either in free form, or else chemically combined as complex.

In this model the nonlinearity arises through the term $k_1 se$, meaning that there is a component of rate of complex change that is proportional to the product of the substrate and enzyme concentrations. The other terms in the model are linear.

Thus, on examining the components of (5.107), we see that there is a negative rate of change of substrate concentration due to the conversion into complex defined by the first nonlinear term on the right-hand side of the equation; and a positive rate of change due to the linear second term corresponding to the conversion of complex back into substrate.

Eq. (5.106) represents the simplest possible enzyme reaction. In practice, enzyme dynamics are usually very much more complex, involving additional layers of nonlinearity through the action of multiple substrates, coenzymes, etc. The nonlinear model considered above is in fact a highly simplified representation of reality, involving many assumptions.

Returning to the model, since the enzyme present at any time is either still a pure substance or has been combined, molecule for molecule, with the substrate as the complex X, a steady state is normally said to exist over the period when the rate of change of substrate concentration, dx/dt is approximately zero. Providing that the initial concentration of substrate, s_0, is very much greater than the initial concentration of enzyme, e_0, then we can write:

$$v = \frac{dp}{dt} = \frac{k_3 e_0 s}{s + \frac{k_1 + k_2}{k_1}} \tag{5.112}$$

which can be rewritten as:

$$v = \frac{V_{max} s}{K_m + s} \tag{5.113}$$

where:

$$V_{max} = k_3 e_0 \tag{5.114}$$

and

$$K_m = \frac{k_2 + k_3}{k_1} \tag{5.115}$$

Eq. (5.113) is the Michaelis–Menten equation that was referred to in Section 5.2. Thus, if the assumption that $s_0 \gg e_0$ is valid, the rate law is completely determined by the two parameters V_{max} and K_m. The former is the limiting velocity as $s \to \infty$ while the latter is the concentration of substrate for which $v = V_{max}/2$. These parameters provide the conventional method for determining the rate law for enzymic reactions.

5.5.3 Baroreceptors

Baroreceptors are specialist cells that monitor blood pressure in certain main arteries of the body and transmit this information to the central nervous system (CNS). As such, these receptors form part of the short-term feedback mechanisms responsible for blood pressure control.

A nonlinear approach to modeling is necessary in order to capture the dynamic behavior of these receptors. The basis of this approach is presented later. The overall relationship between blood pressure, P, and the baroreceptor output function, B, will be developed in the form of the block diagram shown in Fig. 5–37, where $s_A - s_D$ are dummy variables. This block diagram indicates that B is given by a linear combination of a dynamic estimate (s_C) of the positive derivative (s_A) and the dynamic mean pressure estimate (s_B), together with a threshold pressure below which the baroreceptor does not fire. A further constraint is incorporated into the model in order to ensure that the firing rate is always positive (Leaning *et al.*, 1983).

The equations for each baroreceptor area can be developed as follows:

$$s_A = \frac{dP^+}{dt} \tag{5.116}$$

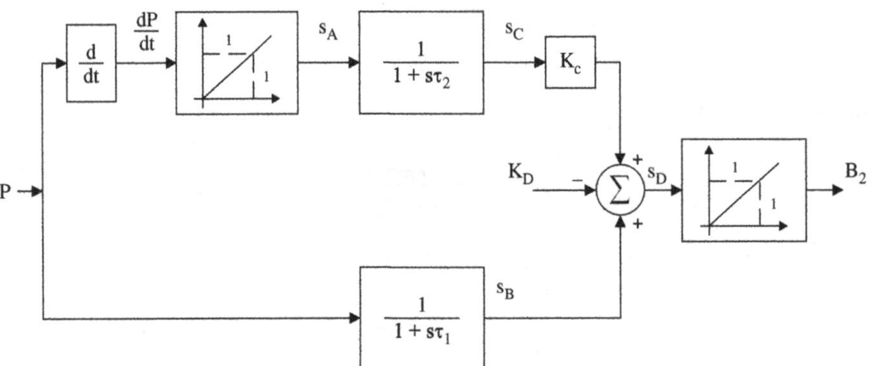

FIGURE 5–37 Block diagram representation of the relationship between blood pressure, P, and the baroreceptor output, B. *Adapted from Leaning et al., 1983.*

that is to say that $s_A = dP/dt$ for $(dP/dt) > 0$ and $s_A = 0$ otherwise.

$$\frac{ds_B}{dt} = \frac{P - s_B}{\tau_1} \quad (5.117)$$

$$\frac{ds_C}{dt} = \frac{sA - sC}{\tau_2} \quad (5.118)$$

$$s_D = s_B + K_C s_C - K_D \quad (5.119)$$

and:

$$B_2 = s_D^+ \quad (5.120)$$

that is to say that there is a firing of the baroreceptor whenever s_D is positive (s_D^+). As depicted in Fig. 5–37, K_D is the threshold below which firing of the baroreceptor does not occur, and K_C is the average contribution of the positive pressure derivative term over one cardiac cycle. In the model, K_C is estimated by assuming that the average value of $K_C s_C$ over one cycle is 60 (Leaning *et al.*, 1983), that is:

$$\frac{1}{T_H}\int_0^{T_H} K_C s_C dt_C = 60$$

or

$$K_C = \frac{60T_H}{\int s_C dt_C} \quad (5.121)$$

where T_H is the heart period, that is, one cardiac cycle. Thus, for normal values of heart rate and blood pressure the value of K_C calculated in this fashion is approximately 1.0.

The effective input to the CNS can then be assumed to be a static linear function of the output of the aortic arch baroreceptor B_{AA} and the carotid sinus baroreceptor B_{CS}, where these are the two baroreceptor locations designated respectively by the subscripts AA and CS. The combination of these two baroreceptor outputs is depicted in Fig. 5–38. Hence:

$$B = \alpha\ B_{CS} + (1 - \alpha)B_{AA} \quad (5.122)$$

where α is typically assumed to be 0.7. In formulating this model it should be noted that the nonlinearity has arisen as a result of the unidirectionality of the baroreceptor response; that is, it fires only when the rate of change of pressure in the blood vessel in question is positive.

5.5.4 Central nervous control of heart rate

This nonlinear approach to modeling can be adopted in a similar manner in relation to the CNS control of heart rate. In this case a two-region dynamic formulation is adopted, one for

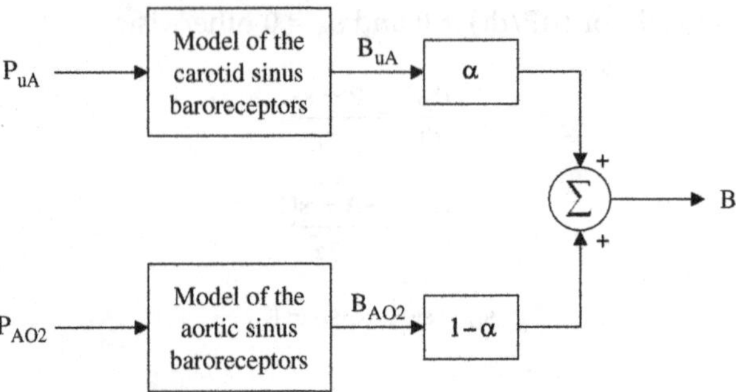

FIGURE 5–38 Combination of two baroreceptor outputs. *Adapted from Leaning et al., 1983.*

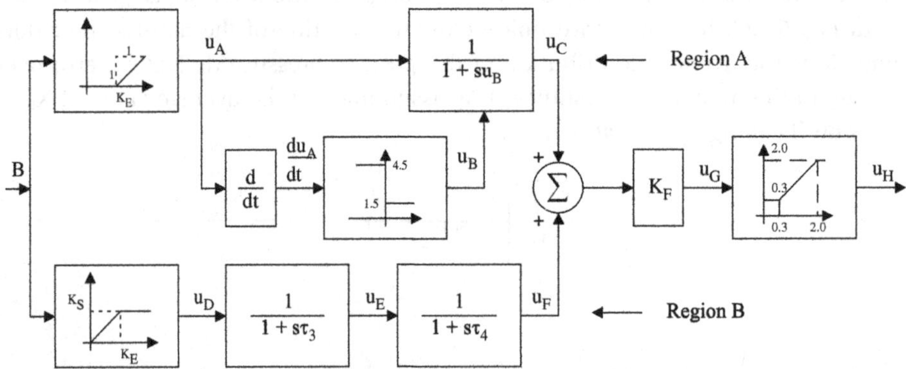

FIGURE 5–39 Block diagram model for central nervous system control of heart rate, relating baroreceptor function as input to the output of the heart period. *Adapted from Leaning et al., 1983.*

blood pressures above normal and the other for pressures below normal. For raised blood pressure, the CNS input function B is greater than a threshold value K_E and the dynamics of this region (region A) are approximated by a first-order system. This is described by the following equations in which U is a CNS variable. These equations form components of the block diagram shown in Fig. 5–39 (Leaning *et al.*, 1983):

$$U_A = \begin{Bmatrix} (B - K_E), & B > K_E \\ 0, & B \leq K_E \end{Bmatrix} \tag{5.123}$$

$$U_B = \begin{Bmatrix} 1.5, & \dfrac{dU_A}{dt} > 0 \\ 4.5, & \dfrac{dU_A}{dt} \leq 0 \end{Bmatrix} \tag{5.124}$$

$$\frac{dU_C}{dt} = \frac{(U_A - U_C)}{U_B} \tag{5.125}$$

For the other region (region B), the dynamics are approximated by a second-order system described by the following equations:

$$U_D = \begin{Bmatrix} K_E, & B > K_E \\ 0, & B \leq K_E \end{Bmatrix} \tag{5.126}$$

$$\frac{dU_E}{dt} = \frac{U_D - U_E}{\tau_3} \tag{5.127}$$

$$\frac{dU_F}{dt} = \frac{U_E - U_F}{\tau_4} \tag{5.128}$$

The overall response of the heart rate controller, which is a linear combination of the outputs of regions A and B, is given by:

$$U_G = K_F(U_C + U_F) \tag{5.129}$$

where U_G represents a continuously varying estimate of the heart rate that is utilized in the next cardiac cycle, subject to the following constraint, which limits the heart rate, f_H, to lie in the range 30–200 beats per minute:

$$U_H = \begin{Bmatrix} 2.0, & U_G \geq 2.0 \\ U_G, & 0.3 < U_G < 2.0 \\ 0.3, & U_G \leq 0.3 \end{Bmatrix} \tag{5.130}$$

Taken together, this set of model equations can be represented by the block diagram depicted in Fig. 5–39 which relates baroreceptor function as input to the output of the heart period.

5.5.5 Compartmental modeling

Compartmental models are a class of dynamic (i.e., differential equation) models derived from mass balance considerations which are widely used for studying quantitatively the kinetics of materials in physiological systems. Materials can be either exogenous, such as a drug or tracer, or endogenous, such as a substrate or hormone, and kinetics include processes such as the production, distribution, transport, utilization, and substrate–hormone control interactions.

Compartmental models have been widely employed for solving a broad spectrum of physiological problems related to the distribution of materials in living systems in research, diagnosis, and therapy at whole-body, organ, and cellular levels. Examples and references can be found in books including Gibaldi & Perrier (1982), Carson *et al.* (1983), Godfrey (1983), Jacquez (1996), Cobelli *et al.* (2000), and Carson & Cobelli (2014). We have already seen some examples of linear compartmental models in Section 5.3. Here we shall define and discuss the general nonlinear compartmental model.

Let us begin with some definitions. A compartment is a quantity of material that acts as though it is well-mixed and kinetically homogeneous. A compartmental model consists of a finite number of compartments with specified interconnections among them. The interconnections represent fluxes of material which physiologically constitute transport from one location to another or a chemical transformation or both. These fluxes of material can be controlled not only by the two interconnected compartments, but also by other system compartments.

Given these introductory definitions, it is useful to consider possible candidates for compartments before explaining well-mixed and kinetic homogeneity. To begin, consider the notion of a compartment as a physical space. Plasma is a candidate for a compartment; a substance such as plasma glucose could be a compartment. Zinc in bone could be a compartment, as could thyroxine in the thyroid gland. In some experiments, different substances could be followed in plasma; plasma glucose, lactate, and alanine provide examples. Thus in the same experiment there can be more than one plasma compartment, one for each of the substances being studied. This notion also extends beyond plasma: glucose and glucose-6-phosphate could be two different compartments inside a liver cell. Thus a physical space may actually represent more than one compartment.

In addition, one must distinguish between compartments that are accessible and those that are nonaccessible for measurement. Researchers often try to assign physical spaces to the nonaccessible compartments. This is a very difficult problem which is best addressed once it is understood that the definition of a compartment is actually a theoretical construct which may, in fact, lump material from several different physical spaces in a system. To equate a compartment with a physical space depends upon the system under study and assumptions about the model.

With these notions of what might constitute a compartment, it is easier to define the concepts of well-mixed and kinetic homogeneity. Well-mixed means that any two samples taken from the compartment at the same time would have the same concentration of the substance being studied, and therefore be equally representative. Thus the concept of well-mixed relates to uniformity of information contained in a single compartment.

Kinetic homogeneity means that every particle in a compartment has the same probability of taking the pathways leaving the compartment. Since, when a particle leaves a compartment, due to metabolic events relating to transport and utilization, it means that all particles in the compartment have the same probability of leaving due to one of these events.

The notion of a compartment, that is, lumping material with similar characteristics into collections that are homogeneous and behave identically, is what allows one to reduce a complex physiological system into a finite number of compartments and pathways. The required number of compartments depends both on the system being studied and on the richness of the experimental configuration. A compartmental model is clearly unique for each system studied, since it incorporates known and hypothesized physiology and

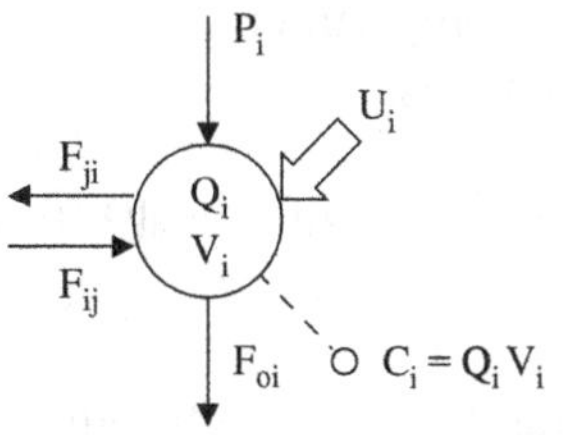

FIGURE 5–40 The i-th compartment with its input and output fluxes and the output measurement of concentration.

biochemistry. It provides the investigator with insights into the system structure and is as good as the assumptions that are incorporated in the model.

5.5.5.1 The model

Let Fig. 5–40 represent the i-th compartment of an n-compartment model, in which $Q_i \geq 0$ denotes the mass of the compartment. The arrows represent fluxes into and out of the compartment. The fluxes into the compartment from outside the system, that is, endogenous (de novo synthesis of material) and exogenous inputs are represented by P_i and U_i respectively. The flux to the environment and therefore out of the system is given by F_{0i}, the flux from compartment i to j by F_{ji}, and the flux from compartment j to i by F_{ij}. All fluxes are ≥ 0. The general equations for the compartmental model are obtained by writing the mass balance equation for each compartment:

$$\dot{Q}_i(t) = \sum_{\substack{j=1 \\ j \neq i}}^{n} F_{ij}(t) - \sum_{\substack{j=1 \\ j \neq i}}^{n} F_{ij}(t) + P_i(t) - F_{0i} + U_i(t) \quad Q_i(0) = Q_{i0} \quad i = 1, 2 \ldots, n \tag{5.131}$$

where Q_{i0} denotes the mass in the compartment at time 0. In (5.131) some terms may be zero, for example, U_i and P_i would be zero if there was no exogenous or endogenous input, respectively.

Fluxes F_{ij} are in general functions of all compartmental masses $Q_1, Q_2, \ldots, Q_n$ and sometimes also of time (for the sake of simplicity we shall ignore this dependency here):

$$F_{ij}(t) = F_{ij}[Q_1(t), Q_2(t), \ldots, Q_n(t)] \quad i = 0, 1, 2, \ldots, n; \; j = 1, 2, \ldots n; \; j \neq i \tag{5.132}$$

A similar dependence on $Q_1, Q_2, \ldots, Q_n$ can also apply for each of the P_i.

Not all compartments are usually accessible to measurement, as already indicated. Let us assume that we can measure the material concentration in M compartments. Then, one can couple (5.131) with the measurement equation:

$$C_i(t) = \frac{Q_i(t)}{V_i} \quad i = 1, 2, \ldots, M \tag{5.133}$$

where V_i denotes the volume of the compartment.

It is always possible to write (5.132) as:

$$F_{ij}[Q_1(t), Q_2(t), \ldots, Q_n(t)] = k_{ij}[Q_1(t), Q_2(t), \ldots, Q_n(t)]Q_j(t) \\ i = 0, 1, 2, \ldots, \; n; \;\; j = 1, 2, \ldots, \; n; \;\; j \neq i \tag{5.134}$$

where k_{ij} is defined as the fractional transfer coefficient from compartment j to i. With this definition one has:

$$k_{ij}[Q_1(t), Q_2(t), \ldots, Q_n(t)] \geq 0 \quad i = 0, 1, 2, \ldots, \; n; \;\; j = 1, 2, \ldots, \; n; \; j \neq i \tag{5.135}$$

Thus by substituting (5.134) into (5.131), the system of equations:

$$\begin{aligned} \dot{Q}_i(t) \; &= \sum_{\substack{j=1 \\ j \neq i}}^{n} k_{ij}[Q_1(t), Q_2(t), \ldots, Q_n(t)]Q_j(t) \\ &- \sum_{\substack{j=1 \\ j \neq i}}^{n} k_{ij}[Q_1(t), Q_2(t), \ldots, Q_n(t)]Q_i(t) + P_i[Q_1(t), Q_2(t), \ldots, Q_n(t)] \\ &- k_{0i}[Q_1(t), Q_2(t), \ldots, Q_n(t), t]Q_i(t) + U_i(t) \quad i = 1, \; 2, \; \ldots, \; n \end{aligned} \tag{5.136}$$

describes the generic n-compartment nonlinear model.

There are several candidate mathematical descriptions of the k_{ij} functional dependencies. The simplest one is that where there is no control on k_{ij}, that is, k_{ij} is a constant:

$$k_{ij}[Q_1(t), Q_2(t), \ldots, Q_n(t)] = k_{ij} \tag{5.137}$$

and thus:

$$F_{ij}(t) = k_{ij}Q_j(t) \tag{5.138}$$

that is, the flux is a linear function of Q_j (Fig. 5–41).

A more realistic description, allowing a saturation control from the source compartment, is that of Michaelis–Menten:

$$k_{ij}[Q_j(t)] = \frac{V_M}{K_m + Q_j(t)} \tag{5.139}$$

and thus:

$$F_{ij}[Q_j(t)] = \frac{V_M Q_j(t)}{K_m + Q_j(t)} \tag{5.140}$$

where V_M is the saturation value and K_M is the value of Q_j giving $V_M/2$ (Fig. 5–41). It is of interest to note that for $Q_j \ll K_M$, (5.139) becomes (5.137) with $k_{ij} = V_M/K_M$. This means that the Michaelis–Menten relation starts linearly for small values of Q_j. This is a potential

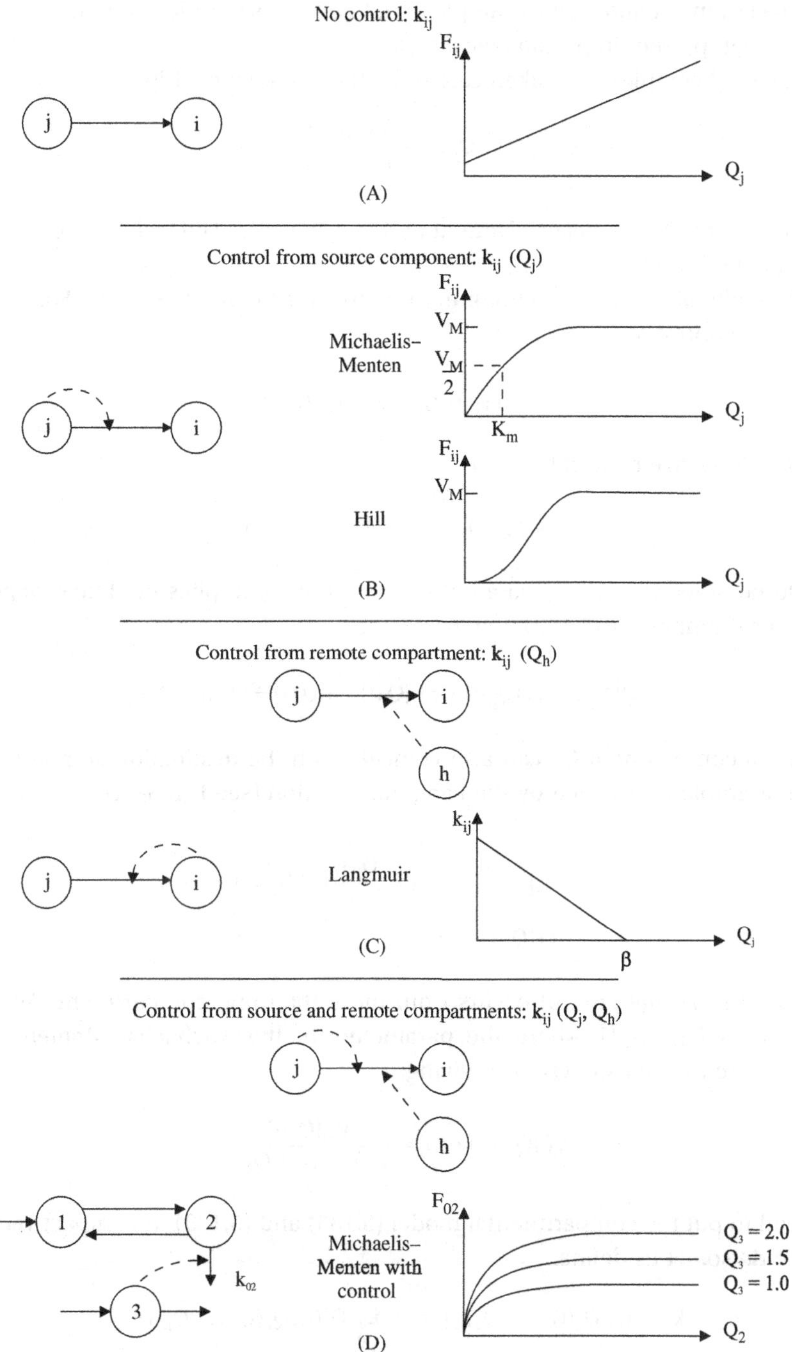

FIGURE 5–41 Four examples of functional dependence of flux between compartments: (A) no control; (B) control from the source compartment; (C) control from the remote compartment; and (D) control from source and remote compartments.

limitation in certain situations, for example, in addition to saturation, the threshold phenomenon is also often present in physiological systems.

This additional complexity is taken care of by the Hill relationship:

$$k_{ij}[Q_j(t)] = \frac{V_M Q_j^{q-1}(t)}{K_m + Q_j^q(t)} \tag{5.141}$$

with q being a positive integer. Note that for $q = 1$ the Hill relation collapses to the Michaelis–Menten form.

Control usually also occurs from compartments other than Q_j, say Q_h. For instance, one can have linear control of k_{ij} from Q_h:

$$k_{ij}[Q_h(t)] = \alpha + \beta Q_h(t) \tag{5.142}$$

or linear plus derivative control from Q_h:

$$k_{ij}[Q_h(t)] = \alpha + \beta Q_h(t) + \gamma \dot{Q}_h(t) \tag{5.143}$$

It should be noted that linear parametric control on k_{ij} implies nonlinear dependence of the flux F_{ij}, for example, for (5.142) one has:

$$F_{ij}[Q_j(t)] = k_{ij}[Q_h(t), Q_j(t)]Q_j(t) = \alpha Q_j(t) + \beta Q_j(t) Q_h(t) \tag{5.144}$$

The control compartment Q_h can also coincide with the destination compartment, Qi. In this case an example is provided by the Langmuir relation (see Fig. 5–41):

$$\begin{aligned} k_{ij}[Q_i(t)] &= \alpha\left[1 - \frac{Q_i(t)}{\beta}\right] \quad && Q_i < \beta \\ k_{ij}[Q_i(t)] &= 0 && Q_i \geq \beta \end{aligned} \tag{5.145}$$

It is also possible that control occurs from more than one compartment. An example of this is shown in Fig. 5–41 where the parameters of the Michaelis–Menten relationship describing k_{02} are functions of Q_3, thus giving:

$$k_{02}[Q_2(t), Q_3(t)] = \frac{V_M[Q_3(t)]}{K_m[Q_3(t)] + Q_2(t)} \tag{5.146}$$

It is useful to put the compartmental model (5.136) and (5.133) in compact vector–matrix notation. To do so, let us define:

$$\begin{aligned} k_{ii}[Q_1(t), Q_2(t), \ldots, Q_n(t)] = &- k_{0i}[Q_1(t), Q_2(t), \ldots, Q_n(t)] \\ &- \sum_{\substack{j=1 \\ j^1 i}}^{n} k_{ji}[Q_1(t), Q_2(t), \ldots, Q_n(t)] \end{aligned} \tag{5.147}$$

Eqs. (5.136) and (5.131) thus become:

$$\dot{Q}_i(t) = \sum_{j=1}^{n} k_{ij}[Q_1(t), Q_2(t), \ldots, Q_n(t)]Q_j(t) + P_i[Q_1(t), Q_2(t), \ldots, Q_n(t)] + U_i(t) \quad (5.148)$$
$$Q_i(0) = Q_{10}$$

and:

$$C_i(t) = \frac{Q_i(t)}{V_i} i \in M \quad (5.149)$$

Now, defining the vectors:

$$Q(t) = [Q_1(t), Q_2(t), \ldots, Q_n(t)]^T \quad (5.150)$$

$$P(t) = [P_1(t), P_2(t), \ldots, P_n(t)]^T \quad (5.151)$$

$$U(t) = [U_1(t), U_2(t), \ldots, U_n(t)]^T \quad (5.152)$$

$$C(t) = [C_1(t), C_2(t), \ldots, C_m(t)]^T \quad (5.153)$$

one has:

$$\dot{Q}(t) = K[Q(t)]Q(t) + P[Q(t)] + U(t) \quad Q(0) = Q_0 \quad (5.154)$$

$$C(t) = HQ(t) \quad (5.155)$$

where $K[Q(t)]$ is the compartmental $n \times n$ matrix and H is the measurement $m \times n$ matrix.

The compartmental matrix has some properties that arise from the mass balance principle upon which compartmental models rely, namely:

$$k_{ii}[Q(t)] \leq 0 \quad \text{for all } i \quad (5.156)$$

$$k_{ij}[Q(t)] \geq 0 \quad \text{for all } i \neq j \quad (5.157)$$

In addition, $K[Q(t)]$ is diagonally dominant with respect to columns, that is:

$$|k_{ii}[Q(t)]| \geq \sum_{\substack{j=1 \\ j \neq i}}^{n} |k_{ji}[Q(t)]| = \sum_{\substack{j=1 \\ j \neq i}}^{n} k_{ji}[Q(t)] \quad \text{for all } i \quad (5.158)$$

$$\text{since} \quad \sum_{j=1}^{n} k_{ji}[Q(t)] = \sum_{\substack{j=1 \\ j \neq i}}^{n} k_{ji}[Q(t)] + k_{ii}[Q(t)] = -k_{oi} \leq 0 \quad (5.159)$$

By using properties of (5.156)–(5.158), one can state some stability properties of nonlinear compartmental models (Jacquez & Simon, 1993).

An interesting class of compartmental models is that where K is a constant matrix, that is, $k_{ij}[Q(t)] = k_{ij}$. In this case one has:

$$\dot{Q}(t) = K \cdot Q(t) + P(t) + U(t) \tag{5.160}$$

and compared to the nonlinear case it is relatively easy to state the stability properties (Jacquez & Simon, 1993). No eigenvalues can have positive real parts and there are no purely imaginary eigenvalues. This means that all the solutions are bounded and if there are oscillations, they must be damped. Also, for particular classes of linear compartmental models, such as mamillary and catenary models (Fig. 5–42), the eigenvalues are always real.

Mamillary

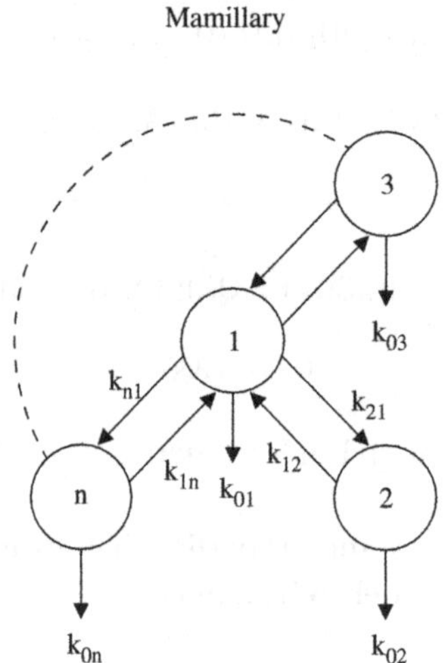

Catenary

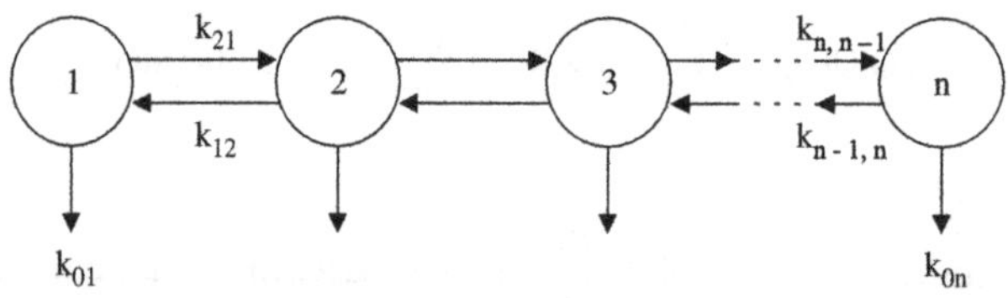

FIGURE 5–42 Examples of mamillary and capillary compartmental models.

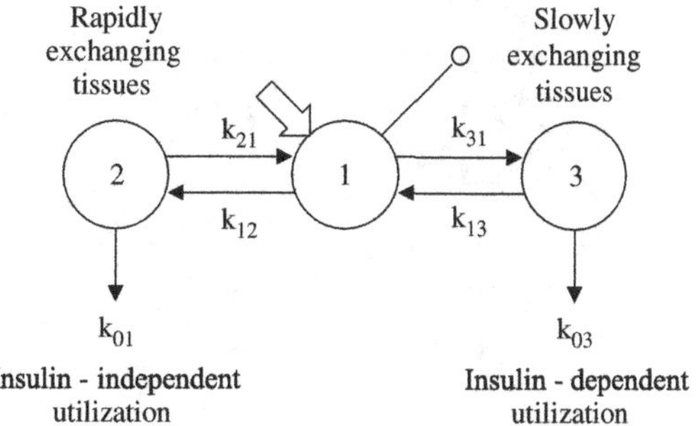

FIGURE 5–43 The linear compartmental model of glucose kinetics.

Physiological systems almost invariably exhibit nonlinear dynamics; the linear dynamic model of equation (5.160) is very useful due to an important result. The kinetics of a tracer in a constant steady-state system, linear or nonlinear, is linear with constant coefficients. An example is shown in Fig. 5–43. This can be used to study tracer glucose kinetics in the steady-state at the whole-body level. Linear compartmental models, in conjunction with tracer experiments, have been used extensively in studying the distribution of materials in living systems at whole-body, organ, and cellular levels. Examples and references can be found by Carson *et al.* (1983), Jacquez (1996), Cobelli *et al.* (2000), and Carson & Cobelli (2014).

An interesting application of linear compartmental models at the organ level is in describing the exchange of materials between blood, interstitial fluid, and cellular tissue from multiple tracer indicator dilution data. Compartmental models provide a finite difference approximation in the space dimension of a system described by partial differential equations which may be more easily resolved from the data. These models are discussed in Jacquez (1985). An example of a model describing glucose transport and metabolism in human skeletal muscle is shown in Fig. 5–44 (Saccomani *et al.*, 1996). This model is, in some sense, the compartmental alternative to the distributed modeling discussed in Section 5.4.1 for describing blood–tissue exchange. The two models clearly rely on different assumptions and exhibit different degrees of parsimony.

5.5.6 Insulin receptor regulation

Representing the dynamics of insulin receptor regulation offers another example of nonlinear modeling. A conceptual representation of the model is given in Fig. 5–45, showing the cell and the processes being modeled (Quon & Campfield, 1991). Surface and intracellular pools of insulin receptors are connected by the rate constants for receptor translocation between the two pools (rates of bound and unbound receptor internalization and receptor recycling); receptor synthesis and the degradation of intracellular receptors. No distinction is made in the model between insertion into the cell membrane of newly synthesized receptors and insertion of receptors which have been internalized, bound or unbound, and then

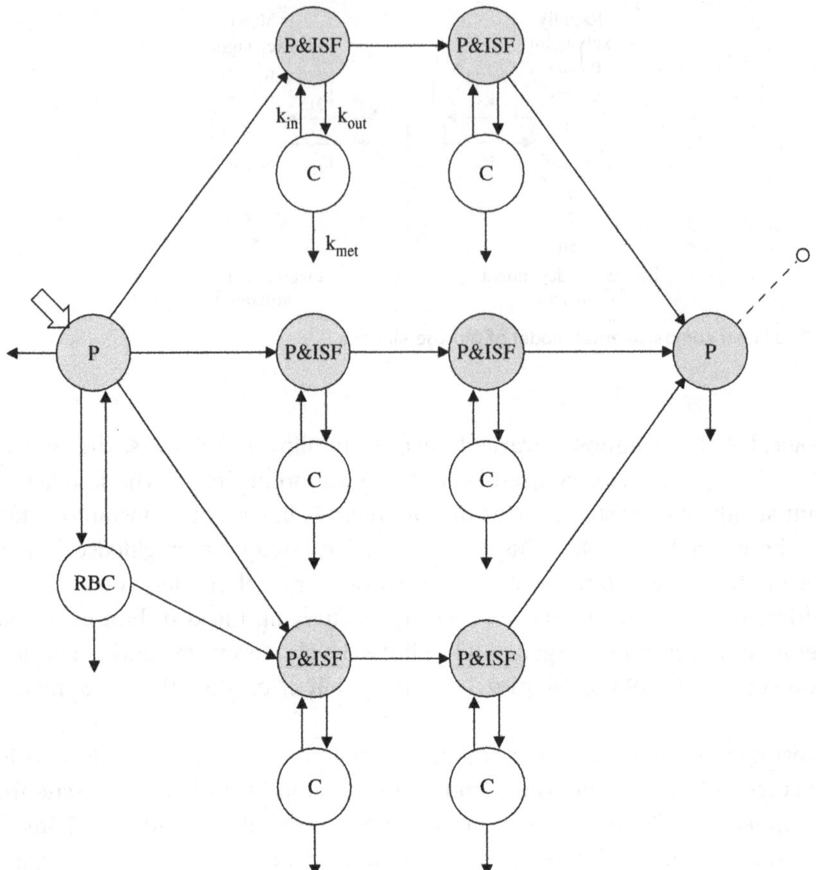

FIGURE 5–44 Compartmental model of transport and metabolism of glucose in skeletal muscle. P denotes plasma; P&ISF denotes plasma and interstitial fluid; C denotes cell; and RBC represents red blood cells. Parameters k_{in}, k_{out}, and k_{met} denote glucose transport into and out of the cell and its metabolism, respectively.

retroendocytosed. In the model it is assumed that all processes are characterized by first-order rate constants, with the exception of receptor synthesis which is modeled as a zero order state dependent process. More complex representations were considered, including higher order rate constants and saturable processes. However, insufficient data were available to justify such complex forms of model representation.

The mathematical realization of this model is as follows:

$$\dot{x}_1(t) = k_{-1}x_2(t) - [k_1(1 - x_3(t) + k)k_1^{'}\ x_3(t)]x_1(t) \quad (5.161)$$

$$\dot{x}_2(t) = [k_1(1 - x_3(t) + k_1^{'}x_3(t)]x_1(t) - k_{-1}x_2(t) + k_2 - k_{-2}x_2(t) \quad (5.162)$$

$$\dot{x}_3(t) = 0 \quad (5.163)$$

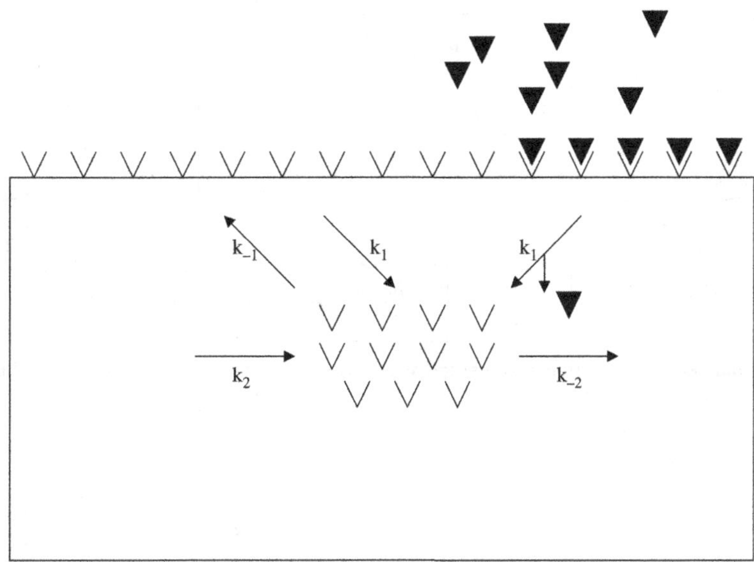

FIGURE 5–45 A schematic diagram of insulin receptor regulation model. The parameter k_1 is the unbound receptor internalization rate constant, k_1' is the bound internalization rate constant, k_{-1} is the receptor recycling rate constant, k_2 is the state dependent receptor synthesis rate constant, and k_{-2} is the intracellular receptor degradation rate constant. The symbol ⊤ denotes a free insulin molecule, V denotes an insulin receptor, and ▼ denotes a bound insulin receptor complex.

where x_1 is the number of surface receptors (% total basal receptors); x_2 is the number of intracellular receptors; x_3 is the fraction of bound receptors; k_1 is the unbound receptor internalization rate; k_1' is the bound receptor internalization rate; k_{-1} is the receptor recycling rate; k_2 is the state dependent synthesis rate; and k_{-2} is the intracellular receptor degradation rate.

The nonlinearity in this model stems from the presence of the multiplicative terms involving the product x_3x_1. There is a component of positive rate of change in the number of intracellular receptors which is proportional both to the number of surface receptors and to the fraction of bound receptors. All of the other terms in the model are linear, but the presence of this one nonlinear effect means that, overall, the model is nonlinear.

5.5.7 Insulin action modeling

The ability to measure *in vivo* insulin action is of great value since it is well established that abnormalities in insulin action are an important determinant of diabetes and other states of glucose intolerance. A model-based noninvasive method to measure insulin action or insulin sensitivity is to resort to an intravenous glucose tolerance test (IVGTT) and to interpret the plasma glucose and insulin concentrations with the minimal model (Bergman *et al.*, 1979). The salient features of this method are discussed later in this chapter, and for a more detailed presentation of the model we refer to Section 11.6. The glucose–insulin system is a

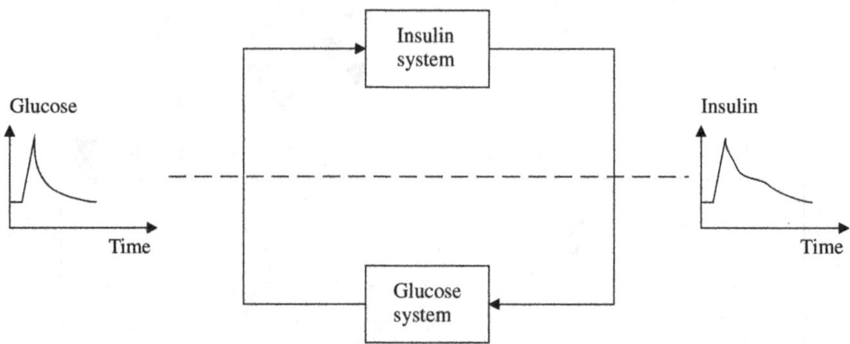

FIGURE 5–46 The glucose–insulin system represented as two interconnected subsystems linked by their measured signals.

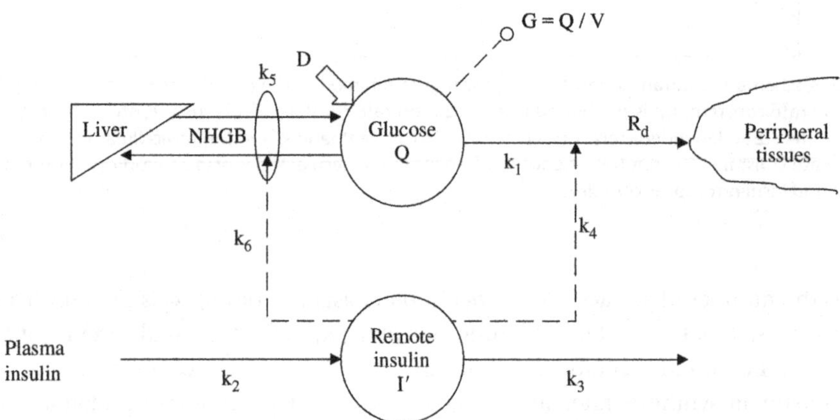

FIGURE 5–47 The glucose minimal model. The rate constants, k, characterize either material fluxes (solid lines) or control actions (dashed lines).

negative feedback system and can be profitably thought of as being composed of the glucose and insulin systems connected by the measured plasma glucose and insulin concentrations (Fig. 5–46).

The rationale behind the glucose minimal model is to treat the measured insulin as a known input and to predict the measured glucose concentration. To do so, a description of the glucose kinetics and insulin action must be incorporated into the model. However, with this system decomposition there is no need to simultaneously describe the upper portion of the system, that is, all processes related to glucose-stimulated insulin secretion, insulin kinetics, and degradation. The physiological scheme of the glucose minimal model is shown in Fig. 5–47 and its mass balance equations are:

$$\dot{Q}(t) = NHGB(t) - R_d(t) \quad Q(0) = Q_b + D \tag{5.164}$$

$$I'(t) = -k_3 I'(t) + k_2[I(t) - I_b] \quad I'(0) = 0 \tag{5.165}$$

$$G(t) = \frac{Q(t)}{V} \tag{5.166}$$

where Q is glucose mass, with Q_b denoting its basal value; D is the glucose dose; NHGB is net hepatic glucose balance; R_d is plasma glucose disappearance rate; I' is insulin concentration (deviation from basal) in a compartment remote from plasma (interstitial fluid—from where insulin action signaling occurs) and I is plasma insulin concentration with I_b denoting its basal value; G is plasma glucose concentration, with G_b denoting its basal value; and V is the distribution value. Clearly G_bV equals Q_b.

NHGB is controlled by glucose and remote insulin:

$$NHGB(t) = NHGB_0 - [k_5 + k_6 I'(t)]Q(t) \tag{5.167}$$

where $NHGB_0$ is net endogenous glucose balance at zero glucose.

R_d is controlled by glucose and remote insulin:

$$R_d(t) = \left[k_1 + k_4 I'(t)\right]Q(t) + R_{d_0} \tag{5.168}$$

where R_{d_0} is glucose disappearance rate at zero glucose. Thus by incorporating (5.167) and (5.168) into (5.164), the following expressions are obtained:

$$\dot{Q}(t) = -\left[(k_5 + k_1) - (k_6 + k_4)I'(t)\right]Q(t) + \left(NHGB_0 - R_{d_0}\right) \quad Q(0) = Q_b + D \tag{5.169}$$

$$\dot{I}'(t) = -k_3 I'(t) + k_2[I(t) - I_b] \quad I'(0) = 0 \tag{5.170}$$

$$G(t) = \frac{Q(t)}{V} \tag{5.171}$$

where the term $(NHGB - R_{d_0})$ can be written as $(k_3 + k_1)Q_b$ by using the basal constraint $dQ/dt = 0$. The model is nonlinear due to the presence of the product of Q and I' in (5.169).

Unfortunately, the model has too many parameters to be resolved, assuming plasma insulin concentration (I) as a known input, from plasma glucose concentration data (G), that is, the model is *a priori* unidentifiable (see Chapter 7: Parametric modeling—the identifiability problem). To be resolved numerically, the model must be made more parsimonious by the following reparameterization which is the classic minimal model representation:

$$\dot{Q}(t) = -\left[p_1 + X(t)\right]Q(t) + p_1 Q_b \quad Q(0) = Q_b + D \tag{5.172}$$

$$\dot{X}(t) = -p_2 X(t) + p_3[I(t) - I_b] \quad X(0) = 0 \tag{5.173}$$

$$G(t) = \frac{Q(t)}{V} \tag{5.174}$$

This parameterization has new parameters, the p's, and a new variable, X, which are related to the parameters and variable of the original scheme of Fig. 5–47 as follows:

$$X(t) = (k_4 + k_6)I'(t) \tag{5.175}$$

$$p_1 = k_1 + k_5 \tag{5.176}$$

$$p_2 = k_3 \tag{5.177}$$

$$p_3 = k_2(k_4 + k_6) \tag{5.178}$$

The model can thus predict the time course of X, a variable related to insulin action by an unknown scale factor $(k_4 + k_6)$. However, it can also provide an index of insulin action called insulin sensitivity. To do this one needs to formally define insulin sensitivity. Let us first define glucose effectiveness, that is, the ability of glucose per se to enhance its own disappearance:

$$S_G = -\frac{\partial \dot{Q}}{\partial Q}\Big|_{ss} \tag{5.179}$$

where ss denotes steady state. Then, insulin sensitivity is simply the ability of insulin to enhance glucose effectiveness:

$$S_I = \frac{\partial S_G}{\partial I}\Big|_{ss} \tag{5.180}$$

By applying these definitions, S_I can be calculated as:

$$S_I = \frac{p_3}{p_2} = \frac{k_2(k_4 + k_6)}{k_3} \quad \frac{\text{min}^{-1}}{(\mu\text{U/mL})} \tag{5.181}$$

The intuitive meaning of S_I is clear from the right-hand side of the expression in terms of the k_i parameters: it is directly proportional to the stimulatory action on the periphery (k_4) and inhibitory action on the liver (k_6), but it is also proportional to the insulin input magnitude (k_2) and to the time constant of action $(1/k_3)$.

The choice of an intravenous test like the IVGTT facilitates the system modeling since the system is perturbed by a known input. However, the IVGTT is nonphysiological, that is, in real-life one does not encounter such a dramatic increase of glucose in a few minutes. It would be important to be able to model a more physiological and easier to perform test with glucose given orally. The more real-life test is a mixed meal test, but also an OGTT is of great interest given its easier standardization. Modeling however becomes more difficult because one has to describe the transit of glucose through the gastrointestinal tract which is a complex process and would require the use of a nonlinear model.

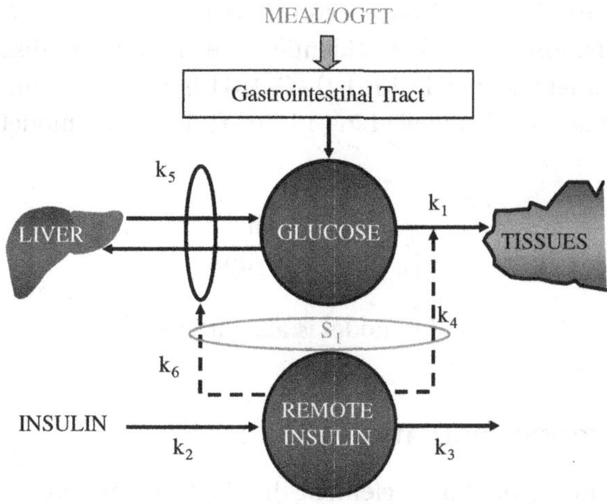

FIGURE 5–48 The oral glucose minimal model. R_a is the rate of appearance of the glucose in plasma after an oral ingestion.

An alternative is to abandon the idea of describing the fate of glucose from the mouth, to the stomach and to the intestine and concentrate on the rate of appearance of glucose in plasma (R_a) which, at variance with the IVGTT know dose, is now unknown. The idea of the oral minimal model is to couple the model with a parametric description of R_a and estimate the unknown R_a parameters together with the other model parameters (Fig. 5–48).

The general formulation of the oral minimal model after an oral glucose perturbation is:

$$\dot{Q}(t) = -\left[p_1 + X(t)\right]Q(t) + p_1 Q_b + R_a(t, \alpha) \quad Q(0) = Q_b + D \tag{5.182}$$

$$\dot{X}(t) = -p_2 X(t) + p_3[I(t) - I_b] \quad X(0) = 0 \tag{5.183}$$

$$G(t) = \frac{Q(t)}{V} \tag{5.184}$$

where G is plasma glucose concentration, I plasma insulin concentration, suffix "b" denotes basal (pretest) values, (X) insulin action on glucose production and disposal, (V) distribution volume, and (p_1, p_2, and p_3) model parameters. R_a can be described with a piecewise-linear function with a given number of break points. Since the rate of glucose absorption varies more rapidly in the first portion of the test, intervals will be shorter at the beginning and longer toward the end: seven/eight break points have been shown to be a good compromise between model flexibility and the number of parameters to be estimated from the data. This is discussed in more detail in Section 11.6. The expression for R_a is thus given by:

$$R_a(t, \alpha) = \begin{cases} \alpha_{i-1} + \dfrac{\alpha_i - \alpha_{i-1}}{t_i - t_{i-1}} \cdot (t_i - t_{i-1}) & \text{for } t_{i-1} \le t < t_i, \; i = 1, \ldots, 7/8 \\ 0 & \text{otherwise} \end{cases} \tag{5.185}$$

The model, due to the increased number of parameters, is *a priori* nonidentifiable, and the additional information needed to identify the model is discussed in detail in Section 11.6. The parameterization in (5.182)–(5.184) is related to the parameters k's and variable I′ of Fig. 5–48 as already detailed in (5.175)–(5.178). The model provides the insulin sensitivity index as:

$$S_I = \frac{p_3}{p_2} \quad \frac{\min^{-1}}{(\mu U/mL)} \tag{5.186}$$

In Section 11.6 the validation of the model is also discussed.

5.5.8 Thyroid hormone regulation

Another model containing a nonlinear element that is developed to increase understanding of physiological mechanisms regulating the thyroid hormones focusing on the relationships between the anterior pituitary and thyroid glands. The basic features of the thyroid hormone regulating system are shown in Fig. 5–49. The regulated variables are assumed to be the free concentrations of the two thyroid hormones, thyroxine T_4 and triiodothyronine T_3 in the plasma. Regulation is assumed to take place through feedback of information relating to these two hormones to the anterior pituitary. In this manner the secretion of thyrotrophin (TSH), the thyroid-stimulating hormone, by the anterior pituitary can be modified. TSH is secreted in response to TRH, the thyrotrophic-releasing hormone that is produced by the hypothalamus. Stimulation of the thyroid gland by TSH brings about the secretion of T_3 and T_4. These hormones undergo reversible binding to three plasma proteins (thyroid hormone–binding globulin, thyroid hormone–binding prealbumin, and albumin). Free (i.e., unbound) hormone is distributed into extravascular sites where breakdown of T_3 and T_4 is assumed to occur. A proportion of T_4 is converted to T_3.

To gain increased quantitative understanding of the nature of the feedback regulatory system, a number of models have been developed, based on the early work of Saratchandran *et al.* (1976). The fundamental postulates underpinning these models are as follows:

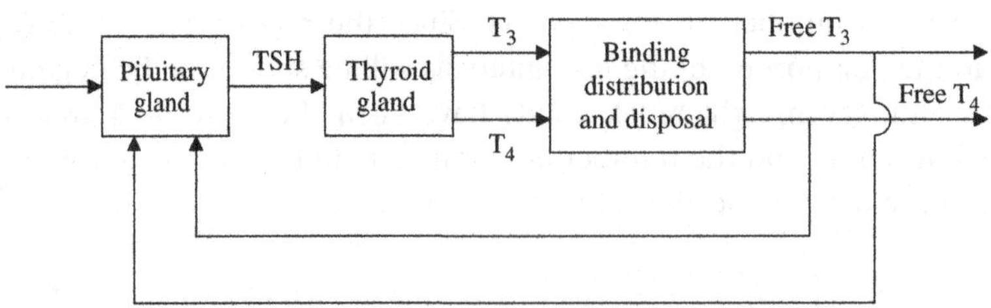

FIGURE 5–49 Conceptual model of the principal features of the thyroid–pituitary axis of the hormone regulatory system.

a. Feedback signals act by altering the secretion rate of the hormones produced by the regulated organ.
b. TSH secretion is inhibited by T_3 or T_4 or both. Secretion is proportional to the logarithm of the current level of TRH in the pituitary portal circulation (introducing a nonlinear component here).
c. The secretion rates of T_3 and T_4 are dependent on TSH, there being no autonomous secretion of either thyroid hormone.
d. Destruction of all hormones occurs by means of first-order processes.
e. Less than 20% of T_3 production is by direct secretion in the basal state. The remainder is produced by peripheral deiodination of T_4.
f. Circulatory mixing dynamics are sufficiently rapid to be ignored.

Let us first consider the mathematical description of the portion of the model describing the dynamics of binding, distribution, and disposal of T_3 and T_4 (DiStefano *et al.*, 1975). Each of the hormones are described in terms of a three compartment model representing plasma and two extravascular sites, those with fast and slow dynamics, respectively (Fig. 5–50). A linearized model can be adopted in terms of the following equations that can be written defining the rate of change of concentration of the hormone:

$$\frac{dx_1}{dt} = a_1x_1 + a_2x_2 + a_3x_3 + \frac{u_1}{V} \tag{5.187}$$

$$\frac{dx_2}{dt} = a_4x_1 + a_5x_2 + a_6x_5 \tag{5.188}$$

$$\frac{dx_3}{dt} = a_7x_1 + a_8x_3 + a_9x_6 \tag{5.189}$$

$$\frac{dx_4}{dt} = a_{10}x_4 + a_{11}x_5 + a_{12}x_6 + \frac{u_2}{V} \tag{5.190}$$

$$\frac{dx_5}{dt} = a_{13}x_4 + a_{14}x_5 \tag{5.191}$$

$$\frac{dx_6}{dt} = a_{15}x_4 + a_{16}x_6 \tag{5.192}$$

where x_1 is the plasma total T_3 concentration; x_2 the fast compartment total T_3 concentration; x_3 the slow compartment total T_3 concentration; x_4 the plasma total T_4 concentration; x_5 the fast compartment total T_4 concentration; x_6 the slow compartment total T_4 concentration; u_1 the rate of secretion of T_3; u_2 the rate of secretion of T_4; V the plasma volume. $a_1, a_2, \ldots, a_{16}$ are constant parameters reflecting the various rates of material transfer. Some of these are composite parameters so that, for instance, a_1 reflects transport of T_3 from plasma to both fast and slow compartments.

Since it is assumed that the free fractions of T_3 and T_4 are involved in feedback regulation, equations are required relating free concentration to the total (i.e., free and protein-bound

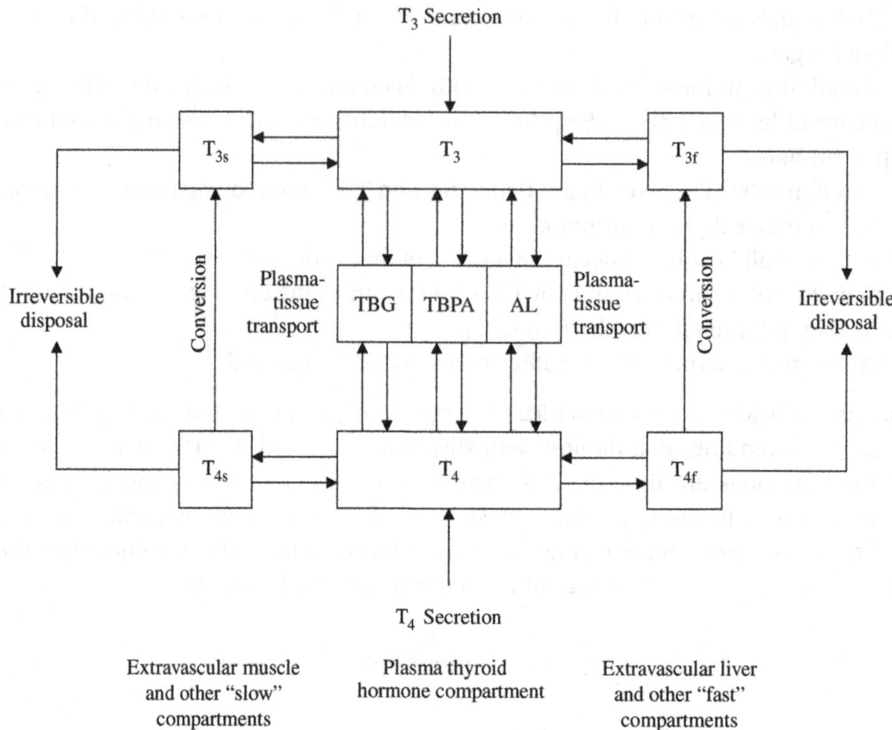

FIGURE 5–50 A six compartment model depicting the coupled dynamics of the binding, distribution, and disposal of T_3 and T_4. The thyroid hormone binds to the three proteins: thyroid hormone–binding globulin (TBG), thyroid hormone–binding prealbumin (TBPA), and albumin (AL). *Adapted from DiStefano, III J. J. et al., 1975.*

fractions) concentration. The following two algebraic equations provide an approximate description of these dynamics:

$$x_7 = a_{17}x_1 \tag{5.193}$$

$$x_8 = a_{18}x_4 \tag{5.194}$$

In its first form, the following descriptions were assumed for the rates of secretion of T_3 and T_4 and for the dynamics of TSH:

$$u_1 = k_1x_9 \tag{5.195}$$

$$u_2 = k_2x_9 \tag{5.196}$$

$$\frac{dx_9}{dt} = k_3 \log u_3 - k_4x_7 - k_5x_9 \tag{5.197}$$

where x_9 is theconcentration of TSH in plasma; u_2 the perceived secretion rate of TRH in portal plasma; k_1, k_2 the parameters representing the stimulatory effect of TSH on the thyroid gland; k_3 the parameter representing the stimulatory effect of TRH on the rate of TSH secretion; k_4 the parameter representing the inhibitory effect of free T_3; k_5 the rate constant for loss of TSH in plasma.

With values inserted for the various parameters, simulation studies can then be undertaken with the model in order to gain quantitative insights regarding the regulatory processes. However, on the basis of such simulation studies it was found that with the model assumptions of proportional control for the rate of release of T_3, acceptable model responses could not be achieved with the adoption of parameter values which were physiologically plausible. The model was therefore extended by assuming that the rate of release of T_3 is not only proportional to the current concentration of TSH, but also to the cumulated past excess of TSH concentration (compared with the steady-state level). This assumption of proportional and what is known as integral control did lead to results that were plausible with the adoption of physiologically acceptable parameters. In other words, in terms of the model, (5.195) is replaced by (5.198):

$$u_1 = k_1 x_9 + k_6 \int_0^t \left(x_9 - x_{9_s}\right) dt \tag{5.198}$$

where x_{9s} is the steady-state concentration of TSH and k_6 is a positive parameter.

5.5.9 Modeling the chemical control of breathing

Large scale mathematical models of the human respiratory system can play an important role in testing hypotheses concerning the control of breathing. The example presented here incorporates the inspiratory and expiratory processes of breathing and has been used to explore the relationships between the elements of the breathing pattern (inspiratory, TI, and expiratory, TE, times, and tidal volume, VT). By assuming a triangular waveform pattern of breathing, separate controllers are provided for inspiratory and expiratory times. This enables a variety of hypotheses relating to the chemical control of breathing to be investigated.

In developing the model, the respiratory system is presented in conventional control system terms with its two major components of the controlled system and the controller (Sarhan *et al.*, 1988).

5.5.9.1 The controlled system

The model adopted for the controlled system is depicted in Fig. 5–51. This consists of four major compartments: lung, brain tissue, muscle, and other tissues connected by the circulatory bloodstream. The lung is represented as a single chamber of variable volume, thus permitting the generation of oscillating blood gas concentrations and pH in the arterial blood. The model incorporates a dead space corresponding to the portion of the lung in which gas exchange does not occur. This is partly fixed volume (the anatomical dead space $V_{D\ anat}$) and

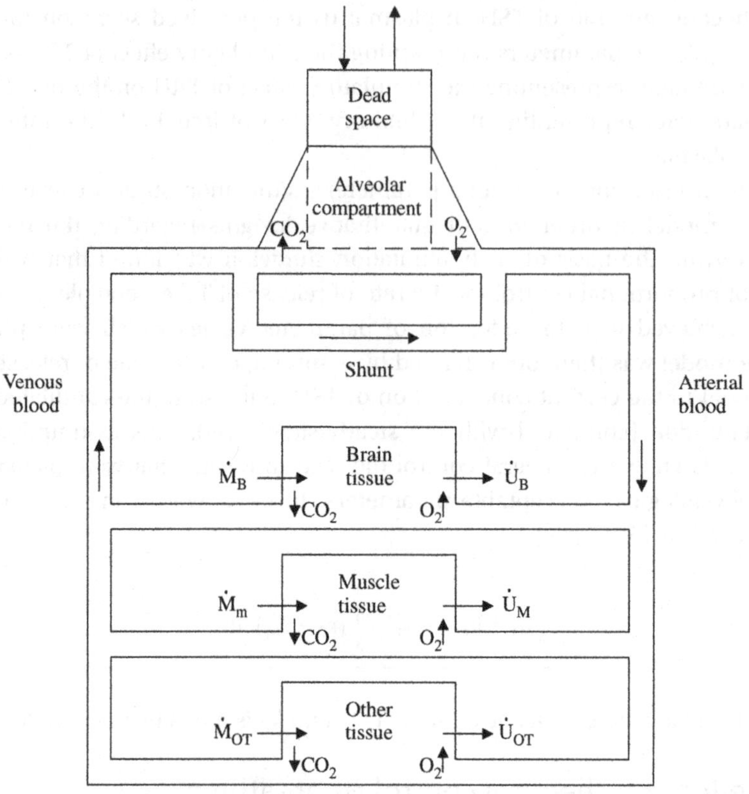

FIGURE 5–51 The model structure of the controlled respiratory system. The rates of change of M and U represent CO_2 production and O_2 utilization; with the subscripts B, M, and OT corresponding to brain tissue, muscle tissue, and other tissues respectively. *Adapted from Sarhan et al., 1988.*

partly expansible, the alveolar dead space $V_{D\ alv}$ which encroaches on the lung volume V_L. Thus alveolar gas exchanging volume V_A is equal to V_L minus $V_{D\ alv}$.

The model also includes a shunt, whereby a portion of mixed venous blood can bypass the lung. It is assumed that the alveolar gas equilibrates perfectly with end-capillary blood, and that similarly the partial pressures of gases in the tissue compartments are equal to the pressures in the venous blood from that compartment. Mixing within compartments is assumed to be instantaneous and complete.

The full equations for the controlled system describe the rate of change of the blood gases in each of the compartments. They are not given here since the emphasis in this example is in showing how the model can be developed for the controller. They can be found by Sarhan *et al.* (1988). The equations correspond to: the alveolar gas exchanging and dead space compartments; the tissue compartments; CO_2 and O_2 dissociation curves in blood and tissues; hydrogen ion concentration equations; control of cardiac output and brain blood flow equations; calculation of lag times due to circulatory delays; mixed venous blood; and dead space and shunt. The equations defining gas exchange and metabolism are restricted to carbon dioxide and oxygen.

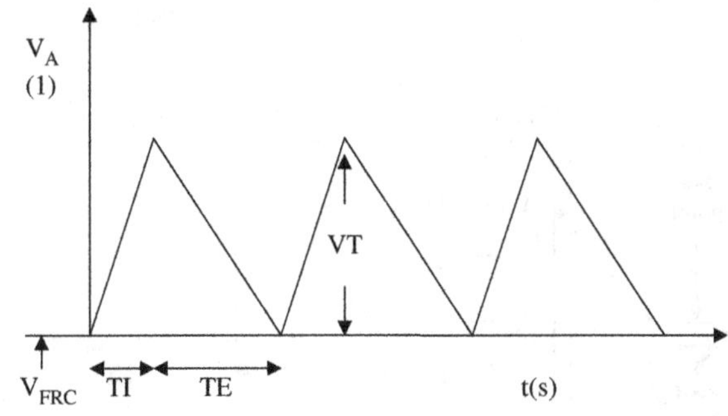

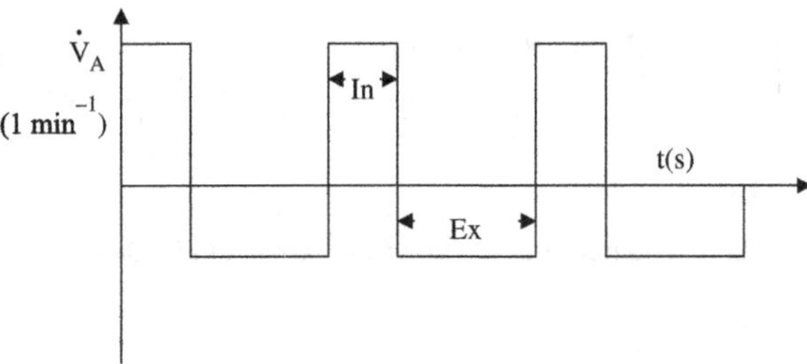

FIGURE 5–52 Pattern of breathing. *Adapted from Sarhan et al., 1988.*

By representing the pattern of breathing with a triangular waveform (as shown in Fig. 5–52), separate controllers can be provided for inspiration and expiration; thus enabling relations between the components of the respiratory cycle and chemical drive to be investigated. The instantaneous lung volume is therefore defined by two equations.

Inspiration

$$V_A = V_{FRC} + \frac{VT(t - t_0)}{TI} \tag{5.199}$$

where V_{FRC} is the functional residual capacity, VT is the tidal volume, TI is the inspiratory time, t is time, and t_0 is the starting time of the current breath. The rate of change of lung volume, dV_A/dt is given by:

$$\frac{dV_A}{dt} = \frac{VT}{TI} \tag{5.200}$$

Expiration

$$V_A = \frac{V_{FRC} + VT - VT(t - t_0)}{TE} \tag{5.201}$$

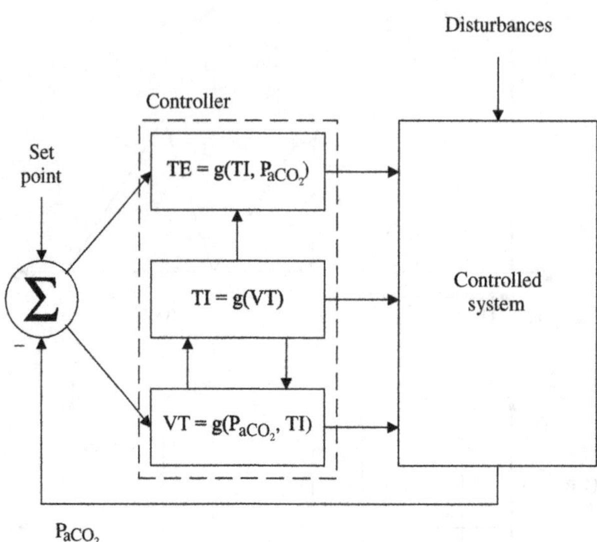

FIGURE 5–53 Controller of the breathing pattern. *Adapted from Sarhan et al., 1988.*

where TE is the expiratory time and dV_A/dt during expiration is given by:

$$\frac{dV_A}{dt} = -\frac{VT}{TE} \tag{5.202}$$

5.5.9.2 The controller

The form of the controller for the pattern of breathing is shown in Fig. 5–53. The equations are derived partly on an empirical basis using data derived from Cunningham and Gardner (1977).

Inspiratory flow controller

$$\frac{VT}{TI} = p_1 \left(P_{aCO_2} - p_2\right) \tag{5.203}$$

where P_{aCO_2} is the arterial partial pressure of CO_2.

Inspiratory time controller

$$TI = p_3 - p_4\ VT \quad (\text{for } VT < 2.08\ L) \tag{5.204}$$

$$TI = p_5\left(VT - p_6\right) + p_7 \quad (\text{for } VT \geq 2.08\ L) \tag{5.205}$$

Expiratory time controller

$$TE = p_8\ TI + \frac{p_9}{(P_{aCO_2} - p_2) - p_{10}} \tag{5.206}$$

where p_1–p_{10} are parameters evaluated from the data of Cunningham and Gardner (1977) with values: $p_1 = 0.11$, $p_2 = 35.2$, $p_3 = 1.29$, $p_4 = 0.07$, $p_5 = 0.65$, $p_6 = 0.88$, $p_7 = 0.59$, $p_8 = 0.64$, $p_9 = 11.1$, and $p_{10} = -2.73$.

Tidal volume is evaluated from:

$$VT = \left(\frac{VT}{TI}\right) \cdot TI \tag{5.207}$$

where (VT/TI) is taken from (5.203) and TI from (5.204) or (5.20), and the total time for one respiratory cycle, TT, is:

$$TT = TI + TE \tag{5.208}$$

so that the respiratory frequency (f) and lung ventilation (dV/dt) are given by:

$$f = \frac{60}{TT\ min^{-1}} \tag{5.209}$$

$$\frac{dV}{dt} = f \cdot VT \tag{5.210}$$

thus providing a definition of ventilation as the product of the separately calculated variables, respiratory frequency, and tidal volume.

Having developed the basic form of this complex model, it can then be used in simulation studies to test hypotheses and gain quantitative insight regarding the control of breathing in situations such as exercise.

5.6 Time-varying modeling

There is a correspondence between nonlinear modeling and model elements that are time-varying. In the examples of nonlinear models presented earlier, the nonlinear terms were an attempt to incorporate the inherently nonlinear structural effects occurring within the underlying physiology. An alternative means of producing the same effects, in terms of dynamic response, is to incorporate into a model components that are treated as if they were time-varying.

5.6.1 An example in cardiac modeling

An illustration of this time-varying approach to modeling can be seen in a representation of the short-term dynamics of the cardiovascular system (Leaning *et al.*, 1983). The basic

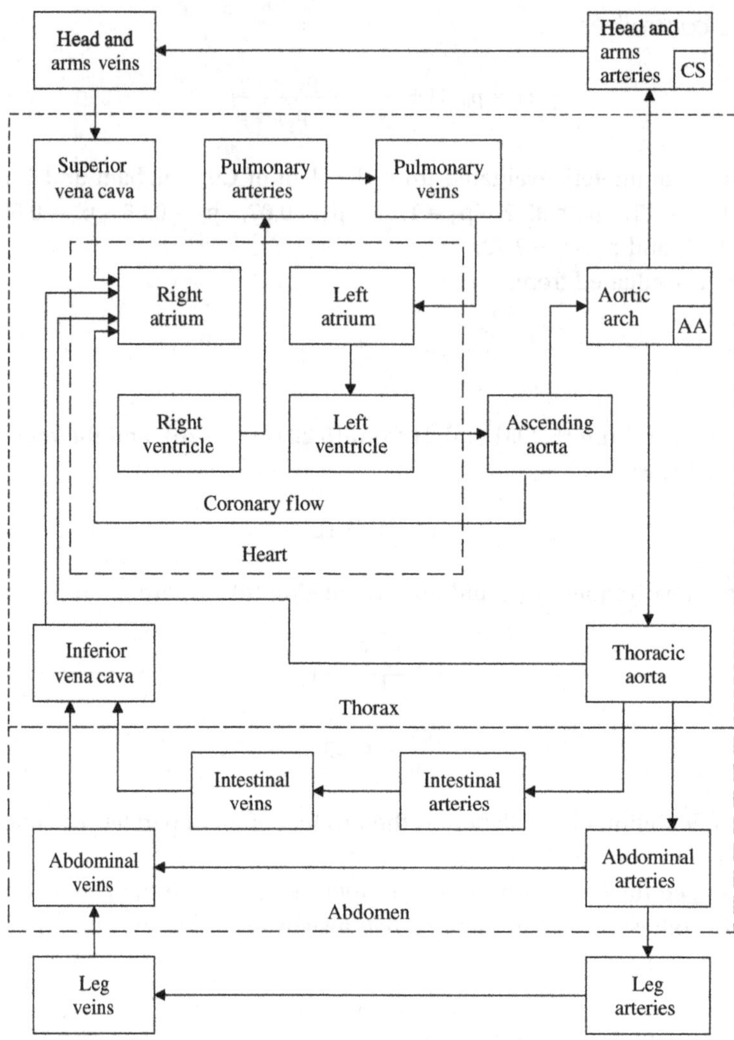

FIGURE 5–54 Structure of the uncontrolled hemodynamics. *Adapted from Leaning et al., 1983.*

structure of the model is depicted in Fig. 5–54. The mathematical model incorporates differential equations which describe the blood flow dynamics. In arriving at these equations, time-varying representations are adopted for the elastic properties of the heart chambers. In other words, rather than treating such parameters as being constant (as was the case earlier in this chapter), here that simplifying assumption is dispensed with, given that the time scale of this model is seconds and minutes; a time frame in which the time-varying nature of these parameters must be incorporated. The assumption of time-invariance would result in an invalid model, in contrast to a time frame of tens of minutes or hours in which case the simplifying assumption would be valid.

The heart is considered as a set of four separate unidirectional pumps. Cardiac timing events are described by linear approximations based on earlier research of Beneken and DeWit (1967):

$$T_{AS} = 0.1 + 0.09T_H \tag{5.211}$$

$$T_{AV} = T_{AS} - 0 \tag{5.212}$$

$$T_{VS} = 0.16 + 0.2T_H \tag{5.213}$$

where T_{AS} is the duration of the arterial systole, T_{AV} is the time between the onset of arterial systole and the onset of ventricular systole, T_{VS} is the duration of ventricular systole, and T_H is the heart period.

For a heart period, T_H, of 0.8 second, corresponding to a heart rate of 75 beats per minute, $T_{AS} = 0.172$ second, $T_{AV} = 0.132$ second, and $T_{VS} = 0.32$ second.

The pumping action of the heart is described by the equation relating pressure and volume:

$$P = a(t)[V - V_u] \tag{5.214}$$

where a(t) is the time-varying elastance function (elastance being the reciprocal of compliance).

The elastance functions for the four heart chambers are given by the equations derived using the time courses of the four elastances shown in Fig. 5–55.

$$a_{RA} = x(a_{RAS} - a_{RAD}) + a_{RAD} \tag{5.215}$$

$$a_{RV} = y(a_{RVS} - a_{RVD}) + a_{RVD} \tag{5.216}$$

$$a_{LA} = x(a_{LAS} - a_{LAD}) + a_{LAD} \tag{5.217}$$

$$a_{LV} = y(a_{LVS} - a_{LVD}) + a_{LVD} \tag{5.218}$$

where the subscripts RA, RV, LA, and LV refer to the right and left atria and ventricles, and the S and D subscripts correspond to systolic and diastolic values respectively. In (5.215)–(5.218):

$$\begin{aligned} x &= \sin\left(\frac{\pi t_c}{T_{AS}}\right), & 0 < t_c < T_{AS} \\ x &= 0, & t_c \geq T_{AS} \\ y &= 0, & t_c \leq T_{AV} \end{aligned} \tag{5.219}$$

$$\begin{aligned} y &= \sin\left[\frac{\pi(t_c - T_{AV})}{T_{VS}}\right], & T_{AV} < t_c < (T_{AV} + T_{VS}) \\ y &= 0, & t_c \geq (T_{AV} + T_{VS}) \end{aligned} \tag{5.220}$$

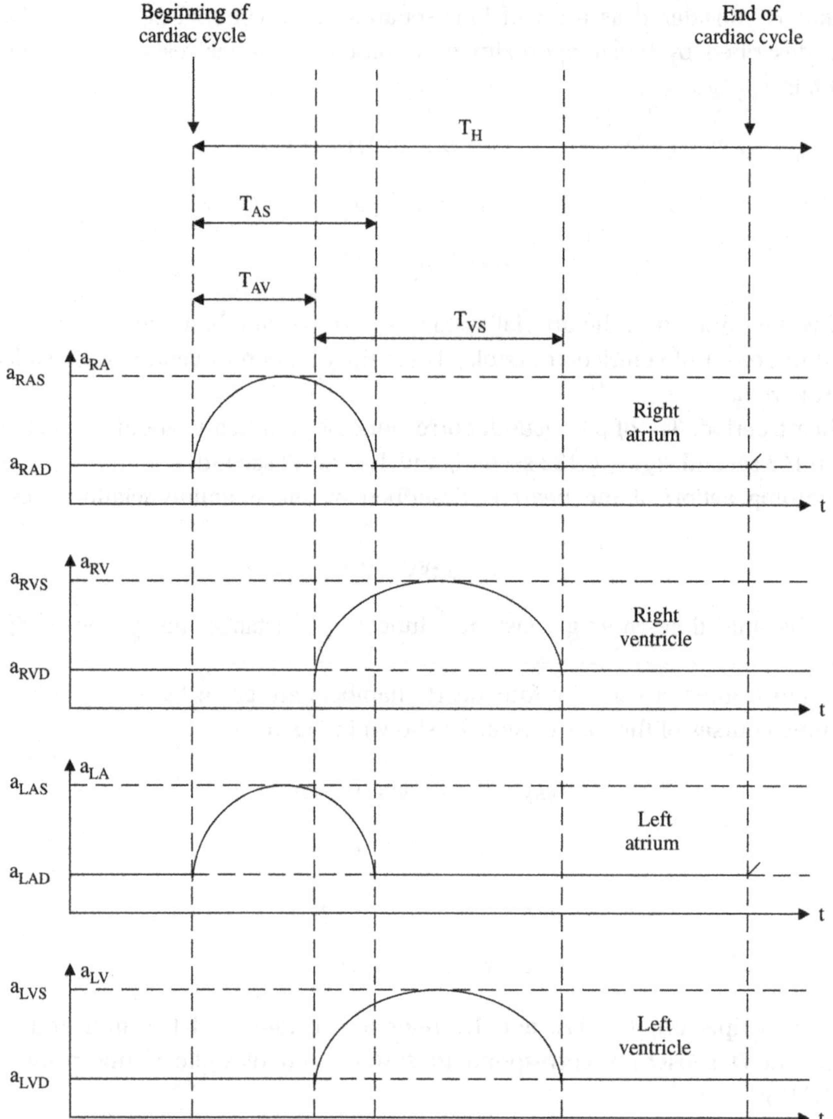

FIGURE 5–55 Elastances of the four heart chambers. *Adapted from Leaning et al., 1983.*

The minimum (diastolic) and maximum (systolic) values of elastance are given by:

$$a_D = \frac{P_D}{V_D - V_u}; \quad a_S = \frac{P_S}{V_S - V_u} \tag{5.221}$$

where t_c is the elapsed time during each cardiac cycle ($0 \leq t_c \leq T_H$), V is volume, and the subscript u denotes its unstressed value.

These time-varying components can then be incorporated into the differential equations to describe the pressure/flow dynamics during the cardiac cycle. As an illustration, consider the right atrium. This can be modeled by the following set of equations:

$$P_{RA} = a_{RA}(t)[V_{RA} - V_{uRA}] \tag{5.222}$$

$$\frac{dV_{RA}}{dt} = F_1 - F_{RARV}, \quad V_{RA} \geq 0 \tag{5.223}$$

$$\begin{aligned} F_{RARV} &= \frac{P_{RA} - P_{RV}}{R_{RARV}}, && P_{RA} > P_{RV} \\ F_{RARV} &= 0, && P_{RA} \leq P_{RV} \end{aligned} \tag{5.224}$$

$$F_1 = F_{SVCRA} + F_{IVCRA} + F_{BRONC} + F_{COR} \tag{5.225}$$

Double subscripts relate to flow, F, and resistance, R, between heart chambers, for example, F_{RARV} corresponds to flow from right atrium to right ventricle. The four terms on the right of (5.225) are the flows from superior vena cava to right atrium, inferior vena cava to right atrium, bronchial flow and coronary flow, respectively.

Eq. (5.224) approximates the action of the tricuspid valve with R_{RARV} being the resistance of the fully opened valve. F_1 represents the total inflow of the right atrium.

The basic flows through the coronary and bronchial vascular beds are given by:

$$F_{COR} = \frac{P_{AO1} - P_{RA}}{R_{COR}} \tag{5.226}$$

$$F_{BRONC} = \frac{P_{AO3} - P_{RA}}{R_{BRONC}} \tag{5.227}$$

where the subscripts AO1 and AO3 correspond to ascending aorta and thoracic aorta respectively.

The right atrial inlet contraction which assists the pumping action introduces resistance to the inflow. While this is negligible in the case of bronchial and coronary flow, it is a significant effect in the case of blood flow from the inferior and superior venae cavae, represented in the model by (5.228) and (5.229).

$$\begin{aligned} F_{IVCRA} &= F_9, && F_9 \geq 0 \\ F_{IVCRA} &= 0.1F_9, && F_9 < 0 \end{aligned} \tag{5.228}$$

$$\begin{aligned} F_{SVCRA} &= F_{10}, && F_{10} \geq 0 \\ F_{SVCRA} &= 0.1F_{10}, && F_{10} < 0 \end{aligned} \tag{5.229}$$

where F_9 and F_{10} are the respective flows, assuming no contraction.

In a similar manner, we can write equations describing the dynamics occurring in the left atrium, taking into consideration the action of the mitral valve.

Thus we have demonstrated an example of how time-varying behavior can be incorporated into model parameters. This illustration in the context of the short-term dynamics of the cardiovascular system has also demonstrated some of the physiological complexity that may need to be included in the model if it is to provide a valid representation of what is undoubtedly complex physiology.

5.7 Stochastic modeling

Deterministic models are widely, and successfully, used to provide quantitative descriptions of the dynamics of a wide variety of types of physiological systems. All of the models considered so far in this chapter have been of a deterministic form, whether the mathematical realization was lumped or distributed, linear or nonlinear. In some cases, however, particularly when modeling physiological phenomena at the cellular level, a purely deterministic approach is not adequate. Such an approach fails to take account of probabilistic effects. Probabilistic (random) effects that are particularly important in the modeling of metabolic processes are those that evolve over time, and are known as stochastic processes.

Stochastic processes can be incorporated into models of physiological systems in a number of ways. One particular class of deterministic model that has been extended to embrace certain forms of stochasticity is the one where the formulation involves a description in terms of a number of interconnected compartments. In this case the stochasticity is incorporated into the basic elements of the compartmental model in one of two ways. The first is to treat the compartmental variables as being stochastic variables, with the time-invariant or time-varying transport rate parameters defining flux between compartments as being deterministic. The alternative approach is to incorporate the intrinsic stochasticity into the transfer rate parameters. In this second case, the stochasticity in the transfer rate parameters can arise from a number of factors, including interindividual variability; variation of system parameters as functions of time, drug concentrations, cell membrane volume/area ratios; measurement and sampling conditions; environmental effects; and so on. It is also possible to combine the two types of representation of stochasticity, in both variables and parameters, into a single model.

5.7.1 Cellular modeling

For a classic example of the formulation of a stochastic model, let us consider the processes occurring at the cellular level by which granulocyte-macrophage progenitor cells proliferate and differentiate. Francis & Leaning (1985) produced a model that included all the major processes associated with such proliferation and differentiation such that it could be validated quantitatively using data from *in vitro* experiments.

5.7.1.1 The conceptual model

The conceptual basis of the proposed mathematical model is shown in Fig. 5–56. In this, the population of cells in the granulocyte-macrophage differentiation pathway is partitioned into a set of distinct generations. The model also incorporates the observed association between

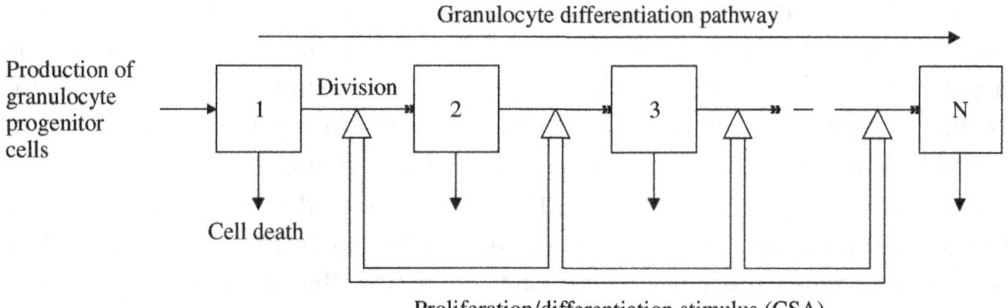

FIGURE 5–56 Conceptual form of the cellular stochastic model. The boxes represent successive generations in the granulocyte differentiation pathway, from the first generation (1) of committed progenitor cells, to the final generation (N), incapable of further division, corresponding to mature granulocytes. Proliferation and differentiation (double-headed arrows) are induced by the specific growth stimulus gm-CSA (open arrows). Vertical arrows indicate loss of cells from each generation by death rather than transition to the next generation. *Adapted from Francis & Leaning, 1985.*

the proliferation and differentiation processes, in that movement between successive generations occurs through cell division (shown as double-headed arrows).

The input to this system of cell production is the first generation of granulocyte-macrophage progenitor cells, which is treated as a time-dependent supply rate. The final generation of cells in the model is mature neutrophil granulocytes which can divide no further. Between these extremes lie intermediate stages corresponding to later progenitors and recognizable granulocyte precursors (including myeloblasts, promyeloblasts, and myelocytes).

The processes of proliferation and differentiation are under the control of at least one agent. Operationally this is termed granulocyte-macrophage colony-stimulating activity (gm-CSA), and this is required at each stage for progression down the pathway of the conceptual model shown in Fig. 5–56.

An important implication of the model is when a sample of marrow cells are seeded, *in vitro* cells of different generations have a different capacity with respect to the size of clone that they are able to produce. Clone size is a function of the number of cell divisions before the mature cell generation is reached. For a cell seeded in generation I, the theoretical maximum size of a clone is $2^{(N-i)}$, where N is the number of generations between the first and final generations of cells.

The occurrence of a proliferation/differentiation event depends monotonically on the level of gm-CSA, but is subject to random variations. The system is therefore modeled as a stochastic process, adopting probability distributions which are functions of the concentration of gm-CSA. In the model, the level of gm-CSA determines the probability that a cell will divide per unit time into the next generation. Since the process of DNA replication and cell division occupies a certain minimum time, the model adopts an 8-hour time unit, so that two successive divisions could not take place within this time span (Francis & Leaning, 1985). It is also assumed in the model that at each stage there is a small but finite probability of cell death.

The division of granulocyte-macrophage progenitor cells is not totally synchronous. The fate of any individual cell in a particular generation within the model is either to divide to the next generation, to die, or to remain in the same cell generation for later action. The model is thus asynchronous despite the fact that discrete time points are adopted. In addition to cell differentiation giving to each successive generation of cells a change limiting the number of cell divisions before mature end cell production, the model also incorporates a graduated change in the sensitivity of the cell to gm-CSA; so, in the model, for each generation of cells, the greater the level of gm-CSA the larger the probability of proliferation/differentiation. Also, as each new stage in the pathways is reached, the cells become increasingly sensitive to CSA and, thus, are more likely to reach completion.

5.7.1.2 The mathematical model

An annotated version of Fig. 5–56 is shown as Fig. 5–57, where the parameters used in the mathematical formulation are included. The variable k represents each discrete time unit of 8 hours. Hence values of k of 0, 1, 2, etc. correspond to real times of 0, 8, 16 hours, etc. The stochastic nature of the model is governed by two sets of probabilities: p_i is the probability that a cell in generation *i* divides to become two cells in generation $i+1$ during the time interval from k to $k+1$, and α_i is the probability that a cell in generation *i* dies in the same time interval k to $k+1$.

Since a cell must either divide, die, or do nothing, it follows that $p_i + \alpha_i \leq 1$. The probability that a cell remains in the same generation for the next time period is thus $1 - p_i - \alpha_i$. The dependency upon age in the processes of proliferation and differentiation and death within a generation is neglected except in that there is a delay of 8 hours before any event occurs. When cells reach generation N, they are mature neutrophil granulocytes which are incapable of proliferation and, thus, $p_N = 0$.

A(k) is the supply rate of generation 1 cells over the time interval k to $k+1$. This is used only in calculating the proportions of cells in each generation *in vivo*. It is not used in *in vitro* simulations.

Fig. 5–58 shows the relationship between the probability of proliferation/differentiation and gm-CSA dose for each cell generation. This set of probability functions incorporates the two main features of the conceptual model, namely increasing probability of proliferation/differentiation with increasing gm-CSA for each individual generation, and increasing sensitivity to gm-CSA with transition to each successive generation.

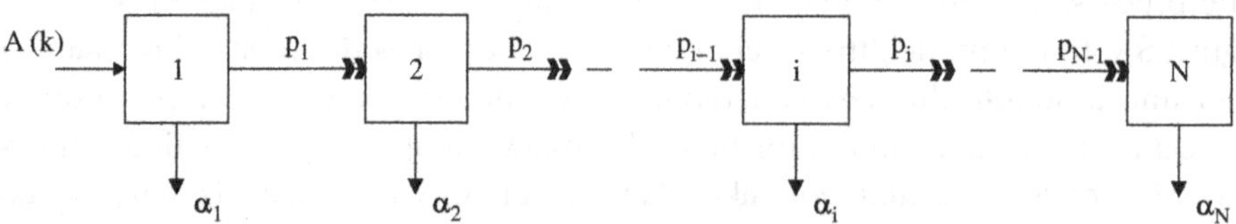

FIGURE 5–57 The mathematical model. *Adapted from Francis & Leaning, 1985.*

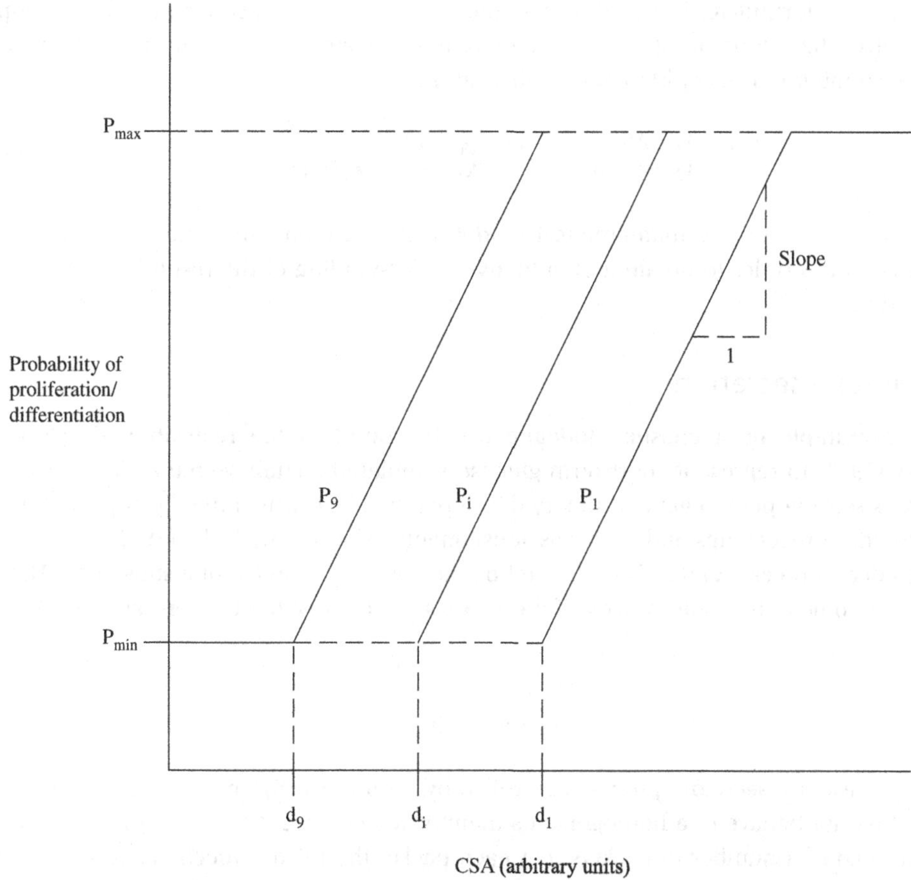

FIGURE 5–58 Relationship between the probability of a proliferation/differentiation event and gm-CSA level for different cell generations (gm-CSA in arbitrary units); p_1-p_9 are the probability functions for generations one to nine, respectively ($p_{10} = 0$); p_{max} is the maximum probability of a proliferation/differentiation event within any one time interval, p_{min} the minimum. For simplicity, the slopes of the probability functions over their operating ranges are assumed to be equal. The threshold sensitivities of the generations to CSA are given by d_1-d_9. *Adapted from Francis & Leaning, 1985.*

It should be noted that in Fig. 5–58 the maximum probability of proliferation/differentiation over a single time interval is less than unity. This allows for a distribution of cell survival times before proliferation/differentiation even when there is maximal CSA stimulation. For example, if $p_{max} = 0.3$, approximately 59% of cells will have undergone a proliferation/differentiation event in 24 hours, and 72% in 48 hours under conditions of maximal gm-CSA stimulation. This allows for 10% cell death per unit time.

In order to provide a complete stochastic description of the system of interest, it would be necessary to incorporate difference equations for the probability distributions of the number of cells in each generation at any time. Such a representation would be extremely complicated to formulate. In this example, therefore, a simpler approach has been adopted. This involves the setting up of a set of recursive difference equations in terms of the mean or expected number of cells $n_i(k)$ in generation i at time k:

$$\begin{aligned} n_i(k+1) &= A(k) + N_1(k)(1 - p_i - \alpha_i) \\ n_i(k+1) &= 2n_{i-1}(k)p_{i-1} + n_i(k)(1 - p_i - \alpha_i) \quad i = 2, 3, \ldots, N \end{aligned} \tag{5.230}$$

Having formulated the mathematical model in this fashion, simulation studies can then be carried out in order to obtain a quantitative understanding of the results of *in vitro* cellular experiments.

5.7.2 Insulin secretion

A classic example of stochastic modeling can be found in the realization developed by Grodsky (1972) to represent short-term glucose-stimulated insulin secretion. This realization took as its starting point a general theory developed by Licko which initally appeared in a set of conference proceedings and then was subsequently reported by Licko (1973).

Consider a process (v) that is controlled by the concentration (S) of a substance. The process is said to be a threshold process if there exists a value θ of the concentration such that:

$$v = 0, \quad \text{if } S < \theta \tag{5.231}$$

$$v = f(S, \theta), \quad \text{if } S \geq \theta \tag{5.232}$$

Now consider a secretory process controlled by a stimulus (S) for the case where the substance does not behave in a homogeneous manner with respect to S, but can be regarded as being formed of a number of packets. For each packet the release mechanism is a threshold process. With each packet a value of concentration θ may be associated so that:

If $S < \theta$, the packet cannot release the substance (it is closed).
If $S \geq \theta$, the packet can release the substance (it is open).

Under these conditions, there exists a probability density function of the threshold, $\xi(\theta,t)$, so that $\xi(\theta,t)\, d\theta$ represents the quantity of substance contained in the packets, the threshold of which lies between θ and $\theta + d\theta$, which can be released when the stimulus passes from θ to $\theta + d\theta$. The quantity of substance, X, that can be released for a certain value of the stimulus at time t, S(t) is given by:

$$X(S, t) = \int_0^{S(t)} \xi(\theta, t)\, d\theta \tag{5.233}$$

This theory has been used by Grodsky (1972) as the basis of a more comprehensive model to represent first-phase and second-phase secretion of insulin by the pancreas which will be discussed in Section 11.5.

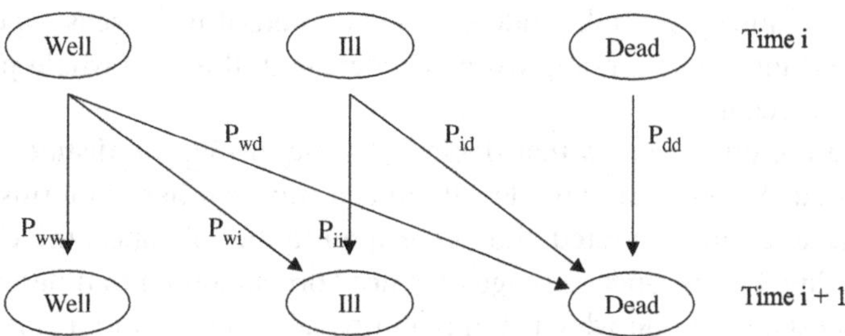

FIGURE 5–59 A simple Markov model depicting patient transitions between the three states WELL, ILL, and DEAD. *Adapted from Beck & Pauker, 1983.*

5.7.3 Markov model

As a final example of stochastic modeling we shall consider Markov processes. These are models in which the system of interest, say the state of health of a patient, is characterized by a finite number of distinct states of health, and with the likelihood of the patient making a transition from one state of health to another being defined by a set of transition probabilities.

A simple example of such a model is depicted in Fig. 5–59. In this case the patient is classified as being in one of three categories: WELL, ILL, and DEAD. At any time (i), he or she resides in just one of these states. The possible changes of state, or transitions, that occur over the fixed time interval from i to i + 1 are represented in Fig. 5–59 by arrows leading to the states at time i + 1. In this Markov model the passage of time is represented by cycles on an implicit clock, where i denotes the cycle count. Transitions between states occur instantaneously at each of these finite time intervals. In this simple example, the state DEAD can be defined as an absorbing state, since once reached it is not possible to make a transition to any other state. In contrast, WELL and ILL are nonabsorbing states since transitions are possible from those states to other states.

In Fig. 5–59 each change of state is represented by a single transition from one health status to another. This implies that the process has no memory of prior states. In other words, a transition is dependent only upon the transition probability and does not in any way depend on how the patient arrived in his or her current state.

Two types of the Markov model are used in clinical decision making. The first is those in which the state transition probabilities are constant and these are known as Markov chains. The second allows for the transition probabilities to vary over time according to preset regular rules, these being the more general Markov processes in which transition probabilities are time-dependent.

The simpler Markov chain models can be applied to clinical problems only if the chances of moving among clinical states can be assumed to be constant. The assumption of such constant transition probabilities is reasonable only for diseases with a short time horizon. In situations of chronic disease, the annual mortality of a healthy population increases with age. Given that clinical Markov models use death as the absorbing state, the population mortality needs to be built into the model. For conditions with short time horizons an approximate average annual mortality rate can be adopted. If the disease-specific probabilities of mortality and morbidity are approximately constant, then the whole problem may be modeled as a Markov chain.

In constructing a model such as that depicted in Fig. 5–59, the distinct states of health must first be defined. As with many models there is a trade-off here in terms of the number of states which are to be incorporated; the larger the number of states, the closer the model corresponds to reality. For instance, a range of states corresponding to different gradations of illness is more realistic than one which simply lumps all illnesses into a single state. On the other hand, a larger number of states mean that there will be a larger number of transition probabilities which need to be estimated.

Having specified the states of the model, all of the allowable transitions need to be defined. In the example shown, from WELL it is possible to move to each of the other states in addition to remaining in the WELL state. Transitions from ILL to WELL are not permitted in this particular case, but may in general be allowed in a Markov model where recovery from illness is a possibility.

There is then the need to specify the probabilities associated with allowable state transitions. In the clinical literature, state transitions are often expressed as rates (Beck & Pauker, 1983). Rates can range from zero to infinity and are expressed as per unit time (e.g., the mortality rate associated with disease X is 5% per year). Probabilities, on the other hand, vary from zero to one, having time built in to them implicitly. So, for a rate r, the probability that an event will occur over a time interval of t time units is:

$$P(t) = 1 - e^{-rt} \tag{5.234}$$

By way of example, suppose that in a published study of the clinical problem being modeled in Fig. 5–59, 100 well patients were followed over a 3-year period, and that 70 became ill during that period. The data represent 70 transitions from WELL to ILL per 100 patients over a 3-year period or (70/100/3) which equals to 0.233 transitions per patient year. This is the annual rate associated with the transition from WELL to ILL. Hence, if the cycle length chosen for the Markov model is 1 year, the transition probability from WELL to ILL, P_{wi}, would be $1 - e^{-0.233}$ or 0.208. On the other hand, if the cycle length had been chosen to be 1 month, then P_{wi} would be $1 - e^{-0.233/12}$ or 0.019. Thus the rate, while unchanged on an annual basis, leads to very different transition probabilities with differing cycle lengths for the Markov model.

Using a model such as this, the dynamics of a patient population can be calculated over time as they make their allowable transitions between the set of patient states (Beck & Pauker, 1983).

5.8 Summary

This chapter has focused on the situation in which the model should correspond to the relevant physiology, in contrast to the data-driven approach described in Chapter 4, Modeling the data. The extent to which the model reflects this underlying physiology is dependent on the *a priori* knowledge that is available, and the extent to which it is reasonable to make simplifying assumptions regarding the physiology. Examples have been presented which compare and contrast a range of approaches to formulating models that correspond to the underlying physiology. These have included static and dynamic, deterministic and stochastic, time-invariant and time-varying, lumped and distributed, linear and nonlinear, and continuous and discrete forms. Between them they have illustrated different levels of model complexity. This chapter concludes the part of the book that has focused on the formulation of mathematical models. Chapter 6, Model identification, provides a framework for the model identification process, by means of which estimates can be made for unknown model parameters.

5.9 Exercises and assignment questions

1. Discuss the benefits of developing mathematical models that are based on the underlying physiology of the relevant system.
2. Give examples of the way in which assumptions can be made in relation to a particular physiological system's impact on the approach to be adopted in formulating the mathematical model of that system.
3. What are the key different assumptions behind lumped and distributed linear dynamic system models? What are the mathematical consequences? Illustrate these concepts by using an appropriate example.
4. Compartmental models are a widely used class to describe nonlinear dynamic physiological systems based on the mass balance principle. First, define a compartment and a compartmental model, and then describe the equations of the general nonlinear compartment model and of the measurements made upon it.
5. Deterministic, either lumped or distributed, linear or nonlinear, models are powerful quantitative tools to describe physiological system dynamics. Why and when does stochastic modeling become important? Illustrate your answer using an appropriate example.

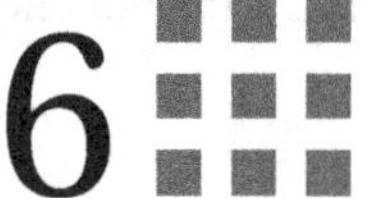

6 Model identification

6.1 Introduction

To complete the transformation from system to model (the essence of the modeling process), we must have both a model structure and a fully determined set of parameters corresponding to that structure. In other words, we require a complete model.

By this stage of the modeling process we have at least one candidate model. It is equally possible, however, that we could have more than one, with the need to choose between them as to which is the most appropriate. Focusing on a single model, if it is incomplete this will be due to some of the parameter values being unknown. This is true whether the modeling approach has been driven by data or by the physiology of the system. We may be dealing with the whole model or just part of it. This chapter aims to provide a framework for dealing with this situation. The basic concepts are depicted in Fig. 6–1 and these will be explained further as the chapter proceeds.

6.2 Data for identification

To solve this identification problem, as it is known, we need data. Data sometimes occur from the intrinsic dynamics of the system; for instance, in the form of spontaneous oscillations or noise. The signals recorded as the electrocardiogram would be an example of this. More usually, however, we need to design experiments. So the question arises: what experiments should be designed in order to yield appropriate data?

In essence, the experiment will involve applying some type of test signal to our system and measuring the response of one or more variables. In doing this it is vital to ensure that the resulting input/output data contain that part of the model which has the unknown parameter values that we are trying to estimate.

6.2.1 Selection of test signals

The selection of appropriate test signals is of essential importance to the identification process. There are a number of general criteria that we can list in this regard:

1. The test signals should be convenient to generate. Examples would be the administration of a drug or metabolic compound in the form of an injection, or applying a step change in the concentration of oxygen being inhaled by a subject in an investigation of the respiratory system dynamics.

Introduction to Modeling in Physiology and Medicine. DOI: https://doi.org/10.1016/B978-0-12-815756-5.00006-0

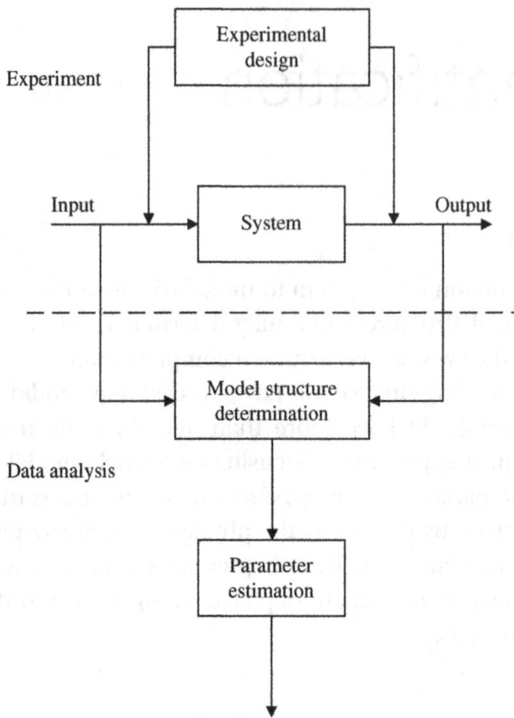

FIGURE 6–1 The overall basis of model identification.

2. The signals should be as large as possible so as to produce a high output signal-to-noise ratio. However, the magnitude of the test signal is limited by practical constraints. First, the extent of perturbation of the system under test must not be excessive. Thus for example, the dose of a drug administered in a pharmacokinetic test, or the quantity of radioactivity in tracer kinetic trials, is restricted by health and safety considerations. Furthermore, the extent of the disturbance to the system posed by the test signal must not move it outside the region for which the assumed model is valid. For example, in the case of a linearized model the disturbance must conform to the assumption that disturbances are small.
3. The test signal should, as far as possible, minimize the time required for the identification process.
4. The test signal should, when taken together with the model to be identified, result in a convenient and accurate identification procedure. This issue will be discussed further later in the chapter.

In general, test signals can be classified into those that result in a transient response, those that result in harmonic signal analysis (frequency response), and those that involve random signal analysis.

6.2.2 Transient test signals

The most commonly applied test signals in metabolic and endocrine studies and in studies on physiological organ systems are those that result in a transient response of one or more system variable. Impulse (e.g., injection) or step (e.g., infusion or step change in concentration of a gas inhaled) inputs are the usual form of input in this context. When applied and the time course of the appropriate output variable is observed, the impulse response or the step response is obtained for the corresponding portion of the system as shown in Fig. 6–2.

The information yielded by the impulse and step tests is theoretically the same for linear systems. Since the step (infusion) is the integral of the impulse (injection), the step response is correspondingly the integral of the impulse response. The choice of input should be such that any effects on the experimental data due to constraints on the perturbation are minimized. For example, in tracer studies, if the radioactivity content of specimens used to define the terminal portion of the impulse response is low (e.g., not more than twice background radioactivity), substantial errors may arise because of the inefficiency of radioactivity counting. Errors due to this cause would be much less significant if a step (infusion) test was carried out, in which case the specific activity would in most instances tend to a finite, readily measurable value rather than to zero, as in the case of the impulse test.

Transient testing offers the advantages of simplicity and short duration of test, since it is the transient and not the steady state that contains the information relating to the system behavior.

Although impulse testing is straightforward in application, in practice a disadvantage can arise because of the restrictions imposed on the magnitude of the impulse. This can result in inadequate excitation of some system modes. Although the impulse should be of such a magnitude as to provide adequate stimulation, it must not be so large as to drive the system into a nonlinear mode of operation.

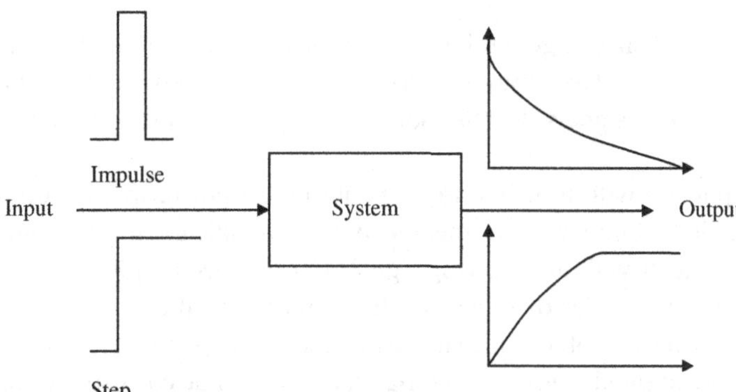

FIGURE 6–2 Diagrammatic representation of using transient test signals in model identification for impulse (e.g., injection) and step (e.g., infusion) inputs.

Equally, no noise filtering is provided in transient testing and hence there is the possibility of high errors, including interference from other system inputs.

The number of sites at which test signals can be applied is generally restricted. For instance, often it is only possible (in the case of metabolic systems) to inject material into the bloodstream. Constraints are particularly rigorous in the case of clinical studies. Here the number of accessible sites is severely restricted. Moreover, where output measurement is made by removing blood samples on a discrete basis in order to measure the metabolite concentration in the blood, the number of samples and the frequency of their withdrawal is limited keeping in mind patient well-being. In physiological studies, however, greater freedom may be available to the experimenter in terms of both the number of accessible sites and the form of permitted test signals. It is worth noting that in some instances it may be possible to overcome some of the limitations of blood sampling by utilizing new healthcare technology. For example, by using appropriate imaging modalities, it may be possible to achieve continuous measurement of the time source of radioactivity concentration in one body organ. This assumes that the imaging technology is sufficiently able to precisely define the particular organ in question, for example, the liver.

6.2.3 Harmonic test signals

As an alternative to transient testing, in some situations harmonic test signals can be applied. Frequency response testing involves applying harmonic (sinusoidally varying) signals of various frequencies and observing the amplification or attenuation and phase shift of the corresponding frequency components in the output variables of the system under test.

For a stable linear system , if an input signal of the form $A \sin \omega t$ is applied; once any transient components have died away, the "steady-state" output will be form $A\,|G(j\omega)| \sin(\omega t + \angle G(j\omega))$. In other words, the output exhibits oscillations of the same frequency as the applied input, but the magnitude is amplified or attenuated by the factor $|G(j\omega)|$ and the oscillations are phase shifted by $\angle G(j\omega)$. $|G(j\omega)|$ and $\angle G(j\omega)$ vary with change in the frequency of the applied sine wave in a manner that is dependent upon the intrinsic dynamics of the system under test.

Harmonic test signals are, in general, less convenient to apply in our physiological context than transient test signals. They may require special instrumentation for output measurement. However, such test signals do offer some advantages in terms of accuracy and convenience of identification.

Firstly, in comparison with transient testing, all the test power in harmonic testing is concentrated at a single frequency. This means that all significant modes can be adequately excited in a series of tests without applying signals of excessive amplitude.

However, a consequent disadvantage is the duration of the test since, in general, the experiment needs to be repeated with sine wave inputs for some 10–15 different frequencies, with the lowest applied frequency being well below that corresponding to the longest time constant in the system. Also, in each test it is necessary to wait for the transient effects to decay and then carry out the harmonic test for 5–10 cycles of the test frequency. On the other hand, frequency response testing has the merit of effectively filtering noise which may be present in the data, since one is only seeking that frequency component in the output that corresponds to the frequency of the sine wave applied as the input.

The frequency response forms, for a linear system, a complete nonparametric model of the system. Parametric models of the frequency response may be fitted to the experimental data obtained in order to estimate parameters.

One area of physiology where frequency response testing has been applied over the past 30 years is in relation to the respiratory system. For example, pioneering experiments were those of Swanson and Belville (1974) who sought to identify the dynamics of a linear mathematical model of the respiratory system. They did so by applying sinusoidally varying inputs of alveolar CO_2 and O_2 over a range of frequencies, and plotting the variation of output amplitude as a function of frequency.

6.2.4 Random signal testing

Random signals, or signals constructed to approximate to random signals (e.g., pseudorandom binary sequences), may be used as test inputs. We now consider a linear, time-invariant system to which an input m(t) is applied, resulting in an output y(t). If that system is characterized by a unit impulse response g(t), then it can be shown that:

$$R_{my}(\tau) = \int_{-\infty}^{\infty} g(t) R_{mm}(t - \tau)\ dt \tag{6.1}$$

That is, the cross-correlation function between the input and the output, $R_{my}(\tau)$, is equal to the convolution of the autocorrelation function of the input, $R_{mm}(t - \tau)$, and the unit impulse response of the system, g(t).

Now, if the input to the system is white noise, a random signal in which all frequency components are present at equal power levels, the cross-correlation function, $R_{my}(\tau)$, is equal to the unit impulse response of the system.

$$R_{my}(\tau) = g(\tau) \tag{6.2}$$

Random signal testing consists then of applying to the system a test signal approximating to white noise and then cross-correlating input and output. The cross-correlation function then gives the unit impulse response.

Random fluctuations approximating to white noise may occur spontaneously on one of the variables of the physiological system and they may be used as a test signal without introducing an external stimulus. Such a situation is convenient, but in practice does not often occur. Hence, in general, it is necessary to generate the random test signals specially. They often take the form of pseudorandom binary sequences, a sequence of pulses of equal duration and taking the values of zero (no disturbance for the pulse duration) or one (a pulse of fixed amplitude). The sequence of zero and unity pulses, which is cyclically repeatable, is such that over one cycle it has white noise properties. White noise analysis has found application particularly in the electrophysiology domain; for example, in the work of Marmarelis and Marmarelis (1978).

Random signals represent the simultaneous injection of all frequencies into a system and thus lead to shorter test times than harmonic signals. Test duration must, however, be sufficiently long for the time averaging in the autocorrelation function to be accurate. The output of the random test procedure is a cross-correlation function corresponding to the unit impulse response of the system. This correlation process effectively filters out noise present in the data.

6.3 Errors

In the identification process, data are mapped into parameter values by means of the model. However, problems can arise in estimating the values of unknown parameters due to a number of sources of errors. These are shown schematically in Fig. 6–3. The four types of error are:

- imperfections in the test signal that do not correspond to the form assumed in the interpretation of the result;
- errors due to imperfections in measurement of output variables;
- influence on observed output of variables other than the test signal; and
- model error, which is the effect of using, in the identification process, a model that does not satisfactorily represent the system being identified.

Clearly, if the values of some of the model parameters are obtained from independent sources (either direct measurement or from *a priori* knowledge), rather than from estimation schemes, then the errors associated with these parameter values must be taken into account.

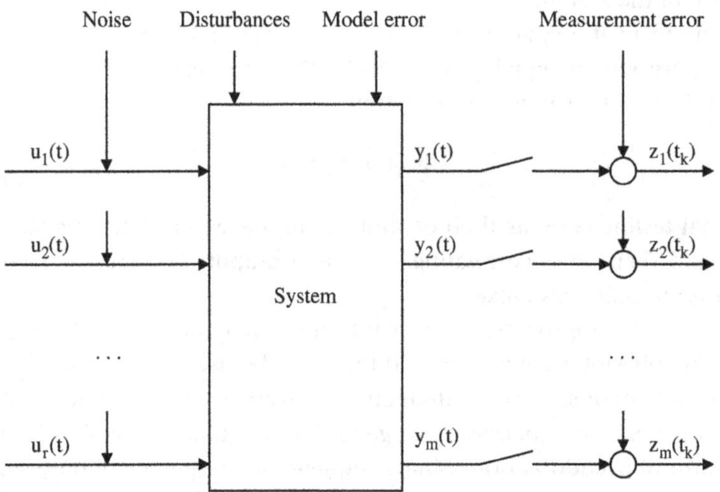

FIGURE 6–3 Practical experimental design, indicating a number of sources of error.

From a theoretical point of view, considerable difficulties arise when trying to account simultaneously for more than one type of error. Measurement errors are always present. Hence, this is the problem that has received the most attention.

With regard to errors in the test signal, normally these are either known explicitly, in which case this information can be directly taken into account, or can often be neglected. Consider, for example, an injection of material (an impulse) applied to a metabolic system that is of finite duration. One possibility is to treat it as a pulse input (i.e., a step increase followed by a step decrease). The alternative is that it might be neglected if its duration is short compared to the most rapid dynamics that one is seeking to identify from the experimental data.

Disturbances may be neglected if, for example, they have only minimal effect on the experimental data that are being obtained in a short-term study on the particular physiological system. Alternatively, it may be assumed that the disturbance simply results in a component of error in the measured variable.

Having proposed a false or inappropriate model constitutes an important source of error. In general, there are few theoretical approaches available for dealing with this type of uncertainty. It is usually only at the stage of model validation that consideration can be given to assessing whether or not a given model structure is appropriate. In some instances the problem may be approached by considering a number of candidate identifiable model structures and carrying out the parameter estimation procedure for each of them. The results of estimating the parameters of these alternative configurations can then be compared in terms of a set of validity criteria as will be outlined in Chapter 10, Model validation. Normally, this will lead to a ranking of the candidate model structures in relation to the given experimental data.

The only error that can be dealt with in a rigorous manner is that which arises due to imperfections in the measurement process. In most practical situations it is reasonable and normal to assume that any errors are additive.

$$z_l(t_i, \mathbf{p}) = y_l(t_i, \mathbf{p}) + v_l(t_i), \quad i = 1, 2, \ldots, N_l; \quad l = 1, 2, \ldots, m \tag{6.3}$$

Eq. (6.3) thus describes, for each of the m measured variables, the relation between the actual noisy, discrete-time measurement z_l and the noise-free measurable output y_l, with v_l being the error associated with the measurement performed at time t_i.

To carry out the parameter estimation process, it is highly desirable to be able to provide a statistical description of the errors. In some instances it may be possible to assume that the errors are characterized by either a Gaussian or a Poisson distribution. In other cases it may only be possible to assume, for instance, that the errors are white; that is to say uncorrelated. The extent of such statistical information, which is available *a priori* regarding these errors, is closely related to the goodness of the results of the parameter estimation procedure. The more complete the statistical description, the more desirable the properties of the estimation algorithm will be, and the greater the confidence that can be placed in the results obtained. Equally, good *a priori* statistical information can provide evidence leading to the rejection of unsuitable models.

6.4 The way forward

Since errors in model structure cannot be dealt with explicitly, they can only be solved by considering each competing model in turn. Thus it is customary to focus on a single model, and concentrate on the impact of measurement errors that are assumed to be additive as indicated earlier. The available approaches can be divided into two groups; situations with parametric models and those with nonparametric models. These are considered briefly below under the headings of parameter estimation and signal estimation. A full treatment for these two cases is given in Chapter 8, Parametric models—the estimation problem, and Chapter 9, Nonparametric models—signal estimation.

6.4.1 Parameter estimation

In relation to parametric models, as discussed in Chapter 7, Parametric modeling—the identifiability problem, the first consideration is identifiability. This involves asking the question as to whether it is theoretically possible to make unique estimates of all the unknown parameters on the assumption that the data we have available for the identification process are complete and noise-free. In other words, we are examining the balance between the availability of experimental data and the number of unknown parameters to be estimated. Are the data rich enough for the parameter estimation problem? Difficulties arise where there is a mismatch between the complexity of the model (as evidenced by the number of unknown parameters) and the richness of the data. The problem can be viewed as there being either too many parameters to be estimated or the data are not sufficient in relation to the model in question.

If this problem arises, there are two possible approaches. The first is to consider whether it might be possible to reduce the complexity of the model, including reducing the number of unknown parameters needing to be estimated. There would, however, be the need to ensure that the reduced model was still valid in relation to the purpose of the modeling activity. The second would be to examine whether it was possible to enrich the available experimental data; for instance, by making measurements of an additional variable.

If the model is uniquely identifiable, on the assumption that the data are perfect, it is possible to proceed with the process of estimating the parameters as discussed in Chapter 8, Parametric models—the estimation problem. In some situations multiple solutions may be theoretically possible for some of the parameters. This means two or more, but a finite number of solutions. In cases such as this, it might be possible to choose between alternative solutions at the stage of validating the complete model by considering which parameter values are most plausible in a physiological sense. Where an infinite number of values are theoretically possible for one or more parameters, there is the need to tackle the mismatch between model and data as indicated earlier.

Once the model has passed the identifiability test, there are a number of techniques available for estimating the parameters. Most commonly adopted are linear or nonlinear least squares estimation. These are least demanding in terms of the quantity of *a priori* information needed. Other techniques available include maximum likelihood and Bayesian estimation. However, both of these require *a priori* knowledge regarding the statistics of the situation being modeled.

6.4.2 Signal estimation

The other type of estimation problem relates to models that do not explicitly contain parameters and hence are referred to as nonparametric models. What we are seeking to estimate here is not parameters, but rather a signal. As described in Section 4.9, we are dealing with an overall input/output model that is specified as an integral equation. Such a description has three main ingredients: the input, the output, and the impulse response that provides the connection between them. In our signal identification problem we know two out of the three, and we need to determine the third.

The most usual situation is that in which the output signal is known, and we need to identify one of the other two ingredients. The techniques available for solving this problem can be classified as raw deconvolution and deterministic regularization. Further details are given in Chapter 9, Nonparametric models—signal estimation. The electrophysiology domain is an example where this is often the identification problem which must be solved. For instance, the evoked electrical response may be measured in response to a known sensory stimulation. In this case the identification problem is determining the impulse response that maps the known applied stimulus into the measured evoked response.

6.5 Summary

This chapter has described an overall framework for model identification. This process enables us to achieve a complete model; that is to say that we have both a model structure and a fully determined set of parameters corresponding to that structure. The following two chapters deal with the identification of parametric models in full detail. Chapter 7, Parametric modeling—the identifiability problem, begins this process by addressing the problem of identifiability.

6.6 Exercises and assignment questions

1. What are the desirable characteristics of physiological measurements in order to provide appropriate test signals for system identification?
2. What are the relative merits of transient, harmonic, and random signals in the context of system identification?
3. Discuss the relationship between experimental design and system identifiability if the process of estimating the unknown parameters of a physiological model is to be successfully completed.
4. Give an account of the different types of error that can arise in the identification process and the means by which such errors might be treated in order to achieve successful parameter estimation.

7

Parametric modeling—the identifiability problem

7.1 Introduction

Once a parametric model has been formulated, the next fundamental step in its development is the assignment of numerical values to its unknown parameters $p_1, p_2, \ldots, p_P$. This parametric model might be an input/output one; say the sum of three decaying exponentials describing the disappearance of a substance in the body after an impulse dose. Examples of such data models are discussed in Chapter 4, Modeling the data. Alternatively, it might be a structural model of a system such as that described in Chapter 5, Modeling the system; for instance, a resistance-compliance model describing the dynamic pressure–flow relationships of respiratory mechanics. In the case of the data model the unknown parameters $p_1, p_2, \ldots,$ p_P would be the coefficients of the exponential function. In the latter case, they would be the resistance and compliance parameters of the differential equation model.

In practice, this assignment of numerical values is done by exploiting the information contained in the measurements performed on the physiological system, which are functions of time t and of the parameter vector $\mathbf{p} = [p_1, p_2, \ldots, p_P]^T$. Let us consider, for the sake of argument the case where a single measurement signal is available. This has the general form:

$$y(t) = g(t, \mathbf{p}) \tag{7.1}$$

where $g(t,\mathbf{p})$ is a function that links the model to the measurement. In the examples discussed above y(t) could be a plasma concentration or a flow signal, respectively.

In practice the signal y(t) is not available. What is measured is a noise-corrupted signal, usually at a number of discrete time points $t_1, t_2, \ldots, t_N$, which can be described as:

$$z(t_i) = z_i = y_i + v_i = g(t_i, \mathbf{p}) + v_i \tag{7.2}$$

where v_i denotes the error on the i-th measurement (Fig. 7–1) which can be viewed as a random variable having its expected value equal to zero. Usually some statistical information on $v_1 \cdots v_N$ is available, for example, they are usually uncorrelated, with either a constant variance σ^2 or with different variances σ_i^2 for the various v_i.

The function $g(t,\mathbf{p})$ is related to the model of the system. As anticipated in the examples above, this can be an input/output (data driven) or a structural model. Let us clarify this with a simple example and consider the data shown in Fig. 7–2. These data refer to the

Introduction to Modeling in Physiology and Medicine. DOI: https://doi.org/10.1016/B978-0-12-815756-5.00007-2

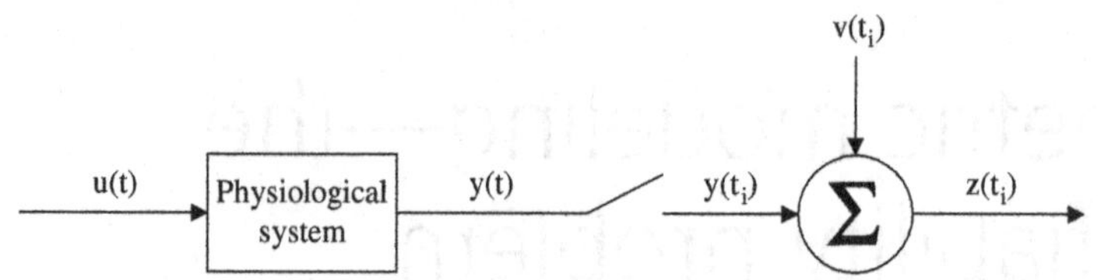

FIGURE 7–1 The physiological system, the input (u) and the output (y). Measurements $z(t_i)$ are taken at discrete times and are corrupted by noise $v(t_i)$.

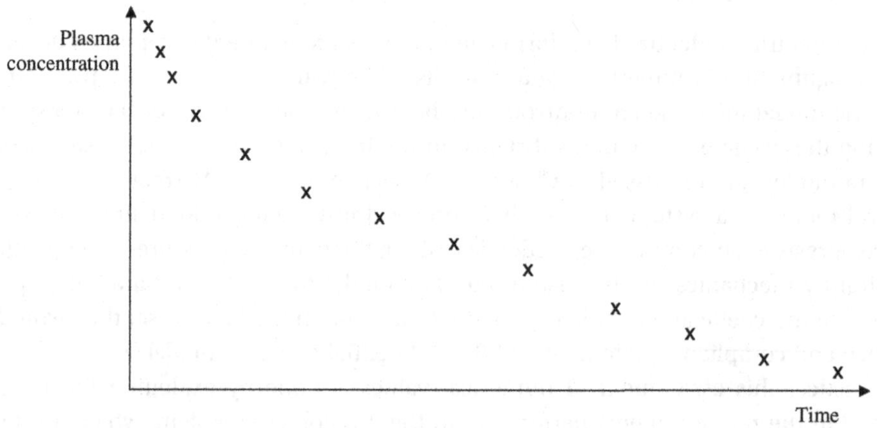

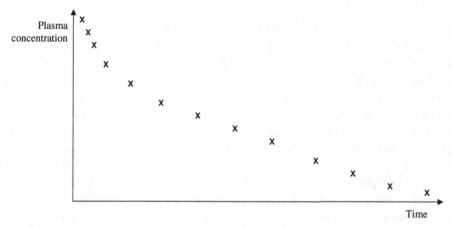

FIGURE 7–2 The plasma concentration disappearance curve of a drug after a bolus injection.

concentration of a drug disappearing from blood after an intravenous unit dose bolus injection given at time 0. The data $z_1 \cdots z_N$ of Fig. 7–2 can be described by (7.2) with $g(t,\mathbf{p})$ of (7.1) expressed either as an input/output model or a structural model. An input/output model would typically be of the form:

$$y(t,\mathbf{p}) = A_1 e^{-\lambda_1 t} + A_2 e^{-\lambda_2 t} \tag{7.3}$$

and the model identification problem becomes that of estimating from the measurements $z_1 \cdots z_N$ the parameters A_1, λ_1, A_2, λ_2, that is, $\mathbf{p} = [A_1, \lambda_1, A_2, \lambda_2]^T$.

The same data can also be described by a structural model of the kinetics of the drug in the body. A candidate model is the one shown in Fig. 7–3. Linear kinetics are assumed and the existence in the body of two compartments with irreversible elimination of the drug taking place from compartment one is postulated. Compartment one is the accessible compartment, that is, the one where the drug is injected and where the concentration is measured at discrete times. The model equations are:

$$\dot{Q}_1(t) = (k_{01} + k_{21})Q_1(t) + k_{12}Q_2(t) + U(t) \quad Q_1(0) = 0 \tag{7.4}$$

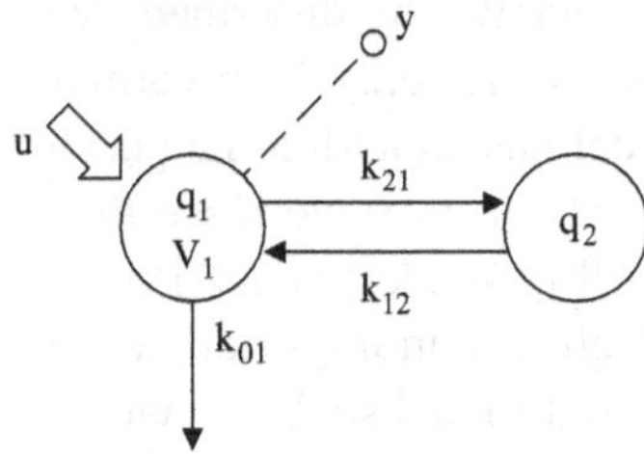

FIGURE 7–3 A two-compartment model of the kinetics of a drug.

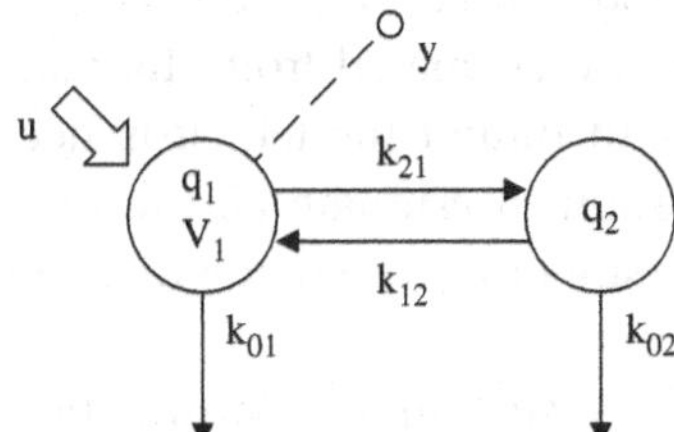

FIGURE 7–4 Another two-compartment model of the kinetics of the drug.

$$\dot{Q}_2(t) = k_{21}Q_1(t) - k_{12}Q_2(t) \quad Q_2(0) = 0 \tag{7.5}$$

$$y(t) = \frac{Q_1(t)}{V_1} \tag{7.6}$$

where Q_1 and Q_2 denote the masses of drug in compartments 1 and 2, respectively; u is the drug input, for example, $U(t) = D \cdot \delta(t)$ where d is the dose and $\delta(t)$ is the Dirac function; V_1 is the distribution volume of compartment 1; k_{21}, k_{12}, and k_{01} are rate parameters describing the transfer of drug between compartments and to the outside of the system, respectively. In this case the model identification problem becomes that of estimating from the measurements $z_1, z_2, \ldots, z_N$ the parameters k_{21}, k_{01}, k_{02}, V_1, that is, $\mathbf{p} = [k_{21}, k_{01}, k_{12}, V_1]^T$.

It is important to note that, when choosing a structural model in order to understand the system, there is, in general, the possibility of describing the data with more than one model, even without changing the model order. For instance, the data of Fig. 7–2 can also be described by the model shown in Fig. 7–4:

$$\dot{Q}_1(t) = -(k_{01} + k_{21})Q_1(t) + k_{12}Q_2(t) + U(t) \quad Q_1(0) = 0 \tag{7.7}$$

$$\dot{Q}_2(t) = k_{21}Q_1(t) - (k_{02} + k_{12})Q_2(t) \quad Q_2(0) = 0 \tag{7.8}$$

$$y(t) = \frac{Q_1(t)}{V_1} \tag{7.9}$$

This model is similar to the previous one described by (7.4) and Fig. 7–3, but postulates that the drug is irreversibly removed not only from compartment 1, but also from compartment 2. This means that the model has an additional parameter, that is, k_{02}, and the identification problem becomes more difficult to solve since the parameters to be estimated from the data are now five, that is, $\mathbf{p} = [k_{21}, k_{01}, k_{12}, k_{02}, V_1]^T$.

This example also serves to highlight an important issue that will be discussed in the next section. While (with an input/output model such as that of 7.3) it is always possible to obtain an estimate of all its unknown parameters from the data, this is generally not true for a structural model. For instance, while the experiment that has been designed (i.e., injection into compartment 1 and measurement of its concentration) is sufficiently informative to estimate all the four parameters of the model of Fig. 7–3; this is not true for the model of Fig. 7–4. Not all of its five parameters can be estimated from the data. In other words, in the case of structural models, but not of input/output models, it is necessary to assess if the designed experiment has enough information to estimate all the unknown parameters of the postulated model structure. This assessment can be made by resorting to a data-independent test that is called *a priori* identifiability.

A priori identifiability is a key step in the formulation of a structural model whose parameters are going to be estimated from a set of data. The question that *a priori* identifiability addresses is the following: do the data contain enough information to estimate all of the unknown parameters of the postulated model structure? This question is usually referred to as the *a priori* identifiability problem. It is set in the ideal context of an error-free model structure and noise-free, continuous-time measurements, and is an obvious prerequisite for well-posed parameter estimation from real data. In particular, if it turns out that the postulated model structure is too complex for the particular set of ideal data (i.e., some model parameters are not identifiable from the data) there is no possibility that a real situation—where there is error in the model structure and noise in the data—the parameters can be identified. The *a priori* identifiability problem is also referred to as the *structural identifiability* problem because it is set independently of a particular set of values for the parameters. For the sake of simplicity, in what follows, only the term *a priori* will be used to qualify the problem.

Only if the model is *a priori* identifiable is it meaningful to use the techniques to estimate the numerical values of the parameters from the data discussed in Section 7.4. If the model is *a priori* nonidentifiable, a number of strategies can be considered. One would be to enhance the information content of the experiment by adding, when feasible, inputs and/or measurements. Another possibility would be to reduce the complexity of the model by simplifying its model structure, for example, by lowering the model order, or by aggregating some parameters. These simple statements allow one to foresee the importance of *a priori* identifiability also in relation to qualitative experiment design, for example, definition of an experiment which allows one to obtain an *a priori* identifiable model with the minimum number of inputs and measurements.

Before discussing the problem in depth and the methods available for its solution, it is useful to illustrate the fundamentals through some simple examples. Then some formal definitions will be given, using these simple examples where the identifiability issue can be easily addressed.

7.2 Some examples

Example 1:

Consider a single-compartment model shown in Fig. 7–5, where the input is a bolus injection of a drug given at time zero, and the measured variable is the drug concentration. The model and measurement equations are:

$$\dot{Q}(t) = -kQ(t) + U(t), \quad Q(0) = 0 \tag{7.10}$$

$$y(t) = \frac{Q(t)}{V} \tag{7.11}$$

where $U(t) = D \cdot \delta(t)$, that is D is the magnitude of the bolus dose. The unknown parameters for the model are the rate constant k and the volume V.

Eq. (7.11) defines the observation on the system, that is, drug concentration, in an ideal context of noise-free and continuous-time measurements. In other words, (7.11) is the *model output* describing what is measured continuously and without errors; it does not represent the noisy discrete times measurements. The word output is used here in the information sense. Specifically, in the context of Fig. 7–5, U(t) and y(t) define an input/output experiment, and should not be confused with the material output or outflow from the compartment.

To see how the experiment can be used to obtain estimates of these parameters, note that the solution of (7.10) is the mono-exponential:

$$Q(t) = De^{-kt} \tag{7.12}$$

The model output y(t) can thus be given by:

$$y(t) = \frac{D}{V}e^{-kt} \equiv Ae^{-\lambda t} \tag{7.13}$$

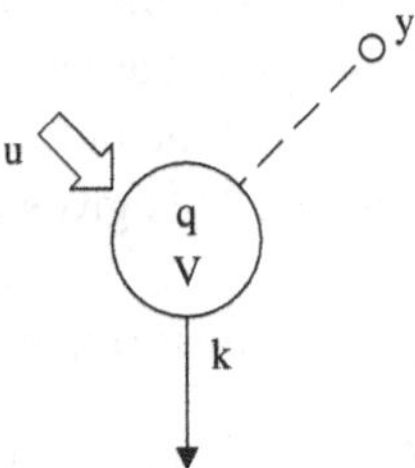

FIGURE 7–5 A single-compartment model.

The model output or ideal data are thus described by a function of the form $Ae^{-\lambda t}$, and the parameters that can be determined by the experiment are A and λ. These parameters are called the *observational parameters.*

What is the relationship between the unknown model parameters k and V, and the observational parameters A and λ? From (7.13) one sees immediately:

$$A = y(0) = \frac{D}{V} \tag{7.14}$$

$$\lambda = k \tag{7.15}$$

In the above example, the unknown parameters k and V of the model are *a priori* uniquely or *globally identifiable* from the designed experiment since they can be evaluated uniquely from the observational parameters A and λ. Since all model parameters are uniquely identifiable, the model is said to be *a priori* uniquely or *globally identifiable* from the designed experiment.

This first example was limited to a bolus injection input. The same identifiability results hold for different inputs as well. This is a general result of dealing with linear, time-invariant models such as the one described above: the identifiability properties of a model are the same irrespective of the shape of the inputs. This is true for a single input situation, but is no longer true in a general multiple input experiment or in nonlinear models.

So far we have analyzed the identifiability properties of the model by inspecting the expression of the model output in order to derive the relationships between the observational parameters and the unknown model parameters. The method is easy to understand, since it only requires some fundamentals of differential calculus. However, the approach is not practicable in general, since it works easily only for some simple linear models of order one and two. For linear models of a higher order the method becomes quite cumbersome and its application is practically impossible. It is worth noting that in these introductory examples emphasis has been placed on linear dynamic models: for nonlinear models it is usually simply impossible to obtain the expression of the model output.

Returning to linear models, a simpler method is available to derive the desired relationships between observational parameters and unknown model parameters. It consists of writing the Laplace transform for the model output and is known as the *transfer function method.* Briefly, the advantage of the Laplace transform method is that there is no need to use the analytical solution of the system of linear differential equations. By writing the Laplace transform of the state variables (e.g., masses) and then of the model outputs (e.g., concentrations), one obtains an expression that defines the observational parameters as a function of the unknown model parameters. This gives a set of nonlinear algebraic equations in the original parameters.

For the model of Fig. 7–5, the Laplace transforms of (7.10) and (7.11) are, respectively:

$$\begin{cases} sQ(s) = -kQ(s) + D \\ Y(s) = \dfrac{Q(s)}{V} \end{cases} \tag{7.16–7.17}$$

where s is the Laplace variable and the capital letter denotes the Laplace transform of the corresponding lower case letter variable.

The transfer function is:

$$H(s) \equiv \frac{Y(s)}{U(s)} = \frac{Q(s)/V}{D} = \frac{[D/(s+k)]/V}{D} = \frac{1/V}{s+k} \equiv \frac{\beta}{s+\alpha} \tag{7.18}$$

The coefficients α and β are determinable from the experiment, that is, they are the observational parameters and thus one has:

$$\begin{cases} \beta = \dfrac{1}{V} \\ \alpha = k \end{cases} \qquad (7.19-7.20)$$

that is, the model is *a priori* uniquely identifiable.

For this simple model the advantage of the Laplace transform method is not evident, but its power will be appreciated when we consider the next example.

Example 2:

Consider next the two-compartment model of the kinetics of a substance in the body shown in Fig. 7–6, where a bolus injection of material is given into compartment 1. The accessible compartment is compartment 2. Assume the measured variable is the concentration $y(t) = Q_2(t)/V_2$.

The equations describing this model, assuming a bolus input, are:

$$\dot{Q}_1(t) = -k_{21}Q_1(t) + U(t), \quad Q_1(0) = 0 \tag{7.21}$$

$$\dot{Q}_2(t) = k_{21}Q_1(t) - k_{02}Q_2(t), \quad Q_2(0) = 0 \tag{7.22}$$

$$y(t) = \frac{Q_2(t)}{V_2} \tag{7.23}$$

where $U(t) = D \cdot \delta(t)$.

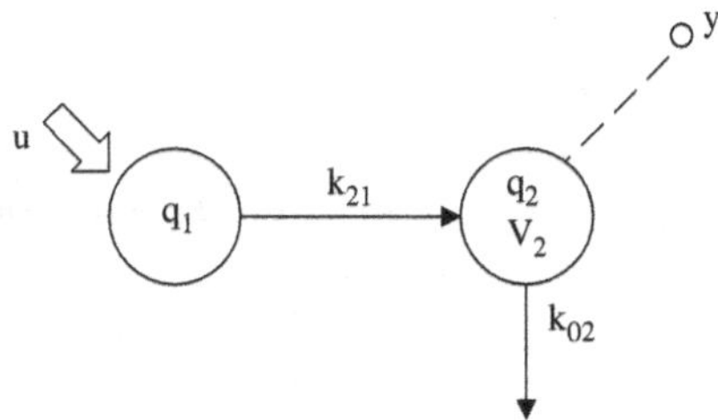

FIGURE 7–6 A two-compartment model.

The unknown model parameters are k_{21}, k_{02}, and V_2. To see how the experiment can be used to obtain estimates of these parameters, one can use either the time domain solution of (7.22) (a sum of two exponentials) or the transfer function method which is much more straightforward. The transfer function is:

$$H(s) = \frac{Y(s)}{U(s)} = \frac{k_{21}/V_2}{(s + k_{21})(s + k_{02})} \equiv \frac{\beta_1}{s^2 + \alpha_2 s + \alpha_1} \tag{7.24}$$

where the coefficients α_1, α_2, β_1, are the observational parameters (known from the experiment) linked to the unknown model parameters by:

$$\begin{cases} \beta_1 = \dfrac{k_{21}}{V_2} \\ \alpha_2 = k_{21} + k_{02} \\ \alpha_1 = k_{21}k_{02} \end{cases} \tag{7.25 – 7.27}$$

Eqs. (7.25)–(7.27) are nonlinear and it is easy to verify that it is not possible to obtain a unique solution for the unknown parameters. In fact, from (7.26) and (7.27) parameters k_{21} and k_{02} are interchangeable and thus each has two solutions, say k_{21}^{I}, k_{21}^{II} and k_{02}^{I}, k_{02}^{II}. As a result, from (7.25) V_2 has two solutions also, V_2^{I} and V_2^{II}. The two solutions provide the same expression for the model output y(t). When there is a finite number of solutions (more than one; two in this case), the unknown parameters are said to be *a priori nonuniquely* or *locally identifiable* from the designed experiment. When all the model parameters are identifiable (uniquely or nonuniquely) and at least one of the model parameters is nonuniquely identifiable (in this case, all three are), the model is said to be *a priori nonuniquely* or *locally identifiable.*

In Fig. 7–7 we show the two curves defined by equations $k_{21} + k_{02} = \alpha_2$ and $k_{21}k_{02} = \alpha_1$: the existence of two solutions is confirmed by the presence of two points of intersection.

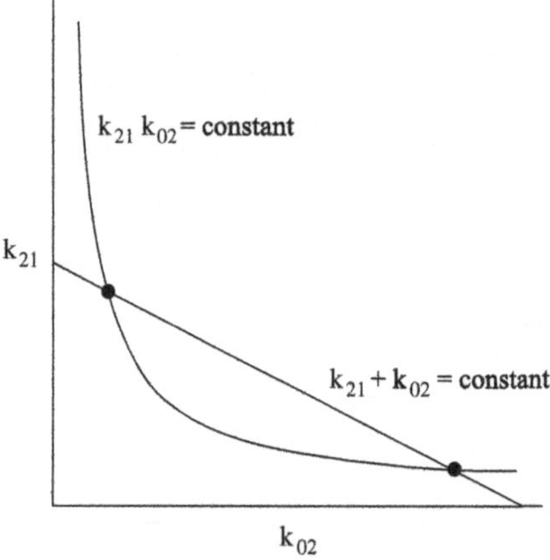

FIGURE 7–7 A plot of $k_{21}k_{02} = \alpha_1$ and $k_{21} + k_{02} = \alpha_2$.

Also, in this case, one has parameters that are *a priori* uniquely identifiable, but these are not the original parameters of interest. They are combinations of the original parameters, in particular $k_{21}k_{02}$, $k_{21} + k_{02}$, and k_{21}/V_2.

To achieve unique identifiability of this nonuniquely identifiable model, one could design a more complex experiment or, if available, exploit additional independent information available on the system. In this particular case, knowledge of V_2, or a qualitative relationship between k_{21} and k_{02}, that is, k_{21} greater or less than k_{02} (see Fig. 7–7), allows one to achieve unique identifiability of all model parameters.

Example 3:

Consider next the two-compartment model shown in Fig. 7–8 where a bolus injection of a drug is given at time zero and where the measured variable is the concentration of drug in plasma. The equations describing this model are:

$$\dot{Q}_1(t) = -(k_{01} + k_{21})Q_1(t) + U(t), \quad Q_1(0) = 0 \tag{7.28}$$

$$\dot{Q}_2(t) = k_{21}Q_1(t), \quad Q_2(0) = 0 \tag{7.29}$$

$$y(t) = \frac{Q_1(t)}{V_1} \tag{7.30}$$

The unknown model parameters are k_{21}, k_{01}, and V_1.

To see how the experiment can be used to obtain estimates of these parameters, one notes that the transfer function is:

$$H(s) = \frac{Y(s)}{U(s)} = \frac{1/V_1}{s + k_{21} + k_{01}} \equiv \frac{\beta}{s + \alpha} \tag{7.31}$$

and thus

$$\beta = \frac{1}{V_1} \tag{7.32}$$

$$\alpha = k_{21} + k_{01} \tag{7.33}$$

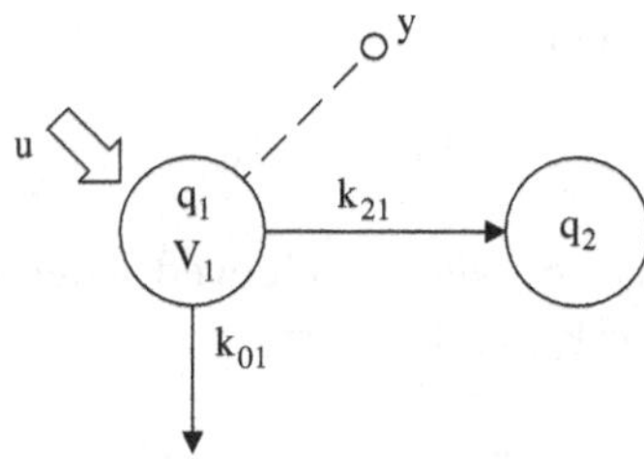

FIGURE 7–8 A two-compartment model.

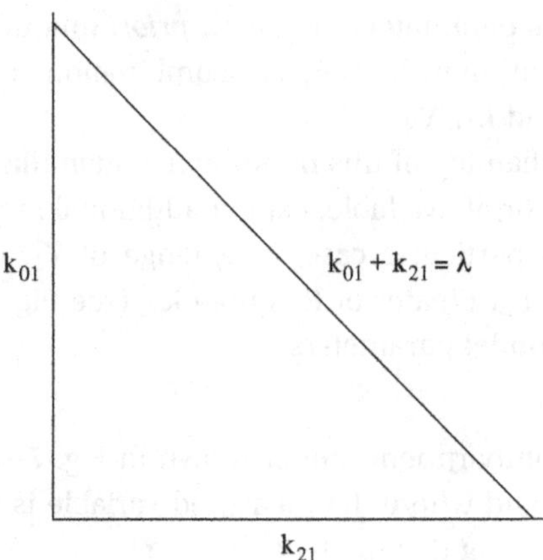

FIGURE 7–9 A plot of $k_{21} + k_{01} = \alpha$.

It is easy to see that, while V_1 is uniquely identifiable, k_{01} and k_{21} are not. In fact, as illustrated in Fig. 7–9, there are an infinite number of solutions lying on the straight line $k_{01} + k_{21} = \alpha$.

When there are an infinite number of solutions for a parameter, one says that the parameter is *a priori nonidentifiable* from the designed experiment. When there is at least one of the model parameters that is nonidentifiable (in this case, there are two), the model is said to be *a priori nonidentifiable.*

As with the previous example, one can find a uniquely identifiable parameterization, that is, a set of parameters that can be evaluated uniquely. In this case, the parameter is the sum $k_{01} + k_{21}$ (V_1 has been seen to be uniquely identifiable). Again to achieve unique identifiability of k_{01} and k_{21}, either a more informative experiment is needed, for example, measuring also in compartment 2, or additional information on the system such as a relationship between k_{01} and k_{21} is required.

When a model is nonidentifiable, however, it is usually possible to obtain for the nonidentifiable parameters upper and lower bounds for their values, that is, to identify an interval of values in which the parameters may lie. The reasoning is the following. Since by definition k_{01} and k_{21} are greater than zero, one sees immediately from (7.33) that the upper bound for each is α. For instance, for k_{21}, one has:

$$k_{21} = \alpha - k_{01} \tag{7.34}$$

and thus the upper bound for k_{21}, α, will be achieved when k_{01} is zero. Similar results hold for k_{01}. The parameter bounds for k_{01} and k_{21} are:

$$k_{01}^{min} = 0 \le k_{01} \le \alpha = k_{01}^{max} \tag{7.35}$$

$$k_{21}^{min} = 0 \le k_{21} \le \alpha = k_{21}^{max} \tag{7.36}$$

In this example, the intervals are the same; normally, this is not the case.

When there is an upper and lower bound for the values that a nonidentifiable parameter can assume, one says the parameter is *a priori* interval identifiable. When all of the nonidentifiable model parameters are interval identifiable (in this case, all are), the model is said to be *a priori interval identifiable.*

7.3 Definitions

The simple examples of linear dynamic models in the previous section emphasized the importance of understanding the *a priori* identifiability problem, and provided a means of introducing, in an appropriate context, some basic definitions. In this section, generic definitions will be given which also hold for more general model structures, that is, nonlinear dynamic models. A general nonlinear model is a system of n-first-order nonlinear ordinary differential equations, depending on a set of P unknown constant parameters $\mathbf{p} = [p_1, p_2, \ldots, p_P]^T$ which can be written conveniently in vector notation as:

$$\dot{\mathbf{x}}(t,\mathbf{p}) = \mathbf{f}[\mathbf{x}(t,\mathbf{p}), \mathbf{u}(t), t; \mathbf{p}], \quad \mathbf{x}_0 = \mathbf{x}(t,\mathbf{p}) \tag{7.37}$$

$$\mathbf{y}(t,\mathbf{p}) = \mathbf{g}[\mathbf{x}(t,\mathbf{p}); \mathbf{p}] \tag{7.38}$$

where the n state variables of the model are denoted by the vector $\mathbf{x} = [x_1, x_2, \ldots, x_n]^T$; $\mathbf{u} = [u_1, u_2, \ldots, u_r]^T$ is the vector of r known inputs; $\mathbf{y} = [y_1, y_2, \ldots, y_m]^T$ is the vector of m outputs (measurements); the observation interval is $t_0 \le t \le T$ and the initial state $\mathbf{x}_0 = \mathbf{x}(t_0) = \mathbf{x}(t_0, \mathbf{p})$ is allowed to depend on $\mathbf{p}$; $\mathbf{f}$ is the vector of n nonlinear functions that defines the structure of the model, that is, the input-state coupling parameterized by $\mathbf{p}$; $\mathbf{g}$ is a vector of m nonlinear functions which defines the state-output coupling, also parameterized by $\mathbf{p}$. Often the $\mathbf{g}$ functions are linear functions of the state variables, so that the output equation becomes:

$$\mathbf{y}(t,\mathbf{p}) = C(\mathbf{p})\mathbf{x}(t,\mathbf{p}) \tag{7.39}$$

where C is an $m \times n$ matrix.

Define the observational parameter vector $\Phi = [\phi_1, \ldots, \phi_R]^T$ having the observational parameters ϕ_j, $j = 1, \ldots, R$ as entries. Each particular input/output experiment will provide a particular value $\hat{\Phi}$ of the parameter vector Φ, that is, the components of $\hat{\Phi}$ can be estimated uniquely from the data by definition. Moreover, the observational parameters are functions of the basic model parameters p_i which may or may not be identifiable:

$$\Phi = \Phi(\mathbf{p}) \tag{7.40}$$

Thus to investigate the *a priori* identifiability of model parameters p_i, it is necessary to solve the system of nonlinear algebraic equations in the unknown p_i obtained by setting the polynomials $\Phi(\mathbf{p})$ equal to the observational parameter vector $\hat{\Phi}$:

$$\Phi(\mathbf{p}) = \hat{\Phi} \tag{7.41}$$

These equations are called the *exhaustive summary.*

Examples of this have already been provided in working out Examples 1, 2, and 3 in (7.14), (7.15) and (7.19), (7.20); (7.25)–(7.27), and (7.32), (7.33), respectively.

One can now generalize definitions. First we shall define a single parameter of the model, and then for the model as a whole.

The single parameter p_i is *a priori—uniquely or globally identifiable* if and only if the system of (7.41) has one and only one solution:

- *nonuniquely or locally identifiable* if and only if the system of (7.41) has for p_i more than one but a finite number of solutions;
- *nonidentifiable* if and only if the system of (7.41) has for p_i infinite solutions; and
- *interval identifiable* if it is nonidentifiable and has finite upper and lower bounds that can be calculated from the system of (7.41).

The model is *a priori*:

- *uniquely or globally identifiable* if all of its parameters are uniquely identifiable;
- *nonuniquely or locally identifiable* if all of its parameters are identifiable, either uniquely or nonuniquely, and at least one is nonuniquely identifiable;
- *nonidentifiable* if at least one of its parameters is nonidentifiable; and
- *interval identifiable* if all its nonidentifiable parameters are interval identifiable.

7.4 Linear models: the transfer function method

The problem now is to assess, only on the basis of knowledge of the assumed model structure and of the chosen experimental configuration, whether the model is *a priori* nonidentifiable, nonuniquely identifiable, or uniquely identifiable.

A linear dynamic model as specified by the linear case of (7.37) is described by:

$$\dot{\mathbf{x}}(t) = A(\mathbf{p})\mathbf{x}(t) + B(\mathbf{p})\mathbf{u}(t), \quad \mathbf{x}_0 = \mathbf{x}(t_0, \mathbf{p}) \tag{7.42}$$

$$\mathbf{y}(t, \mathbf{p}) = \mathbf{g}[\mathbf{x}(t, \mathbf{p}); \mathbf{p}] \tag{7.43}$$

where A and B are constant coefficient matrices of suitable dimensions. Again, one often has an output equation linear in the states [see (7.39)], that is:

$$\mathbf{y}(t, \mathbf{p}) = C(\mathbf{p})\mathbf{x}(t, \mathbf{p}) \tag{7.44}$$

For sake of simplicity it will be assumed in the following that $\mathbf{x}_0(t_0,\mathbf{p}) = 0$, but all comments and results, which will be presented, hold for the general case.

The most common method to test *a priori* identifiability of linear models described by (7.42) and (7.43) or (7.44) is the transfer function method. The approach is based on the analysis of the $r \times m$ transfer function matrix:

$$\mathbf{H}(s, \mathbf{p}) = \left[H_{ij}(s, \mathbf{p})\right] = \frac{Y_i(s, \mathbf{p})}{U_j(s)} = C(\mathbf{p})\left[sI - A(p)\right]^{-1}B(\mathbf{p}) \tag{7.45}$$

where each element H_{ij} of $\mathbf{H}$ is the Laplace transform of the response in the measurement variable at port i, $y_i(t,\mathbf{p})$ to a unit impulse at port j, $u_j(t) = \delta(t)$, and I is the identity matrix. Thus each element $H_{ij}(s,\mathbf{p})$ reflects an experiment performed on the system between input port j and output port i.

The transfer function approach makes reference to the coefficients of the numerator and denominator polynomials of each of the $m \times r$ elements $H_{ij}(s,\mathbf{p})$ of the transfer function matrix, respectively, $\beta_1^{ij}(\mathbf{p}), \ldots, \beta_n^{ij}(\mathbf{p})$ and $\alpha_1^{ij}(\mathbf{p}), \ldots, \alpha_n^{ij}(\mathbf{p})$. These coefficients are the $2n \times (r \times m)$ observational parameters φ_1^{ij}. Therefore the exhaustive summary can be written as:

$$\begin{aligned}
\beta_1^{11}(p) &= \phi_1^{11} \\
\vdots \quad & \quad \vdots \\
\alpha_n^{11}(p) &= \phi_{2n}^{11} \\
\vdots \quad & \quad \vdots \\
\beta_1^{rm}(p) &= \phi_1^{rm} \\
\vdots \quad & \quad \vdots \\
\alpha_n^{rm}(p) &= \phi_{2n}^{rm}
\end{aligned} \tag{7.46}$$

This system of nonlinear algebraic equations needs to be solved for the unknown parameter vector ($\mathbf{p}$) to define the identifiability properties of the model.

Let us consider two examples of physiological systems, one dealing with the glucose–insulin control system and one with respiratory mechanics.

Example 4: A model of glucose–insulin control

Consider the linear model discussed in Section 5.3.5 [(5.43)–(5.46), Fig. 5.10] and assume for the moment that only glucose concentration is measured after an impulse input, that is, the model is:

$$\dot{q}_1(t) = -p_1 q_1(t) - p_2 q_2(t) + \delta(t), \quad q_1(0) = 0 \tag{7.47}$$

$$\dot{q}_2(t) = -p_3 q_2(t) + p_4 q_1(t), \quad q_2(0) = 0 \tag{7.48}$$

$$c_1(t) = \frac{q_1}{V_1} \tag{7.49}$$

The unknown parameter vector is $\mathbf{p} = [p_1, p_2, p_3, p_4, V]^T$.

Let us study the identifiability properties of this model. The transfer function is:

$$H_{11}(s) = \frac{c_1(s)}{u(s)} = \frac{(s + p_3)/V_1}{s^2 + (p_1 + p_2)s + p_1p_3 + p_2p_4}$$
$$\equiv \frac{\beta_2 s + \beta_1}{s_2 + \alpha_2 s + \alpha_1} \tag{7.50}$$

and the exhaustive summary is given by:

$$\begin{cases} \frac{p_3}{V_1} = \phi_1 \\ \frac{1}{V_1} = \phi_2 \\ p_2p_4 + p_1p_3 = \phi_3 \\ p_1 + p_3 = \phi_4 \end{cases} \tag{7.51 – 7.54}$$

Therefore the model is *a priori* nonidentifiable and the set of *a priori* uniquely identifiable parameters is p_1, p_3, V_1, and p_2p_4.

If, however, the plasma concentration of insulin is also measured, that is, one has:

$$c_2(t) = \frac{q_2(t)}{V_2} \tag{7.55}$$

then a second transfer function can be defined:

$$H_{21}(s) = \frac{c_2(s)}{u(s)} = \frac{p_4/V_2}{s^2 + (p_1 + p_3)s + p_1p_3 + p_2p_4} \tag{7.56}$$

and the identifiability properties improve. In fact, a new equation can now be added to the exhaustive summary of (7.51)–(7.54):

$$\frac{p_4}{V_2} = \phi_5 \tag{7.57}$$

This means that the set of *a priori* uniquely identifiable parameters becomes p_1, p_3, V_1, p_2V_2, and p_4/V_2. Note that if the assumption can be made that V_2 is known or that $V_1 = V_2$, the model becomes *a priori* uniquely identifiable.

Example 5: A model of respiratory mechanics

Many techniques for estimating respiratory system mechanics are based on the assumption that the lungs can be described by the general equation of motion, a linear first order system:

$$P(t) = R\dot{V}(t) + \frac{1}{C}V(t) + I\ddot{V}(t) \tag{7.58}$$

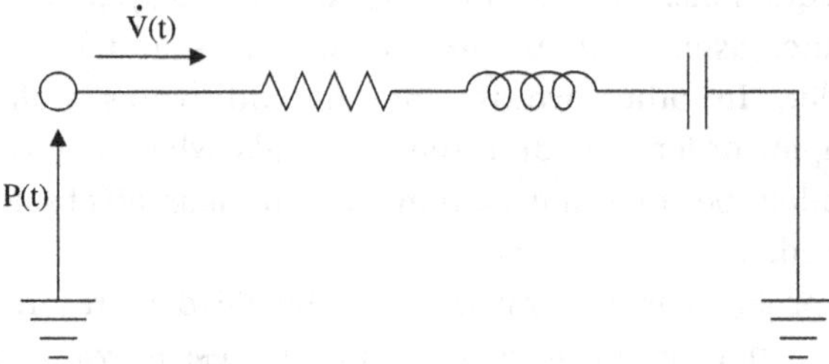

FIGURE 7–10 The resistance-elastance first-order model of respiratory mechanics.

where P denotes airway pressure, $\dot{V}$ airflow, V lung volume, $\ddot{V}$ volume acceleration, R total breathing resistance, C respiratory compliance, and I inertial effects. The electric analog of the model is shown in Fig. 7–10.

For most practical applications the inertial components are negligible and can be ignored. Thus (7.58) reduces to:

$$P(t) = R\dot{V}(t) + \frac{1}{C}V(t) \tag{7.59}$$

Taking ventilatory airflow, $\dot{V}(t)$, as input and pressure at the airway opening, P(t), as output we can rewrite (7.59) in terms of the pair of differential equations:

$$\begin{cases} \dot{x}(t) = \dfrac{\dot{V}(t)}{C} \\ P(t) = R\dot{V}(t) + x(t) \end{cases} \qquad (7.60-7.61)$$

where x(t) is the elastic component of pressure. The unknown parameter vector is $\mathbf{p} = [R, C]^T$. The transfer function is:

$$H(s) = \frac{Y(s)}{U(s)} = \frac{P(s)}{\dot{V}(s)} = R + \frac{1}{sC} = \frac{sRC + 1}{sC} \equiv \frac{\beta s + 1}{\alpha s} \tag{7.62}$$

Thus the exhaustive summary is given by:

$$RC = \phi_1 \tag{7.63}$$

$$C = \phi_2 \tag{7.64}$$

Therefore the model is *a priori* uniquely identifiable.

We have discussed the Laplace transform method to generate the exhaustive summary of the models. The method is simple to use even for system models of an order greater than two. What becomes more and more difficult is the solution, that is, to determine which of the original parameters of the model are uniquely determined by the system of nonlinear algebraic equations. In fact, one has to solve a system of nonlinear algebraic equations which is increasing both in number of terms and in degree of nonlinearity with the model order. In other words, the method works well for models of low dimension, for example, order two or three, but fails when applied to relatively large, general structure models because the system of nonlinear algebraic equations becomes too difficult to be solved.

To deal with the problem in general there is the need to resort to computer algebra methods. In particular, there is the need for a tool to test *a priori* identifiability of linear compartmental models of general structure which combines the transfer function method with a computer algebra method. Such a tool, named the Gröbner basis, is available (Audoly *et al.*, 1998).

7.5 Nonlinear models: the Taylor series expansion method

For a nonlinear model described by (7.37) and (7.38) or (7.39), the problem becomes even more difficult. Below, we illustrate a method based on the analysis of the coefficients of the Taylor series expansion in t_0 of the output variable **y** (Pohjanpalo, 1978).

For sake of simplicity, let us consider the scalar case and more precisely the i-th measurement variable y_i. The Taylor series expansion in t_0 of y_i is:

$$y_i(t) = y_i(t_0) + t\dot{y}_i(t_0) + \frac{t^2}{2!}\ddot{y}_i(t_0) + \frac{t^3}{3!}\dddot{y}_i(t_0) + L \tag{7.65}$$

where $y_i(t_0)$, $\dot{y}(t_0), \ldots$ are known and are the observational parameters ϕ_j. By expressing $y_i(t_0)$, $\dot{y}_i(t_0), \ldots$, as functions of the unknown parameters (**p**) of the model, one has the exhaustive summary of the model as:

$$y_i^k(t_0, \mathbf{p}) = \phi_k, \quad k = 0, 1, 2, \ldots \tag{7.66}$$

where k denotes the derivative order.

The system of nonlinear algebraic (7.66) needs to be solved for **p**. If it has a unique solution, then one can conclude that the model is uniquely identifiable. Unfortunately, nothing can be said about the identifiability properties of the model if this is not the case, for example, if one is not able to prove, due to the complexity of (7.66), that the system of (7.66) has a unique solution. However, this does not necessarily mean that the model is nonidentifiable. In other words, the method only provides necessary and sufficient conditions for *a priori* unique identifiability.

In addition to this limitation, it should also be noted that one does not know how many coefficients of the power series expansion are needed to study *a priori* identifiability of a given model and experiment. In other words, theory does not provide the value of k, that is, the order of the derivatives, at which one can stop. This makes the analysis even more difficult.

The power series expansion method also holds for linear models. In this case one knows (from the Cayley Hamilton theorem) that one can stop at $k = 2n-1$, that is, there is no independent information in the derivatives of an order higher than $2n-1$. To illustrate this point, let us consider an example of a receptor model.

Example 7: A Langmuir receptor model

Let us consider the model in Fig. 7–11. Assume that the material is injected at time 0 as a bolus of dose d, that is, $U(t) = D \cdot \delta(t)$, in plasma (compartment 1) and its concentration is measured. While irreversible elimination occurs linearly, that is, it is characterized by parameter k_{01}, transfer of material into the nonaccessible compartment 2 takes place with Langmuir saturation kinetics (see Fig. 5–41c), that is, the parameter k_{21} decreases linearly as the material is accumulated into 2.

The model equations are:

$$\begin{cases} \dot{Q}_1(t) = -k_{01}Q_1(t) - k_{21}\left(1 - \dfrac{Q_2(t)}{s_2}\right)Q_1(t) + U(t) & Q_1(0) = 0 \\ \dot{Q}_2(t) = k_{21}\left(1 - \dfrac{Q_2(t)}{s_2}\right)Q_1(t) & Q_2(0) = 0 \\ y(t) = \dfrac{Q_1(t)}{V_1} \end{cases} \quad (7.67-7.69)$$

The unknown parameter vector is $\mathbf{p} = [V_1, k_{01}, k_{21}, s_2]^T$.

To study *a priori* identifiability one now has to obtain the various $y(0)$, $\dot{y}(0)$, $\ddot{y}(0)$, $\dddot{y}(0)$.... (Note that 0 is a 0^+, i.e., an instant immediately after the impulse.) Let us thus calculate $y(0)$, $\dot{y}(0)$, $\ddot{y}(0)$, and $\dddot{y}(0)$. $Q_1(0)$ is easy to calculate:

$$Q_1(0) = D \quad (7.70)$$

For $\dot{Q}_1(0)$ one has from (7.67):

$$\dot{Q}_1(0) = -(k_{01} + k_{21})Q_1(0) \quad (7.71)$$

since $Q_2(0) = 0$.

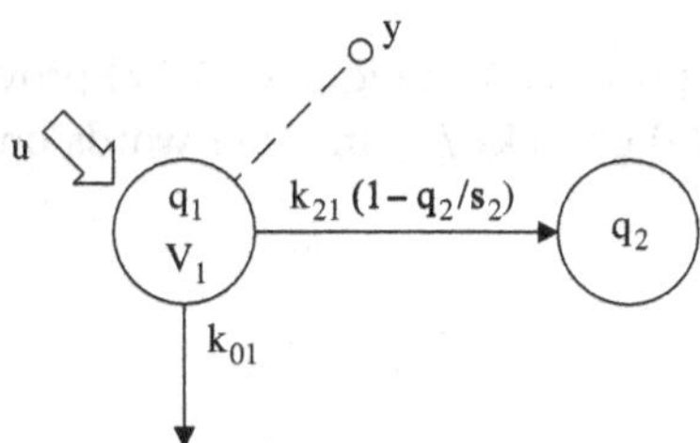

FIGURE 7–11 A two-compartment with the flux from compartments 1 to 2 described by a Langmuir relationship.

For $\ddot{Q}_1(0)$ one has:

$$\ddot{Q}_1(t) = -\left[k_{01} + k_{21}\left(1 - \frac{Q_2(t)}{s_2}\right)\right]\dot{Q}_1(t) + k_{21}\frac{\dot{Q}_2(t)}{s_2}Q_1(t) \tag{7.72}$$

and thus:

$$\ddot{Q}_1(0) = -(k_{01} + k_{21})\dot{Q}_1(0^+) + \frac{k_{21}}{s_2}k_{21}Q_1^2(0^+) \tag{7.73}$$

For $\dddot{Q}_1(0)$ one has:

$$\dddot{Q}_1(t) = -\left[k_{01} + k_{21}\left(1 - \frac{Q_2(t)}{s_2}\right)\right]\ddot{Q}_1(t) + k_{21}\frac{\dot{Q}_2(t)}{s_2}\dot{Q}_1(t) + \frac{k_{21}}{s_2}\dot{Q}_2(t)\dot{Q}_1(t) + \frac{k_{21}}{s_2}\ddot{Q}_2(t)Q_1(t) \tag{7.74}$$

and thus:

$$\dddot{Q}_1(0) = \frac{k_{21}^2}{s_2}\left(\frac{k_{21}}{s_1}Q_1^2(0^+) - 3\dot{Q}_1(0^+)\right)Q_1(0^+) - (k_{01} + k_{21})\ddot{Q}_1(0^+) \tag{7.75}$$

Now it is easy from (7.71) to obtain $y(0)$, $\dot{y}(0)$, $\ddot{y}(0)$, $\dddot{y}(0)$ from (7.70), (7.71), (7.73), and (7.75), respectively. The exhaustive summary of (7.65) is:

$$\frac{D}{V_1} = \phi_1 \tag{7.76}$$

$$\frac{1}{V_1}[-(k_{01} + k_{21})Q_1(0^+)] = \phi_2 \tag{7.77}$$

$$\frac{1}{V_1}\left[-(k_{01} + k_{21})Q_1(0^+) + \frac{k_{21}^2}{s_2}Q_1^2(0^+)\right] = \phi_3 \tag{7.78}$$

$$-\frac{k_{21}^2}{s_2}\left(\frac{k_{21}}{s_2}Q_1^2(0) - 3\dot{Q}_1(0)\right)Q_1(0) - (k_{01} + k_{21})\ddot{Q}_1(0) = \phi_4 \tag{7.79}$$

It is easy to see that (7.76) provides V_1 uniquely, (7.77) provides $k_{01} + k_{21}$ uniquely, (7.78) gives k_{21}^2/s_2 uniquely, and (7.79) gives k_{21}/s_2. In other words one has:

$$V_1 = c_1 \tag{7.80}$$

$$k_{01} + k_{21} = c_2 \tag{7.81}$$

$$\frac{k_{21}^2}{s_2} = c_3 \tag{7.82}$$

$$\frac{k_{21}}{s_2} = c_4 \tag{7.83}$$

where c_1, c_2, c_3, c_4 are known constants. Since one has $s_2 = k_{21}/c_4$, then $k_{21} = c_3/c_4$ and thus $k_{01} = c_1 - (c_3/c_4)$. Therefore the model is *a priori* uniquely identifiable.

It is interesting to note that if we consider a linearized version of the model, that is, with $Q_2 \ll s_2$ one has $k_{21}(1-Q_2/s_2) \simeq k_{21}$; the model becomes nonidentifiable. In fact, the equations for $Q_1(0)$, $\dot{Q}_1(0)$ become:

$$Q_1^k(0) = -(k_{01} + k_{21})Q_1^{k-1}(0), \quad k = 1, 2, \ldots \tag{7.84}$$

that is, only the aggregated parameter $k_{01} + k_{21}$ is uniquely identifiable (in addition to V_1). Note that in this case the model of Fig. 7–11 reduces to that of Fig. 7–8, and we have already proven the above in Section 7.2.

7.6 Qualitative experimental design

7.6.1 Fundamentals

Having defined a model structure and an input/output experiment for its identification, *a priori* identifiability analysis permits one to avoid doing an experiment if the parameters of interest are not identifiable, or conversely to define which would be the uniquely identifiable parameter combinations of the model. This is particularly important in physiological and clinical studies where ethical as well as practical issues come into play. For instance, if the general two-compartment model of Fig. 7–4 is the model of choice for the system under study, but only compartment 1 is accessible for input and measurement, *a priori* identifiability analysis can show that k_{21}, k_{12}, k_{01}, and k_{02} are nonidentifiable. However, some combinations of them are uniquely identifiable, that is, $k_{11} = k_{21} + k_{01}$, $k_{22} = k_{12} + k_{02}$, and $k_{21}k_{12}$.

A priori identifiability is also an essential ingredient of *qualitative experiment design*. Qualitative experiment design consists of selecting the site of inputs and outputs, among those that are experimentally feasible, which will guarantee *a priori* unique identifiability of the model parameters. Since severe constraints exist on experiment design when dealing with *in vivo* studies, that is, the number of inputs and outputs is severely limited for both ethical and practical reasons, it is of great interest to define a minimal input/output configuration; that is, necessary and sufficient to guarantee *a priori* unique identifiability. Minimal here means minimum number of inputs and outputs: obviously more than one minimal input/output configuration can exist, that is, having the same minimum number of inputs and outputs that take place in different compartments.

The definition of a minimal input/output configuration thus relies on *a priori* identifiability. For instance, the minimal input/output configuration of the general two-compartment model of Fig. 7–4 is not the most general two input/four output configuration, but a two input/three output one. There are thus four minimal configurations available in this case.

7.6.2 An amino acid model

An example of qualitative experiment design and minimal input/output configuration can be provided using a model of leucine metabolism, which is an essential amino acid (Saccomani & Cobelli, 1992). Leucine metabolism can be described in the context of the unit processes shown in Fig. 7–12. The first metabolite in the degradation via transamination is a-ketoisocaproate (Kic). Leucine and Kic are interconvertible via the transamination process. Irreversible oxidation occurs with the next step in metabolism which releases CO_2. Leucine can enter the system from protein breakdown, and be incorporated into protein.

To quantitate the steps in leucine metabolism outlined in Fig. 7–12, knowledge of leucine, Kic, and bicarbonate kinetics is required. To develop a model of this complex system, a pilot two-stage (A and B) tracer experiment described in Fig. 7–13 was performed.

Stage A

This is a two input/five output experiment where carbon labeled leucine and tritium—or deuterium labeled Kic are simultaneously administered into plasma (e.g., as a bolus). The corresponding four plasma leucine and Kic tracer concentration curves are measured; in addition, the carbon labeled CO_2 is measured in expired air.

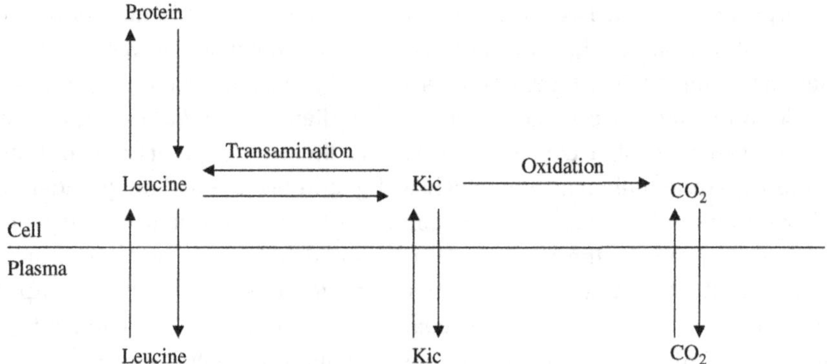

FIGURE 7–12 Schematic representation of the major unit processes of leucine metabolism. *Adapted from Saccomani, M. P., & Cobelli, C. (1992). Qualitative experiment design in physiological system identification.* IEEE Control Systems Magazine, 12, *18–23.*

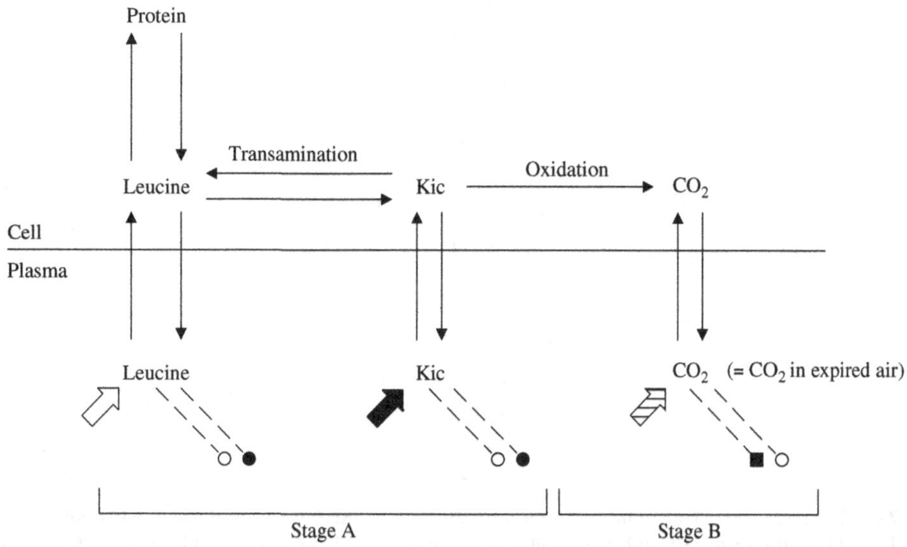

FIGURE 7–13 Two-stage pilot tracer experiment designed for model formulation and identification. Tracer inputs and measurements are denoted by large arrows and dashed lines with a bullet, respectively. The open and closed bullets correspond to the labeled leucine (*open*) and Kic (*closed*) inputs, respectively. The closed square bullet corresponds to the bicarbonate input. *Adapted from Saccomani, M. P., & Cobelli, C. (1992). Qualitative experiment design in physiological system identification.* IEEE Control Systems Magazine, 12, *18–23.*

Stage B

This is a single input/single output experiment performed on a separate occasion where labeled bicarbonate is administered into plasma, for example, as a bolus, and labeled CO_2 is measured in expired air.

The modeling strategy employed to describe the pilot experimental data was as follows. First, the single input/single output data of bicarbonate kinetics (Stage B) were interpreted using the known three-compartment model of bicarbonate kinetics shown in Fig. 7–14. Then, assuming the bicarbonate model is known in each individual (from Stage B), the Stage A two input/five output data were interpreted using the model shown in Fig. 7–15 where, besides assuming a known bicarbonate system, the model is subject to the constraint $k_{03} = k_{05}$.

Having postulated a plausible model structure, both in terms of physiology and consistency with the pilot experimental data, the first question is: do the Stage A and Stage B experiments ensure *a priori* unique identifiability of the leucine–Kic–bicarbonate model? The answer is yes. In fact, one can show first that the Stage B single input/single output experiment allows *a priori* unique identifiability of all the unknown parameters of the model in Fig. 7–15, that is, k_{89}, k_{98}, $k_{8,10}$, $k_{10,8}$, k_{08}^{R}, and k_{08}^{NR}, once the structural symmetry problem is resolved by labeling compartments 9 and 10 as fast and slow, respectively. Then it can be shown that the Stage A two input/five output experiment allows *a priori* unique identifiability of all the remaining 16 unknown parameters. These are the remaining k_{ij} together with

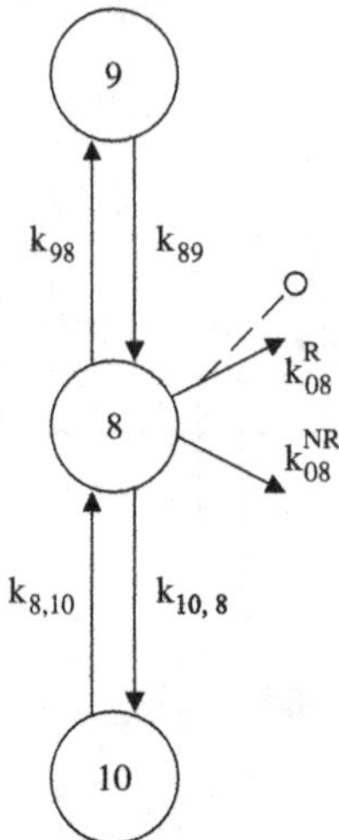

FIGURE 7–14 The three-compartment model of bicarbonate kinetics used to interpret the single input/single output data of the Stage B experiment. The number of compartments has been chosen to be consistent with the leucine metabolism model shown in Fig. 7–12. Irreversible loss from compartment 8 is comprised of a respiratory k_{08}^{R} and nonrespiratory k_{08}^{NR} component. The large arrow denotes tracer input while the dashed line with the bullet denotes the measurement of labeled bicarbonate in the expired air, that is, $k_{08}^{R}Q_8$.

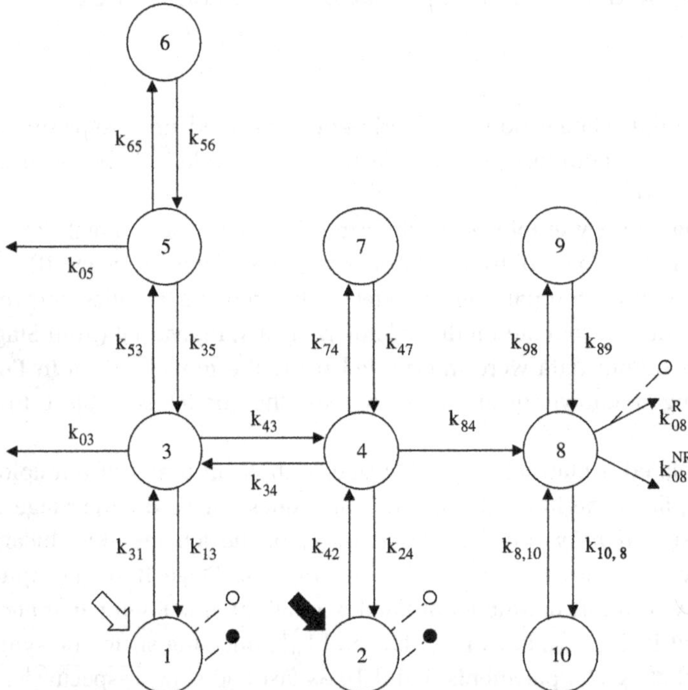

FIGURE 7–15 Ten-compartment model of leucine–Kic–bicarbonate kinetics used to interpret the Stage A tracer experiment. The bicarbonate model shown in Fig. 7–14 has been appended to the intracellular Kic compartment. Two tracer inputs (*large arrows*) and five measured variables are indicated: three measured variables (*open bullets*) refer to the labeled leucine input, and the two closed bullets refer to labeled Kic. The model is subject to the constraint that $k_{03} = k_{05}$.

V_1 and V_2, of the model shown in Fig. 7–14 (subject to the constraint $k_{03} = k_{05}$ and assuming the bicarbonate system parameters are known from the Stage B experiment).

Knowing that the model is *a priori* uniquely identifiable, the minimal input/output configuration problem can be addressed. In particular, the following qualitative experiment design questions must be addressed: is the two-stage pilot experiment a minimal one which guarantees *a priori,* unique identifiability? In particular, is Stage B necessary? If not, are all the four plasma outputs of Stage A necessary? Which are the sufficient ones? In particular, is the expired CO_2 measurement of Stage A needed?

To answer these questions, it is necessary to analyze the *a priori* identifiability of the model from the Stage A experiment only.

Stage B is not necessary

A priori identifiability analysis of the leucine–Kic–bicarbonate model of Fig. 7–15 from data of only Stage A experiment, that is, without assuming the parameters of the bicarbonate portion of the model to be known, shows the unique *a priori* identifiability of all the parameters including those related to the bicarbonate model. This theoretical result indicates that the independent assessment of bicarbonate kinetics (Stage B) is not necessary since the information content of the five curves of Stage A is sufficient to solve for all the unknown parameters of the leucine–Kic–bicarbonate model. In terms of experiment design, this theoretical result is of particular interest since it shows that the model is *a priori* identifiable with a reduced experimental effort. The two-stage pilot tracer experiment originally designed for model identification is *a priori* not necessary; in particular, the single input/single output experiment (Stage B) performed on a separate occasion from the dual input/five output one (Stage A) is not required.

Dual input/four output experiment

So far the sufficiency of the dual input/five output experiment for *a priori* unique identifiability of the leucine–Kic–bicarbonate model shown in Fig. 7–15 has been demonstrated. Is this experiment design also necessary? In other words, is it a minimal experiment design for model identifiability? An examination of the Stage A exhaustive summary reveals that measurements of labeled leucine concentration after a labeled leucine injection and of labeled Kic concentration after a labeled Kic injection are necessary. However, either the measurement of leucine concentration after a labeled Kic injection or the measurement of labeled Kic after labeled leucine injection is redundant. Thus not all four plasma curves are necessary for the *a priori* unique identifiability of the model. Only three of them are needed, that is, the two disappearance curves of leucine and Kic plus one of the two appearance curves are required. So far, we have proved that the two input/four output experiment, that is, the measurement of the three plasma curves described above and of the labeled CO_2 in the expired air, is sufficient.

Two input/three output experiment

Now remaining to be proved is the necessity of the two input/four output experiment. Having demonstrated the necessity of three plasma curves, one must examine the necessity of the measurement of expired CO_2. This is of particular interest since it would allow the model to be identified with less experimental effort, that is, from plasma measurements only.

With such a two input/three output experiment, the model is that of Fig. 7–15 without the bicarbonate portion of the model, and with k_{84} replaced by k_{04}. Examination of the exhaustive summary shows that all of the parameters of the leucine–Kic portion of the model are *a priori* uniquely identifiable from the two input/three output tracer experiment, an experiment based on plasma measurement only.

7.7 Summary

This chapter has explored the nature of the identifiability problem in relation to parametric models and discussed methods which are available for addressing it. In essence this involved asking the question as to whether or not it is theoretically possible to make unique estimates of all the unknown model parameters on the basis of data obtained from particular input/output experiments. This is an exercise that needs to be undertaken prior to performing any actual experiment, thereby avoiding unnecessary resource expenditure that would be ineffective in terms of securing useful parameter estimates. The various approaches to addressing the problem have been illustrated by many examples. Having considered this issue of identifiability, Chapter 8, Parametric models—the estimation problem, will now go on to consider the next step in dealing with parametric models, namely ways of estimating the model parameters.

7.8 Exercises and assignment questions

1. Discuss the role of the assessment of *a priori* identifiability in the overall problem of parameter estimation.
2. Why does the *a priori* identifiability problem become more and more difficult to solve when the model order increases?
3. A model of a given physiological system has been shown to be *a priori* nonidentifiable. Discuss possible strategies to cope with nonidentifiability.
4. The kinetics of a drug in the body are described by the model shown below:

$$\begin{cases} \dot{Q}_1(t) = -(k_{21} + k_{01}) \cdot Q_1(t) + U_1(t), \quad Q_1(0) = 0 \\ C_1(t) = \dfrac{Q_1(t)}{V_1} \end{cases}$$

- Show that the model is *a priori* nonidentifiable and derive the uniquely identifiable parametrization.
- Examine the *a priori* identifiability of this model if it now includes an additional output from compartment 2:

$$\begin{cases} \dot{Q}_1(t) = -(k_{21}+k_{01})\cdot Q_1(t) + U_1(t), & Q_1(0)=0 \\ \dot{Q}_2(t) = -k_{02}\cdot Q_2(t) + k_{21}\cdot Q_1(t), & Q_2(0)=0 \\ C_1(t) = \dfrac{Q_1(t)}{V_1} \\ C_2(t) = \dfrac{Q_2(t)}{V_2} \end{cases}$$

Consider the two cases, V_2 unknown and V_2 known.

- Examine *a priori* identifiability of the model with an additional input in compartment 2 simultaneous with that into compartment 1:

$$\begin{cases} \dot{Q}_1(t) = -(k_{21}+k_{01})\cdot Q_1(t) + U_1(t), & Q_1(0)=0 \\ \dot{Q}_2(t) = -k_{02}\cdot Q_2(t) + k_{21}\cdot Q_1(t) + U_2(t) & Q_2(0)=0 \\ C_1(t) = \dfrac{Q_1(t)}{V_1} \end{cases}$$

5. Assume that the kinetics of a drug are described by the nonlinear model shown below:

$$\begin{cases} \dot{Q}(t) = -\dfrac{V_M}{K_M + Q(t)}\cdot Q(t) + U(t) \quad Q_1(0)=0 \\ C(t) = \dfrac{Q(t)}{V} \end{cases}$$

where V_M and K_M are the parameters of the Michaelis–Menten description of irreversible drug elimination.

Examine the *a priori* identifiability problem.

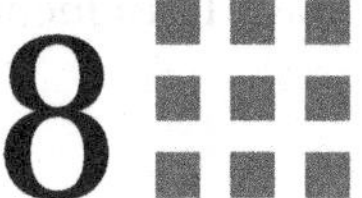

Parametric models—the estimation problem

8.1 Introduction

The focus of this chapter is the estimation problem in the context of mathematical models that explicitly include unknown parameters. Having formulated the basic estimation problem, descriptions are given of the major approaches which include linear and nonlinear least squares, maximum likelihood, and Bayes. Additionally, the basis of the related problem of optimal experimental design is discussed. For a more detailed account of estimation methods, including least squares, maximum likelihood, and Bayesian methods, Walter and Pronzato (1997) provide a good description.

A model of the system—whether an input/output or a structural one—has now been formulated. The model contains a set of unknown parameters to which we would like to assign numerical values from the data of an experiment. For a structural model we assume that we have checked its *a priori* identifiability. However, this is not necessary for an input/output model because, by definition, its unknown parameters are the observational ones. The experimental data are available, for example, they have been obtained after a qualitative experiment design phase. In mathematical terms the ingredients we have are the model output [as shown earlier in (7.1)]:

$$y(t) = g(t, \mathbf{p}) \tag{8.1}$$

where $g(t, \mathbf{p})$ is related to the model of the system, for example, a structural or an input/output one, and the discrete-time noisy output measurements, z_i [as shown earlier in (7.2)]:

$$z(t_i) = z_i = y_i + v_i = g(t_i, p) + v_i \tag{8.2}$$

where $\mathbf{v}_i$ is the measurement error of the i-th measurement.

The problem is to assign a numerical value to $\mathbf{p}$ from the data z_i. As an example, suppose the model of data:

$$y(t) = p_1 + p_2 t + p_3 t^2 \tag{8.3}$$

is used to describe the data z_i: in this case one needs to assign a numerical value to $\mathbf{p} = [p_1, p_2, p_3]^T$. On the other hand, suppose that the model of data:

$$y(t) = A_1 e^{-\alpha_1 t} + A_2 e^{-\alpha_2 t} \tag{8.4}$$

Introduction to Modeling in Physiology and Medicine. DOI: https://doi.org/10.1016/B978-0-12-815756-5.00008-4

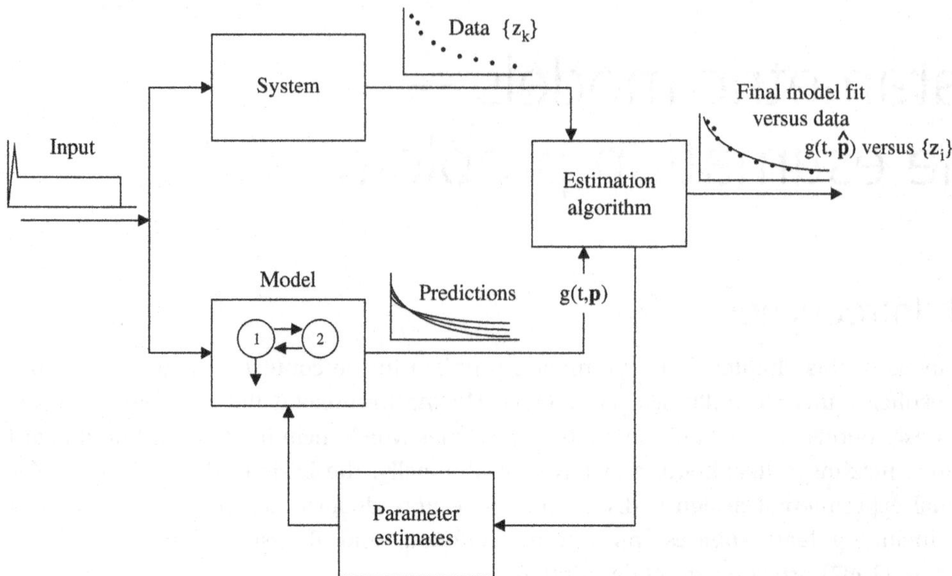

FIGURE 8–1 The parameter estimation scheme showing its iterative nature.

is the candidate one for describing z_i: in this case one needs to assign a numerical value to $\mathbf{p} = [A_1, \lambda_1, A_2, \lambda_2]^T$. The same also holds for models of systems, for example, consider the model of Figs. 7.3 and 7.4 in Chapter 7, Parametric modeling—the identifiability problem. In this case one needs to assign a numerical value to $\mathbf{p} = [k_{21}, k_{12}, k_{01}, V_1]^T$ or $\mathbf{p} = [k_{21}, k_{12}, k_{01}, k_{02}, V_1]^T$, respectively.

If either of these models were being used to describe a set of data, the parameters characterizing them need to be adjusted until a set of values for them is obtained which provides the best fit to the data (Fig. 8–1). Regression analysis, which is defined and described in detail below, is the most widely used method to adjust the parameters characterizing a particular function to obtain the best fit scenario to a set of data.

There are fundamentally two kinds of regression: linear and nonlinear. The theory of linear regression is mathematically precise with the formulae for the parameters characterizing the function specifically defined. Nonlinear regression is more complex and results only in approximations for the estimates of the parameters. In addition to the parameter estimates, for both linear and nonlinear regression, one usually wants information on the errors of the parameter estimates. To obtain estimates of these errors, one moves to weighted regression. In weighted regression, knowledge of the error structure of the data is needed. These errors are used to calculate the weight assigned to a datum during the regression process. The importance of understanding the nature of the error in the data and how this relates to weighted and unweighted regression is an essential ingredient of the regression problem as will be made clear later. Thus there are several ingredients to the regression problem. These will be isolated and explained in detail with examples provided.

8.2 Linear and nonlinear parameters

What constitutes a linear or nonlinear parameter? It is important to understand the answer to this since, as will be seen in Section 8.4, there is an exact solution when the model contains only linear parameters. In contrast, as will be seen in Section 8.5, the solution is only approximate if the model contains a nonlinear parameter.

There are many kinds of functions that are linear in their parameters. Polynomials such as the following one are an example:

$$y(t) = p_1 + p_2 \cdot t + p_3 \cdot t^2 + \cdots + p_n \cdot t^{n-1} \tag{8.5}$$

This polynomial y(t) is characterized by the coefficients $p_1, p_2, \ldots, p_n$ which are the parameters to be estimated in data fitting, and the independent variable is t. Why are polynomials linear? The reason why can be illustrated by using this simple polynomial:

$$y(t) = pt = y(p, t) \tag{8.6}$$

When $y(t) = y(p, t)$ is written in this manner, it indicates that y is a function of the independent variable (t) and of the value assigned to the parameter (p). That is, y(t) will assume different values depending upon a specific value for p. The function y(t) is linear in the parameter p, or equivalently the parameter p in (8.6) is linear because if the value $p + p'$ is considered, then:

$$y(p + p', t) = (p + p')t = pt + p't = y(p, t) + y(p', t) \tag{8.7}$$

For example, doubling the value for the parameter p will double the value for the function y (t).

If y(t) is nonlinear in at least one of its parameters, or equivalently if not all parameters describing y(t) are linear, then y(t) is nonlinear. Nonlinearity is seen when the counterpart of (8.7) cannot be written for a particular function. For example, the exponential function y(t) given in (8.4) is nonlinear since $y(A_1 + A'_1, \lambda_1 + \lambda'_1, A_2 + A'_2, \lambda_2 + \lambda'_2, t)$ is not equal to the sum of $y(A_1, \lambda_1, A_2, \lambda_2, t)$ and $y(A_1', \lambda_1', A_2', \lambda_2', t)$. This function is linear in A_1 and A_2 and nonlinear in λ_1 and λ_2.

For a linear model in the parameters, exact solutions are available based on linear regression theory. However, for a nonlinear model in the parameters, only approximate solutions are available based on the linear theory. That is why an understanding of the linear theory is essential to discuss the nonlinear problem.

One final remark that is worth emphasizing relates to the difference between linearity in the parameters and linearity of the dynamics. To exemplify this, consider the simplest linear dynamic model, for example, a one compartment model:

$$\dot{q}(t) = -kq(t) + d\delta(t) \quad q(0) = 0 \tag{8.8}$$

In terms of parameter estimation, this is a nonlinear model in the parameters since the solution of (8.8) is:

$$q(t) = de^{-kt} \tag{8.9}$$

and, thus, the parameter estimation problem is nonlinear in k (d is known).

8.3 Regression: basic concepts

Here we examine one by one the essential ingredients of regression.

8.3.1 The residual

The basic notions of regression, that is, finding a set of parameter values which define a function that will provide the best fit for a set of data, can be described using Fig. 8–2. Suppose an investigator wishes to obtain the best fit of the data to the straight line.

$$y(t) = pt \tag{8.10}$$

How can this fit be obtained?

To solve the problem, one sees that, for different values of p, different straight lines will be generated. How does one find the particular value for p which provides the best fit? Note that for each point at time t_i where there is a datum, denoted z_i, there is a corresponding prediction from y(t), y_i. Once a value for p is chosen, the difference between the experimentally observed datum and the calculated value, that is, $z_i - y_i$, can be calculated; this is called the *residual*. In general, if y(t) is a function to be fitted to a set of data, and if z_i is the ith observation, the residual is written:

$$res_i = z_i - y_i \tag{8.11}$$

8.3.2 The residual sum of squares

The expression:

$$RSS = \sum_{i=1}^{N} (z_i - y_i)^2 = \sum_{i=1}^{N} res_i^2 \tag{8.12}$$

where N is the number of observations is called the *residual sum of squares*, RSS, or *sum of squares of errors* since $z_i - y_i$ can be considered as the error between the observed and predicted value for each sample time t_i.

The residual sum of squares, RSS, can be considered a measure of how good the fit is to the given set of data. For different numerical values of the parameter characterizing (8.10), that is, for different numerical values for p, one will obtain a different RSS. Therefore, RSS

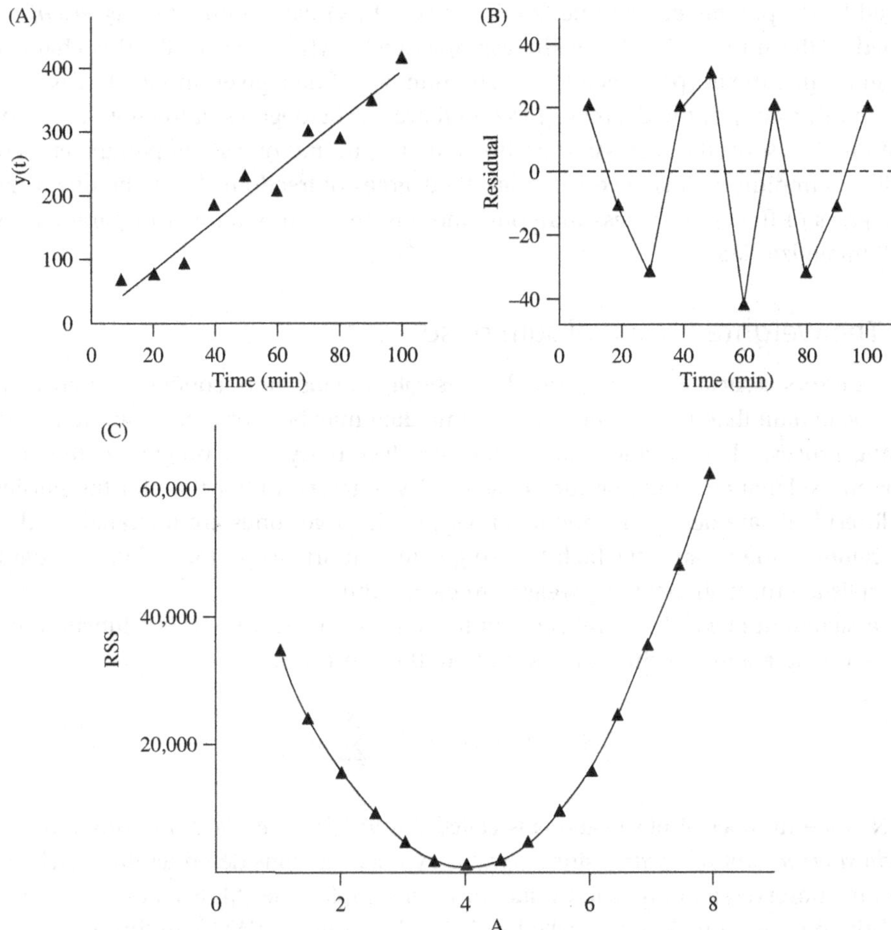

FIGURE 8–2 (A) A set of data with a straight line through them obtained by linear regression. (B) A plot of the residuals illustrating the pattern of above or below zero. (C) Plot of WRSS(**p**) versus p which shows that there is a unique value of p for which WRSS(p) is minimal. *Adapted from Cobelli et al., 2001.*

itself can be considered as a function of the parameter characterizing the linear function chosen to describe a set of data. One can write RSS = RSS(p) for (8.12) to emphasize this fact.

The idea behind regression is to minimize RSS with respect to the parameter values characterizing the function to be fitted to the data, that is, to find a set of parameter values for y(t) which minimizes RSS. The process is called *least squares*. In the case of the function defined in (8.10), the problem would be to find a value for p which minimizes RSS for the set of data given in Fig. 8–2.

The theory behind this minimization utilizes differential calculus. It also depends upon a number commonly encountered in statistics: degrees of freedom. Suppose a function y(t) described by (P) parameters is to be fitted to a set of (N) data points; *the degrees of freedom* is defined as the number N−P. For the example above, y(t) given in (8.10) is characterized by the single parameter (p), hence P = 1. The number of data given in Fig. 8–2 is 10, hence N = 10. In this example, the degrees of freedom are 9. The degrees of freedom are important since in order to solve the regression problem, that is, to find one set of parameter values for which RSS is minimum, it is necessary that the degrees of freedom should be one or greater. If the degrees of freedom are less than one, there is an infinite number of parameter values that will minimize RSS.

8.3.3 The weighted residual sum of squares

Data have errors associated with them. This basically means more confidence may be placed in one type of data than in another, that is, some data may be more important than others in the fitting process. For instance, some data are less noisy than others, so the preferred description/explanation would be for the less noisy outcome rather than for the noisier, that is, small residuals are desired for the less noisy, while larger ones are tolerated for the noisier. Therefore, some means by which to give greater importance to these data is sought. This is accomplished through assigning weights to each datum.

The assignment of weights is reflected in the sum of squares. If y(t) is a function to be fitted to a set of data and z_i is the i-th observation, the expression:

$$\mathrm{WRSS} = \sum_{i=1}^{N} w_i(z_i - y_i)^2 = \sum_{i=1}^{N} \mathrm{wres}_i^2 \tag{8.13}$$

where N is the number of observations is called the *weighted residual sum of squares*, WRSS, or *weighted error sum of squares* since $\sqrt{w_i}(z_i - y_i)$ can be considered as the weighted error between the observed and predicted value for each sample time (t_i). Extending the above, the theory behind minimizing WRSS is called *weighted least squares* (WLS). In this expression w_i is the weight assigned to the i-th datum, and the *weighted residual* is written:

$$\mathrm{wres}_i = \sqrt{w_i}(z_i - y_i) \tag{8.14}$$

RSS and WRSS are functions of the parameters characterizing a function, y(t). They are examples of what in the theory of optimization are called an *objective or cost function.* While there are other objective functions that can be used, RSS and WRSS are most commonly used in the modeling of physiological systems. Other objective functions will be briefly described in Section 8.7 where the maximum likelihood and Bayes estimators are discussed.

8.3.4 Weights and error in the data

It is natural to link the choice of weights to what is known about the precision of each individual datum. In other words, it is necessary to give more credibility, or weight, to those data whose precision is high, and less credibility, or weight, to those data whose precision is small.

Suppose that fitting a function y(t) to a set of data is required. In what follows, it will be assumed that the function y(t) is the correct model for the data being considered. As part of the theory to be developed, information is recovered from the fitting process to test if this assumption is correct.

To start, for each datum (z_i) at sample time (t_i), there is an error term (v_i). It is usually assumed that this term is additive, that is, can be expressed as:

$$z_i = y_i + v_i \tag{8.15}$$

v_i is a random variable and assumptions about its characteristics must be made. The most common assumption is that the sequence of v_i is a random process with zero mean (i.e., no systematic error) independent samples and variance known. This can be formalized in the statistical setting using the notation E, Var, and Cov to represent, respectively, mean, variance, and covariance. Then:

$$E(v_i) = 0 \tag{8.16}$$

$$\mathrm{Cov}(v_i,\ v_j) = 0 \quad \text{for } t_i \neq t_j \tag{8.17}$$

$$\mathrm{Var}(v_i) = \sigma_i^2 \tag{8.18}$$

Eq. (8.16) indicates that the errors v_i have zero mean; (8.17) signifies that they are independent, and (8.18) shows that the variance is known. A standardized measure of the error is provided by the *fractional standard deviation* (FSD) or *coefficient of variation* (CV):

$$\mathrm{FSD}(v_i) = \mathrm{CV}(v_i) = \frac{\mathrm{SD}(v_i)}{z_i} \tag{8.19}$$

where SD is the standard deviation of the error:

$$\mathrm{SD}(v_i) = \sqrt{\mathrm{Var}(v_i)} \tag{8.20}$$

The FSD or CV is often expressed as a percentage, that is, the percentage fractional standard deviation or percentage coefficient of variation, by multiplying $\mathrm{SD}(v_i)/z_i$ in (8.19) by 100.

Three remarks are in order here. First, if the errors v_i are Gaussian, then (8.16)–(8.18) specify completely the probability distribution; otherwise they provide a description based on the first two moments (mean and variance). Second, using the fact that if Y is a random variable, and α and β are constants, $\mathrm{Var}(\alpha + \beta Y) = \beta^2\ \mathrm{Var}(Y)$; one has from (8.15) that, since y_i is constant, $\mathrm{Var}(z_i) = \mathrm{Var}(v_i)$, that is, the variance of an individual datum and of its error are equal.

Finally, we have considered the case where the variance is known [see Eq. (8.18)]. However, one can also easily handle the case where the variance is known up to a proportionality constant, that is, $\mathrm{Var}(v_i) = b_i\sigma^2$ with b_i known and σ^2 unknown. It is beyond the scope of this book to consider this case further. For more details the reader is referred to Cobelli *et al.*, 2001 (Chapter 10: Model validation).

Knowing the error structure of the data, how are the weights w_i chosen? The natural choice is to weight each datum according to the inverse of the variance, that is:

$$w_i = \frac{1}{\sigma_i^2} \tag{8.21}$$

It can be shown that this natural choice of weights is optimal in the linear regression case, that is, it produces the minimum variance of the parameter estimates. Therefore, it is very important to have correct knowledge of the data error , and to weight each datum according to this error.

The problem now is how to estimate the error variance. Ideally one would like to have a direct estimate of the variance of all error sources. This is a difficult problem. For instance, the measurement error is just one component of the error; it can be used as an estimate of the error only if the investigator believes that the major error source arises after the sample is taken. To have a more precise estimate of the error, the investigator should have several independent replicates of the measurement (z_i) at each sampling time (t_i) from which the sample variance (σ_i^2) at t_i can be estimated. If there is a major error component before the measurement process (for instance, an error related to drawing a plasma sample or preparing a plasma sample for measurement), then it is not sufficient to repeat the measurement *per se* on the same sample several times. In theory, in this situation it would be necessary to repeat the experiment several times. Such repetition is not often easy to handle in practice. Finally, there is the possibility that the system itself can vary during the different experiments.

In any case, since the above-mentioned approach estimates the variance at each sampling time(t_i), it requires several independent replicates of each measurement. An alternative more practical approach consists of postulating a model for the error variance and estimating its unknown parameters from the experimental data.

A flexible model that can be used for the error variance is:

$$\sigma_i^2 = \alpha + \beta(y_i)^\gamma \tag{8.22}$$

which can be approximated in practice by:

$$\sigma_i^2 = \alpha + \beta(z_i)^\gamma \tag{8.23}$$

where α, β, and γ are nonnegative model parameters relating the variance associated with an observation to the value of the observation itself. Values can usually be assigned to these parameters, or they can also be estimated from the data themselves.

8.4 Linear regression

The fundamental ideas of linear regression are discussed by fitting a straight line through the data of Fig. 8–2. The concepts introduced here, based on least squares theory, carry over to any linear function. The equation for the straight line used here is:

$$y = y(p,\ t) = pt \tag{8.24}$$

where t is the independent variable. The parameter describing this line, p, is linear as described above. Different values for p will produce different lines. Hence, for each value of p there is a different calculated value of RSS, or RSS(p) to denote the functional relationship with p; this is shown in Fig. 8–2. What one seeks is the value of $\hat{p}$, which minimizes RSS(p). This point is indicated in Fig. 8–2. As part of the theory of linear regression, when the degrees of freedom are greater than one, there is a unique value for p which will minimize RSS(p).

8.4.1 The problem

It is important to take into account measurement errors. This is done by WLS which takes errors in the data explicitly into account through weights. The expression to be minimized is WRSS:

$$WRSS(p) = \sum_{i=1}^{N} wres_i^2 = \sum_{i=1}^{N} w_i(z_i - y_i)^2 = \sum_{i=1}^{N} \frac{1}{\sigma_i^2}(z_i - pt_i)^2 \tag{8.25}$$

To find the unique value for p which minimizes WRSS(p), one takes the derivative of WRSS(p) with respect to p, sets the resulting expression equal to zero, and solves this equation for p:

$$\frac{d(WRSS(p))}{dp} = -2\sum_{i=1}^{N} \frac{t_i}{\sigma_i^2}(z_i - pt_i) = 0 \tag{8.26}$$

From differential calculus, it is known that the value of p which is a solution of (9.26), $\hat{p}$, will minimize WRSS(p). This is given by:

$$\hat{p} = \frac{\left(\sum_{i=1}^{N}(z_i \cdot t_i)/\sigma_i^2\right)}{\left(\sum_{i=1}^{N} t_i^2/\sigma_i^2\right)} \tag{8.27}$$

It is also possible to obtain an expression for the precision of $\hat{p}$, Var($\hat{p}$). Since data z_i are affected by a measurement error v_i as specified in (8.15), one has that $\hat{p}$ is also affected by an error which we call estimation error. The estimation error can be defined as:

$$\tilde{p} = p - \hat{p} \tag{8.28}$$

$\tilde{p}$ is a random variable because $\hat{p}$ is random. One can measure the ability of the estimation error to vary through its variance:

$$\mathrm{Var}(\tilde{p}) = E(\tilde{p}^2) = \frac{1}{\sum_{i=1}^{N}(t_i^2/\sigma_i^2)} = \frac{1}{\sum_{i=1}^{N}\sigma_i^2 t_i^2} = \mathrm{Var}(\hat{p}) \tag{8.29}$$

The precision of the estimate $\hat{p}$ of p is often expressed in terms of standard deviation, that is, the square root of the variance $\mathrm{Var}(\hat{p})$:

$$\mathrm{SD}(\hat{p}) = \sqrt{\mathrm{Var}(\hat{p})} \tag{8.30}$$

It can also be given in terms of the fractional standard deviation FSD or the coefficient of variation CV, which measures the relative precision of the estimate:

$$\mathrm{FSD}(\hat{p}) = \mathrm{CV}(\hat{p}) = \mathrm{SD}(\hat{p})\hat{p} \tag{8.31}$$

As noted previously, FSD and CV can be expressed as a percent by multiplying it by 100.

From (8.27) and (8.29), one sees that both $\hat{p}$ and $\mathrm{VAR}(\hat{p})$ depend upon the σ_i^2. This is why it is essential that the investigator appreciates the nature of the error in the data.

8.4.2 Test on residuals

Up to this point, an assumption has been made that the model is correct, that is, that $y(t) = pt$ provides the correct functional description of the data. In this case, from the comparison between the equation describing the data:

$$z_i = y_i + v_i = pt_i + v_i \tag{8.32}$$

and from the definition of the residual (8.11):

$$\mathrm{res}_i = z_i - y_i = z_i - \hat{p}t_i \tag{8.33}$$

it can immediately be concluded that residuals res_i must reflect the measurement errors v_i. For this in fact to be true, two conditions must hold: (1) the correct model or functional description of the data has been selected, and (2) the parameter estimation procedure has converged to values close to the true values. The sequence of residuals can thus be viewed as an approximation of the measurement error sequence.

We can check if the above two conditions hold by testing on the sequence of residuals the assumptions made regarding the measurement error. As discussed in previous sections, the measurement error is usually assumed to be a zero mean, the independent random process having a known variance. These assumptions can be checked on the residuals by means of statistical tests. This analysis can reveal the presence of errors in the model structure, that is, in the above example if $y(t) = pt$ is not an appropriate model for a given set of data, or the failure of the parameter estimation procedure to converge, that is, if $\hat{p}$ are not close to the true values for p.

Independence of the residuals can be tested visually by using a plot of residuals versus time. It is expected that the residuals will oscillate around their mean, which should be close to zero, in an unpredictable way. Systematic residuals, that is, a long run sequence of residuals above or below zero, suggests that the model is an inappropriate description of the system since it is not able to describe a nonrandom component of the data. In Fig. 8–3 a typical plot is shown for a sequence of independent and correlated residuals.

A formal test of nonrandomness of residuals is called the run test. A run is defined as a subsequence of residuals having the same sign (assuming the residuals have zero mean); intuitively a very small or very large number of runs in the residual sequence is an indicator of nonrandomness, that is, of systematic errors in the former and of periodicity in the latter case. For details and examples we refer the reader to Cobelli *et al.* (2001; Chapter 8: Parametric models—the estimation problem).

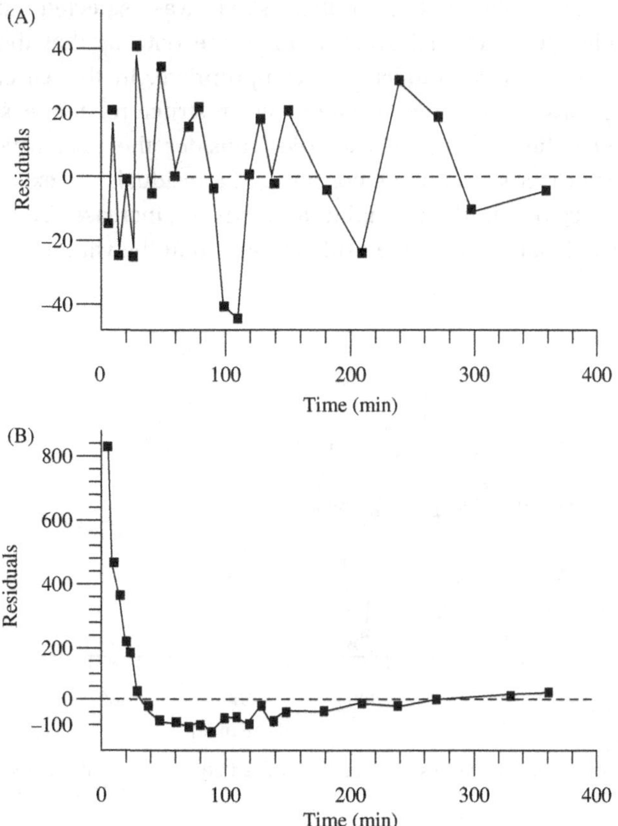

FIGURE 8–3 Plot of residuals versus time: (A) shows a pattern of independent residuals; (B) of correlated residuals. *Adapted from Cobelli et al., 2001.*

In WLS estimation a specific assumption on the variance of the measurement errors has been made. If the model is correct, the residuals must reflect this assumption.

Since:

$$\mathrm{Var}\left(\frac{v_i}{\sigma_i}\right) = \frac{1}{\sigma_i^2}\mathrm{Var}(v_i) = 1 \tag{8.34}$$

if we define the weighted residuals as:

$$\mathrm{wres}_i = \frac{\mathrm{res}_i}{\sigma_i} \tag{8.35}$$

there should be a realization of a random process having unit variance. By plotting the weighted residual versus time, it is thus possible to visually test the assumption on the variance of the measurement error: weighted residuals should lie in a $-1, +1$ wide band. A typical plot of weighted residuals is shown in Fig. 8–4.

A pattern of residuals different from that which was expected, indicates either the presence of errors in the functional description of the data or that the model is correct, but that the measurement error model is not appropriate. In this case, it is necessary to modify the assumptions on the measurement error structure. Some suggestions can be derived by examining the plot. As an example, consider the case where the variance of the measurement error is assumed to be constant. The residuals are expected to be confined in a $-1, +1$ wide region. If their amplitude tends to increase in absolute value with respect to the observed value, a possible explanation is that the variance of the measurement

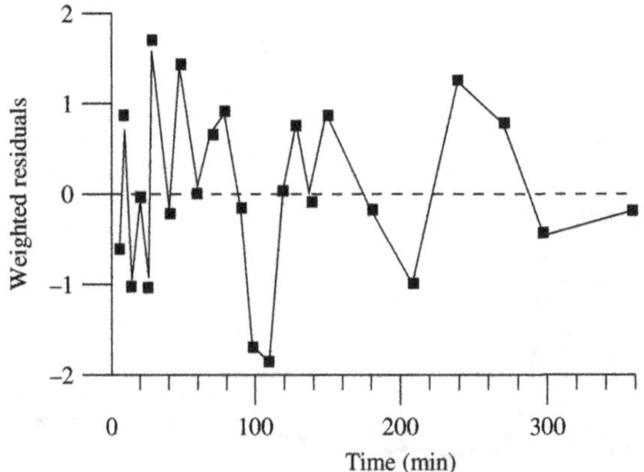

FIGURE 8–4 Plot of weighted residuals versus time. See text for additional explanation. *Adapted from Cobelli et al., 2001.*

error is not constant, thus suggesting a modification of the assumption on the measurement error variance.

A formal test on the variance of weighted residuals based on χ^2 statistics can also be applied; this test is exact for linear regression with Gaussian measurement errors, while it is approximate in the general case. For details and examples we refer the reader to Cobelli *et al.* (2001; Chapter 8: Parametric models—the estimation problem).

8.4.3 An Example

Consider the data shown in Fig. 8–5 (these data have already been shown in Fig. 8–2). Assume that the linear function to be fitted to the data is $y(t) = pt$ and let us consider two different weighting schemes. The fitted data and the linear function prediction are shown in Fig. 8–6A.

In the first weighting scheme, σ^2 was constant and equal to 100, hence the weights (w_i) were constant and equal to 0.01. In the second weighting scheme, $Var(v_i) = z_i \cdot 0.01$.

The assignment of weights has a substantial effect upon the estimate $\hat{A}$ and its estimated standard deviation. The effect of the two weighting schemes can be evaluated by using (8.27) and (8.29). The results are summarized below in Table 8–1.

The plot of residuals for testing independence is shown in Fig. 8–6B: residuals are randomly scattered around the origin. The plot of weighted residuals to test the assumption on the variance of the measurement error is shown in Fig. 8–6C: most weighted residuals lie between −1 and 1, indicating that they are consistent with the above assumption.

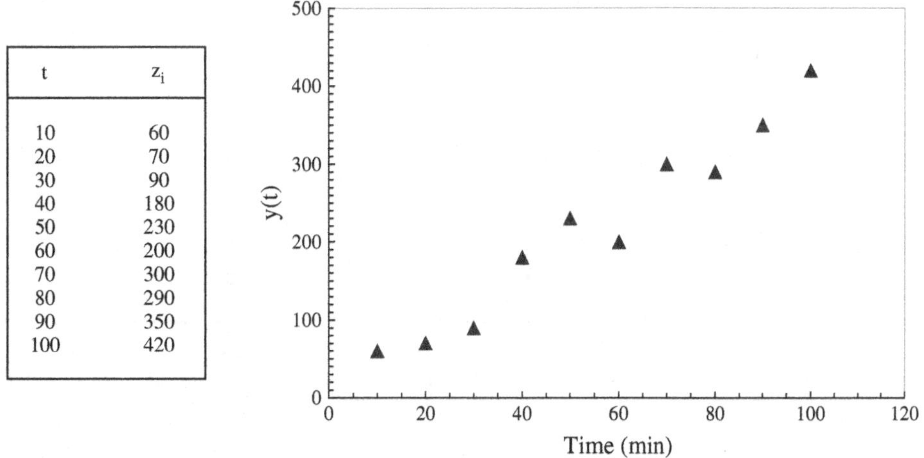

t	z_i
10	60
20	70
30	90
40	180
50	230
60	200
70	300
80	290
90	350
100	420

FIGURE 8–5 A set of data (those of Fig. 8–2) to be fitted with a linear function. *Adapted from Cobelli et al., 2001.*

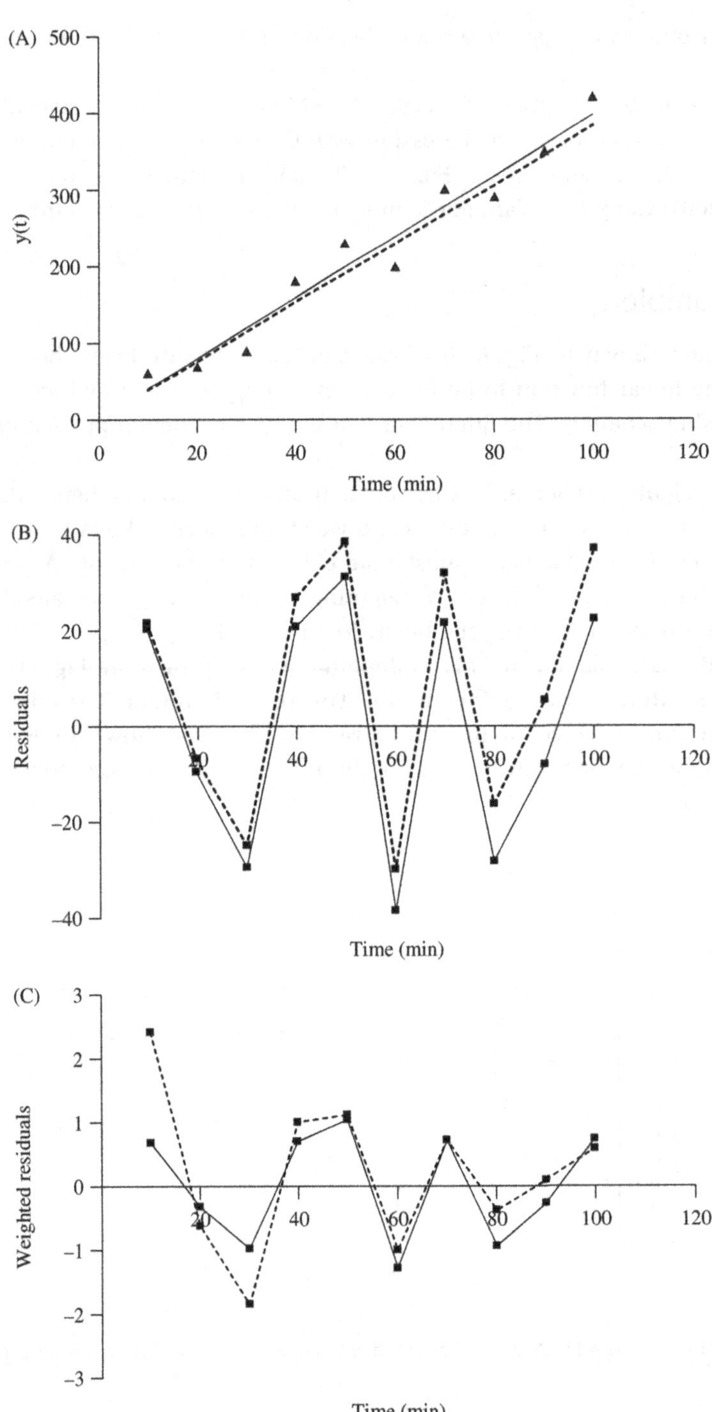

FIGURE 8–6 Effect of two different weighting schemes on parameter estimation. (A) Plot of data versus model fits. The solid line is a plot of $y(t) = 3.977t$ and the dotted line is $y(t) = 3.845t$. (B) Plot of residuals. (C) Plot of weighted residuals. *Adapted from Cobelli et al., 2001.*

Table 8–1 Estimation results for two weighting schemes.

	Constant variance $Var(v_i) = 100$ $w_i = 1/100$	**Constant FSD** $Var(v_i) = z_i^2 \cdot 0.01$ $w_i = 1/(z_i^2 \cdot 0.01)$
$\hat{p}$	3.89	3.75
$Var(\hat{p})$	0.011	0.025
$SD(\hat{p})$	0.105	0.157
$FSD(\hat{p})$	3%	4%
WRSS	41.9	28.58

8.4.4 Extension to the vector case

We have seen in detail the simple case with one parameter:

$$y(t) = p \cdot t \tag{8.36}$$

An easy extension, (and one that will allow us a straightforward handling of the general case), is to two model parameters:

$$y(t) = pt + q \tag{8.37}$$

The measurement equation is:

$$z_i = y_i + v_i = pt_i + q + v_i \tag{8.38}$$

In this case, the weighted residual sum of squares, WRSS, is given by:

$$WRSS = \sum_{i=1}^{N} \frac{1}{\sigma_i^2}(z_i - pt_i - q)^2 \tag{8.39}$$

To get $\hat{p}$ and $\hat{q}$ we follow the same line of reasoning discussed for the model (8.36), and so calculate:

$$\frac{\partial WRSS(p, q)}{\partial p} = 0 \tag{8.40}$$

$$\frac{\partial WRSS(p, q)}{\partial q} = 0 \tag{8.41}$$

and obtain explicit expressions for $\hat{p}$ and $\hat{q}$. We can also calculate $Var(\hat{p})$ and $Var(\hat{q})$, but this time there will be the covariance between $\hat{p}$ and $\hat{q}$ available, $cov(\hat{p}, \hat{q}) = cov(\hat{p}, \hat{q})$.

Let us put this example in compact matrix-vector notation. By writing the measurement Eq. (8.38) for all measurements i = 1,2,. . .,N we get:

$$\begin{bmatrix} z_1 \\ z_2 \\ \cdots \\ \cdots \\ z_{N-1} \\ z_N \end{bmatrix} = \begin{bmatrix} y_1 \\ y_2 \\ \cdots \\ \cdots \\ y_{N-1} \\ y_N \end{bmatrix} + \begin{bmatrix} v_1 \\ v_2 \\ \cdots \\ \cdots \\ v_{N-1} \\ v_N \end{bmatrix} = \begin{bmatrix} t_1 & 1 \\ t_2 & 1 \\ \cdots & \cdots \\ \cdots & \cdots \\ t_{N-1} & 1 \\ t_N & 1 \end{bmatrix} \begin{bmatrix} m \\ q \end{bmatrix} + \begin{bmatrix} v_1 \\ v_2 \\ \cdots \\ \cdots \\ v_{N-1} \\ v_N \end{bmatrix} \tag{8.42}$$

and thus:

$$\mathbf{z} = \mathbf{y} + \mathbf{v} = \mathbf{Gp} + \mathbf{v} \tag{8.43}$$

with:

$$\mathbf{z} = [z_1, z_2, \ldots, z_N]^T \tag{8.44}$$

$$\mathbf{y} = [y_1, y_2, \ldots, y_N]^T \tag{8.45}$$

$$\mathbf{v} = [v_1, v_2, \ldots, v_N]^T \tag{8.46}$$

$$\mathbf{p} = [mq]^T \tag{8.47}$$

$$\mathbf{G} = \begin{bmatrix} t_1 & \cdots & 1 \\ t_2 & \cdots & 1 \\ \vdots & & \vdots \\ t_N & \cdots & 1 \end{bmatrix} \tag{8.48}$$

The measurement error (**v**), assuming a second order description, that is, mean and covariance matrix (N × N), is:

$$E[\mathbf{v}] = 0 \tag{8.49}$$

$$E[\mathbf{v}\mathbf{v}^T] = \mathbf{\Sigma_v} \tag{8.50}$$

Since independence is assumed, $\mathbf{\Sigma_v}$ is diagonal:

$$\mathbf{\Sigma_v} = \mathrm{diag}(\sigma_1^2, \sigma_2^2, \cdots, \sigma_N^2) \tag{8.51}$$

Now it is straightforward to generalize. We can write:

$$\mathbf{v} = \mathbf{y} + \mathbf{v} = \mathbf{Gp} + \mathbf{v} \tag{8.52}$$

$$\begin{bmatrix} z_1 \\ z_2 \\ \cdots \\ \cdots \\ z_N \end{bmatrix} = \begin{bmatrix} y_1 \\ y_2 \\ \cdots \\ \cdots \\ y_N \end{bmatrix} + \begin{bmatrix} v_1 \\ v_2 \\ \cdots \\ \cdots \\ v_N \end{bmatrix} = \begin{bmatrix} g_{11}, g_{12}, \ldots, g_{1M} \\ g_{21}, g_{22}, \ldots, g_{2M} \\ \cdots \\ g_{N1} \qquad g_{NM} \end{bmatrix} \begin{bmatrix} \mathbf{p}_1 \\ \mathbf{p}_2 \\ \cdots \\ \mathbf{p}_M \end{bmatrix} + \begin{bmatrix} \mathbf{v}_1 \\ \mathbf{v}_2 \\ \cdots \\ \cdots \\ \mathbf{v}_N \end{bmatrix} \tag{8.53}$$

with:

$$p = [p_1, p_2 \ldots p_M]^T \tag{8.54}$$

$$\mathbf{G} = \begin{bmatrix} g_{11} & \cdots & g_{1M} \\ \vdots & & \vdots \\ g_{N1} & \cdots & g_{NM} \end{bmatrix} \tag{8.55}$$

Now, if we define the residual vector **r**:

$$\mathbf{r} = \mathbf{z} - \mathbf{Gp} \tag{8.56}$$

the weighted residual sum of squares is:

$$\text{WRSS}(\mathbf{p}) = \sum_{i=1}^{N} \frac{1}{\sigma_i^2} r_i^2 = \mathbf{r}^T \boldsymbol{\Sigma}_v^{-1} \mathbf{r} = (\mathbf{z} - \mathbf{Gp})^T \boldsymbol{\Sigma}_v^{-1} (z - \mathbf{Gp}) \tag{8.57}$$

The WLS estimate of **p** is that which minimizes WRSS(**p**):

$$\hat{\mathbf{p}}_{\text{WLS}} = \arg\min_{p} \text{WRSS}(\mathbf{p}) = \arg\min_{p} \, (\mathbf{z} - \mathbf{Gp})^T \boldsymbol{\Sigma}_v^{-1} (\mathbf{z} - \mathbf{Gp}) \tag{8.58}$$

and we get the expression:

$$\hat{\mathbf{p}}_{\text{WLS}} = (\mathbf{G}^T \boldsymbol{\Sigma}_v^{-1} \mathbf{G})^{-1} \mathbf{G}^T \boldsymbol{\Sigma}_v^{-1} \mathbf{z} \tag{8.59}$$

We can also extend the test of residuals to the vector case and the estimation of the precision of parameter estimates.

As far as the residuals are concerned, since we now have $\hat{\mathbf{p}}$, we can obtain the residuals and the weighted residuals, respectively, as:

$$\mathbf{r} = \mathbf{z} - \mathbf{G}\hat{\mathbf{p}} \tag{8.60}$$

$$\mathbf{wr} = \boldsymbol{\Sigma}_v^{-1} \mathbf{r} \tag{8.61}$$

As far as the precision is concerned, the covariance matrix is:

$$\boldsymbol{\Sigma}_{\tilde{\mathbf{p}}} = \mathrm{cov}(\tilde{\mathbf{p}}) = \mathrm{E}\left[\tilde{\mathbf{p}}\tilde{\mathbf{p}}^T\right] = \boldsymbol{\Sigma}_{\hat{\mathbf{p}}} \tag{8.62}$$

with $\tilde{\mathbf{p}} = \mathbf{p} - \hat{\mathbf{p}}$.

Since $\hat{\mathbf{p}}_{WLS} = (\mathbf{G}^T\boldsymbol{\Sigma}_v^{-1}\mathbf{G})^{-1}\mathbf{G}^T\boldsymbol{\Sigma}_v^{-1}\mathbf{z}$, we get:

$$\tilde{\mathbf{p}} = \mathbf{p} - \hat{\mathbf{p}} = \underbrace{\left[\mathbf{I}_M - (\mathbf{G}^T\boldsymbol{\Sigma}_v^{-1}\mathbf{G})^{-1}\mathbf{G}^T\boldsymbol{\Sigma}_v^{-1}\mathbf{G}\right]\mathbf{p}}_{\text{deterministic}} - \underbrace{(\mathbf{G}^T\boldsymbol{\Sigma}_v^{-1}\mathbf{G})^{-1}\mathbf{G}^T\boldsymbol{\Sigma}_v^{-1}\mathbf{v}}_{\text{random}} \tag{8.63}$$

Where $\boldsymbol{\Sigma}$ is the identity matrix.

By using the definition (8.62), $\boldsymbol{\Sigma}_{\tilde{\mathbf{p}}}$ can be immediately obtained as the covariance of the random addendum:

$$\boldsymbol{\Sigma}_{\tilde{\mathbf{p}}} = (\mathbf{G}^T\boldsymbol{\Sigma}_v^{-1}\mathbf{G})^{-1} = \boldsymbol{\Sigma}_{\hat{\mathbf{p}}} \tag{8.64}$$

8.5 Nonlinear regression

What happens in the case where y(t), instead of being described by a set of linear parameters, has nonlinear parameters as well? The problem of how to estimate the parameters becomes more complex.

In the previous section, the major points were illustrated using the function $y(\mathbf{p},t) = pt$. In this section, the major points will be illustrated using the mono-exponential function $y(t) = g(t, \alpha) = e^{-\alpha t}$ where α is the nonlinear parameter to be estimated. Later in this section, the function $y(t) = g(A, \alpha, t) = Ae^{-\alpha t}$ will be used to then generalize to the vector case. How is the nonlinear case handled? The problem is solved through a number of iterations that draws on the linear regression theory discussed previously.

8.5.1 The scalar case

In this section, the same notation from the previous section will be used where $w_i = 1/\sigma_i^2$ is the weight assigned to each datum (z_i), and the expression to be minimized is:

$$\mathrm{WRSS}(\alpha) \sum_{i=1}^{N} w_i(z_i - y_i)^2 = \sum_{i=1}^{N} w_i(z_i - e^{-\alpha t_i})^2 \tag{8.65}$$

In order to keep the formulae as simple as possible we shall retain w_i in the derivation instead of $1/\sigma_i^2$. As noted previously, y(t) is a nonlinear function of the parameter (α), so an explicit analytical solution for α analogous to (8.27) is not possible. In fact if one takes the derivative of WRSS with respect to α and sets it equal to zero:

$$\frac{dWRSS(\alpha)}{d\alpha} = \frac{d\left(\sum_{i=1}^{N} w_i(z_i - e^{-\alpha t_i})^2\right)}{d\alpha} = 0 \tag{8.66}$$

one obtains:

$$-2\sum_{i=1}^{N} w_i t_i e^{-\alpha t_i}(z_i - e^{-\alpha t_i}) = 0 \tag{8.67}$$

which does not yield an explicit expression for α as a function of the known quantities z_i, t_i, and w_i.

To arrive at an estimate of α, one possible strategy is based on iterative linearizations of the model, that is, the Gauss-Newton method. Let us consider the expression of y(t) obtainable through its Taylor series expansion around a specific value of α, say α^0:

$$y(t) = g(\alpha, t) = g(\alpha^0, t) + \left.\frac{dg(\alpha, t)}{d\alpha}\right|_{\alpha=\alpha^0}(\alpha - \alpha^0) + \frac{1}{2}\left.\frac{d^2g(\alpha, t)}{d\alpha^2}\right|_{\alpha=\alpha^0}(\alpha - \alpha^0)^2 + \cdots \tag{8.68}$$

where the derivatives are evaluated at $\alpha = \alpha^0$. The Taylor series is an infinite series, that is, the expression on the right hand side of (8.68) contains an infinite number of terms. Normally, however, a truncated version of this expression can be used, for example, a finite number of terms of the series given on the right-hand side of (8.68). When this is done, the right-hand side of (8.68) no longer equals y(t) exactly, but approximates it with an approximation that generally improves as more terms of the series are retained.

Now assume that an initial estimate α^0 of α is available. The idea behind linearizing the problem is to assume that the terms in (8.68) which contain derivatives of second order and higher, are small and can be neglected. This means that (8.68) can be re-written as:

$$y_i(t) \approx \left.g(\alpha, t)\right|_{\alpha=\alpha^0} + \left.\frac{dg(\alpha, t)}{d\alpha}\right|_{\alpha=\alpha^0}(\alpha - \alpha^0) = e^{-\alpha^0 t} - te^{-\alpha^0 t}(\alpha - \alpha^0) \tag{8.69}$$

Notice that this equation is now linear in α, since α^0 is known as the assumed initial estimate of α. Define:

$$\Delta\alpha = \alpha - \alpha^0 \tag{8.70}$$

Eq. (8.69) can be re-written for the generic time t_i as:

$$y_i(t) \approx \left.g(\alpha, t)\right|_{\substack{\alpha=\alpha^0 \\ t=t_i}} + \left.\frac{dg(\alpha, t)}{d\alpha}\right|_{\substack{\alpha=\alpha^0 \\ t=t_i}}\Delta\alpha = e^{-\alpha^0 t_i} - t_i e^{-\alpha^0 t_i}\Delta\alpha \tag{8.71}$$

which is an equation linear in $\Delta\alpha$. Assuming that the weights w_i for the data (z_i) are known, one can write the following expression for WRSS(α):

$$\begin{aligned}
\text{WRSS}(\alpha) &= \sum_{i=1}^{N} w_i(z_i - y_i)^2 \\
&\approx \sum_{i=1}^{N} w_i\left(z_i - g(\alpha, t)\Big|_{\substack{\alpha=\alpha^0\\ t=t_i}} - \frac{dg(\alpha, t)}{d\alpha}\Big|_{\substack{\alpha=\alpha^0\\ t=t_i}} \cdot \Delta\alpha\right)^2 \\
&= \sum_{i=1}^{N} w_i(z_i - e^{-\alpha^0 t_i} + t_i \cdot e^{-\alpha^0 t_i}\Delta\alpha)^2
\end{aligned} \tag{8.72}$$

For convenience, define a new term:

$$\Delta z_i = z_i - y(\alpha^0,\ t_i) = z_i - e^{-\alpha^0 t_i} \tag{8.73}$$

Eq. (8.72) can be re-written:

$$\text{WRSS}(\alpha) = \sum_{i=1}^{N} w_i\left(\Delta z_i - \frac{dg(\alpha, t)}{d\alpha}\Big|_{\substack{\alpha=\alpha^0\\ t=t_i}} \Delta\alpha\right)^2 = \sum_{i=1}^{N} w_i(\Delta z_i t_i e^{-\alpha^0 t_i}\Delta\alpha)^2 \tag{8.74}$$

WRSS can now be considered as a linear function of $\Delta\alpha$, and hence $\Delta\alpha$ can be estimated using the linear regression machinery. Briefly, in (8.27), Δz_i is substituted for z_i, and $dg(\alpha,\ t)/d\alpha\Big|_{\substack{\alpha=\alpha^0\\ t=t_i}}$ for t_i. Then, one obtains:

$$\begin{aligned}
\Delta\hat{\alpha} &= \frac{\sum_{i=1}^{N} w_i \Delta z_i (dg(\alpha,\ t)/d\alpha)\Big|_{\substack{\alpha=\alpha^0\\ t=t_i}}}{\sum_{i=1}^{N} w_i\left(dg(\alpha,\ t)/d\alpha\Big|_{\substack{\alpha=\alpha^0\\ t=t_i}}\right)^2} \\
&= \frac{-\sum_{i=1}^{N} w_i \Delta z_i t_i e^{-\alpha^0 t_i}}{\sum_{i=1}^{N} w_i t_i^2 e^{-2\alpha^0 t_i}} \\
&= \frac{-\sum (1/\sigma_i^2)\Delta z_i t_i e^{-\alpha^0 t_i}}{\sum (1/\sigma_i^2) t_i^2 e^{-2\alpha^0 t_i}}
\end{aligned} \tag{8.75}$$

At this stage, a new estimate for α can be obtained:

$$\alpha^1 = \alpha^0 + \Delta\hat{\alpha} \tag{8.76}$$

and the process repeated using α^1 instead of α^0 in the above formulae. WRSS(α^1) is obviously smaller than WRSS(α^0) since $\Delta\alpha$ was chosen to minimize WRSS in the neighborhood of α^0. At each iteration, both the model function $y(t) = g(\alpha, t)$ and its derivative with respect to the parameter (α) need to be evaluated at the sample times.

The iterative process, which technically could go on forever, usually stops when some preset criterion, for example, comparing two consecutive values of WRSS, is satisfied.

The linear regression machinery used to obtain an estimate for α can also be used to obtain an estimate of the precision of this estimate. The extension of the linear WLS equation, (8.62) to the nonlinear case provides [using the rationale behind (8.75)] an estimate of $\text{Var}(\hat{\alpha})$:

$$\text{Var}(\hat{\alpha}) \approx \frac{1}{\sum_{i=1}^{N} \frac{1}{\sigma_i^2} \left(dg(\alpha, t)/d\alpha \Big|_{\substack{\alpha=\hat{\alpha} \\ t=t_i}} \right)^2} \tag{8.77}$$

The derivative term is known:

$$dg(\alpha, t)/d\alpha \Big|_{\substack{\alpha=\hat{\alpha} \\ t=t_i}} = -t_i e^{-\hat{\alpha} t_i} \tag{8.78}$$

Therefore, one has:

$$\text{Var}(\hat{\alpha}) \approx \frac{1}{\sum_{i=1}^{N} (t_i^2/\sigma_i^2) e^{-2\hat{\alpha} t_i}} \tag{8.79}$$

In the case of linear regression, the expressions for $\text{Var}(p)$ is exact, whereas in the case of nonlinear regression, the expression given in (8.77) only provides an approximation for $\text{Var}(\hat{\alpha})$. As far as the residuals and weighted residuals are concerned, the treatment of the linear case in Section 8.4.2 also holds here, with model prediction being produced by $g(\hat{\alpha}, t)$.

The linear machinery has been used to solve the nonlinear case. However, it is worth remarking that the nonlinear case is more complex to handle than the linear case. This is true not only from a computational point of view (see Section 8.5.3), but also conceptually due to presence of local minima of $\text{WRSS}(\alpha)$ and the necessity of specifying an initial estimate of α, and α^0. To graphically illustrate this additional complexity, let us consider $\text{WRSS}(\alpha)$ as a function of α as shown in Fig. 8–7. There is more than one minimum for WRSS, and this is distinctly different from the linear case where there is only one (unique) minimum. The minima shown in Fig. 8–7 are called *local minima.* The difference, then, between the linear and nonlinear case is that in linear regression there is a unique minimum for WRSS, while in the nonlinear case there may be several local minima for WRSS. Among the local minima, the smallest is called the *global minimum.* This has obvious implications for the choice of α^0. Generally, to be sure one is not ending up at a local minimum, several tentative values of α^0 are used as starting points.

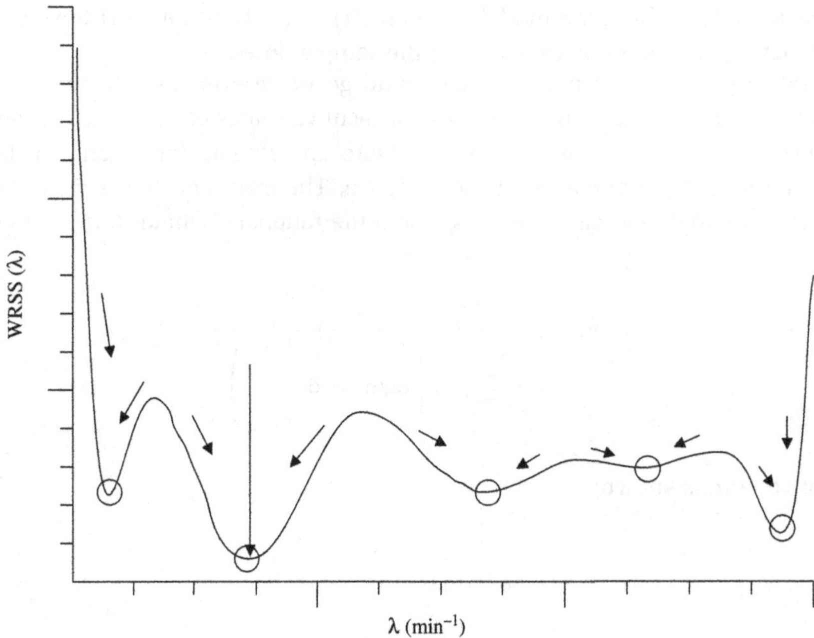

FIGURE 8–7 Plot of WRSS(α) as a function of α illustrating several local minima but only one global minimum over the domain of the function. Notice also that some of the minima are quite well-defined, or sharp, while others are much more gradual. *Adapted from Cobelli et al., 2001.*

8.5.2 Extension to the vector case

Let us now extend the machinery to the case where there is more than one unknown parameter. This will accommodate functions y(t) such as:

$$y(t) = Ae^{-\alpha t} \tag{8.80}$$

or

$$y(t) = A_1 e^{-\alpha_1 t} + A_2 e^{-\alpha_2 t} \tag{8.81}$$

where, in (8.80) there are two parameters, A and α, and in (8.81) there are four, A_1, A_2, α_1, and α_2; the ideas carry over to arbitrary functions y(t) described by a set of parameters $\mathbf{p} = [p_1, p_2, \ldots, p_p]^T$.

To set the scene, let us consider the model of (8.80), that is:

$$y(t) = g(t, \mathbf{p}) = g(t, A, \alpha) = Ae^{-\alpha t} \tag{8.82}$$

Let us assume we have an initial estimate $\mathbf{p}^0 = [A^0, \alpha^0]$. For A and α in the neighborhood of A^0, α^0 one has:

$$g(t, A, \alpha) \cong g(t, A^0, \alpha^0) + \left.\frac{\partial g(t, A, \alpha)}{\partial \alpha}\right|_{\substack{A=A^0 \\ \alpha=\alpha^0}} (\alpha - \alpha^0) + \left.\frac{\partial g(t, A, \alpha)}{\partial A}\right|_{\substack{A=A^0 \\ \alpha=\alpha^0}} (A - A^0) \tag{8.83}$$

where now partial derivatives are used in the Taylor series since we have more than a single parameter, and so we have:

$$g(t, A^0, \alpha^0) = A^0 e^{-\alpha^0 t} \tag{8.84}$$

$$\left.\frac{\partial g(t, A, \alpha)}{\partial \alpha}\right|_{\substack{A=A^0 \\ \alpha=\alpha^0}} = -A^0 t e^{-\alpha^0 t} \tag{8.85}$$

$$\left.\frac{\partial g(t, A, \alpha)}{\partial A}\right|_{\substack{A=A^0 \\ \alpha=\alpha^0}} = e^{-\alpha^0 t} \tag{8.86}$$

Thus, we can write (8.83) as:

$$g(t, A, \alpha) \cong A^0 e^{-\alpha^0 t} - A^0 t e^{-\alpha^0 t}(\alpha - \alpha^0) + e^{-\alpha^0 t}(A - A^0) \tag{8.87}$$

Let us now consider the data:

$$z_i = g(t_i, A, \alpha) + v_i = Ae^{-\alpha t_i} + v_i \tag{8.88}$$

and by using (8.87) one has:

$$z_i = A^0 e^{-\alpha^0 t_{ik}} - A^0 t_i e^{-\alpha^0 t_{ik}} (\alpha - \alpha^0) + e^{-\alpha^0 t_{ik}}(A - A^0) + v_i \tag{8.89}$$

Now, by defining:

$$\Delta z_i = z_i - A^0 e^{-\alpha^0 t_i} \tag{8.90}$$

one has:

$$\Delta z_i = A^0 t_i e^{-\alpha^0 t_i}(\alpha - \alpha^0)\, e^{-\alpha^0 t_i}(A - A^0) + v_i \tag{8.91}$$

If we now further define:

$$\Delta\alpha = \alpha - \alpha^0 \qquad \Delta A = A - A^0 \tag{8.92}$$

one has:

$$\Delta z_i = -A^0 t_i e^{-\alpha^0 t_i} \Delta\alpha + e^{-\alpha^0 t_i} \Delta A + v_i \tag{8.93}$$

and thus, by considering all measurements, we have the matrix vector formulation:

$$\begin{bmatrix} \Delta z_1 \\ \Delta z_2 \\ \cdots \\ \cdots \\ \Delta z_{N-1} \\ \Delta z_N \end{bmatrix} = \begin{bmatrix} e^{-\alpha^0 t_1} & -A^0 t_1 e^{-\alpha^0 t_1} \\ e^{-\alpha^0 t_2} & -A^0 t_2 e^{-\alpha^0 t_2} \\ \cdots & \cdots \\ \cdots & \cdots \\ e^{-\alpha^0 t_{N-1}} & -A^0 t_{N-1} e^{-\alpha^0 t_{N-1}} \\ e^{-\alpha^0 t_N} & -A^0 t_N e^{-\alpha^0 t_N} \end{bmatrix} \begin{bmatrix} \Delta A \\ \Delta \alpha \end{bmatrix} + \begin{bmatrix} v_1 \\ v_2 \\ \cdots \\ \cdots \\ v_{N-1} \\ v_N \end{bmatrix} \tag{8.94}$$

We have now the linear model formulation:

$$\Delta \mathbf{z} = \mathbf{G}\Delta \mathbf{p} + \mathbf{v} \tag{8.95}$$

where $\Delta\mathbf{z}$ is known and $\Delta\mathbf{p}$ unknown. The WLS solution (see 8.59):

$$\Delta \hat{\mathbf{p}} = (\mathbf{G}^T \boldsymbol{\Sigma}_\mathbf{v}^{-1} \mathbf{G})^{-1} \mathbf{G}^T \boldsymbol{\Sigma}_\mathbf{v}^{-1} \Delta \mathbf{z} \tag{8.96}$$

Now, having estimated $\Delta\hat{\mathbf{p}}$, the initial estimate can be improved (we have moved in the parameter space by decreasing WRSS):

$$\mathbf{p}^1 = \mathbf{p}^0 + \Delta \hat{\mathbf{p}} \tag{8.97}$$

and the procedure can be iterated till WRSS (A, α) stops decreasing according to some preset criterion.

Now we are in a position to extend the machinery to the generic nonlinear model $y(t) = g(t,\mathbf{p})$. Paralleling the general linear model development (as described in Section 8.4.4) we have:

$$\mathbf{z} = \mathbf{y} + \mathbf{v} = \mathbf{G}(\mathbf{p}) + \mathbf{v} \tag{8.98}$$

where:

$$\mathbf{z} = [z_1, z_2, \ldots, z_N]^T \tag{8.99}$$

$$\mathbf{y} = [y_1, y_2, \ldots, y_N]^T \tag{8.100}$$

$$p = [p_1, p_2, \ldots, p_N]^T \tag{8.101}$$

$$\mathbf{G}(\mathbf{p}) = [g(t_1,\ \mathbf{p}),\ g(t_2,\ \mathbf{p}), \ldots, g(t_N,\ \mathbf{p})]^T \tag{8.102}$$

$$\mathbf{v} = [v_1, v_2, \ldots, v_N]^T \text{ with } \boldsymbol{\Sigma}_\mathbf{v} = \text{cov}(\mathbf{v}) \tag{8.103}$$

The WLS estimate of $\mathbf{p}$ is the one that minimizes WRSS($\mathbf{p}$):

$$\hat{\mathbf{p}}_{WLS} = \arg\min_p\ [\mathbf{z} - \mathbf{G}(\mathbf{p})]^T \boldsymbol{\Sigma}_\mathbf{v}^{-1} [\mathbf{z} - \mathbf{G}(\mathbf{p})] \tag{8.104}$$

Let us denote with $\mathbf{p}_0$, the initial estimate of $\mathbf{p}$:

$$\mathbf{p}^0 = [p_1^0, p_2^0, \ldots, p_M^0]^T \tag{8.105}$$

The model prediction at time (t_i) is:

$$g(t_i, \mathbf{p}) \cong g(t_i, p^0) + \left[\frac{\partial g(t_i, p^0)}{\partial p_1} \frac{\partial g(t_i, p^0)}{\partial p_2} \cdots \frac{\partial g(t_i, p^0)}{\partial p_M}\right] \begin{bmatrix} p_1 - p_1^0 \\ p_2 - p_2^0 \\ \cdots \\ p_M - p_M^0 \end{bmatrix} \tag{8.106}$$

where notation has been compacted with respect to (8.83) by bringing the $|_{\substack{p=p^0 \\ t=t_i}}$ inside the argument of $g(t, \mathbf{p})$. The data relate with $g(t_k, \mathbf{p})$ as:

$$z_i = g(t_i, \mathbf{p}) + v_i \quad i = 1, 2, \ldots, N \tag{8.107}$$

Thus, using (8.106) and moving to vector notation one has:

$$\begin{bmatrix} z_1 - g(t_1, p^0) \\ z_2 - g(t_2, p^0) \\ z_3 - g(t_3, p^0) \\ \cdots \\ z_N - g(t_N, p^0) \end{bmatrix} = \begin{bmatrix} \frac{\partial g(t_1, p^0)}{\partial p_1} & \frac{\partial g(t_1, p^0)}{\partial p_2} & \cdots & \frac{\partial g(t_1, p^0)}{\partial p_M} \\ \frac{\partial g(t_2, p^0)}{\partial p_1} & \frac{\partial g(t_2, p^0)}{\partial p_2} & \cdots & \frac{\partial g(t_2, p^0)}{\partial p_M} \\ \cdots & \cdots & \cdots & \cdots \\ \cdots & \cdots & \cdots & \cdots \\ \cdots & \cdots & \cdots & \cdots \\ \frac{\partial g(t_N, p^0)}{\partial p_1} & \frac{\partial g(t_N, p^0)}{\partial p_2} & \cdots & \frac{\partial g(t_N, p^0)}{\partial p_M} \end{bmatrix} \begin{bmatrix} p_1 - p_1^0 \\ p_2 - p_2^0 \\ \cdots \\ p_M - p_M^0 \end{bmatrix} + \begin{bmatrix} v_1 \\ v_2 \\ v_3 \\ \cdots \\ v_N \end{bmatrix} \tag{8.108}$$

and thus:

$$\mathbf{\Delta z} = \mathbf{S}\mathbf{\Delta p} + \mathbf{v} \tag{8.109}$$

with obvious definition of $\mathbf{\Delta z}$, **S, and** $\mathbf{\Delta p}$ from (8.109).

Now since $\mathbf{\Delta z}$ ($\mathbf{p}^0$ is given, $\mathbf{z}$ is measured) and $\mathbf{S}$ can be computed, one can use WLS to estimate $\mathbf{\Delta p}$ with the linear machinery:

$$\mathbf{\Delta \hat{p}} = (\mathbf{S}^T \mathbf{\Sigma}_v^{-1} \mathbf{S})^{-1} \mathbf{S}^T \mathbf{\Sigma}_v^{-1} \mathbf{\Delta z} \tag{8.110}$$

Hence, a new estimate of $\mathbf{p}$ can be obtained as:

$$\mathbf{p}^1 = \mathbf{p}^0 + \mathbf{\Delta \hat{p}} \tag{8.111}$$

Now, with $\mathbf{p}^1$, which is by definition a better estimate than $\mathbf{p}^0$, the process can restart: the model is linearized around $\mathbf{p}^1$, a new estimate ($\mathbf{p}^2$) is obtained and so on until the cost function stops decreasing significantly, for example, when two consecutive values of WRSS($\mathbf{p}$) are within a prescribed tolerance.

Once $\Delta\hat{\mathbf{p}}$ has been obtained, by paralleling the general linear model case discussed in Section 8.4.4, one can obtain the covariance of the parameter estimates as:

$$\boldsymbol{\Sigma}_{\hat{\mathbf{p}}} \cong (\mathbf{S}^T\boldsymbol{\Sigma}_v^{-1}\mathbf{S})^{-1} = \boldsymbol{\Sigma}\hat{\mathbf{p}} \tag{8.112}$$

with:

$$\mathbf{S} = \begin{bmatrix} \frac{\partial g(t_1,\hat{p})}{\partial p_1} & \frac{\partial g(t_1,\hat{p})}{\partial p_2} & \cdots & \frac{\partial g(t_1,\hat{p})}{\partial p_M} \\ \frac{\partial g(t_2,\hat{p})}{\partial p_1} & \frac{\partial g(t_2,\hat{p})}{\partial p_2} & \cdots & \frac{\partial g(t_2,\hat{p})}{\partial p_M} \\ \cdots & \cdots & \cdots & \cdots \\ \cdots & \cdots & \cdots & \cdots \\ \cdots & \cdots & \cdots & \cdots \\ \frac{\partial g(t_N,\hat{p})}{\partial p_1} & \frac{\partial g(t_N,\hat{p})}{\partial p_2} & \cdots & \frac{\partial g(t_N,\hat{p})}{\partial p_M} \end{bmatrix} \tag{8.113}$$

Residuals and weighted residuals are defined as for the linear case in Section 8.4.4 (Eqs. 8.60 and 8.61) with model prediction provided by $\mathbf{G}(\hat{\mathbf{p}})$.

8.5.3 Algorithms

The steps of nonlinear least squares estimation have been illustrated using the Gauss–Newton iterative scheme. This outlines the principles of that class of algorithms, which require the computation of derivatives contained in matrix **S**. This is usually done numerically, for example, using central difference methods, albeit other strategies are also available, for example, the sensitivity system (Cobelli *et al.*, 2001; Chapter 10: Model validation). This class is referred to as gradient-type (derivative) algorithms. Numerically refined and efficient algorithms, for example, the Levenberg–Marquardt technique, based on the Gauss-Newton principle, are available and are implemented in many software tools.

Another category of algorithms for minimizing WRSS, which has been applied in physiological model parameter estimation, is one that does not require the computation of the derivatives. These algorithms are known as direct search methods, and both deterministic and random search algorithms are available and implemented in software tools. An efficient deterministic direct search algorithm is the simplex method. It is worth emphasizing that with a direct search method, the computation of the derivatives is not required. Albeit a direct comparison of gradient versus direct search methods is difficult and may be problem dependent, available experience in physiological model parameter estimation tends to favor the gradient type methods.

8.5.4 An example

Consider next the data given in Table 8–2 and assume that a mono-exponential function is to be fitted to the data, $y(t) = Ae^{-\alpha t}$, that is, both A and α need to be estimated from the

Table 8–2 Test data with two descriptions of measurement error.

t_i	z_i	$Var(v_i) = 0.0025w_i$	$Var(v_i) = (0.1 \cdot z_i)^2$
15	0.856	400	136
30	0.797	400	157
60	0.538	400	345
120	0.318	400	989
240	0.133	400	5653
360	0.069	400	21003

Table 8–3 Estimation results with two weighting schemes.

	$Var(v_i) = 0.0025$	$Var(v_i) = (0.1 \cdot z_i)^2$
α	0.00923	0.00808
$Var(\alpha)$	0.593×10^{-6}	0.576×10^{-7}
$SD(\alpha)$	0.77×10^{-3}	0.24×10^{-3}
$FSD(\alpha)$	8%	3%
WRSS	1.94	11.0

data. Consider two situations for the variance of measurement error. In the first there is a constant standard deviation of 0.05 assigned to each datum, while in the second a constant fractional standard deviation equal to 10% is assigned to each datum. The weights are calculated as $w_i = 1/\sigma^2 (t_i)$. The two situations are summarized in Table 8–2.

When the function $y(t) = Ae^{-\alpha t}$ is fitted to these data using the two weighting schemes, estimates of A, α, SD(A), and SD(α) are obtained. Table 8–3 and Fig. 8–8 summarize the results. The estimates of A and α and their precision clearly depend upon the weighting scheme. This observation underlines the importance of having a good knowledge of the error structure in the data.

8.6 Tests for model order

Up to this point, only the problem of testing whether or not a specific model is an appropriate description of a set of data has been examined. Consider now the case where different candidate models are available, and the problem is to select the model that provides the best description of the data. For example, when performing multiexponential modeling of a decay curve:

$$y(t) = \sum_{i=1}^{n} A_i e^{-\lambda_i t} \tag{8.114}$$

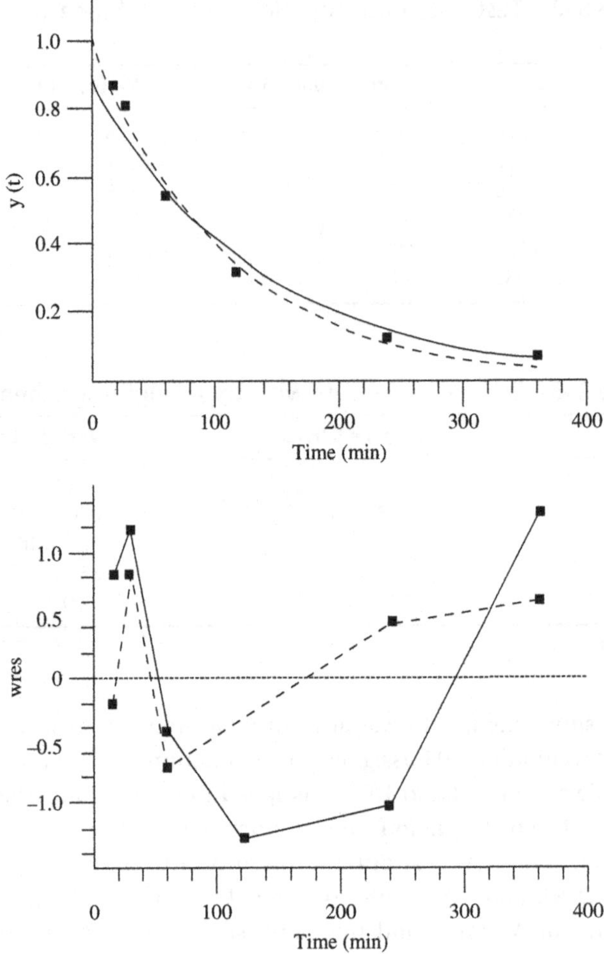

FIGURE 8–8 Upper panel: A plot of a function $y(t) = Ae^{-\alpha t}$ for the case of constant variance (*dashed line*) and constant FSD (*solid line*). Lower panel: A plot of the weighted residuals. *Adapted from Cobelli et al., 2001.*

the model order, that is the number (n) of exponentials, is not known *a priori*. A mono-, bi- and tri-exponential model are usually fitted to the data, and the results of parameter estimation evaluated so as to select the optimum order, that is, the best' value for n.

Relying solely upon WRSS and an examination of the weighted residuals to determine the optimum model order is not appropriate since, as the model order increases, WRSS will decrease. For example, in dealing with a tracer decay curve following a bolus injection, each additional exponential term added to the sum of exponentials will decrease WRSS. Similarly, the pattern of residuals will become more random. However, each time an exponential term is added, two parameters are added (a coefficient and an exponential), and the degrees of freedom are decreased by two. Thus intuitively, when comparing different model structures, both WRSS and the degrees of freedom should be evaluated. This is in order to check whether or not the reduction of WRSS truly reflects a more accurate representation of the data, or whether it is merely the result of the increase in the number of parameters. Hence additional tests are required.

The two tests which are frequently used to compare model structures are the F-test and tests based on the principle of parsimony. We briefly describe below only the latter and refer the readers for illustration of the F-test to Cobelli *et al.* (2001; Chapter 8: Parametric models—the estimation problem).

The most commonly employed tests that implement the principle of parsimony, that is, choose the model which is best able to fit the data with the minimum number of parameters, are the *Akaike information criterion* (AIC) (Akaike, 1974) and the *Schwartz criterion* (SC) (Schwartz, 1978). More than two models can be compared and the model that has the smallest criterion value is chosen as the best.

These criteria have been derived for linear dynamic models in a maximum likelihood estimation context, the principles of which are discussed in the next Section 8.7. However, if one assumes that errors in the data are uncorrelated and Gaussian, then the criteria can also be computed for WLS and are:

$$\mathrm{AIC} = \mathrm{WRSS} + 2\mathrm{P} \tag{8.115}$$

$$\mathrm{SC} = \mathrm{WRSS} + \mathrm{P}\ln\mathrm{N} \tag{8.116}$$

where P is the number of parameters in the model and N are the number of data. While having different derivations, AIC and SC are similar as they are made up of a goodness-of-fit measure plus a penalty function proportional to the number of parameters (P) in the model. Note that in SC, P is weighted ln(N), that is, with large N; this may become important.

To illustrate the use of the criteria based on the parsimony principle let us consider a two- and a three-exponential model as candidates to describe a set of data. Model predictions against data and weighted residuals are shown in Fig. 8–9. Parameter estimates with their precision and WRSS values of the two models are shown in Table 8–4. As expected from theory, the value of WRSS and residuals of the three are lower than those of the two-exponential model, while the parameter estimates that the two-exponential model are more precisely estimated than those of the three-exponential model. Which is the model to adopt? The principle of parsimony tests comes in to play, and in Table 8–4 AIC and SC values are shown: the more parsimonious model is the three-exponential one (lower AIC and SC).

8.7 Maximum likelihood estimation

The least squares approach to estimation requires comparatively little *a priori* knowledge. Apart from having the model and the data, all that is required for full probabilistic treatment is information regarding the measurement errors; that is, the noise model. In contrast, a

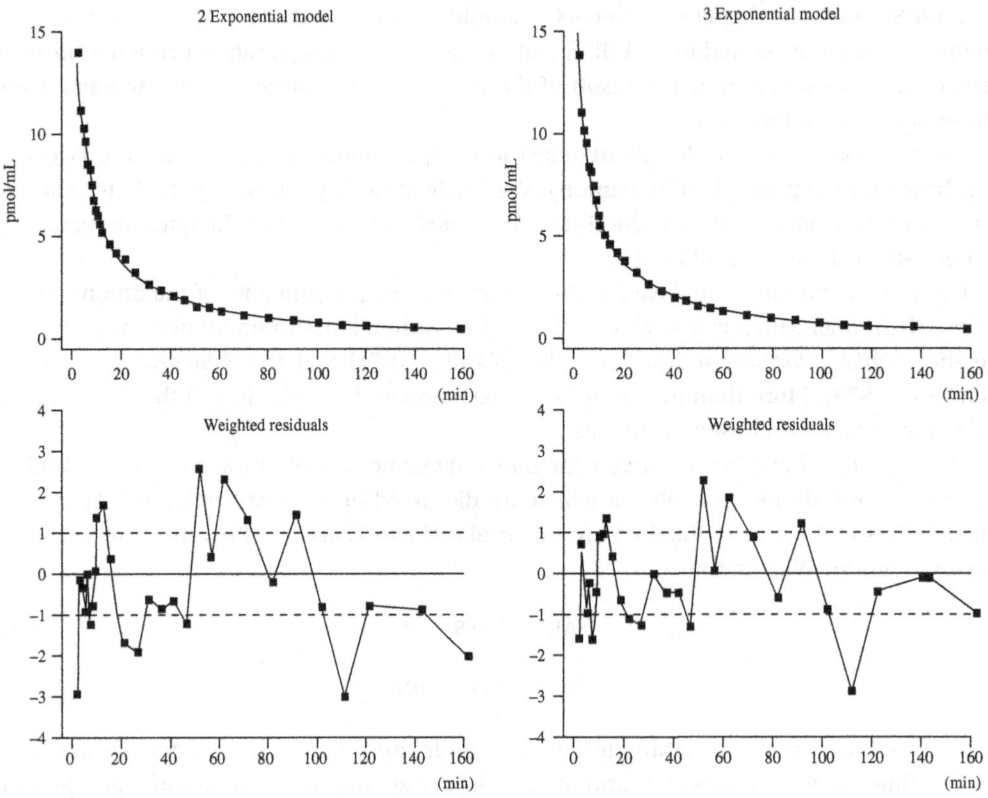

FIGURE 8–9 Left panel: Two-exponential model fit of the data and weighted residuals. Right panel: Three-exponential model fit of the data and weighted residuals. *Adapted from Sparacino et al., 2000.*

Table 8–4 Model order choice based upon the principle of parsimony.

	A_1 (mL)$^{-1}$	A_2 (mL)$^{-1}$	A_3 (mL)$^{-1}$	α_1 (min)$^{-1}$	α_2 (min)$^{-1}$	α_3 (min)$^{-1}$	WRSS	AIC	SC
2 Exponentials	1.79×10^{-4}	0.90×10^{-4}	–	0.141	0.025	–	61	69	75
	(7.2)	(4.8)		(9.2)	(2.5)				
3 Exponentials	1.29×10^{-4}	0.88×10^{-4}	0.81×10^{-4}	0.253	0.085	0.024	40	52	60
	(39)	(66)	(9)	(49)	(40)	(3)			

maximum likelihood (ML) estimation has additional requirements of *a priori* knowledge. Not only is a noise model required, but also a probability density function, defining the generation of the experimental data. ML estimation makes use of this additional information so as to maximize the probability that the parameter estimates achieved would enable the actual experimental data to be recreated.

Let us consider the model of (8.98):

$$\mathbf{z} = \mathbf{y} + \mathbf{v} = \mathbf{G}(\mathbf{p}) + \mathbf{v} \tag{8.117}$$

and assume the probability density function of **v**, $f_{\mathbf{v}}(\mathbf{v})$ is known. Since **v** is random, **z** will also be random with probability density function $f_{\mathbf{z}}(\mathbf{z})$.

To clarify, let us now consider the case where **v** is independent and normally distributed, that is, $\mathbf{v} \in N(0, \Sigma_{\mathbf{v}})$ with $\Sigma_{\mathbf{v}}$ diagonal. Then **z** is also normal:

$$\mathbf{z} \in N(\mathbf{G}(\mathbf{p}), \Sigma_{\mathbf{v}}) \tag{8.118}$$

and:

$$f_{\mathbf{z}}(\mathbf{z}) = \frac{1}{\left[(2\pi)^N \det(\Sigma_{\mathbf{v}})\right]^{1/2}} \exp\left(-\frac{1}{2}[\mathbf{z} - \mathbf{G}(\mathbf{p})]^T \Sigma_{\mathbf{v}}^{-1} [\mathbf{z} - \mathbf{G}(\mathbf{p})]\right) \tag{8.119}$$

It should be noted that $f_{\mathbf{z}}(\mathbf{z})$ is partially unknown since it depends on $\mathbf{G}(\mathbf{p})$, which is unknown and also reflects randomness of **v** through its $f_{\mathbf{v}}(\mathbf{v})$.

What then is the rationale on which ML estimation is based? Let us consider the random vector **z** of (8.117). Since $f_{\mathbf{v}}(\mathbf{v})$ is known, for a given value of **p**, $f_{\mathbf{z}}(\mathbf{z})$ is completely determined as measurements are also known. In other words, for a generic value of **p**, $f_{\mathbf{z}}(\mathbf{z})$ gives the *a priori* probability that the random vector **z** can have as its realization the exact measurements. This quantity, which is called the likelihood of the measurements, varies with **p** and is denoted by $L(\mathbf{p})$. The principle of ML estimation is to choose the value that maximizes the likelihood of the measurements as an estimate of **p**, that is, it renders most plausible the available measurements:

$$\hat{\mathbf{p}}_{ML} = \underset{\mathbf{p}}{\operatorname{argmax}}\, L(\mathbf{p}) \tag{8.120}$$

The solution of (8.120) is normally tackled numerically and it is usual for computational reasons to maximize $\ln L(\mathbf{p})$ instead of $L(\mathbf{p})$ (see below for an example).

It is of interest to see what $L(\mathbf{p})$ becomes if **v** is Gaussian. Consider (8.119) and fix **z** to the measurements. Then the likelihood of the measurements as a function of **p** becomes:

$$L(\mathbf{p}) = \frac{1}{\left[(2\pi)^N \det(\Sigma_{\mathbf{v}})\right]^{1/2}} \exp\left(-\frac{1}{2}[\mathbf{z} - \mathbf{G}(\mathbf{p})]^T \Sigma_{\mathbf{v}}^{-1} [z - G(p)]\right) \tag{8.121}$$

Thus the ML estimate is:

$$\hat{\mathbf{p}}_{ML} = \underset{p}{\operatorname{argmax}} \frac{1}{\left[(2\pi)^N \det(\Sigma_{\mathbf{v}})\right]^{1/2}} \exp\left(-\frac{1}{2}[\mathbf{z} - \mathbf{G}(\mathbf{p})]^T \Sigma_{\mathbf{v}}^{-1} [\mathbf{z} - \mathbf{G}(\mathbf{p})]\right) \tag{8.122}$$

Since $e^{-f(x)}$ is monotonically decreasing, the argument which maximizes $e^{-f(x)}$ is that which minimizes f(x), so one has:

$$\hat{\mathbf{p}}_{ML} = \underset{\mathbf{p}}{\operatorname{argmin}} [\mathbf{z} - \mathbf{G}(\mathbf{p})]^T \Sigma_v^{-1} [\mathbf{z} - \mathbf{G}(\mathbf{p})] \tag{8.123}$$

It is then simple to recognize that (8.122) is the same as (8.104). In other words, for Gaussian and independent measurement errors, the ML and WLS estimates coincide.

The maximum likelihood estimation context allows one to set the precision of parameter estimates within a rigorous framework. Let us define the Fisher information matrix as:

$$\mathbf{F}(\mathbf{p}) = E\left[\frac{\partial \ln L(\mathbf{p})}{\partial \mathbf{p}} \frac{\partial \ln L(\mathbf{p})}{\partial \mathbf{p}}^T\right] \tag{8.124}$$

Then, one has from the Cramér-Rao inequality that:

$$\operatorname{cov}(\tilde{\mathbf{p}}) = \operatorname{cov}(\hat{\mathbf{p}}) \geq [\mathbf{F}(\mathbf{p})|_{\mathbf{p}=\hat{\mathbf{p}}}]^{-1} \tag{8.125}$$

In other words, there is a limit on the achievable precision of parameter estimates which is given by the inverse of the Fisher information matrix.

What kind of expression do we then have for $\mathbf{F}(\mathbf{p})$? Let us consider the case of Gaussian and independent measurement noise $\mathbf{v}$. In this case it is easy to show that:

$$[\mathbf{F}(\mathbf{p})]_{ij} = \sum_{i=1}^{N} \frac{1}{\sigma_i^2} \frac{\partial g(\mathbf{p}, t_i)}{\partial \mathbf{p}_i} \frac{\partial g(\mathbf{p}, t_i)}{\partial \mathbf{p}_j} \tag{8.126}$$

and, thus, in matrix form:

$$\mathbf{F}(\mathbf{p})|_{\mathbf{p}=\hat{\mathbf{p}}} = \mathbf{S}^T \Sigma_v^{-1} \mathbf{S} \tag{8.127}$$

with:

$$\mathbf{S} = \begin{bmatrix} \frac{\partial g(t_1, \mathbf{p})}{\partial \mathbf{p}_1}\big|_{\mathbf{p}=\hat{\mathbf{p}}} & \frac{\partial g(t_1, \mathbf{p})}{\partial \mathbf{p}_2}\big|_{\mathbf{p}=\hat{\mathbf{p}}} & \cdots & \frac{\partial g(t_1, \mathbf{p})}{\partial \mathbf{p}_M}\big|_{\mathbf{p}=\hat{\mathbf{p}}} \\ \frac{\partial g(t_2, \mathbf{p})}{\partial \mathbf{p}_1}\big|_{\mathbf{p}=\hat{\mathbf{p}}} & \frac{\partial g(t_2, \mathbf{p})}{\partial \mathbf{p}_2}\big|_{\mathbf{p}=\hat{\mathbf{p}}} & \cdots & \frac{\partial g(t_2, \mathbf{p})}{\partial \mathbf{p}_M}\big|_{\mathbf{p}=\hat{\mathbf{p}}} \\ \cdots & \cdots & \cdots & \cdots \\ \cdots & \cdots & \cdots & \cdots \\ \cdots & \cdots & \cdots & \cdots \\ \frac{\partial g(t_N, \mathbf{p})}{\partial \mathbf{p}_1}\big|_{\mathbf{p}=\hat{\mathbf{p}}} & \frac{\partial g(t_N, \mathbf{p})}{\partial \mathbf{p}_2}\big|_{\mathbf{p}=\hat{\mathbf{p}}} & \cdots & \frac{\partial g(t_N, \mathbf{p})}{\partial \mathbf{p}_M}\big|_{\mathbf{p}=\hat{\mathbf{p}}} \end{bmatrix} \tag{8.128}$$

As a result one has that:

$$\text{cov}(\tilde{\mathbf{p}}) = \text{cov}(\hat{\mathbf{p}}) \geq (\mathbf{S}^T \Sigma_v^{-1} \mathbf{S})^{-1} \tag{8.129}$$

Thus, approximating the covariance matrix of parameter estimates with $(\mathbf{S}^T \Sigma_v \mathbf{S})^{-1}$, as in WLS, underestimates the effective uncertainty of the parameter estimates.

The ML estimator has important asymptotic (i.e., as $N \rightarrow \infty$) properties for the case of independent and Gaussian measurement error. In particular it is unbiased, normal and efficient, that is, the equality holds in (8.125) and (8.129). Given the equivalence of ML and WLS for independent and Gaussian measurement error, these properties also carry over to WLS. The above are asymptotic properties; in practice the number of measurements is limited and one has to perform Monte Carlo simulation to assess the reliability of the estimator.

8.8 Bayesian estimation

So far we have discussed two methods—nonlinear least squares and maximum likelihood—of the Fisherian approach to parameter estimation. This means that only the data **z** of (8.117) are supplied to the estimator, together with the noise characteristics, in order to estimate the unknown model parameters **p** (Fig. 8–10, upper and middle panels). Here we briefly discuss the Bayesian approach to parameter estimation which takes into account not only the data **z**, but also some *a priori* information available on the unknown parameter vector **p**.

A Bayesian estimation assumes that the *a priori* probability distribution of **p**, $f_{\mathbf{p}}(\mathbf{p})$, is available (Fig. 8–10, lower panel). This knowledge is independent of the data. The basic idea is to exploit the actual data to refine our *a priori* knowledge and obtain the a posteriori probability distribution of **p**, that is, the probability distribution of **p** given the data, $f_{\mathbf{p}|\mathbf{z}}(\mathbf{p}|\mathbf{z})$. How

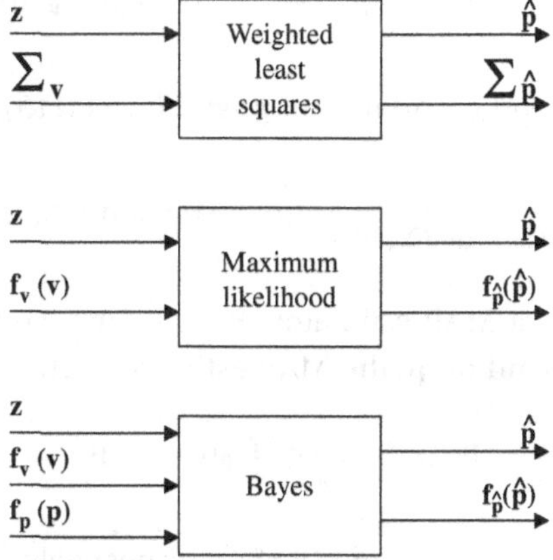

FIGURE 8–10 Comparison of the requirements for weighted least squares, maximum likelihood and Bayesian estimation.

can we obtain $f_{p|z}(\mathbf{p}|\mathbf{z})$? Since the model $\mathbf{G}(\mathbf{p})$ is known (8.117), as is the probability distribution of the noise vector $\mathbf{v}$, $f_v(\mathbf{v})$, we can calculate the probability distribution of the data $\mathbf{z}$ as a function of the parameters $\mathbf{p}$, that is, the likelihood function, $f_{z|p}(\mathbf{z}|\mathbf{p})$. Now, since we know $f_p(\mathbf{p})$ and $f_{z|p}(\mathbf{z}|\mathbf{p})$, Bayes' theorem can be used to obtain $f_{p|z}(\mathbf{p})$:

$$f_{p|z}(\mathbf{p}|\mathbf{z}) = \frac{f_{z|p}(\mathbf{z}|\mathbf{p})f_p(\mathbf{p})}{f_z(\mathbf{z})} = \frac{f_{z|p}(\mathbf{z}|\mathbf{p})f_p(\mathbf{p})}{\int f_{z|p}(\mathbf{z}|\mathbf{p})f_p(\mathbf{p})d\mathbf{p}} \tag{8.130}$$

Once $f_{p|z}(\mathbf{p}|\mathbf{z})$ has been obtained, several point estimators can be defined. Two that are widely used are maximum a posteriori (MAP) and mean square (MS) estimates which are given, respectively, by:

$$\hat{\mathbf{p}}_{MAP} = \arg\max_{\mathbf{p}} f_{p|z}(\mathbf{p}|\mathbf{z}) \tag{8.131}$$

and:

$$\hat{\mathbf{p}}_{MS} = E[\mathbf{p}|\mathbf{z}] = \int \mathbf{p} f_{p|z}(\mathbf{p}|\mathbf{z})) \tag{8.132}$$

In general, an analytic expression for $f_{p|z}$ is either not available or else it is simply intractable. Hence one has to resort to sophisticated numerical simulation techniques known as Markov chain Monte Carlo (Gilks *et al.*, 1995). The description of these techniques is outside the scope of this book but we refer the interested readers to Pillonetto *et al.* (2002a), Pillonetto *et al.* (2006), for an appreciation of these techniques in relation to biomedical modeling.

The expression for $f_{p|z}(\mathbf{p}|\mathbf{z})$ in (8.130) is simplified considerably if specific assumptions regarding the distributions of $\mathbf{v}$, $f_v(\mathbf{v})$, and $\mathbf{p}$, $f_p(\mathbf{p})$, are made. For instance, let us assume that both $\mathbf{v}$ and $\mathbf{p}$ are independent and normally distributed (8.118). Then we have:

$$f_p(\mathbf{p}) = \frac{1}{[(2\pi)^N \det(\Sigma_p)]^{1/2}} \exp\left(-\frac{1}{2}(\mathbf{p}-\mu_p)^T \Sigma_p^{-1}(\mathbf{p}-\mu_p)\right) \tag{8.133}$$

with μ_p and Σ_p as the mean and covariance of $\mathbf{p}$, and (see 8.119):

$$f_{z|p}(\mathbf{z}|\mathbf{p}) = \frac{1}{[(2\pi)^N \det(\Sigma_v)]^{1/2}} \exp\left(-\frac{1}{2}[\mathbf{z}-\mathbf{G}(\mathbf{p})]^T \Sigma_v^{-1}[\mathbf{z}-\mathbf{G}(\mathbf{p})]\right) \tag{8.134}$$

Suppose now that we choose a MAP estimator (8.131). First we note that since the denominator of (8.130) does not depend on $\mathbf{p}$, the MAP estimate is given by:

$$\hat{\mathbf{p}}_{MAP} = \underset{\mathbf{p}}{\operatorname{argmax}}\, f_{z|p}(\mathbf{z}|\mathbf{p}) \cdot f_p(\mathbf{p}) \tag{8.135}$$

with $f_{z|p}(\mathbf{z}|\mathbf{p})$ and $f_p(\mathbf{p})$ given by (8.134) and (8.133), respectively.

By using a reasoning similar to that used and adopted in deriving the ML estimate (8.123), we get:

$$\hat{\mathbf{p}}_{MAP} = \underset{p}{\arg\min}\, [\mathbf{z}-\mathbf{G}(\mathbf{p})]^T \boldsymbol{\Sigma}_v^{-1}[\mathbf{z}-\mathbf{G}(\mathbf{p})] + (\mathbf{p}-\mu_\mathbf{p})^T \boldsymbol{\Sigma}_\mathbf{p}^{-1}(\mathbf{p}-\mu_\mathbf{p}) = \underset{p}{\arg\min}\, \mathbf{J}(\mathbf{p}) \tag{8.136}$$

where the first addendum in the argument is an *a posteriori* information term (the data) and the second an *a priori* one (our expectation on **p**).

The MAP estimator thus realizes a compromise between *a priori* and *a posteriori* information. For instance, if *a priori* information is poor, that is, $\boldsymbol{\Sigma}_\mathbf{p}$ is large, the second term becomes negligible and one has the situation in which the MAP estimate coincides with ML:

$$\hat{\mathbf{p}}_{MAP} = \underset{p}{\arg\min}\, [\mathbf{z}-\mathbf{G}(\mathbf{p})]^T \boldsymbol{\Sigma}_v^{-1}[\mathbf{x}-\mathrm{G}(\mathbf{p})] = \hat{\mathbf{p}}_{ML} \tag{8.137}$$

This is also true in general (above we have made the assumption of normality). In fact, if we consider the definition of the MAP estimate (8.131) and consider a situation of poorer and poorer *a priori* information, $\mathbf{f_p(p)}$ will tend to a uniform distribution (Fig. 8–11). In other words, it is like not having *a priori* information, and the MAP estimate of (8.136) then coincides with the ML estimate of (8.123).

The statistical information characterizing a MAP estimate is similar to that considered in the Fisherian approach; that is, confidence intervals for the parameter estimates can be derived to assess precision, and parsimony principle criteria for model order selection are available. One that is frequently used is the generalized information criterion (GEN-IC):

$$\text{GEN-IC} = \frac{2M}{N} + \mathbf{J}(\hat{\mathbf{p}}_{MAP}) \tag{8.138}$$

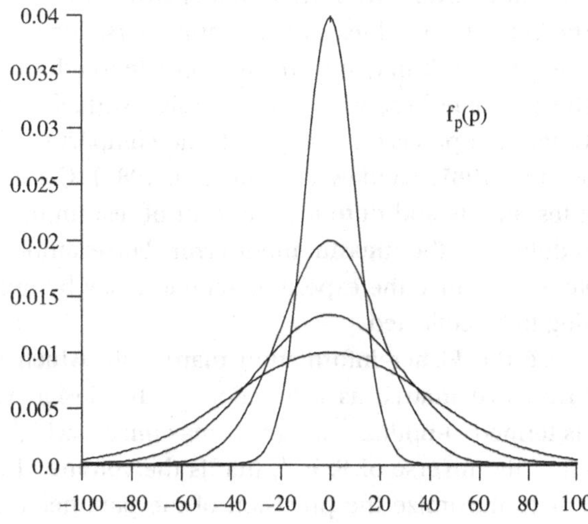

FIGURE 8–11 Distribution of $f_p(p)$ as affected by poorer *a priori* information (a scalar case is considered).

Table 8–5 Comparison of ML and MAP estimation.

	A_1 (mL)$^{-1}$	A_2 (mL)$^{-1}$	A_3 (mL)$^{-1}$	α_1 (min)$^{-1}$	α_2 (min)$^{-1}$	α_3 (min)$^{-1}$	WRSS
WLS	1.29×10^{-4}	0.88×10^{-4}	0.81×10^{-4}	0.253	0.085	0.024	40
(ML)	(39)	(66)	(9)	(49)	(40)	(3)	
MAP	1.51×10^{-4}	0.93×10^{-4}	0.74×10^{-4}	0.283	0.074	0.023	48
	(13)	(10)	(7.5)	(12)	(11.8)	(2.9)	

In general, with respect to ML, MAP estimation worsens the fit [the second term in (8.136) is positive], but precision improves.

As a case in point, we can revisit the example that was considered in Section 8.6. The three-exponential model performance can be improved if we have some *a priori* knowledge regarding the parameters. Table 8–5 shows the MAP results for the three-exponential model obtained by assuming that $\boldsymbol{\mu}_\mathbf{p}$ and $\boldsymbol{\Sigma}_\mathbf{p}$ were known from previous population studies. Also shown for comparison are the WLS results (or ML since we assumed measurement errors to be independent and Gaussian) which were already reported in Table 8–4. Precision improves with point estimates remaining very similar. Weighted residuals are shown in Fig. 8–12, demonstrating that they are virtually the same as those obtained by WLS/ML estimation.

Examples of situations in which the Bayesian approach is particularly helpful are presented in Chapter 11, Case studies.

8.9 Optimal experimental design

We have now reached the stage where we have a model structure, a description of the measurement error, and the numerical values of our parameters, together with the precision with which they can be estimated. It may now be appropriate to address the issue of *optimal experimental design*. The rationale here is to act on design variables in order to maximize, according to some criterion, the precision with which the compartmental model parameters can be estimated (DiStefano, 1981; Landaw & DiStefano, 1984). Candidate design variables include the number of test inputs and outputs, the form of test inputs, the number of samples and sampling schedule, and the measurement error. For example, in clinical studies it may be highly desirable to minimize the experimental effort, say by minimizing the number of blood samples needing to be collected.

The approach is to use the Fisher information matrix (**F**), which is the inverse of the lower bound of the covariance matrix, as a function of the design variables. Usually the determinant of **F** (this is termed D-optimal design) is maximized, which corresponds to minimizing the determinant of the inverse of **F**, $\mathbf{F}^{-1}$, that is the volume of the asymptotic confidence region for **p**, so as to maximize the precision of the parameter estimates, and hence numerical identifiability.

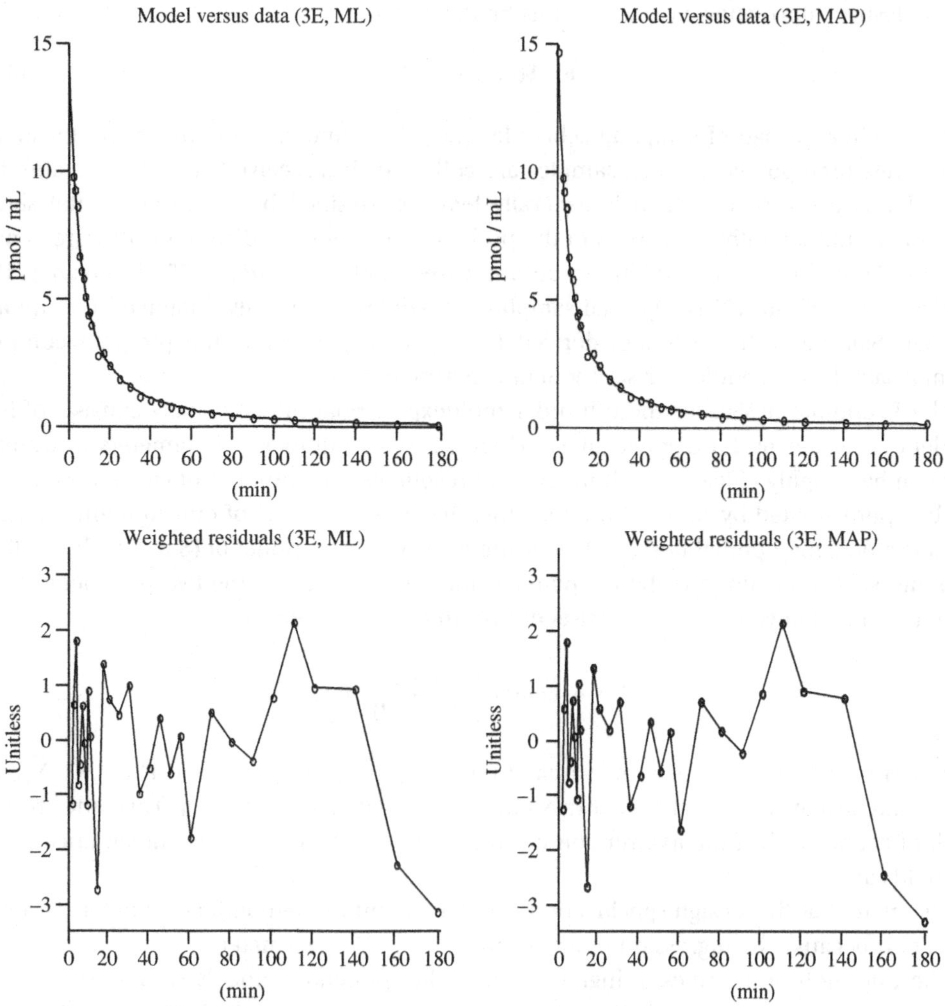

FIGURE 8–12 Example of the fitting of data to a three-exponential (3E) model demonstrating the patterns of weighted residuals obtained with ML (left) and MAP (right) estimation.

Let us define the principal variables of the experimental design, considering the scalar case, as follows:

a) the form of the test signal u (e.g., injection, infusion, or combination of such signals);
b) the duration of the time over which the output variable is measured T;
c) the number of samples, N, obtained during T;
d) the sampling schedule SS, that is where the samples are located in T (i.e., the choice of $t_1, t_2, \ldots, t_k, \ldots, t_N$); and
e) the variance of the measurement errors, Σ_v.

The Fisher information matrix can thus be defined as:

$$\mathbf{F} = \mathbf{F}(u, T, N, SS, \boldsymbol{\Sigma}_v) \tag{8.139}$$

The optimal design of sampling schedules (i.e., determining the number and location of the discrete time points at which samples are collected) has received considerable attention, since this is the variable which is generally least constrained by the experimental setting. Theoretical and algorithmic aspects of the problem have been studied, and software is available for both the single- and multi-output cases (Cobelli *et al.*, 1985; DiStefano, 1981; Landaw & DiStefano, 1984). Optimal sampling schedules are usually obtained in an iterative manner. Starting with the model derived from pilot experiments, the program computes optimal sampling schedules for subsequent experimentation.

The D-optimal design for the nth order multiexponential model usually consists of independent replicates at 2M distinct times, where M is the number of parameters to estimate. This can be a highly efficient result in terms of resources. In a number of cases these designs can be approximated by rules of thumb, which have become part of our intuition for selecting and modifying optimal designs. Under the error variance model of (8.22), with $\alpha = 0$ and time interval from t_0 up to t_f, the D-optimal sampling schedule for the two-parameter monoexponential model $y(t) = A_1 e^{\lambda 1t}$ consists of two times $t_1^* = t_o$ and:

$$t_2^* = \text{minimum}\left\{\frac{t_0 + 2}{(\lambda_1(\gamma - 2))}, t_f\right\}.$$

Note that for $\gamma = 0$ (constant error variance), the spacing between t_1^* and t_2^* is $(-1/\lambda_1)$, and for $\gamma = 2$ (constant CV error) t_2^* is always chosen at the maximum time t_f. This latter result is valid, of course, only if the assumption of no constant background constant variance $(\alpha = 0)$ still holds at t_f.

Also note that this design specification is independent of the nominal value for parameter A_1, in part because the regression model is linear in the A_1 parameter.

The extension of the rules to higher-order multiexponential models is more difficult, but hints are given in Landaw and DiStefano (1984). In general for a single input-single output, linear dynamic model with M parameters, the D-optimal design consists of M distinct samples with independent replicates at the M points. This allows improvement to be made in the precision by a factor (m) for the variance and $\sqrt{m}$ for the CV.

The adoption of optimal sampling schedule design has been shown to enhance the precision of estimated parameters as compared to designs that have been arrived at by intuition or some other means. The approach has also been shown to enhance the cost-effectiveness of a dynamic clinical test by reducing the number of blood samples withdrawn from a patient without significantly reducing the precision with which model parameters have been obtained.

For instance, in Cobelli and Ruggeri (1989), the four parameters of a glucose tracer kinetic model have been estimated in humans with a frequent sampling schedule consisting of 19/35 samples (considered as the reference) and compared with those obtained with an optimal population four sample schedule. In each individual the parameters estimated using the four sample and the 19/35 samples schedule were fairly close: the mean absolute percentage difference from the reference of the four estimated parameters was 18%, 15%, 9%, and 4%. The precision of the estimated parameters was obviously lower with the four sample as compared to the reference schedule, but still satisfactory: mean coefficient of variation was for the four parameters 20 versus 12 (reference), 21 versus 11, 17 versus 9 and 4 versus 3, respectively. This means that with four replicates at the four optimal points, it is possible to achieve a precision virtually identical to that obtained with the full 19/35 sample reference schedule.

8.10 Summary

This chapter has focused on the problem of assigning numerical values to the unknown parameters of a structural model, given that relevant experimental data are available for this purpose. The concept of linear and nonlinear parameters has been introduced, followed by a discussion of the basic concepts of regression analysis. This led on to a consideration of linear and nonlinear least squares estimation. Discussion of maximum likelihood and Bayesian estimation then followed. The chapter concluded with a discussion of the related issue of optimal experimental design. Having dealt with structural models in this chapter, Chapter 9, Nonparametric models—signal estimation, will go on to consider signal estimation in the context of nonparametric models.

8.11 Exercises and assignment questions

a) Discuss the relative advantages of weighted least squares and least squares parameter estimation.
b) Weighted least squares parameter estimation for a model that is nonlinear in the parameters is more difficult than for models that are linear in the parameters. Discuss why this is the case.
c) The first criterion with which to judge whether or not a specific system model is a reliable description of the data is the test on residuals. Discuss why residuals should be independent, and why weighted residuals should lie in a $-1, +1$ wide band.
d) Discuss the relative merits of least squares, maximum likelihood and Bayesian approaches to parameter estimation in the context of physiological modeling.
e) Discuss the rationale of optimal experiment design and formalize it.

9 Nonparametric models—signal estimation

9.1 Introduction

Just as many parameters (the subject of Chapter 8: Parametric models—the estimation problem) are not directly measurable *in vivo*, the same is true of many signals that are of interest for the quantitative understanding of physiological systems. Examples include the secretion rate of a gland, the production rate of a substrate, or the appearance rate of a drug in plasma after an oral administration. Very often, it is only possible to measure the causally-related effects of these signals in the circulation, for example, the time course of plasma concentrations. Thus, there must be reconstruction of the unknown causes, for example, hormone secretion rate, from the measured effects, for example, hormone plasma concentration.

This is referred to as an inverse problem. If the unknown signal is the input of the system, the inverse problem is an input estimation problem (refer back to Fig. 4–29), which in the case of a linear time-invariant system is called deconvolution. As already discussed in Chapter 4, Modeling the data, Section 4.9.2, deconvolution is known to be an ill-posed and ill-conditioned problem and dealing with physiological signals adds to the complexity of the problem. In this chapter we discuss these difficulties in a formal manner and describe a classic nonparametric regularization method to handle these difficulties.

9.2 Why is deconvolution important?

One could argue that the measurement of a concentration time series in plasma provides sufficient information on the system of interest, for example, for understanding its basic mechanisms or for diagnostic and therapeutic purposes. In other words, there would be no need to solve for u(t) in the integral (Eq. (4.29)):

$$c(t) = \int_0^t g(t-\tau)u(\tau)d\tau \tag{9.1}$$

since the samples of c(t) would do the job. There is no question that concentration time series, that is, the samples of c(t), contain precious information; we discussed in Chapter 4, Modeling the data a number of methods to extract important quantitative information from them. However, these concentration signals also reflect, in addition to the substance secretion/production process of interest, its distribution and metabolism in the organism, that is, its kinetics. In fact, the substance kinetics can play a very important role since they can

Introduction to Modeling in Physiology and Medicine. DOI: https://doi.org/10.1016/B978-0-12-815756-5.00009-6

render the measured plasma concentration signal very different from that of the signal we are interested in, that is, the secretion/production flux, with obvious consequences on inference from data analysis.

Let us illustrate this aspect with the simulated example of Fig. 9–1. The input u(t) is common to two systems, one characterized by a fast impulse response, $g(t) = e^{-\alpha t}$ with $\alpha = 12$

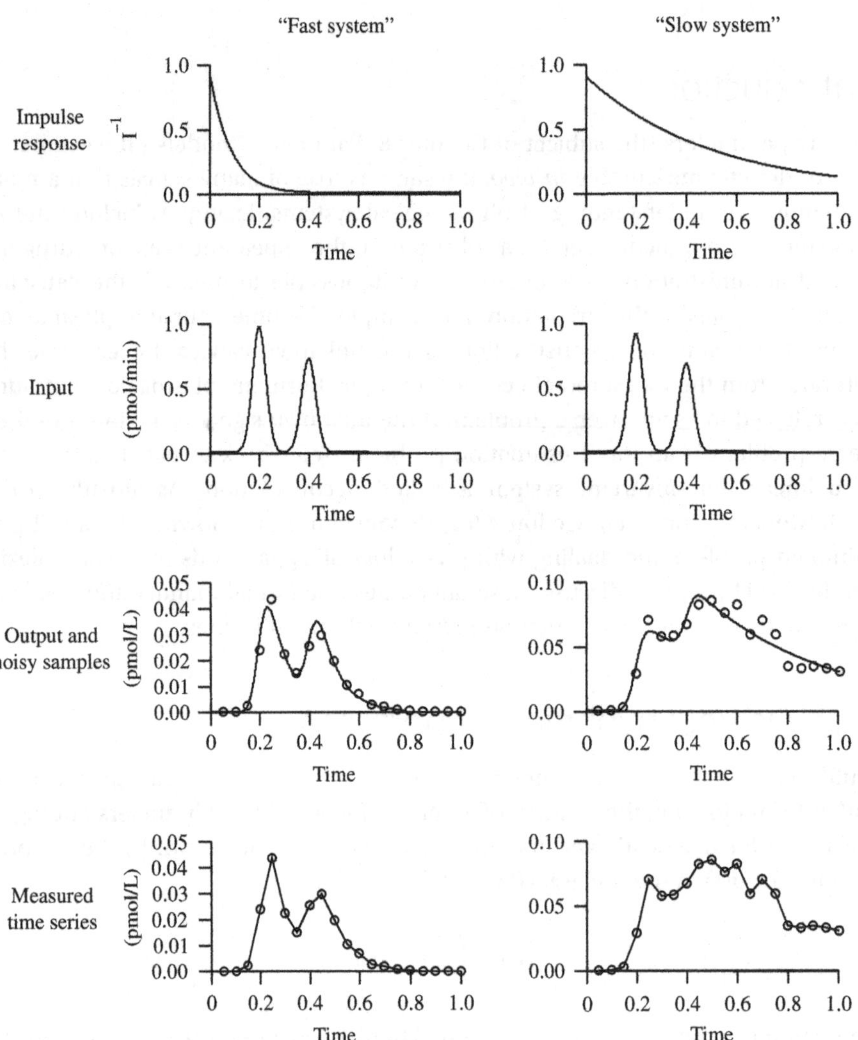

FIGURE 9–1 Influence of substance kinetics on concentration time series. *Left and right panels* describe a fast and a slow system, respectively. From *top to bottom panels*: impulse response, input, continuous output (*continuous line*), noisy samples (*open circles*), and measurement time series (*open circles*, interpolation also shown) are shown, respectively. *Adapted from Sparacino, G., Pillonetto, G., De Nicolao, G., & Cobelli, C. (2004). Deconvoluzione per l'analisi di segnali fisiologici. In S. Cerutti & C. Marchesi (Eds.),* Metodi Avanzati di Elaborazione di Segnali Biomedici *(pp. 163–188). Bologna: Patron.*

(left panels), and the other by a slow one, that is, $g(t) = e^{-\alpha t}$ with $\alpha = 2$ (right panels). This makes the two outputs c(t) calculated by convolution from u(t) and g(t) very different (central panels, continuous lines): the slow system shows a second peak higher than the first one, while the true input shows the opposite. The situation is further worsened if we consider discrete sampling and measurement noise (central panels, open circles). The investigator only "sees" the measured time series redrawn and interpolated in the bottom panels: the "fast" system shows the two original peaks while the "slow" system only shows a single bell-shaped peak. The lesson of the simulated example shown in Fig. 9–1 is pretty clear: there is a need to remove the distortion introduced by the kinetics of the substance by estimating the input.

9.3 The problem

We solve (9.1) for the unknown input, u(t), from the knowledge of the output of the system, c(t), and the impulse response of the system, g(t). In real world problems, only a finite number of output samples can be measured; and the impulse response g(t) is a model (often a sum of exponentials) either identified through a specific input-output experiment or obtained from population studies.

In (9.1) it is implicitly assumed that u(t) is causal, that is, $u(t) = 0$ for $t < 0$. In several cases, this is not true, as when a basal spontaneous hormone secretion also occurs for $t < 0$. There are several ways to approach this problem, see for instance Sparacino *et al.* (2001).

It is worth noting that due to the symmetry of (9.1) with respect to g(t) and u(t), a deconvolution problem also arises whenever the impulse response g(t) of the system given the input u(t) and the output c(t) is estimated. For instance, the transport function of a substance through an organ can be estimated by deconvolution of the inlet and outlet concentrations (Sparacino *et al.*, 1998). Hereafter, we address only the input estimation problem.

Finally, we will assume the system to be linear and time invariant. There are situations where this is not the case; that is, the system is linear time-varying. In such situations the input estimation problem becomes that of solving a Fredholm integral equation of the first kind:

$$c(t) = \int_0^t g(t, \tau)u(\tau)d\tau \tag{9.2}$$

The function $g(t,\tau)$ is called the kernel of the system and depends on both t and τ and not on their difference as in (9.1). In particular, the function $g(t, \tau_0)$ describes the time course of the output when the system is forced by a unitary pulse input $\delta(\tau_0)$ given at time τ_0. For instance, the reconstruction of hepatic glucose production after a glucose perturbation can be stated as a Fredholm integral equation of the first kind, where the kernel $g(t,\tau)$ is described by a linear two-compartment model of glucose kinetics with time-varying parameters (Caumo & Cobelli, 1993; Vicini *et al.*, 1999). In the literature, the solution of the Fredholm integral equation of the first kind is usually also called (albeit improperly) deconvolution.

9.4 Difficulty of the deconvolution problem

In the mathematics/physics/engineering literature, deconvolution is known to be difficult because such problems tend to be ill-posed and ill-conditioned. Here, we discuss these analytical difficulties of input estimation by using a classic example of the literature (Hunt, 1971), hereafter referred to as the *Hunt simulated problem.* Consider the input given by:

$$u(t) = e^{-[(t-400/75)]^2} + e^{-[(t-600/75)]^2}, \quad 0 \le t \le 1025 \tag{9.3}$$

and the impulse response of the system given by:

$$g(t) = \begin{Bmatrix} 1, & t \le 250 \\ 0, & t > 250 \end{Bmatrix} \tag{9.4}$$

These functions do not necessarily have a physiological counterpart. Knowing u(t) and g(t), c(t) can be obtained, assume that N samples of c(t), $\{c_k\}$ where $c_k = c(t_k)$, are measured without error on the uniform sampling grid $\Omega_s = \{kT\}$, $k = 1, \ldots, N$, with $T = 25$ and $N = 41$. The input u(t), the impulse response g(t), and the output c(t) together with the samples $\{c_k\}$ are shown in Fig. 9–2 upper panel: left and right; middle: right, respectively.

The problem of reconstructing the continuous-time function u(t) from the time series $\{c_k\}$ can be shown not to result in a unique solution (Bertero, 1989). This will be illustrated below by making reference to the least squares deconvolution technique. Thus the problem has, in addition to the true solution, others such as the staircase function (Fig. 9–2, middle panel, left), the convolution of which with the impulse response g(t) perfectly describes the output data $\{c_k\}$. More precisely, there is an infinite number of continuous-time functions that, once convoluted with the impulse response, perfectly describe the sampled data. Therefore the deconvolution problem is an *ill-posed* problem.

To tackle ill-posedness, any deconvolution approach must in some way restrict the field of the functions among which the solution of the problem is sought. For instance, in *discrete deconvolution* the signal u(t) is assumed to be a piecewise constant within each interval of the sampling grid $\Omega_s = [t_1, t_2, \ldots, t_N]$, that is, $u(t) = u_i$; for $t_{i-1} \le t \le t_i$, $i = 1, 2, \ldots, N$, where $t_0 = 0$. From (9.1) it follows that:

$$c(t_k) = \int_0^{t_k} g(t_k - \tau) \cdot u(\tau) \cdot d\tau = \sum_{i=1}^{k} u_i \cdot \int_{t_{i-1}}^{t_i} g(t_k - \tau) \cdot d\tau \tag{9.5}$$

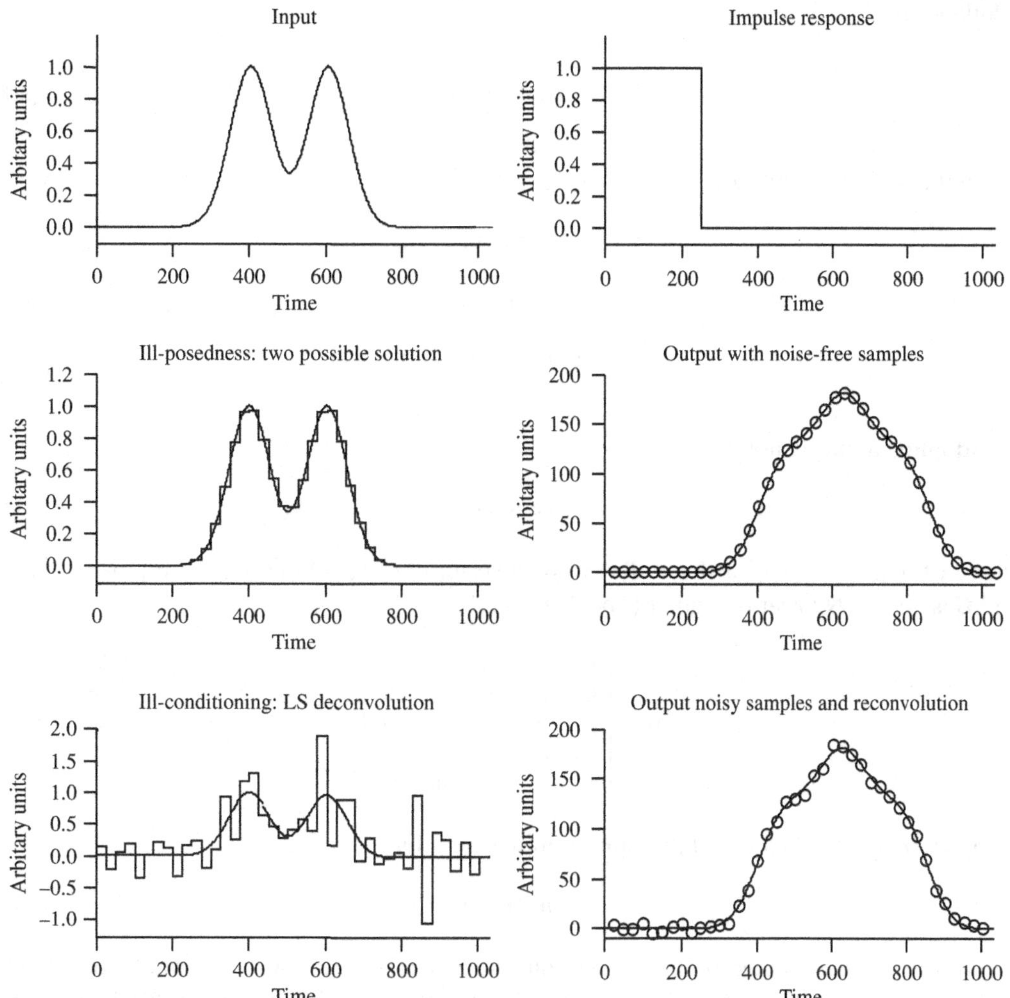

FIGURE 9–2 The Hunt simulated problem. *Upper panels*: True input (*left*) and impulsive response (*right*). Middle panels: Ill-posedness. The staircase function (*left, thick line*) is a solution of the problem with error-free data like the true input (*left, thin line*), that is, it perfectly describes the sampled data (*right, open circles*, N = 41). The true continuous output is also shown (*right, continuous line*). *Lower panels*: Ill-conditioning. Solution provided by LS deconvolution versus true input (*left, thick* vs *thin line*) from the noisy (SD = 3) sampled data (*right, open circles*). Also shown is reconvolution (*right, continuous line*). *Adapted from Sparacino, G., Pillonetto, G., De Nicolao, G., & Cobelli, C. (2004). Deconvoluzione per l'analisi di segnali fisiologici. In S. Cerutti & C. Marchesi (Eds.),* Metodi Avanzati di Elaborazione di Segnali Biomedici *(pp. 163–188). Bologna: Patron.*

One may also think of u_i as being the mean level of u(t) during the ith sampling interval. By letting:

$$g_{k-i} = \int_{t_{i-1}}^{t_i} g(t-\tau) \cdot d\tau \tag{9.6}$$

it follows that:

$$c_k = c(t_k) = \sum_{i=1}^{k} u_i \cdot g_{k-i} \tag{9.7}$$

So that the first terms are:

$$c_1 = g_0 \cdot u_1 \tag{9.8}$$

$$c_2 = g_0 \cdot u_2 + g_1 \cdot u_1 \tag{9.9}$$

$$c_3 = g_0 \cdot u_3 + g_1 \cdot u_2 + g_2 \cdot u_1 \\ \vdots \tag{9.10}$$

Adopting a matrix notation:

$$\mathbf{c} = \mathbf{G}\mathbf{u} \tag{9.11}$$

where $\mathbf{c} = [c_1, c_2, \ldots, c_N]^T$ is the N-dimensional vector of sampled output, $\mathbf{u} = [u_1, u_2, \ldots, u_N]^T$, and $\mathbf{G}$ is an $N \times N$ lower triangular (Toeplitz) matrix:

$$\mathbf{G} = \begin{bmatrix} g_0 & 0 & 0 & 0 & 0 \\ g_1 & g_0 & 0 & 0 & 0 \\ g_2 & g_1 & g_0 & 0 & 0 \\ \cdots & \cdots & \cdots & \cdots & \cdots \\ g_N & \cdots & g_2 & g_1 & g_0 \end{bmatrix} \tag{9.12}$$

Since $\mathbf{G}$ is invertible, (9.11) provides a unique solution:

$$\hat{\mathbf{u}} = \mathbf{G}^{-1}\mathbf{c} \tag{9.13}$$

For the Hunt simulated problem, this solution is displayed in Fig. 9–2, middle panel: left. It should be noted that, given the ill-posed nature of the problem, this profile is only one possible solution of the deconvolution problem with noise-free data. Once convoluted with g (t), the staircase function perfectly describes the output samples just as the true input, providing an accurate approximation, apart from the staircase approximation.

Eq. (9.11) addresses the noise-free situation. However, output samples are usually affected by measurement error (Fig. 9–3), and this dramatically enhances the difficulty of the deconvolution problem. Let z_k denote the kth measurement:

$$z_k = c_k + v_k \quad k = 1, 2, \ldots, N \tag{9.14}$$

where v_k is the error. Thus, in vector notation:

$$\mathbf{z} = \mathbf{G} \cdot \mathbf{u} + \mathbf{v} \tag{9.15}$$

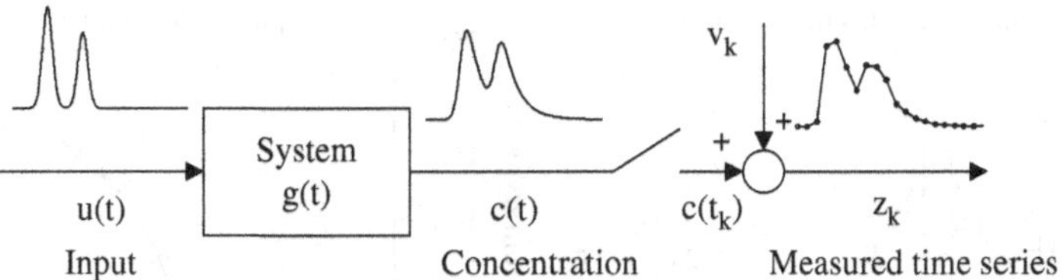

FIGURE 9–3 Output samples and measurement error.

where $\mathbf{z} = [z_1, z_2, \ldots, z_N]^T$ and $\mathbf{v} = [v_1, v_2, \ldots, v_N]^T$. Let us assume $\mathbf{v}$ to be of zero mean and independent with covariance matrix Σ_v given by (8.50). The simplest estimate of $\mathbf{u}$ from data $\mathbf{z}$ is achieved by resorting to least squares parameter estimation, that is, to solve the least-squares (LS) problem:

$$\min_u (\mathbf{z} - \mathbf{G}\,\mathbf{u})^T \textstyle\sum_v^{-1} (\mathbf{z} - \mathbf{G} \cdot \mathbf{u}) \tag{9.16}$$

The solution of (9.16) is [see Chapter 8: Parametric models—the estimation problem (8.59)]:

$$\hat{\mathbf{u}}_{LS} = \left(\mathbf{G}^T \textstyle\sum_v^{-1} \mathbf{G}\right)^{-1} \mathbf{G}^T \textstyle\sum_v^{-1} \mathbf{z} = \mathbf{G}^{-1} (\mathbf{G}^T \textstyle\sum_v^{-1})^{-1} \mathbf{G}^T \textstyle\sum_v^{-1} \mathbf{z} = \mathbf{G}^{-1} \mathbf{z} \tag{9.17}$$

since $\mathbf{G}$ is square and invertible.

In this case reconvolution, that is, the prediction of the output z(t) in (9.1) by using $\hat{u}_{LS}(t)$:

$$z(t) = \int_0^t g(t - \tau) \cdot \hat{u}_{LS}(\tau) \cdot d\tau \tag{9.18}$$

perfectly describes the sampled data, that is, the residual vector $\mathbf{r} = \mathbf{z} - \mathbf{G}\ \hat{\mathbf{u}}_{LS}$ is identically zero.

The presence of noise in the measurement vector ($\mathbf{z}$) (9.15) has a dramatic effect on the quality of the estimate. In Fig. 9–2 (lower panel: right) Gaussian noise (standard deviation SD = 3) was added to the data of the Hunt simulated problem and LS deconvolution was performed (Fig. 9–2, lower panel: left). Note that wide, spurious, and unrealistic oscillations contaminate the estimated input, which also takes on negative values. The reason for this deterioration is that deconvolution is not only ill-posed but is also an ill-conditioned problem. Small errors in the observed data can be amplified, thus yielding much larger errors in the estimates.

It could be hypothesized that increasing the number of samples would be beneficial to the solution of the problem. On the contrary, both theory and practice show that increasing the sampling rate worsens the ill-conditioning. In addition, the slower the system (i.e., the smoother the impulse response), the worse the ill-conditioning for the same sampling frequency. This is well-exemplified in Fig. 9–4 again on the Hunt simulated problem. For the sake of clarity, we report in the top panels and the lower panels of Fig. 9–2, that is, those corresponding to a sampling period of T = 25. The middle panels refer to the same impulsive

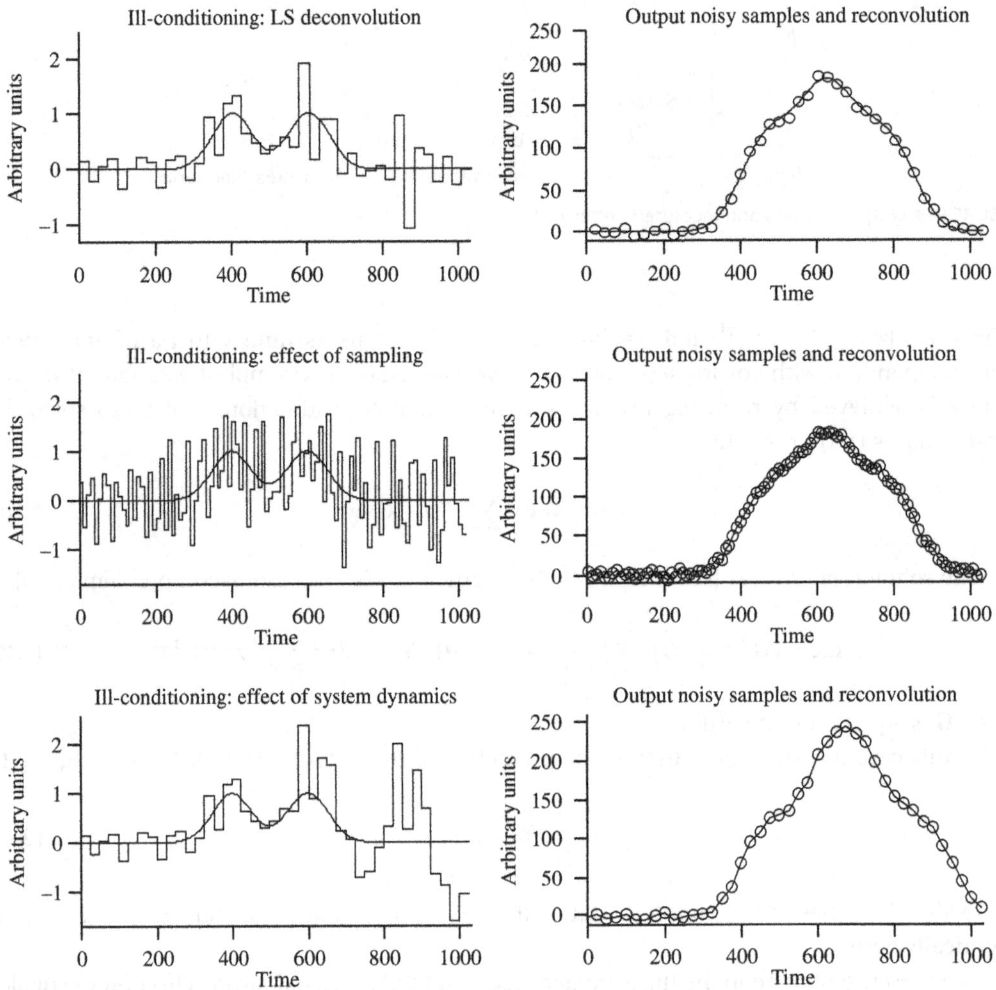

FIGURE 9–4 The Hunt simulated problem. Effect of sampling frequency and system dynamics. *Upper panels*: Lower panels of Fig. 9–2 are reported for sake of comparison. *Middle panels*: Effect of an increased sampling frequency. LS deconvolution versus true input (*left, thick* vs *thin line*) from noisy (SD = 3) samples (*right, open circles*, N = 102). Also shown is reconvolution (*right, continuous line*). *Lower panels*: Effect of a slower dynamics. LS deconvolution versus true input (*left, thick* vs *thin line*) from noisy (SD = 3) samples (*right, open circles*, N = 41). Also shown is reconvolution (*right, continuous line*). *Adapted from Sparacino, G., Pillonetto, G., De Nicolao, G., & Cobelli, C. (2004). Deconvoluzione per l'analisi di segnali fisiologici. In S. Cerutti & C. Marchesi (Eds.),* Metodi Avanzati di Elaborazione di Segnali Biomedici *(pp. 163–188). Bologna: Patron.*

response and measurement error (SD = 3) of the top panels, but the sampling period is now T = 10 (vs 25). The lower panels refer to a slower system (g(t) lasts 400 instead of 250) with the original sampling period (T = 25) and measurement error (SD = 3). This means, for example, that the longer the hormone half-life and the higher the sampling rate, the more difficult the reconstruction of the hormone secretion rate by deconvolution.

The conceptual difficulties described above made the deconvolution problem a classic of the engineering/mathematics/physics literature. Unfortunately, dealing with physiological signals adds to the complexity of the problem. For instance, parsimonious sampling schemes are needed to cope with technical and budget limitations as well as patient comfort. Consequently, the data are often collected with infrequent and nonuniform sampling schedules. Among other things, nonuniform sampling hinders the possible use of frequency domain techniques such as Wiener filtering. Furthermore, physiological inputs are often intrinsically nonnegative (e.g., hormone secretion or substrate production rate). Thus, negative input estimates due to ill-conditioning are physiologically implausible. Finally, physiological systems are sometimes time-varying, for example, the glucose-insulin system during a glucose perturbation.

Least square deconvolution is appealingly simple but weak because it is too sensitive to ill-conditioning. In the literature many methods have been developed to circumvent ill-conditioning. Broadly speaking, these methods can be divided into two categories. The first, named *parametric deconvolution*, assumes the analytical expression of the input to be known except for a small number of parameters, so that the deconvolution problem becomes one of parameter estimation. A second, often referred to as *nonparametric deconvolution*, does not require an analytical form of the input to be postulated. The best known nonparametric approach is the regularization method. A deterministic version of this will be described in detail in the next section.

9.5 The regularization method

9.5.1 Fundamentals

The regularization method is a nonparametric approach (Phillips, 1962; Tikhonov, 1963). The idea of the method is to identify a solution that provides not a perfect fit to the data (like LS deconvolution) but rather a good data fit and one that simultaneously enjoys a certain degree of smoothness. This is done by solving the optimization problem:

$$\min_{\mathrm{u}} (\mathbf{z}-\mathbf{G}\cdot\mathbf{u})^{\mathrm{T}} \sum\nolimits_{\mathrm{v}}^{-1} (\mathbf{z}-\mathbf{G}\cdot\mathbf{u}) + \gamma \mathbf{u}^{\mathrm{T}}\mathbf{F}^{\mathrm{T}}\mathbf{F}\mathbf{u} \tag{9.19}$$

where $\mathbf{\Sigma_v}$ is the covariance matrix of the measurement error, $\mathbf{F}$ is a $\mathrm{N} \times \mathrm{N}$ penalty matrix (see below), and γ is a real nonnegative parameter (see below).

The problem posed in (9.19) is quadratic and its solution is:

$$\hat{\mathbf{u}} = \left(\mathbf{G}^{\mathrm{T}} \sum_{\mathbf{v}}^{-1} \mathbf{G} + \gamma \mathbf{F}^{\mathrm{T}}\mathbf{F}\right)^{-1} \mathbf{G}^{\mathrm{T}} \sum_{0}^{-1} (\mathbf{z}-\mathbf{G}\cdot\mathbf{u}) + \gamma \mathbf{u}^{\mathrm{T}}\mathbf{F}^{\mathrm{T}}\mathbf{F}\mathbf{u} \sum_{\mathbf{v}}^{-1} \mathbf{z} \tag{9.20}$$

which depends linearly on the vector data $\mathbf{z}$.

Note that, if $\gamma = 0$, (9.19) and (9.20) coincide with (9.16) and (9.17), respectively, and the LS solution is obtained. When $\gamma > 0$, the cost function (9.19) is made up of two terms. The first one penalizes the distance, weighted by the inverse of $\mathbf{\Sigma_v}$, between the model prediction

Gu (the reconvolution vector) and the data. The second contribution $\mathbf{u}^T\mathbf{F}^T\mathbf{F}\mathbf{u}$, is a term that penalizes the 'roughness' of the solution. The standard choice is to penalize the energy of the m-th order time derivative, with m being an integer parameter. Usually the energy of the first or second derivatives is considered. How is F built in order to achieve this? Let us consider the case of uniform sampling (in what follows we shall remove this assumption). **F** is built so that **Fu** gives the m-th differences of **u** (m = 1, 2, ...), that is, one has:

$$\mathbf{F} = \mathbf{D}^m \tag{9.21}$$

$$\mathbf{D} = \begin{bmatrix} 1 & 0 & 0 & \cdots & 0 \\ -1 & 1 & 0 & \cdots & 0 \\ 0 & -1 & 1 & \cdots & 0 \\ \cdots & \cdots & \cdots & \cdots & \cdots \\ 0 & \cdots & \cdots & -1 & 1 \end{bmatrix} \tag{9.22}$$

As an illustration let us consider the case where the energy of the first derivatives is penalized, that is, m = 1. In this case:

$$\mathbf{F} = \begin{bmatrix} 1 & 0 & 0 & \cdots & 0 \\ -1 & 1 & 0 & \cdots & 0 \\ 0 & -1 & 1 & \cdots & 0 \\ \cdots & \cdots & \cdots & \cdots & \cdots \\ 0 & \cdots & \cdots & -1 & 1 \end{bmatrix} \tag{9.23}$$

and thus **Fu** with **F** = **D** gives the first differences of **u**:

$$\mathbf{D}\mathbf{u} = \begin{bmatrix} 1 & 0 & 0 & \cdots & 0 \\ -1 & 1 & 0 & \cdots & 0 \\ 0 & -1 & 1 & \cdots & 0 \\ \cdots & \cdots & \cdots & \cdots & \cdots \\ 0 & \cdots & \cdots & -1 & 1 \end{bmatrix} \begin{bmatrix} u_1 \\ u_2 \\ u_3 \\ \cdots \\ u_N \end{bmatrix} = \begin{bmatrix} u_1 \\ u_2 - u_1 \\ u_3 - u_2 \\ \cdots \\ u_N - u_{N-1} \end{bmatrix} \tag{9.24}$$

If the energy of the second derivatives is penalized, that is, m = 2, one has:

$$\mathbf{F} = \begin{bmatrix} 1 & 0 & 0 & \cdots & 0 \\ -2 & 1 & 0 & \cdots & 0 \\ 1 & -2 & 1 & \cdots & 0 \\ \cdots & 1 & -2 & \cdots & 0 \\ \cdots & \cdots & \cdots & \cdots & \cdots \\ 0 & \cdots & 1 & -2 & 1 \end{bmatrix} \tag{9.25}$$

and thus **Fu** with $\mathbf{F} = \mathbf{D}^2$ gives the second differences of **u**:

$$\mathbf{D}^2\mathbf{u} = \mathbf{D}(\mathbf{D}\mathbf{u}) = \begin{bmatrix} 1 & 0 & 0 & \dots & 0 \\ -1 & 1 & 0 & \dots & 0 \\ 0 & -1 & 1 & \dots & 0 \\ \dots & \dots & \dots & \dots & \dots \\ 0 & \dots & \dots & -1 & 1 \end{bmatrix} \begin{bmatrix} u_1 \\ u_2 - u_1 \\ u_3 - u_2 \\ \dots \\ u_N - u_{N-1} \end{bmatrix} = \begin{bmatrix} u_1 \\ u_2 - 2u_1 \\ u_3 - 2u_2 + u_1 \\ \dots \\ u_N - 2u_{N-1} + u_{N-2} \end{bmatrix} \tag{9.26}$$

The relative weight given to data and solution regularity is governed by the so-called *regularization parameter,* γ. By increasing γ, the cost of roughness increases and the data match becomes relatively less important. Conversely, by decreasing the value of γ the cost of roughness is lowered, and the fidelity to the data becomes relatively more important. The choice of regularization parameter is a crucial problem: values of γ that are too large will lead to very smooth estimates of $\hat{\mathbf{u}}$ which may not be able to explain the data (over-smoothing), while values of γ that are too small will lead to ill-conditioned solutions of $\hat{\mathrm{u}}$ that accurately fit the data but exhibit spurious oscillations due to their sensitivity to noise (for $\gamma \to 0$ the LS solution is approached).

The importance of the choice of γ is demonstrated by the profiles reported in Fig. 9–5 (left panels) for the Hunt simulated problem (right panels display how well the estimated input, once convoluted with the impulse response, matches the data). Too small of a value of γ produces an input estimate $\hat{\mathbf{u}}$ which suffers from noise amplification due to ill-conditioning (under-smoothing) while too high of a value produces an estimate of $\hat{\mathbf{u}}$ that is, too regular and hence is not able to explain the data (over-smoothing).

9.5.2 Choice of the regularization parameter

In the literature, several criteria have been proposed for the choice of the regularization parameter γ such as: discrepancy; cross-validation and generalized cross-validation; unbiased risk; minimum risk; and L-curve (see Sparacino *et al.*, 2001 for references). Below we only describe the popular discrepancy criterion (Twomey, 1965) which suggests the following. Let us compare the residual vector:

$$\mathbf{r} = \mathbf{z} - \mathbf{G}\hat{\mathbf{u}} \tag{9.27}$$

where **r** depends on γ.

Since from (9.15) one has:

$$\mathbf{v} = \mathbf{z} - \mathbf{G}\mathbf{u} \tag{9.28}$$

the residual vector **r** can be thought of as an estimate of the measurement error vector (**v**), that is,

$$\hat{\mathbf{v}} = \mathbf{r} \tag{9.29}$$

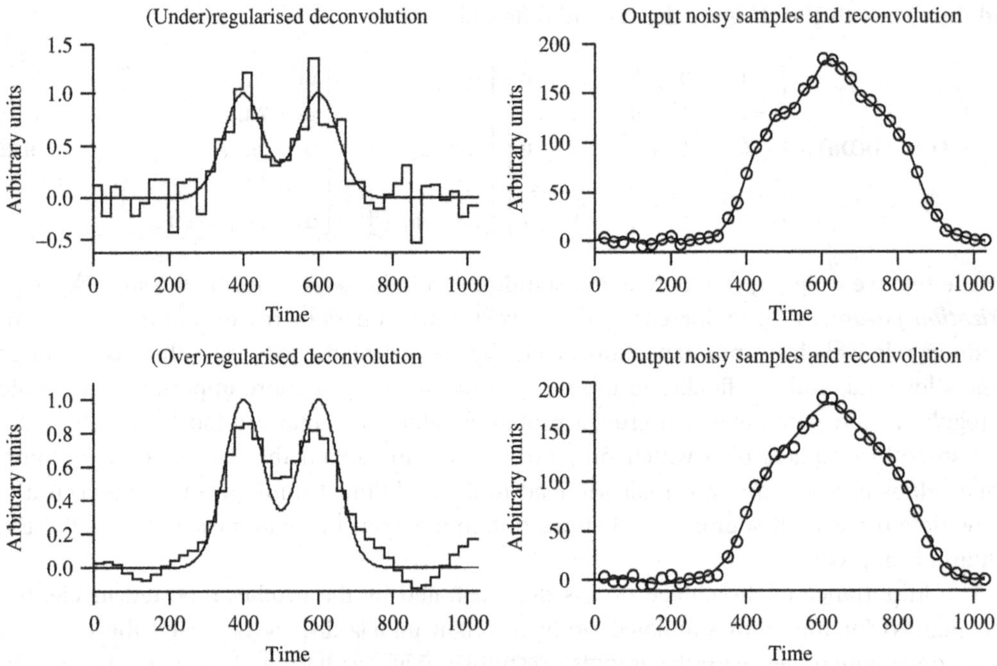

FIGURE 9–5 The Hunt simulated problem. *Upper panels*: Regularized deconvolution versus true input (*left, thick* vs *thin line*) obtained with too small a value of the regularization parameter ($\gamma = 5$) from the noisy data (*right, open circles*). Also shown is reconvolution (*right, continuous line*). *Lower panels*: Regularized deconvolution versus true input (*left, thick* vs *thin line*) obtained with too large a value of the regularization parameter ($\gamma = 400$) from the noisy data (*right, open circles*). Also shown is reconvolution (*right, continuous line*). *Adapted from Sparacino, G., Pillonetto, G., De Nicolao, G., & Cobelli, C. (2004). Deconvoluzione per l'analisi di segnali fisiologici. In S. Cerutti & C. Marchesi (Eds.),* Metodi Avanzati di Elaborazione di Segnali Biomedici *(pp. 163–188). Bologna: Patron.*

Thus it is logical to expect that:

$$\mathbf{r}^T\mathbf{r} \cong E[\mathbf{v}^T\mathbf{v}] \tag{9.30}$$

Since $\mathbf{r}^T\mathbf{r}$ depends on γ, one has to adjust γ iteratively until:

$$\sum_{i=1}^{N} r_i^2 \cong \text{trace}\left(\sum_v\right) = \sum_{i=1}^{N} \sigma_i^2 \tag{9.31}$$

Examples of the use of the Phillips-Tikhonov regularization method with the discrepancy criterion are shown in Figs. 9–6–9–8 (left panels). In Fig. 9–6, results of the Hunt simulation problem are shown, which are definitely better than those of Fig. 9–5 where the regularization parameter γ was chosen empirically. Figs. 9–7 and 9–8 are two physiological case studies on insulin and LH oscillations, respectively.

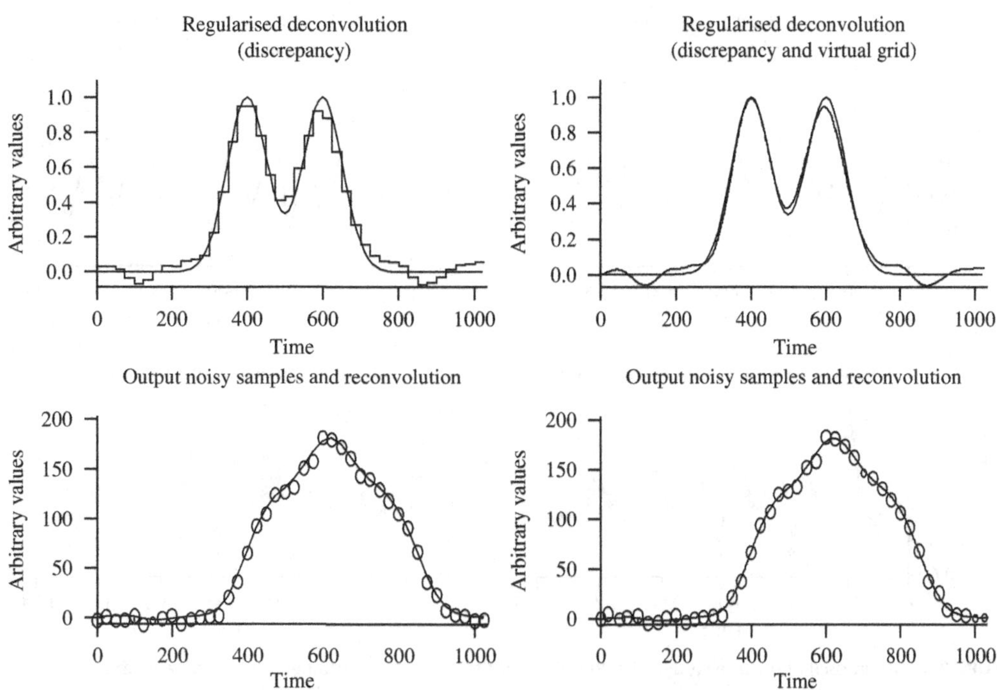

FIGURE 9–6 The Hunt simulated problem. *Left panels*: Regularized deconvolution versus true input (*upper, thick* vs *thin line*) obtained with the value of the regularization parameter determined by the discrepancy criterion ($\gamma = 105$) from the noisy samples (*lower, open circles*). Also shown is reconvolution (*lower, continuous line*). *Right*: Same as left by employing the virtual grid ($\gamma = 1237455$).

9.5.3 The virtual grid

Physiological signals are often sampled at a low and often nonuniform rate. The regularization method is based on the discrete model, (9.7), which was derived assuming that the unknown input is constant during each sampling interval, no matter how long. In the infrequent sampling case, this results in a poor approximation of the signal. For instance, consider the problem of estimating insulin secretion rate from an intravenous glucose tolerance test. Fig. 9–9 (left, upper panel) shows the secretion profile obtained by deconvolution from plasma C-peptide data (left, bottom panel) using the C-peptide impulse response. Due to the infrequent sampling, the staircase approximation is hardly acceptable. The roughness of the staircase approximation can also be appreciated by examining the deconvoluted profiles obtained for the Hunt simulated problem, in both the ideal (Fig. 9–2, middle panel, left) and noisy case (Fig. 9–2, bottom panel, left and Fig. 9–5, left panels).

Such an unsatisfactory performance is due to the fact that the number of components of the unknown vector (**u**) is assumed to be equal to the number (N) of measurements. To remove this assumption, a different discretization grid can be used for the input and the output. Let Ω_S be the (experimental) sampling grid and $\Omega_V = \{T_1, T_2, \ldots, T_k, \ldots, T_V\}$ a finer

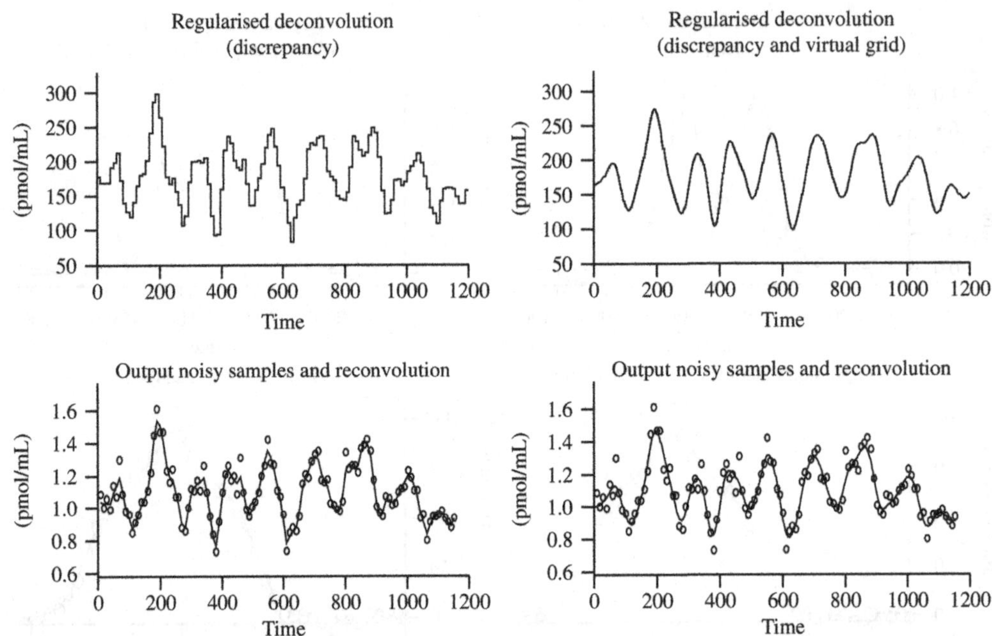

FIGURE 9–7 Insulin oscillation case study. *Left*: Regularized deconvolution obtained with a value of the regularization parameter determined by the discrepancy criterion ($\gamma = 0.0015$) from the noisy samples (*lower, open circles*). Also shown is reconvolution (*lower, continuous line*). *Right*: Same as left by employing the virtual grid ($\gamma = 0.588$).

($V \gg N$) grid (possibly uniform) over which the unknown input u(t) is described as a piecewise constant function. Ω_V must contain Ω_S but, apart from this, it is arbitrary and has no experimental counterpart. For this reason, Ω_V is called a *virtual grid*. Let $c_V(T_k)$ denote the (noise-free) output at the virtual sampling times T_k. Assuming that u(t) is a piecewise constant within each time interval of the virtual grid, it follows that:

$$c_V(T_k) = \int_0^{T_k} g(T_k - \tau)u(\tau)d\tau = \sum_{i=1}^{k} u_i \int_{T_{i-1}}^{T_i} g(T_k - \tau)d\tau \tag{9.32}$$

where $T_0 = 0$. Adopting the usual matrix notation one has:

$$\mathbf{c_V} = \mathbf{G_V u} \tag{9.33}$$

where V stands for virtual, $\mathbf{c_V}$ and $\mathbf{u}$ are V-dimensional vectors obtained by sampling c(t) and u(t) on the virtual grid, and $\mathbf{G_V}$ is a $V \times V$ lower-triangular matrix. Times belonging to the virtual grid Ω_V have no counterpart in the sampled output data. We can regard them as (virtually) missing data.

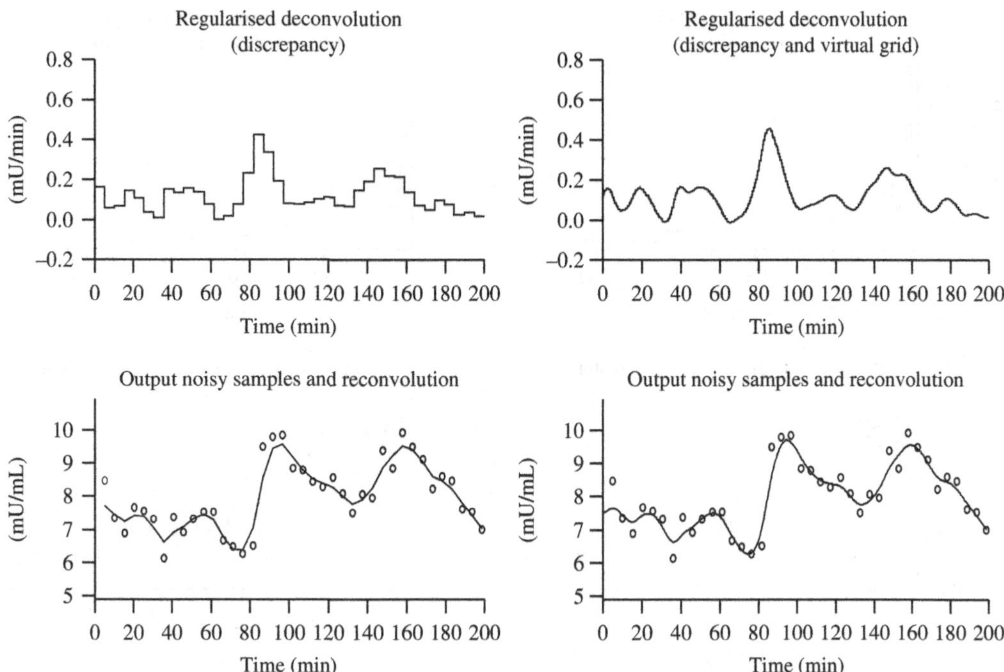

FIGURE 9–8 Luteinizing hormone oscillation case study. *Left*: Regularized deconvolution obtained with a value of the regularization parameter determined by the discrepancy criterion ($\gamma = 130$) from the noisy samples (*bottom, open circles*). Also shown is reconvolution (*lower panel, continuous line*). *Right*: Same as left by employing the virtual grid ($\gamma = 776$).

Let us denote by **G**, the $N \times V$ matrix obtained by removing those rows that do not correspond to sampled output data from G_V. The measurement vector is thus:

$$\mathbf{z} = \mathbf{G}\,\mathbf{u} + \mathbf{v} \tag{9.34}$$

where **v** is the N-dimensional vector of the measurement error, and **u** is the V-dimensional vector of the input discretized over the virtual grid. If Ω_V is uniform (note that a uniform Ω_V can always be chosen), **G** has a near-to-Toepliz structure, meaning that it misses some of the rows of the Toepliz matrix $\mathbf{G}_V$.

The estimate $\hat{\mathbf{u}}$ is given by (9.20), where **G** and **u** are those of (9.34) and F has magnitude of $V \times V$. In fact, in (9.20) the matrix $(\mathbf{G}^T\, \Sigma_V^{-1}\, \mathbf{G} + \gamma \mathbf{F}^T\mathbf{F})$ is invertible because it is the sum of $\mathbf{G}^T\Sigma_V^{-1}\,\mathbf{G}$ (semidefinite positive) and $\mathbf{F}^T\mathbf{F}$ (positive). Provided that Ω_V has a fine time detail (in other words the time points are not widely spaced), this method yields a stepwise estimate that is virtually indistinguishable from a continuous profile.

To clarify the mechanics of the virtual grid rationale, an illustrative example that can help. Let us consider a nonuniform and infrequent sampling grid (five samples, time is arbitrary):

1 ? 3 ? ? 6 ? ? ? 10 ? ? ? ? 15

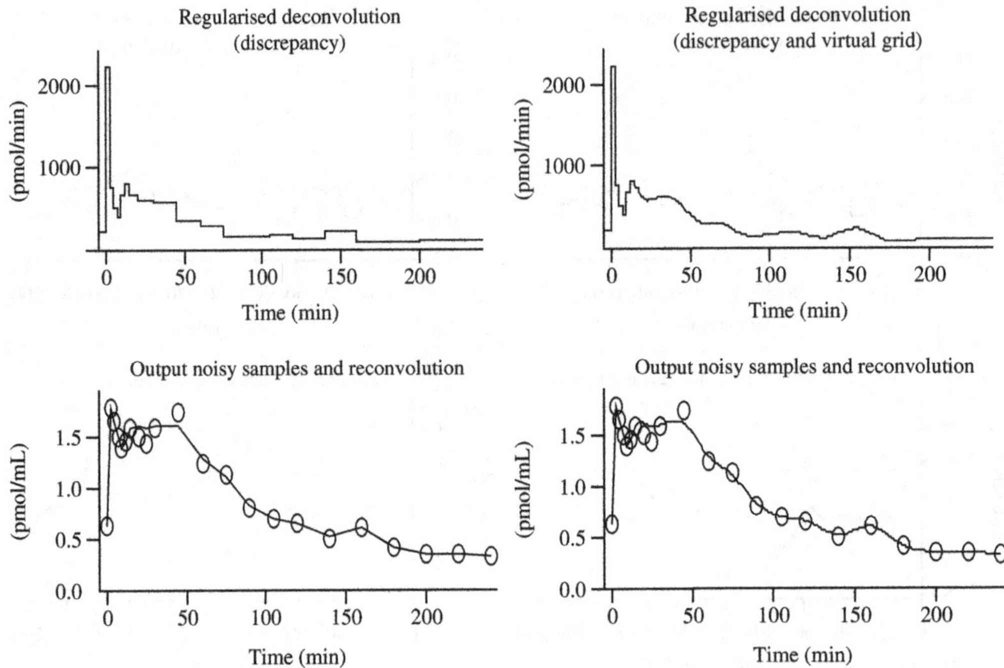

FIGURE 9–9 IVGTT insulin secretion case study. *Left*: Regularized deconvolution obtained with a value of the regularization parameter determined by the discrepancy criterion ($\gamma = 0.0012$) from the noisy samples (*lower panel, open circles*). Also shown is reconvolution (*lower panel, continuous line*). *Right*: Same as left by employing the virtual grid ($\gamma = 0.25$). *Adapted from Sparacino, G., De Nicolao, G., & Cobelli, C. (2001). Deconvolution. In: E. Carson & C. Cobelli (Eds.),* Modelling methodology for physiology and medicine *(pp. 45–75). New York: Academic Press.*

and define a virtual grid as:

$$\underline{1\ \ 2\ \ 3\ \ 4\ \ 5\ \ 6\ \ 7\ \ 8\ \ 9\ \ 10\ \ 11\ \ 12\ \ 13\ \ 14\ \ 15}$$

then one has:

$$\begin{bmatrix} c(1) \\ c(3) \\ c(6) \\ c(10) \\ c(15) \end{bmatrix} = \begin{bmatrix} g_0 & 0 & 0 & 0 & 0 & 0 & 0 & 0 & 0 \\ g_2 & g_1 & g_0 & 0 & 0 & 0 & 0 & 0 & 0 \\ g_5 & g_4 & g_3 & \cdots & g_0 & 0 & 0 & 0 & .0 \\ g_9 & g_8 & g_7 & \cdots & \cdots & \cdots & g_0 & 0 & 0 \\ g_{14} & g_{13} & g_{12} & \cdots & \cdots & \cdots & \cdots & g_1 & g_0 \end{bmatrix} \begin{bmatrix} u_1 \\ u_2 \\ u_3 \\ u_4 \\ \cdots \\ \cdots \\ \cdots \\ u_{15} \end{bmatrix} \tag{9.35}$$

If all samples of the virtual grid are available, then we have:

$$\begin{bmatrix} c(1) \\ c(2) \\ c(3) \\ c(4) \\ \cdots \\ \cdots \\ c(14) \\ c(15) \end{bmatrix} = \begin{bmatrix} g_0 & 0 & 0 & 0 & 0 & 0 & 0 & 0 & 0 \\ g_1 & g_0 & 0 & 0 & 0 & 0 & 0 & 0 & 0 \\ g_2 & g_1 & g_0 & 0 & 0 & 0 & 0 & 0 & 0 \\ g_3 & g_2 & g_1 & g_0 & 0 & 0 & 0 & 0 & 0 \\ & & \cdots & \cdots & \cdots & & & & \\ & & & & & & & & \\ g_{13} & g_{12} & \cdots & \cdots & \cdots & \cdots & g_1 & g_0 & 0 \\ g_{14} & g_{13} & g_{12} & \cdots & \cdots & \cdots & \cdots & g_1 & g_0 \end{bmatrix} \begin{bmatrix} u_1 \\ u_2 \\ u_3 \\ u_4 \\ \cdots \\ \cdots \\ \cdots \\ u_{15} \end{bmatrix} \tag{9.36}$$

We can now remove those rows that do not correspond to the sampled output data and have:

$$\begin{bmatrix} c(1) \\ \cancel{c(2)} \\ c(3) \\ \cancel{c(4)} \\ \cdots \\ \cdots \\ \cancel{c(14)} \\ c(15) \end{bmatrix} = \begin{bmatrix} g_0 & 0 & 0 & 0 & 0 & 0 & 0 & 0 & 0 \\ \cancel{g_1} & \cancel{g_0} & \cancel{0} & \cancel{0} & \cancel{0} & \cancel{0} & \cancel{0} & \cancel{0} & \cancel{0} \\ g_2 & g_1 & g_0 & 0 & 0 & 0 & 0 & 0 & 0 \\ \cancel{g_3} & \cancel{g_2} & \cancel{g_1} & \cancel{g_0} & \cancel{0} & \cancel{0} & \cancel{0} & \cancel{0} & \cancel{0} \\ & & \cdots & \cdots & \cdots & & & & \\ & & & & & & & & \\ \cancel{g_{13}} & \cancel{g_{12}} & \cancel{\cdots} & \cancel{\cdots} & \cancel{\cdots} & \cancel{\cdots} & \cancel{g_1} & \cancel{g_0} & \cancel{0} \\ g_{14} & g_{13} & g_{12} & \cdots & \cdots & \cdots & \cdots & g_1 & g_0 \end{bmatrix} \begin{bmatrix} u_1 \\ u_2 \\ u_3 \\ u_4 \\ \cdots \\ \cdots \\ \cdots \\ u_{15} \end{bmatrix} \tag{9.37}$$

and thus:

$$\begin{bmatrix} c(1) \\ c(3) \\ c(6) \\ c(10) \\ c(15) \end{bmatrix} = \begin{bmatrix} g_0 & 0 & 0 & 0 & 0 & 0 & 0 & 0 & 0 \\ g_2 & g_1 & g_0 & 0 & 0 & 0 & 0 & 0 & 0 \\ g_5 & g_4 & g_3 & \cdots & g_0 & 0 & 0 & 0 & 0 \\ g_9 & g_8 & g_7 & \cdots & \cdots & \cdots & g_0 & 0 & 0 \\ g_{14} & g_{13} & g_{12} & \cdots & \cdots & \cdots & \cdots & g_1 & g_0 \end{bmatrix} \begin{bmatrix} u_1 \\ u_2 \\ u_3 \\ u_4 \\ \cdots \\ \cdots \\ \cdots \\ u_{15} \end{bmatrix} \tag{9.38}$$

In matrix notation:

$$\underset{5\times 1}{\mathbf{z}} = \underset{5\times 15}{\mathbf{G}} \; \underset{15\times 1}{\mathbf{u}} + \underset{5\times 1}{\mathbf{v}}$$

Results obtained with a 1-minute virtual grid and employing the discrepancy criterion are shown in Figs. 9–6–9–9 (right panels), where the corresponding, already discussed, estimates obtained with the sampling grid are shown on the left panels. The estimates are able to describe both the true continuous-time input of the Hunt simulated problem (Fig. 9–6) and the physiological case studies data (Figs. 9–7 and 9–9) much better than staircase functions.

9.6 Summary

In this chapter we have discussed the importance, and also the difficulties, of the deconvolution problem for estimating an unknown input, for example, the secretion rate of a gland or a substrate production rate of an organ. We have presented in detail a regularization method which can cope with most of the difficulties. However, one can do much better. For instance, as concerns the choice of the regularization parameter, albeit the discrepancy criterion has an intuitive rationale, it has no solid theoretical foundation. In particular, it can be shown to be at risk of oversmoothing, that is, it provides too high a value of γ (De Nicolao *et al.*, 1997). Another shortcoming is the impossibility, within the deterministic context of the regularization method as presented, of obtaining the confidence intervals of the reconstructed input. This is a very important point, since deconvolution provides an indirect way of measuring a nonaccessible variable. Hence, it is important to assess the reliability of such a measurement. In physiological systems analysis, confidence limits are particularly useful when one has to make inferences, such as choosing a threshold for detecting the number of pulses present in a hormone secretory pulsatile profile or deciding if a secretory profile is a pathological one. Another drawback is that sometimes, albeit the input u(t) is known to be intrinsically nonnegative, for example, hormone secretion rates and drug absorption rates, due to the measurement errors and impulse response model mismatch, the solution provided may take on negative values.

All of the above aspects can be handled by more sophisticated approaches. For instance, by setting the deconvolution problem within a stochastic embedding (De Nicolao *et al.*, 1997; Sparacino *et al.*, 2001), we can derive a statistically-based choice of the regularization parameter, improving on the discrepancy criterion and putting statistically-based confidence limits on the reconstructed input. Also, nonnegativity constraints can be handled by considering constrained deconvolution (De Nicolao *et al.*, 1997; Pillonetto *et al.*, 2002a; Pillonetto *et al.*, 2002b; Sparacino *et al.*, 2001). Finally, it is worth mentioning that a user-friendly software tool, WINSTODEC (Sparacino *et al.*, 2002) is available, which implements both the deterministic version of the regularization method described in this chapter as well as its stochastic embedding.

9.7 Exercises and assignment questions

1. Hormonal concentration time series reflect both secretion by the gland and its distribution and metabolism in the body. Discuss why deconvolution is important if the study goal is to reconstruct the secretion rate of the gland.

2. Discuss the difficulties of the deconvolution problem in general and the additional complexity involved when dealing with physiological signals.
3. Least squares deconvolution generally performs poorly when attempting to reconstruct the unknown input. Discuss why this is the case.
4. Discuss the rationale of the regularization method.
5. The regularization method guarantees a certain degree of smoothness of the reconstructed input. Discuss how this is achieved.

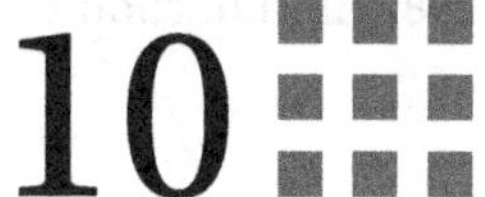

Model validation

10.1 Introduction

Model validation involves assessing the extent to which a model is well-founded and tractable, while fulfilling the purpose for which it was formulated (valid—from the Latin *validus*, "strong, vigorous"). This assumes that, in a Popperian (General attitude and practice of critical rationalism—Karl Popper) sense, it can be tested. Clearly, no model can have absolute, unbounded validity given that, by definition, a model is an approximation of reality. When dealing with a set of competing, candidate models, the validation process involves determining which of them is best in relation to its intended purpose. A valid model is one that has successfully passed through the validation process.

The aim of this chapter is to consider the nature of model validity and provide a framework, with associated methods, for the model validation process. First, we consider model validation and the domain of validity of models. This is followed by an examination of validation strategies; this involves considering both the validation of a single model as well as the situation in which there is a need to choose amongst a number of competing models. The chapter concludes with some thoughts on what constitutes good practice in the overall context of good modeling methodology.

10.2 Model validation and the domain of validity

Validation is integral to the overall modeling process. It is an activity that needs to be performed both during model building, and upon completion of the model. Let us consider each of these in turn.

10.2.1 Validation during model formulation

As already explained, model validation involves assessing the model in order to check that it is well-founded and fulfills the purpose for which it was intended. Validation is something that needs to be considered all the way through the modeling process. It begins when specifying the purpose of the modeling activity and continues right on to the completed model as discussed below.

Here we wish to consider the validation process as it should be applied during the formulation of the model. First of all we need to think very carefully about the purpose of the model. This needs to be specified very precisely and clearly. Validation involves assessing the goodness or the worth of the model in relation to its intended purpose. If this purpose

Introduction to Modeling in Physiology and Medicine. DOI: https://doi.org/10.1016/B978-0-12-815756-5.00010-2

has not been clearly defined, then it will not be possible to make the required judgment as to whether the model is fit for its purpose.

The building of a model normally proceeds by postulating a conceptual model and then proceeding to a mathematical realization of this conceptual form. In putting up a conceptual framework, care needs to be taken to ensure that all the relevant physical and chemical concepts are properly described. This is important when it comes to producing the mathematical realization. For example, it might be assumed that the air flow in a portion of the respiratory system is to be considered, conceptually, as including a turbulent component. This means that the mathematics used to describe that flow must be appropriate as a description of the process of turbulent flow. More generally, the particular mathematical formulation adopted must be consistent with the physics, chemistry, and physiology that are relevant to the situation being modeled.

As was discussed in Chapter 5, Modeling the system, different degrees of assumption can be built into the model. In reality, most physiological systems exhibit the complexities of nonlinearity, distributed phenomena, stochasticity, etc. Yet, in appropriate circumstances, it may be acceptable (in relation to the intended purpose) to adopt a linear, time-invariant, deterministic, lumped parameter model. Such simplifications imply assumptions being made, and it is essential to be sure that such assumptions are valid. This is a key component of the validation process during the formulation of a model. For example, is an assumption of laminar air flow in the portion of the respiratory system being modeled valid? Is the perturbation being modeled in relation to an oral glucose tolerance test sufficiently small that it is valid to adopt a linear model of glucose metabolism?

Not only should the mathematical model be consistent with the relevant physical and chemical principles and laws that are being represented, but the model should also be consistent in other ways. It is important to ensure that the proposed set of differential equations, say representing some of the dynamics of lipid metabolism, is compatible with a feasible steady state. To carry out this check, the derivative terms in all the differential equations of the model are set equal to zero. Solving what is now a set of algebraic equations gives the values of all the variables that correspond to that steady state. If the equations had been compiled in an inconsistent manner, it might be found that one or more of the variables had an infinite or zero value in the steady state, clearly providing evidence of model invalidity.

10.2.2 Validation of the completed model

The essence of the validation process once the model is complete is shown in Fig. 10–1. In other words, by this stage all of the previously unknown parameters will have been estimated.

It is important to stress that, in examining the validity of the complete model, the process is dependent on model purpose. In other words, the task is problem-specific. Validity is a multidimensional concept reflecting model purpose, current theories, and experimental data relating to the particular physiological system of interest, together with other relevant knowledge. Thus, as new theories are developed and additional data become available, the

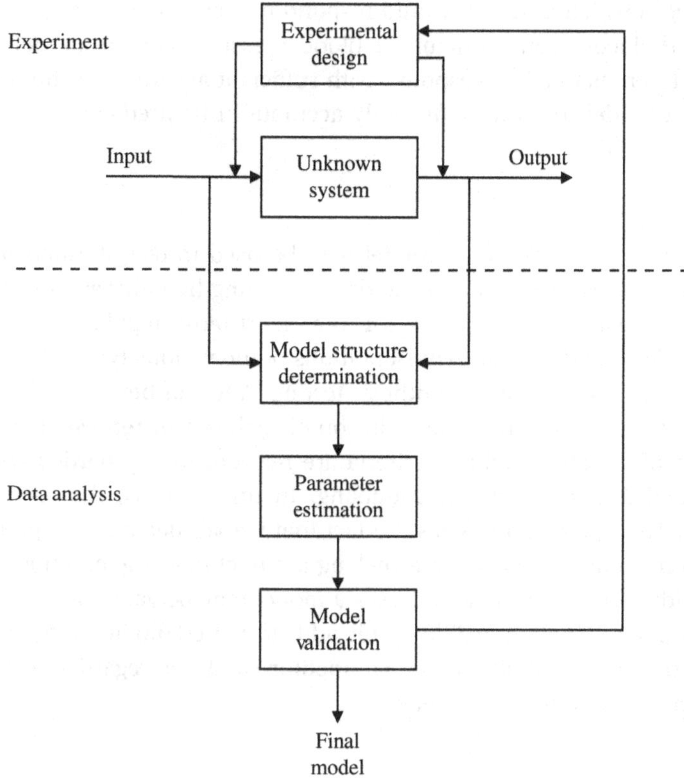

FIGURE 10–1 Validating the complete model.

requirements for a model to be deemed valid can change although its validity is still assessed in terms of the same criteria.

In general, for a model to be valid it will need to satisfy one or more of the criteria of: empirical, theoretical, pragmatic, and heuristic validity.

Empirical

Empirical validity is assessed by examining how well the model corresponds to available data.

Theoretical

Theoretical validity, on the other hand, is concerned with ensuring that the model is consistent with accepted physiological theories.

Pragmatic

Pragmatic validity particularly comes into play in the context of a model that is to be used to support clinical decision making. For instance, consider the case of a model being used to predict the way in which a patient would respond to a change in therapy as evidenced by a change in blood glucose concentration or blood pressure. For the model to be useful, it needs to be able to predict patient response with sufficient accuracy for the predictions to be clinically useful. A model that was sufficiently accurate in its predictions would be deemed to be pragmatically valid.

Heuristic

Heuristic validity is important when a model is to be used to test physiological hypotheses. For instance, if a model is to be used to explore competing hypotheses as to the type of sensors involved in providing information for the short-term regulation of cardiovascular dynamics, the model would include representations of the various types of sensor being considered if it was to be used in such hypothesis testing. A test of heuristic validity in this connection would be an examination of the inclusion of such sensor representations.

Clearly, which of the above validity criteria are relevant in any particular case is dependent on the intended purpose of the modeling. In other words, the issue is very much problem-specific. This again emphasizes the fact that we are dealing in a particular instance with a specific domain of validity. We are seeking a model that is good enough in relation to its domain of validity. However, in some cases a model may be valid for some situations that lie outside the original domain of validity. This adds to the credibility of the model. A model that has a wider domain of validity than a competitor would be regarded as a more credible model, if all other considerations were equal.

10.3 Validation strategies

10.3.1 Validation of a single model—basic approach

The strategy to be adopted in the validation of a single model has as its essence a comparison of the behavior of the model with that of the physiological system being considered. This will involve assessing any mismatch between the system output, as evidenced principally by experimental data, and the model output. In addition, the model should be checked for plausibility of behavior.

Examining system and model responses has two ingredients. The first involves comparison of overall patterns of response. The second focuses on particular features of response.

Overall patterns of response

In terms of overall patterns of response, the usual measure is the fit of the model response to the response of the physiological system as evidenced by the data collected from input/output experiments. Typically we are examining the residual sum of squares, SS_R, corresponding to the final parameter estimates of the model, $\mathbf{p}$. This is the expression, as shown in (10.1) that we wish to make as small as possible, or at least not greater than some agreed threshold value. In other words, we are seeking to ensure that the model response must fit the experimental test data with sufficient accuracy.

$$SS_R = \sum_{i=1}^{N} \left(\frac{1}{\sigma^2(t_i)}\right) [z(t_i) - y(t_i, \mathbf{p})]^2 \tag{10.1}$$

In (10.1), $z(t_i)$ is the measured experimental value of the output variable of the physiological system made at time t_i, σ is the standard deviation of that measurement, $y\ (t_i)$ is the value of the corresponding model output variable for time t_i, and $\mathbf{p}$ is the vector of parameter estimates.

Features of response

In assessing the validity of a model, it may be useful to examine the occurrence of certain patterns of features to be observed in the dynamic behavior produced by the model. In essence, we are asking the question as to whether or not certain response features, which are to be seen in experimental data, are reproduced by the model.

In many physiological systems, the normal or abnormal response is characterized by the presence or absence of such features. Therefore a qualitative assessment of the occurrence or nonoccurrence of features can be an important ingredient of the validation process. Such features, which can be said to represent a subset of the information contained in the available data, may be simple or complex. Simple features might include the rise or fall of a particular variable following the application of a particular physiological stimulus. More complex features might include the occurrence and specific timing of a peak value of a variable, a biphasic response pattern, or particular patterns of oscillatory behavior. The model must be capable of reproducing such qualitative features if it is to be deemed valid.

As well as undertaking such a qualitative analysis, it may be useful to quantify the occurrence of such distinctive features. Typically this will involve setting up an appropriate measure of distance between the features as predicted by the model and those exhibited in available experimental test data. The setting up of such quantitative measures of features such as distance can be regarded as a form of error function that should be reduced to an adequate level if a model is to be valid.

For instance, suppose $\mathbf{x_D}$ is a vector of quantitative features in the data and $\mathbf{x_M}$ is the vector of the corresponding model features. The distance between $\mathbf{x_M}$ and $\mathbf{x_D}$ in feature space can be used to provide a measure of the error of fit between model and data. Let us define a figure of merit or measure of model adequacy (F) in terms of the error between the data features $\mathbf{x_D}(k)$ and the model features $\mathbf{x_M}(k)$, $k = 1, \ldots, N$:

$$F = \frac{1}{\left(1 + \left(\frac{1}{N}\right) \sum_{k=1}^{N} \omega_k \delta_k\right)}, \quad F \in [0, 1] \tag{10.2}$$

where:

$$\delta_k = \left(\frac{(x_M(k) - x_D(k))}{x_D(k)}\right) \tag{10.3}$$

and ω_k are weighting factors ($\omega_k \in [0, 1]$). δ_k is the fractional error of the kth model feature. If there is no error, $F = 1$, whereas an average error of $\pm 50\%$ between model and data fives $F = 0.67$.

A figure of merit such as this thus provides an indicator of how closely important features of dynamic response in the physiological system are mimicked by those in the model. As well as being a useful tool in the validation of a single model, this measure can also be very helpful when deciding between two or more competing models as discussed below. An assessment of such quantitative measures of features may equally enable deficiencies in the individual model to be revealed, requiring a return to model formulation.

10.3.2 Validation of a single model—additional quantitative tools for numerically identified models

In the case of validating a complete, single model, a number of other quantitative tools are available. Let us consider the case where parameters have been estimated using the methods that were described in Chapter 8, Parametric models—the estimation problem. These tools enable us to investigate the precision of the estimated parameters, the residuals of the mismatch between model and data, and the plausibility of the parameter estimates for the situation in which the parameters should have some explicit correspondence to physiological concepts.

Parameter precision

An important test of model validity involves assessing the precision of the parameters that have been estimated. In general terms, this can be achieved by determining the covariance matrix of the parameter estimates, $\mathbf{V}(\hat{\mathbf{p}})$. In the case of nonlinear least squares estimation as considered in Chapter 8, Parametric models—the estimation problem, the diagonal elements $v_{ii}(\hat{p})$ of $\mathbf{V}(\hat{\mathbf{p}})$, provide the variances of the parameter estimates. Hence, the precision with which the parameter p_i can be estimated may be expressed in terms of the standard deviation by:

$$\hat{p}i \pm \sqrt{(v_{ii}(\hat{p}_i)} \tag{10.4}$$

Very often in judging parameter precision (*a posteriori* identifiability) a percentage measure is employed. This is the coefficient of variation (CV) or fractional standard deviation (FSD):

$$CV(\hat{p}_i) = FSD(\hat{p}_i) = \left(\frac{\sqrt{(v_{ii}(\hat{p}_i))}}{\hat{p}_i}\right) \times 100 \tag{10.5}$$

Residuals of the mismatch between model and data

As indicated above, for the model to be deemed valid, there must be an adequately good fit of the model to the data which will have been assessed through the residual sum of squares. Following on from this should be an investigation of the statistics of the residual errors of this fitting process.

For example, it may have been assumed *a priori* that the measurement noise is white, Gaussian, and of zero mean. The residual errors of the fitting process must be examined for bias, normality, and whiteness, wherever possible using appropriate statistical tests. For instance, whiteness can be examined by the use of correlation techniques, and normality by the application of a χ^2 test. If, however, the data are small in number, empirical visual methods may need to be adopted in examining the residuals. This would typically involve plotting them against time in order to detect possible inconsistencies; for example, outliers or systematic deviations between experimental data and predicted model response.

Parameter plausibility

After assessing these other quantitative methods, we can finally turn to examining the plausibility of the parameters in particular, as well as the plausibility of the model overall. If the estimated parameters of a model correspond to some specific physical or physiological properties, then those parameter estimates must accord with the known values of such properties. In other words, if estimated parameters of a model take on values that are absurd (e.g., fractional transfer rate constants in a metabolic system or compliance of a blood vessel in the circulatory system lying outside the physiologically feasible range), the model must be deemed invalid and is rejected.

In the case of a model that is identifiable, but not uniquely so (i.e., there are two possible values for one or more of the parameters), this criterion may enable one to be selected on the grounds that it is plausible whereas the other one is not.

In addition to the specific issues of parameter plausibility just examined, other features of model plausibility may be used in assessing validity. For instance, wherever possible, the validity of the model should be tested against data independent of those used in the fitting process, but obtained from other tests that are nevertheless within the chosen domain of validity. For example, in the context of a metabolic system, the model may enable values to be estimated for parameters such as volume of distribution and clearance rate; parameters not directly estimated in the identification process. The values estimated for such parameters from the model should then be compared with the corresponding parameter values obtained from independent experiments. Such parameters can be used in assessing the validity of the model under consideration.

Another useful test is to examine the prediction provided by the model of variables other than those measured in the available input/output identification experiments. Again, such predictions may support or refute a specific model. Finally, there is the need to consider the extent to which model is compatible with current physiological knowledge.

10.3.3 Validation of competing models

Goodness of fit

If there is a set of two or more candidate models, comparisons between them of their ability to fit the available data as one measure of model validity should be made. In this way the best model, in terms of a good fit, may be selected. However, the improvement in predictability of the data by one model over a competing model should not be obtained purely as a result of an increase in the number of parameters. It must truly reflect a more accurate representation of data corrected for the increase in the degrees of freedom in fitting. This is sometimes referred to as the *principle of parsimony*.

In the case of linear dynamic models, the Akaike information criterion takes into account both goodness of fit and number of parameters when comparing models (Akaike, 1974). This criterion, AIC, is given by:

$$AIC = N \ln SS_R + 2P \tag{10.6}$$

where N is the number of data points, P is the number of parameters, and SS_R is the residual sum of squares defined in (10.1) as:

$$SS_R = \sum_{i=1}^{N} \left(\frac{1}{\sigma^2(t_i)}\right) [z(t_i) - y(t_i, p)]^2 \tag{10.7}$$

Features of response

The role of feature comparison has already been discussed above in the context of a single model. However, this aspect of testing for model validity can also play an important role in the situation in which a choice amongst two or more competing models is sought. The figure of merit, F, such as that defined in (10.2), can be very useful as an objective measure for deciding among competing models, enabling one or more to be rejected without having to proceed further in the validation process.

Model plausibility

The considerations of plausibility, described above in relation to a single model, are equally applicable when choosing the best out of a number of candidate models. Examination of the plausibility of the parameter estimates achieved should help when choosing the most appropriate model.

Having examined the plausibility of the parameters of the competing models, other aspects of plausibility should be investigated, as for the case above when considering the validity of just a single model. So again this involves exploring the plausibility of other features such as structure, parameters, and behavior, as well as overall physiological plausibility compatible with current physiological knowledge.

10.4 Good practice in good modeling

Let us conclude this chapter by offering a few remarks that should be helpful in ensuring good practice. First of all, remain critical of your model. Do not love it too much! Remember that, by definition, a model is an approximation of reality. As such, it cannot be perfect. So always be prepared to take account of new facts and observations with a view to including them in your model.

A good model, in a Popperian sense, is one that is clearly falsifiable and therefore is capable of bringing about its own downfall. In other words, it should be possible to devise critical experiments to perform on the model which will provide a rigorous test of its validity and provide clues as to where improvement is needed.

It should also be remembered that in situations of complexity, it might be appropriate to think in terms of a suite of models, where each would have its own distinct domain of validity. It is then a case of choosing which is most appropriate for the specific context. This may reflect the particular level in the physiological hierarchy that is being represented and the time scale of interest in relation to dynamic response, for instance short-term or long-term. For example, the model chosen to examine breath-by-breath control in the human respiratory system is likely to be significantly different, both in terms of structure and parameters, from that needed to investigate day-by-day changes in the asthmatic patient.

In summary, we have examined what is required in order to produce a model that can be deemed valid. This requires the adoption of good modeling methodology, with its ingredients that have been discussed in detail in this book. What should be clear, as captured in Fig. 10–2, is that a successful outcome to the modeling process is critically dependent on both the quality of the model and the quality of the experimental data. Neither by itself is sufficient. We hope that by explaining good methodology, and demonstrating its application in a variety of physiological settings, we have given you the confidence to embark on this fascinating and important arena of scientific endeavor.

Now that we have established a framework for considering the validity of one or more models, the final chapter will look at a number of case studies to demonstrate how these methods and techniques can be applied in practice.

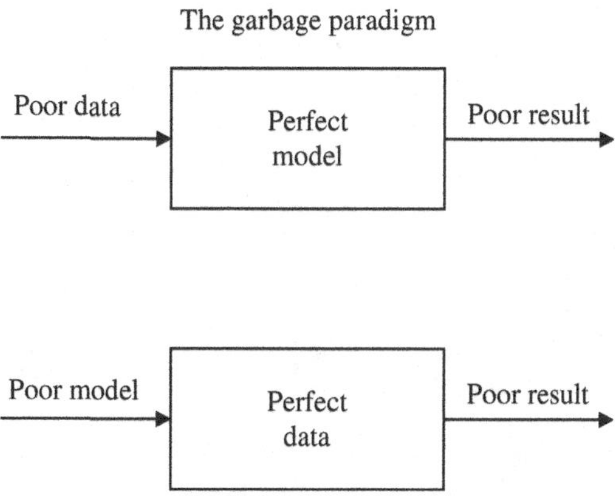

FIGURE 10–2 The garbage paradigm.

10.5 Summary

This chapter has provided an overview of the process of model validation. It has been shown to be a process that pervades the whole modeling process, from initial thinking about model purpose to consideration of the worth or value of the completed model. Strategies for validation have been outlined, both for the case of a single model and also for the situation in which one is seeking to judge between competing models. Suggestions have also been offered as to what constitutes good modeling practice. The final chapter of the book will put these concepts and methods into practice, offering a number of detailed case studies of model validation in action.

10.6 Exercises and assignment questions

1. Describe how the process of model validation is influenced by the purpose for which a physiological model is intended.
2. Discuss how issues of validation need to be considered during the process of formulating a mathematical model of a physiological system.
3. Give an account of the criteria that can be used to assess the validity of a single model, where the model might be developed for use in the context of (a) physiological research, or (b) clinical decision support.
4. Two competing models have been developed as possible representations of the dynamic processes within a particular area of human metabolism. Indicate ways by means of which it might be possible to judge which model is the more appropriate.

Case studies

The previous chapters have outlined concepts, methods and techniques relevant to the development of mathematical models of physiological systems. This final chapter now presents a number of case studies which will demonstrate how such approaches have been applied in tackling a number of real physiological and medical situations. Taken together, these case studies cover the application of a wide range of modeling methods and techniques.

11.1 Case study 1: a sum of exponentials tracer disappearance model

As a first case study let us consider a set of data that have been collected during a tracer experiment. These data represent the time course of radioactive glucose tracer concentration following an injection of tracer at time zero. The data, which were collected from a normal subject, are depicted in Table 11–1 where the plasma measurements are dpm/mL and the measurement times are minutes following the injection.

From a modeling perspective, our aim is to fit these data to a set of exponential terms. The number of exponentials required to fit the data would give us a clue as to how many compartments would be needed should we wish to model our physiological system explicitly in terms of a number of interconnected compartments.

In order to select the order of the multiexponential model which is best able to describe these data, one, two and three-exponential models can be considered as represented by Eqs. (11.1)–(11.3):

$$y(t) = A_1 e^{-\alpha_1 \cdot t} \tag{11.1}$$

$$y(t) = A_1 e^{-\alpha_1 \cdot t} + A_2 e^{-\alpha_2 \cdot t} \tag{11.2}$$

$$y(t) = A_1 e^{-\alpha_1 \cdot t} + A_2 e^{-\alpha_2 \cdot t} + A_3 e^{-\alpha_3 \cdot t} \tag{11.3}$$

It is assumed that the measurement error is additive:

$$z_i = y_i + v_i \tag{11.4}$$

where the errors v_i are assumed to be independent, Gaussian with a mean of zero, and having an experimentally determined standard deviation of:

$$SD(v_i) = 0.02 \cdot z_i + 20 \tag{11.5}$$

Introduction to Modeling in Physiology and Medicine. DOI: https://doi.org/10.1016/B978-0-12-815756-5.00011-4

Table 11–1 Plasma data from a tracer experiment.

Time	Plasma		Time	Plasma	
2	3993.50	99.87	28	2252.00	65.04
4	3316.50	86.33	31	2169.50	63.39
5	3409.50	88.19	34	2128.50	62.57
6	3177.50	83.55	37	2085.00	61.70
7	3218.50	84.37	40	2004.00	60.08
8	3145.00	82.90	50	1879.00	57.58
9	3105.00	82.10	60	1670.00	53.40
10	3117.00	82.34	70	1416.50	48.33
11	2984.50	79.69	80	1333.50	46.67
13	2890.00	77.80	90	1152.00	43.04
14	2692.00	73.84	100	1080.50	41.61
15	2603.00	72.06	110	1043.00	40.86
17	2533.50	70.67	120	883.50	37.67
19	2536.00	70.72	130	832.50	36.65
21	2545.50	70.91	140	776.00	35.52
23	2374.00	67.48	150	707.00	34.14
25	2379.00	67.58			

Source: Adapted from Cobelli *et al*., (2000).

These values are shown associated with each datum in Table 11−1. The three models are to be fitted to the data by applying weighted nonlinear regression, as discussed in Chapter 8, Parametric models – the estimation problem, with the weights chosen equal to the inverse of the variance. The plots of the data and the model predictions, together with the corresponding weighted residuals, are shown in Fig. 11−1. The model parameters, that is to say the coefficients of the exponential terms and their corresponding rate constants (eigenvalues), are given in Table 11−2.

On examination of the parameter values presented in Table 11−2, it can be observed that all those corresponding to the one (1E) and two-exponential (2E) models can be estimated with acceptable precision. However, some of the parameters of the 3E model are very uncertain. This means that the 3E model cannot be resolved with precision from the data.

This arises from the fact that the first exponential is so rapid, $\alpha_1 = 4.6\ \text{min}^{-1}$, that it has practically vanished by the time of the first available datum at 2 minutes. The other two exponential terms have values similar to those obtained for the 2E model. In addition, the final estimates of A_1 and α_1 are also dependent upon the initial estimates; that is, starting from different initial points in parameter space, the nonlinear regression procedure yields different final estimates while producing similar values of the weighted residual sum of squares (WRSS). Therefore the 3E model is not numerically identifiable, and hence can be rejected at this stage.

The next step is to compare the fit of the 1E and 2E models. It can be seen by inspection that the residuals of the 1E model are not random because the plot reveals long runs of

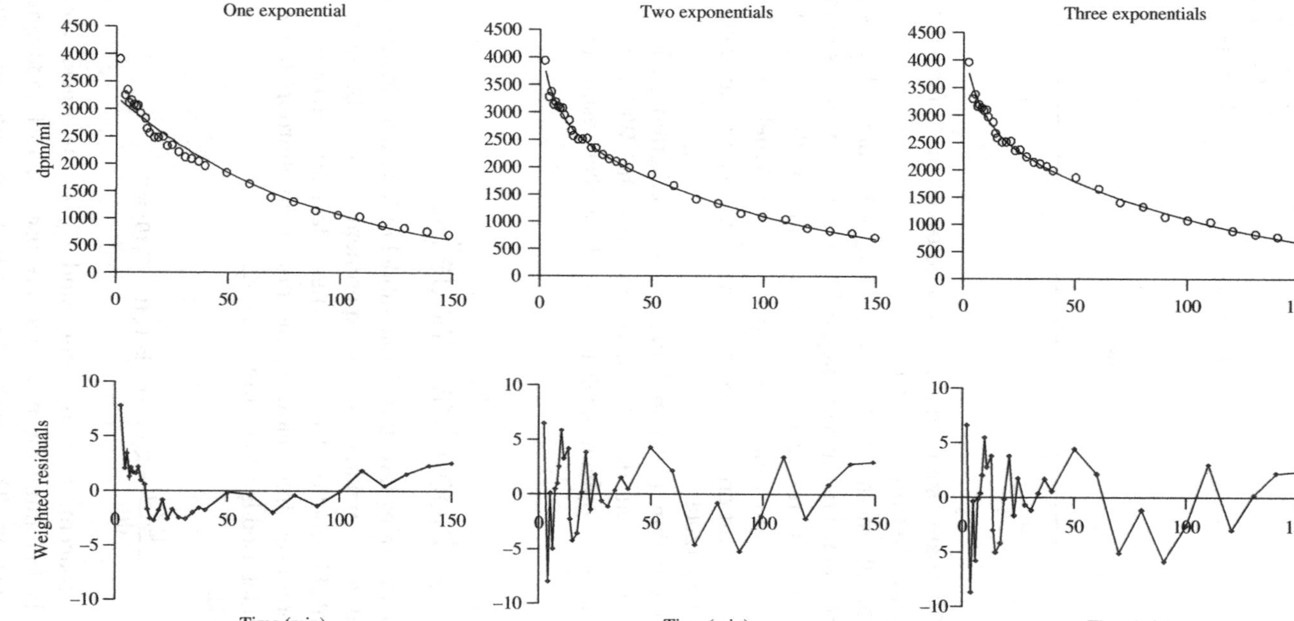

FIGURE 11–1 The best fit of the data given in Table 11–1 to a single-, a two-, and three-exponential models, together with a plot of the weighted residuals for each case. The exponential coefficients and rate constants (eigenvalues) for each model are given in Table 11–2.

Table 11–2 One, two, three-exponential model parameter estimates.

	One exponential	Two exponentials	Three exponentials
A_1	3288 (1%)	1202 (10%)	724,866 (535,789%)
α_1	0.0111 (1%)	0.1383 (17%)	4.5540 (7131%)
A_2		2950 (2%)	1195 (14%)
α_2		0.0098 (3%)	0.1290 (14%)
A_3			2925 (2%)
α_3			0.0097 (3%)
AIC	171.10	40.98	
SC	174.09	46.97	

consecutive residuals of the same sign. This can also be tested more formally using the statistical runs test. For details, see Cobelli *et al.* (2000).

Most residuals for the 2E model lie between -1 and 1. This indicates that they are compatible with the assumptions made regarding the variance of the measurement error. On the other hand, only a few of the residuals of the 1E model fall in this range. To formally test if the weighted residuals have unit variance, as expected if the model and/or assumptions on the variance of the measurement error are correct, the X^2-test can be applied. Again, details can be found in Cobelli *et al.* (2000).

Applying the Akaike criterion (AIC) and the Schwarz criterion [refer to (8.115) and (8.116)], Table 11–2 shows that the 2E model reduces the WRSS significantly when compared with the 1E model. Applying an F test reveals similar results (see Cobelli *et al.*, 2000).

11.2 Case study 2: blood flow modeling

This next case study demonstrates how the classic model of Kety and Schmidt (1948) can be used to measure blood flow, making use of experimental data obtained from positron emission tomography (PET) functional imaging. These data are measures of radioactivity concentration in the blood over time following injection of an appropriate radioactive tracer substance. The basic model used is shown in Fig. 11–2.

The model equation is:

$$\frac{dC_t(t)}{dt} = K_1 C_p(t) - k_2 C_t(t) \quad C_t(0) = 0 \tag{11.6}$$

where C_t is the tracer concentration in tissue, and C_p is the tracer concentration in arterial plasma. K_1 and k_2 (adopting the nomenclature used in PET modeling) are the two first-order kinetic rate constants. The tracer concentrations are often measured in units of μCi/mL or in kBq/mL, and the acquisition time in minutes. Consequently, K_1 has units of

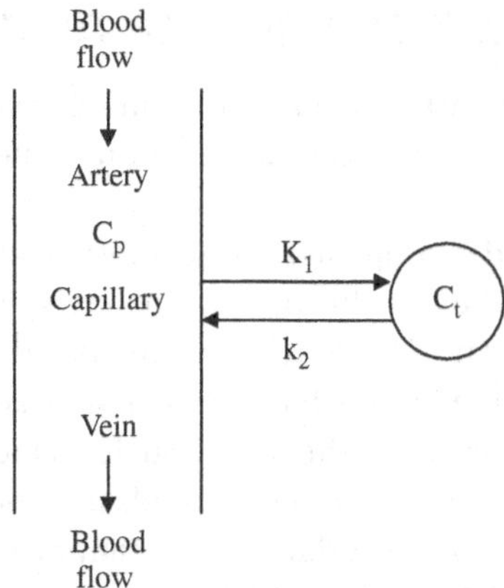

FIGURE 11–2 Blood flow model incorporating a single tissue compartment.

$mL_{plasma}/mL_{tissue}/min$ (or in abbreviated form, mL/mL/min or mL/100 g/min) and k_2 has units of min^{-1}.

At any time following the introduction of the PET tracer, the total radioactivity concentration measured by a PET scanner, C(t), is the sum of the tissue activity in a region of interest (ROI), or in a voxel, and a certain fraction of blood tracer concentration:

$$C(t) = (1 - V_b) \cdot C_t(t) + V_b \cdot C_b(t) \tag{11.7}$$

where V_b is the fraction of the measured volume occupied by blood and C_b the tracer concentration in the whole blood. The three model parameters are *a priori* uniquely identifiable and can be estimated by weighted nonlinear least squares.

In PET neuroimaging, because blood volumes in the human brain are small, typically constituting only 5% of the total blood volume, the blood volume term is often omitted. Adopting this simplified model structure, together with experimental data obtained following the injection of freely diffusible $[^{15}O]H_2O$ PET tracer, blood flow can be quantified by making use of the assumptions:

$$K_1 = F \tag{11.8}$$

$$k_2 = \frac{F}{\lambda} \tag{11.9}$$

where F is the rate of blood flow per unit mass of tissue and λ is the tissue–blood partition coefficient. The partition coefficient was originally defined as the ratio of the tissue to venous blood concentration. In PET studies the partition coefficient refers to the concentration ratio between a tissue compartment and arterial plasma at equilibrium, that is, $\lambda = C_t/C_p|_{equilibrium} = K_1/k_2$ which is more correctly termed volume of distribution, generally represented by V_d. However, traditionally in $[^{15}O]H_2O$ PET quantification, the ratio $\lambda = K_1/k_2$ is named partition coefficient.

11.3 Case study 3: cerebral glucose modeling

Experimental data obtained by PET functional imaging can also be used in order to study glucose metabolism in the brain. In this case a two-compartment model is adopted as shown in Fig. 11–3.

This two-compartment model proposed by Sokoloff *et al.* (1977) was originally developed for autoradiographic studies in the brain, but has subsequently been used for PET studies of glucose utilization with $[^{18}F]$fluorodeoxyglucose, $[^{18}F]$FDG. $[^{18}F]$FDG is an analog of glucose that crosses the blood–brain barrier by a saturable carrier-mediated transport process and competes with glucose for the same carrier. Once in the tissue, $[^{18}F]$FDG, like the glucose, can either be transported back to plasma or can be phosphorylated. In the model, C_p is $[^{18}F]$FDG plasma arterial concentration, C_e is $[^{18}F]$FDG cerebral tissue concentration, and C_m is $[^{18}F]$FDG-6-P cerebral concentration in tissue. K_1 [mL/100 g/min or mL/mL/min] and k_2 (min^{-1}) are the rate constants of $[^{18}F]$FDG forward and reverse transcapillary membrane transport, respectively, and k_3 (min^{-1}) is the rate constant of $[^{18}F]$FDG phosphorylation.

The model equations are:

$$\frac{dC_e(t)}{dt} = K_1 C_p(t) - (k_2 + k_3) C_e(t) \quad C_e(0) = 0 \tag{11.10}$$

and

$$\frac{dC_m(t)}{dt} = k_3 C_m(t) \quad C_m(0) = 0 \tag{11.11}$$

The total concentration of radioactivity measured by a PET scanner, C(t), is the sum of the tissue activity in a ROI, or in a voxel, and a certain fraction of blood tracer concentration:

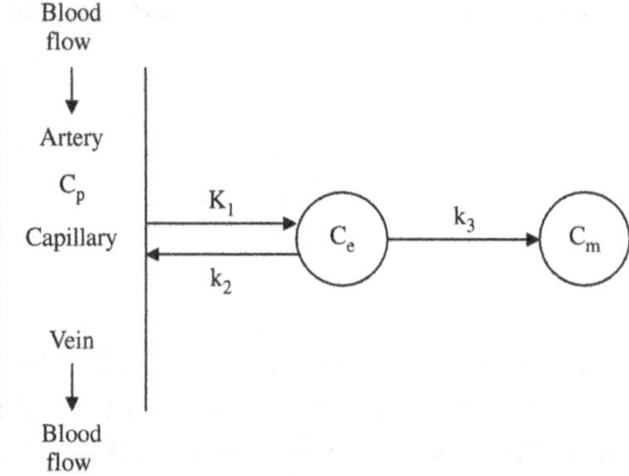

FIGURE 11–3 Cerebral $[^{18}F]$FDG model incorporating two tissue compartments.

$$C(t) = (1 - V_b) \cdot (C_e(t) + C_m(t)) + V_b \cdot C_b(t) \tag{11.12}$$

where V_b is the fraction of the measured volume occupied by blood, and C_b is the tracer concentration in whole blood. All four parameters, $[K_1, k_2, k_3, V_b]$ are *a priori* uniquely identifiable. It should be noted that the model parameters reflect [^{18}F]FDG kinetics and not those of glucose. However, from [^{18}F]FDG parameter estimates it is possible to also derive the cerebral metabolic rate of glucose utilization, CMR_{glu} from:

$$CMR_{glu} = \frac{K_1 k_3}{k_2 + k_3} \frac{C_p^{glu}}{LC} \tag{11.13}$$

where C_p^{glu} is the arterial plasma glucose concentration (mg/dL). LC is a lumped constant (unitless) that describes the relationship between the glucose analog [^{18}F]FDG and glucose itself. LC is given by:

$$LC = \frac{E^{FDG}}{E^{GLU}} \tag{11.14}$$

where E^{FDG} and E^{GLU} are, respectively, the extraction of [^{18}F]FDG and glucose. The value of LC for the human brain under normal physiological conditions has been reported to be 0.85 (Graham *et al.*, 2002). From the model parameter estimates obtained, it is also possible to derive the distribution volume for the C_e compartment as:

$$V_d = \frac{K_1}{k_2 + k_3} \left(\frac{mL}{100\ g}\right) \text{or} \left(\frac{mL}{mL}\right) \tag{11.15}$$

11.4 Case study 4: models of the ligand–receptor system

Advances in PET imaging also make it possible to study receptor density and radioligand affinity in the brain and in the myocardium. Quantification of the ligand–receptor system is of fundamental importance not only in understanding how the brain works, for example, how it performs the various commands and reacts to stimuli, but also in the investigation of the pathogenesis of important diseases such as Alzheimer's and Parkinson's. In recent years PET has become an increasingly used tool to quantitate important parameters such as the receptor density and the binding affinity of radioligands. A number of models have been proposed for specific ligand–receptor interactions, including those of Mintun *et al.* (1984) which will be discussed below.

The most widely adopted model in this context is one that incorporates two tissue compartments as shown in Fig. 11–4.

In this model Cp is the plasma arterial plasma concentration corrected for metabolites, C_{f+ns} is the free and the nonspecifically bound tissue concentration of the PET ligand, and C_s is the tissue concentration of specifically bound ligand. The parameters K_1 (mL/mL/min)

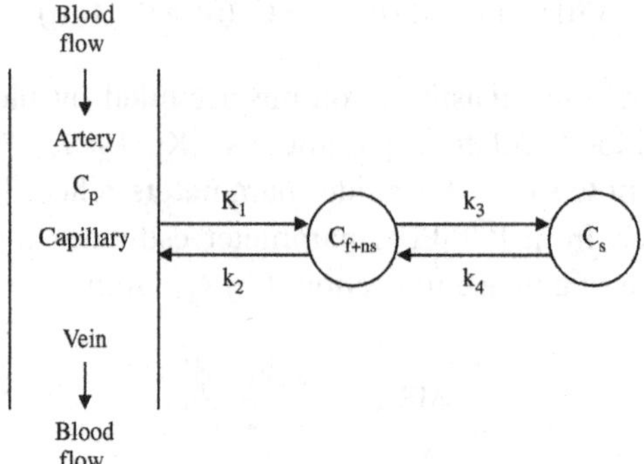

FIGURE 11–4 Model incorporating two tissue compartments.

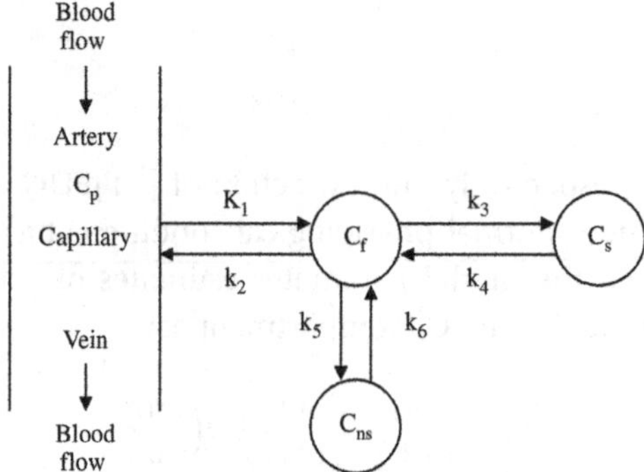

FIGURE 11–5 Model incorporating three tissue compartments.

and k_2 (min^{-1}) represent rate constants for the ligand transfer from plasma to tissue and vice-versa, while k_3 (min^{-1}) represents the transfer of tracer to the specifically bound compartment and k_4 (min^{-1}) relates to the return from the specifically bound compartment to the free and nonspecifically bound compartment.

Whilst the two-tissue compartment model is the one that is most widely employed, it is in fact a simplification of the true tissue distribution space which should be more realistically represented by three compartments. This structure is depicted in Fig. 11–5.

In this model, C_p is the arterial plasma concentration corrected for metabolites, C_f is the concentration of free ligand, C_{ns} is the concentration of nonspecifically bound ligand, and C_s is the concentration of specifically bound ligand. The model equations are thus:

$$\frac{C_f(t)}{dt} = K_1 C_P(t) - (k_2 + k_3 + k_5) C_f(t) + k_4 C_S(t) + k_6 C_{ns}(t) \tag{11.16}$$

$$\frac{C_s(t)}{dt} = k_3 C_f(t) - k_4 C_S(t) \tag{11.17}$$

$$\frac{C_{ns}(t)}{dt} = k_5 C_f(t) - k_6 C_{nS}(t) \tag{11.18}$$

with initial conditions $C_f(0) = C_s(0) = C_{ns}(0) = 0$. K_1 (mL/mL/min) is the rate constant for the transfer from plasma to the free ligand tissue compartment, and k_2, k_3, k_4, k_5, k_6 (min^{-1}) are the rate constants for ligand transfer from tissue to plasma and within the tissue space.

In order to have a better understanding of the physiological meaning of parameters k_3 and k_4, let us assume that the binding of the ligand to the receptor site can be described by a bimolecular reaction:

$$L + R \underset{k_{off}}{\overset{k_{on}}{\rightleftharpoons}} LR \tag{11.19}$$

where L represents the ligand, R the receptor site, LR the binding product, k_{on} is the association rate of the ligand with the receptor sites, and k_{off} is the dissociation rate of the specifically bound reaction product. In terms of the notation of Fig. 11–5, C_f and C_s represent L and LR, respectively, hence:

$$\frac{dC_s(t)}{dt} = k_{on} C_f(t) C_r(t) - k_{off} C_S(t) \tag{11.20}$$

where C_r denotes the concentration of receptors. If B_{max} is the total number of available reaction sites, then:

$$B_{max} = C_s + C_r \tag{11.21}$$

and, if the ligand is present in tracer concentration, then the concentration C_s is negligible and thus:

$$B_{max} \approx C_r \tag{11.22}$$

Hence (11.20) becomes:

$$\frac{dC_f(t)}{dt} = k_{on} B_{max} C_f(t) - k_{off} C_S(t) = k_3 C_f(t) - k_4 C_S(t) \tag{11.23}$$

with $k_3 = k_{on} B_{max}$ and $k_4 = k_{off}$.

Another important parameter is the equilibrium binding constant K_d which is defined with the ligand–receptor reaction in steady state as:

$$K_d = \frac{C_s}{C_r C_f} = \frac{k_{on}}{k_{off}} \tag{11.24}$$

The PET measurement is the result of the tracer present in the tissue and of that present in the blood of the ROI. Consequently the measurement equation for the three-tissue compartment model is:

$$C(t) = (1 - V_b)(C_f(t) + C_{ns}(t) + C_s(t)) + V_b C_b(t) \tag{11.25}$$

where C_b is whole blood tracer concentration including metabolites, and V_b is the fraction of the volume occupied by blood. However, the three-tissue model is *a priori* only nonuniquely identifiable, allowing two solutions for each parameter. To ensure unique identifiability, it is usually assumed that the exchange rates between the free tissue and nonspecific binding pools are sufficiently rapid (compared with the other rates of the model) so that the three-tissue compartment model reduces to the two-tissue model, where $C_{f+ns}(t) = C_f(t) + C_{ns}(t)$ is the free and nonspecific binding tracer concentration. It is for this reason that the two-tissue compartment model is the most widely adopted in studies, designed to quantify receptor binding. The model equations for the two-tissue compartment model are:

$$\begin{aligned} \frac{C_{f+ns}(t)}{dt} &= k_1 C_P(t) - (k_2 + k_3) C_{f+ns}(t) + k_4 C_S(t) \\ \frac{C_s(t)}{dt} &= k_3 C_{f+ns}(t) - k_4 C_S(t) \end{aligned} \tag{11.26 – 11.27}$$

with initial conditions $C_{f+ns}(0) = C_s(0) = 0$ and with:

$$k_3 = k_{on} B_{max} f \tag{11.28}$$

where f is given by:

$$f = \frac{C_f}{C_{f+ns}} = \frac{C_f}{C_f + C_{ns}} = \frac{C_f}{C_f\left(1 + \frac{C_{ns}}{C_f}\right)} = \frac{1}{1 + \frac{k_5}{k_6}} \tag{11.29}$$

The measurement equation thus becomes:

$$C(t) = (1 - V_b)(C_{f+ns}(t) + C_s(t)) + V_b C_b(t) \tag{11.30}$$

The model is now *a priori* uniquely identifiable. Moreover, in addition to k_1, k_2, k_3, k_4, and V_b, it is also possible to estimate the binding potential, BP:

$$BP = f \cdot \frac{B_{max}}{K_d} = \frac{k_3}{k_4} \tag{11.31}$$

and the distribution volumes:

$$V_{d-C_{f+ns}} = \left.\frac{C_{f+ns}}{C_p}\right|_{equilibrium} = \frac{K_1}{k_2} \tag{11.32}$$

$$V_{d-C_s} = \left.\frac{C_s}{C_p}\right|_{equilibrium} = \frac{K_1 k_3}{k_2 k_4} \tag{11.33}$$

$$V_d = \frac{C_S + C_{f+ns}}{C_p}\bigg|_{equilibrium} = \frac{K_1}{k_2} + \frac{K_1 k_3}{k_2 k_4} = \frac{K_1}{k_2}\left(1 + \frac{k_3}{k_4}\right) \tag{11.34}$$

11.5 Case study 5: A model of insulin secretion from a stochastic cellular model to a whole-body model

In this case study we first describe the insulin secretion model developed in the rat by Grodsky (1972) following the packet storage theory of Licko (1973) and briefly anticipated in Section 5.5.7. Then, starting from this model we will move to a whole-body model and discuss its clinical use in the context of an intravenous glucose tolerance test (IVGTT) test.

11.5.1 The stochastic cellular model

The perfused rat pancreas, which allowed the collection of the insulin response in the portal vein after a variety of glucose stimuli, is shown in Fig. 11–6; and the data are shown in Fig. 11–7.

The data propose a number of interesting features on insulin secretion:

- The response to a step increase of glucose concentration is instantaneous, and subsequently, the secretion decreases in a manner independent of the stimulus magnitude.
- If the stimulus is weak, there is no response; the magnitude of the response increases with stimulus magnitude and the response is biphasic: first phase with instantaneous increase and subsequent decay independent of the stimulus magnitude, and second phase slower and delayed.
- The secretion stops immediately after the stimulus stops.
- A prolonged stimulation with an elevated glucose level renders the pancreas hypersensitive to a subsequent stimulus.

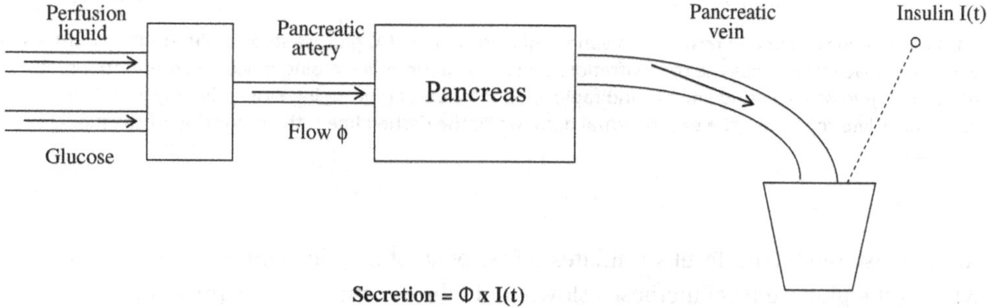

FIGURE 11–6 The perfused rat pancreas allowing estimation of insulin secretion from the perfusion flow and insulin concentration.

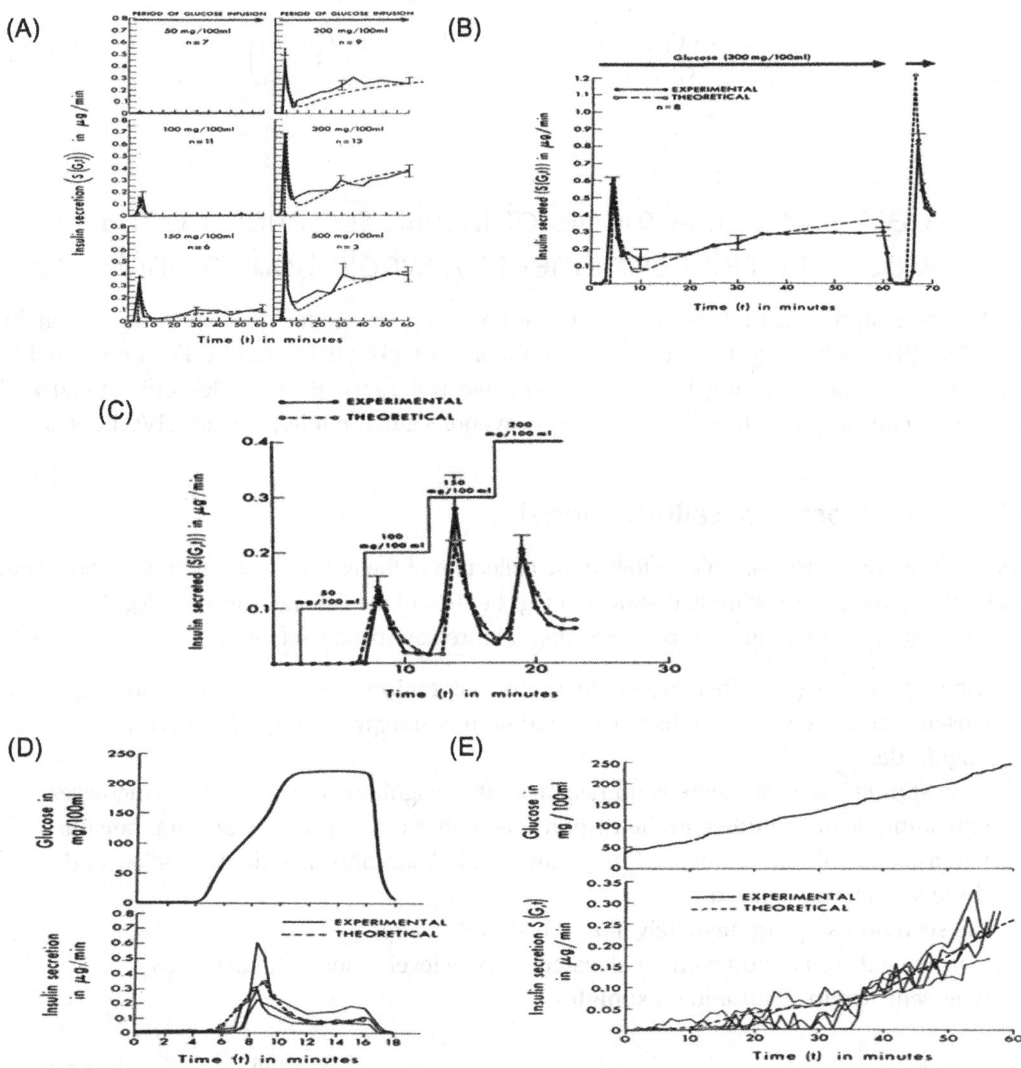

FIGURE 11–7 Insulin secretion in response to various glucose stimuli. (A) glucose steps of different concentrations; (B) two consecutive steps of glucose concentration; (C) step infusion of increasing glucose concentrations; (D) infusion of glucose increasing linearly and rapidly; (E) infusion of glucose increasing linearly and slowly. The continuous line represents the experimental data, while the dashed line is the prediction of the model described later.

- An increase of glucose level stimulates a first peak of insulin secretion only if it is rapid, while if the glucose level increases slowly only the second phase is present.
- Insulin secretion is additive, that is, it is the same whether glucose moves from zero to an elevated level or it reaches the elevated level through a number of increasing intermediate steps.

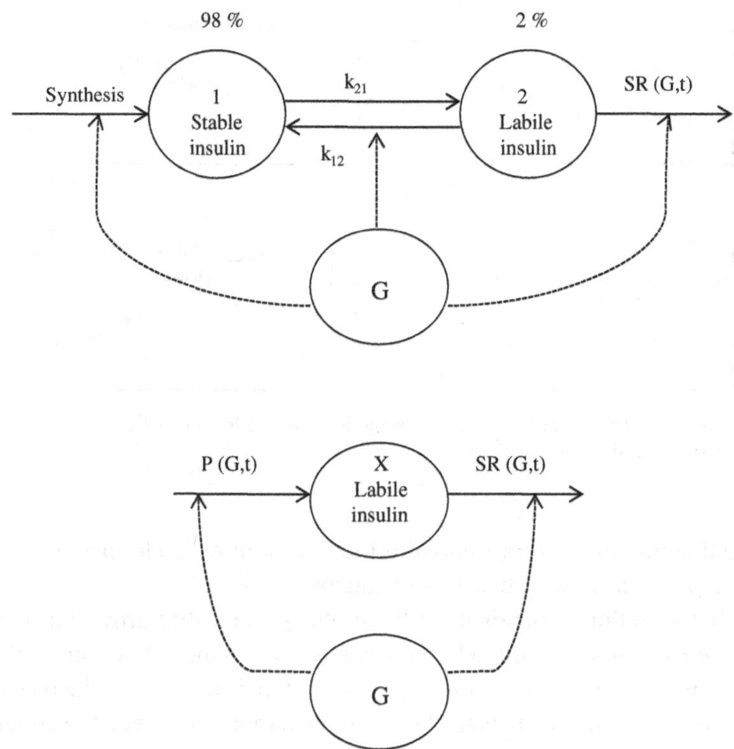

FIGURE 11–8 Tentative models of insulin secretion. A two compartment model is shown in the upper panel, while a simplified single compartment is shown in the bottom panel. k_{21} and k_{12} are the exchange parameters between the two compartments; P and SR denote production and secretion of insulin, both controlled by glucose G, which also controls the conversion from stable to labile insulin.

On the basis of the first three observations, the models of Fig. 11–8 were first proposed by Grodsky (1972). The model in Fig. 11–8 (top panel) has two compartments associated with the two forms of insulin in the pancreas: a stable insulin compartment which accounts for 98% of the pancreatic insulin and a labile insulin compartment of promptly releasable insulin which accounts for the remaining 2%. The two compartments exchange insulin with time constants of the order of 100 minutes for k_{12} and 1000 minutes for k_{21}.

The model describes the ability of glucose to increase the promptly releasable insulin with two control actions, one related to enhance the transformation of stable insulin into labile and one to stimulate the synthesis of new insulin. Taking into account the time constants for stable-labile exchanges, the model can be simplified into that of Fig. 11–8 (bottom panel). By denoting with X the amount of releasable insulin and with SR(G,t) and P (G,t) the processes of insulin secretion and provision, respectively, both controlled by glucose concentration G, the model equation is:

$$\dot{X}(t) = -SR(G,t) + P(G,t) \quad X(0) = X_0 \tag{11.35}$$

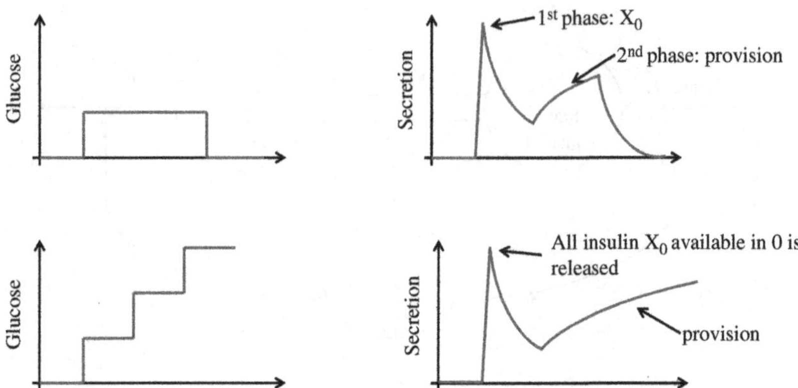

FIGURE 11–9 The prediction of the single compartment model to a step increase of glucose (*upper panel*) and to subsequent glucose steps (*lower panel*).

where the initial condition X_0 represents the total amount of labile insulin contained in the beta-cells of the pancreas in the absence of a glucose stimulus.

Assuming that secretion depends linearly on glucose and that provision of new insulin is slowly increasing over time, the model above is able to qualitatively describe the experimentally observed insulin secretion in the case of a step increase of glucose concentration (Fig. 11–7, panel A) as shown in Fig. 11–9 (upper panel). However the model is not able to describe the secretion data in response to subsequent glucose steps (Fig. 11–7, panels B and C) as shown for the staircase stimulus in Fig. 11–9 (lower panel). In fact, the first step causes the complete emptying of the compartment, after that there is a second phase of which only P(G,t) is responsible. The subsequent, more elevated glucose level of the second step only affects P(G,t) and the model cannot produce the characteristic more elevated new peak of the secretion.

Three lessons can be learned from the above exercise:

a. For a given stimulus, only a fraction of labile insulin is released (staircase experiment). This means that a certain amount of labile insulin remains available for subsequent glucose stimuli. The labile insulin compartment is nonhomogeneous.

b. To subsequent glucose steps of the staircase experiment, the amount of the first phase released insulin which is different and depends on the glucose level. This means that the released amount depends on glucose.

c. The first-phase insulin secretion is present only if the glucose stimulus varies rapidly. This means that the description of insulin secretion should include a glucose derivative control mechanism.

To be able to account for these features the theory of packet storage, Licko (1973) briefly anticipated in Section 5.5.7, was used. The basic assumptions are:

i. Labile insulin is formed by packets that do not behave in an homogeneous manner.

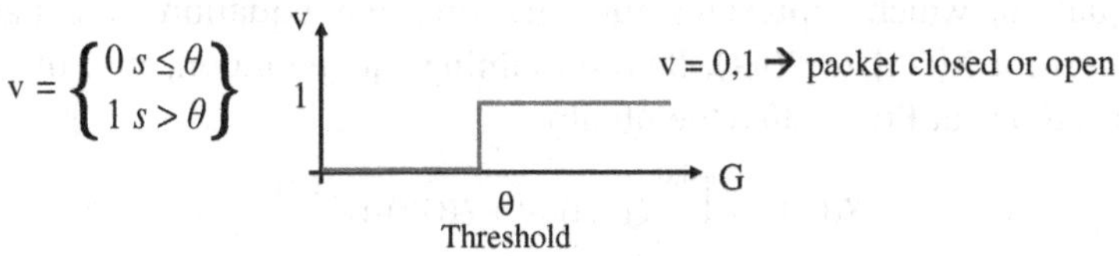

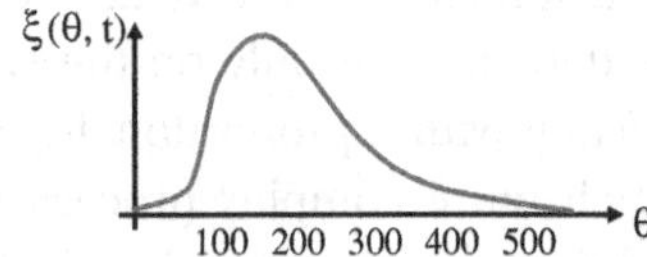

FIGURE 11–10 The threshold process (*upper panel*) and the threshold density function (*lower panel*).

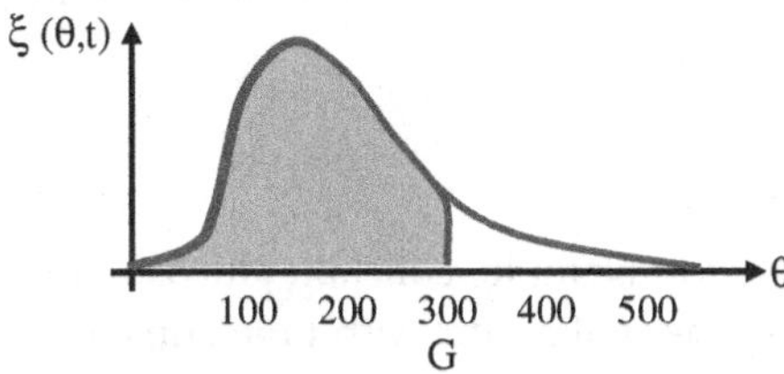

FIGURE 11–11 The amount of insulin releasable at time (t) for a stimulus (G).

ii. Each packet has its own sensitivity to glucose, that is, a threshold θ, so that if the stimulus above it opens up insulin can be released; if it is below, the packet remains closed, as depicted in Fig. 11–10 (upper panel).

The threshold density function ξ(θ,t), shown in Fig. 11–10 (lower panel), describes how insulin is distributed among packets, in particular ξ(θ,t) dθ is the amount of insulin releasable at time (t) in the packets with a threshold between θ and θ + dθ.

It is important to note that ξ depends on time since the amount of insulin in the packets will vary in time being dependent on secretion, provision, and exchanges among packets.

The stimulus acts only on the packets that have a threshold less than the glucose level (G), so that the amount of insulin which can be released at time (t) for a given level of the stimulus (G) is:

$$X(G,t) = \int_0^{G(t)} \xi(\vartheta, t)d\theta \tag{11.36}$$

as shown in Fig. 11–11.

Insulin secretion is assumed to be proportional to this quantity:

$$SR(G,t) = m(G)X(G,t) = m(G)\int_0^{G(t)} \xi(\vartheta, t)d\theta \tag{11.37}$$

where the constant m is in principle depending on G.

For this equation, which represents the measurement equation, one has to couple a dynamic equation for X(G,t) or $\xi(\theta,t)$. Before defining this equation, it is of interest to take the derivative of X(G,t) of Eq. 11.36. One obtains:

$$\dot{X}(G,t) = \int_0^{G(t)} \dot{\xi}(\vartheta,t)d\vartheta + \xi(G(t),t)\frac{dG(t)}{dt} \tag{11.38}$$

which defines the dynamics of X as a function of the dynamics of $\xi(\theta,t)$. The interesting observation is that the derivative of X depends not only on the stimulus (G), but also on its derivative; the derivative term is not acting with a proportionality constant but depends on ξ and time, ξ (G(t),t), that is, it is a much more complex process than a purely proportional and derivative control where the coefficients are constant in time. Often models of secretion of substances and hormones include a proportional and derivative control, but this assumption is often made only to describe the data. Here Eq. 11.38 shows that these two control actions arise naturally if the secretion process is a threshold process and the packets have different thresholds.

11.5.1.1 First-phase secretion

Looking at experimental data, for example, constant glucose infusion, one can describe insulin secretion with a single exponential model with time constant in principle being a function of G:

$$\dot{S}R = -m(G)SR \tag{11.39}$$

Thus,

$$d\,\dot{S}\,R = -m(G)\,dSR \tag{11.40}$$

Remembering that $dSR = m(G)\ \xi(\vartheta,t)\ d\vartheta$, one has that the packet differential equation due to secretion only (no provision) is:

$$\dot{\xi}(\vartheta,t) = -m(G)\xi(\vartheta,t) \tag{11.41}$$

and thus,

$$\xi(\vartheta,t) = \xi(\vartheta,0)e^{-m(G)t} \tag{11.42}$$

describes the dynamics of packets with threshold $\theta < G$.

Remark 1: $\xi(\vartheta,t) \to 0$ for $t \to \infty$ (with no provision all packets become empty).

Remark 2: $\xi(\vartheta,0)$ gives the subdivision among packets at time 0.

We can now write SR(G,t):

$$SR(G,t) = m(G)X(G,t) = m(G)\int_0^G \xi(\vartheta,t)\,d\vartheta = m(G)\,e^{-m(G)t}\int_0^G \xi(\vartheta,0)\,d\vartheta = m(G)\,e^{-m(G)t}X(G,0) \tag{11.43}$$

where

$$X(G,0) = \int_0^G \xi(\vartheta,0)d\vartheta \tag{11.44}$$

11.5.1.2 Second-phase secretion

We have to account now for two processes:

a. labile insulin provision P(G,t), which comprises new insulin synthesis and transformation of stable to labile, and its distribution among packets;

b. the exchange of insulin between packets.

i. Refilling process

Assuming G constant P(G,t) is described by first order dynamics:

$$\dot{P}(G,t) = -\alpha(G)[P(G,t) - P(G,\infty)] \quad P(G,0) = 0 \tag{11.45}$$

where $\alpha(G)$ is the time constant and $P(G,\infty)$, which depends on G, is the steady state level. To describe the distribution of P(G,t) among packets, we hypothesize that the packets, which at time 0 were more full, will receive more insulin; that is, P(G,t) distributes among packets according to the initial threshold density function. For a given packet with threshold (ϑ), the refilling process can be described by:

$$\dot{\xi}(\vartheta,t) = fP(G,t)\xi(\vartheta,0) \tag{11.46}$$

and posing $\gamma(\vartheta) = f\,\xi(\vartheta,0)$ one has:

$$\dot{\xi}(\vartheta,t) = \gamma(\vartheta)P(G,t) \tag{11.47}$$

ii. Exchange between packets

To describe this process we make two assumptions:

a. consider the generic packet λ, λ transfers insulin at time (t) in proportion to $\xi(\lambda,t)$,

b. insulin received by packet σ at time (t) is proportional to $\xi(\sigma,0)$.

Thus, the generic packet (ϑ) will have an input flux (ξ) in and an output flux ($\dot{\xi}_{out}$). $\dot{\xi}_{in}$ from packet σ the flux to ϑ is:

$$f'\xi(\sigma,t)\xi(\vartheta,0) \tag{11.48}$$

and thus

$$\dot{\xi}_{in}(\vartheta,t) = \int_0^\infty f'\xi(\vartheta,0)\xi(\sigma,t)\,d\sigma = f'\xi(\vartheta,0)\int_0^\infty \xi(\sigma,t)\,d\sigma \tag{11.49}$$

and posing $f'\xi(\vartheta,0) = \gamma'(\vartheta)$ one has:

$$\dot{\xi}_{in}(\vartheta,t) = \gamma'(\vartheta)\int_0^\infty \xi(\sigma,t)\,d\sigma \tag{11.50}$$

$\dot{\xi}_{out}$: from packet ϑ to σ the flux is:

$$f'\xi(\vartheta, t)\xi(\sigma, 0) \tag{11.51}$$

and thus,

$$\dot{\xi}_{out}(\vartheta, t) = -\int_0^\infty f'\xi(\vartheta, t)\xi(\sigma, 0)\,d\sigma = -\xi(\vartheta, t)\int_0^\infty f'\xi(\sigma, 0)\,d\sigma \tag{11.52}$$

and posing,

$$f'\xi(\sigma, 0) = \gamma'(\sigma) \tag{11.53}$$

one has:

$$\dot{\xi}_{out}(\vartheta, t) = -\xi(\vartheta, t)\int_0^\infty \gamma'(\sigma)\,d\sigma \tag{11.54}$$

and with:

$$\int_0^\infty \gamma'(\sigma)d\sigma = \Gamma'_\infty \tag{11.55}$$

one has:

$$\dot{\xi}_{out}(\vartheta, t) = -\Gamma'_\infty\xi(\vartheta, t) \tag{11.56}$$

We are now in a position to write the model equations: each packet has its own differential equation with all the various contributions described above.

For $\vartheta < G$:

$$\dot{\xi}(\vartheta, t) = \underbrace{-m(G)\xi(\vartheta, t)}_{\text{release}} + \underbrace{\gamma(\vartheta)P(G, t)}_{\text{provision}} - \underbrace{\Gamma'_\infty\xi(\vartheta, t)}_{\text{exchange out}} + \underbrace{\gamma'(\vartheta)\int_0^\infty \xi(\sigma, t)\,d\sigma}_{\text{exchange in}} \tag{11.57}$$

For $\vartheta > G$:

$$\dot{\xi}(\vartheta, t) = \underbrace{\gamma(\vartheta)P(G, t)}_{\text{provision}} - \underbrace{\Gamma'_\infty\xi(\vartheta, t)}_{\text{exchange out}} + \underbrace{\gamma'(\vartheta)\int_0^\infty \xi(\sigma, t)\,d\sigma}_{\text{exchange in}} \tag{11.58}$$

with initial condition $\xi(\vartheta,0)$ and $\gamma(\vartheta) = f\,\xi(\vartheta,0)$, $\gamma'(\vartheta) = f'\xi(\vartheta,0)$ and

$$\Gamma'_\infty = \int_0^\infty \gamma'(\vartheta)d\vartheta \tag{11.59}$$

There is an infinite number of differential equations, one for each value of ϑ.

$$\begin{aligned} &\dot{P}(G,t) = -\alpha(G)[P(G,t) - P(G,\infty)] \\ &SR(G,t) = m(G)\int_0^{G(t)} \xi(\vartheta,t)\,d\vartheta \end{aligned} \tag{11.60}$$

We still have to define the dependence of m and α from G and a functional description for $\xi(\vartheta,0)$ and $P(G,\infty)$. To do so the model has been compared to the experimental data. However, to arrive at a workable model we consider the case of a constant glucose stimulus by focusing on first-phase secretion.

Let us consider $m(G)$.

Measurements are average values of secretion at 1 minute intervals:

$$SR_M(G,n) = \int_n^{n+1} SR(G,t)\,dt \tag{11.61}$$

At time 0 one has thus:

$$SR_M(G,0) = \int_0^1 SR(G,t)\,dt = \int_0^1 m(G)X(G,0)\,e^{-m(G)t}dt = X(G,0)[1 - e^{-m(G)}] \tag{11.62}$$

Thus,

$$m'(G) = 1 - e^{-m(G)} = \frac{SR_M(G,0)}{X(G,0)} \tag{11.63}$$

$SR_M(G,0)$ is the height of the secretion peak, while $X(G,0)$ is the area under the first-phase secretion curve: both these values can be derived from the data. $m'(G)$ can be calculated for various of values of G as shown in Fig. 11–12, and thus one can conclude that $m = \text{constant} = 0.622\ \text{min}^{-1}$.

Let us focus now on $\xi(\vartheta,0)$.

One notes that $X(G,0)$ is the amount of insulin released during the first-phase insulin secretion stimulated by the instant step (G). It can thus be calculated as the area under the

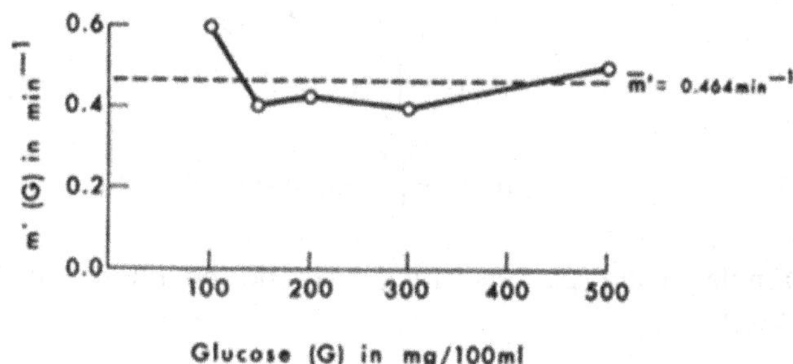

FIGURE 11–12 Parameter m′(G) calculated for various values of the stimulus (G).

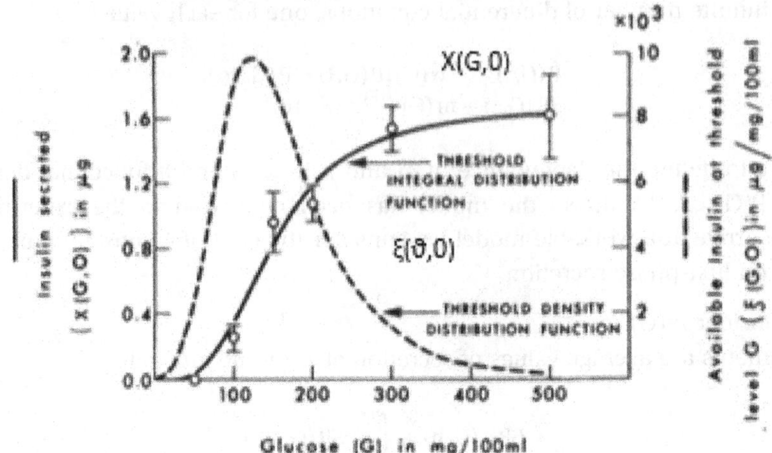

FIGURE 11–13 X(G,0), the amount of insulin released during the first-phase insulin secretion stimulated by the instant step G, and ξ(ϑ,0), its derivative with respect to G, plotted for various levels of the stimulus (G).

curve of SR(G,t) during the first phase (neglecting the second phase) for various levels of the stimulus (G) as shown in Fig. 11–13:

The data X(G,0) can be described by:

$$X(G,0) = X_{max}\frac{G^k}{C+G^k} \tag{11.64}$$

with $X_{max} = 1.65$ pg; $C = 1.51\ 10^7$ and $k = 3.3$.

Thus, ξ(ϑ,0) can be determined by taking the derivative of X(G,0) with respect to G:

$$\xi(\vartheta,0) = kX_{max}\frac{C\vartheta^{k-1}}{(C+\vartheta^k)^2} \tag{11.65}$$

and is plotted in Fig. 11–13.

Consider now $P(G,\infty)$.

Posing:

$$X_1(G,t) = \int_0^G \xi(\vartheta,t)\,d\vartheta \tag{11.66}$$

$$X_2(G,t) = \int_0^\infty \xi(\vartheta,t)\,d\vartheta \tag{11.67}$$

the amount of releasable insulin (packets with $\vartheta < G$) and the amount of nonreleasable insulin (packets with $\vartheta > G$).

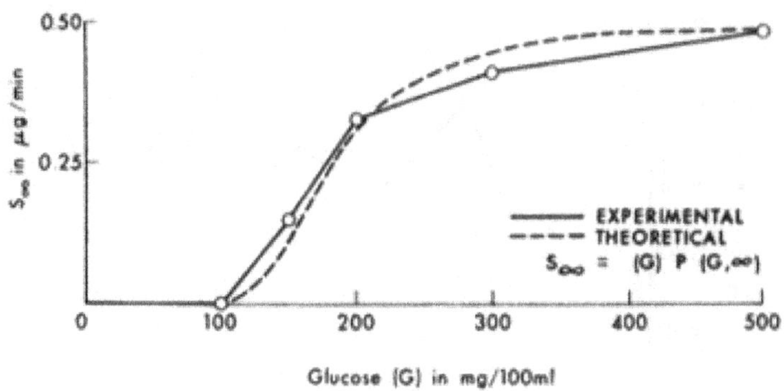

FIGURE 11–14 The steady state insulin secretion plotted for various values of the stimulus (G).

Integrating the differential equations of Eqs. (11.57) and (11.58) one has:

$$\dot{X}_1(G,t) = -mX_1(G,t) + \Gamma(G)P(G,t) + \Gamma'(G)[X_1(G,t) + X_2(G,t)] - \Gamma'_\infty X_1(G,t) \tag{11.68}$$

$$\dot{X}_2(G,t) = [\Gamma_\infty - \Gamma(G)]P(G,t) + [\Gamma'_\infty - \Gamma'(G)][X_1(G,t) + X_2(G,t)] - \Gamma'_\infty X_2(G,t) \tag{11.69}$$

and posing:

$$\Gamma(G) = \int_0^G \gamma(\vartheta)\, d\vartheta \tag{11.70}$$

$$\Gamma'(G) = \int_0^G \gamma'(\vartheta)\, d\vartheta \tag{11.71}$$

In the steady state, that is, $\dot{X}_1 = \dot{X}_2 = 0$, and one obtains:

$$mX_1(G,\infty) = \Gamma_\infty P(G,\infty) \tag{11.72}$$

The left hand term member represents the steady state secretion which can be measured from the data for various values of G. Thus, one has the values of $\Gamma_\infty P(G,\infty)$ which are plotted in Fig. 11–14 and can be approximated by the equation:

$$SR_\infty = SR(G,\infty) = \Gamma_\infty P(G,\infty) = \frac{0.5 \cdot G^{10}}{8.75 \cdot 10^{21} + 2.25 \cdot 10^{15} \cdot G^3 + 3.5 \cdot 10^6 \cdot G^7 + G^{10}} \tag{11.73}$$

Finally, let us consider $\alpha(G)$. This parameter has been estimated from the constant glucose infusion data by weighted least squares and it has been shown (see Fig. 11–15) to not depend on G:

$$\alpha(G) = \alpha = 0.0377 \text{ min}^{-1} \tag{11.74}$$

Thus, it characterizes a slow dynamics, that is, $1/\alpha$ is approximately 30 minutes.

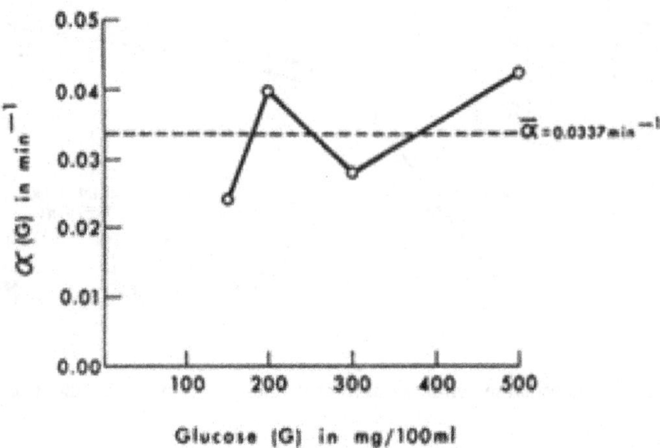

FIGURE 11–15 Parameter $\alpha(G)$ plotted for various values of the stimulus (G).

Before proceeding, it is useful to summarize where we have arrived at, that is, the *two-state variable model*:

$$\dot{X}_1(G,t) = -mX_1(G,t) + \Gamma(G)P(G,t) + \Gamma'(G)[X_1(G,t) + X_2(G,t)] - \Gamma'_{\infty}X_1(G,t) \tag{11.75}$$

$$\dot{X}_2(G,t) = [\Gamma_{\infty} - \Gamma(G)]P(G,t) + [\Gamma'_{\infty} - \Gamma'(G)][X_1(G,t) + X_2(G,t)] - \Gamma'_{\infty}X_2(G,t) \tag{11.76}$$

where

$$X_1(G,0) = \int_0^G \xi(\vartheta,0)\,d\vartheta; \quad X_2(G,0) = \int_0^{\infty} \xi(\vartheta,0)\,d\vartheta; \tag{11.77}$$

$$\dot{P}(G,t) = -\alpha[P(G,t) - P(G,\infty)] \tag{11.78}$$

$$SR(G,t) = mX_1(G,t) \tag{11.79}$$

This two-state variable model with all the parameters obtained above has been used to describe the data (dashed line in Fig. 11–7) and to formulate theories on the cellular mechanisms of insulin secretion.

This model can be further simplified into a *one-state variable model* for elevated levels of G ($>$300 mg/100 mL). In this case (see Fig. 11–11), only a few packets are not available for release, and thus:

$$\Gamma(G) = \int_0^G \gamma(\vartheta)\,d\vartheta \cong \Gamma_{\infty} \qquad \Gamma'(G) = \int_0^G \gamma'(\vartheta)\,d\vartheta \cong \Gamma'_{\infty} \tag{11.80}$$

The model becomes:

$$\dot{X}_1(G,t) = -mX_1(G,t) + \Gamma_\infty P(G,t) + \Gamma'_\infty[X_1(G,t) + X_2(G,t)] - \Gamma'_\infty X_1(G,t) \tag{11.81}$$

$$\dot{X}_2(G,t) = -\Gamma'_\infty X_2(G,t) \tag{11.82}$$

with

$$X_1(G,0) = \int_0^G \xi(\vartheta,0)\,d\vartheta; \quad X_2(G,0) \cong 0 \tag{11.83}$$

$X_2(G,t)$, however, can be neglected because it decreases exponentially from an almost zero initial condition (a few packets have a threshold $\vartheta > G$), thus the model becomes a one-state variable model:

$$\dot{X}_1 = -mX_1(G,t) + \Gamma_\infty P(G,t) \quad X_1(G,0) = \int_0^G \xi(\vartheta,0)\,d\vartheta \tag{11.84}$$

$$P'(G,t) = -\alpha[P(G,t) - P(G,\infty)] \tag{11.85}$$

$$SR(G,t) = mX_1(G,t) \tag{11.86}$$

It is interesting to also analyze the performance of the one-state model.

i. Step glucose infusion (see Fig. 11–16)
In the first minutes the major role is played by the insulin available at time 0. $X_1(G,t)$ and $SR(G,t) = mX_1(G,t)$ follow first order dynamics with time constant (m) (see (11.84)). Once first-phase secretion has been exhausted, the packets restart their replenishment due to P(G,t) which, by starting from 0, tends with time constant $1/\alpha$ to the steady state level $P(G,\infty)$ by increasing again the amount $X_1(G,t)$ which is responsible for insulin secretion.

ii. Double step glucose infusion (see Fig. 11–17)
After the first glucose step, the packets close ($X_1(G,t)$ the releasable quantity, tends to zero in the absence of stimulus, and secretion stops immediately ($SR(G,t) = mX(G,t) = 0$). The packets however are continuously replenished thanks to P(G,t) which, starting from $P(G,\infty)$, tends to zero with time constant $1/\alpha$ (steady state level in the absence of a stimulus). Thus, even in the presence of virtually no secretion, the replenishment of the packets continues allowing a second peak greater than the first once the stimulus arrives at a value allowing secretion to occur.

iii. Staircase glucose infusion (additivity of first-phase insulin secretion) (see Fig. 11–18)
Let us consider a first case where glucose increases from level 0 to level G_2 in one step. Insulin release during the first phase is:

$$X_3 = \int_0^{G_2} \xi(\vartheta,0)\,d\vartheta \tag{11.87}$$

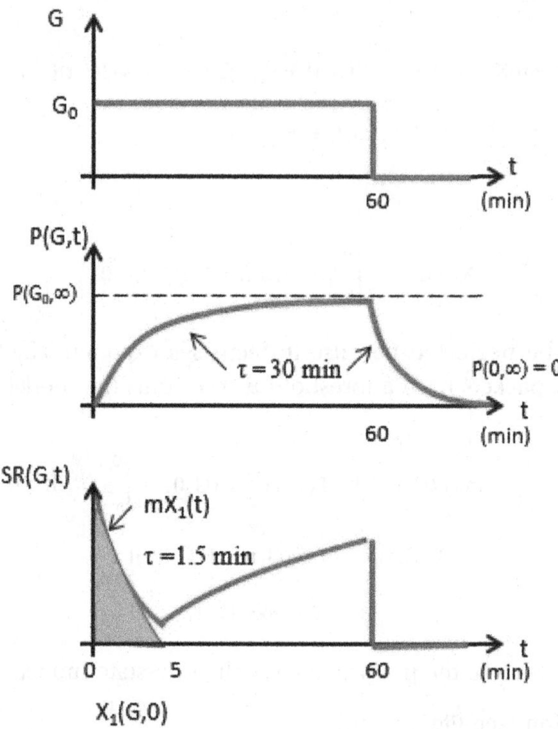

FIGURE 11–16 Performance of the one-state variable model for a step glucose infusion.

Consider now the case where glucose increases from level 0 to an intermediate level G_1: insulin released during the first phase is:

$$X_1 = \int_0^{G_1} \xi(\vartheta, 0)\, d\vartheta \tag{11.88}$$

Let us assume now that at time t*, for example, t* = 5 minutes, glucose stimulus increases from G_1 to the final level G_2. The packets with threshold ϑ between 0 and G_1 are almost empty because a time interval greater than three times the constant $T = 1/m \cong 1.5$ minutes has elapsed. In addition, both the provision which has started at time 0 with a time constant $T = 1/\alpha \cong 30$ minutes, and the exchange between packets provide a negligible contribution in the first minutes. Therefore, the amount released during the first phase in response to the second step is almost equal to that present in the packets with a threshold between G_1 and G_2 at time t*,

$$X_2 \cong \int_{G_1}^{G_2} \xi(\vartheta, t^*)\, d\vartheta \tag{11.89}$$

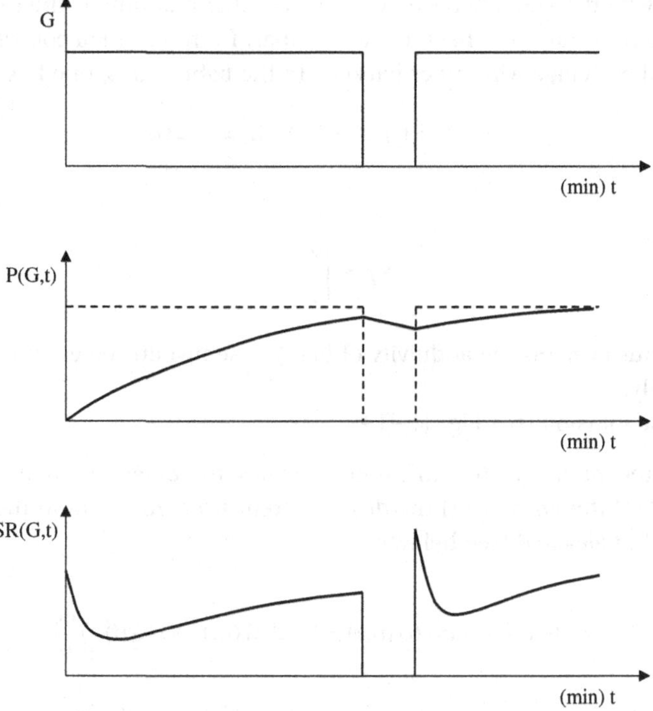

FIGURE 11–17 Performance of the one-state variable model for a double step glucose infusion.

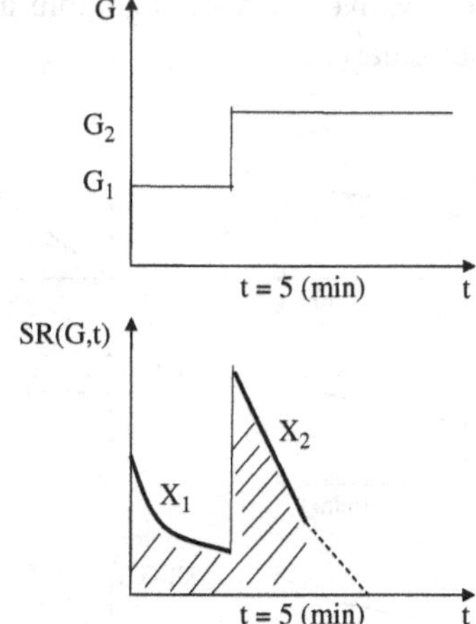

FIGURE 11–18 Performance of the one-state variable model for a staircase glucose infusion.

The packets with threshold between G_1 and G_2 contain at time t^* the same insulin they had at time 0 (they have not been released) apart from the small contribution of provision and exchange with other packets. In the light of this, one has:

$$\xi(\vartheta, t^*) \cong \xi(\vartheta, 0) \quad G_1 \leq \vartheta \leq G_2 \tag{11.90}$$

and thus

$$X_2 \cong \int_{G_1}^{G_2} \xi(\vartheta, 0)\, d\vartheta \tag{11.91}$$

The model thus explains the additivity of first-phase insulin secretion observed experimentally.

iv. Ramp glucose infusion (see Fig. 11–19)

To describe the ramp glucose infusion, one has to remember that in the differential equation for $X_1(G,t)$ the term $\xi(\vartheta,t)\, dG/dt$ is different from zero due to the fact that G is no longer constant, but elevated (see below):

$$\dot{X}_1(G, t) = -mX_1(G(t), t) + \Gamma_\infty P(G(t), t) + \xi(G(t), t)\frac{dG}{dt} \tag{11.92}$$

If glucose concentration increases rapidly, for example, a value of 250 mg/100 mL is reached in 5 minutes, the derivative term is large and the model can reproduce the first peak of secretion observed experimentally due to the rapid release of insulin contained in all packets that can release insulin; in contrast if glucose increases slowly, for example, it reaches an elevated value at 60 minutes, the derivative term is negligible and secretion increases in time but without showing a first phase release.

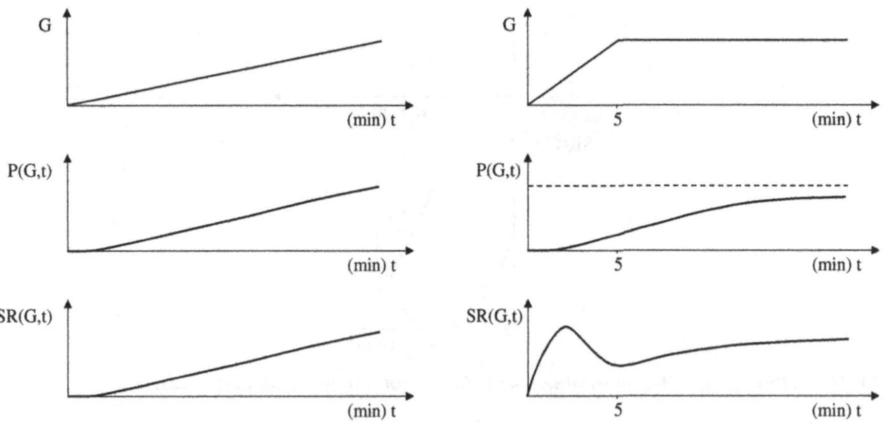

FIGURE 11–19 Performance of the one-state variable model for a ramp glucose infusion.

To arrive at the Eq. 11.92, one starts from:

$$\dot{\xi}(\vartheta, t) = -m\xi(\vartheta, t) + \gamma(\vartheta)P(G, t) - \Gamma'_{\infty}\xi(\vartheta, t) + \gamma'(\vartheta)\int_0^{\infty}\xi(\sigma, t)\,d\sigma \tag{11.93}$$

Integrating with respect to $d\vartheta$ from 0 and G(t) one has at the left member:

$$\int_0^{G(t)}\dot{\xi}(\vartheta, t)\,d\vartheta = \dot{X}(G(t), t) + \xi(G(t), t)\frac{dG}{dt} \tag{11.94}$$

and the right hand term, after simplifications, becomes:

$$-mX(G(t), t) + \Gamma_{\infty}P(G(t), t) \tag{11.95}$$

Thus,

$$\dot{X}(G(t), t) - \xi(G(t), t)\frac{dG}{dt} = -mX(G(t), t) + \Gamma_{\infty}P(G(t), t) \tag{11.96}$$

$$\dot{X}(G(t), t) = -mX(G(t), t) + \Gamma_{\infty}P(G(t), t) + \xi(G(t), t)\frac{dG}{dt} \tag{11.97}$$

11.5.2 The whole-body model

We will now derive from the cellular model a minimal (parsimonious) whole-body model of insulin secretion which can be used in a clinical context in conjunction with an intravenous (IVGGT) and an oral (MTT/OGTT) test, already discussed in Section 5.5.7. The derivation below holds for the IVGTT test, while the MTT/OGTT requires a modification since the time course of glucose is much slower than with an IVGTT (interested readers can consult Breda *et al.*, 2001; Cobelli *et al.*, 2014).

Since at whole-body level insulin is measured in plasma, a model of insulin kinetics is needed. However, since insulin is degraded by the liver (typically 50–60%), only a fraction of insulin secretion will reach the plasma (Fig. 11–20). Therefore only posthepatic secretion from insulin data, that is, insulin secretion and liver extraction, can be inferred. Fortunately, a substance exists, C-peptide (CP), which is secreted equimolarly with insulin but is not degraded by the liver. CP plasma concentrations reflect, apart from the small delay introduced by the liver, the pancreatic secretion of CP, and thus of insulin. A typical IVGTT data set, where also CP concentrations are measured in plasma, is shown in Fig. 11–21.

Several studies have shown that CP kinetics are linear and time invariant also in the presence of changing glucose and insulin concentrations; and can be described by the two compartment model shown in Fig. 11–22, where compartment 1 represents plasma and

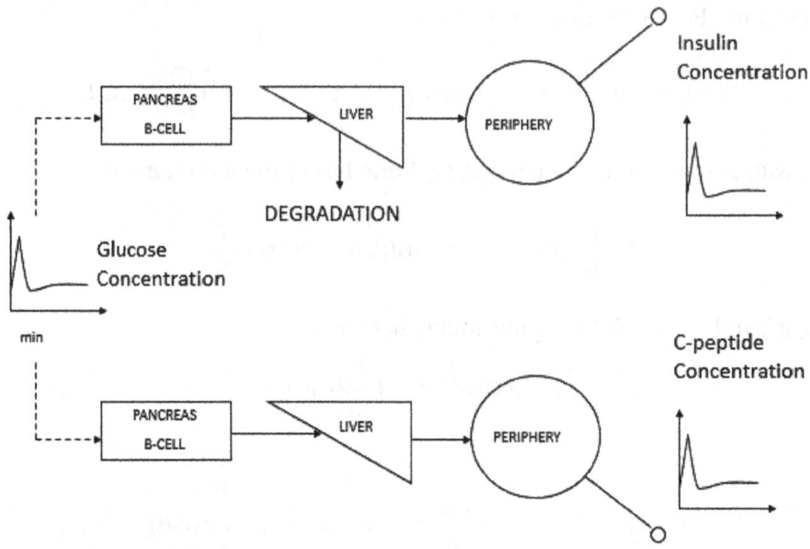

FIGURE 11–20 Relation between insulin and C-peptide. The two substances, equimolarly cosecreted by the pancreas, reach the liver where insulin, but not C-peptide, is degraded. Thus, the measurement of C-peptide in plasma reflects insulin secretion, while insulin is only a fraction of the secretion, that is, the posthepatic delivery.

rapidly equilibrating tissues and compartment 2 represents the other tissues. Assuming that secretion enters compartment 1, the model equations are:

$$\dot{Q}_1(t) = -(k_{01} + k_{21}) \cdot Q_1(t) + k_{12} \cdot Q_2(t) + SR(t) \quad Q_1(0) = Q_{1b} \tag{11.98}$$

$$\dot{Q}_2(t) = -k_{12} \cdot Q_2(t) + k_{21} \cdot Q_1(t) \quad Q_2(0) = Q_{2b} \tag{11.99}$$

$$C_1(t) = \frac{Q_1(t)}{V} \tag{11.100}$$

where Q_1 and Q_2 denote the mass of CP in compartments 1 and 2, respectively; k_{12} and k_{21} the transfer rate constants (min^{-1}) between the two compartments; $k_{01}(min^{-1})$, the parameter responsible for the irreversible elimination; SR (pmol/min), the pancreatic secretion; and V (l), the distribution volume in the accessible compartment.

Now we have to propose a parametric description of SR(t). The starting point is the cellular model (described in Section 11.5.1) in which we will introduce a number of simplifying assumptions to adapt the model to IVGTT and arrive at a minimal (parsimonious) model, that is, robust and with a minimal number of model parameters which can be estimated from the data.

The starting point to describe SR(G,t) is the cellular model we have developed:

$$\dot{\xi}(\vartheta, t) = -m\xi(\vartheta, t) + \gamma(\vartheta)P(G, t) + \gamma' \int_0^{\infty} \xi(\sigma, t)d\sigma - \Gamma'_{\infty}(\vartheta, t) \tag{11.101}$$

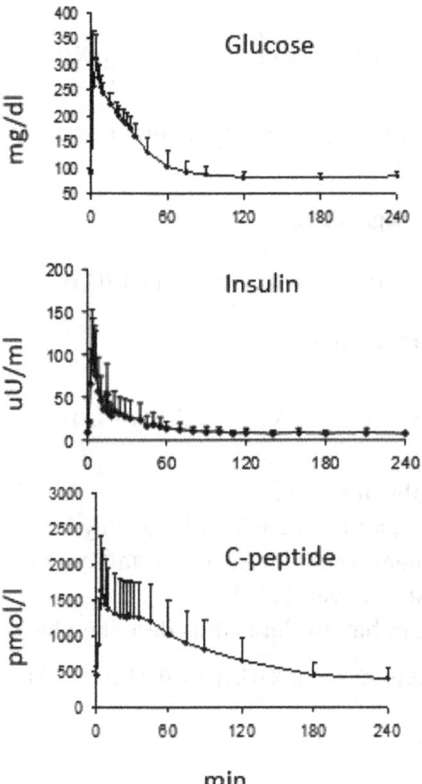

FIGURE 11–21 An intravenous glucose tolerance test (IVGTT) data set in seven normal individuals with measurement of glucose, insulin, and C-peptide concentrations (mean ± SD are reported).

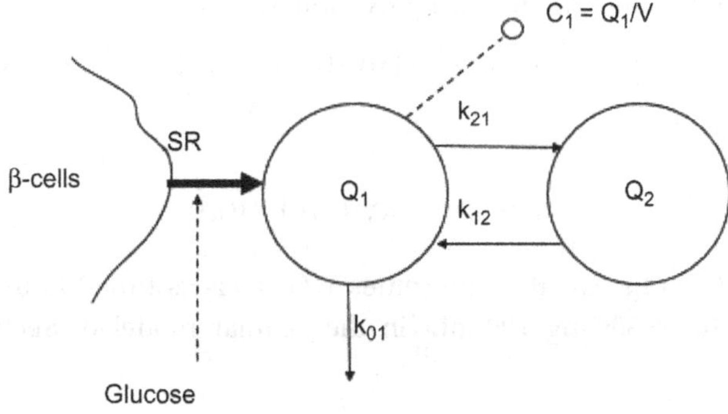

FIGURE 11–22 A two-compartment model of C-peptide kinetics.

$$SR(G,t) = m\int_0^{G(t)} \xi(\vartheta,t)\,d\vartheta = mX(G,t) \tag{11.102}$$

We will develop a number of simplifications in order to arrive at a tractable whole-body model:

i. packet insulin exchange negligible:

$$\dot{\xi}(\vartheta,t) = -m\xi(\vartheta,t) + \gamma(\vartheta)P(G,t) \quad \vartheta < G \tag{11.103}$$

ii. integrating from 0 to G(t) one has:

$$\dot{X}(G,t) = -mX(G,t) + \Gamma(G)P(G,t) + \xi(G,t)\frac{dG}{dt} \tag{11.104}$$

iii. derivative term is negligible for $t > 0$.

The dG/dt term during an IVGTT is very large only in $t = 0+$. Thus, one can put the derivative term in the initial condition $X(0) = X_0$ and neglect it during the second phase $(t > 0+)$ (details in Licko & Silver, 1975).

The dynamics of releasable insulin is thus described by:

$$\dot{X}(G,t) = -mX(G,t) + \Gamma(G)P(G,t) \quad X(0) = X_0 \tag{11.105}$$

iv. Description of provision

Let us suppose:

$$Y(G,t) = \Gamma(G)P(G,t) \tag{11.106}$$

Y(G,t) describes the fraction of provision P(G,t), which distributes among packets with a threshold less than G, and is thus releasable.

We assume that Y(G,t) follows first order dynamics:

$$\dot{Y}(G,t) = -\alpha[Y(G,t) - Y(G,\infty)] \tag{11.107}$$

The model becomes:

$$\dot{X}(G,t) = -mX(G,t) + Y(G,t) \tag{11.108}$$

The dependence of G on the steady state values $Y(G,\infty)$ is assumed to be linear in the range of interest, that is, $100 \div 300$ mg/100 mL (in the cellular model of Section 11.5.1 it was a rational function):

$$Y(G,\infty) = \begin{cases} Y_\infty & G < h \\ \beta[G-h] + Y_\infty & h < G < 300 \end{cases} \tag{11.109}$$

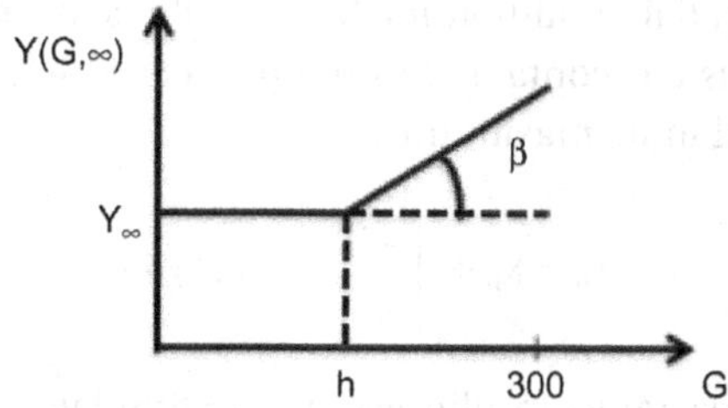

FIGURE 11–23 Y(G,t) plotted as a function of the stimulus (G).

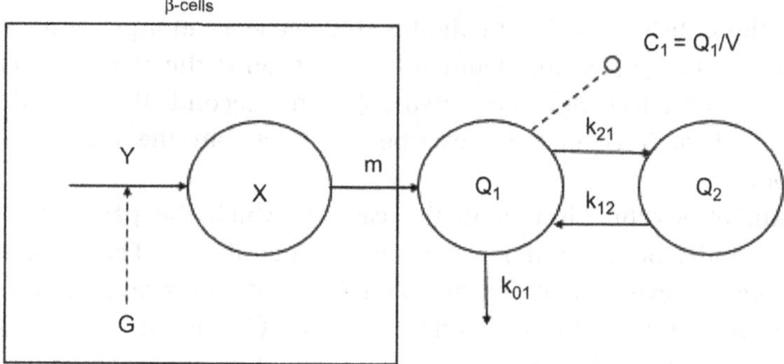

FIGURE 11–24 The C-peptide oral minimal model.

Here, as shown in Fig. 11–23, h is a threshold above which Y is stimulated (usually very similar to the basal value), β represents the beta-cell responsivity to a glucose stimulus, and $Y(G, \infty)$ accounts for the fact that there is an insulin provision also in basal conditions due to other secretagogues, for example, amino acids.

Summarizing, one has:

$$\dot{Y}(G,t) = -\alpha[Y(G,t) - \beta(G-h) - Y_{\infty}] \tag{11.110}$$

The model is shown in Fig. 11–24 and the model equations are:

$$\dot{Q}_1(t) = -(k_{01} + k_{21}) \cdot Q_1(t) + k_{12} \cdot Q_2(t) + m \cdot X(t) \quad Q_1(0) = Q_{1b} \tag{11.111}$$

$$\dot{Q}_2(t) = -k_{12} \cdot Q_2(t) + k_{21} \cdot Q_1(t) \quad Q_2(0) = Q_{2b} \tag{11.112}$$

$$\dot{X}(t) = -m \cdot X(t) + Y(G,t) \quad X(0) = X_0 \tag{11.113}$$

$$\dot{Y}(G,t) = -\alpha[Y(G,t) - Y(G,\infty)] \quad Y(0) = Y_{\infty} \tag{11.114}$$

$$C_1(t) = \frac{Q_1(t)}{V} \tag{11.115}$$

It is worth noting that the initial condition for X, X_0, is the sum of releasable insulin in basal conditions, X_b, and of the insulin contained in the packets which open up at time zero when glucose increases from basal to its maximum value:

$$X_0 = X_b + \int_{G_b}^{G_b+G^{max}} \xi(\vartheta, 0)\, d\vartheta \tag{11.116}$$

X_0 is responsible for the first rapid insulin secretion stimulated by the increase of glucose immediately after the test, while provision of insulin Y is responsible for the slower second-phase secretion.

The model is linear but is too complex for the data. First, *a priori* identifiability, assessed using the transfer function method with glucose as an input and CP as an output, shows that the volume (V) is nonidentifiable and, even if the model is reparameterized with β/V, four model parameters have two solutions; second, if the model is identified from the IVGTT data, it is able to describe the data, but the precision of parameter estimates is poor.

An important observation is that in the case in which the parameters of CP would be known, the model becomes *a priori* uniquely identifiable. The ideal strategy would be to add a second experiment to the IVGTT by administering to the subject a CP bolus with a concomitant somatostatin infusion to inhibit insulin secretion and identify the two-compartment CP model; clearly this approach is rather invasive. Fortunately, there is an alternative noninvasive strategy that allows one to eliminate this additional invasive experiment: one can use the results reported in Van Cauter *et al.* (1992), where CP kinetics after a bolus of CP have been studied in three populations of normal, obese, and diabetic subjects of different ages. Due to the modest interindividual variability of CP kinetics, the kinetic parameters of CP in an individual can be calculated with good approximation from a population model, which can be personalized on the basis of anthropometric measurements (sex, age, weight, and height of the person). In Table 11–3 the individual versus population strategy is compared in seven subjects,

Table 11–3 C-peptide kinetics: individual versus population model.

#	k_{01} (min^{-1})	k_{21} (min^{-1})	k_{12} (min^{-1})	V_1 (mL/kg)	k_{01} (min^{-1})	k_{21} (min^{-1})	k_{12} (min^{-1})	V_1 (mL/kg)
1	0.074	0.050	0.056	56.7	0.060	0.052	0.050	60.9
2	0.071	0.049	0.052	47.1	0.060	0.051	0.050	55.3
3	0.053	0.045	0.047	76.9	0.058	0.053	0.049	71.5
4	0.069	0.061	0.056	52.3	0.061	0.051	0.050	59.7
5	0.051	0.062	0.056	71.6	0.059	0.052	0.050	67.8
6	0.071	0.067	0.065	53.0	0.060	0.051	0.050	51.3
7	0.055	0.047	0.064	54.3	0.060	0.051	0.050	58.7
Mean	0.064	0.054	0.056	58.8	0.060	0.052	0.050	60.7
SD	0.011	0.011	0.005	11.1	0.0008	0.0008	0.0003	6.9

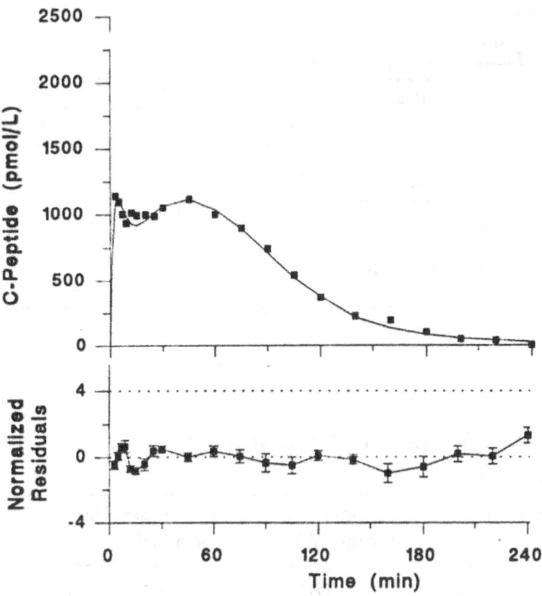

FIGURE 11–25 The fit of the C-peptide oral minimal model to data of a representative normal subject.

and the good approximation provided by the population approach slide is numerically documented.

An example of model fit is shown in Fig. 11–25 for a representative normal subject. The model provides two important indices of beta-cell function, one related to the first-phase insulin secretion, Φ_1, and one related to the second-phase secretion, Φ_2. They can be expressed as:

$$\Phi_1 = \frac{X_0}{\Delta G}. \tag{11.117}$$

$$\Phi_2 = \beta \tag{11.118}$$

The structure of the model evidencing the beta-cell function parameters is redrawn in Fig. 11–26.

It is of interest to compare the individual versus population strategy also in relation to the beta-cell model parameters. This is done in Table 11–4 in the same seven subjects where the CP kinetics were assessed (Table 11–3).

The model also provides the time course of insulin secretion is shown in (11.120):

$$SR(t) = k_{01} \cdot Q_{1b} + m \cdot X(t) \tag{11.119}$$

which is shown in Fig. 11–27 as an example for the same subject of Fig. 11–25.

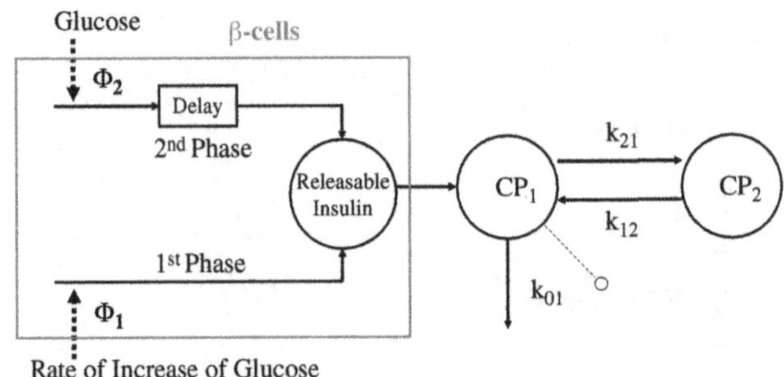

FIGURE 11–26 The C-peptide oral minimal model evidencing the beta-cell function first and second-phase responsivity indices.

Table 11.4 Beta-cell parameters: individual (A) versus population (B) model (mean ± SD are reported).

	m (min^{-1})	α (min^{-1})	Φ_1 (pmol per mg/dL)	$\Phi_2 = \beta$ (pmol/min per mg/dL)	h (mg/dL)	X_0 (pmol)
A	**0.58 ± 0.09 (33%)**	0.075 ± 0.0082 (24%)	5.03 ± 0.81 (7%)	0.604 ± 0.072 (16%)	88 ± 3 (18%)	1786 ± 353 (7%)
B	**0.640 ± 0.11 (39%)**	0.087 ± 0.017 (27%)	4.69 ± 0.66 (7%)	0.568 ± 0.046 (17%)	90 ± 3 (19%)	1662 ± 298 (7%)

Mean ± SD.

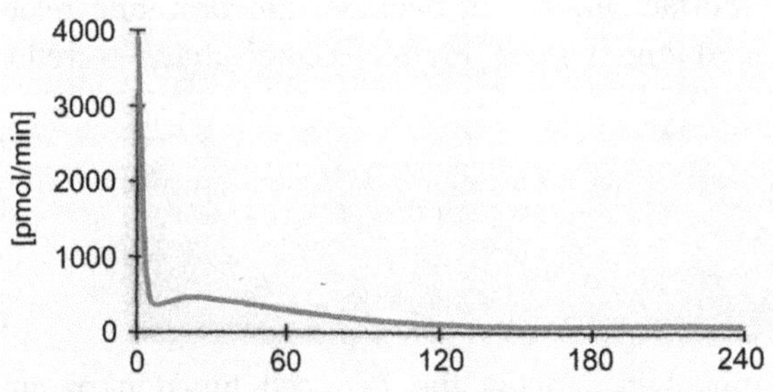

FIGURE 11–27 The prediction of insulin secretion by the C-peptide oral minimal model for the same subject of Fig. 11–25.

11.6 Case study 6: a model of insulin control

In pathophysiology it is of the utmost importance to quantitatively measure the control that insulin exerts on glucose metabolism. In fact, insulin stimulates glucose utilization and inhibits glucose production (Fig. 11–28) and it is easily appreciated that derangement

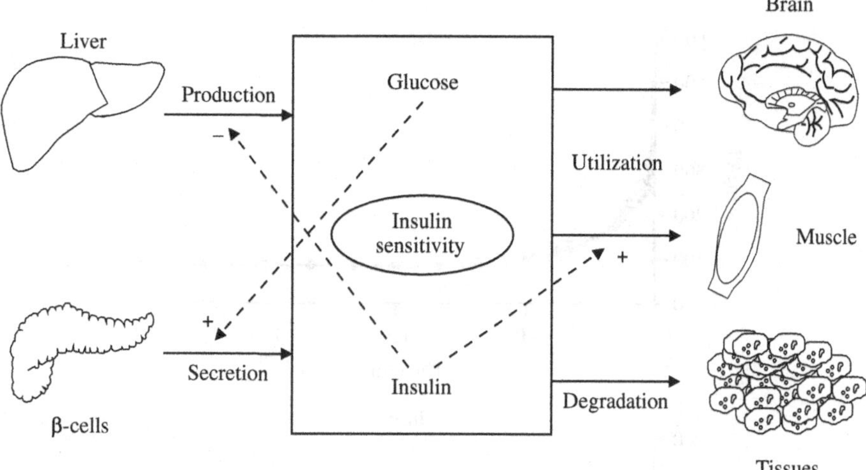

FIGURE 11–28 The glucose–insulin control system.

of these two control features can lead to glucose intolerance and type 2 diabetes. In this case study we discuss a widely adopted model. This is the glucose minimal model that is used to measure insulin action from an intravenous glucose tolerance test (IVGTT) (see Fig. 11–29).

The feedback nature of the glucose-insulin system poses major difficulties. A closed-loop model must be postulated, thus possible inaccuracies in modeling insulin action and secretion can compensate for each other. To avoid this, the feedback loop can be opened conceptually by partitioning the whole system into two subsystems (Fig. 11–30) linked by the measured variables, insulin and glucose concentration. The two subsystems can be separately modeled. For the model of insulin action on glucose production and utilization, insulin is the (known) input and glucose the output (Fig. 11–31).

Since the whole model is intended for clinical use, another important attribute is its parsimony, in other words the model must be simple; this is to enable all the parameters to be estimated with acceptable precision from the data of an individual subject. At the same time the model must not be simplistic, since it needs to be able to provide a reliable description of the relevant physiological processes. It is in this context that the term, minimal model, was coined (Bergman *et al.*, 1979).

The model is shown in Fig. 11–32.

Its key features are as follows: (1) glucose kinetics are described by a single-compartment model; (2) glucose inhibition of production and stimulation of utilization are proportional to glucose plasma concentration; and (3) insulin inhibition of glucose production and

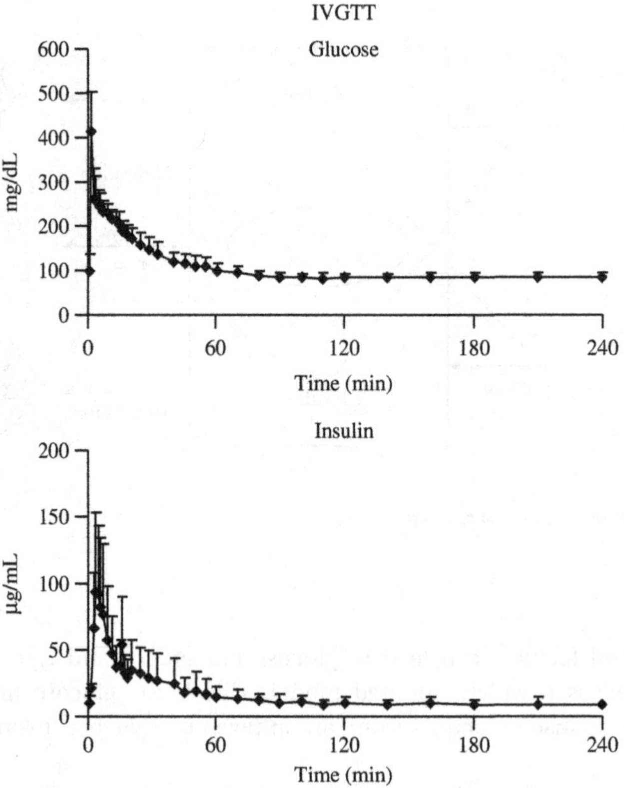

FIGURE 11–29 Glucose and insulin concentrations after an intravenous glucose tolerance test (IVGTT) in thirteen normal subjects (mean ± SD are reported).

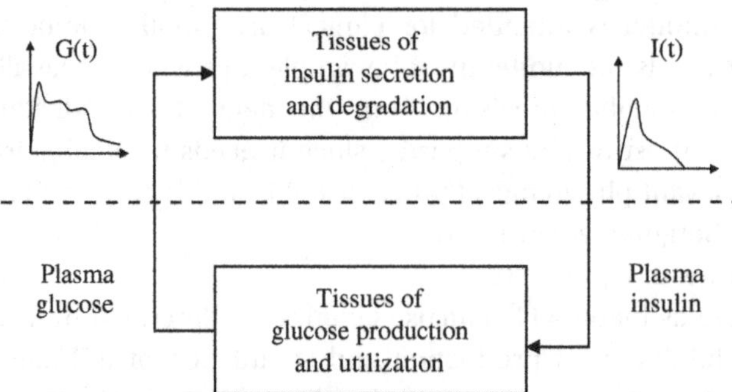

FIGURE 11–30 Partitioning of the feedback system into glucose and insulin subsystems, linked by plasma measurements.

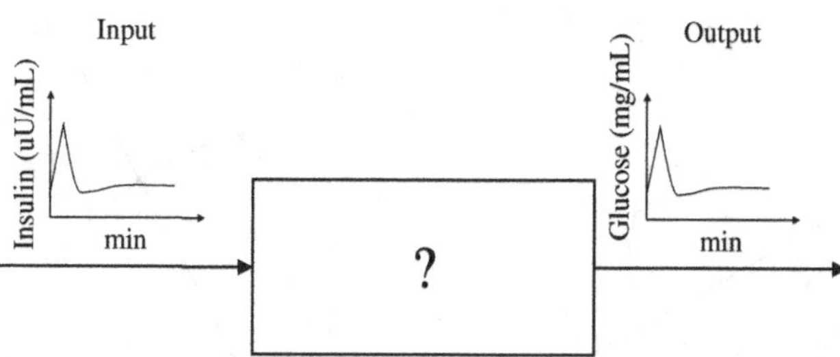

FIGURE 11–31 Model of insulin action to be determined using insulin as the input variable and glucose as the output.

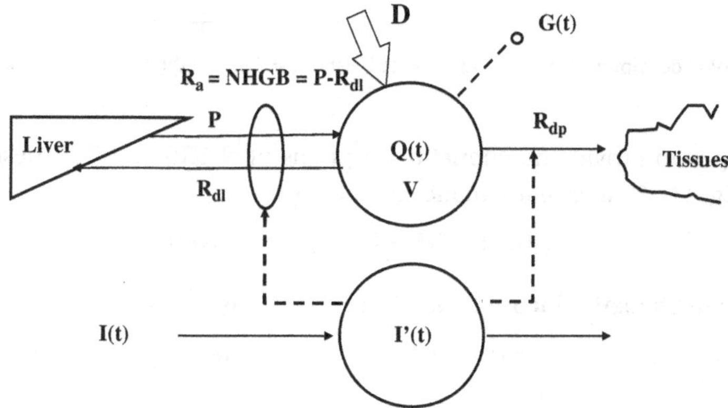

FIGURE 11–32 The glucose minimal model. *Continuous lines* denote flux of material and *dashed lines* denote control signals. *Adapted from Bergman et al. (1979).*

stimulation of glucose utilization are proportional to insulin concentration in a compartment remote from plasma. Mathematically one has:

$$\begin{aligned}\dot{Q}(t) &= R_a\,(Q\,(t), I'(t)) - R_d\,(Q\,(t), I'(t)) + D \cdot \delta\,(t) \quad Q\,(0) = Q_b \\ &= \mathrm{NHGB}\,(Q(t),\ I'(t)) - R_d\,(Q\,(t),\ I'(t)) + D \cdot \delta(t)\end{aligned} \tag{11.120}$$

$$\dot{I}'(t) = -\,k_3 \cdot I'(t) + k_2 \cdot I(t) \quad I'(0) = I'_b \tag{11.121}$$

$$G\,(t) = \frac{Q\,(t)}{V} \tag{11.122}$$

where Q is the mass of glucose, with Q_b denoting its basal value; D is the glucose dose, $\delta(t)$ is the Dirac function, R_a is the rate of appearance of glucose in plasma which is equal to NHGB, the net hepatic glucose balance; R_d is plasma glucose disappearance rate. I′(t) is insulin concentration in a compartment remote from plasma, that is, interstitial fluid, and I (t) is plasma insulin concentration with I_b denoting its basal value; G is plasma glucose concentration; and V is the glucose distribution volume.

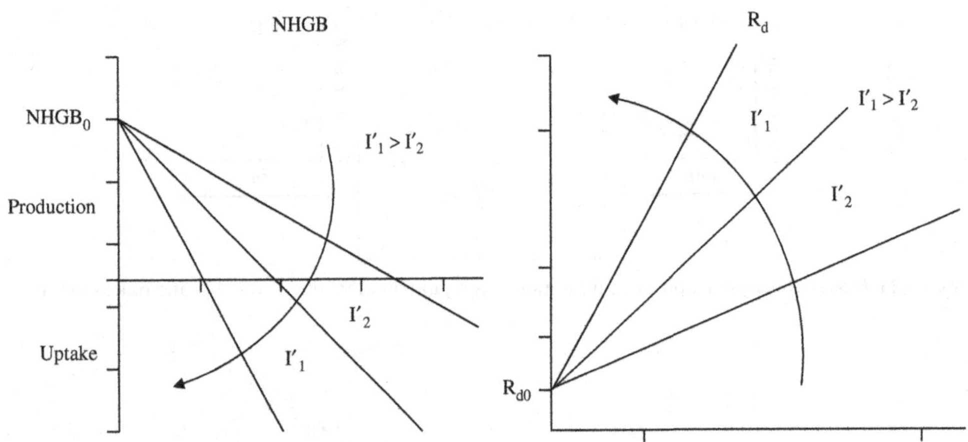

FIGURE 11–33 Graphical description of net hepatic glucose balance (NHGB) and the rate of appearance of glucose (R_d).

The next step is to provide functional descriptions of NHGB and R_d. These are displayed graphically in Fig. 11–33 and mathematically one has:

$$NHGB\,(t) = NHGB_0 - [k_5 + k_6 I'(t)]\,Q(t) \tag{11.123}$$

where $NHGB_0$ is net hepatic glucose balance at zero glucose, and:

$$R_d\,(t) = [k_1 + k_4 I'(t)]\,Q(t) + R_{d0} \tag{11.124}$$

where R_{d0} is glucose disappearance rate at zero glucose.

Sigmoidal shaped relationships would be more realistic but one has to remember that during an IVGTT glucose is usually confined in a range, say 90–350 mg/dL, so one has to regard these linear relationships as a reasonable approximation in the observed glucose range, and $NHGB_0$ and R_{d0} are the result of these approximations.

Now, incorporating (11.123) and (11.124) into (11.120) enables us to write:

$$\dot{Q}\,(t) = [(k_5 + k_1) - (k_6 + k_4)\,I'(t)]\,(Q\,(t) + (NHGB_0 - R_{d0}) \quad Q\,(0) = Q_b + D \tag{11.125}$$

$$\dot{I}'\,(t) = -\,k_3 \cdot I'(t) + k_2\,[I(t) - I_b] \quad I'(0) = 0 \tag{11.126}$$

$$G\,(t) = \frac{Q\,(t)}{V} \tag{11.127}$$

where the term ($NHGB_0 - R_{d0}$) can be written as $(k_5 + k_1)Q_b$ by using the steady-state constraint $\dot{Q}(t) = 0$, and the impulse dose has been incorporated into the initial condition.

Unfortunately, the model has too many parameters to be resolved, assuming plasma insulin concentration as a known input, from plasma glucose concentration data. By testing *a priori* identifiability with the Taylor series expansion method (the model is nonlinear) of Section 7.5, one can show that the model is *a priori* nonidentifiable since all the k parameters are nonidentifiable (only V is uniquely identifiable). The uniquely identifiable parametrization of the model is:

$$\dot{Q}(t) = -\left[p_1 + X(t)\right]Q(t) + p_1 Q_b \quad Q(0) = Q_b + D \tag{11.128}$$

$$\dot{X}(t) = -p_2 X(t) + p_3[I(t) - I_b] \quad X(0) = 0 \tag{11.129}$$

$$G(t) = \frac{Q(t)}{V} \tag{11.130}$$

This parametrization includes new parameters p_1, p_2, p_3, and a new variable, X, where these are related to the original parameters as follows:

$$X(t) = (k_4 + k_6)\, I'(t) \tag{11.131}$$

$$p_1 = k_1 + k_5 \tag{11.132}$$

$$p_2 = k_3 \tag{11.133}$$

$$p_3 = k_2\,(k_4 + k_6) \tag{11.134}$$

From the uniquely identifiable model parameters p_1, p_2, p_3, and V, one can calculate indices of glucose effectiveness (S_G) and insulin sensitivity (S_I) as follows.

Glucose effectiveness

$$\begin{aligned} S_G &= -\left.\frac{\partial \dot{Q}}{\partial Q}\right|_{ss} = -\left[-(p_1 + X(t))\right]_{ss} = p_1 + X_b \\ &= p_1 + \frac{p_3}{p_2} \cdot I_b = k_1 + k_5 + \frac{k_2 \cdot (k_4 + k_6)}{k_3} \cdot I_b \end{aligned} \tag{11.135}$$

Insulin sensitivity

$$S_I = -\left.\frac{\partial^2 \dot{Q}}{\partial Q \cdot \partial I}\right|_{ss} = \left.\frac{\partial\left[p_1 + X(t)\right]}{\partial I}\right|_{ss} = \left.\frac{\partial X}{\partial I}\right|_{ss} \tag{11.136}$$

In the steady state:

$$0 = -p_2 \cdot X_{ss} + p_3 \cdot I(t) \tag{11.137}$$

$$X_{ss} = \frac{p_3}{p_2} \cdot I(t) \tag{11.138}$$

and thus:

$$S_I = \left.\frac{\partial X}{\partial I}\right|_{ss} = \frac{p_3}{p_2} = \frac{k_2 \cdot (k_4 + k_6)}{k_3} \tag{11.139}$$

S_G and S_I reflect both the effect of glucose and insulin on R_d and NHGP. In fact, S_G is a function not only of k_1 but also of k_5, and thus measures the ability of glucose per se, at basal insulin, to stimulate R_d and inhibit NHGB. Similarly, S_I is a function not only of k_2, k_3, k_4, but also of k_6, and thus measures the ability of insulin to enhance the glucose per se stimulation of R_d and the glucose per se inhibition of NHGB.

The model of (11.128–11.130) can be identified for instance by weighted nonlinear least squares assuming that the measurement error is independent, zero mean and with a coefficient of variation (CV) = 2%. To favor the single compartment approximation, the first 8–10 minutes samples are usually neglected. A typical identification result is shown in Fig. 11–34.

This model also allows discussion of issues related to model validation. For instance, is the value of S_I reliable? In fact, there is an alternative, albeit rather invasive and labour intensive technique to measure S_I. This technique is the euglycemic hyperinsulinemic clamp (Fig. 11–35). In this case, the feedback loop is opened experimentally by maintaining glucose concentration at basal level in spite of an elevated insulin concentration:

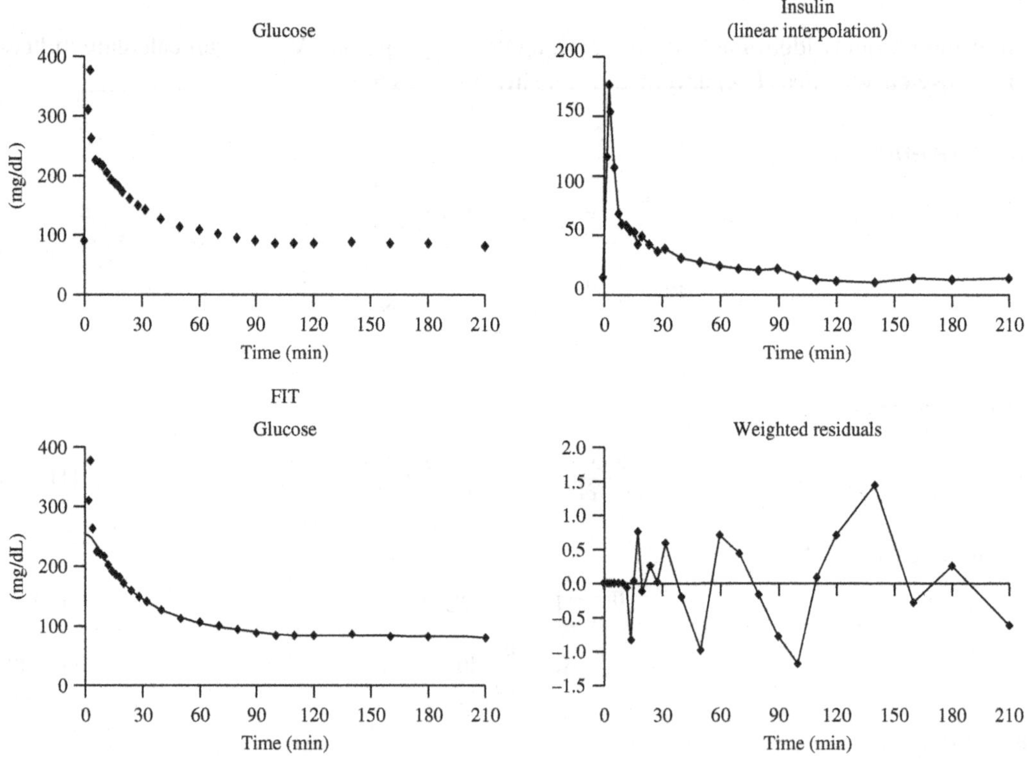

FIGURE 11–34 *Upper panel*: data (left—glucose; right—insulin) of an individual subject. *Lower panel*: left—model fit to glucose data; right—weighted residuals.

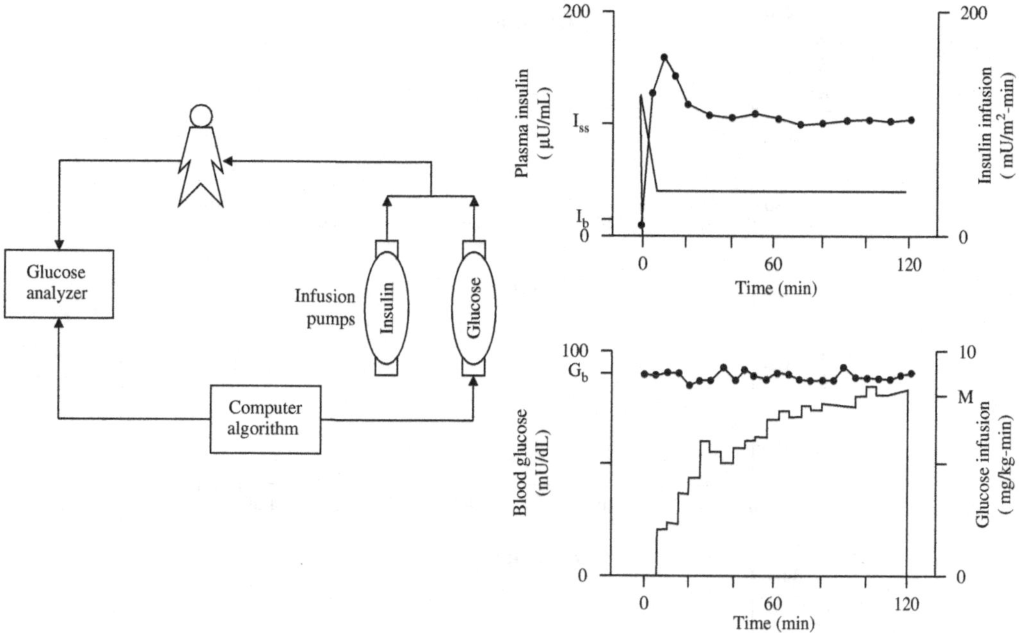

FIGURE 11–35 The glucose clamp technique.

$$S_I = \frac{M}{\Delta I \cdot G_b} \tag{11.140}$$

where $\Delta I = I_{ss} - I_b$.

The minimal model (S_I) has been validated against the clamp (S_I) in numerous studies with correlation ranging from 0.79 to 0.92.

It is important to have a similar model for a more physiological test, like a meal (MTT) or an oral (OGTT) glucose tolerance test. A typical data set of an MTT is shown in Fig. 11–36.

The rationale of the oral glucose minimal model has been discussed in Section 5.5.7. The model is shown again for convenience in Fig. 11–37 and its dynamic equations are reported below:

$$\dot{Q}(t) = -\left[p_1 + X(t)\right]Q(t) + p_1 Q_b + R_a(t, \alpha) \quad Q(0) = Q_b + D \tag{11.141}$$

$$\dot{X}(t) = -p_2 X(t) + p_3\left[I(t) - I_b\right] \qquad X(0) = 0 \tag{11.142}$$

$$G(t) = \frac{Q(t)}{V} \tag{11.143}$$

As anticipated in Section 5.5.7, the model can be shown to be *a priori* nonidentifiable; since the model is nonlinear one has to resort to the Taylor series expansion method discussed in

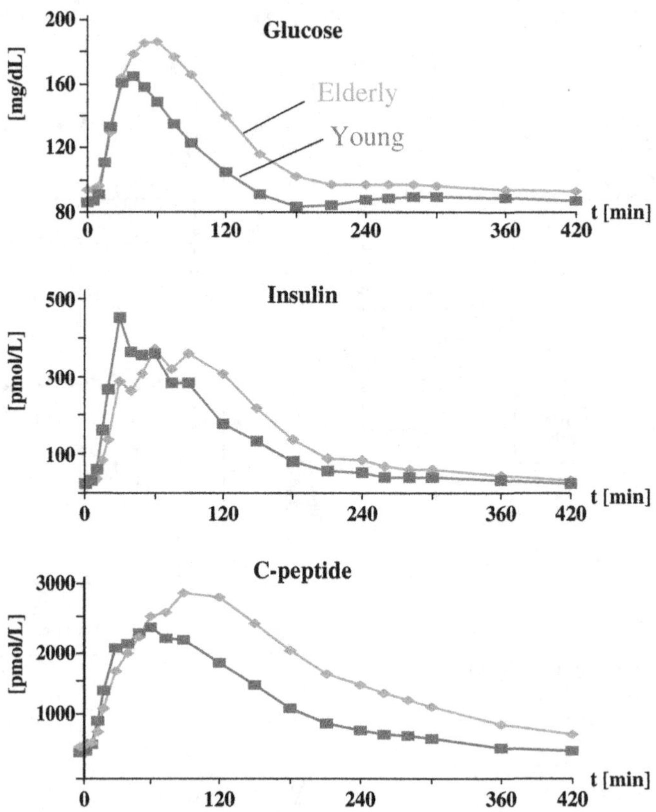

FIGURE 11–36 Glucose and insulin plasma concentrations after a meal in healthy, young ($n = 59$) and elderly ($n = 145$) subjects (mean values are shown).

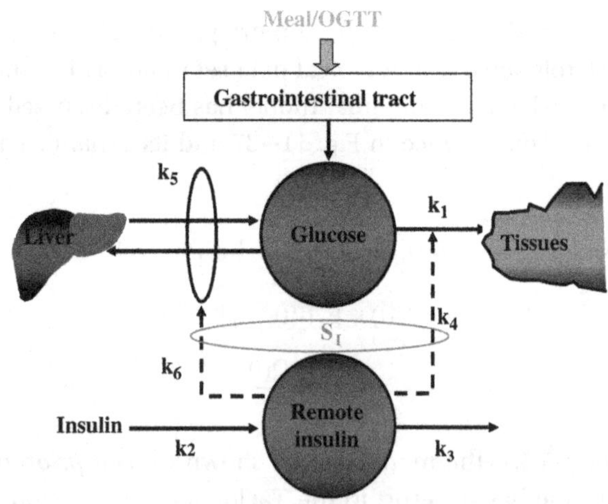

FIGURE 11–37 The oral glucose minimal model. *Adapted from Cobelli, et al. (2014).*

Table 11–5 Reference values of the nonidentifiable parameters for MTT and OGTT.

	MTT		OGTT	
Parameter	**Value**	**Unit**	**Value**	**Unit**
V	1.45	dL/kg	1.34	dL/kg
p_1	0.025	min^{-1}	0.028	min^{-1}
f	0.9	Dimensionless	0.9	Dimensionless

Section 7.5. The additional *a priori* knowledge necessary for the model identification is detailed in Table 11–5

In addition a Bayesian prior on p_2 is needed to improve numerical identifiability of the model. A constraint is also imposed to guarantee that the area under the estimated R_a equals the total amount of ingested glucose, (D), multiplied by the fraction that is actually absorbed f (see Table 11–5), and divided by the body weight (BW):

$$\int_{\infty}^{\infty} R_a(t) \cdot dt = \frac{D \cdot f}{BW} \tag{11.144}$$

By solving Eq. (11.144) for one of the α_i describing R_a, the number of unknowns is reduced by one.

With this additional knowledge and constraint, the model can be identified for instance by weighted nonlinear least squares with insulin plasma concentration (the known input), and assuming that the glucose measurement error is independent, zero mean and with a CV = 2%. If the data are those of an MTT like those of Fig. 11–36, the break points can be allocated at 0, 13, 25, 35, 60, 90, 120, 180, and 420 minutes and one can estimate insulin sensitivity by using S_I by using Eq. (11.140).

Since for the identification of the oral minimal model there is the need to fix some parameters to population values, it is important to assess the validity of S_I with that obtained using an independent method. Two validation strategies have been used (Fig. 11–38).

First, the euglycemic hyperglycemic clamp was used, and provided a correlation similar to that observed for the IVGTT, R = 0.81. Then, it was also possible to use for validation the oral reference model method: this consists of the use of the IVGTT minimal model of Eqs. (11.128)–(11.130) driven, in each subject, by a model-independent estimate of R_a (R_a^{ref}) obtained by the triple tracer protocol, and provided in healthy subjects a correlation of 0.86.

It is of interest, in the light of a possible clinical application of the model, to discuss using the oral minimal model in the case of a reduced oral test protocol in which the observation period, originally, for example, of 300 and 420 minutes for OGTT and MTT, respectively, was shortened to 180 or 120 minutes. This results in a reduction of samples from 11 in the OGTT and 21 in the MTT to 8 or 7, respectively. The major obstacle to overcome when applying the model to a short protocol is that there is a need to know the fraction of the ingested dose which is absorbed in the first 180 or 120 minutes (f_{180}, f_{120}) to correctly apply the constraint

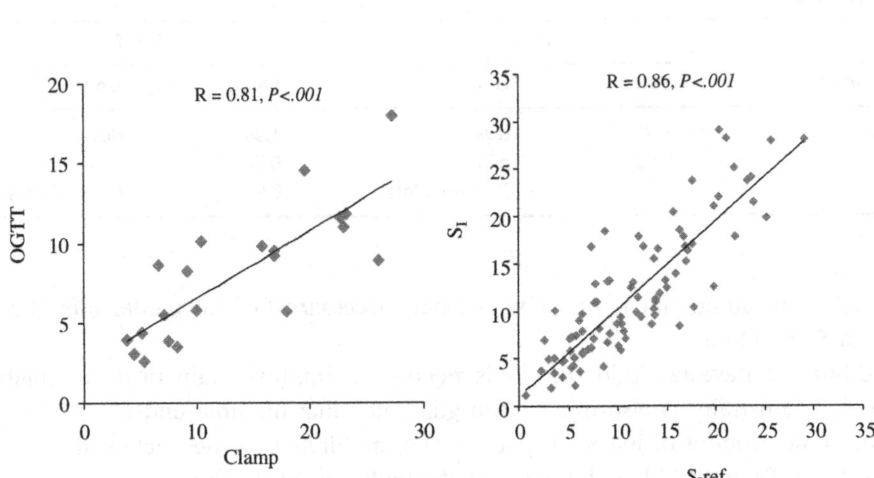

FIGURE 11–38 Validation of oral minimal model SI against the euglycemic hyperinsulinemic clamp (*left panel*) and the oral reference model method (*right panel*).

of (11.144). Unfortunately, in the literature, knowledge regarding these parameters is scarce, also due to their high intra- and intersubject variability. The need to fix these values in each subject was solved using a strategy often adopted in pharmacokinetics, that is, to assume that from 120 minutes onwards, in other words beyond the shortened observation period, R_a decays exponentially at a known rate.

$$R_a(t) = \begin{cases} \alpha_{i-1} + \dfrac{\alpha_i - \alpha_{i-1}}{t_i - t_{i-1}} \cdot (t - t_{i-1}) & \text{for } t_i - 1 \leq t < t_i \ \ i = 1 \ldots 5, \text{ and } t \leq 120 \text{ min} \\ \alpha_5 \cdot e^{-\frac{(t-t_5)}{T}} & \text{for } t > 120 \text{ min} \end{cases} \tag{11.145}$$

where the breakpoints where chosen at 0, 10, 30, 60, 90 and 120 minutes, and T is the time constant of the exponential function.

As a matter of fact, the area under R_a for $t > 120$ minutes only depends on α_5 and T, with α_5 estimated from 0 to 120 minutes data and (T) fixed to a population value, depending on oral dose composition (T = 120 minutes for MTT, T = 60 minutes for OGTT):

$$\int_{120}^{\infty} R_a(t) \cdot dt = \alpha_5 \cdot T \tag{11.146}$$

S_I estimated from a reduced protocol (120 minutes, seven samples) was successfully compared with that obtained with the full protocol in healthy subjects studied with MTT, healthy and impaired glucose tolerant subjects studied with OGTT, and Type 2 diabetic subjects studied with MTT, as discussed in detail in Dalla Man & Cobelli (2014).

11.7 Case study 7: a simulation model of the glucose-insulin system

This case study describes a model of the glucose-insulin control system that is to be used to examine dynamic effects both during meals and in normal daily life. Such a model is useful for testing glucose sensors, algorithms for the infusion of insulin and, more generally, decision support systems for diabetes. This simulation model enables computer-based experiments to be performed which would be too difficult, too dangerous or unethical to perform in real life.

One of the key factors for success in any modeling study is the availability of experimental data. In this case data were available from 204 normal subjects who received a triple tracer, mixed meal. The resultant data allowed estimates to be made for a number of glucose and insulin fluxes as well as measures of glucose and insulin concentration. Fig. 11–39 depicts the mean ± SD values over a time course of 7 hours.

11.7.1 Model formulation

The basic structure of the glucose-insulin control system is shown in Fig. 11–40 This depicts the uptake of the ingested glucose via the gastrointestinal tract, the distribution of glucose in the liver and in muscle and adipose tissue, together with the various regulating mechanisms. However, on the basis of experimental data that are limited to measures of glucose and insulin concentrations, it would not be possible to identify the parameters of a mathematical model that encompassed the full complexity of the system as shown. For instance, a good model representation of the plasma glucose and insulin concentrations would be compatible with a wide range of descriptions of endogenous glucose production by the liver, its rate of appearance in the plasma from the gut, and its rate of utilization.

Fortunately, an approach can be adopted which is based on developing structural models corresponding to each unit process. Reliable parametric models can be formulated this way. For example, in order to model the rate of glucose utilization, we can make use of our knowledge of endogenous glucose production, glucose rate of appearance, and insulin concentration as known inputs, and as model outputs—glucose utilization and plasma glucose concentration.

11.7.1.1 Glucose subsystem

The two-compartment model used to describe glucose kinetics is shown in the upper panel of Fig. 11–41 (Vicini *et al.*, 1997). The model equations are:

$$\dot{G}_p(t) = EGP(t) + Ra(t) - U_{ii}(t) - E(t) - k_1 \cdot G_p(t) + k_2 \cdot G_t(t) \quad G_p(0) = G_{pb} \tag{11.147}$$

$$\dot{G}_t(t) = -U_{id}(t) + k_1 \cdot G_p(t) - k_2 \cdot G_t(t) \quad G_t(0) = G_{tb} \tag{11.148}$$

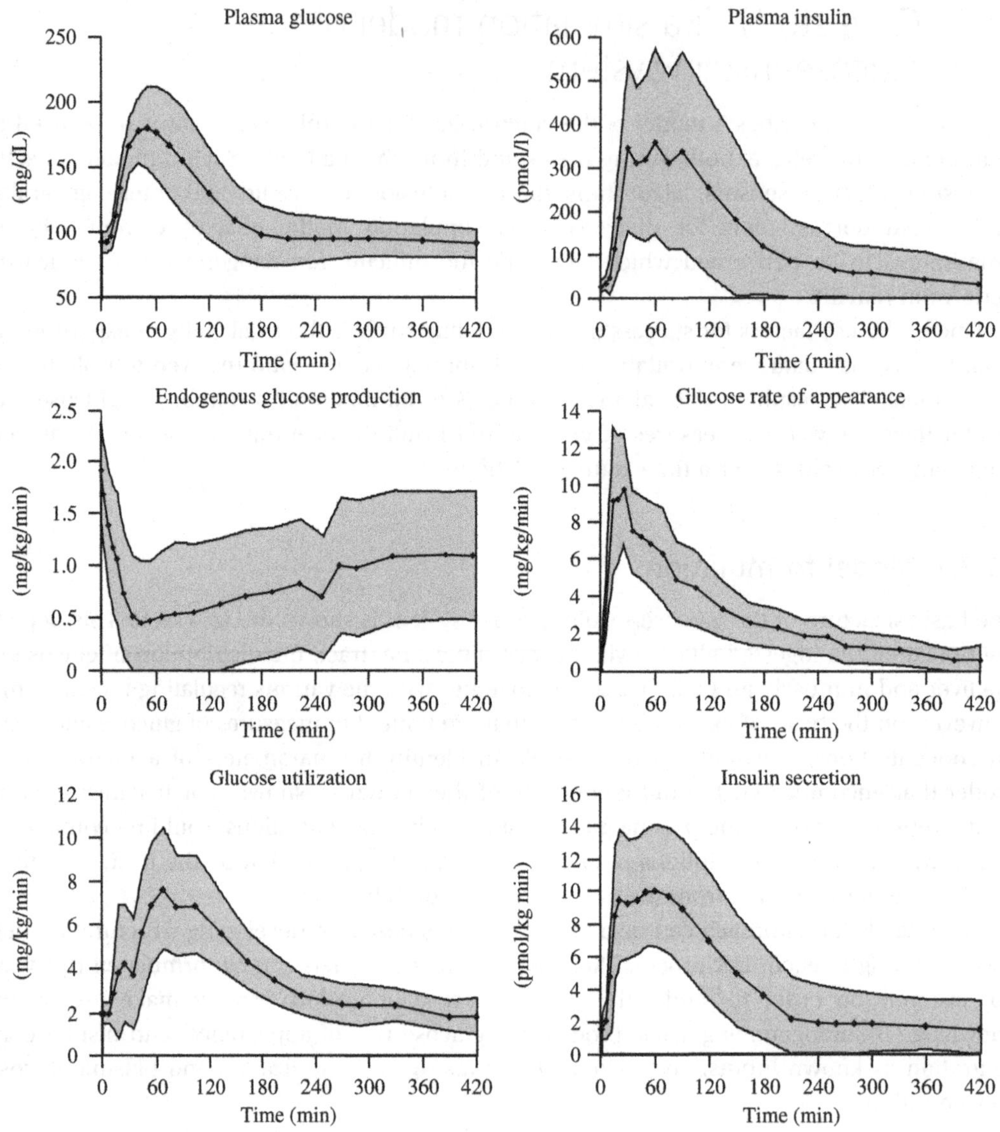

FIGURE 11–39 Glucose and insulin database corresponding to 204 normal subjects. *Adapted from Dalla Man et al. (2007b).*

$$G(t) = \frac{G_p}{V_G} \qquad G(0) = G_b \tag{11.149}$$

where G_p and G_t (mg/kg) are glucose masses in plasma and rapidly-equilibrating tissues, and in slowly-equilibrating tissues, respectively, G (mg/dL) plasma glucose concentration,

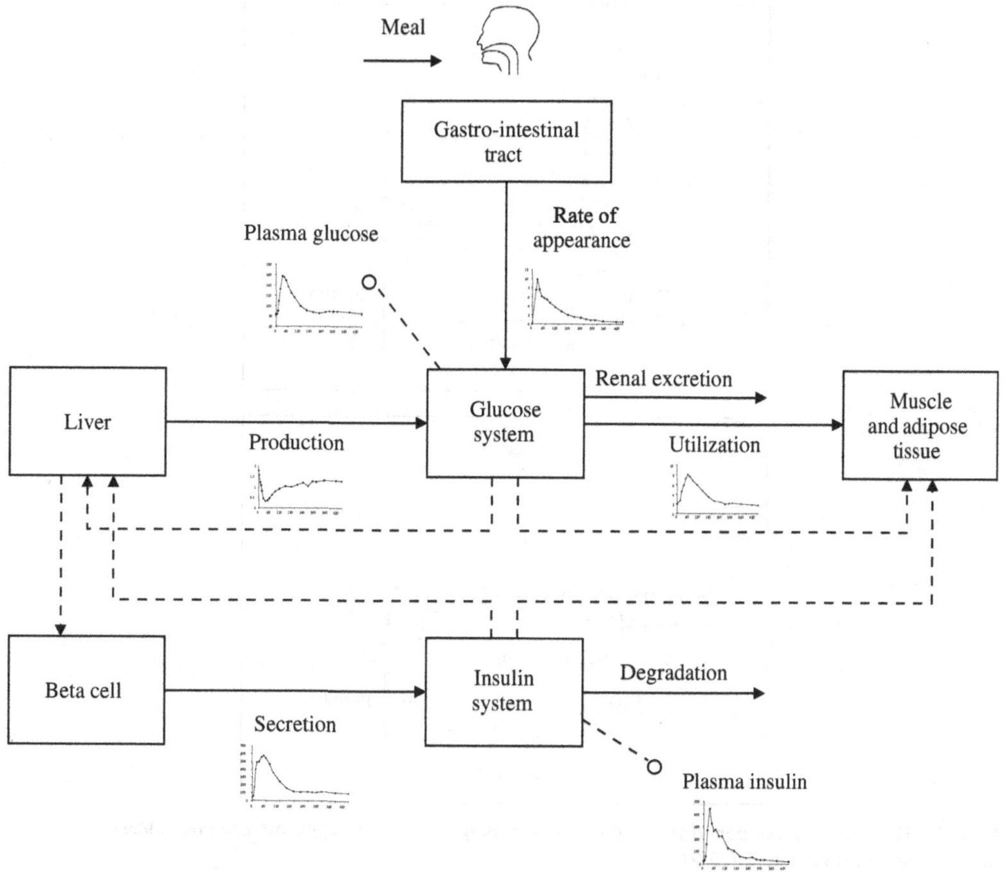

FIGURE 11–40 Basic structure of the glucose–insulin control system.

with the suffix b denoting the basal state. EGP is the endogenous glucose production (mg/kg/min), R_a is the glucose rate of appearance in plasma (mg/kg/min), E is renal excretion (mg/kg/min), and U_{ii} and U_{id} are the insulin-independent and dependent glucose utilizations, respectively (mg/kg/min). V_G is the distribution volume of glucose (dL/kg), and k_1 and k_2 (min^{-1}) are rate parameters.

In the basal steady-state endogenous production, EGP_b, equals glucose disappearance, that is, the sum of glucose utilization and renal excretion (which is zero in the normal subject), $U_b + E_b$.

$$EGP_b = U_b + E_b \tag{11.150}$$

Parameter values of V_G, k_1, k_2 are reported in Table 11–6 (Glucose kinetics) for both the normal and the type 2 diabetic subject.

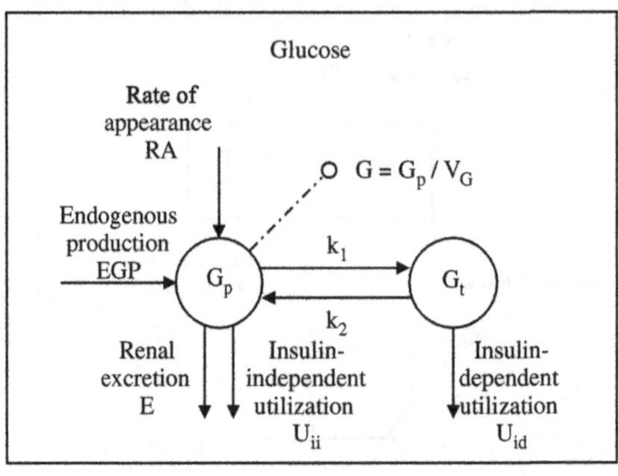

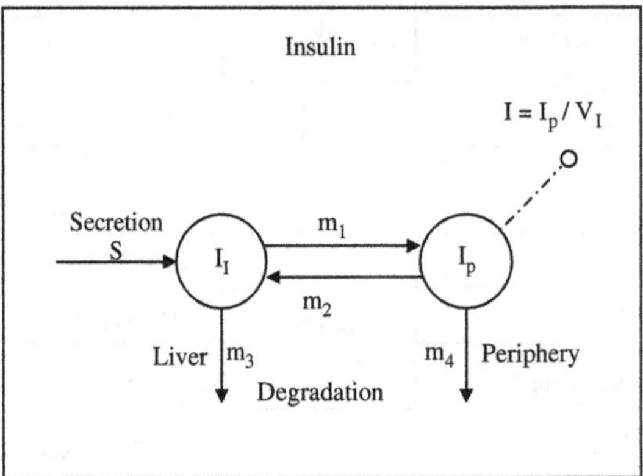

FIGURE 11–41 Glucose (*upper panel*) and insulin (*lower panel*) subsystem models. *Adapted from Vicini et al. (1997). and Ferrannini, E., & Cobelli, C. (1987).*

11.7.1.2 Insulin subsystem

The lower panel of Fig. 11–41 depicts the two-compartment model used to describe insulin kinetics (Ferrannini & Cobelli, 1987). The model equations are:

$$\{\dot{I}_l(t) = -(m_1 + m_3(t)) \cdot I_l(t) + m_2 I_p(t) + S(t) \quad I_l(0) = I_{lb} \tag{11.151}$$

$$\dot{I}_p(t) = -(m_2 + m_4) \cdot I_p(t) + m_1 \cdot I_l(t) \quad I_p(0) = I_{pb} \tag{11.152}$$

$$I(t) = \frac{I_p}{V_I} \quad I(0) = I_b \tag{11.153}$$

where I_p and I_l (pmol/kg) are insulin masses in plasma and in liver respectively, I (pmol/L) is plasma insulin concentration, with the suffix b denoting basal state. S is insulin secretion (pmol/kg/min), V_I is the distribution volume of insulin (l/kg), and m_1, m_2, m_4 (min^{-1}) are rate parameters. Degradation, D, occurs both in the liver and in the periphery. Peripheral degradation has been assumed to be linear (m_4). Hepatic extraction of insulin, HE, is defined as the insulin flux that leaves the liver irreversibly divided by the total insulin flux leaving the liver. Thus, we get:

$$m_3(t) = \frac{HE(t) \cdot m_1}{1 - HE(t)} \tag{11.154}$$

Experimental evidence suggests that the time course of HE is related to the secretion of insulin, S, as:

$$HE(t) = -m_5 \cdot S(t) + m_6 \quad HE(0) = HE_b \tag{11.155}$$

In the basal steady state we have:

$$m_6 = m_5 \cdot Sb + HE_b \tag{11.156}$$

$$m_3(0) = \frac{HE_b \cdot m_1}{1 - HE_b} \tag{11.157}$$

$$S_b = m_3(0) \cdot I_{1b} + m_4 \cdot I_{pb} = D_b \tag{11.158}$$

with S_b and D_b being basal secretion and degradation, respectively.

Moreover, given that the liver is responsible for 60% of insulin clearance in the steady state, one has:

$$m_2 = \left(\frac{S_b}{I_{pb}} - \frac{m_4}{1 - HE_b}\right) \cdot \frac{1 - HE_b}{HE_b} \tag{11.159}$$

and,

$$m_4 = \frac{2}{5} \cdot \frac{S_b}{I_{pb}} \cdot (1 - HE_b) \tag{11.160}$$

HE_b was fixed to 0.6, and is reported together with V_I, m_1, m_2, m_4, m_5, and m_6 in Table 11–6 (Insulin kinetics) for both the normal and type 2 diabetic subject.

11.7.1.3 Unit process models and identification

The model is divided into the unit processes of the glucose and insulin subsystems: *endogenous glucose production, glucose rate of appearance, glucose utilization, glucose renal excretion,* and *insulin secretion.* The model for each of them was identified from average data with a forcing function strategy; that is to say that some variables, considered to be the input of the unit process, were assumed to be known without error.

Endogenous glucose production

The functional description of EGP in terms of glucose and insulin signals is described in Dalla Man *et al.* (2006); it comprises a direct glucose signal and both delayed and anticipated insulin signals:

Table 11–6 Parameter values of the simulator for normal and type 2 diabetic subjects.

Process	Parameter	Normal value	Type 2 diabetic value	Unit
Glucose kinetics	V_G	1.88	1.49	dL/kg
	k_1	0.065	0.042	min^{-1}
	k_2	0.079	0.071	min^{-1}
Insulin kinetics	V_I	0.05	0.04	l/kg
	m_1	0.190	0.239	min^{-1}
	m_2	0.484	0.302	min^{-1}
	m_4	0.194	0.477	min^{-1}
	m_5	0.0304	0.0690	min kg/pmoL
	m_6	0.6471	0.8778	Dimensionless
	HE_b	0.6	0.6	Dimensionless
Rate of appearance	k_{max}	0.0558	0.0465	min^{-1}
	k_{min}	0.0080	0.0076	min^{-1}
	k_{abs}	0.057	0.023	min^{-1}
	k_{gri}	0.0558	0.0465	min^{-1}
	f	0.90	0.90	Dimensionless
	a	0.00013	0.00006	min^{-1}
	b	0.82	0.68	Dimensionless
	c	0.00236	0.00023	min^{-1}
	d	0.010	0.09	Dimensionless
Endogenous production	k_{p1}	2.70	3.09	mg/kg/min
	k_{p2}	0.0021	0.0007	min^{-1}
	k_{p3}	0.009	0.005	mg/kg/min per pmol/L
	k_{p4}	0.0618	0.0786	mg/kg/min per pmol/kg
	k_i	0.0079	0.0066	min^{-1}
Utilization	F_{cns}	1	1	mg/kg/min
	V_{m0}	2.50	4.65	mg/kg/min
	V_{mx}	0.047	0.034	mg/kg/min per pmol/L
	K_{m0}	225.59	466.21	mg/kg
	p_{2U}	0.0331	0.0840	min^{-1}
Secretion	K	2.28	1.38	pmol/kg per (mg/dL)
	α	0.050	0.014	min^{-1}
	β	0.11	0.05	pmol/kg/min per (mg/dL)
	γ	0.5	0.5	min^{-1}
Renal excretion	k_{e1}	0.0005	0.0007	min^{-1}
	k_{e2}	339	269	mg/kg

$$EGP(t) = k_{p1} - k_{p2} \cdot G_p(t) - k_{p3} \cdot I_d(t) - k_{p4} \cdot I_{po}(t) \quad EGP(0) = EGP_b \tag{11.161}$$

where I_{po} is the quantity of insulin in the portal vein (pmol/kg), and I_d (pmol/L) is a delayed insulin signal realized with a chain of two compartments:

$$\dot{I}_1(t) = -k_i \cdot [I_1(t) - I(t)] \quad I_1(0) = I_b \tag{11.162}$$

$$\dot{I}_d(t) = -k_i \cdot [I_d(t) - I_1(t)] \quad I_d(0) = I_b \tag{11.163}$$

In terms of the parameters, k_{p1} (mg/kg/min) is the extrapolated EGP at zero glucose and insulin, k_{p2} is (min^{-1}) liver glucose effectiveness, k_{p3} (mg/kg/min per pmol/L) is the parameter governing amplitude of insulin action on the liver, k_{p4} [mg/kg/min/(pmol/kg)] is the parameter governing amplitude of portal insulin action on the liver, and k_i (min^{-1}) is the rate parameter accounting for delay between insulin signal and insulin action. EGP is also constrained to be nonnegative.

In the basal steady state we have:

$$k_{p1} = EGP_b + k_{p2} \cdot G_{pb} + k_{p3} \cdot I_b + k_{p4} \cdot I_{pob} \tag{11.164}$$

The model of (11.161) was identified by nonlinear least squares using mean EGP data with the forcing function strategy of: mean insulin, portal insulin, and glucose concentrations as the model inputs, assumed to be known without error and EGP is the model output. The measurement error of the EGP data was assumed to be independent, with zero mean and unknown constant standard deviation (constant SD assumes relatively more precise values when the signal is higher). A satisfactory model fit was obtained and parameters were estimated with precision for both normal and type 2 diabetic subjects. They are reported in Table 11–6 (Endogenous glucose production).

Glucose rate of appearance

The physiological model of glucose intestinal absorption, as proposed in Dalla Man *et al.* (2006), was used to describe the glucose transit through the stomach and intestine; it assumes that the stomach is represented by two compartments (one for solid and one for the triturated phase), while a single compartment is used to describe the gut:

$$Q_{sto}(t) = Q_{sto1}(t) + Q_{sto2}(t) \quad Q_{sto}(0) = 0 \tag{11.165}$$

$$\dot{Q}_{sto1}(t) = -k_{gri} \cdot Q_{sto1}(t) + D \cdot \delta(t) \quad Q_{sto1}(0) = 0 \tag{11.166}$$

$$\dot{Q}_{sto2}(t) = -k_{empt}(Q_{sto}) \cdot Q_{sto2}(t) + k_{gri} \cdot Q_{sto1}(t) \quad Q_{sto2}(0) = 0 \tag{11.167}$$

$$\dot{Q}_{gut} = -k_{abs} \cdot Q_{gut}(t) + k_{empt}(Q_{sto}) \cdot Q_{sto2}(t) \quad Q_{gut}(0) = 0 \tag{11.168}$$

$$R_a(t) = \frac{f \cdot k_{abs} \cdot Q_{gut}(t)}{BW} \quad R_a(0) = 0 \tag{11.169}$$

where Q_{sto} (mg) is quantity of glucose in the stomach (solid, Q_{sto1}, and liquid phase, Q_{sto2}), Q_{gut} (mg) is the glucose mass in the intestine, k_{gri} (min^{-1}) is the rate of grinding, and k_{abs} (min^{-1}) is the rate constant of intestinal absorption, and f is the fraction of intestinal absorption which actually appears in plasma. D (mg) is the quantity of ingested glucose, BW (kg) is the body weight, and R_a (mg/kg/min) is the appearance rate of glucose in plasma; $k_{empt}(Q_{sto})$ (min^{-1}) is the rate constant of gastric emptying which is a nonlinear function of Q_{sto}:

$$k_{empt}(Q_{sto}) = k_{min} + \frac{k_{max} - k_{min}}{2} \cdot \left\{ \tanh\left[a(Q_{sto} - b \cdot D)\right] - \tanh\left[c(Q_{sto} - d \cdot D)\right] + 2 \right\} \tag{11.170}$$

The model of (11.165–11.170) was identified using R_a data with the forcing function strategy. A good model fit was achieved. The parameters k_{gri}, a and c were fixed as follows:

$$k_{gri} = k_{max} \tag{11.171}$$

$$a = \frac{5}{2 \cdot D \cdot (1 - b)} \tag{11.172}$$

$$c = \frac{5}{2 \cdot D \cdot d} \tag{11.173}$$

while the remaining parameters were estimated with precision. They are reported in Table 11–6 (Glucose rate of appearance) for both normal and type 2 diabetic subjects.

Glucose utilization

The model of glucose utilization by body tissues during a meal assumes that glucose utilization is made up of two components: insulin-independent and insulin-dependent.

Insulin-independent utilization takes place in the first compartment, is constant, and represents glucose uptake by the brain and erythrocytes (F_{cns}):

$$U_{ii}(t) = F_{cns} \tag{11.174}$$

Insulin-dependent utilization takes place in the remote compartment and depends nonlinearly (Michaelis-Menten) upon glucose in the tissues:

$$U_{id}(t) = \frac{V_m(X(t)) \cdot G_t(t)}{K_m(X(t)) + G_t(t)} \tag{11.175}$$

where $V_m(X(t))$ and $K_m(X(t))$ are assumed to be linearly dependent upon a remote insulin, X(t):

$$V_m\,(X(t)) = V_{m0} + V_{mx} \cdot X\,(t) \tag{11.176}$$

$$K_m\,(X(t)) = K_{m0} + K_{mx} \cdot X\,(t) \tag{11.177}$$

It should be noted that, when fitting this model to available data, K_{mx} collapsed to zero, so that K_m is no longer dependent upon X.

X (pmol/L) is insulin in the interstitial fluid (deviation from basal) described by:

$$\dot{X}(t) = -p_{2U} \cdot X(t) + p_{2U}\left[I(t) - I_b\right] \quad X(0) = 0 \tag{11.178}$$

where I is plasma insulin, with the suffix (b) denoting basal state, and p_{2U} (min^{-1}) is a rate constant defining insulin action on peripheral glucose utilization.

Total glucose utilization, U, is therefore:

$$U\,(t) = U_{ii}\,(t) + U_{id}\,(t) \tag{11.179}$$

In the basal steady state one has:

$$G_{tb} = \frac{F_{cns} - EGP_b + k_1 \cdot G_{pb}}{k_2} \tag{11.180}$$

and:

$$U_b = EGP_b = F_{cns} + \frac{V_{m0} \cdot G_{tb}}{K_{m0} + G_{tb}} \tag{11.181}$$

from which:

$$V_{mo} = \frac{(EGP_b - F_{cns}) \cdot (K_{m0} + G_{tb})}{G_{tb}} \tag{11.182}$$

This model and that of (11.147–11.149) were simultaneously identified using U and G data with the forcing function strategy. A good model fit was achieved and the parameters were estimated with precision, and are reported in Table 11–6 (Glucose utilization) for both normal and type 2 diabetic subjects.

Insulin secretion

The model used to describe pancreatic insulin secretion is:

$$S(t) = \gamma \cdot I_{po}(t) \tag{11.183}$$

$$\dot{I}_{po}(t) = -\gamma \cdot I_{po}(t) + S_{po}(t) \quad I_{po}(0) = I_{pob} \tag{11.184}$$

$$S_{po}(t)\begin{cases} Y(t) + K \cdot \dot{G}(t) + S_b & \text{for } \dot{G} > 0 \\ Y(t) + S_b & \text{for } \dot{G} \leq 0 \end{cases} \tag{11.185}$$

and:

$$\dot{Y}(t) = \begin{cases} -\alpha \cdot [Y(t) - \beta \cdot (G(t) - h)] & \text{if } \beta \cdot (G(t) - h) \geq -S_b \\ -\alpha \cdot Y(t - \alpha \cdot S_b) & \text{if } \beta \cdot (G(t) - h) < -S_b \end{cases}; \quad Y(0) = 0 \tag{11.186}$$

where γ (min^{-1}) is the transfer rate constant between portal vein and liver. K (pmol/kg per mg/dL) is the pancreatic responsivity to glucose rate of change, α (min^{-1}) is the delay between glucose signal and insulin secretion, β (pmol/kg/min per mg/dL) is the pancreatic responsivity to glucose, and h (mg/dL) is the threshold level of glucose above which the beta-cells initiate the production of new insulin (h has been set to the basal glucose concentration (G_b) to guarantee system steady state in basal condition).

This model and that of (11.152–11.154) were simultaneously identified using S and I data with the forcing function strategy. A good model fit was achieved and the parameters were estimated with precision and are reported in Table 11–6 (Insulin secretion) for both normal and type 2 diabetic subjects.

Glucose renal excretion

Glucose excretion by the kidney occurs if plasma glucose exceeds a certain threshold and can be modeled by a linear relationship with plasma glucose:

$$E(t) = \begin{cases} k_{e1} \cdot \lfloor G_p(t) - k_{e2} \rfloor & \text{if } G_p(t) > k_{e2} \\ 0 & \text{if } G_p(t) \le k_{e2} \end{cases} \quad (11.187)$$

where k_{e1} (min^{-1}) is glomerular filtration rate and k_{e2} (mg/kg) is the renal threshold for glucose. The parameters are reported in Table 11–6 (Glucose renal excretion).

11.7.2 Results

Meal in normal subject

A normal subject receiving a mixed meal was simulated first using parameters reported in Table 11–6 (Normal value). Fig. 11–42 shows the predicted glucose and insulin concentrations and glucose/insulin fluxes (continuous line) against ±1 SD confidence limits (gray area, Fig. 11–39). The model also enables prediction of the effect of the various control signals on glucose production (Fig. 11–43, upper panel), as well as the insulin-independent and -dependent components of glucose utilization (Fig. 11–43, right panel); in addition, hepatic insulin extraction can be predicted (Fig. 11–43, lower panel).

Meal in type 2 diabetic subject

The model was also numerically identified for the type 2 diabetic subject, although in this case the database was much smaller and involved a triple tracer meal. The model structure that had been proposed for the normal subject turned out to be robust and data were fitted well. In other words the type 2 diabetic subject can be described quantitatively using the same model structure, but with different parameter values (Table 11–6, Type 2 diabetic value). In particular, gut absorption, k_{abs}, was slower than in the normal case; parameters quantifying insulin action, both peripheral, V_{mx}, and hepatic, k_{p3}, were lower; hepatic glucose effectiveness, k_{p2}, was lower; even though the maximum utilization by the tissue at basal insulin, V_{m0}, was higher, it was reached at higher glucose levels, K_{m0}. Finally, both dynamic, K, and static beta-cell responsivity, β, as well as the rate of response, α, were lower. This different parametric portrait is reflected in the predictions of the model. It can be seen that there are important derangements in both glucose and insulin concentration as well in glucose and insulin fluxes as compared to the normal situation (Fig. 11–42, dashed line).

Daily life for a normal subject

The model can also be used to simulate the dynamic patterns occurring during the day in the case of a normal subject: 24 hours with breakfast at 8:00 a.m. (45 g), lunch at 12:00 p.m. (70 g) and dinner at 6:00 p.m. (70 g). Fig. 11–44 (continuous line) shows the predictions of concentrations and fluxes in the normal subject during the day.

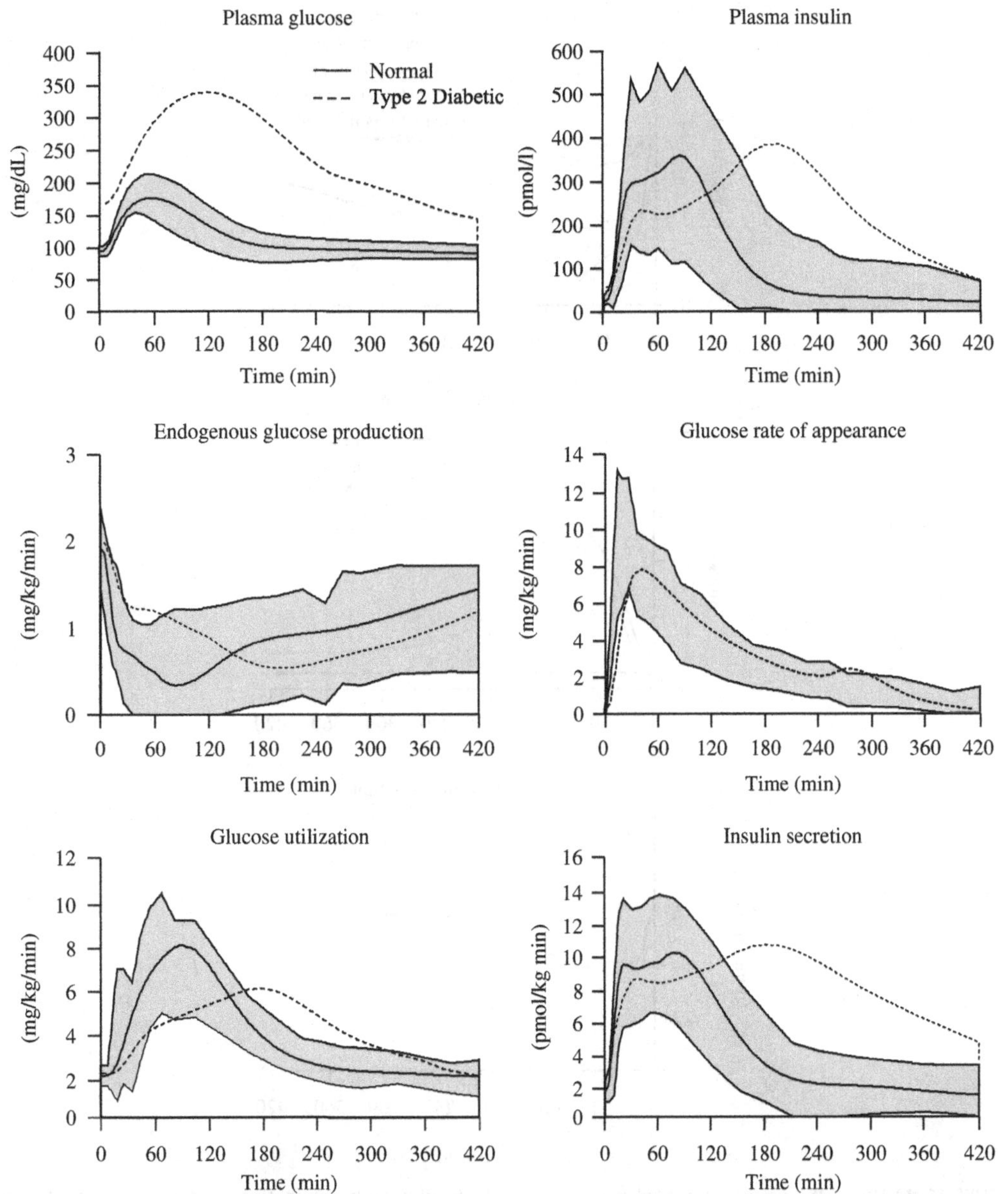

FIGURE 11–42 Simulation results following the administration of a meal for both normal (*continuous line*) and type 2 diabetic subjects (*dashed line*). *Adapted from Dalla Man et al. (2007b).*

Daily life for a subject with impaired glucose tolerance

Glucose intolerance can also be simulated. In particular, an impairment in insulin sensitivity (with both V_{mx} and k_{p3} halved) is considered for the cases both compensated, and not by

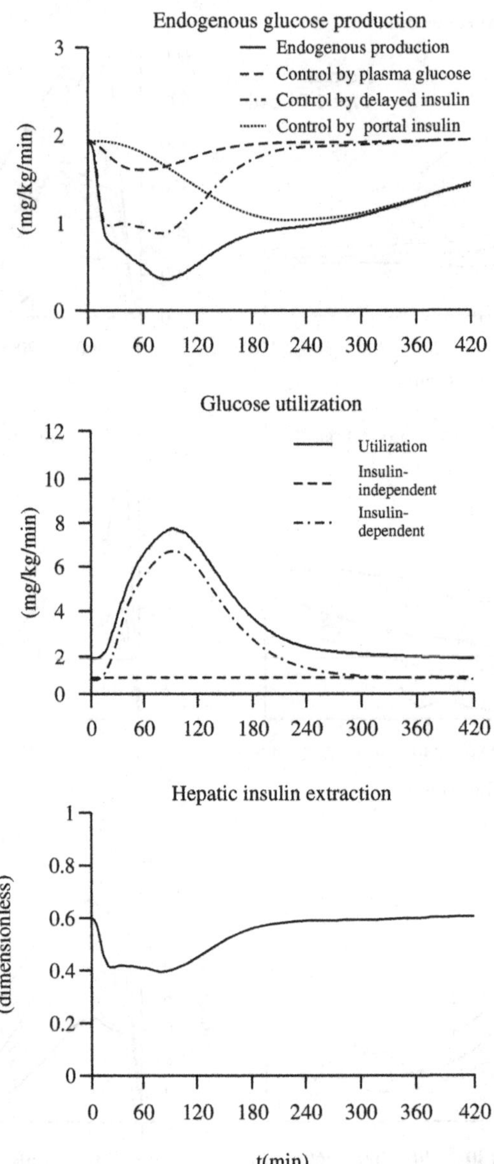

FIGURE 11–43 Use of the simulation model to predict the effects of various control signals on endogenous glucose production (*upper left panel*), glucose utilization (*upper right*), and hepatic insulin extraction (*lower panel*). *Adapted from Dalla Man, et al. (2007b).*

higher beta-cell response to glucose. For instance, if the parameters (V_{mx} and k_{p3}) are halved without a significant increase in beta-cell responsivity, glucose concentration exhibits a higher peak and returns to basal level almost 2 hours later than in the normal subject (Fig. 11–44, dashed line).

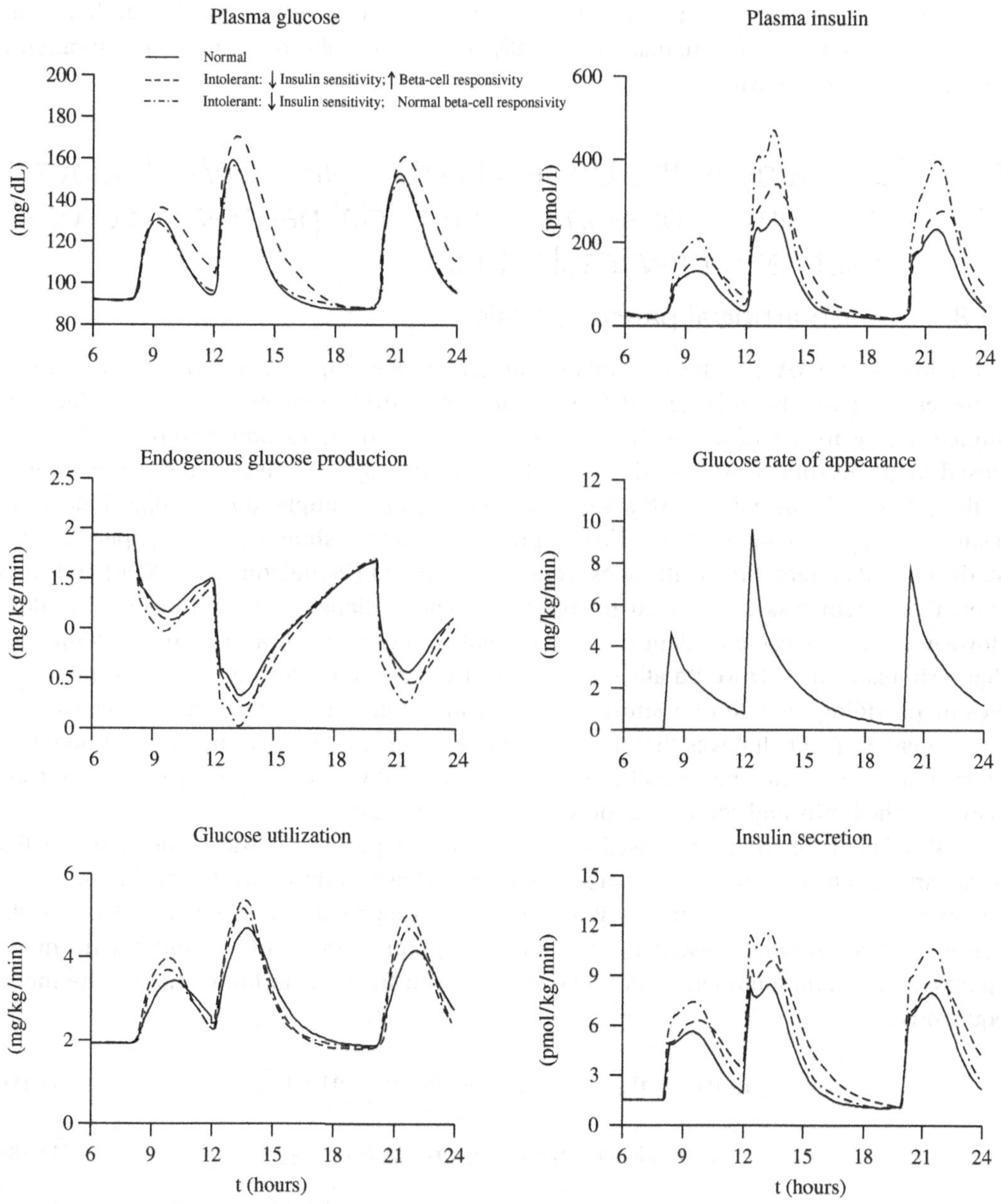

FIGURE 11–44 Model predictions for both the normal subject and the subject with impaired glucose tolerance. *Adapted from Dalla Man. et al. (2007b).*

Conversely, if the parameters (K and β) are both doubled, glucose concentration basically does not differ significantly from the normal case. However, plasma insulin concentration is doubled (Fig. 11–44, dashed-dotted line). Finally, if K and β are halved with insulin action remaining normal, glucose concentration peaks at a higher value and returns to its basal level almost 3 hours later than in the normal subject. However, if V_{mx} and k_{p3} are both doubled, glucose concentration remains essentially normal, but plasma insulin concentration is halved (results not shown).

11.8 Case study 8: the University of Virginia (UVA)/Padova type 1 simulator – *in silico* artificial pancreas, glucose sensors and new insulin trials

11.8.1 *In silico* artificial pancreas trials

The story of the UVA/Padova simulator started in September 2006 when the Juvenile Diabetes Research Foundation (JDRF) initiated the artificial pancreas (AP) project and funded a consortium of university centers in the United States and Europe to carry out closed-loop control research. At the time, the regulatory agencies mandated demonstration of the safety and feasibility of AP systems in animals, for example, dogs or pigs, before any testing could begin in humans. This approach is clearly shown in two papers for the Medtronic AP system: first, eight dogs were safely studied (Pantaleon *et al.*, 2006) and then, later, the system was used in 10 people with Type 1 diabetes (T1D) (Stei *et al.*, 2006). However, it also became evident that the animal studies were slow and cumbersome, and that a simulator of T1D would allow a cost-effective preclinical testing of AP control strategies by providing direction for subsequent clinical research and ruling out ineffective control scenarios. The belief was that a reliable, large-scale simulator would account better for inter-subject variability than small-size animal trials, and would allow for fast and extensive testing of the limits and robustness of AP control algorithms.

A simulation environment based on the data and past work was built, and the first necessary modification of the simulator discussed in Case study 7 was the substitution of an endogenous insulin secretion subsystem with an exogenous subcutaneous (sc) insulin delivery. This required describing insulin absorption with a two-compartment model approximating nonmonomeric and monomeric insulin fractions in the sc space. The model equations are:

$$\dot{I}_{sc1}(t) = -(k_d + k_{a1}) \cdot I_{sc1}(t) + IIR(t) \quad I_{sc1}(0) = I_{sc1ss} \tag{11.188}$$

$$\dot{I}_{sc2}(t) = k_d \cdot I_{sc1}(t) - k_{a2} \cdot I_{sc2}(t) \quad I_{sc2}(0) = I_{sc2ss} \tag{11.189}$$

with I_{sc1}, I_{sc2} amounts of the nonmonomeric and monomeric insulin in the subcutaneous space, respectively, IIR exogenous insulin infusion rate, k_d rate constant of insulin dissociation, and k_{a1} and k_{a2} rate constants of nonmonomeric and monomeric insulin absorption, respectively. The rate of appearance of insulin in plasma (R_i) is thus:

$$R_i(t) = k_{a1} \cdot I_{sc1}(t) + k_{a2} \cdot I_{sc2}(t) \tag{11.190}$$

Given the absence in 2006 of tracer studies in T1D similar to those described in case study 7 for healthy subjects, a more difficult task was the description of inter-individual variability. In order to obtain the joint model parameter distributions in T1D it was assumed that inter-subject variability was the same as for the healthy state (same covariance matrix), but certain clinically-relevant modifications were introduced in the average vector, for example, higher basal glucose concentration, lower insulin clearance, higher glucose production. The resulting T1D simulation model included 13 differential equations and 35 parameters, 26 of which were free and 9 were derived from steady-state constraints (Kovatchev *et al.*, 2009).

Once the T1D model was built, its validity was tested using a number of T1D data sets including adults, adolescents, and children. The UVA/Padova simulator is equipped with 300 virtual subjects: 100 adults, 100 adolescents, and 100 children, spanning the variability of the T1D population observed *in vivo*. In addition, the simulator is equipped with a model of a glucose sensor and of an insulin pump. With this technology, any meal and insulin delivery scenario can be tested efficiently *in silico*, prior to its clinical application (Fig. 11–45).

After extensive testing, in January 2008, this simulator was accepted by the U.S. Food and Drug Administration (FDA) as a substitute to animal trials for the pre-clinical testing of control strategies in AP studies, and has been adopted by the JDRF AP consortium as a primary test bed for new closed-loop control algorithms. The simulator was immediately put to its intended use with the *in silico* testing of a new model predictive controller, and in April 2008 an investigational device exemption (IDE) was granted by the FDA for a closed-loop control clinical trial. This IDE was issued solely on the basis of *in silico* testing of the safety and efficacy of AP control algorithm, an event that set a precedent for future clinical studies (Kovatchev *et al.*, 2009). In brief, to test the validity of the computer simulation environment independently from the data used for its development, a number of experiments were

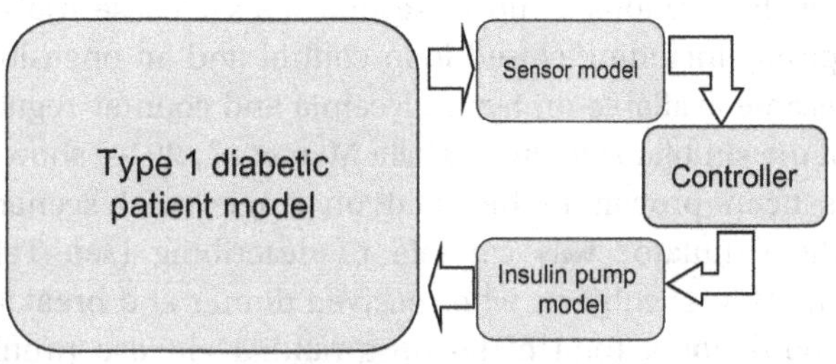

FIGURE 11–45 The UVA/Padova Type 1 diabetes simulator for artificial pancreas research equipped with a model of a glucose sensor, of an insulin pump and a controller.

conducted, aiming to assess the model's capability to reflect the variety of clinical situations as closely as possible. These experiments included:

a. reproducing the distribution of insulin correction factors in the T1D population of children and adults, which tests that the variability in the action of insulin administered by control algorithms will reflect the variability in observed insulin action;
b. reproducing glucose traces in children with T1D observed in clinical trials performed by the Diabetes Research in Children Network (DirecNet) consortium;
c. reproducing glucose traces of induced moderate hypoglycemia observed in adults in clinical trials at the University of Virginia, which provides comprehensive evaluation of control algorithms during hypo-glycemia.

Thus, the following paradigm has emerged: (1) *in silico* modeling could produce credible pre-clinical results that could substitute certain animal trials, and, (2) *in silico* testing yields these results in a fraction of the time and the cost required for animal trials. This was a paradigm shift in the field of T1D research: for the first time a computer model has been accepted by a regulatory agency as a substitute for animal trials in the testing of insulin treatments.

Since its introduction, this simulator enabled an important acceleration of AP studies, with a number of regulatory approvals obtained using *in silico* testing. A total of 140 candidate control algorithms have been formally evaluated from March 2008 to August 2014: 4 in 2008, 86 in 2009, 32 in 2010, 2 in 2011, 6 in 2012, 3 in 2103, and 7 in 2014. These 140 evaluations represented 16 AP projects, which typically resulted in IDEs being submitted to the FDA after final algorithm validation. However, one needs to emphasize that good *in silico* performance of a control algorithm does not guarantee *in vivo* performance; it only helps to test the robustness of the algorithm in extreme situations and to rule out inefficient scenarios. Thus, computer simulation is only a prerequisite to, but not a substitute for, clinical trials.

Since 2012, the AP studies successfully moved to the outpatient, free-living environment and became longer, with durations of up to several weeks. These trials are collecting large amounts of data, typically including closed-loop control and an open-loop mode as a comparator. New data became available on hypo-glycemia and counter-regulation as well, which allowed an update of the simulator in 2014 (Dalla Man *et al.*, 2014) shown in Fig. 11–46.

This version has been proven to be valid on single-meal scenarios; in fact, it has been shown that the simulator was capable of describing (see Table 11–7), glucose variability observed in 24 T1D subjects who received dinner and breakfast in two occasions (open- and closed-loop), for a total of 96 postprandial glucose profiles (Visentin *et al.*, 2014).

The simulator domain of validity was then extended by the introduction of diurnal patterns of insulin sensitivity based on data in 19 T1D subjects who underwent a triple-tracer study at breakfast, lunch, and dinner. This has allowed the incorporation of a circadian time-varying insulin sensitivity into the simulator, thus making this technology suitable for running multiple-meal scenarios and enabling a more robust design of AP control algorithms

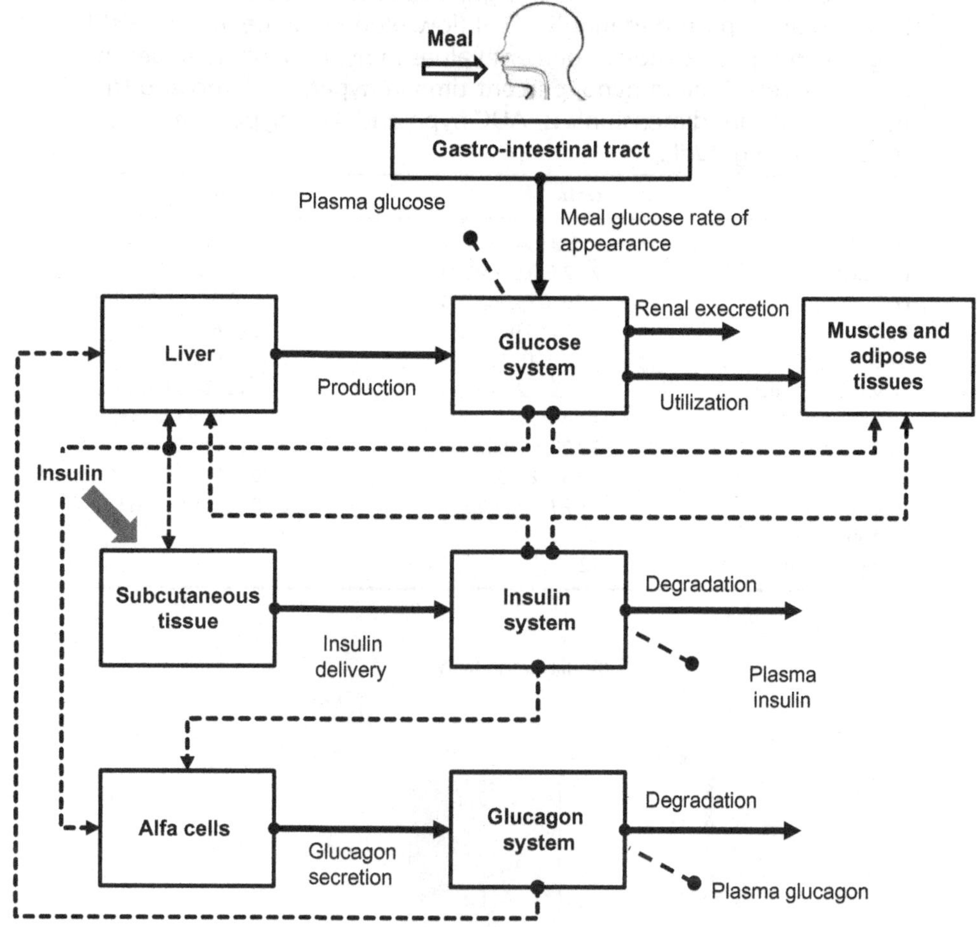

FIGURE 11–46 The single meal UVA/Padova Type 1 diabetes simulator updated in 2014 (Dalla Man *et al.*, 2014).

(Visentin *et al.*, 2015). In particular, seven empirical classes (see Fig. 11–47) were identified, each one associated with a particular pattern of SI at breakfast, lunch, and dinner; each virtual subject was randomly assigned to one of the above classes according to the estimated probability.

The fact that a subject belongs to the i-th class means that the SI daily pattern of that subject is on average the one associated with the i-th class. However, deviations from this nominal profile are allowed, by modulating the nominal pattern with a multiplicative random noise. The actual SI pattern is then transformed in the corresponding time-varying parameter SI(t) (i.e., an almost stepwise-like signal that varies three times a day [at 4:00 a.m., 11:00 a.m., and 5:00 p.m.]). Fig. 11–48 shows the procedure described above for an illustrative subject of class 5.

Table 11–7 Comparison between data and simulations: values are mean ± SD for normally distributed variables (*P*-value from paired *t*-test) or median [interquartile range] for nonnormally distributed variables (*P*-value from Wilcoxon signed rank test). Mean (BG) and IQR (BG) are reported in mg/dL, LBGI (low blood glucose index,) HBGI (high blood glucose index), percent values in hypo, percent values in hyper, percent time in hypo, percent time in hyper, Nr. hypo and Nr. hyper events are dimensionless, AUC hypo and AUC hyper are reported in mg · h/dL.

	Data	Simulator
Mean (BG)	156.9 ± 41.3	157.3 ± 43.3 (n.s.)
IQR (BG)	71.2 (50.9 – 96.1)	66.0 (47.8 – 89.2) (n.s.)
LBGI	0.59 (0.02 – 2.22)	0.36 (0.00 – 3.00) (n.s.)
HBGI	4.85 (1.79 – 8.34)	4.63 (1.60 – 8.24)
% Values in hypo	6.47 ± 10.19	7.98 ± 13.21 (n.s.)
% Values in hyper	28.78 ± 24.75	27.64 ± 24.93 (n.s.)
% Time in hypo	4.04 ± 7.93	6.22 ± 11.81 (0.006)
% Time in hyper	33.90 ± 29.02	33.44 ± 30.99 (n.s.)
AUC hypo	2.65 ± 8.99	5.00 ± 14.50 (0.019)
AUC hyper	88.23 ± 111.15	80.82 ± 112.44 (n.s.)
Nr. hypo events	37	32
Nr. hyper events	72	67

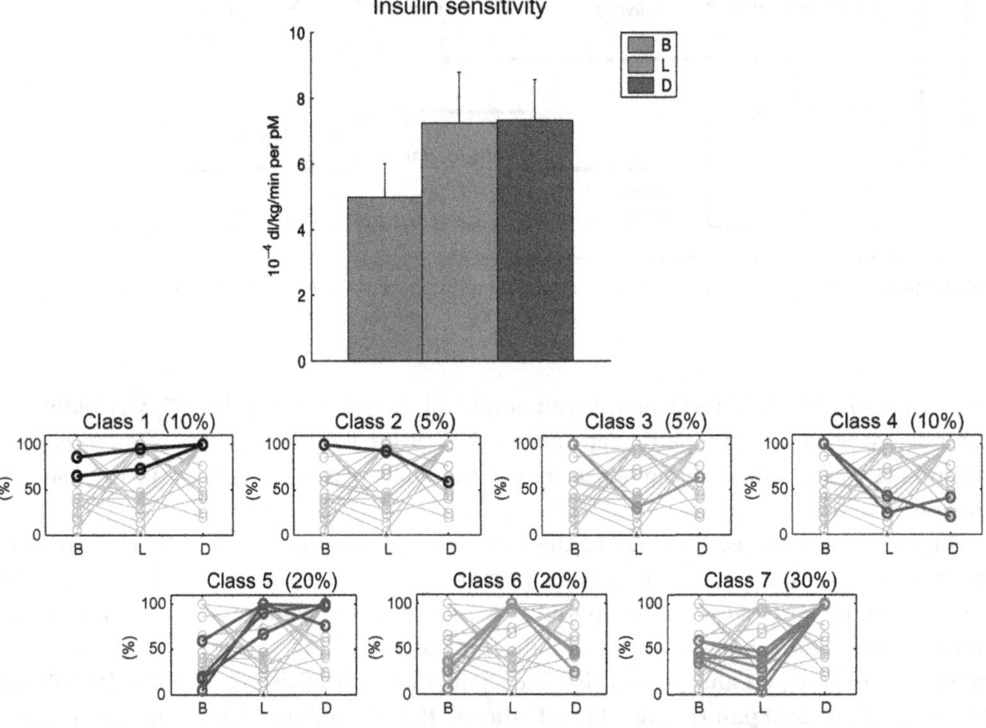

FIGURE 11–47 Upper panel: Average insulin sensitivity at the different diurnal portions (*B*, breakfast; *L*, lunch;and *D*, dinner). Data are mean ± SE values. *Lower panel*: Seven classes of insulin sensitivity pattern at *B*, breakfast; *L*, lunch; and *D*, dinner.

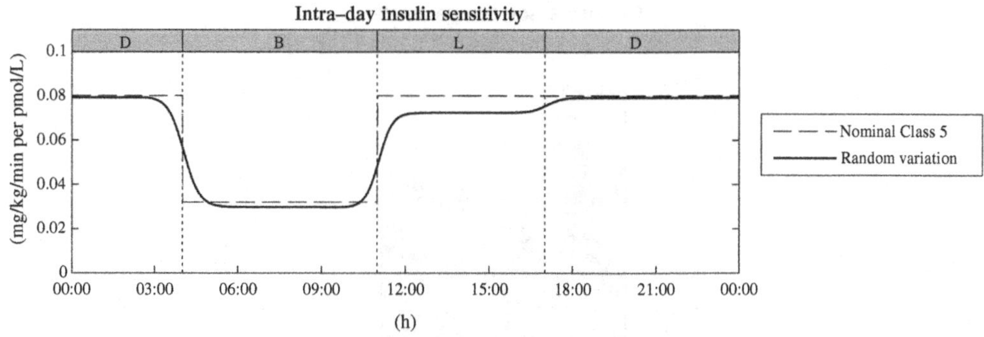

FIGURE 11–48 Intra-day insulin sensitivity profile for a virtual subject belonging to class 5: the final time-varying insulin sensitivity (*continuous line*) is obtained as a smoothed random variation of the nominal profile (*dashed line*), of which the 100% is the original time-invariant value, here set at 0.08 mg/kg/min per pmol/L. *B* Breakfast; *L* lunch; *D* dinner.

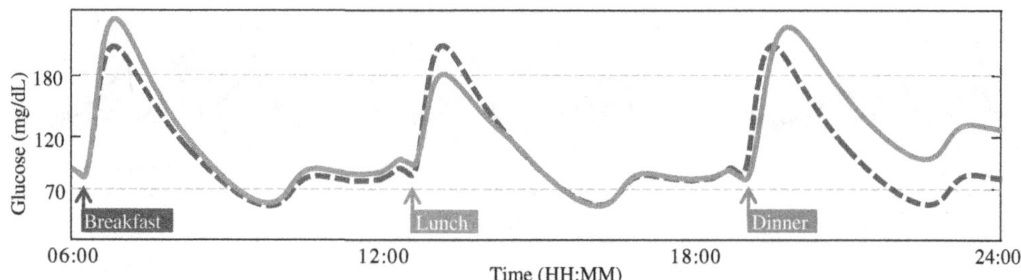

FIGURE 11–49 Plasma glucose profile in response to three identical meals, simulated with a time-invariant (*dashed red line*) or a time-varying model (*continuous green line*), respectively. A time-varying model provides more realistic behavior, for which the glucose response to the same meal perturbation can be different during the day.

The importance of accounting for intra-day variabilty of insulin sensitivity is clearly shown in Fig. 11–49: the glucose profile in response to three identical meals at breakfast, lunch, and dinner is different.

Finally, another validation of the simulator was carried out by comparing *in silico* output to data of 47 T1D subjects from six clinical centers, who underwent three randomized 23-hour admissions, one open-loop and two closed-loop. The protocol approximated real-life with breakfast, lunch, and dinner and collected 141 daily traces of glucose and insulin concentrations. A Maximum *a Posteriori* Bayesian approach was used, which exploited both the information provided by the experimental data and the *a priori* knowledge on model parameters represented by the joint parameter distribution incorporated in the simulator. Plasma insulin concentrations were used as model-forcing functions, that is, assumed to be known without error. The identification of the simulator on a specific person provided an *in silico* "clone" of this person; thus, the possibility emerged to clone a large number of T1D

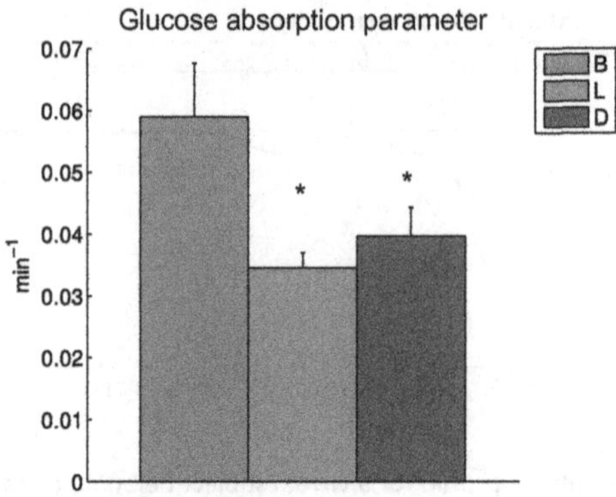

FIGURE 11–50 Absorption parameter (k_{max}, see Eq. 11.178, case study 11.7) at *B*, breakfast; *L*, lunch; and *D*, dinner [*vertical bars* represent SE]. **P* < .05 with respect to B.

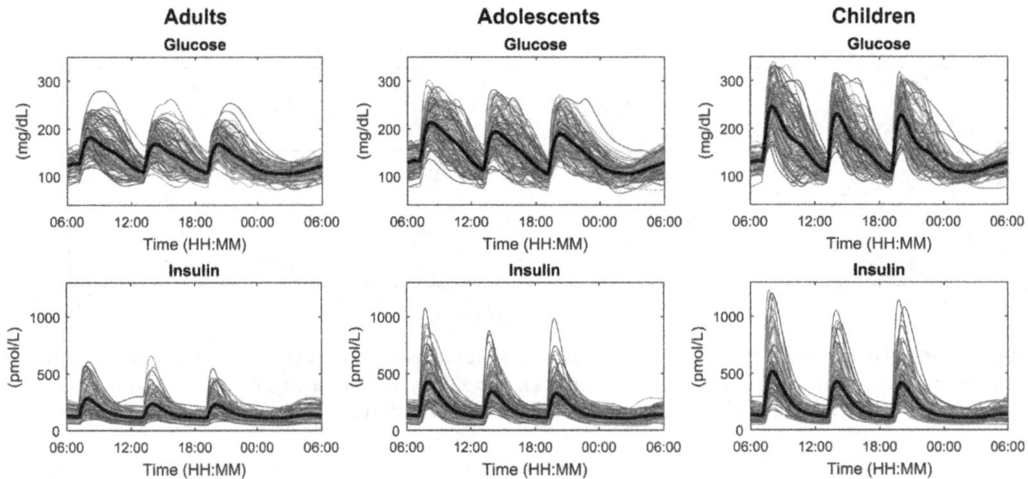

FIGURE 11–51 Simulated plasma glucose (*upper*) and insulin (*lower panels*) in the 100 *in silico* adults (*left*), adolescents (*middle*), and children (*right panels*) undergoing a 24-h scenario with three identical meals (60 g of CHO) at 7:00 a.m., 1:00 p.m., and 7:00 p.m., respectively, and receiving optimal subcutaneous insulin basal and bolus.

individuals and to move from single-meal to breakfast/lunch/dinner scenario, thus accounting for intra-subject variation not only on insulin sensitivity, but also on glucose absorption parameters as shown in Fig. 11–50 (Visentin *et al.*, 2016).

All these new features have been incorporated in the latest version of the T1D simulator, which has moved from single meal to single day (Visentin *et al.*, 2018)

Fig. 11–51 shows 24-hour profiles of plasma glucose and insulin concentrations of 100 adults, adolescents, and children receiving 60 g of CHO at 7:00 a.m., 1:00 p.m., 7:00 p.m., and the optimal insulin bolus. The observed inter-subject glucose variability is larger in children and adolescents compared to adults, in agreement with the knowledge that glucose control is more challenging in these groups of subjects. Moreover, in all the cohorts the postprandial glucose and insulin excursions at breakfast (B) are higher, on average, with respect to those at lunch (L), and dinner (D). This reflects that several subjects are insulin resistant in that portion of the day.

This new version of the simulator is extensively used in designing and testing the new generation of closed-loop control algorithms, in particular those aiming at individualization, that is, tuning the control algorithm to a specific person (Messori *et al.*, 2017) and those making the AP adaptive, that is, learning from the behavior in time of a specific person (Toffanin *et al.*, 2017, 2018).

11.8.2 *In silico* glucose sensors trials

In the past 10 years, the accuracy of glucose sensing has moved from MARD [mean absolute relative difference, a common metric used to compare continuous glucose sensors (CGS) to reference blood glucose] of 19.7% of the Medtronic RT-Guardian to a 9% of the Dexcom G4 Platinum (with software 505). Does this improved accuracy make sc glucose sensors reliable for insulin treatment decisions in place of self-monitoring of blood glucose? A clinical trial addressing this question would be almost impossible since the required number of patients to ensure exploration of the tail of the sensor MARD distribution would be huge. Also, retrospective data are not useful because it is impossible to see what would have happened of the insulin dosing was based on CGS rather than self-monitored blood glucose. Determining if CGS is safe and effective enough to substitute self-monitoring of blood glucose in diabetes management has therefore become a hot topic of investigation for the diabetes research community and regulatory agencies. Computer simulation is of critical importance because it allows *in silico* clinical trials to be performed [see also the outcome of a recent FDA panel meeting (FDA, 2016) and commentary (Edelman, 2016)]. The simulator used in this case is in the context of a patient decision-making model (Fig. 11–52).

By describing the blocks B, C, and D, and defining *in silico* scenarios to recreate real-life conditions, for example, 100 adults and 100 pediatric patients, 3 meals/day with variability in timeand amount and meal bolus behavior, we have evaluated standard outcome metrics, for example, time in severe hypo, time in hypo, time in target, hypo or hyperglycemic events, for both CGS and self-monitored blood glucose scenarios. The results based on 40,000 simulated virtual subjects in adults supported the noninferiority of CGS versus self-monitored blood glucose; moreover, time below 50 mg/dL and time below 70 mg/dL are significantly improved, time between 70 and 180 mg/dL and time above 180 mg/dL are slightly improved, and the number, extent, and duration of hypoglycemic events are significantly reduced (Vettoretti *et al.*, 2018).

11.8.3 *In silico* inhaled insulin trials

The delayed onset of action inherent to the current sc injected insulin analogs makes their optimal administration difficult, particularly in the presence of real-life perturbations, such

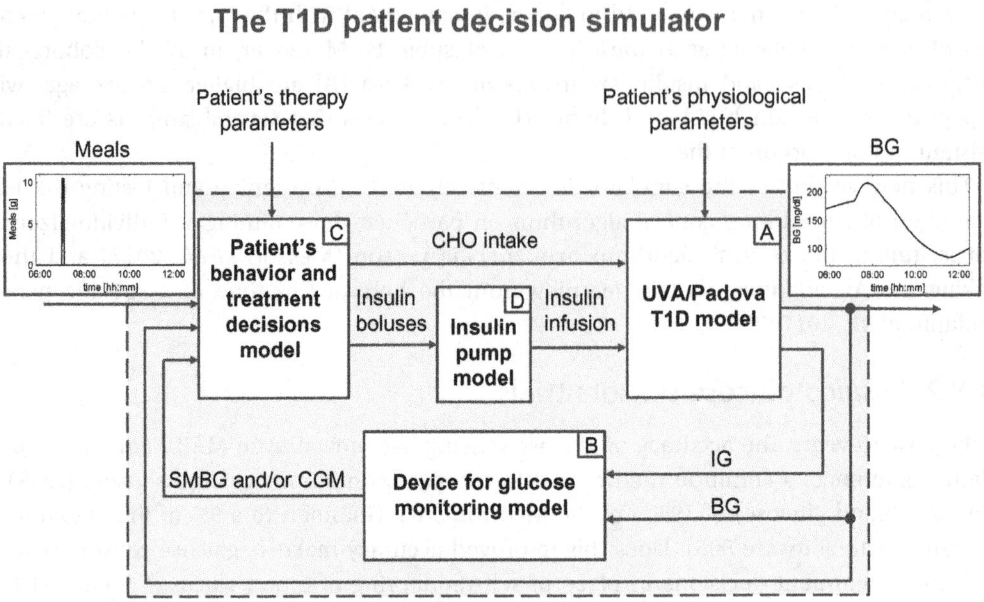

FIGURE 11–52 The T1D patient decision-making model.

as meals. Inhaled prandial insulin with rapid kinetics may overcome some of these delays, but also introduces new challenges. Technosphere insulin (TI) (MannKind Corporation; Valencia, CA) is a dry powder formulation of recombinant human insulin adsorbed onto Technosphere microparticles. Upon inhalation, these microparticles can reach the deep lung, allowing absorption into the systemic circulation with a time to maximum serum insulin concentration of 12–15 minutes (Boss *et al.*, 2012). In a phase III trial in T1D, TI demonstrated noninferiority to sc prandial insulin Aspart (Novolog) (Bode *et al.*, 2015). However, because of the fast onset and short duration of action, the dosing regimen of TI in this study may have been suboptimal. Designing a clinical trial to identify the optimal dosing regimen and the optimal titration rule would be prohibitively expensive because countless combinations would need to be tested. Thus, *in silico* trials were performed translating the known pharmacokinetic profile of TI (and insulin Lispro as comparator) into the expected postprandial glucose response following a meal tolerance test (Visentin *et al.*, 2016). The simulator and the *in silico* trials are shown in Figs. 11–53 and 11–54, respectively.

The simulations suggested that postmeal dosing (at 15 or 30 minutes after the start of the meal) and split dosing (with 15 or 30 minutes split times) result in a flatter postprandial glucose profile than at meal dosing (Fig. 11–55)

In several virtual patients the flatter profile allowed for a higher TI dose without increasing the risk for hypoglycemia events. In addition, the simulations revealed that the selection of the titration rule is crucial to achieve optimal treatment benefit. Simulated uptitrations

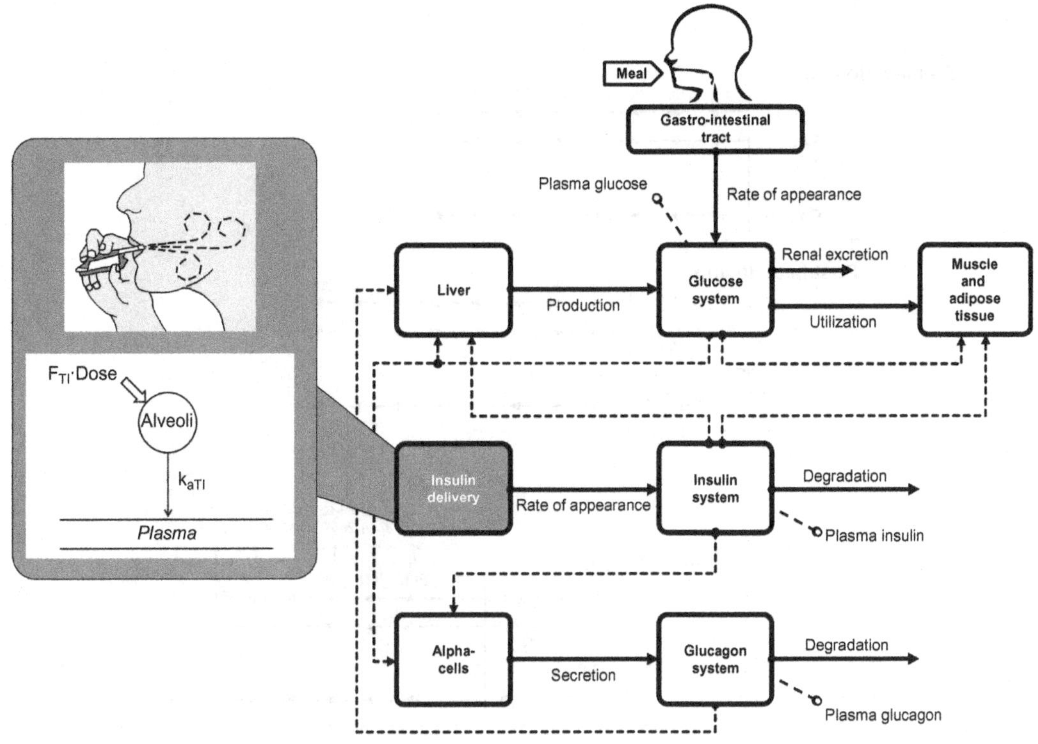

FIGURE 11–53 The T1D simulator incorporating Afrezza insulin delivery.

using 20 titration rules identified that the best time to measure postprandial glucose is 150 minutes after the meal, and the upper threshold for the glucose target should be 150–160 mg/dL. These optimized titration rules can considerably improve the efficacy of TI on postprandial glucose control.

11.9 Case study 9: illustrations of Bayesian estimation

A key step in developing both structural and input/output models of physiological systems is parameter estimation. That is, assigning numerical values to the unknown model parameters from the experimental data. Maximum Likelihood (ML) is probably the most used parameter estimation approach, also given its connection, in the Gaussian case, to least squares estimation. A more sophisticated but less adopted approach is Maximum *a Posteriori* (MAP) estimation.

The major difference between these two approaches lies in the fact that MAP estimation exploits not only the experimental data, but also the *a priori* available statistical information on the unknown parameter vector; for example, its expected value and covariance matrix in the Gaussian case. In other words, while ML is a Fisherian approach (i.e., to say that experimental data are the only information supplied to the estimator) MAP is a Bayesian approach

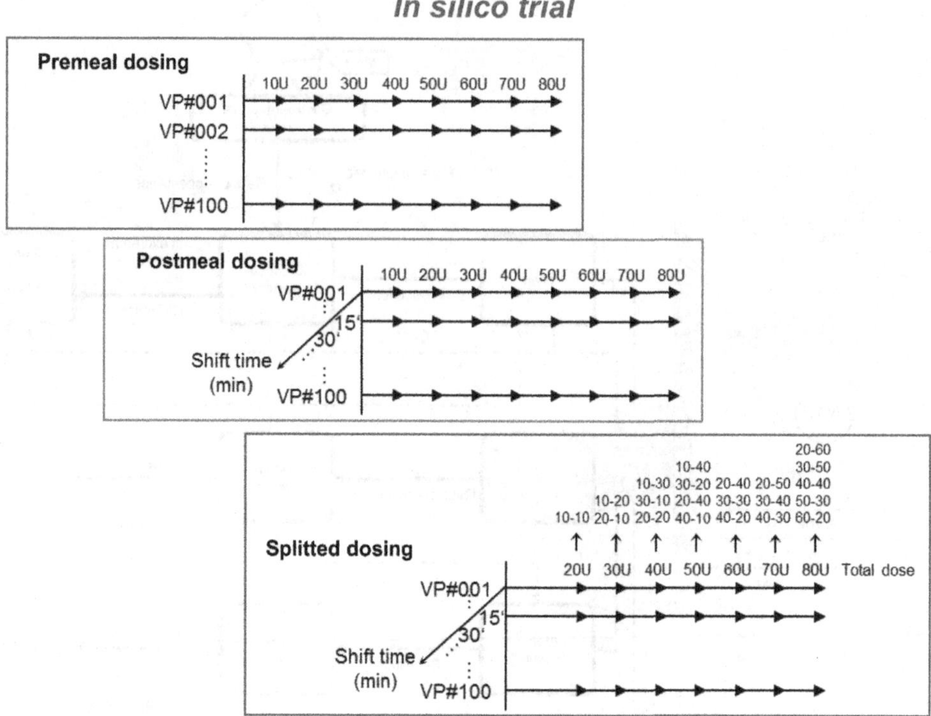

FIGURE 11–54 *In silico* trial on premeal, postmeal, and splitted meal dosing.

(i.e., *a priori* information is used) in addition to the information contained in the data (therefore termed *a posteriori* information), in the determination of the numerical values of the model parameters. Often, the *a priori* information needed to implement Bayesian estimation is available, for instance from population studies.

In this case study a comparison will be performed between ML and MAP estimators in the determination of the parameters of a sum of exponentials model which describes the impulse response of C-peptide (CP), using the results obtained by Sparacino *et al.* (2000).

CP is a peptide co-secreted with insulin on an equimolar basis, but is not extracted by the liver and exhibits linear kinetics over a large range of concentrations. Therefore CP plays a key role in quantitative studies of the insulin system, since its impulse response (but not that of insulin) allows the reconstruction of prehepatic beta-cell insulin secretion rate by deconvolution.

In particular, it will be shown that, when *a priori* information on the unknown model parameters is available, Bayesian estimation can be of particular interest since it can significantly improve the precision of parameter estimates with respect to Fisher estimation. This enables more complex models to be adopted than would be the case with a Fisherian

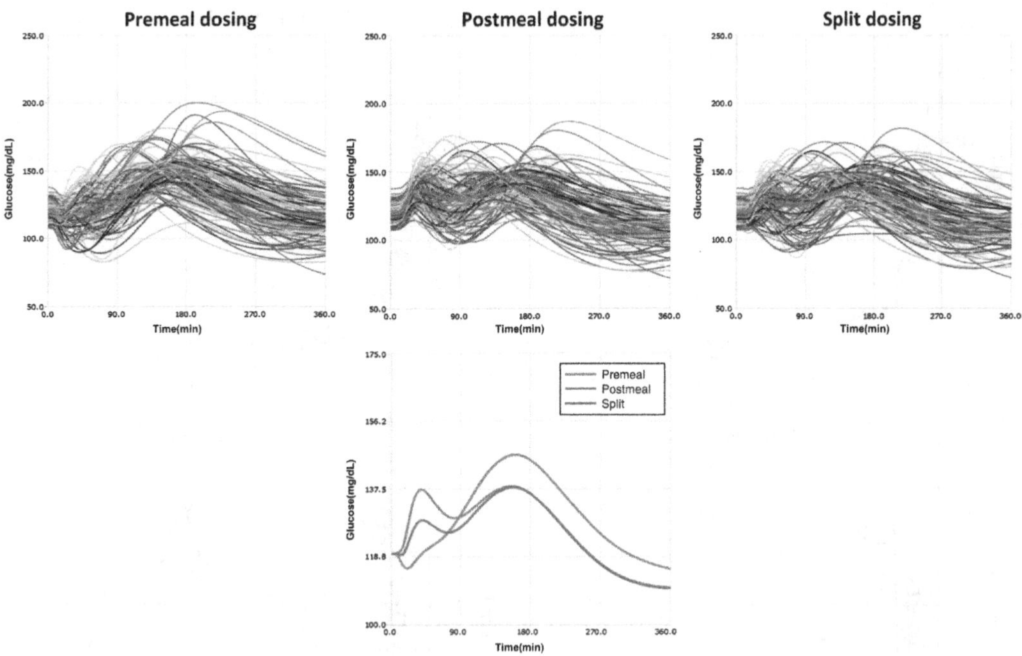

FIGURE 11–55 *Upper panel*: Glucose time courses obtained by simulating meal test in 100 virtual subjects receiving an individualized premeal dose of TI, an individualized postmeal dose, and an individualized split dose. *Lower panel*: Average postprandial glucose profiles with premeal, postmeal, and split TI dose.

approach. Moreover, it also enables a model to work in a data-poor situation, for instance with reduced sampling schedules and large errors in the measurements that constitute the data.

11.9.1 Database

In 14 normal humans, a bolus of biosynthetic CP was administered intravenously. Blood samples were collected at 2, 3, 4, 5, 6, 7, 8, 9, 10, 11, 14, 17, 20, 25, 30, 35, 40, 45, 50, 55, 60, 70, 80, 90, 100, 110, 120, 140, 160, and 180 minutes following the bolus administration, and CP plasma concentration was measured. The measurement noise was assumed Gaussian and independent, that is, the covariance matrix $\boldsymbol{\Sigma}_{\mathbf{v}}$ was diagonal, with zero mean, and with constant CV equal to 5%. A representative decay curve (subject # 1) is shown in Fig. 11–56 (top panels, open bullets).

11.9.2 The two-exponential model: ML versus MAP

The unknown vector is $\mathbf{p} = [A_1, A_2, \alpha_1, \alpha_2]^T$. Table 11–8 shows the estimates obtained by ML and MAP together with their precision.

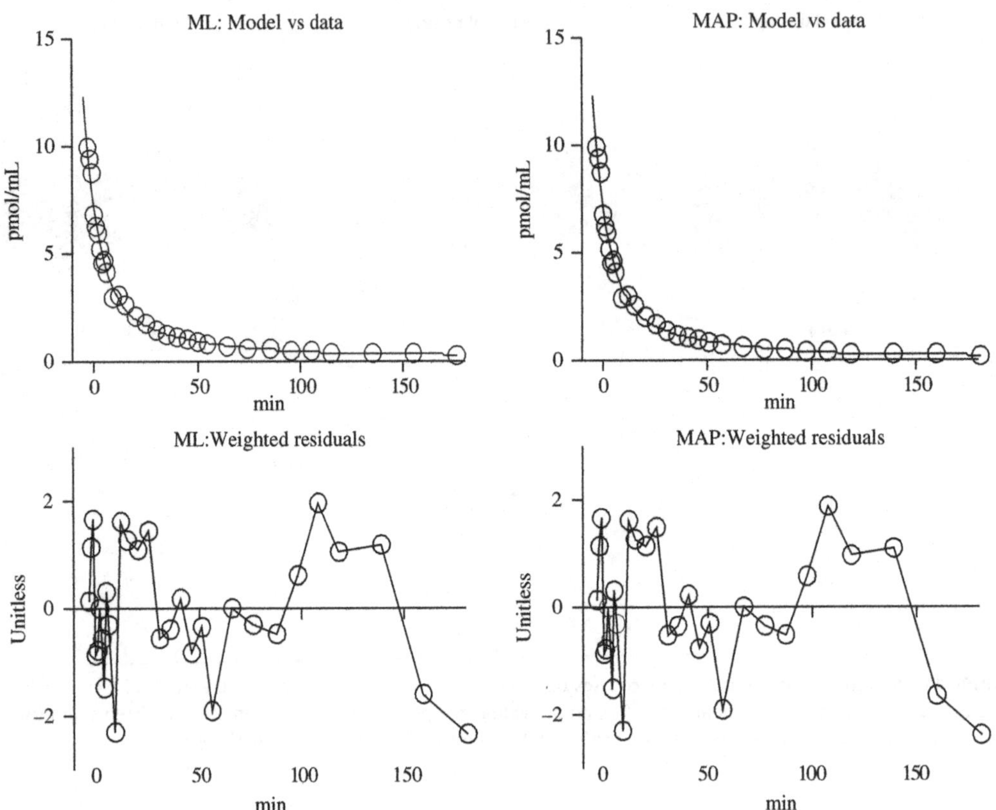

FIGURE 11–56 The 2E model identified by ML (*left*) and MAP (*right*) estimators from C-peptide concentration samples following the administration of a bolus at t = 0 (subject #1). Top: model predictions (*continuous line*) versus data (*open bullets*). Bottom: weighted residuals. *Adapted from Sparacino et al. (2000).*

The values of μ and $\Sigma_{\mathbf{p}}$ needed for MAP estimation have been obtained from:

$$\mu = \frac{1}{M}\sum_{i=1}^{M} \mathbf{p}^{(i)} \tag{11.191}$$

$$\Sigma_{\mathbf{p}} = \frac{1}{M-1}\sum_{i=1}^{M} \left(\mathbf{p}^{(i)} - \mu\right)\left(\mathbf{p}^{(i)} - \mu\right)^T \tag{11.192}$$

where $\mathbf{p}^{(i)}$ is the parameter vector of the ith subject of the population. First, individual ML estimates of the parameters of the CP impulse response model are obtained for the 14 subjects. Then, μ and $\Sigma_{\mathbf{p}}$ are calculated from these estimates by applying (11.191) and (11.192).

The values of ML and MAP estimates are very similar. In all subjects, the WRSS is lower for ML. This should not be surprising since, while the ML estimator only weights the distance of the model predictions from the data, the MAP estimator also weights the distance of the parameters from their *a priori* expected values. However, the WRSS difference is very

Table 11–8 Parameter estimates of the two-exponential (2E) model with their precision [expressed as percentage coefficient of variation (CV), in parenthesis] obtained by ML and MAP.

		$A_1 \times 10^{-4}$ (mL^{-1})	$A_2 \times 10^{-4}$ (mL^{-1})	α_1 (min^{-1})	α_2 (min^{-1})	WRSS
#1	ML	1.894 (4.7)	0.5564 (4.6)	0.1443 (5.6)	0.0262 (2.2)	55.56
	MAP	1.896 (4.3)	0.5518 (4.3)	0.1436 (5.0)	0.0261 (2.1)	55.58
#2	ML	1.996 (4.7)	0.5612 (4.4)	0.1470 (5.5)	0.0251 (2.3)	43.88
	MAP	1.991 (4.3)	0.585 (4.2)	0.1461 (5.0)	0.0250 (2.2)	43.88
#3	ML	1.908 (4.5)	0.6444 (4.0)	0.1256 (5.9)	0.0204 (2.1)	76.67
	MAP	1.956 (4.4)	0.6634 (3.6)	0.1328 (5.4)	0.0206 (1.9)	77.23
#4	ML	2.210 (5.2)	0.6747 (3.7)	0.1625 (5.8)	0.0240 (1.9)	47.99
	MAP	2.167 (4.7)	0.6662 (3.6)	0.1579 (5.1)	0.0239 (1.9)	48.17
#5	ML	1.913 (6.3)	0.7551 (3.0)	0.1750 (6.9)	0.0196 (1.8)	77.91
	MAP	1.875 (5.4)	0.7489 (2.9)	0.1692 (5.7)	0.0195 (1.7)	78.05
#6	ML	1.443 (5.8)	0.5222 (4.0)	0.1691 (6.7)	0.0257 (2.2)	89.15
	MAP	1.413 (5.1)	0.5058 (3.8)	0.1595 (5.6)	0.0253 (2.1)	89.44
#7	ML	1.777 (5.7)	0.8846 (4.1)	0.1353 (7.7)	0.0245 (2.0)	45.15
	MAP	1.842 (5.2)	0.8856 (3.7)	0.1407 (6.5)	0.0244 (1.8)	45.61
#8	ML	2.444 (5.4)	0.8595 (3.3)	0.1552 (6.1)	0.0222 (1.7)	59.75
	MAP	2.410 (4.8)	0.8555 (3.2)	0.1529 (5.3)	0.0222 (1.7)	59.88
#9	ML	2.309 (3.8)	0.6049 (5.7)	0.1186 (5.1)	0.0273 (2.4)	96.37
	MAP	2.313 (3.6)	0.6032 (5.3)	0.1191 (4.7)	0.0272 (2.3)	96.47
#10	ML	2.271 (4.3)	0.4515 (3.8)	0.1555 (4.5)	0.0220 (2.1)	128.85
	MAP	2.229 (4.0)	0.4506 (3.7)	0.1527 (4.1)	0.0220 (2.0)	129.03
#11	ML	2.605 (5.1)	0.6719 (3.5)	0.1705 (5.2)	0.0237 (1.8)	39.56
	MAP	2.497 (4.5)	0.6614 (3.4)	0.1625 (4.7)	0.0235 (1.7)	40.29
#12	ML	2.046 (7.1)	1.037 (3.2)	0.1720 (8.1)	0.0215 (1.8)	70.65
	MAP	2.042 (5.8)	1.023 (2.9)	0.1681 (6.3)	0.0214 (1.7)	70.86
#13	ML	2.104 (3.7)	0.4548 (4.0)	0.1214 (4.4)	0.0195 (2.1)	130.90
	MAP	2.143 (3.7)	0.4724 (3.7)	0.1273 (4.2)	0.0198 (1.9)	131.49
#14	ML	1.243 (5.3)	0.4691 (3.9)	0.1431 (6.8)	0.0231 (2.0)	44.44
	MAP	1.265 (4.9)	0.4717 (3.6)	0.1459 (5.9)	0.0232 (1.9)	44.53

WRSS, Weighted residuals sum of squares; Amplitudes of exponentials are divided by the bolus dose.
Source: Adapted from Sparacino *et al.* (2000).

small. Turning to precision of parameter estimates (CV, reported in parentheses), it can be noted that it always improves by using Bayesian estimation. This is again in line with theoretical expectations, given the incorporation of *a priori* knowledge into the algorithm. However, here the improvement is almost undetectable, since the parameters estimated by ML, exploiting only the *a posteriori* information, already have very good precision.

To give a quantitative flavor of the extent of this modest improvement, by averaging the percentage CV of the estimates of $[A_1, A_2, \alpha_1, \alpha_2]^T$ reported in Table 11–8, the values are $[5.1, 3.9, 6.0, 2.0]^T$ with ML and $[4.6, 3.7, 5.2, 1.9]^T$ with MAP. On average, the uncertainty is thus reduced by approximately 10%.

Fig. 11−56 shows the model fit and the weighted residuals for a representative subject, obtained by ML and MAP estimation. In agreement with the small gap in WRSS, no significant differences can be detected by inspecting the two fits.

11.9.3 The three-exponential model: ML versus MAP

The unknown vector is $\mathbf{p} = [A_1, A_2, A_3, \alpha_1, \alpha_2, \alpha_3]^T$. The ML and MAP estimates are shown in Table 11−9. The *a priori* information supplied to the MAP estimator, is the same for the 2E model. Again, by looking at Table 11−9, only small differences between the values of the parameters estimated by ML or MAP can be detected. Also, the WRSS of ML estimation is only slightly better than that of that MAP estimation. In contrast with the 2E model, a significant improvement in the precision of the parameter estimates now occurs with MAP in comparison with ML estimation. For instance, for subject #7 the CV of the parameter A_2 is 59.3% with ML estimation, and 16.1% with MAP estimation. By averaging the percentage CV of the estimates of $[A_1, A_2, A_3, \alpha_1, \alpha_2, \alpha_3]^T$ reported in Table 11−9, the values are $[16.4, 29.4, 20.8, 24.2, 27.7, 8.4]^T$ with ML and $[9.7, 12.4, 13.5, 12.2, 11.8, 5.6]^T$ with MAP. On average, the uncertainty is thus reduced by approximately 50%.

Fig. 11−57 shows the model fit and weighted residuals (bottom) obtained by the two estimation techniques. As with the 2E model, no significant differences can be detected by inspection, again given the fact that the WRSS values are very close.

By comparing the results presented in Tables 11−8 and 11−9, it is evident that the improvement in parameter precision obtained by using MAP in place of ML estimation is now much more significant. This can be explained by noting that in MAP estimation a trade-off is established between *a priori* and *a posteriori* information. Thus, the improvement in the precision obtained by MAP estimation is more significant for those parameters related to the fastest eigenvalues (A_1 and α_1 and A_2 and α_2) than for those related to the slowest mode (A_3 and α_3), since their estimation is based on fewer data (i.e., less *a posteriori* information).

11.9.4 Two versus three-exponential model order choice

In each subject (see, e.g., Figs. 11−56 and 11−57) both the 2E and the 3E models describe the data satisfactorily. The 3E model obviously fits the data better than the 2E one, especially in the first portion of the experiment (0−20 minutes), where the 2E model exhibits larger and correlated residuals in contrast with the assumptions on measurement error. As a consequence, the WRSS is significantly lower for the 3E model. For instance, by looking at Tables 11−8 and 11−9 it can be seen that, for the representative subject, WRSS is approximately 55.5 with the 2E model (Fig. 11−56) and 47 with the 3E model (Fig. 11−57), thus showing a 15% difference. Even greater WRSS differences can be detected in other subjects (e.g., more than 100% for subject #10). However, the 3E parameter estimates always exhibit worse precision, especially those associated to the fastest eigenvalue. Therefore the question of selecting the better model needs to be addressed.

Table 11–9 Parameter estimates of the three-exponential (3E) model with their precision [expressed as percentage coefficient of variation (CV), in parenthesis] obtained by ML and MAP.

		$A_1 \times 10^{-4}$ (mL^{-1})	$A_2 \times 10^{-4}$ (mL^{-1})	$A_3 \times 10^{-4}$ (mL^{-1})	α_1 (min^{-1})	α_2 (min^{-1})	α_3 (min^{-1})	WRSS
#1	ML	1.304 (32.0)	1.093 (47.1)	0.4929 (10.2)	0.2998 (48.2)	0.0998 (26.4)	0.0251 (4.0)	46.83
	MAP	1.525 (12.0)	0.9294 (13.1)	0.4593 (8.2)	0.2799 (13.8)	0.0859 (9.7)	0.0245 (3.5)	47.82
#2	ML	1.712 (17.2)	0.8711 (37.0)	0.441 (14.9)	0.2659 (28.0)	0.0793 (26.8)	0.0229 (5.6)	29.29
	MAP	1.750 (10.5)	0.8808 (13.3)	0.4217 (10.5)	0.2723 (13.1)	0.0760 (11.2)	0.0225 (4.3)	29.48
#3	ML	2.266 (13.5)	1.007 (9.0)	0.3597 (20.6)	0.3283 (17.6)	0.0520 (13.8)	0.0161 (8.5)	21.21
	MAP	2.239 (9.3)	0.9495 (8.0)	0.3786 (17.7)	0.3068 (11.4)	0.0522 (12.3)	0.0165 (7.3)	21.89
#4	ML	2.313 (13.2)	0.9013 (22.1)	0.5118 (12.9)	0.3273 (21.8)	0.0742 (21.3)	0.0216 (4.9)	21.19
	MAP	2.125 (9.6)	0.8745 (12.3)	0.4918 (9.9)	0.2989 (12.1)	0.0706 (11.6)	0.0213 (4.1)	21.91
#5	ML	2.112 (15.6)	0.7661 (17.6)	0.5657 (11.8)	0.3576 (22.4)	0.0641 (22.1)	0.0173 (5.2)	46.45
	MAP	2.024 (9.8)	0.6872 (12.5)	0.5541 (9.1)	0.3120 (11.8)	0.0591 (13.3)	0.0171 (4.2)	47.14
#6	ML	1.648 (15.5)	0.6683 (13.7)	0.3332 (18.5)	0.3677 (21.2)	0.0675 (18.8)	0.0215 (7.0)	47.60
	MAP	1.522 (11.2)	0.6474 (10.7)	0.3444 (12.2)	0.3347 (12.0)	0.0695 (12.0)	0.0218 (5.0)	48.44
#7	ML	1.331 (35.5)	0.8817 (59.3)	0.7765 (12.7)	0.2471 (47.8)	0.0790 (41.1)	0.0233 (4.5)	38.57
	MAP	1.525 (11.9)	0.7974 (16.1)	0.7672 (6.7)	0.2465 (14.8)	0.0743 (11.2)	0.0232 (2.8)	39.08
#8	ML	2.428 (9.0)	0.9118 (12.8)	0.3980 (47.0)	0.2311 (14.7)	0.0424 (24.0)	0.0170 (15.5)	28.30
	MAP	2.375 (8.5)	0.9143 (10.9)	0.5013 (19.7)	0.2469 (11.8)	0.0498 (15.7)	0.0183 (7.0)	28.92
#9	ML	1.998 (13.7)	1.280 (18.7)	0.3907 (20.8)	0.2597 (23.5)	0.0695 (16.1)	0.0236 (6.9)	64.54
	MAP	2.047 (10.1)	1.234 (10.2)	0.3908 (17.1)	0.2534 (13.1)	0.0689 (10.9)	0.0235 (5.9)	64.82
#10	ML	2.494 (7.5)	0.7363 (9.1)	0.1382 (36.6)	0.2490 (10.1)	0.0455 (13.5)	0.0134 (16.9)	51.73
	MAP	2.441 (6.8)	0.7527 (8.8)	0.1574 (27.3)	0.2534 (9.0)	0.0479 (11.8)	0.0142 (12.2)	52.07
#11	ML	2.598 (9.8)	0.7882 (24.2)	0.4661 (16.7)	0.2673 (16.7)	0.0640 (24.3)	0.0207 (6.0)	12.85
	MAP	2.380 (8.4)	0.8812 (13.1)	0.4561 (11.0)	0.2712 (11.4)	0.0662 (12.0)	0.0205 (4.3)	14.18
#12	ML	1.876 (20.0)	0.4559 (79.1)	0.9092 (17.4)	0.2186 (29.3)	0.0618 (80.5)	0.0204 (6.1)	66.90
	MAP	1.871 (9.7)	0.5914 (21.5)	0.8633 (6.6)	0.2393 (13.6)	0.0618 (13.2)	0.0200 (3.0)	67.53
#13	ML	2.457 (7.9)	0.8876 (6.9)	0.1101 (38.7)	0.2458 (10.4)	0.0405 (10.4)	0.0103 (21.8)	11.68
	MAP	2.484 (7.1)	0.9007 (6.8)	0.1528 (26.0)	0.2596 (9.2)	0.0442 (9.5)	0.0123 (12.7)	12.75
#14	ML	1.100 (19.4)	0.3997 (51.6)	0.3808 (19.6)	0.2104 (26.4)	0.0636 (46.0)	0.0215 (6.7)	37.64
	MAP	1.103 (12.0)	0.5149 (17.6)	0.3915 (7.4)	0.2571 (14.3)	0.0728 (11.5)	0.0216 (3.2)	38.32

WRSS, Weighted residuals sum of squares; Amplitudes of exponentials are divided by the bolus dose.
Source: Adapted from Sparacino *et al.* (2000).

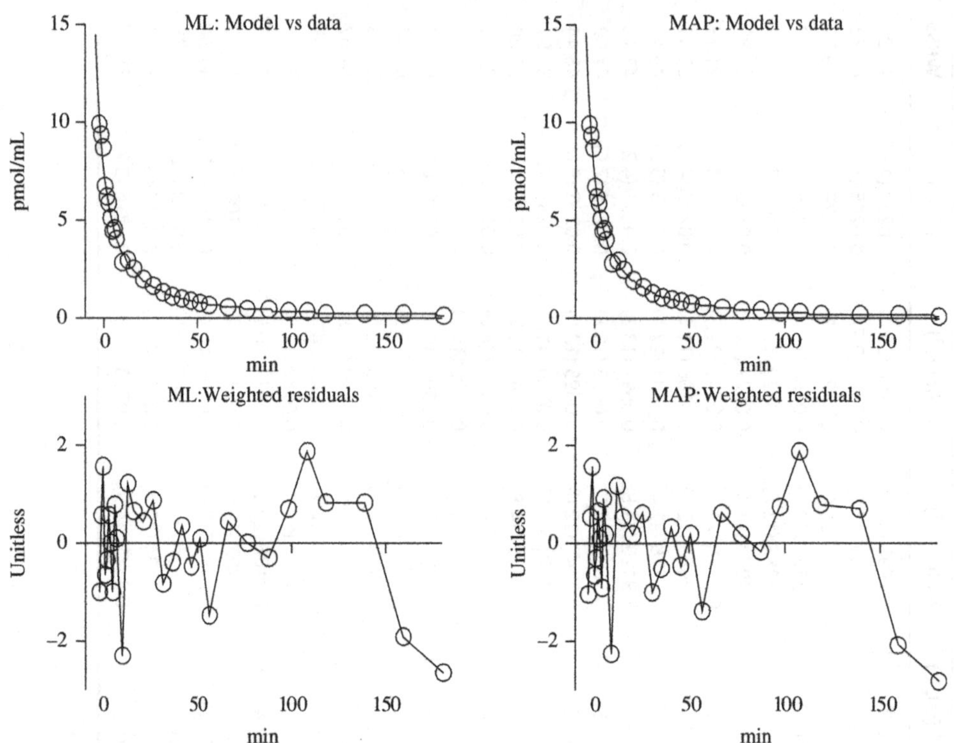

FIGURE 11–57 3E model identified by ML (*left*) and MAP (*right*) estimators in the same subject of Fig. 11–56. *Top*: model predictions (*continuous line*) versus data (*open bullets*). *Bottom*: weighted residuals. *Adapted from Sparacino et al. (2000).*

The AIC and GEN-IC indexes are the tools for resolving this issue.

Table 11–10 shows the differences in AIC, ΔAIC, and GEN-IC, ΔGEN-IC, between the 3E and the 2E models in the 14 subjects. As far as an ML estimation is concerned, for all the subjects with the exception of #12, ΔAIC is negative, suggesting that the 3E model is the one of choice. For subject #12 the slightly positive ΔAIC value reflects the similar performance of the two models.

As far as MAP is concerned, ΔGEN-IC is negative in all subjects. Therefore in the context of a Bayesian estimation, the superiority of the 3E model is more clear cut than in the deterministic embedding.

11.9.5 Data-poor situation: ML versus MAP

To understand the ML versus MAP situation in a data-poor context, let us consider two simulations which depict such a data-poor situation. In both cases, the response of a 3E system to a CP bolus was simulated using the parameters reported in Table 11–11. In

Table 11–10 Values of the difference of AIC (ΔAIC) and GEN-IC (ΔGEN-IC) between 3E and 2E by ML and MAP.

Subject	ΔAIC	ΔGEN-IC
#1	− 4.75	− 6.80
#2	− 10.56	− 13.90
#3	− 51.78	− 55.47
#4	− 22.89	− 25.77
#5	− 27.63	− 31.70
#6	− 37.62	− 39.91
#7	− 2.60	− 7.12
#8	− 27.57	− 30.10
#9	− 27.94	− 31.05
#10	− 73.45	− 76.67
#11	22.79	− 26.15
#12	0.27	− 2.30
#13	− 116.0	− 120.12
#14	− 2.80	− 4.95

Source: Adapted from Sparacino *et al.* (2000).

Table 11–11 True parameters and parameter estimates with precision obtained by ML and MAP from the simulated bolus responses displayed in Fig. 11–52 (simulation #1) and Fig. 11–53 (simulation #2).

		$A_1 \times 10^{-4}$ (mL^{-1})	$A_2 \times 10^{-4}$ (mL^{-1})	$A_3 \times 10^{-4}$ (mL^{-1})	α_1 (min^{-1})	α_2 (min^{-1})	α_3 (min^{-1})	WRSS	$E \times 10^{-10}$
True		1.304	1.093	0.4929	0.2998	0.0998	0.0251	–	–
Sim # 1	ML	1.632 (38.7)	0.6443 (80.7)	0.3084 (88.4)	0.1997 (63.4)	0.0545 (82.5)	0.0217 (24.5)	21.5	9.979
	MAP	1.663 (18.8)	0.9001 (15.9)	0.3830 (19.7)	0.2798 (16.9)	0.0744 (13.7)	0.0229 (7.2)	21.9	0.654
Sim # 2	ML	1.690 (31.4)	0.5522 (108.3)	0.4976 (12.5)	0.2212 (37.7)	0.0772 (57.3)	0.0251 (3.4)	9.6	2.876
	MAP	1.530 (12.7)	0.8206 (15.5)	0.4845 (6.4)	0.2738 (14.9)	0.0839 (9.3)	0.0249 (2.0)	10.7	1.493

WRSS, Weighted residuals sum of squares; *E*, estimation error.
Source: Adapted from Sparacino *et al.* (2000).

simulation #1, we created a situation with a normally-frequent sampling schedule (the grid was the same as that described in the database above) and a large measurement error, that is, a constant CV of 20%. The simulated, noisy data are displayed in Fig. 11–58 (open bullets). The ML and MAP estimates are shown in Table 11–11. The differences between the values of the parameters estimated by ML or MAP are now much larger than in Table 11–9 (where a 5% CV measurement error affected the data).

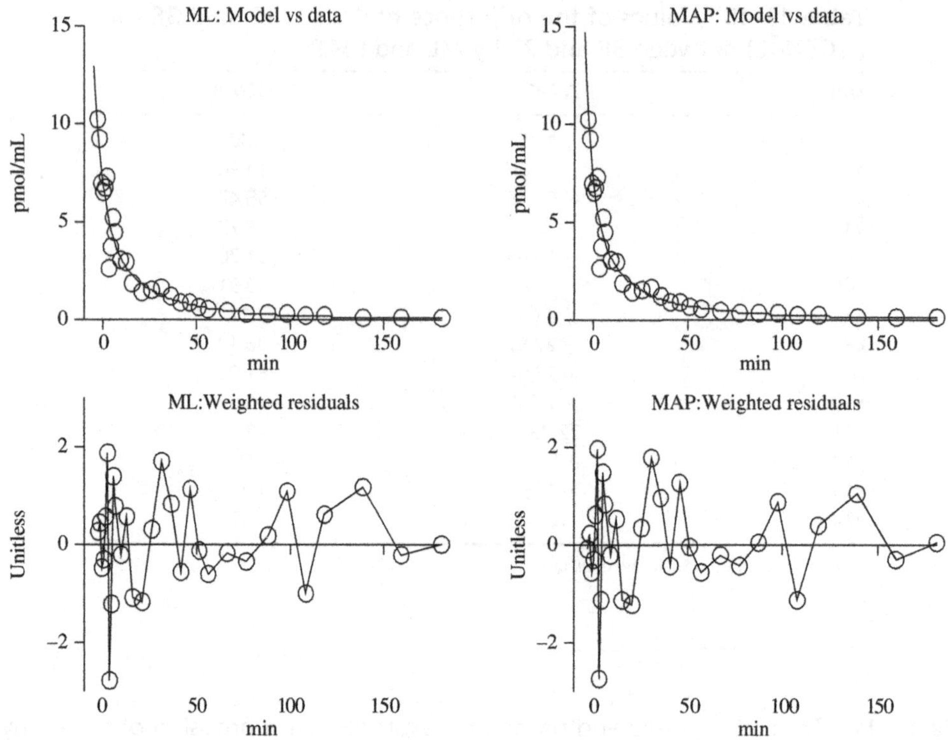

FIGURE 11–58 Simulation #1 for large measurement error situation. The 3E model identified by ML (*left*) and MAP (*right*) estimators. *Top*: model predictions (*continuous line*) versus data (*open bullets*). *Bottom*: weighted residuals. *Adapted from Sparacino et al. (2000).*

Moreover, the values of the model parameters estimated by MAP are much closer to the true ones than those estimated by ML. Even if the WRSS of the ML estimation is (only slightly) better than that of the MAP estimation, the realization of the impulse response estimation error E (defined as the integral from zero to infinity of the squared difference between the true and the estimated impulse response) is much lower in the MAP case. As expected, a large improvement in the precision of parameter estimates now occurs with MAP in comparison with the ML estimation. For instance, the CV of parameter A_2 is 88.4% with the ML estimation, and 19.7% with the MAP estimation. On average, the uncertainty is reduced by 75%.

In simulation #2, we create a situation with the same noise as found in the real data, CV = 5%, but with a much reduced sampling schedule: 2, 4, 6, 9, 14, 25, 40, 60, 80, 100, 120, 140, 160, 180 minutes. It is worth noting that this grid is a subset of the rich grid, but, although sparse, is frequent enough to make all three modes of the impulse response resolvable. The ML and MAP results are shown in Table 11–11 and Fig. 11–59.

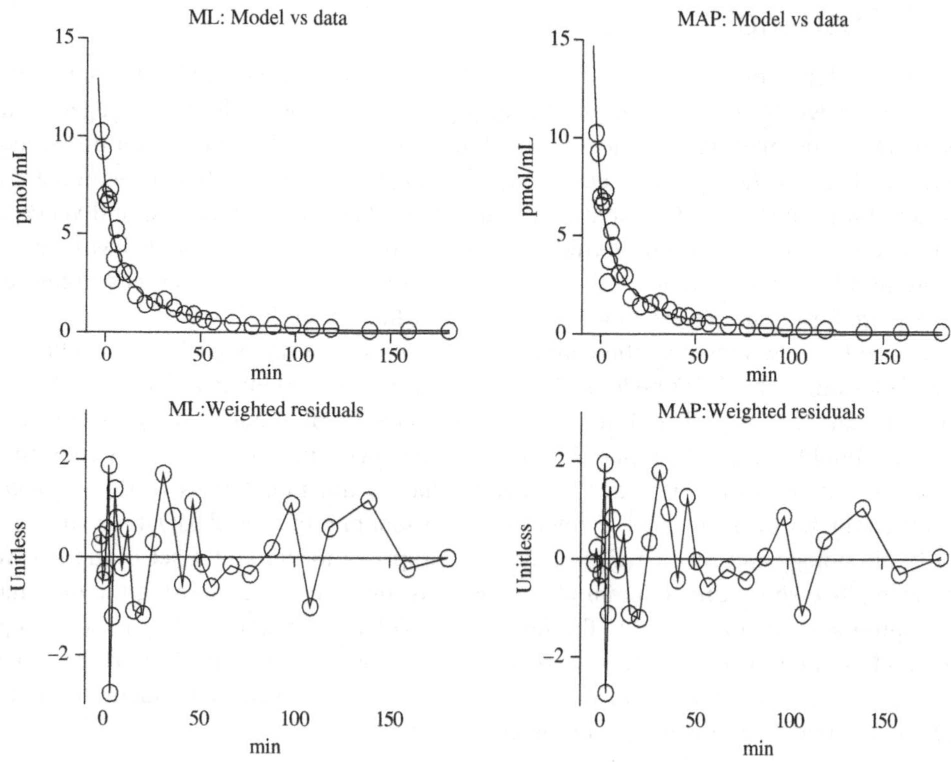

FIGURE 11–59 Simulation #2 for the reduced sampling situation. The 3E model is identified by ML (*left*) and MAP (*right*) estimators. Top: model predictions (*continuous line*) versus data (*open bullets*). *Bottom*: weighted residuals. *Adapted from Sparacino et al. (2000).*

Again, the differences between the values of the parameters estimated by ML or MAP are much larger than in Table 11–9 (where a rich sampling grid was used). The values of the model parameters estimated by MAP are, on average, much closer to the true ones than those estimated by ML, and the lowest estimation error (E) is obtained using MAP estimation. More importantly, the improvement in the precision of parameter estimates with MAP in comparison with ML estimation is now really impressive: for instance, the CV of parameter A_2 is 108.3% with ML and 15.5% with MAP estimation. In both simulations the uncertainty of the ML estimates is unacceptable. In contrast, MAP estimation leads to reasonable confidence intervals.

In summary, the general lesson which emerges is that the improvement obtained by a Bayesian estimation with respect to a Fisher estimation is, that the more significant the result, the more the *a priori* information supports the *a posteriori* information. The examples that have been discussed here cover three typical situations in which taking into account, *a priori* information can be crucial: the model is too complex for being identifiable with satisfactory precision by a Fisherian approach (see real case studies); data are very noisy (i.e., *a posteriori* information is not sufficiently reliable, see simulation #1); and data are few in number (i.e., there is only a small amount of *a posteriori* information, see simulation #2).

11.10 Postscript

This final chapter, with its set of seven case studies, has provided illustrations of some of the varied ways in which modeling of physiological systems can be undertaken. Together they cover many of the main ingredients of modeling methodology that have been described in the earlier chapters. As has been emphasized throughout, good modeling methodology is made up of a number of components, including formulation, identification, and validation. This text has set out to provide a guide to such modeling methodology. It has essentially been an introductory exploration, but we hope that we have encouraged at least some readers to explore further in this exciting interdisciplinary field of study.

As a final thought, repeating the comment that we make at the end of the first chapter of our more advanced book (Cobelli & Carson, 2014), it is important that one should always remain critical of a model and not view it as perfect. All models are approximations; hence one should always be prepared to include new facts and observations. A good model (in a Popperian sense) is one that is clearly falsifiable, and therefore is readily capable of bringing about its own downfall. Remember, in situations of complexity (very much the norm in physiology and medicine), it may be appropriate to think of a set of models, with each having its own, distinct domain of validity. It is then a case of choosing the one that is most appropriate; for instance, for the level of physiological hierarchy that is being represented and the time scale of interest in relation to the dynamic response. As summarized in Fig. 10–2, a successful outcome to the modeling process is critically dependent on both the quality of the model and the quality of the experimental data.

References

Ackerman, E., Rosevear, J. W., & McGuckin, W. F. (1964). A mathematical model of the glucose tolerance test. *Physics in Medicine and Biology, 9*(2), 203–213.

Akaike, H. (1974). A new look at the statistical model identification. *IEEE Transactions on Automatic Control, AC-19*, 716–723.

Atkins, G. L. (1969). *Multicompartment models for biological systems*. London: Methuen.

Audoly, S., D'Angio, L., Saccomani, M. P., & Cobelli, C. (1998). Global identifiability of linear compartmental models. A computer algebra algorithm. *IEEE Transactions on Biomedical Engineering, 45*, 36–41.

Bassingthwaighte, J. B., Chan, I. S., & Wang, C. Y. (1992). Computationally efficient algorithms for convection-permeation-diffusion models for blood-tissue exchange. *Annals of Biomedical Engineering, 20*, 687–725.

Bassingthwaighte, J. B., & Goresky, C. A. (1984). Modeling in the analysis of solute and water exchange in the microvasculature. In E. M. Renkin (Ed.), *Handbook of physiology – The cardiovascular system. Microcirculation*. Bethesda, MD: American Society of Physiology.

Bassingthwaighte, J. F., Ackerman, E., & Wood, E. (1996). Applications of the lagged normal density curve as a model for arterial dilution curves. *Circulation Research, 18*, 398–415.

Basu, R., Di Camillo, B., Toffolo, G., Basu, A., Shah, P., Vella, A., . . . Cobelli, C. (2003). Use of a novel triple-tracer approach to assess postprandial glucose metabolism. *American Journal of Physiology Endocrinology and Metabolism, 284*, E55–E69.

Bates, J. T. H. (1991). Deconvolution of tracer and dilution data using the Wiener filter. *IEEE Transactions on Biomedical Engineering, 38*, 1262–1266.

Beck, J. R., & Pauker, S. G. (1983). The Markov process in medical prognosis. *Medical Decision Making, 3*(4), 419–458.

Beneken, J. E. W., & DeWit, B. (1967). A physical approach to hemodynamic aspects of the human cardiovascular system. In E. B. Reeve, & A. C. Guyton (Eds.), *Physical bases of circulatory transport: Regulation and exchange*. Philadelphia, PA: WB Saunders.

Bequette, W. (2005). A critical assessment of algorithms and challenges in the development of a closed-loop artificial pancreas. *Diabetes Technology & Therapeutics, 7*, 28–47.

Bergman, R. N., Ider, Y. Z., Bowden, C. R., & Cobelli, C. (1979). Quantitative estimation of insulin sensitivity. *American Journal of Physiology, 236*, E667–E677.

Bertero, M. (1989). Linear inverse problems and ill-posed problems. *Advances in Electronics and Electron Physics, 75*, 1–120.

Bode, B. W., McGill, J. B., Lorber, D. L., Gross, J. L., Chang, P. C., Bregman, D. B., & Affinify 1 Study Group. (2015). Inhaled technosphere insulin compared with injected prandial insulin in type 1 diabetes: A randomized 24-week trial. *Diabetes Care, 38*, 2266–2273.

Bolie, V. W. (1961). Coefficients of normal blood glucose regulation. *Journal of Applied Physiology, 16*, 783–788.

Boss, A. H., Petrucci, R., & Lorber, D. (2012). Coverage of prandial insulin requirements by means of an ultra-rapid-acting inhaled insulin. *Journal of Diabetes Science and Technology, 6*, 773–779.

Box, G. E. P., & Jenkins, G. M. (1976). *Time series analysis, forecasting and control* (2nd ed.). San Francisco, CA: Holden-Day.

Breda, E., Cavaghan, M. K., Toffolo, G., Polonsky, K. S., & Cobelli, C. (2001). Oral glucose tolerance test minimal model indexes of beta-cell function and insulin sensitivity. *Diabetes, 50,* 150–158.

Bronikowsky, T., Lawson, C., & Linehan, J. (1983). Model-free deconvolution techniques for estimation of vascular transport functions. *International Journal of Biomedical Computing, 14,* 411–429.

Bronzino, J. D. (Ed.), (2000). *The biomedical engineering handbook* (2nd ed.). Boca Raton, FL: CRC Press.

Bruce, E. (2000). *Biomedical signal processing and signal modeling.* New York: Wiley.

Cage, P. E., Carson, E. R., & Britton, K. E. (1977). A model of the human renal medulla. *Computers in Biomedical Research, 10,* 561–584.

Carson, E. R., & Cobelli, C. (Eds.), (2014). *Modelling methodology for physiology and medicine* (2nd ed.). Amsterdam: Elsevier.

Carson, E. R., Cobelli, C., & Finkelstein, L. (1983). *The mathematical modeling of metabolic and endocrine systems: Model formulation, identification and validation.* New York: John Wiley & Sons.

Carson, E. R., & Cramp, D. G. (Eds.), (1985). *Computers and control in clinical medicine.* New York: Plenum.

Caumo, A., & Cobelli, C. (1993). Hepatic glucose production during the labelled IVGTT: Estimation by deconvolution with a new minimal model. *American Journal of Physiology, 264,* E829–E841.

Ceresa, F., Ghemi, F., Martini, P. F., Martino, P., Segre, G., & Vitelli, A. (1973). Control of blood glucose in normal and in diabetic subjects. *Diabetes, 17,* 570–578.

Charter, M. K., & Gull, S. F. (1991). Maximum entropy and drug absorption. *Journal of Pharmacokinetics and Biopharmaceutics, 19,* 497–520.

Clifton, D. K., Aksel, S., Bremner, W. J., Steiner, R. A., & Soules, M. R. (1988). Statistical evaluation of coincident prolactin and luteinizing hormone pulses during the normal menstrual cycle. *Journal of Clinical Endocrinology and Metabolism, 67,* 832–838.

Clough, A., Cui, D., Linehan, J. H., Krenz, G. S., Dawson, C. A., & Maron, M. B. (1993). Model-free numerical deconvolution of recirculating indicator concentration curves. *Journal of Applied Physiology, 75,* 1444–1453.

Cobelli, C., & Carson, E. (2014). Introduction to modelling methodology. In E. Carson, & C. Cobelli (Eds.), *Modelling methodology for physiology and medicine* (2nd ed., pp. 1–11). Amsterdam: Elsevier.

Cobelli, C., Dalla Man, C., Toffolo, G., Basu, R., Vella, A., & Rizza, R. (2014). The oral minimal model method. *Diabetes, 63,* 1203–1213.

Cobelli, C., & DiStefano, J. J., III (1980). Parameter and structural identifiability concepts and ambiguities: A critical review and analysis. *American Journal of Physiology, 239,* R7–R24.

Cobelli, C., Foster, D. M., & Toffolo, G. (2000). *Tracer kinetics in biomedical research: From data to model.* New York: Kluwer.

Cobelli, C., Mari, A., Del Prato, S., De Kreutzenberg, S., Nosadini, R., & Jensen, I. (1987). Reconstructing the rate of appearance of subcutaneous insulin by deconvolution. *American Journal of Physiology, 252,* E549–E556.

Cobelli, C., & Ruggeri, A. (1989). Optimal design of sampling schedules for studying glucose kinetics with tracers. *American Journal of Physiology: Endocrinology and Metabolism, 257,* E444–E450.

Cobelli, C., Ruggeri, A., DiStefano, J. J., III, & Landaw, E. M. (1985). Optimal design of multioutput sampling schedules: Software and applications to endocrine-metabolic and pharmacokinetic models. *IEEE Transactions on Biomedical Engineering, 32,* 249–256.

Commenges, D., & Brendel, A. J. (1982). A deconvolution program for processing radiotracer dilution curves. *Computer Methods and Programs in Biomedicine, 14,* 271–276.

Crone, C., & Lassen, N. A. (Eds.), (1970). *Capillary permeability: The transfer of molecules and ions between capillary blood and tissue.* New York: Academic Press.

Cunningham, D. J. C., & Gardner, W. N. (1977). A quantitative description of the pattern of breathing during steady-state CO_2 inhalation in man with special emphasis on expiration. *Journal of Physiology (London), 272,* 613–632.

Cutler, D. J. (1978). Numerical deconvolution by least squares: Use of polynomials to represent the input function. *Journal of Pharmacokinetics and Biopharmaceutics, 6,* 243–263.

Dalla Man, C., Caumo, R., Basu, R., Rizza, R. A., Toffolo, G., & Cobelli, C. (2004). Minimal model estimation of glucose absorption and insulin sensitivity from oral test: Validation with a tracer method. *American Journal of Physiology Endocrinology and Metabolism, 287,* E637–E643.

Dalla Man, C., & Cobelli, C. (2014). Glucose modelling. In E. R. Carson, & C. Cobelli (Eds.), *Modelling methodology for physiology and medicine* (2nd ed., pp. 355–380). Amsterdam: Elsevier.

Dalla Man, C., Micheletto, F., Lv, D., Breton, M., Kovatchev, B., & Cobelli, C. (2014). The UVA/Padova type 1 diabetes simulator: New features. *Journal of Diabetes Science and Technology, 8,* 26–34.

Dalla Man, C., Rizza, R. A., & Cobelli, C. (2006). A system model of oral glucose absorption: Validation on gold standard data. *IEEE Transactions on Biomedical Engineering, 53,* 2472–2478.

Dalla Man, C., Rizza, R. A., & Cobelli, C. (2007). Meal simulation model of the glucose-insulin system. *IEEE Transactions on Biomedical Engineering, 54,* 1740–1749.

Dalla Man, C., Yarasheski, K. E., Caumo, A., Robertson, H., Toffolo, G., Polonsky, K. S., & Cobelli, C. (2005). Insulin sensitivity by oral glucose minimal models: Validation against clamp. *American Journal of Physiology Endocrinology and Metabolism, 289,* E954–E959.

De Nicolao, G., & Liberati, D. (1993). Linear and nonlinear techniques for the deconvolution of hormone time series. *IEEE Transactions on Biomedical Engineering, BME-40,* 440–455.

De Nicolao, G., Liberati, D., & Sartorio, A. (1995). Deconvolution of infrequently sampled data for the estimation of growth hormone secretion. *IEEE Transactions on Biomedical Engineering, 42,* 678–687.

De Nicolao, G., Sparacino, G., & Cobelli, C. (1997). Nonparametric input estimation in physiological systems: Problems, methods, case studies. *Automatica, 33,* 851–870.

Deutsch, T., Lehmann, E. D., Carson, E. R., Roudsari, A. V., Hopkins, K. D., & Sönksen, P. H. (1994). Time series analysis and control of blood glucose levels in diabetic patients. *Computer Methods and Programs in Biomedicine, 41,* 167–182.

DiStefano, J. J., III (1981). Optimized blood sampling protocols and sequential design of kinetic experiments. *American Journal of Physiology, 9,* R259–R265.

DiStefano, J. J., III (2013). *Dynamic systems biology modeling and simulation.* New York: Elsevier.

DiStefano, J. J., III, Wilson, K. C., Jang, M., & Mak, P. H. (1975). Identification of the dynamics of thyroid hormone metabolism. *Automatica, 11,* 149–159.

Dix, L., Frazier, D., Cooperstein, M., & Riviere, J. (1986). Exponential intravenous infusion in toxicological studies: Achieving identical serum drug concentration profiles in individuals with altered pharmacokinetic states. *Journal of Pharmaceutical Science, 75,* 448–451.

Edelman, S. V. (2016). Regulation catches up to reality: Nonadjunctive use of continuous glucose monitoring data. *Journal of Diabetes Science and Technology, 10,* 1–5.

Edelstein-Kehset, L. (2004). *Mathematical models in biology.* Philadelphia, PA: SIAM.

Enderle, J., Blanchard, S., & Bronzino, J. (2000). *Introduction to biomedical engineering.* San Diego, CA: Academic Press.

FDA (2016). Brief summary of the clinical chemistry and clinical toxicology devices panel meeting July 21, 2016. Department of Health and Human Services, Food and Drug Administration. <http://www.fda.gov/downloads/AdvisoryCommittees/CommitteesMeeting Materials/MedicalDevices/MedicalDevicesAdvisoryCommittee/ClinicalChemistryandClinicalToxicologyDevices/UCM513025.pdf>.

Ferrannini, E., & Cobelli, C. (1987). The kinetics of insulin in man. I. General aspects. *Diabetes and Metabolism Review, 3,* 335–363.

Finkelstein, L., & Carson, E. R. (1985). *Mathematical modelling of dynamic biological systems* (2nd ed.). Chichester: Wiley.

Flenley, D. C., & Warren, P. M. (1988). Clinical measurement in respiratory medicine. In D. G. Cramp, & E. R. Carson (Eds.), *The respiratory system* (pp. 97–144). London: Croom Helm.

Flood, R. L., & Carson, E. R. (1993). *Dealing with complexity: An introduction to the theory and application of systems science* (2nd ed.). New York: Plenum.

Forker, E. L., & Luxon, B. (1978). Hepatic transport disappearance curves – Distributed modeling versus the conventional approach. *American Journal of Physiology, 235,* E648–E660.

Francis, G. E., & Leaning, M. S. (1985). Stochastic model of human granulocyte-macrophage progenitor cell proliferation and differentiation. I. Setting up the model. *Experimental Hematology, 13,* 92–98.

Gatewood, L. C., Ackerman, A., Rosevear, J. W., & Molnar, J. D. (1968a). Tests of a mathematical model of the blood-glucose regulatory system. *Computers and Biomedical Research, 2,* 1–14.

Gatewood, L. C., Ackerman, A., Rosevear, J. W., & Molnar, J. D. (1968b). Simulation studies of blood-glucose regulation: Effect of intestinal glucose absorption. *Computers and Biomedical Research, 2,* 15–27.

Gibaldi, M., & Perrier, D. (1982). *Pharmacokinetics* (2nd ed.). New York: Marcel Dekker.

Gilks, W. R., Richardson, S., & Spiegelhalter, D. (Eds.), (1995). *Markov chain Monte Carlo in practice.* London: Chapman and Hall.

Gillespie, W., & Veng-Pedersen, P. (1985). A polyexponential deconvolution method. Evaluation of the "gastrointestinal bioavailability" and mean in vivo dissolution time of some ibuprofen dosage forms. *Journal of Pharmacokinetics and Biopharmaceutics, 13,* 289–307.

Godfrey, K. R. (1983). *Compartmental models and their application.* New York: Academic Press.

Goresky, C. A., Bach, G. G., & Nadeau, B. E. (1973). On the uptake of materials by the intact liver. The transport and net removal of galactose. *Journal of Clinical Investigation, 52,* 991–998.

Graham, M. M., Muzi, M., Spence, A. M., O'Sullivan, F., Lewellen, T. K., Link, J. M., & Krohn, K. A. (2002). The FDG lumped constant in normal human brain. *Journal of Nuclear Medicine, 43,* 1157–1166.

Grodsky, G. M. (1972). A threshold distribution hypothesis for packet storage of insulin and its mathematical modeling. *Journal of Clinical Investigation, 51,* 2047–2059.

Guardabasso, V., Genazzani, A. D., Veldhuis, J. D., & Rodbard, D. (1991). Objective assessment of concordance of secretory events in two endocrine time series. *Acta Endocrinologica, 124,* 208–218.

Hartman, M., Pincus, S., Johnson, M., Matthews, D. H., Faunt, L., Vance, M. L., . . . Veldhuis, J. (1994). Enhanced basal and disorderly growth hormone secretion distinguish acromegalic from normal pulsatile growth hormone release. *Journal of Clinical Investigation, 94,* 1277–1288.

Harvey, A. C. (1989). *Forecasting, structural time series models and the Kalman filter.* Cambridge: Cambridge University Press.

Hodgkin, A. L., & Huxley, A. F. (1952). A quantitative description of membrane current and its application to conduction and excitation in nerve. *Journal of Physiology, 117,* 500–544.

Hoppensteadt, F. C., & Peskin, C. (2002). *Modeling and simulation in medicine and the life sciences.* New York: Springer-Verlag.

Hovorka, R., Chappell, M. J., Godfrey, K. R., Madden, F. N., Rouse, M. K., & Soons, P. A. (1998). CODE: A deconvolution program implementing a regularization method of deconvolution constrained to non-negative values: Description and pilot evaluation. *Biopharmaceutical Drug Disposition, 19,* 39–53.

Hunt, B. R. (1970). The invese problem of radiography. *Mathematical Biosciences, 8,* 161–179.

Hunt, B. R. (1971). Biased estimation for nonparametric identification of linear systems. *Mathematical Biosciences, 10*, 215–237.

Iga, K., Ogawa, Y., Yashiki, T., & Shimamoto, T. (1986). Estimation of drug absorption rates using a deconvolution method with nonequal sampling times. *Journal of Pharmaceutical Biology, 14*, 213–225.

Jacquez, J. A. (1972). *Compartmental analysis in biology and medicine: Kinetics of distribution of tracer-labeled materials*. Amsterdam: Elsevier.

Jacquez, J. A. (1985). *Compartmental analysis in biology and medicine* (2nd ed.). AnnArbor, MI: University of Michigan Press.

Jacquez, J. A. (1996). *Compartmental analysis in biology and medicine* (3rd ed.). AnnArbor, MI: BioMedware.

Jacquez, J. A., & Simon, C. P. (1993). Qualitative theory of compartmental systems. *SIAM Review, 35*, 43–79.

Janes, F. R., & Carson, E. R. (1971). Modelling biological systems. *IEE Electronics and Power, 17*, 110–116.

Keener, J., & Sneyd, J. (1998). *Mathematical physiology*. New York: Springer-Verlag.

Kety, S. S., & Schmidt, C. F. (1948). The nitrous oxide method for the quantitative determination of cerebral blood flow in man: Theory, procedure, and normal values. *Journal of Clinical Investigation, 27*, 476–483.

Khoo, M. C. K. (2000). *Physiological control systems*. New York: IEEE Press.

King, R. B., Raymond, G. M., & Bassingthwaighte, J. B. (1996). Modeling blood flow heterogeneity. *Annals of Biomedical Engineering, 24*, 352–372.

Knopp, T. J., Dobbs, W. A., Greenleaf, J. F., & Bassingthwaighte, J. B. (1976). Transcoronary intravascular transport functions obtained via a stable deconvolution technique. *Annals of Biomedical Engineering, 4*, 44–59.

Kovatchev, B. P., Breton, M. D., Dalla Man, C., & Cobelli, C. (2009). *In silico* preclinical trials: A proof of concept in closed-loop control of type 1 diabetes. *Journal of Diabetes Science and Technology, 3*, 44–55.

Kuikka, J., Levin, M., & Bassingthwaighte, J. B. (1986). Multiple tracer dilution estimates of D- and 2-deoxy-D-glucose uptake by the heart. *American Journal of Physiology, 250*, H29–H42.

Landaw, E. M., & DiStefano, J. J., III (1984). Multiexponential, multicompartmental and noncompartmental modelling. II Data analysis and statistical considerations. *American Journal of Physiology, 246*, R665–R677.

Leaning, M. S., Pullen, H. E., Carson, E. R., & Finkelstein, L. (1983). Modelling a complex biological system: The human cardiovascular system. I. Methodology and model description. *Transactions of the Institute of Measurement and Control, 5*, 71–86.

Licko, V. (1973). Threshold secretory mechanism; model of derivative element in biological control. *Bulletin of Mathematical Biology, 35*(1), 51–58.

Licko, V., & Silver, A. (1975). Open-loop glucose insulin control with threshold secretory mechanism: Analysis of intravenous glucose tolerance tests in man. *Mathematical Biosciences, 27*, 319–332.

Linkens, D. A. (Ed.), (1979). *Biological systems, modelling and control*. Stevenage: Peter Peregrinus Press.

Marmarelis, P. Z., & Marmarelis, V. Z. (1978). *Analysis of physiological systems: The white noise approach*. New York: Plenum.

McIntosh, J. E. A., & McIntosh, R. P. (1980). *Mathematical modelling and computers in endocrinology*. Berlin: Springer-Verlag.

Meneilly, G. S., Ryan, A. S., Veldhuis, J. D., & Elahi, D. (1997). Increased disorderliness of basal insulin release, attenuated insulin secretory burst mass, and reduced ultradian rhythmicity of insulin secretion in older individuals. *Journal of Clinical Endocrinology and Metabolism, 82*, 4088–4093.

Merriam, G., & Wachter, K. (1982). Algorithms for the study of episodic hormone secretion. *American Journal of Physiology, 243*, E310–E318.

Messori, M., Kropff, J., Del Favero, S., Place, J., Visentin, R., Calore, R., . . . Cobelli, C. (2017). Individually adaptive artificial pancreas in subjects with type 1 diabetes: A one-month proof-of-concept rial in free-living conditions. *Diabetes Technology and Therapeutics, 19,* 560–571.

Milhorn, H. T. (1966). *The application of control theory to physiological systems.* Philadelphia, PA: WB Saunders Company.

Milsum, J. H. (1966). *Biological control systems analysis.* New York: McGraw-Hill.

Mintun, M. A., Raichie, M. E., Martin, W. R., & Herscovitch, P. (1984). Brain oxygen utilization measured with O-15 radiotracers and positron emission tomography. *Journal of Nuclear Medicine, 25,* 177–187.

Nakai, M. (1981). Computation of transport function using multiple regression analysis. *American Journal of Physiology, 240,* H133–H144.

Northrop, R. B. (2000). *Endogenous and exogenous regulation and control of physiological systems.* Boca Raton, FL: Chapman and Hall/CRC Press.

O'Meara, N. M., Sturis, J., Blackman, J. D., Roland, D. C., Van Cauter, E., & Polonsky, K. S. (1993). Analytical problems in detecting rapid insulin secretory pulses in normal humans. *American Journal of Physiology, 264,* E231–E238.

O'Meara, N. M., Sturis, J., Van Cauter, E., & Polonsky, K. S. (1993). Lack of control by glucose of ultradian insulin secretory oscillations in impaired glucose tolerance and in non-insulin-dependent diabetes mellitus. *Journal of Clinical Investigation, 92,* 262–271.

Ottesen, J. T., Olufsen, M. S., & Larsen, J. K. (2004). *Applied mathematical models in human physiology.* Philadelphia: SIAM.

Pantaleon, A. E., Loutseiko, M., Steil, G. M., & Rebrin, K. (2006). Evaluation of the effect of gain on the meal response of an automated closed-loop insulin delivery system. *Diabetes, 55,* 1995–2000.

Phillips, D. L. (1962). A technique for the numerical solution of certain integral equations of the first kind. *Journal of the Association of Computational Machinery, 9,* 97–101.

Pillonetto, G., Caumo, A., Sparacino, G., & Cobelli, C. (2006). A new dynamic index of insulin sensitivity. *IEEE Transactions on Biomedical Engineering, 53*(3), 369–379.

Pillonetto, G., Sparacino, G., & Cobelli, C. (2001). Reconstructing insulin secretion rate after a glucose stimulus by an improved stochastic deconvolution method. *IEEE Transactions on Biomedical Engineering, 48,* 1352–1354.

Pillonetto, G., Sparacino, G., & Cobelli, C. (2002a). Handling non-negativity in deconvolution of physiological signals: A nonlinear stochastic approach. *Annals of Biomedical Engineering, 30,* 1077–1087.

Pillonetto, G., Sparacino, G., Magni, P., Bellazzi, R., & Cobelli, C. (2002b). Minimal model S(I) = 0 problem in NDDM subjects: Nonzero Bayesian estimates with credible confidence intervals. *American Journal of Physiology: Endocrinology and Metabolism, 282*(3), E564–E573.

Pilo, A., Ferrannini, E., & Navalesi, R. (1977). Measurement of glucose-induced insulin delivery rate in man by deconvolution analysis. *American Journal of Physiology, 233,* E500–E508.

Pincus, S. M. (1991). Approximate entropy as a measure of system complexity. *Proceedings of the National Academy of Sciences of the United States of America, 88,* 2297–2301.

Pincus, S. M., Gevers, E. F., Robinson, I. C., Van Den Berg, G., Roelfsema, F., Hartman, M. L., & Veldhuis, J. D. (1996). Females secrete growth hormone with more process irregularity than males in both humans and rats. *American Journal of Physiology, 270,* E107–115.

Pincus, S. M., Mulligan, T., Iranmanesh, A., Gheorghiu, S., Godschalk, M., & Veldhuis, J. D. (1996). Older males secrete luteinizing hormone and testosterone more irregularly, and jointly more asynchronously, than younger males. *Proceedings of the National Academy of Sciences of the United States of America, 93,* 14100–14105.

Pohjanpalo, H. (1978). System identifiability based on the power series expansion of the solution. *Mathematical Biosciences, 41*, 21–34.

Polonsky, K. S., Licinio-Paixao, J., Given, B. D., Pugh, W., Rae, P., Galloway, J., . . . Frank, B. (1986). Use of biosynthetic human C-peptide in the measurement of insulin secretion rates in normal volunteers and type 1 diabetic patients. *Journal of Clinical Investigation, 51*, 98–105.

Quon, M. J., & Campfield, L. A. (1991). A mathematical model and computer simulation study of insulin receptor regulation. *Journal of Theoretical Biology, 150*(1), 59–72.

Richards, T. G., Tindall, V. R., & Young, A. (1959). A modification of the bromosulphtalein liver function test to predict the dye content of the liver and bile. *Clinical Science, 18*, 499–511.

Riggs, D. S. (1963). *The mathematical approach to physiological problems*. Baltimore, MD: Williams & Wilkins.

Rose, C. P., & Goresky, C. A. (1976). Vasomotor control of capillary transit time heterogeneity in the canine coronary circulation. *Circulation Research, 39*, 541–554.

SAAM User Guide (1998). Seattle, WA: University of Washington.

Saccomani, M. P., Bonadonna, R. C., Bier, D. M., DeFronzo, R. A., & Cobelli, C. (1996). A model to measure insulin effects on glucose transport and phosphorylation in muscle: A three tracer study. *American Journal of Physiology, 270*, E170–E185.

Saccomani, M. P., & Cobelli, C. (1992). Qualitative experiment design in physiological system identification. *IEEE Control Systems Magazine, 12*, 18–23.

Sangren, W. C., & Sheppard, C. W. (1953). A mathematical derivation of the exchange of a labeled substance between a liquid flowing in a vessel and an external compartment. *Bulletin of Mathematical Biophysics, 15*, 387–394.

Saratchandran, P., Carson, E. R., & Reeve, J. (1976). An improved mathematical model of human thyroid hormone regulation. *Clinical Endocrinology, 5*, 473–483.

Sarhan, N. A. S., Leaning, M. S., Saunders, K. B., & Carson, E. R. (1988). Development of a complex model: Breathing and its control in man. *Biomedical Measurement, Informatics and Control, 2*, 81–100.

Sartorio, A., De Nicolao, G., Pizzini, G., & Liberati, D. (1997). Nonparametric deconvolution provides an objective assessment of GH responsiveness to GH releasing stimuli in normal subjects. *Clinical Endocrinology, 46*, 387–400.

Schmitz, O., Porksen, N., Nyholm, B., Skjaerbaer, P. C., Butler, P. C., Veldhuis, J. D., & Pincus, S. M. (1997). Disorderly and nonstationary insulin secretion in relatives of patients with NIDDM. *American Journal of Physiology, 272*, E218–E226.

Schwartz, G. (1978). Estimating the dimension of a model. *Annals of Statistics, 6*, 461–464.

Segre, G., Turco, G. L., & Vercellone, G. (1973). Modelling blood glucose and insulin kinetics in normal, diabetic and obese subjects. *Diabetes, 22*, 94–103.

Sheppard, C. W. (1962). *Basic principles of the tracer method.* New York: Wiley.

Slate, J. B., & Sheppard, L. C. (1982). Automatic control of blood pressure by drug infusion. *IEEE Proceedings, 129*(part A), 639–645.

Sokoloff, L., Reivich, M., Kennedy, C., Des Rosiers, M. H., Patlak, C. S., Pettigrew, K. D., . . . Shinohara, M. (1977). The [^{14}C] deoxyglucose method for the measurement of local cerebral glucose utilization: Theory, procedure, and normal values in the conscious and anesthetized albino rat. *Journal of Neurochemistry, 28*, 897–916.

Sparacino, G., Bonadonna, R., Steinberg, H., Baron, A., & Cobelli, C. (1998). Estimation of organ transport function from recirculating indicator dilution curves. *Annals of Biomedical Engineering, 26*, 128–135.

Sparacino, G., & Cobelli, C. (1996). A stochastic deconvolution method to reconstruct insulin secretion rate after a glucose stimulus. *IEEE Transactions on Biomedical Engineering, 42*, 512–529.

Sparacino, G., & Cobelli, C. (1997). Impulse response model in reconstruction of insulin secretion by deconvolution. Role of input design in the identification experiment. *Annals of Biomedical Engineering, 25*, 398–416.

Sparacino, G., & Cobelli, C. (1998). Analisi di serie temporali. In C. Cobelli, & R. Bonadonna (Eds.), *Bioingegneria dei Sistemi Metabolici* (pp. 109–136). Bologna: Patron.

Sparacino, G., De Nicolao, G., & Cobelli, C. (2001). Deconvolution. In E. Carson, & C. Cobelli (Eds.), *Modelling methodology for physiology and medicine* (pp. 45–75). New York: Academic Press.

Sparacino, G., Pillonetto, G., Capello, M., De Nicolao, G., & Cobelli, C. (2002). WINSTODEC: A stochastic deconvolution interactive program for physiological and pharmacokinetic systems. *Computer Methods and Programs in Biomedicine, 67*, 67–77.

Sparacino, G., Pillonetto, G., De Nicolao, G., & Cobelli, C. (2004). Deconvoluzione per l'analisi di segnali fisiologici. In S. Cerutti, & C. Marchesi (Eds.), *Metodi Avanzati di Elaborazione di Segnali Biomedici* (pp. 163–188). Bologna: Patron.

Sparacino, G., Tombolato, C., & Cobelli, C. (2000). Maximum likelihood versus maximum *a posteriori* parameter estimation of physiological system models: The C-peptide impulse response case study. *IEEE Transactions on Biomedical Engineering, 47*, 801–811.

Sparacino, G., Vicini, P., Bonadonna, R. C., Marraccini, P., Lehtovirta, M., Ferrannini, E., & Cobelli, C. (1997). Removal of catheter distortion in multiple indicator dilution studies: A deconvolution-based method and case studies on glucose blood-tissue exchange. *Medical and Biological Engineering and Computer, 35*, 337–342.

Stapleton, D. D., Moffett, T. C., Baskin, D. G., & Bassingthwaighte, J. B. (1995). Autoradiographic assessment of blood flow heterogeneity in the hamster heart. *Microcirculation, 2*, 277–282.

Stark, L., & Sherman, P. (1957). A servo-analytical study of consensual pupil light reflex to light. *Journal of Neurophysiology, 20*, 17–26.

Steil, G. M., Rebrin, K., Darwin, C., Hariri, F., & Saad, M. F. (2006). Feasibility of automating insulin delivery for the treatment of type 1 diabetes. *Diabetes, 55*, 3344–3350.

Sturis, J., Polonsky, K., Shapiro, T., Blackman, J. D., O'Meara, N., & Van Cauter, E. (1992). Abnormalities in the ultradian oscillations of insulin secretion and glucose levels in Type 2 diabetic patients. *Diabetologia, 35*, 681–689.

Sturis, J., Van Cauter, E., Blackman, J. D., & Polonsky, K. S. (1991). Entrainment of pulsatile insulin secretion by oscillatory glucose infusion. *Journal of Clinical Investigation, 87*, 439–445.

Swanson, G. D., & Belville, J. W. (1974). Hypoxic hypercapnic interactions in human respiratory control. *Journal of Applied Physiology, 36*, 480–487.

Talbot, S. A., & Gessner, U. (1973). *Systems physiology*. New York: Wiley.

Tett, S. E., Cutle, D., & Day, R. (1992). Bioavailability of hydroxychloroquine tablets assessed with deconvolution techniques. *Journal of Pharmaceutical Science, 81*, 155–159.

Tikhonov, A. N. (1963). Solution of incorrectly formulated problems and the regularization method. *Soviet Mathematics Doklady, 4*, 16–24.

Toates, F. M. (1975). *Control theory in biology and experimental psychology*. London: Hutchinson.

Toffanin, C., Messori, M., Cobelli, C., & Magni, L. (2017). Automatic adaptation of basal therapy for type 1 diabetic patients: A run-to-run approach. *Biomedical Signal Processing and Control, 31*, 539–549.

Toffanin, C., Visentin, R., Messori, M., Di Palma, F., Magni, L., & Cobelli, C. (2018). Toward a run-to-run adaptive artificial pancreas: *In silico* results. *IEEE Transactions on Biomedical Engineering, 65*, 479–488.

Twomey, S. (1965). The application of numerical filtering to the solution of integral equations of the first kind encountered in indirect sensing measurements. *Journal of the Franklin Institute, 279*, 95–109.

Ultrainen, T., Nuutila, P., Takala, T., Vicini, P., Ruotsalainen, U., Rönnemaa, T., ... Yki-Järvinen, H. (1997). Intact insulin stimulation of skeletal muscle blood flow, its heterogeneity and redistribution but not of glucose uptake in non-insulin dependent diabetes mellitus. *Journal of Clinical Investigation, 100*, 777–785.

Van Cauter, E. (1988). Estimating false-positive and false-negative errors in analysis of hormone pulsatility. *American Journal of Physiology, 254*, E786–E794.

Van Cauter, E. (1990). Computer assisted analysis of endocrine rhythms. In G. Forti, V. Guardabasso, & D. Rodbard (Eds.), *Computers in Endocrinology: Recent Advances* (pp. 59–70). New York: Raven Press.

Van Cauter, E., Mestrez, F., Sturis, J., & Polonsky, K. S. (1992). Estimation of insulin secretion rates from C-peptide levels. Comparison of individual and standard kinetic parameters for C-peptide clearance. *Diabetes, 41*, 368–377.

Veldhuis, J. D., Carlson, M. L., & Johnson, M. L. (1987). The pituitary gland secretes in bursts: Appraising the nature of glandular secretory impulses by simultaneous multiple-parameter deconvolution of plasma hormone concentration. *Proceedings of the National Academy of Sciences of the United States of America, 4*, 7686–7690.

Veldhuis, J. D., & Johnson, M. L. (1988). Operating characteristics of the hypothalamo-pituitary-gonodal axis in men: Circadian, ultradian and pulsatile release of prolactin and its temporal coupling with luteinizing hormone. *Journal of Clinical Endocrinology and Metabolism, 67*, 116–123.

Veldhuis, J. D., King, J. C., Urban, R. J., Rogol, A. D., Evans, W. S., Kolp, L. A., & Johnson, M. L. (1987). Operating characteristics of the male hypothalamo-pituitary-gonadal axis: Pulsatile release of testosterone and follicle-stimulating hormone and their temporal coupling with luteinizing hormone. *Journal of Clinical Endocrinology and Metabolism, 65*, 929–941.

Verotta, D. (1996). Concepts, properties and applications of linear systems to describe the distribution, identify input, and control endogenous substances and drugs in biological systems. *Critical Reviews in Bioengineering, 24*, 73–139.

Vettoretti, M., Facchinetti, A., Sparacino, G., & Cobelli, C. (2018). Type-1 diabetes patient decision simulator for *in silico* testing safety and effectiveness of insulin treatments. *IEEE Transactions on Biomedical Engineering, 65*, 1281–1290.

Viceconti, M., Cobelli, C., Haddad, T., Himes, A., Kovatchev, B., & Palmer, M. (2017). *In silico* assessment of biomedical products: The conundrum of rare but not so rare events in two case studies. *Proceedings of the Institution of Mechanical Engineers H, 231*, 455–466.

Vicini, P. (2001). Blood-tissue exchange modelling. In E. R. Carson, & C. Cobelli (Eds.), *Modelling methodology for physiology and medicine* (pp. 373–401). San Diego: Academic Press.

Vicini, P., Bonadonna, R. C., Lehtovirta, M., Groop, L., & Cobelli, C. (1998). Estimation of blood flow heterogeneity in human skeletal muscle using intravascular tracer data: Importance for modeling transcapillary exchange. *Annals of Biomedical Engineering, 26*, 764–774.

Vicini, P., Bonadonna, R. C., Ultrianen, T., Nuutila, P., Raitakari, M., Yki-Järvinen, H., & Cobelli, C. (1997). Estimation of blood flow heterogeneity distribution in human skeletal muscle from positron emission tomography. *Annals of Biomedical Engineering, 25*, 906–910.

Vicini, P., Caumo, A., & Cobelli, C. (1997). The hot IVGTT two-compartment minimal model: Indexes of glucose effectiveness and insulin sensitivity. *American Journal of Physiology, 273*, E1024–E1032.

Vicini, P., Zachwieja, J. J., Yarasheski, K. E., Bier, D. M., Caumo, A., & Cobelli, C. (1999). Glucose production during an IVGTT by deconvolution: Validation with the tracer-to-tracee clamp technique. *American Journal of Physiology, 276*, E285–E294.

Visentin, R., Campos-Nánez, E., Schiavon, M., Lv, D., Vettoretti, M., Breton, M., ... Cobelli, C. (2018). The UVA/Padova type 1 diabetes simulator goes from single meal to single day. *Journal of Diabetes Science and Technology, 12*, 273–281.

Visentin, R., Dalla Man, C., & Cobelli, C. (2016). One-day Bayesian cloning of type 1 diabetes subjects: Towards a single-day UVA/Padova type 1 diabetes simulator. *IEEE Transactions on Biomedical Engineering, 63,* 2416–2424.

Visentin, R., Dalla Man, C., Kovatchev, B., & Cobelli, C. (2014). The University of Virginia/Padova type 1 diabetes simulator matches the glucose traces of a clinical trial. *Diabetes Technology and Therapeutics, 16,* 428–434.

Visentin, R., Dalla Man, C., Kudva, Y. C., Basu, A., & Cobelli, C. (2015). Circadian variability of insulin sensitivity: Physiological input for *in silico* artificial pancreas. *Diabetes Technology and Therapeutics, 17,* 1–7.

Visentin, R., Giegerich, C., Jäger, R., Dahmen, R., Boss, A., Grant, M., . . . Klabunde, T. (2016). Improving efficacy of inhaled technosphere insulin (Afrezza) by post-meal dosing: *In silico* clinical trial with the University of Virginia/Padova type 1 diabetes simulator. *Diabetes Technology and Therapeutics, 18,* 574–585.

Walter, E., & Pronzato, L. (1997). *Identification of parametric models from experimental data.* Berlin: Springer.

Westwick, D. T., & Kearney, R. E. (2003). *Identification of nonlinear physiological systems.* New York: IEEE Press.

Whiting, B., Kelman, A., & Struthers, A. D. (1984). Prediction of response to theophylline in chronic bronchitis. *British Journal of Clinical Pharmacology, 17,* 1–8.

Yates, F. E. (1978). Complexity and the limits to knowledge. *American Journal of Physiology, 4,* R201–R204.

Young, P. (1984). *Recursive estimation and time-series analysis: An introduction.* Berlin: Springer.

Index

Note: Page numbers followed by "*f*" refer to figures.

D

E

F